Books by Tom Ainslie

Ainslie's Jockey Book
The Compleat Horseplayer

Ainslie's Complete Guide to
THOROUGHBRED RACING

by
TOM AINSLIE

SIMON AND SCHUSTER • NEW YORK—————————————

Contents

Ainslie's Complete Guide to Thoroughbred Racing

Preface: In Which We Name the Game

THIS BOOK seeks to fill an enormous void in the literature of American Thoroughbred racing.

Other volumes celebrate the romance of the turf, the feats of champions, the distinctiveness of the breed, the exploits of horsemen dead and gone. This one occupies different territory. It is an encyclopedic review of handicapping theory and technique—the first such work in the long history of the game. Its sole concerns are (1) the competition among horsemen for purse winnings and (2) the competition among horsemen and fans for pari-mutuel winnings. Its goal is to place the fan on approximately equal footing with the horseman by revealing the strategy and tactics that lead to the winner's circle and the mutuel cashier's window.

Racing is unique in American sport. Its paying customer is more than a spectator. He is a participant. He goes to the track not only to see something but to do something. Specifically, he goes to bet. In these pages I propose to enhance his pleasure in the game by helping him to become good at it.

I hasten to concede that one need not be a winning bettor to enjoy an occasional outing at the track. Horse races are incomparably exciting. Moreover, these are prosperous times. Millions of men and women can afford the very minor misfortunes with which racing penalizes innocence. Unless the racegoer gambles insanely, his losing excursion to the track costs no more than a night on the town.

Nevertheless, it is more fun to win than to lose. Nobody with normal emotions can possibly be indifferent to the outcome of the races on which he bets. I therefore find it preposterous that no serious effort has been made (until now) to undress, dissect and analyze this multibillion-dollar pastime for those whose wagers are its main source of revenue.

Rank-and-file players should know the percentages and probabilities of the game. They should know how horsemen decide what to do with their animals, and when, and why. They should know the criteria on which professional handicappers and successful bettors base their judgments. They should, in other words, be made privy to the what's what, who's who and how come of the game they play.

Inasmuch as human beings tend to concentrate on pastimes in which they are skilled and to avoid those in which they take a thumping, one might fairly ask why racing has been so remiss about educating its own clientele. Why the huge omissions from the tons of literature issued by the racing industry and its able publicists? Has Thoroughbred racing's eminence as our largest "spectator" sport blinded it to the fact that most of its customers, however enthusiastic they may be, are transients? And that, aside from a small minority of neurotically compulsive losers, persons who attend racing regularly do so only because they have learned how to avoid serious financial loss? And that the way to increase the popularity of any game, no matter how popular it may be to begin with, is to teach people how to play it?

The reason that racing fails to grasp such opportunities is that it is afraid to. The fear is understandable. It derives from the sport's checkered past.

Not more than two generations ago, it was taken for granted that the only reputable persons at the track were the high-society types who owned the best horses. Their excuse for having all that fun was that they were perpetuating the glorious traditions of their class, improving the breed. They all bet, of course. But any commoner who went to the track to bet was a practitioner of evil. It surprised nobody when he turned out to be the black sheep of someone's family, or an absconding bookkeeper, or a stage-door johnny, or a degenerate gambler, or some kind of nut. The tracks were overrun with pickpockets and bunco steerers. Anyone with half a brain knew that many races were fixed. Victorian moral standards, or the instinct of self-preservation, or both, discouraged ordinary folk from entering such an environment. The sport was too seamy to mess with.

Great changes have occurred. Victorian morality has all but vanished. People no longer equate excitement with sin. Racing, an excitement if ever there was one, has responded by tidying its house. It now draws customers by the millions from the arts, the sciences, the professions and the upper reaches of the country's business and political establishments. The clientele of racing has become a representative cross section of the American public, as respectable as any other. And the act of going to the track to bet has achieved social acceptance. This is not quite as comfortable as social approval, but is a lap ahead of social toleration. In my opinion, the game will cross the threshold of approval as soon as it recognizes that it deserves to. It has become an industry of immense importance.

Every year, tens of millions of Thoroughbred racing enthusiasts deposit more than $3 billion in the pari-mutuel betting pools at United States tracks. The tracks remit over $250 million to state treasuries, which get another $125 million from harness and quarter-horse racing.

To put it mildly, the state governments welcome these tax contributions. They also enjoy the political jobs made possible by establishment and expansion of commissions charged with supervision of the sport. And they seem to appreciate the highly moral flavor of racing's communications with the voting public. The owners and managers of the game are careful to thwart anti-vice elements and other moralizers by playing down the lure of betting. So that neither they nor their political protectors will be mauled for "encouraging gambling," the tracks promote the spectator aspects of their business. They pretend that the pari-mutuel machines are not the main attraction in the store.

Which returns me to the original point. A major book explaining the game of racing to the bettor should have been published long before now. It might have come from the industry itself, as a goodwill effort to educate the customers toward wiser, less costly betting. Yet one searches in vain for printed matter in which racing officials or active horsemen emit so much as a hint about the art of selecting winners.

So sensitive is the industry to the hostility of anti-gambling fanatics that it even discourages the use of words like "horseplayer." The purple-necked gentleman tearing up a fistful of losing mutuel tickets and bawling abuse at the jockey is not to be called "horseplayer." He is a "racing fan." If it is bad taste to call a horseplayer a horseplayer, what shall we call a poker player?

Let us grant that the sport's modest garb, woven of 100 percent pure, virgin fig leaves, shields it from charges that it promotes vice. Let us applaud anything that frustrates the bluenoses who oppose racing. But let us question whether it is necessary any longer to appease the bluenoses. And let us recognize that the timid failure of racing experts to explain the art of handicapping actually encourages gambling. Their secretiveness is a primary reason why millions of floundering fans waste money on unintelligent bets!

The viewpoint of this book is that few racegoers are emotionally crippled gamblers, hell-bent to make themselves miserable by squandering the milk money. Most horseplayers are capable of learning how to function more effectively at the track—if someone would only do them the honor of showing them how.

How Experts Get That Way

From long experience in a variety of games, I feel qualified to make a most unusual but absolutely valid statement about the handicapping of horse races: It demands no less mental prowess than bridge, poker or chess. The skills of the expert handicapper are, in fact, closely comparable to those of the good bridge, poker or chess player. In any such competition, the player who depends on instinct, trial-and-error, inexpert advice, superstition or reckless guesses is at a disadvantage. He cannot hope to hold his own against persons who have acquired an understanding of the game as a whole.

The bedside table or living-room bookcase of every serious bridge player holds encyclopedic volumes by Charles Goren, Alfred Sheinwold and Louis Watson. Chess players make endless use of comprehensive texts by Reuben Fine, Emanuel Lasker, Fred Reinfeld. Mediocre poker players become tough propositions after studying Oswald Jacoby, Herbert O. Yardley and Irwin Steig. But horseplayers get no such aid and comfort.

Armed only with unreliable tips, insubstantial systems and hope, most horseplayers take a cruel battering in a game that really is not all that tough. Not, that is, for the few players lucky enough to know its theory and technique.

In response to the racing enthusiast's need, this book offers him what Goren, Sheinwold and Watson have given the bridge player. It dismantles the barriers that traditionally separate the paying customer from the professional horseman and professional handicapper. It presents the entire story, the full range of possibilities. Truths about Thoroughbreds and the men who race them are revealed here for the first time. These truths are the essence of sound handicapping, sound wagering.

Above all, the book equips its reader with standards whereby he may judge the relevance of the dizzyingly diverse items of coded technical information which are the handicapper's stock in trade. Believe it or not (and, if you have been going to the races for a while, you will believe it), most players consciously avoid that information, because they don't know what to make of it. Which is like trying to navigate without looking at the map.

The Importance of Predictability

Apart from its neglect of handicapping, published information about Thoroughbred racing is abundant, detailed and accurate. Two superb daily newspapers, several monthly magazines and a yearly encyclopedia offer to horsemen, officials and fans a range of news, statistics and commentary unsurpassed in any sport.

These easily available materials are more than merely interesting. They are essential to the orderly conduct of the game. They help the horseman make decisions about his horses. They help the expert fan make decisions about his bets. For both individuals the name of the game is prediction. And published information is the raw material from which prediction is made. Moreover, it provides the background against which errors in prediction may be diagnosed and corrected.

Certain patterns have become well established in centuries of Thoroughbred racing. The running condition of horses improves and declines in cycles familiar enough to make sudden reversals of form both noticeable and suspect. The class, or quality, of horses is also patterned, as is their ability to cope with high weights or unfamiliar distances, or with races in which the early stages are run at unusually fast or slow speeds. For these reasons and many others, race results themselves follow what might be termed a pattern of reasonable predictability.

A limitation on predictability is the unalterable fact that the race is a contest among mute animals of impermanent quality and unstable temperament. Nobody can interview a horse. The creature reveals the truth about itself only after the race has begun and the bets have become irrevocable. Moreover, its ability to do its best is affected by the handling it gets from humans of varying competence and integrity—trainers, grooms, stablehands and jockeys. These circumstances explain why any player able to win 40 percent of his bets in the course of a year is probably a genuine expert. And a marvel of self-discipline. He achieves his winning average by picking his spots with great care. Only a rare day finds him making more than three bets. On some days he makes no bets at all.

Another aspect of racing's predictability is more melancholy, and is closely linked to what I have just said. Anyone who tries to pick a winner in every race will be unable to predict the outcome of more than three races in ten if he persists in the practice for a year.

A third aspect is that racetrack crowds do better than that. The crowds function on a blend of hunch, horoscope, hot tip, individual handicapping, the motley forecasts of newspapers and tip sheets (which somehow name almost every horse in most races), and the dubious predictions of innumerable selection systems. Yet the crowds pick the winner of one race in every three. That statistic, which holds up year after year, is, of course, the percentage of victories by betting favorites.

Opening day at Aqueduct   **UPI PHOTO**

TOP: *Railbirds at Aqueduct*   UPI PHOTO

BOTTOM: *"Getting down" on the daily double at Santa Anita*   UPI PHOTO

The public's consistency is one of the inexplicable mysteries of the sport.

If these aspects of predictability seem to impose a ceiling on success at the track, they also suggest the possibility of a floor under failure. The racing industry recognizes this. It understands all too clearly that its hold on public confidence would become infirm if race results were to depart from the established patterns of reasonable predictability. The industry expends much money and a good deal of ingenuity to prevent and/or punish hanky-panky.

Here again, published information is vital. In deciding whether a suspect race was honestly contested, officials have access to movies of it and of previous races involving the same horses and riders. They also avail themselves of the published record about those past races. They do so knowing that the expert fan uses the same information. His ability to interpret the information is a spur to the authorities. The penalty for official laxness is public indignation—a first step toward desertion.

Horsemen, Handicappers and Information

For an example of how horsemen use public information, let us consider a trainer. He has a pretty nice kind of four-year-old sprinter which he regards as ready to win a race for $10,000 animals at three quarters of a mile. But his arch rival, the wily Trainer Doe, has just imported a large, bright-eyed colt from Illinois. If our horseman had to wait and see Doe's colt in a race or two before learning anything about him, his ability to manage the affairs of his own horse would be seriously impaired. Indeed, such a plight would mean that he and Doe and everyone else in racing had been transported, science-fiction style, to the beginning of the century, when published information was sparse and horsemen resolved their problems by collusion, chicanery and simple assault.

Our modern horseman can learn a great deal about Doe's import without budging from his desk. Chart books and past-performance records offer an almost photographic profile of the creature. Its quality, its running style, its favorite distances, its ability to carry high weight, its liking for wet or muddy running surfaces, and even its capacity for retaining top form after a long journey are all there in the records. If the colt was losing to $5,000 horses in Illinois it had better not jump up and beat $10,000 ones in its debut here, or Doe will find himself in trouble. Such reversals of form were common in the bad old days but, as suggested earlier, are too noticeable to be tolerated now that fans and officials are equipped to recognize them.

The practiced fan has a remarkably accurate bead on every horse in most races. With exceptions that we shall discuss in full detail later, he is able to foretell which entrants are likely to be in contention and which have only negligible chances. The minutely specific information contained in result charts and past-performance records is the foundation of his judgment. He supplements that data by consulting periodic public tabulations that summarize the success or failure of jockeys, trainers, owners and breeders. He also keeps abreast of news about breeding transactions, livestock sales, personnel shifts, owners' and trainers' plans, and equine injury and illness.

His regular presence at the track and the large amounts of money he bets (horsemen and expert customers are the biggest bettors) suggest that the published information works for him. He apparently is able to hold his betting losses at an endurable level—low enough to justify his continued attendance.

Or he may even be a winner. Thousands of fans combine intelligence, knowledge and self-control in proportions adequate to win money for themselves year after year, and even season after season or month after month. In all such cases, including that of the enthusiast whose pleasure in the game outweighs the pain of his small losses, it can be seen that Thoroughbred racing is reasonably predictable.

Yet of the 47 million persons who paid their way into American Thoroughbred racetracks and fed $3.6 billion into the machines during 1967, I doubt that one in 500 qualified as an expert. I doubt, in short, that more than a handful were able to exploit the predictability of racing by putting available information to profitable use.

Confessions of an Author

My own interest in racing arose more than three decades ago. I was fascinated by the commotion of the break from the starting barrier, the skill of the jockeying on the turns, the tension and suspense of the sprint down the homestretch. But I was a serious-minded type, with a thin billfold. I saw no profit in betting on something about which I knew nothing. I decided to buy some books.

No such thing was to be had. I was appalled. Nostalgic volumes about the history of the turf were available for nine cents on the remainder counter of every bookshop, but a book about the art of picking winners was available at no price.

"The reason they don't publish books for horseplayers," explained one merchant, "is that horseplayers can't read."

Certain magazines contained fragmentary articles extolling the un-demonstrated advantages of various handicapping angles or outlining equally unsubstantiated selection systems. Advertisements in the same periodicals hawked pamphlets revealing alleged "secrets" of successful "turf speculation." The pamphlets were similar in quality and substance to the magazine pieces. They offered a glimmering of what might have been wisdom, but nothing remotely like a comprehensive view of the overall problem with which they purported to deal. Also, the mail-order promoters who published these tracts invariably turned out to be tipsters and touts who kept one's mailbox cluttered with promises of riches beyond belief—for a $5 bill. I was young and naive, but it never occurred to me to patronize the touts. I wondered uneasily about the age and worldliness of those who did.

The Morning Telegraph and *Racing Form* published, as they still do, full instructions on how to decipher the notations in their result charts and past-performance records. This was helpful. But mastery of the cipher left one with the fundamental problem of how to *interpret* the decoded information. What was important? What was not? Which end was up?

I remained interested in racing for years, without betting a nickel on any race. In spare time I tested various systems on paper, much as a would-be stock investor might attempt dry runs with theories of market analysis. A few bookmakers and several professional horsemen supplied some lore, guiding me toward a beginning grasp of the game. In time, by dint of lonesome, laborious study of a sort so dedicated as to raise questions about the mental hygiene of anyone willing to undertake it, I reached a point where I could go to the track without fear of losing my shirt. It had taken me fifteen years of intermittent study to learn what a decent book could have taught me in a few weeks.

When racing entered its boom period of expansion after World War II, volumes of advice to horseplayers began to materialize in the bookshops. Persons who had never gone near a track now began drop-ping around to try the daily double. The books were an understandable effort to grab this new market. They continue to appear. I have at least forty of them and am sure that twenty more must have escaped my attention. With few exceptions, the ones I have seen pose no challenge to the theory that "horseplayers can't read."

Most of them are unreadable, whether one be a horseplayer or not. The worst are not only unreadable but fraudulent. The best, including the very few that have been written by authentic experts, outline system-atic methods of prediction. They are serviceable in the limited sense that any more-or-less sound method is superior to no method at all. Their chief weakness is that they leave the reader in the dark about the multitudinous possibilities untouched by their systems. Lacking the time, space, knowledge or willingness to do otherwise, their authors seek to imprison the reader in procedures which, while of some use in special situations, neglect the infinite variety of the game. Also, no single system is likely to be compatible with the temperament, mentality and bankroll of the individual player.

Fond of racing and offended by the book-length material offered to my companions in the audience, I finally decided to write books of my own. In 1966, *The Compleat Horseplayer** explained a handicapping method based on a more than ordinarily comprehensive view of the total problem. Its illustrative examples were the records of, and reasoning behind, wagers made during a successful week at Monmouth Park, New Jersey. In 1967 came *Ainslie's Jockey Book,†* another version of the same method, emphasizing certain previously unpublicized truths about the relationship of the rider to the winning or losing of the race.

These books quickly became the best-selling handicapping manuals in the history of the pastime. They met with unprecedented praise from professional horsemen and other racing experts. But, in my opinion and in that of insiders whose views I respect, both books were too fragmentary to fill the void.

What the racing follower needs is not someone else's method of handicapping, but his own. A book containing a procedure highly esteemed by Tom Ainslie is only a partial help. The chances are that its value derives less from its explanation of Ainslie's method than from what Ainslie discloses about the nature of the game itself.

To evaluate a handicapping procedure, whether he finds it in print or dreams it up himself, the player must understand what the other possibilities are. What other procedures exist? What fundamental principles must be taken into account in the development of any sound approach? Having reviewed the entire array, the individual is well situated to determine his preferences, test them at his leisure and amend them as events and his own developing knowledge may dictate.

To make that possible for its readers is the business of this book.

Anyone who has ever spent a precious summer Saturday afternoon watching his five "best bets" run out of the money will agree, I think, that it's high time.

* (Trident Press, New York, $4.95.)
† (Trident Press, New York, $4.95.)

Beginners are also welcome. Anything one might need to launch one-self into the fascinating game of racing will be found in these pages.

How We're Going To Operate

The book begins with a description and explanation of the materials necessary, or useful, to development and maintenance of expert skill.

We then take a good look at the physical layout of racetracks. One should know more than the location of one's seat, the finish line, the $2 window, the cashier's window, the frankfurter stand, the bathroom and the parking lot.

Next we analyze the arithmetic of racing. We start with the percentages of the game—figures with which every expert reckons. We proceed to the pari-mutuel system and how its deductions from winnings affect expert methods of play. We then examine the economics of the industry itself, a kind of arithmetic which has much to do with the outcome of races. We conclude the section with some of the most important arithmetic of all—the cost of the hobby, and how this influences the size of the bet.

We come now to the horse itself. We strip breeding of the hocus-pocus that has mystified and confused generations of players. We discuss the size, weight and appearance of the Thoroughbred, explaining what he should look like, and why.

The central section of the book explores the arts of handicapping. After a summary review of the accepted schools of thought, we describe and analyze each fundamental of theory and method. Under appropriate headings, the reader will find concrete information about factors such as distance, form, class, age, sex, consistency, weight, speed, pace, post position, the owner, the trainer, the jockey. And ways to recognize play-able-beatable races. And the secrets of the paddock and post parade. And a huge array of supplementary "angles" or "plus factors." And the names of, and strategic differences among, leading tracks; an assortment of professional speed charts and speed-weight formulas; methods of calculating daily track-speed variants; pace-rating procedures; the principles of class handicapping, form handicapping, speed handicapping and pace handicapping; the form cycle and how to recognize improvement or deterioration; the usefulness of workouts; the truth about the drugging and "stiffing" of horses; the names and characteristics of the nation's leading trainers; the names and specialties of leading riders; the names of leading owners and breeders; methods of recognizing soreness, lameness and illness. And much, much more, with explicit instructions on how to use it all.

The next section contains seventy-seven outstanding selection systems. Some have been sold to players for as much as $500 each. We offer them not as substitutes for actual handicapping but as sources of ideas. Presented as they are—with advice as to how they can be altered or combined—they should provide the fan with endless entertainment, plus unlimited opportunity to practice his growing skills as an analyst of the game.

The final sections of the book contain the official rules of racing; complete instructions on how to read result charts and past-performance records in both *The Morning Telegraph* and *Racing Form*, and, at the very end, a full glossary of racing terminology.

Acknowledgments

I am indebted to Triangle Publications, Inc., for permission to reproduce copyrighted materials from *The Morning Telegraph, Racing Form, American Racing Manual* and from booklets explaining result charts and past-performance records.

Mr. Henry Bomze, publisher of *American Turf Monthly,* has been most gracious in allowing me to use photographs and other materials that have appeared in his magazine. Howard A. Rowe, editor-in-chief of the magazine, and one of the most astute journalists in the field, has given me numerous invaluable suggestions. I thank him warmly and hasten to absolve him of responsibility for the content or tone of the book.

Because much of the information in the book has never been made public before, the reader will deduce that I have been interviewing jockeys, trainers and other experts. That is true, in a sense. The book's insights are the fruit of many years of observation, conversation and successful play. I doubt it would be a kindness to name any of the professional horsemen who, during the years, have contributed (usually unwittingly) to the development of those insights.

1 The Tools of the Trade

Most thoroughbred races are at distances of three quarters of a mile or more, around at least one turn, from a standing start. The margin of victory often is narrow enough to be measurable in inches or hundredths of a second. The best horse usually wins, but not always. Bad luck and human error are factors in the running of every race. They can make an abject loser of an animal that should have won easily. Considering the influence of luck and error in a game of inches and split seconds, it is remarkable that the best horse wins as often as it does.

The horse may be of distinctly higher quality than its rivals. It may also be in peak physical condition. But it may lose its race in the paddock, before it ever gets to the starting gate. A clumsy trainer or groom may fasten the saddle too tightly, or not tightly enough, causing sufficient discomfort to throw the animal hopelessly out of sorts. Or the horse may be upset by the nervousness of another horse, or the sudden roar of a low-flying airplane, or the frightening whiteness of a windblown newspaper. If the handlers misunderstand this and react with more harshness or less firmness than the situation demands, the ensuing fracas can deplete the horse of its winning energy.

If the horse is not familiar with its rider, or does not like him, or if the rider is not attuned to the animal, the race can be lost during the post parade. Some horses resent being busted with a whip during a pre-race warm-up. In trying to run away from the whip, such a horse may get more exercise than is good for him.

If he is a fast-breaking, front-running animal, eager for action, he may lose the race in the starting gate. The start may be delayed by the sulkiness or unruliness of other entrants, or by this horse's own highstrung behavior. When the bell finally sounds, it may catch him standing cross-legged. Or his jockey may have lapsed into a daydream. The effort of recovering the lost ground may empty the horse of the stamina it needs for the homestretch.

Another nervous type, whose disposition has suffered in the paddock, post parade or gate, may express himself by running rankly, frantically, uncontrollably, exhausting himself in the first half-mile.

A horse may break nicely from the gate and be jarred off stride by a careening neighbor. Bumps and brushes can cost precious split seconds of running time at any stage of a race, especially on the turns. Or an animal's new shoes may fit improperly, throwing his gait into imbalance and crippling him as soon as he attempts to lengthen stride.

Saving ground on the rail, a jockey may find himself without running room in the stretch, hemmed in by horses fore, aft and starboard. If daylight appears, the rider's hesitation for only a fraction of a second may prevent his mount from seizing an opportunity to run to the wire. Or the jockey may ride into a blind switch, swinging a few widths to the inside or outside for room on the turn—and racing straight into a pocket. Or he may be forced to check the animal's stride to avoid a pile-up with tiring horses that are backing up to him. Or he may be a timid rider, or a fatigued rider, or a rider weakened by dieting and dehydration, and may be unable to muster the whoop-de-doo necessary to get the horse's head up at the finish. Or he may use the whip too soon and too much, or too late and not enough. Or the horse may stumble on a clod of earth or a hoofprint.

The list of mishaps and errors could be prolonged for pages but need not be. The message is clear: The best horse can be beaten in a multitude of ways. Which is one of the reasons why sages declare, "You can't beat the races." Other sages modify this. "You can beat a race," they say, "but you can't beat the races." A more precise description of the situation is that some players beat the races, and most do not. For those who do not, the chief problem is lack of know-how. Yet some persons with know-how are insufficiently motivated to use the knowledge. They'd rather eat hot dogs and drink beer and have fun in the sun and lose a few hundred dollars a year than expend the effort necessary to catch the extra few winners that would put their accounts into the black. It is their sovereign right. They'd rather cream you on the golf course, or beat you at the poker or bridge table. It's all a matter of taste.

Persons who beat the races are, on the very face of it, knowledgeable players, motivated to use the knowledge. They enjoy winning so much that they are willing to work at it. Yet they may be unable to understand why an expert poker player will lie in ambush at the table for two and a half hours before sandbagging his companions. Again, it's a matter of taste.

As far as I know, horseplayers who win more money than they lose are almost invariably persons who have learned to be expert handicappers. To be sure, a medical friend of mine, who does not know which end kicks or which end bites, financed the establishment of his practice with $60,000 he won on hot tips. He was an intern at the time. The tips came from underworld characters who were grateful for a kindness he had rendered one of their relatives. The horses all won. Every month or two would come a tip on a horse at some small track. And every tip paid off—$60,000 worth in two or three years. It can be assumed that the mob continues to rig a few races at various minor-league tracks and that anyone with access to the information can beat such races. The rest of us are obliged to work for our winnings. We are obliged to learn how to handicap.

Some of the most consistent losers at any track are insiders, or friends of insiders, who depend on stable information. It is nice to know for certain that a certain stable plans to "go" with its horse, and is not simply sending the animal out for exercise. Unfortunately, three or four other stables are also likely to be all-out to win the same race, and may have the horseflesh to do it with. Which is why the player who knows how to handicap does not need stable information or, if he gets it, will not be misled by it.

As a class, professional horsemen are much better handicappers than the paying customers are. But an individual customer can be as effective a handicapper as any horseman. The expert customer's judgment is free of the pressures that result from loyalty to a stable owner or enthusiasm about a particular horse. He learns to mistrust and avoid all enthusiasms except his delight in lining up at the cashier's window to collect the rewards of his judgment.

By the same token, the accomplished player resists the emotional squalls that might be induced by ill fortune. He knows that he can't win every bet. He expects to lose more than half of them. Like the competitive golfer, the homicidal poker player and the expert bridge player— all of whom he resembles in many other particulars—he takes his reverses in stride. When, as happens all too often, the best horse in the race not only loses but loses a bet for him, the handicapper presses onward and upward. There will be other races today, or the next time. And every now and then, as he knows full well, he will bet on a horse, discover during the running of the race that it is not the best horse after all, and will cash the bet anyhow, racing luck or human fallibility having made a loser into a winner.

Knowledge, motivation to use the knowledge, self-control and composed self-confidence. These, then, are the primary attributes of the good player. Anyone who begins with the motivation, and enjoys maintaining

They're off at Churchill Downs
UPI PHOTO

Traffic jam on home turn at Aqueduct
UPI PHOTO

OPPOSITE: *Eddie Arcaro boots Bold Ruler (inside) to new track record in 1957 Wood Memorial at Jamaica, nosing out John Choquette on Gallant Man.*
UPI PHOTO

it, can develop the knowledge, the self-control and the confidence. The latter two qualities are products of experience—successful experience based on knowledge.

In acquiring the necessary experience, the reader probably will use this volume as home base, a primary source of essential knowledge. But he will want additional materials with which to check and test his knowledge and make it firmly his own. Still other materials will help him to replenish and expand what he knows, in light of new developments in the game.

Such materials are the tools of the handicapper's trade. Some are indispensable. Others can be omitted, depending on the amount of effort the player is willing to give to his pastime.

Here are the materials most useful to the hobby of handicapping Thoroughbreds:

"The Morning Telegraph" or "Racing Form" [INDISPENSABLE]

It is impossible to handicap a field of horses without one of these newspapers. Most players rely exclusively on the individual past-performance records which the papers publish every racing day. Some also keep files of the official result charts which appear in those papers. The charts are far more detailed than past-performance records. They are especially useful in establishing the actual class of competition against which a horse has been competing. As shall be demonstrated later in this book, among three or four horses that have been winning in $5,000 claiming races, one may actually have been defeating animals of decisively superior quality. The result charts show this—and much else that we shall notice in due course.

Because the hobbyist is likely to be an infrequent visitor to the track, he may find the acquisition of official result charts a greater chore and expense than he wants to incur. Rather than buy the *Telegraph* or *Form* every day to get the charts, he may prefer to rely on the past-performance records available on the day he goes to the track. Many winning players survive this way, although it must be assumed that they would win somewhat more if they had access to a file of charts.

Another sort of file is almost mandatory, however. To test the concepts and procedures and selection systems he finds in this book or elsewhere, or generates from his own expanding awareness, the player must have a file of *Telegraphs* or *Forms*. A month of back issues would be good. Six months would be twenty times as good. An angle might show a profit in a month's trial simply by accident. But if it holds up well over a six month's trial, it may be worth trying in real life with real money. Back issues are obtainable from the papers themselves, or from mail-order firms that advertise in racing magazines.

The "American Racing Manual" [IMPORTANT]

Every year this magnificent, encyclopedic by-product of the *Telegraph* and *Form* gives last year's record of every horse, rider, owner, trainer and breeder. Plus track diagrams; track and world speed records; charts of the principal races; lengthy articles summarizing and analyzing the chief developments and accomplishments of the year; tabulations showing who did best in every department of the game; other tabulations showing how often the betting favorites won at every track, and how much purse money was paid out at every track. And several hundred other items, all of keen interest to handicappers.

Magazines [USEFUL]

The most useful are these:

American Turf Monthly, 505 Eighth Avenue, New York, 10018. Frankly addressed to horseplayers, with liberal helpings of the pie-in-the-sky that nourishes their hopes, this monthly contains more handicapping advice than other racing periodicals. Its best column, "Increase Your Horsepower," offers timely inside information about the maneuverings of trainers. Monthly articles by the popular handicapping teacher, Ray Taulbot, cover a wide range of angles and techniques. Every issue contains three or four selection systems, some of which are ingenious enough to merit experimental, self-educational study by the budding player.

Blood-Horse, P.O. Box 1520, Lexington, Kentucky. A splendid weekly that views the game through the eyes of the breeder and will fascinate the player.

Thoroughbred Record, P.O. Box 580, Lexington, Kentucky. Breeding, training, economics, who's doing what. Another well-edited weekly, worth keeping up with.

Turf and Sport Digest, 511-513 Oakland Avenue, Baltimore, 21212. The most valuable section of this monthly lists the fastest recent times at all distances at each track. Also keeps tabs on the winning percentages of public race selectors. In addition, it rates jockeys and horses, publishes feature articles about riders and other horsemen, and produces an occasional selection system, usually with adequate documentation of results. Well worth subscribing to.

Monthly Chart Books [USEFUL]

The official result charts of all races on all American tracks, in convenient book form. Available from Triangle Publications, Inc., 731 Plymouth Court, Chicago, 60605, or 525 West 52 Street, New York, 10019. Triangle is the parent corporation of *Telegraph* and *Form*.

Notebooks [ESSENTIAL]

Written records are the only reliable means of telling whether one's handicapping is good or not. Notebooks provide a continuous record of what you do and how it works. Some players, as we shall see, use notebooks to record daily track variants, or the actual class of every race, or to keep tabs on horses whose imminent improvement has been noticed in the result charts or at the track.

Local Newspapers [USEFUL]

Few papers ever mention handicapping, much less discuss any of its ramifications, but racing columnists often give significant news of horses and horsemen.

Gadgets [DOUBTFUL]

Advertisers peddle a stupefying variety of metal, cardboard and laminated plastic devices, guaranteed to relieve the player of the need to use his own brain. None is a substitute for handicapping. Most are variants of the slide-rule principle, highly simplified to include the two or three or four factors built into the inventor's system. Those that calculate a horse's percentage of winning or in-the-money races may save enough arithmetical effort to seem worthwhile. For fanciers of pace handicapping, Ray Taulbot's Reliable Pace Calculator, sold by Amerpub, Inc., 505 Eighth Avenue, New York 10018, saves a bit of labor.

Binoculars [IMPORTANT]

Most players sit or stand where they can see the track. But few see much of the race except the finish. A good pair of seven- or eight-power binoculars with a wide field enables a well-positioned player to see the entire race. This is fun. It also is informative, because it helps the player to approach the full truth about how his choices run, and how their jockeys ride. To that extent, binoculars improve his handicapping.

Leisure [INDISPENSABLE]

Some experts can learn all they want to know about a day's program of races in less than half an hour with the *Form* or *Telegraph*. Others use more elaborate methods which require as much as an hour of careful study per playable race. No matter where one may stand between these extremes, it is safe to assert that only a player of enormous skill and long experience can do his handicapping in the hustle and bustle of the track. The place to figure the horses is in private, on the morning of the race, or—if the racing paper is available—on the previous night. Even with basic handicapping completed before the trip to the track, the player finds plenty to do while there. Eleventh-hour jockey changes, last-minute scratches, unforeseen changes in weights, and the player's all-important visits to the paddock will keep him more than sufficiently busy.

Daily Track Program [INDISPENSABLE]

Not more than eight out of ten persons at the track buy the program, which costs a quarter. Many of those who save the quarter can be seen forking over a couple of dollars for tip sheets. Anybody who cares to be his own master at the track will want a program. It gives all but the final scratches and jockey changes, offers the track's official guess as to what the odds may be (a guess which influences the odds considerably), and lists the leading trainers and jockeys at the current meeting. Expert players do a good deal of pencil work on their programs. To be at the track without one is like playing golf without a putter.

And now some items that every horseplayer should try to do without.

Bookies

Where bookmaking is legal, or otherwise secure from the cops, a player unable to get to the track may sometimes feel like taking a flyer on a horse. The likelihood that the horse will win is somewhat smaller than if the player were at the track. For one thing, no bet is as sound as it should be until the player has seen the horse and has satisfied himself that it is ready to run. Animals that look great on paper often look awful in the paddock.

But the main problem with bookies is that they usually are on the lam from the law. The day you hit them for $700 is the day they vanish over the state line to avoid arrest. I use the sum of $700 because it happened to me many years ago. The guy was not running out on his debt to me. He was literally running from arrest. I suppose he could have mailed me the money, but this obviously was too much to expect.

In more recent years I have had other problems with bookies. They have refused to take my action after discovering that I was a consistent winner with whom they could not catch up. Others have limited the size of my bets, apparently for the same reason. It is possible that old-time, gentleman bookies still exist, accepting wagers from anyone with good credit and settling accounts once a week. Such operatives used to welcome the trade of a winner. In the first place, they had good and sufficient reason to expect that he might turn out in time to be a loser. Secondly, his success was a nice advertisement for the game. It provided incentive to other players, losers all.

I no longer fool with bookies. The ones I meet nowadays smell of penitentiary. I'd sooner travel seventy-five miles to the nearest track, or stay home and read a book.

Old-time bookie parlor—Harold's Club, Reno, Nevada   MODERN PHOTO

Tip Sheets

As far as I am concerned, this category includes selections published in racing papers, scratch sheets, daily papers and the multicolored leaflets peddled at tracks. It also includes the tips obtainable from "turf consultants" and "information services." As we shall see, none of this information is better than any other. Rather than waste time or money or both, the player should handicap his own horses.

Touts

Although pickpockets have been eliminated from most tracks, touts have not. Many trainers, grooms, stable boys, jockeys, jockeys' agents and track employees supplement their incomes by promoting what are known in the trade as "clients"—persons willing to bet substantial sums for them on horses they recommend. All this hustling of hot information (three quarters of which turns cold after the results are posted) heightens the conspiratorial atmosphere at the track.

Most touts are good enough handicappers to know which four or five horses in a race have the best chances. They "give" one horse to each of four or five tourists. After the race they find the winning sucker and demand the proceeds of a $5 or $10 bet.

Although the small-time tout who buttonholes you at the sandwich stand claims to have intimate stable connections, he almost never does. Even if he did, his information would be of small use, because stable information is itself of small use. Furthermore, while many persons with stable connections supplement their incomes through touting, few would dare to tout a stranger. He might turn out to be a private detective in the pay of the Thoroughbred Racing Associations. At major tracks, the penalty for touting is exile.

A kind of "help" as insidious as that of the tout is the advice given by one's companion at the track. If the player has done his homework and is satisfied, on the basis of past experience, that his selections are as good as anyone else's, he should stick with them. If his companion disagrees, the debate should be resolved by a 25-cent side bet on the race. Occasionally, of course, a trusted friend with superior knowledge and experience can point out a flaw in one's handicapping. That's different.

2 Know the Track

A GOOD HANDICAPPER knows something about horses. A superior handicapper is intimately familiar with the ways of horses, trainers and riders. And he knows his track. On his first visit to a strange track, he is likely to turn up hours before the start of the first race, to get the lay of the land.

Here are some of the things he wants to learn about:

Paddock and Walking Ring

As one race ends, the entrants in the next race are led to their covered paddock stalls for final grooming and saddling. They then go to the walking ring, or parade ring. In nice weather they usually parade around the ring twice with their grooms. After the riders mount (in response to the order, "Riders up!"), the horses walk the ring once or twice more and then amble to the track for another parade in front of the stands, followed by pre-race warm-ups which take them to the starting gate.

The design and location of paddock and walking ring are important to the expert player. He needs to see the animals in their paddock stalls. He also needs to see how they look in the walking ring. At most establishments, paddock and walking rings are behind the stands, necessitating a hike. The player is used to this. In a day at the races, pilgrimages from his seat to various other facilities and points of interest will take him at least six furlongs, some of it at a trot. It's the nature of the game.

If paddock and walking ring are behind the stands, they may be rather widely separated. In any case, it is most unusual to find a single spot that commands an unobstructed view of both. On a first visit, the provident player takes such problems into account. He plans as best he can to see whatever he can of the paddock preliminaries and then get to the walking-ring rail before it becomes hopelessly congested. An expert player may be fat, but he's nimble.

Among other things that may concern the player during the minutes

Walking ring at Aqueduct

between races is the trend of betting, as reflected in the shifting odds. Some tracks put electric odds boards where they can be seen from the walking ring. Others do not. If a player is sufficiently dubious about the condition of his horse to want to see how it warms up before the race, he may have no opportunity to study the odds until the warm-up is over, two or three minutes before post-time. This is ample time. The study can be made while standing on line at the mutuel window, where odds boards are always visible. I mention the matter only to demonstrate that a player is likely to become quite busy during the period immediately preceding a playable race. If he does not know where things are, he may be unable to use his time profitably.

Seats

The expert cases the joint to find out where the best seats are. He knows that there is no such thing as a good seat at a racetrack, but that some seats are better than others. In general, the best possible seat is high enough to afford a clear view of the entire race, and close enough to the finish line to permit an accurate guess as to which nose arrived first. At most tracks the very best seats are in the private boxes of the upper crust. If the regular occupants don't show up, the player can sometimes gain admittance by slipping the usher a couple of dollars. First, of course, he has to pay his way into the clubhouse, a ticket to which usually costs two or three dollars more than the general admission to the grandstand.

For some reason, the reserved sections of the grandstand are often in better locations than any but the choicest private clubhouse boxes. And unreserved grandstand seats are often closer to the finish line than unreserved clubhouse ones. A player who does not mind the wrong side of the tracks is far better off in most grandstands than in most clubhouses. The main advantage of the clubhouse (except on summer Saturdays and holidays) is extra elbowroom. Another advantage is the presence of professional horsemen and other sophisticated regulars, who tend to be quieter and more civil than ordinary players. Still another advantage is the comfort of clubhouse dining rooms and bars. But the grandstand has no worse food at better prices. And, unless you happen to sit next to a maniac, you usually have more privacy in the grandstand. They don't know you. You don't know them. They leave you alone to study your figures. In the clubhouse, where you probably know somebody, you talk. The more you talk, the more you miss.

Be all that as it may, it is an excellent idea to get to the track early on one's first day. See where the finish line is situated relative to the grandstand and clubhouse. Then make decisions about seats.

In this connection, the beginning handicapper will find it an excellent idea to plan to leave his seat for the start of at least one race. It should be a race that starts in front of the stands—at mile tracks that would be a race of a mile, or a mile and one sixteenth, or a mile and an eighth. Go to the infield rail, as close to the starting gate as possible. Listen to the commotion. Watch the assistant starters handle the horses. Watch the riders. Especially watch them as the bell rings and the gate opens. An experience or two of that kind is not only interesting but enlightening. It is amazing how the good "gate boys"—jockeys noted for ability to break swiftly at the start—usually get out on top. Their reputations are deserved.

Another place to go during at least one race is all the way to the left of the spectators' area, where you can lean on the rail and watch the horses race around the final turn, their riders maneuvering for favorable position in the stretch drive. Again, the skill, courage and alertness that distinguish the best riders will be compellingly evident.

Racing Secretary's Office

Most horseplayers have never been near the place. But the expert locates it as soon as he can and makes regular visits thereafter. Here, without cost, he picks up the condition books in which the racing secretary prescribes the terms of entry for every race on every program. A player with a complete file of condition books published by his track during the current season is not quite as well off as a player with a complete file of result charts. But he can at least tell with certainty the quality of opposition today's horses faced in their previous starts at the track. The condition book also helps him decide whether he should come back next Wednesday, or whenever. The book tells him exactly what kind of races will be held on each day. He need not wait until the entries are published in his newspaper.

Other useful information published in some condition books includes the names and riding weights of all active jockeys on the grounds; the track's rules; the proportions in which purses are divided among winners and runners-up; track records, and the dates of forthcoming major races.

At or near this office most tracks have a bulletin board on which items of interest are posted. On a Monday, the board contains the names of horses that worked out on Sunday, and the distances they ran, and the speeds at which they were clocked. Because Monday's racing papers are published on Sunday, they cannot report these workouts. The presence or absence of a horse's name on the Sunday list can be a matter of great significance to the player, as we shall explain in a later chapter.

Shoe Board

At modern tracks, a panel on the infield totalisator board tells what kind of shoes each horse is wearing. Elsewhere, the board may be found tucked away near the paddock, or the racing secretary's office, or under the stands. The expert needs this information, and makes sure to find it.

Tracks in General

In a later section of this book, we shall list the names and distinguishing characteristics of all major American tracks. Let us now make sure that the reader knows how to orient himself when he takes his seat and views the course.

The diagram on the opposite page represents a typical Thoroughbred track, one mile in circumference. From a seat in the grandstand, to the left of the finish wire, the fan sees the tote board. It is the electric sign that shows the amounts bet on each horse for win, place and show, and the approximate odds on each horse to win. The first odds posted, before any money is bet, are those printed in the track program. They comprise "the morning line"—the track handicapper's estimate of what the final odds will be. The estimate is never anything to bank on. The horse named as favorite may or may not become the favorite and may or may not deserve to. But the morning line influences many bettors, some of whom actually believe that the horse listed as favorite is the horse to bet, regardless of where his odds finally roost.

The tote board flashes new betting totals, and revised odds, every 90 seconds until post-time. It also shows the time of day, the number of minutes remaining until post-time, and the condition of the running surface (fast or sloppy or muddy or slow or good or heavy). During the race it shows the times in which early stages of the running are clocked. At the end it gives the final time, the program numbers of the leading horses and, at last, the mutuel prices they paid.

The finish line is not a line. It is an overhead wire. The various poles on the infield rail are named in accordance with the distances between each of them and the finish line. For example, horses run three quarters of a mile (six furlongs) from the three-quarter pole to the finish line. Races are run counterclockwise, of course, which means that they pass the stands from left to right on the homestretch and from right to left on the backstretch.

At a one-mile track, the first pole encountered in a mile race is the fifteen-sixteenths pole—seven and a half furlongs to the wire. Next comes the seven-eighths pole, followed by the six-and-a-half-furlong pole. That pole might as well be called the thirteenth-sixteenths pole, but it isn't. Similarly, the three-quarter pole is never referred to as the six-furlong pole. But the pole situated five eighths of a mile from the finish is called, as the diagram shows, the five-furlong pole! And the four-furlong pole is never, but never, alluded to as the four-furlong pole. It's the *half-mile* pole.

The chute in the upper right corner, near the five-and-a-half-furlong and three-quarter poles, is where races of six, six and a half and seven furlongs start. The long straightaway is easier for the horses, permitting them to settle into stride before having to negotiate turns. The chute at the head of the homestretch is where races of a mile and a quarter start.

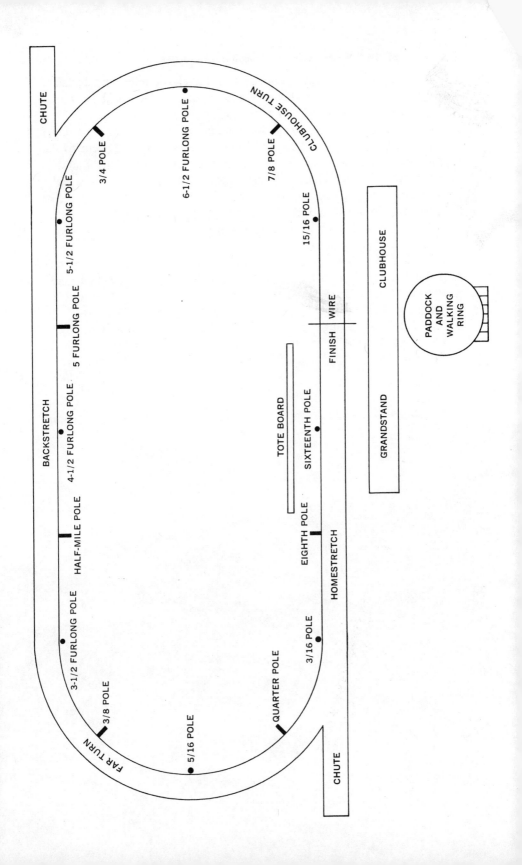

Some tracks are longer or shorter than the classic mile. The distances of races run out of their chutes therefore vary. Full particulars will be found on pages 255–258.

Nowadays, the better tracks are running more races on grass (turf races) than ever before. The turf course is customarily adjacent to the inner perimeter of the regular track. This means that the turf course is always shorter, with sharper turns. Tracks that hold hurdle or steeplechase races sometimes run them over the turf course. But places like Aqueduct, Saratoga and Delaware Park have separate jumping tracks.

If your track is on the following list, it is a mile track, and looks very much like the diagram on page 31:

Ak-Sar-Ben, Bay Meadows, Beulah Park, Bowie, Caliente, Centennial, Churchill Downs, Delaware Park, Del Mar, Detroit, Fair Grounds, Fairmount Park, Finger Lakes, Florida Downs, Fort Erie, Fresno, Garden State, Golden Gate, Gulfstream, Hawthorne, Hollywood Park, Las Vegas, Latonia, Longacres, Monmouth Park, Narragansett Park, Oaklawn Park, Pikes Peak Meadows, Pimlico, Pleasanton, Portland Meadows, Randall, River Downs, Rockingham Park, Sacramento, Santa Anita,

The stretch at Aqueduct   PAUL SCHAFER—NEW YORK RACING ASSN.

Start of the Futurity in 1902 at Sheepshead Bay **JAMES HOLMES**

The world's largest window encloses the stands at Laurel. **UPI PHOTO**

Stockton, Suffolk Downs, Sunland Park, Thistledown, Tropical Park, Turf Paradise, Woodbine, Yakima Meadows.

The following tracks are a mile and an eighth in length:

Aqueduct, Arlington Park, Atlantic City, James C. Ellis Park, Hialeah, Laurel, Saratoga.

The Bull Rings

The major tracks in the United States are those that attract the best stables and jockeys by paying the largest purses. All major American tracks are at least a mile in length. Some minor tracks are also a mile or more in length, but most are shorter. The short ones are known to horsemen as "bull rings," because of the sharpness of their turns. Some, like Shenandoah Downs in West Virginia, offer more comfortable seating, more courteous service and better food than one finds at most major tracks. Although the quality of their horseflesh is inferior, the better minor tracks offer races as formful and honest as can be found anywhere. A good handicapper can keep body and soul together at a half-mile oval. An indifferent handicapper is in trouble wherever he goes.

3 The Arithmetic of Racing

THE HANDICAPPER attempts to unravel a multitude of factors. Some are clear, some obscure. But each relates to all the others in ways that vary from horse to horse, race to race and day to day.

Because the raw materials are numerous, changeable and deceptive, handicapping is a highly personal kind of approximation, closer to an art than to an exact science. Which is why the predictions of experts coincide only part of the time.

Two good handicappers may often play the same horse in the same race. Both may refrain from betting on certain other races. Some races find one of them betting and the other with his wallet buttoned. And, without fail, they frequently bet against each other—picking different horses in the same race. Even if they try to employ identical methods, they reach less than identical conclusions. Differences of this kind are, of course, the fascinating hallmark of any great game.

I enjoyed a demonstration of handicapping's personal aspects after people began reading *The Compleat Horseplayer*. Letters of thanks arrived from racing enthusiasts throughout the United States. Many claimed to have achieved unprecedented success, for which they credited the book. Some of their feats made me drool. Longshots! A Chicagoan gave *The Compleat Horseplayer* full marks for a winner that had paid him more than $90 on a $2 mutuel ticket. I was almost tempted to inquire how he had done it. I have never picked a $90 winner in my life.

Obviously the procedure so painstakingly described in *The Compleat Horseplayer* had been modified by the individual mentality. Some readers had become capable of turning up bonanzas of a magnitude quite beyond my own grasp. No doubt the same readers had also been backing more losers than I could possibly tolerate.

I make these observations about the personal, non-scientific nature of handicapping for several reasons. The first and most urgent is that the reader should harbor no illusions. No matter what theory of handicapping may strike him as most plausible, he will be attempting to predict the future by interpreting past events of uncertain character and inexact significance. Yet his survival at the track will demand predictions of considerable accuracy.

Beating the Percentages

If certainty about the past is so limited, must not certainty about the future be terribly slight? How can anyone wrench a profit from such confusion?

By dealing in probabilities. Or, as they say at the track, working *with* the percentages instead of against them.

It so happens that the old saw "You can beat a race, but you can't beat the races," is quite wrong. It turns reality upside down. The truth is that nobody can be sure of beating an individual race, but lots of people win more money than they lose in a season's activity at the track. There is nothing unusual about this. In any game worth playing, the outcome of any one play (any one race) is rarely a matter of absolute certainty. But someone who plays well finishes ahead in the long run.

Take poker as an example. No matter how expert the player, nothing short of a royal flush provides complete certainty of a winning bet. The expert is lucky if he holds one royal flush in forty years of play. In other words, he can't necessarily beat the race. But he is an expert and he makes out fine, losing a little, winning a little more. He beats the game.

Let us suppose that our poker expert competes with six of his peers in a game of jackpots. After he has been at the table with these sharpers a few times he knows a great deal about their courage, wiles and weaknesses. He undoubtedly knows more about them than any handicapper can know about a field of horses. The usefulness of this knowledge varies from session to session, of course. In poker, last week's tabby is this week's tiger, his mood having modified his style for the time being. A further limitation on the expert's success is that his opponents also are experts and know a good deal about *his* style.

In the end, therefore, the poker expert's main armor against all uncertainties is his knowledge of the game itself—more particularly, his knowledge of the *percentages* that give the game its central character. As long as he is faithful to the laws—the probabilities—embodied in these percentages, he seldom loses. And, when he combines knowledge of the probabilities with accurate guesses about the tactics of his opponents, he becomes a big winner.

Allow me to pursue the matter further. By reminding the reader how the percentages are used in poker, I hope to whet his appetite for discussion of the less familiar, but equally important percentages of racing.

A 52-card poker deck contains slightly less than 2.6 million five-card hands. The exact probability of drawing any specific hand is a matter of established mathematical knowledge. So is the exact probability of improving any hand on the draw. If the expert has a chance to convert his hand into a straight by discarding one card and drawing either a nine or an ace, will he bet the money required for the gamble? It all depends.

He knows that the odds against drawing either an ace or nine are 5 to 1. He may draw the right card and lose the pot to someone who holds a flush or a full house. But he will win in the long run on hands of this kind if he respects the percentages of the game. He will win in the long run if he stays with such a hand *only* when the pot promises to pay him *at least* five times the money he bets. If he draws to the bobtail straight on occasions when the pot pays less than a 5 to 1 gamble should, he eventually will lose. Winning one such hand in every six or seven he plays, he will take in less money than he spends on the losing ones.

Identical principles apply to horseplaying. Certain percentages are as cut-and-dried in racing as in cards, and deserve comparable respect. They occur with astonishing uniformity, year after year. They affect the handicapper's choice of horse. They affect the size and frequency of his bets.

What is more, racing is so patterned that a handicapper's own methods are certain to embody percentages of their own. If his methods are consistent (regardless of whether they are profitable or not), they turn up winning horses at a rate that fluctuates hardly at all from one year to the next. Likewise, his annual rate of profit or loss on each invested dollar varies but slightly from year to year. He may encounter long losing streaks and incredible strings of winners, but in the end his handicapping settles at its own percentage level. When he knows this percentage, and the accompanying rate of profit or loss, he is able to judge the efficiency of his methods. He remains uncertain about the outcome of any individual bet, but he knows with considerable certainty that, in due course, he can expect to win a predictable minimum percentage of bets, with a predictable minimum profit or loss per invested dollar.

A life insurance company does the same kind of thing on an incomparably larger scale. It hitches its treasury to the laws of probability. It does not have the vaguest idea when you will die. But it knows, within the practical limits of earthly certainty, the percentage of people your age who will die this year, or next, or twelve years from now. It designs its premium rates accordingly. In the long run its books show a predictable percentage of "winners" and a predictable rate of profit.

Although good handicappers are respectfully attentive to the established percentages of the game, and to the percentages achieved by their own methods, handicapping is not necessarily a mathematical pastime. Some of the best handicappers use pencil and paper only to cross out the names of horses they think will lose. Other good handicappers do simple arithmetic, but not much of it. Still others devise rather elaborate arithmetical formulas in an attempt to introduce reassuring order into the hodgepodge of information with which they deal. Whatever style is most appealing to the individual, he needs no mathematical skill beyond the ability to add, subtract, multiply and divide.

Even the numbers contained in this chapter need not be committed to memory. Far more important than the numbers are the conclusions they permit about the nature of the game.

The Magic Number

Anybody who bets $1,000 on the races and emerges from the experience with less than $830 is doing something dreadfully wrong. A $2 bettor who selected horses with a hatpin, or by using numerology, or by consulting tea leaves, would almost certainly lose no more than $170 in a series of 500 bets—an investment of $1,000.

It is, of course, more than theoretically possible to go broke at the track. Desperate gamblers do it every day. And victims of inefficient selection methods or wasteful betting systems also manage to run out of cash long before they should.

The shortest route to disaster is to bet too much of one's money at a time. The man with a $1,000 bankroll who plays it all on one horse has a splendid chance of losing it all. The man who bets the $1,000 in five installments of $200 each also risks extinction: In any given series of five bets, no handicapper on earth can be sure of winning so much as one!

How, then, can a less-than-expert player expect to have $830 left after betting $1,000?

The magic number is 17.

Without knowing the slightest thing about horses, and betting entirely at random, the player's long-term losses should not exceed 17 percent of the total amount he bets. To limit his losses to that extent, he need only bet in amounts small enough to assure himself of a large, representative number of bets.

It works like this. Of all money bet on any race, most tracks deduct approximately 17 percent for taxes and their own revenue. The remaining 83 percent is disbursed to the holders of winning mutuel tickets.

This means that, regardless of how the individual player fares with his bet, the crowd as a whole loses 17 percent of its wagered dollar on every race, every day, every week, every year. A random bettor, playing horses at random, should do no worse. A selection system employing daisy petals or playing cards or dice or something else entirely unrelated to handicapping should leave the bettor with close to 83 percent of his wagered money after a series of 500 or more bets.

Any handicapping procedure that results in seasonal losses as high as 17 percent of all money wagered is, therefore, no better than the hatpin method. And anyone who loses more than 17 cents of every dollar he bets in a season is—whether he realizes it or not—going out of his way to find trouble.

The 17 percent "take" of racetracks has been compared unfavorably with the smaller levies imposed by gambling houses. A roulette player, for instance, should lose only slightly more than a nickel of each dollar he bets, assuming that the computation is made after a long, representative series of plays. The difference between roulette and racing is, however, a considerable one. The wheel spins every few seconds, all night. The roulette fanatic makes hundreds of bets in one session. No matter how conservatively he bets, the house "take" of 5 percent-plus nibbles away at his capital, and he finally has nothing left.

But the horseplayer encounters only nine races a day, and a daily double. If he confines his wagering to the smallest possible fraction of his betting capital, he might play for months or years before emptying his pocket. For example, a man who allocates $200 to racetrack wagering, and bets $2 on every race, should have about $114 left after going to the track for 28 days. He might have much more or much less, but the track "take" *should* siphon off only $86 or so from the 252 bets he makes. And, if he knows absolutely nothing about the horses and makes no attempt to learn, he very probably will do just about that well.

It follows that anything useful he learns about the horses should enable him to begin reducing the percentage of loss. In this chapter we shall see how he can begin to reduce that percentage merely by learning some of the probabilities of the game, and without learning a thing about horses themselves!

Betting on Favorites

An infallible guide to the reliability or intelligence, or both, of a racing expert is his attitude toward persons who bet on favorites. All experts know that, in a representatively large sample of races, one of every three will be won by the betting favorite—the horse on which the most money is bet. The conclusions various writers achieve in light of this statistic are a dead giveaway to their knowledge of probabilities. Anyone ignorant of probabilities is not only unable to evaluate his own chances at the track but is hopelessly unqualified to advise anyone else.

It is fashionable to sneer at "chalk players"—the conservative types who play nothing but favorites. Observing that favorites win only one third of the time, many sages proclaim, with flawless arithmetic, that the crowd is wrong two thirds of the time. They insist that the secret of success at the track is to part company with the crowd, avoid favorites and, presumably, begin winning a lion's share of the two races in three which find the crowd wrong. Such advise is crude nonsense. Whatever truth it contains is strictly coincidental.

Any child will understand the reason for this, after a few facts are set forth. At major tracks, the typical race involves nine horses. This means that about 80 horses go to the post on a representative day. The crowd picks nine of these animals as betting favorites. Three of the nine win. Anyone who thinks it easier to find winners among 71 non-favorites than among nine favorites is thinking backwards.

The fact that non-favorites win two thirds of all races does not mean that non-favorites have twice as good a chance of winning as favorites do. Quite the contrary. Until we handicap the entire field and see which horse is probably the best of the lot (a task few players can perform), we know nothing about the non-favorite except that it is one of eight non-favorites in the race. But we know more than that about the favorite. We know that it wins one race in three. This means that the "natural" odds against it are 2 to 1. But the "natural" odds against a random non-favorite in a nine-horse race are 11 to 1! (This figure is obtained by the statistical process of dividing the number of races that non-favorites win ($\frac{2}{3}$) by the number of non-favorites (8).)

We now have established that it is foolish to reject a horse simply because it is the favorite, or to stab at another horse simply because it is a non-favorite. We therefore are in better position to appreciate some interesting statistics. We begin with a blazer:

To cut the magic number of 17 just about in half and bring one's losses within striking distance of the break-even point, one need only confine one's bets to horses that are the favorites in their races!

Several years ago, the resourceful Robert V. Rowe studied a series of 7,301 races. He reported in *American Turf Monthly* that a bet on each of the favorites would have produced a loss of 8.4 percent for each dollar wagered. More recently, Burton P. Fabricand studied 10,035 races and came up with a closely similar figure. In a highly original book —*Horse Sense,** proposing a mathematical approach to the game— Fabricand writes that a flat bet on each favorite would have lost the player nine cents per dollar.

Many selection systems, including Fabricand's and several that I describe later in this book, attempt to convert the 9 percent loss into a profit by applying handicapping principles to the past-performance records of favorites. Because the starting point of such systems finds the player only a hop and a skip from profit's promised land, they are among the best possible procedures for persons unacquainted with the game.

Fabricand found that bets on favorites paying extremely short prices (1 to 2 or less) resulted in a small profit. On such wagers, it would seem that the magic number is reduced to zero or thereabouts before a bit of actual handicapping has been undertaken.

In Praise of the Crowd

I have just said some harsh things about experts who base their theories on disdain for the judgment of the crowd. I have showed that the crowd as a whole does a better job of conserving its money than is likely to be done by someone who refuses in any circumstances to agree with the crowd. The object of this book is, nevertheless, to equip the player to surpass the crowd by means of expert handicapping.

The next step in that direction is to analyze a second accomplishment of the crowd. Insiders have long known that, even though the crowd loses 17 cents on the dollar, it does a rather remarkable job of handicapping. If it bets in such proportions as to make a horse a 3 to 1 shot, that horse is more likely to win than the animal that goes off at 4 to 1. Putting it another way, any long series of 5 to 2 shots will win a higher percentage of races for the bettor than a comparable series of horses that run at higher odds.

Fabricand's study of more than 10,000 races included 93,011 horses. Classifying the animals according to the mutuel prices at which they ran,

* (David McKay Company, New York, $5.95.)

he found the following percentages of winners:

Mutuel Price Range	Percentage of Starts Won	Mutuel Price Range	Percentage of Starts Won
Up to 3.10	71.3	10.00–10.90	16.1
3.20– 3.50	55.3	11.00–11.90	15.5
3.60– 3.90	51.3	12.00–13.90	12.3
4.00– 4.30	47.0	14.00–15.90	11.0
4.40– 4.70	40.3	16.00–17.90	9.9
4.80– 5.10	37.9	18.00–19.90	8.2
5.20– 5.50	35.5	20.00–21.90	8.2
5.60– 5.90	30.9	22.00–31.90	6.0
6.00– 6.90	28.9	32.00–41.90	4.0
7.00– 7.90	23.0	42.00 up	1.4
8.00– 8.90	20.9		
9.00– 9.90	18.6		

The lower the odds, the greater the likelihood that the horse will win.

Fabricand also demonstrates that it is impossible to turn a profit by playing *all* horses in a given odds range. The very shortest-priced horses on his list earned an insignificant profit when played in that way. But all other odds ranges showed a loss.

However, some important lessons are to be learned from the percentages of loss in each odds range:

1. The largest single group of horses on the list were the 25,044 animals that went off at odds of 20 to 1 or more (mutuel prices of $42 and up). A bet on each of those longshots would have meant a loss of 54 cents on every wagered dollar, even though 340 winning tickets would have been cashed!

2. The odds ranges below 5 to 2 (mutuel prices below $7) yielded losses that clustered around 6 percent of the wagered dollar.

3. Only on horses at 5 to 1 and higher did the percentage losses exceed the magic number of 17.

4. These results, mind you, were based on uncritical wagering without recourse to handicapping. The sole basis for the paper bet was the odds at which the horse left the starting gate.

It now is possible to modify an earlier statement about the quality of a handicapping procedure that loses as much as 17 percent. A player not only would do far better to play all favorites indiscriminately, but would do still better if he picked himself an odds range below 2 to 1 and played all horses that fell into that range! He would find himself betting on about half of all races, and would lose only 7 percent of his money in the long run.

If he took the trouble to learn handicapping, he could then move in one of two directions. He could become more sensibly selective about the horses in his pet odds range. Or he could become more selective about horses in general, betting on apparently promising horses regardless of their odds. The test of his method would now be whether or not his bets yielded a loss smaller than 7 percent. His glee at cashing an occasional longshot ticket would remain provisional until he had balanced his books for the season. To hit the dreamed-of longshot or two and end with a loss of 21 cents on the dollar, as many players do, is to carry enjoyment past the point of diminishing returns. For anyone but a person with unlimited means and an uncontrollable yen to gamble, a procedure of that kind is downright foolish.

What Kind of Favorites?

Numerous players believe that certain kinds of races are more formful than others. That is, they believe that the favorites win a substantially higher percentage of one kind of race than of another, producing smaller dollar losses. Statistical surveys that appear to demonstrate the truth of such theories are all based on inadequate studies. More extensive samplings, such as Fabricand's and Robert Rowe's, show that the percentage of winning favorites remains essentially the same in all types of races, and that the profit or loss in each odds range does not vary significantly according to the quality of the race itself.

To show how inflexible the percentages of the game really are, I have just surveyed the results of all races that paid purses of $30,000 or more during 1965. Of the 215 races of that high quality, the favorites won 39 percent. A $2 bet on each favorite would have netted the player a loss of about 8 percent on his wagered dollars. Which is where we came in.

Extra Ways To Lower the Magic Number

Here are some other well-established statistics that enable a player unacquainted with handicapping to keep his long-term losses below 17 percent:

1. Favorites at even money or less produce losses of about 4 percent when bet to win.
2. Odds-on favorites cost about 1 percent when bet to show.
3. All favorites to place cost about 4 percent.
4. Odds-on favorites in major handicaps, stakes races and featured allowance races at major tracks throw off a *profit* of almost 5 percent

when bet to place. This exception to all other rules occurs too infrequently to mean very much in the way of riches, but is worth knowing about. It happens because the horses involved are animals of the highest grade, and seldom run worse than second.

And here is something borne in mind by expert players. It may induce non-experts to brush up on their handicapping: If a handicapper's methods customarily yield about one winner in every three attempts, the "natural" odds against any single one of his selections are about 2 to 1. Therefore, when his handicapping points out a horse running at odds of 4 to 1, he is in an enviable situation. The percentages of the game are with him. His position is comparable to that of the poker player who draws to a bobtail straight when he knows that the pot will pay more than the necessary 5 to 1 odds.

The word "overlay" is heard constantly at the tracks. It describes an animal that runs at higher odds than its winning chances would seem to call for. The very best kind of overlay is the horse we have just discussed—picked by the methods of a competent handicapper, and running at odds more than sufficient to repay the handicapper for the losing bets he makes.

Attainable Results

A successful handicapper with a prejudice against betting on favorites is forced to refrain from betting until he finds a race in which the favorite seems undeserving. He then must be able to find a non-favorite that seems clearly superior to the other entrants.

Another successful handicapper, with no prejudice against favorites, must avoid betting on too many favorites that lose, and must bet on a certain number of winning non-favorites, or he will show no profit.

Regardless of the individual's handicapping style, the percentages of the game govern his results. Generally speaking, the more often he bets on longshots, the less often he wins. And the more often he bets on low-priced horses, the more often he wins. But his rate of profit—the only meaningful index to his success—depends on whether he wins enough bets at prices high enough to compensate for his losses.

It has long been taken for granted in racing that a first-class handicapper can win about four bets in ten if he is extremely conservative, bets on relatively few races, and favors horses whose odds average about 2 to 1. Such a level of play brings a profit of about 20 cents for every dollar he bets, increasing his capital at a tremendous rate. For example, if his capital is $2,000 and he makes an average of two $100 bets a day

for 200 racing days (spread over a period of years, perhaps), his operations return a profit of $8,000, enlarging his capital to $10,000.

A great deal of garbage is published about the 100 percent profits
allegedly yielded by one or another winning system. In every instance,
the high profits were earned (if indeed they were earned at all), over
periods of time too short for significance. During the week of success at
Monmouth Park that I recorded in *The Compleat Horseplayer,* my rate
of profit was 92 cents on the invested dollar. Profits of that magnitude
are entirely beyond reach over the long haul. If I had stayed at Monmouth for the following week I might well have suffered a shellacking.

My usual rate of profit over a period of years has been closer to 30
percent. I employ the word "usual" in a loose sense. Since most of my
excursions to the track are for recreation and do not involve grimly
serious handicapping, the records on which I base the 30 percent statistic are the records of days such as those at Monmouth Park, when the
sole object was to win dough. When I go to the track to laugh and play
and get a sunburned nose, I consider myself extremely lucky to break
even.

Be that as it may, the percentage of the game and the limits of human
capability seem to limit long-range profits to something like 40 cents on
the dollar. A more easily attainable rate would be about 20.

Some handicappers hint that through careful selection of their spots
they manage to win half of all their bets. I suppose this is possible, but
whether it is possible to turn a good profit by doing it is another matter.
A far more realistic objective for the handicapper is a bet-winning
average in the range of 30 to 40 percent, with mutuel prices high enough
for profit.

The reader will be rewarded by a few moments with the following
figures.

To earn a rate of profit of 20 cents on the wagered dollar, a handicapper must:

1. Win half of all his bets, at average odds not lower than 7 to 5, or
2. Win 40 percent of his bets, at average odds of 2 to 1, or
3. Win a third of his bets, at average odds of 13 to 5, or
4. Win 30 percent of his bets, at average odds of 3 to 1.

Anyone who hopes to do twice that well, earning profits at the rate of 40 cents on the wagered dollar, must:

1. Win half of all his bets, at average odds of 9 to 5, or
2. Win 40 percent of all his bets, at average odds of 5 to 2, or
3. Win a third of his bets, at average odds of more than 3 to 1, or
4. Win 30 percent of his bets, at average odds exceeding 7 to 2.

Any of the formulas in those two lists is at least theoretically attainable. But the practicalities of the game, and of human self-control, suggest that the beginning handicapper deserves a medal if he can achieve results in the neighborhood of items 2 and 3 on the first of the lists. If he does that well, he will be able to buy his own medal.

Public Selectors

Among the personalities at the track, few are more colorful than the human foghorns who peddle tip sheets to the crowd. Posted in booths directly inside the entrance gates, they use every form of persuasion but gun, knife and fist. The walls of the booths are plastered with yesterday's editions of their sheets. The names of the winning horses are encircled, their mutuel prices scrawled in heavy ink.

It so happens that some (not many) of the men who publish the tip sheets are topnotch handicappers. It also happens that none of the sheets is worth a damn to the player.

The better sheets can claim with accuracy that they "name" the winners of about half of the races. But "naming" winners is different from picking winners. The sheets *name* as many as four horses per race. Let any of the named horses win and the sheet claims a success for itself.

A player interested in knowing which three or four horses are regarded by one or another expert as the livest in each race can get information of comparable quality from the selection pages of *The Morning Telegraph* or *Daily Racing Form,* and from the handicaps published in newspapers of general circulation.

The weakness of all such advice is that no handicapper can show a profit if he attempts to pick the winner of every race on the card. The best proof of this is that no public selector ever shows a long-term profit. Furthermore, even when the public selector attempts to pick a "Best Bet"—the likeliest horse on the entire program—he also fails to show a profit. He may be a fine handicapper, but two obstacles defeat him. The first is that he picks his "best bet" before the horses have entered the paddock, and he therefore misses the essential opportunity to check their pre-race condition. An equally important reason is that his "best bets" become popular choices and pay woefully low mutuel prices. The prices they pay when they win are insufficient to counterbalance the losses.

I have before me the January, 1967, issue of *Turf and Sport Digest.* It shows that anyone who had bet on every favorite at all tracks from March 15 to November 15, 1966, would have cashed 33 percent of his bets and lost 9 percent of every dollar he bet. These figures, as we

THE ARITHMETIC OF RACING 47

already know, are par for the course. The most successful public selector on the *Digest* list during that lengthy period was "Trackman," who is not an individual but an assemblage of *Telegraph* and *Form* experts, each of whom is posted at a track. Trackman's selections were correct 25 percent of the time. His longest losing streak was 30. Repeat, 30 losers in a row for the most successful group of selections on the list.

The loss suffered by anyone who bet on each of Trackman's choices was 11.5 percent. To have played the choices of others among the surveyed public selectors would have meant losses ranging as high as 19 cents on the wagered dollar, after suffering as many as 33 losers in succession.

I observed earlier that anyone who loses more than 17 cents on the dollar is going out of his way to find trouble. The losses recorded season after season by the nation's most able public selectors seldom exceed the magic percentage of 17, but come close enough. They prove the absolute impossibility of profiting from an attempt to pick a winner in every race.

The disadvantages of trying to pick a "best bet" on the day before its race are equally clear. Trackman, the 1966 champion at handicapping entire programs, was correct on only 35 percent of his "best bets." To have played each of them would have meant a loss of 16.5 cents per dollar. By far the top picker of "best bets" during that period was the handicapper known as Reigh Count. Only 27 percent of his spot selections won, but they paid enough to produce a net loss of but 3.5 cents for every dollar bet on them.

Numerous selection systems, including some to be reviewed in this book, apply handicapping angles to the choices of public selectors. The percentages discussed in this chapter suggest rather strongly that the player would do better with similar systems that concentrate on favorites, inasmuch as favorites lose less money to begin with than newspaper and tip-sheet selections do.

Beware the Law of Averages

Statisticians and others acquainted with the laws of probability try, wherever possible, to measure situations in precise terms. They know that averages are misleading. The classic example is of the man who needs to cross a river. Having learned that the average depth is only five feet, and being six feet tall, he tries to wade across. In midstream he sinks like a stone and drowns. A river can be 12 feet deep at midstream and still have an average depth of only five.

Or take the following series of numbers: 1, 2, 3, 4, 5, 6, 7, 8, 9, 75.

The average of those numbers is 12. But, if the numbers represent the results of something or other—like the odds paid by a series of racing selections—the average distorts reality. Nine of the ten horses ran at odds of 9 or less, yet the striker of averages stumbles around under the delusion that he can expect an "average" return of about 12 on his next series of ten winners. Unless the horse that returned 75—and threw the average out of whack—was a normal, predictable, usual selection, a statistician would prefer to say that the *median* of the series was between 5 and 6. In other words, he would look for the point that falls midway in the series. Five of the numbers in this series were 6 or more. The other five were 5 or less. The median is, therefore, around 5.5. Which ain't 12.

In the handicapping of Thoroughbred horses it is essential to remember the illusory nature of averages. To give an extreme example, the player sometimes encounters a horse that has won over $100,000 in twenty starts—an average of about $5,000 per race. No other animal in the race may show winnings close to that average. To decide that the $100,000 horse is the classiest in the race might be a mistake. It might have won most of its $100,000 in one race last year and have won not a dime since. Indeed, it might have won only two races in its entire career. Another horse in today's race, with average earnings of only $3,000, might have an enormous edge in current class and condition.

Knowing that averages can never be more than rough yardsticks, the good handicapper makes them work for him. He looks beyond them.

Above all, he pays no heed whatsoever to the racetrack superstition known as "the law of averages."

Example: If favorites win one of every three races, and nine races in succession have been won by non-favorites, it is incorrect to suppose that the favorite in the tenth race has a better than ordinary chance to win. The favorite is *not* "due." Aside from what the handicapper may think of the animal's quality, which is quite another matter, its status as a favorite tells only one thing about its winning chances. That one thing is a generality: In the long run, favorites win one race out of three.

But the long run is often a *long* one. Persons who base their play on the inevitability of victory by favorites sometimes increase the amount of their bets after every loss. They lose more than they should. In fact, if they go the route of doubling their bets after each loss, they end in ruin.

It is not unusual for favorites to lose ten races in succession. At Aqueduct during 1966, there was a losing series of 13. At other tracks the losing streaks ran as high as 20. The man who bets $2 on a favorite, loses it, bets $4 on the next, and $8 on the next and continues to double up in hope that the favorite is "due" will have parted with $1,022 after nine successive losses. He will be required to bet another $1,024 on the next race, if he has it. His bet might drive the odds down from the usual 3 to 2 to something like even money. If the horse wins, which is by no means inevitable, the bettor emerges with a profit of $2 on an investment of $2,046.

The law of averages is equally meaningless in connection with the performances of jockeys. Willie Shoemaker and Braulio Baeza may win more than 20 percent of their starts every year, but they also lose as many as 50 races in succession while doing it.

Similarly, the handicapper's carefully recorded knowledge that his selections win almost twice in every five attempts is poor grounds for an assumption that seven losers in a row will be followed by an immediate winner. Or that seven winners in a row make the next selection a sure loser.

Another even more harmful product of this kind of misunderstanding occurs at every track every day. A longshot wins a race. A disappointed bettor consults his *Form* and discovers that the longshot had been timed at 36 seconds in a breezing three-furlong workout a couple of days ago. No other horse in the race had worked so rapidly so recently. Powie! A new system is born! The player now loses eight bets in a row on horses whose records contain that particular workout angle.

Or a player reads a system that seems plausible, tries it on paper for a week and discovers to his delight that it picks eight winners in sixteen attempts for a profit of $1.45 on every hypothetical dollar bet. So he takes it to the track and it hits one winner in the next sixteen races, for a monumental loss. He now discards it. But it might actually be a good system. His first mistake was to assume that it was good without sufficient evidence. His second mistake was to risk money on it. His third was to discard it without sufficient evidence.

To summarize, it is not possible to determine probabilities without a large, representative series of cases. One robin doesn't make a spring. And, even after the probabilities are determined, they remain nothing but long-range probabilities. In no way do they guarantee the outcome of a single, isolated event. Nor do they guarantee the outcome of any short series of events. The feeblest handicapper enjoys winning days and winning weeks. The only inevitability in his situation is that he will end as a heavy loser if he persists in his usual methods. And the best handicapper suffers losing days and weeks, but recovers the ground

OPPOSITE: *Hedley Woodhouse boots one home at Gulfstream.* UPI PHOTO

Dr. Fager and Manuel Ycaza easily win the $100,000 Jersey Derby at Garden State in 1967, only to be disqualified. Second horse, In Reality, was declared the victor.

UPI PHOTO

Kelso, under Milo Valenzuela, beats Gun Bow in the 1964 Washington D.C. International at Laurel. UPI PHOTO

if his methods remain sensible and he plays in his usual style.

As I have insisted before, and as may seem more agreeable by this time, you can't necessarily beat a race, but you may be able to beat the races. To do so you will have to overcome the unfavorable percentages of the game. You will have to confine your play to situations in which (1) your handicapping knowledge tells you that an animal has an especially good chance to win and (2) the gross returns on your winning bets are more than sufficient to repair your losses.

The House Percentage

Our poker player holds four diamonds and a spade. The odds against exchanging the spade for another diamond are 4 to 1. If it has cost $1 to stay in the game until now, and will cost another $1 to discard the spade and draw a new card, he will do so, provided that the total pot contains at least $10. If he succeeds in getting his flush, it probably will win the pot. And the pot—at least $4 of their money to every $1 of his—will more than compensate for the risk.

Suppose, however, that every time the player won a pot, the owner of the card table extracted a cut of about 20 percent of the money? The odds against drawing the flush would remain 4 to 1. But the player no longer would be able to break even on such gambles unless the pots offered at least 5 to 1.

Chances are the player would look elsewhere for a poker game. Or, if this were the only game in town, he would revise his methods. He would play much more conservatively. He would incur fewer risks. Where winning probabilities decrease, losses become more costly, more difficult to overcome.

This is exactly what has happened in Thoroughbred racing. Notwithstanding the unfragrance of old-time racing, when pari-mutuel machines were unheard of, a good handicapper enjoyed idyllic advantages. For instance, he often could get 5 to 2 from a track bookmaker on a horse that finally went off at 9 to 5. Nowadays, he would get no more than 3 to 2 on the same horse, because the house keeps a lot of the money for itself. The arithmetic is worth noting; certain bets on which the player used to make $5 in profit now yield him only $3. His profit on a bet of that kind has been reduced by 40 percent. Or, looking at it another way, that profit used to be 67 percent higher than it is now. He therefore plays much more conservatively now. He has to. The house cuts every pot with a cleaver.

The principle of pari-mutuel betting is eminently fair. The odds paid by the winning horse are—in principle—the ratio between the amount

The Tote Board and the Price

This table shows the mutuel prices represented by the figures posted on racetrack odds boards. Horses posted at 4 to 5 or higher may pay more than the minimum mutuel price, but they never pay less. The computations are revised at frequent intervals until post-time.

Odds	Price	Odds	Price	Odds	Price
1-9	$2.20	2-1	$6.00	18-1	$38.00
1-8	2.20	5-2	7.00	19-1	40.00
1-7	2.20	3-1	8.00	20-1	42.00
1-6	2.20	7-2	9.00	21-1	44.00
1-5	2.40	4-1	10.00	22-1	46.00
1-4	2.40	9-2	11.00	23-1	48.00
1-3	2.60	5-1	12.00	24-1	50.00
2-5	2.80	6-1	14.00	25-1	52.00
1-2	3.00	7-1	16.00	30-1	62.00
3-5	3.20	8-1	18.00	35-1	72.00
3-4	3.40	9-1	20.00	40-1	82.00
4-5	3.60	10-1	22.00	45-1	92.00
1-1	4.00	11-1	24.00	50-1	102.00
6-5	4.40	12-1	26.00	60-1	122.00
7-5	4.80	13-1	28.00	75-1	152.00
3-2	5.00	14-1	30.00	99-1	200.00
8-5	5.20	15-1	32.00		
9-5	5.60	16-1	34.00		
		17-1	36.00		

of money bet on it and the amount bet on all the losers.

Theoretically, if members of the crowd bet $30,000 on Horse "A" and other players bet a total of $60,000 on all other horses in the race, "A" is a 2 to 1 shot (60 to 30). The mutuel price should be $6, representing the bettor's original $2 plus a $4 profit. In actuality, "A" pays nothing like $6. At Aqueduct it pays only $5, having been cut from 2 to 1 to 3 to 2 by the house and the state. Elsewhere it might pay $5.20. But nowhere does it pay $6.

The house deductions are called take and breakage. They finance track operations and provide tax revenues to the state and other governments. Tracks need funds with which to pay purses, hire employees and keep themselves spruce. Governments are undoubtedly entitled to a slice, too. It would be idle to deplore any of this. But certain trends are questionable.

At Aqueduct, for example, the State of New York makes off with more than twice as much of the take and breakage as the track does. Indeed the tendency throughout racing is toward more state taxation, which means higher deductions from betting pools and less profit for the winning bet. Racing editorialists frequently mention the man who killed the goose that laid the golden egg. Sounds plausible. The betting handle at Aqueduct began to decline in 1965, when the latest increase in state levies made it harder than ever for a player to beat the percentages.

The accompanying chart shows what happens to the natural profits of a winning bet at Aqueduct or Saratoga. Charts for other tracks would differ only slightly.

The Big Bite

Natural Odds	Natural Mutuel Price	N.Y. Mutuel Price	Reduction of Profit (%)
7-1	$16.00	$13.60	16
6-1	14.00	11.80	18
5-1	12.00	10.20	18
4-1	10.00	8.40	20
3-1	8.00	6.80	20
2-1	6.00	5.00	25
1-1	4.00	3.40	30
4-5	3.60	3.00	37

By "natural odds" of 6 to 1, the chart means a situation in which the bets on a horse total one seventh of the betting pool. If $1,000 were bet on the horse, and $6,000 on his opponents, he is a natural 6 to 1 shot. The final column of the chart is the gasser. It shows that someone who collects a $5 mutuel has been deprived of fully 25 percent of his natural profit. If take and breakage were less drastic, his profit would be higher, and so would his prospects of staying in the game.

The Truth about Dime Breakage

Let us now return to Horse "A," on which $30,000 has been bet. The other horses in the race have attracted a total of $60,000. The mutuel pool is $90,000.

The first thing that happens is that the track lifts $13,500 from the pool—representing the 15 percent take provided by law in New York and Florida. In California, Illinois, Kentucky and Massachusetts, the take is 14 percent; in New Jersey, 14½; in Maryland, 13; and in Delaware, 12.

After the take, $76,500 remains in the pool, including the $30,000 bet on the winning horse. The remainder of $46,500 is supposed to be the profit for the winning bettors, but is not. Here is what happens:

$$30,000 \mid \frac{46,500.00}{1.55}$$

The $30,000 has been divided into the $46,500 to see how much money in profit is due per dollar bet on "A." Another way of saying it is that the division gives the dollar odds on "A."

Inasmuch as nobody can bet $1 at a track, mutuel prices are always stated in terms of a $2 bet. Therefore, the next step should be to multiply 1.55 by 2. The product, 3.10, would be the profit on a $2 bet —the odds in terms of $2. To compute the actual mutuel payoff, one then would add the bettor's original $2 to the $3.10, giving a mutuel price of $5.10 on "A."

But it is not done that way.

Instead, the dollar odds of 1.55 are reduced to 1.50. If the odds had been 1.51 or anything else up to and including 1.59, they also would have been cut to 1.50. This is known as "dime breakage." Unless dollar odds turn out all by themselves to end in a string of zeros, they are always cut to the next lower dime. Track and state pocket the leftover pennies—millions of dollars a year.

Back again now to Horse "A" and the poor soul who bet on him to win. Now that the dollar odds are only 1.50, the odds on the $2 bet are 3.00 to 2.00 and the mutuel price becomes $5.

There is no logic in the procedure, except as a pretext for raising taxes without seeming to. In New York and California, the state gets the lion's share of the breakage. In New Jersey it takes every penny. In Delaware, Illinois, Maryland, Massachusetts, Michigan and New Hampshire, the state gets half.

This legalized pilferage began years ago, when mutuel prices were computed by a slightly different method. Instead of dividing the amount bet on the *winner* into the amount bet on all the *losers,* and coming up with the basic dollar odds, the tracks worked in terms of $2 units. They divided the amount of the entire betting pool by a figure representing *the number of $2 tickets* sold on the winner. The answer was the winner's mutuel price. This is worth exploring further, since it shows how breakage has developed into the larceny that it now is. Let us therefore take another look at Horse "A," this time using the old-fashioned method of calculating his mutuel price.

The $30,000 bet on him represents 15,000 mutuel tickets. The pool, after take, is $76,500. The arithmetic:

$$15,000 \enclose{longdiv}{76,500.00}$$
$$5.10$$

Under this old method, the track would have paid $5.10 to any holder of a winning $2 ticket on "A." In those days, furthermore, the track take was no higher than 10 percent, so the mutuel would have been $5.40. But that's another story.

Breakage arose because few mutuel prices came out in neat, round figures. The correct payoff on "A" might have been $5.12. Rather than bother their mutuel clerks with the chore of making chicken-feed change, the tracks adopted dime breakage, reducing the $5.12 to $5.10. As I have now shown, dime breakage under the old method was less costly to the player than dime breakage as currently practiced. Under the old method, the winning player collected a higher mutuel on "A" than he does now.

At some point, a procedure called nickel breakage came into vogue. Odds were computed at the dollar level. If a ticket on "A" was worth 1.55 to 1.00, the mutuel remained $5.10. If the ticket was worth 1.59 to 1.00, the odds were cut to 1.55 and the mutuel stayed at $5.10. Dollar odds were always reduced to the next lower nickel.

Which paved the way for dime breakage calculated in terms of the dollar odds. A whopping increase over old-style dime breakage. Take a horse whose dollar odds are 2.19 to 1.00. Under nickel breakage the odds become 2.15 to 1.00 and the mutuel price is $6.30. But the new, unreasonable dime breakage reduces dollar odds of 2.19 to 2.10. The horse pays only $6.20. Breakage that used to be 8 cents has become 18 cents.

Consider what this means to the holder of a ticket on a short-priced horse. If the dollar odds turn out to be .99, they are reduced to .90 and the animal pays 18 cents less on the dollar than it should have. For any horse in the even-money range this means *a profit diminution of about 18 percent on every winning ticket!*

In New York, breakage of that kind adds slightly more than one full percentage point to the total take. At Aqueduct and Saratoga during 1966, breakage exceeded $8 million, of which $6.3 million went to the state. The basic take at the two tracks gave the state another $70 million. Which brings us to the percentages that affect place and show betting.

Place and Show Lunacy

As most players—but not all—understand, the holder of a show ticket collects a profit if the horse wins or runs second or third. A place ticket wins if the horse finishes first or second. A win ticket *loses* unless the horse wins the race.

Obviously, the best horse in the race has a better chance of running second or third than of winning. Some excellent handicappers try to capitalize on this theory. They bet only for place or show. The profits on a successful place or show bet are low, but the players hope to compensate by winning many more bets than they lose.

The profits are low in place betting because the money lost on unsuccessful bets must be divided between two groups of winners—those who hold place tickets on the animal that won the race, and those who backed the horse that ran second. The profits are even lower in show betting because the profits must be divided three ways.

The arithmetical facts are sobering:

1. To win money on horses that pay $2.20, it is necessary to cash 91 of every 100 bets.

2. To win money on horses that pay $2.40, it is necessary to cash more than 83 of every 100 bets.

3. To win money on horses that pay $2.60 it is necessary to cash more than 77 of every 100 bets.

4. To win money on horses that pay $3.00, it is necessary to cash more than 66 of every 100 bets.

Those are large orders.

The following statements about place and show betting can be accepted as absolute maxims. They derive not from my own prejudices but from the facts of racetrack life, the patterns and percentages of the game:

1. It is harder to make money by betting horses for place and show than by betting on them to win.

2. The number of correct predictions necessary to produce a profit in any representative series of place or show bets is unattainable by any but a supremely expert, supremely patient handicapper.

3. The relatively low natural profits on place and show winnings are drastically reduced by take and breakage, making the task of the place or show bettor even more difficult.

4. The guaranteed profits from place bets on odds-on favorites in high-class races are too low and the betting opportunities too infrequent to alter the overall situation.

5. Anyone able to show a profit from a long series of place or show bets has the ability to make important money on straight betting—betting to win.

Calculating Place and Show Odds

The place pool consists of all the money bet on all the horses for place. Like the win pool, it is subject to take and breakage. Unlike the win pool, it is divided (after take and breakage) between two groups of bettors. Those who bet on the winning horse for place share the profits with those who bet on the runner-up for place. Here is an example:

> Total amount in place pool: $48,000
> Remainder after 15 percent take: $40,800
> Total bet on "A" to place: $20,000
> Total bet on "B" to place: $12,000

The total profit to be returned to the successful place bettors on this race is $8,800. That figure is obtained by subtracting from the net pool of $40,800 the $32,000 that was bet on "A" and "B." The remainder is what the losing bettors have lost to the winning bettors.

The $8,800 is now divided in half, leaving $4,400 in profits for distribution to the backers of "A" and $4,400 for those who bet on "B."

We'll take "A" first:

$$20,000 \ | \ \underline{4,400.00}$$
$$.22$$

The correct dollar odds in "A" to place are .22 to 1.00. Breakage transforms this to 20 cents on the dollar, making "A" a 1 to 5 shot for place. The mutuel is $2.40.

If there were no such things as take and breakage, the mutuel would be $2.80. Take and breakage reduce the natural profits on "A" by a full 50 percent!

Now let us see what happens with "B":

$$12,000 \ | \ \underline{4,400.00} \ \text{plus}$$
$$.36 \ \text{plus}$$

Breakage reduces the dollar odds to .30 to 1.00 and makes "B's" mutuel price $2.60 for place. But the natural mutuel, without take and breakage, would be $3.33. The profits have been cut by 55 percent.

The difficulties of place and show betting are even more pronounced than these examples indicate. Most notably, the purchaser of a place or show ticket buys a pig in a poke. He may have reason for confidence in the horse's ability to finish second or third, but he cannot begin to know what the place or show ticket will be worth until after the race is over. If he must share the profits with holders of place tickets on an odds-on favorite, his own ticket will be worth little. If his horse wins the race and a longshot finishes second—or vice versa—the place ticket will be worth more. Thus, his position is comparable to that of a poker player with a bobtail straight who agrees to buy a card without knowing how much money is in the pot. He might as well play a slot machine.

To make this clear, let us now see what happens to the place price on the well-backed "A" if Longshot "C" wins the race or finishes second. The pool remains $40,800, after deduction of the take. The crowd has bet $5,000 on "C" to place. That amount, plus the $20,000 bet on "A," is now deducted from the pool, leaving $15,800 for distribution. Holders of tickets on "A" will get $7,900. So will the supporters of "C." Compute the odds on "A":

$$20,000 \mid \frac{7,900.00}{.39}$$

The correct dollar odds on "A" are slashed to .30 to 1.00 by breakage, making the mutuel price $2.60. This is more than "A" paid when the pool was shared with backers of the fairly well-supported "B." But now that "B" has failed to finish first or second, the $12,000 bet on him for place has been lost, and the losses have increased the profits available for distribution to owners of cashable place tickets.

I doubt that it is necessary to work out the computations on a show pool. After the take, the amounts bet on all three horses are subtracted from the pool. The remainder is divided into three equal parts, and the show price on each horse is then calculated in the usual way.

Since the place or show price on a horse depends only partly on how much has been bet on it for place or show, but depends also on how well other in-the-money horses were supported, a sensible rule can be suggested:

The only time to consider betting on a horse for place or show is when it is

an odds-on favorite and all, repeat all, other likely contenders are longshots. In such circumstances, the horse might pay only $2.40 to win but could pay almost that much—and sometimes more—to place or show. When Roman Brother won the Jockey Club Gold Cup in 1965, he paid $2.40 to win and $2.40 to place. In the Spinaway Stakes that year, Moccasin paid $2.60 to win and $2.60 to place.

Hedging

In this connection, it might be a good idea to analyze the thought processes of players who try to minimize losses by hedging their bets. They bet a horse across the board, or for win and show. Or they bet two horses in the same race, one to win and the other for place or show.

Their results depend, as usual, on handicapping ability and are limited by the effects of take and breakage. And these effects, as we have seen, are most grievous when the odds are short. If a player backs a horse for win and show and the beast finishes third, there is no doubt that the player reduces part of his loss by collecting on the show ticket. Indeed, if he bets about six times as much for show as for win, he may sometimes turn a profit on such a deal.

However, when the horse substantiates the player's handicapping ability by winning the race, the return on combined win and show betting is far less than it would be if the player put all his money on a larger ticket to win.

The inherent problem of all such maneuvering at the mutuel windows is the near-impossibility of making money on place or show bets. Unless the player is able to make such a profit, his attempts to hedge merely prevent him from making as much on his straight bets as he otherwise might. Or, if he also is incapable of making money on straight bets, the hedges will tend to reduce his overall rate of loss to some extent, while increasing his total investment. Finally, if he is good enough to break even or make a small profit on place or show bets, he almost certainly wastes time and money in the effort: He is good enough to make considerably more money than that by betting to win only!

One of the shrewdest handicappers I know often plays two horses in a race. He usually plays one to win and the other to place or show. Occasionally he plays one to win and place, the other to place or show. One of the animals is always a comparative longshot. The other is most often among the top favorites in the race.

My friend wins money, or stays extremely close to neck-and-neck with the game. I happen to think he would do even better if he bought nothing but straight tickets, but his own method of play is more comfortable for him. He is a good enough handicapper to get away with it. And his approach to hedging is the exact opposite of the one most often practiced at the tracks.

Most hedgers play the favorite or near-favorite to win, and the long-shot for place or show. Supposedly, the longshot returns enough for place or show to compensate for the possible loss by the favorite. If the favorite wins and the longshot gets no part of the money, a profit re-mains possible, especially if the player bets at least twice as much on the favorite as on the longshot. If both tickets cash, great.

My friend, who understands what happens in place and show pools, disdains the customary hedging procedure. His handicapping tells him that the longshot has a better than fair chance to finish in the money. *He therefore bets it to win.* He bets the favorite for place or show. When the longshot wins, as it sometimes does, he makes a small fortune, re-gardless of how the favorite fares. If the longshot finishes second or third, which happens more often, the place and show prices on the favorite are better than usual, because of the longshot's presence in those pools!

If bets are to be hedged at all, that is the way to do it. Naturally, the hedger must be a first-rate handicapper, able to recognize an overlayed longshot when he sees it. And I insist that he would make a higher rate of profit in the end by betting overlays to win only, without hedging.

Betting More than One Horse To Win

Jule Fink and his celebrated "Speed Boys" attracted national at-tention years ago with their practice of betting two and three horses to win the same race. As far as I know, Fink and other successful players still make money that way. It is a perfectly reasonable approach for any good handicapper with plenty of capital. If he can narrow the contention in a race to two or three or four animals, and the odds on each are high enough to assure a net profit, such betting makes sense.

Booking Percentages

Before the advent of mutuel machines, a hustler could shop among the trackside bookmakers for the best odds. Good handicappers made money that way by betting on every horse in a race except rank out-siders, overrated favorites and other animals that figured to lose.

The practice was known as "dutching," supposedly in honor of its originator, a player known as Dutch. Its basis was the bookmaker's scale of percentages, which showed how odds varied according to the fraction of the betting pool represented by the total money bet on each horse. For an easy example, if the player felt that an even-money choice could not win, he would operate as if half the betting pool—the proportion represented by the bets on that horse—were up for grabs. Simply by betting on every other horse in the race in amounts equal or proportionate to their booking percentages, he would win a substantial amount.

I understand that some players try to do the same thing at the mutuel machines. Knowing that the mutuel pool adds up to about 117 percent (the extra 17 being take and breakage), they try to eliminate horses whose odds represent 30 or 40 percent of the pool. Then, by betting the remaining horses in proportions indicated by the table of booking percentages, they beat the race.

It is easier in theory than in real life. Bets must be made at the last possible moment, in amounts that require lightning calculation. Enormous capital and outstanding ability as a handicapper are needed. The player cannot employ the method single-handed, because bets have to be made at more than one mutuel window. How could a solo operative get down bets of $33, $19, $11 and $7 in the same race—and all in the final seconds before post-time? To bet any earlier would risk having the entire deal thrown awry by last-minute changes in the odds.

I do not say that mutuel dutching is impossible. But it requires betting partners of such reliability, capital of such magnitude, and handicapping talent so well developed that the rare person able to carry it off would probably do better by playing alone, betting on two or three good horses a day.

Booking Percentages

Odds	Percentage	Odds	Percentage	Odds	Percentage
1-9	90.00	8-5	38.46	13-1	7.14
1-8	88.89	9-5	35.71	14-1	6.66
1-7	87.50	2-1	33.33	15-1	6.25
1-6	85.68	5-2	28.57	16-1	5.88
1-5	83.33	3-1	25.00	17-1	5.55
1-4	80.00	7-2	22.23	18-1	5.26
1-3	75.00	4-1	20.00	19-1	5.00
2-5	71.42	9-2	18.19	20-1	4.76
1-2	66.67	5-1	16.67	25-1	3.85
3-5	62.50	6-1	14.29	30-1	3.23
3-4	57.14	7-1	12.50	40-1	2.44
4-5	55.55	8-1	11.11	50-1	1.96
1-1	50.00	9-1	10.00	60-1	1.64
6-5	45.45	10-1	9.09	75-1	1.32
7-5	41.67	11-1	8.33	99-1	.99
3-2	40.00	12-1	7.69		

Simplifying the Booking Percentages

Persons able to narrow the contention in a race to three or four horses can use the following table to guarantee a profit. By betting on each of the contending horses in the precise proportions called for by the odds, the player wins, no matter which of the horses wins. Naturally, if some other horse wins, the entire amount is lost. The only limit on this adaptation of the old-fashioned booking-percentage table is that the total amount wagered may not exceed $42. Of course, if the player wants to double or triple or quadruple the prescribed amounts, his possible outlay increases to the chosen multiple of $42. Note also that the method is not usable with extremely short-priced horses.

Odds at Post-Time	Bet	Odds at Post-Time	Bet	Odds at Post-Time	Bet
8-5	$19	7-2	$11	7-1	$6
9-5	18	4-1	10	8-1	6
2-1	16	9-2	9	9-1	5
5-2	14	5-1	8	10-1	5
3-1	12	6-1	7	11-1 and up	4

Progressive and System Betting

Most betting systems are poison. They require the player to increase his bet after every losing attempt. Their theory is that the player is "due" to win at some point, and that the increased bet will return enough to make up for prior losses. We have already noted the disaster that awaits anyone who, relying on a "law" of averages, doubles his bet after every loss on a favorite, or on a top jockey. One need not double the bets, of course. Modifications of the double-up method are frequently used. But they only modify the player's losses. They cannot produce profits except briefly and accidentally. Also, they require investment outlays out of all proportion to the returns.

A pet method of some players is known as "due-column betting." The racegoer decides that the track owes him a daily stipend—say, $100. He therefore bets as much on each of his selections as will produce the desired return. Let us say that he likes a horse in the first race. Shortly before post-time, the odds board holds the animal at 4 to 1. The player bets $25. If the horse wins, the player has his $100 and goes home. If the horse loses, the player now must win $125 to make his $100 net profit.

The most evident flaw in that procedure is the underlying supposition that anyone can make a profit at any track on any given day. Or in any given week. Due-column betting thus multiplies the player's losses during a losing streak, requiring him to increase the size of his losing bets. Few players can afford it.

A far more sensible arrangement is to abandon "due-columns" and allocate a fixed percentage of betting capital for each transaction. As the capital increases, so does the size of each bet. As the capital decreases, so does each bet, enabling the player to withstand a long succession of losses, if he has to.

The notion that a player should invest more when he is winning and less when he is losing is accepted as wisdom in every game. Players who bet according to that principle make more money—or lose less—than players who defy the principle. Indeed, if two handicappers are capable of turning a 20 percent profit, and each of them starts with a bankroll of $100, the player who bets 5 percent of capital on each of his selections will end the year with far more money than the player who goes in for due-column betting or progressive betting or other upside-down methods that violate the percentages of the game, the principles of sound investment and, last but not least, the tenets of common sense.

The player who bets 5 percent of his capital can stay in business at the track for months, without winning a dime. If he goes there with $100 and loses from the beginning, he will have $45 left even if he encounters twenty successive losses before hitting a single winner. Assuming that he is the kind who can actually make the 20 percent profit we have mentioned so often, he probably will go for years without a series of losers as grievous as that.

The due-column or progressive bettor would put himself out of business in such circumstances, even though he might be just as good a handicapper as the other guy. By the same token, neither the due-column bettor nor the slave of progressive betting systems makes as much money in a series of winning bets as the man who bets a fixed fraction of capital.

By way of demonstrating this, let us analyze the occasional, but inevitable blessing of five winners in succession. For the sake of argument, we can assume that each horse pays 5 to 2. The due-column bettor has a bankroll of $400 and wants to make $50 per race. He bets $20 on each of these winners, netting $250 in profits and raising his bankroll to $650. He is happy as a clam.

The adherent of progressive betting also has a $400 bankroll. He bets $20 on the first horse, planning to apply his magic formula in such a way as to require a larger bet on the second horse, if the first one loses. But the first one wins, and so do the next four. He ends by making $250 on the series of bets. His bankroll is also $650, and he is perfectly satisfied.

The man who bets 5 percent of capital also has a $400 bankroll. His first bet nets $50, making the capital $450.

His second bet is $22, netting $55. Bankroll is now $505.

His third bet is $25, netting $62.50. Bankroll: $567.50.

His fourth bet is $28, netting $70. Bankroll: $637.50.

His fifth bet is $32, netting $80. Bankroll: $717.50.

He has done better than the others. Even when his next two horses lose, he will remain in better shape.

He will bet $36 on the first loser, reducing his capital to $681.50.

He will bet $34 on the second loser, reducing his capital to $647.50.

The due-column bettor will lose $20 on the first losing bet and, assuming we are still dealing with 5 to 2 shots, will be trying to win $70 on the second bet. He therefore will wager, and lose, $28. His bankroll is now down to $602.

The progressive bettor, no matter how conservative his system, will lose at least $50 on the two bets, reducing his bankroll to $600 or less.

Daily Doubles and Other Lotteries

The daily double, exacta, perfecta, quinella, twin double, and similar pari-mutuel attractions at modern tracks are conclusive evidence that the pooh-bahs of racing have no prejudice against outright gambling, as long as they can cut each pot. For that is what these trick bets are—gambling, impure and simple. Moreover, they are forms of gambling without the slightest incentive for a competent player of horses. They are strictly sucker bait. The only knowing bettors who bother with them are tricky horsemen, including some whose trickiness crosses the border of fraud.

Before discussing the tricks, let us agree that it is hard enough to pick one winner at a time without trying to pick two in succession, as in the double, or the winner and runner-up, as in the exacta. Consider what the player of doubles does. If he is any part of a handicapper, he may actually have reason to like one of the horses entered in the first or second race. So he buys a flock of doubles tickets which pair the horse with as many as twelve animals in the other race. So his horse wins, and pays $7. And he wins the daily double, which pays $26. He has spent $24 on doubles tickets. His profit is $2. But if he had put the $24 on the $7 horse, he would have won $60. It happens all the time. The daily double is a pig in a poke. So are the exacta, perfecta, twin double, quinella and the rest.

The main complaint against these multiple bets, then, is that the player has no way of knowing what his return will be if the bet wins. This is sucker play in any game.

Another complaint against the multiple bets is that they encourage and reward dishonesty. Scandalous revelations about the activities of twin-double betting syndicates at harness-racing tracks have made that particular pari-mutuel wrinkle unfashionable in major Thoroughbred racing.

But the well-accepted daily double opens the way to skulduggery of its own. The only kind of race in which a horseman can stiff his animal with high profit and relative impunity is a daily-double race. If the horse is a short-priced favorite, the horseman is able to enrich himself simply by preventing it from winning, after purchasing daily-double tickets on the other contenders. For a modest outlay, and without confiding in another living soul, he can make more money that way than by collecting the short odds and the wretchedly small winner's share of the purse at the cheap tracks he frequents.

Obviously, his chances of profiting from the defeat of his own horse are much slimmer in a race that is *not* part of the daily double. To ensure a comparable return on his betting investment he must take the risk of collusion with other horsemen in the race. Either that or bet on practically every other horse in the race in an expensive dutching method that produces a low rate of profit. Quite a different proposition from the plum he plucks by stiffing his 6 to 5 shot and paying comfortable amounts for double tickets on all real contenders in both races. Once in a while a non-contender may jump up and win one of the races, spoiling his scheme. But if he tries three such coups a year and guesses right twice, he makes much more than he could from the measly $600 purses paid in races of that kind.

Moral: Shun the daily double and all other gimmick bets. Play horses one at a time, betting as much as you can afford on each. And when the character in the next row boasts about the $400 double he hit last month, rest assured that he has not won one since and has bought $800 worth of tickets in the meantime.

The Economics of Racing

Among the most joyful recollections of any veteran horseman is the time he caught everyone napping and saddled a 70 to 1 shot that romped by four lengths at New Orleans, laughing all the way. Sometimes it was 20 to 1 or 50 to 1 or Empire City or Havre de Grace or Latonia or Havana. It happened over and over again.

"That colt had the tenderest mouth I ever saw," says the old-timer.

"Couldn't stand the bit. When I bought him for $200 he hadn't won any part of a purse in more than a year. Soon as he'd feel the bit he'd sulk. Wouldn't run an inch. So I got him down to Hover de Graw and entered him in a $1,500 race and told the boy, 'Keep a stout hold on him all the way. Don't let him run off with you. He needs a lot of rating. Save his run for the stretch.' They break and the boy takes a tight wrap and the horse feels the bit and props and damned near throws the boy and they get beat by sixty lengths. So the next week I put the horse in a $2,500 race and tell the boy, 'Now boy, all I want you to do is sit there and let them reins hang loose. Let the horse do all the work.' Horse win all by hisself. I got almost a hundred bucks down on the race, all I had in the world. One book give me ninety to one and another give eighty-five and another eighty. I sell the horse for two grand and go to Europe for a year on my winnings."

Times have changed, but not completely. Now, as in the old days, the dream of every journeyman trainer is to find the hole card, the magic formula that converts a losing horse into a winner. The horseman needs to win a purse. He also needs to win some bets. The ideal situation is when the magic formula presents itself after the horse has run out of the money repeatedly, without showing any signs of improvement. The horse wins. The mutuel price looks like the registration number on a freight car. The stewards call in the trainer, to inquire about the miraculous reversal of form.

"The horse was off his feed for months," says the trainer truthfully. "But the other day a kitten wandered into his stall and the bugger perked up. I guess he was lonesome, or something. Him and that kitten are thick as thieves. Horse is real frisky all of a sudden."

Goats and dogs are standard items in Thoroughbred barns. Race horses love the company.   ARLINGTON PARK PHOTO

Hoof, tail and muzzle, the economics of horse racing are tied to the pari-mutuel machines. The purse money comes from the mutuel betting pools. The funds with which struggling horsemen eke out their purses are earned at the betting windows. The horseman's prime object is to win races with his livestock, but he will go to any permissible length to conceal a horse's true form in hope of getting 5 to 1 on a natural 2 to 1 shot. He has to. He needs the dough.

The Phipps family, whose millions originated in steel, entertains itself with Buckpasser and one of the most successful racing stables in history. It does not need to win bets. Neither do Howard "Buddy" Jacobson and H. Allen Jerkens, two of the most competent trainers of all time. Each wins over a hundred races a year—more than one victory in every five attempts. "I don't bet," says Jacobson. "Why should I? Every time I send a horse to the post I'm betting my career."

But Jacobson has called racing "an outdoor Las Vegas," because of the emphasis on betting. "Close the mutuel windows and the tracks wouldn't last a week," he says. Two days would be more like it.

Let it be agreed that certain leading trainers do not rely on bets for any part of their livelihood. Neither do certain glamorous owners. Many jockeys do not bet. But almost everyone else does, from the candy butchers and tip-sheet hawkers and ushers and sweepers and mutuel clerks to the occupants of the nice boxes in the upper tier.

The player may own a desk full of super-scientific speed charts. He may be able to recite Buckpasser's pedigree all the way back to Tregonwell's Natural Barb. He may know at a glance that yonder filly has bad knees. But his handicapping will be a game of blindman's buff unless he appreciates the significance of the winning bet in the life of the average horseman. The following facts are basic:

1. It costs at least $7,500 a year to feed, house, groom, shoe, doctor and train a Thoroughbred in the big leagues of racing. In lesser environments the cost may fall below $5,000, but not by much.

2. Transportation, jockey fees, entry fees, workmen's compensation insurance, equine mortality insurance and accident insurance may increase the costs by thousands of dollars a year.

3. During 1966, a total of 39,604 Thoroughbreds went to the post at racetracks in the United States, Canada and Mexico. They earned net purses of slightly more than $125 million.

4. Sixty horses, the leading money winners of the year, earned about $9 million in purses, leaving $116 million for distribution among 39,544 other starters.

The Growth of Racing

Year	Total Races	Total Horses	Total Purses	State Revenues
1915	5,454	3,700	$ 2,853,037	—
1920	6,897	4,032	7,773,407	—
1925	11,579	6,438	12,577,270	—
1930	11,477	8,791	13,674,160	—
1935	15,830	10,544	12,794,418	$ 8,386,255
1940	16,401	13,257	15,911,167	16,145,182
1945	19,587	14,307	32,300,060	65,265,405
1950	26,932	22,554	50,102,099	98,366,167
1955	31,757	26,056	76,643,696	186,989,588
1960	37,661	29,773	93,741,552	257,510,069
1965	47,335	38,502	126,463,984	369,892,036
1966	46,902	39,604	130,678,231	388,452,125
1967	47,992	40,500*	139,216,005	400,000,000*

* Approximate number.

5. The purse money available to those lesser horses was the equivalent of less than $3,000 apiece—not nearly enough to pay expenses.

6. Of 7,500 licensed trainers, thirty won an aggregate $17 million in purses. The remaining 99.6 percent of the brotherhood scrambled after the remaining prizes. Some won none of them. The average came to $14,500 per trainer, of which his personal share was 10 percent.

7. A handful of jockeys enjoyed a monopoly as impressive as that of the top trainers and top horses. Most jockeys made less than $5,000 in winning bonuses during the year.

8. With the field dominated by a few dozen eminently successful personalities, an estimated 98 percent of racing stables lose money every year. Their deficits are compounded not only of high costs and low purses, but of certain other expenses on which no return is ever possible —the cost of purchasing (or breeding) and feeding and training and doctoring animals that suffer injury or illness and never run in a race.

9. Some owners do not mind. An indeterminate number—far fewer than the losing 98 percent—are hobbyist sportsmen, successful in finance, industry or commerce. They deduct their racing losses from personal or corporate taxes.

10. Sportsmen or not, most owners bet. All welcome an extra point or two in the odds.

11. And horsemen who rely on racing for a living not only welcome higher odds, but usually manipulate their horses in ways that encourage higher odds.

A handicapper will be helpless at the betting windows if he does not keep the foregoing facts in mind. He will be unable to interpret past-performance records accurately.

The maneuvering that results in higher odds—the maneuvering that enables many horsemen to remain in the game—is so widespread that it affects the outcome of an overwhelming majority of races.

Do I imply that racing is dishonest, fixed, rigged? Do I suggest that the best horse in the race is pulled or drugged to build the odds for his next outing?

Not really. In big-time racing, when a horse is in shape to win and is entered against animals it can beat, the stable goes all-out for the purse and the bet, regardless of odds. Few horses retain winning form long enough for the kind of odds-building shenanigans that require a ready animal to lose. Next time, when the odds are "right," it may no longer be able to win.

But something else is done. Every day, horses are entered in races that they cannot win except by sheer accident. They are outclassed, or at the wrong distance, or off their feed, or sore-legged, or short of wind. Two interrelated reasons account for their presence on the track:

1. Tracks have to fill nine or ten races a day. Fields of fewer than eight horses are unpopular, but there are not enough fit and ready horses to go around. The tracks therefore expect (to put it mildly) every horseman to keep his stock active. A trainer who refuses to run his animals as frequently as possible finds that the track would rather give his stall-space to a more cooperative stable. Under these pressures, only the stables owned by the big names of racing are permitted to train horses in the proper way—racing them when ready to run at their best, and not before.

2. Most trainers have adapted to these economic and political realities. They now race their stock into shape. They no longer rely on the workouts, the patient nurture and careful doctoring that are the bases of sound training methods. They ruin numerous horses this way, but they have become used to it. They can't fight city hall. As a matter of fact, they have learned to turn the racing of unready horses to their own advantage. Chiefly, they use it to darken an animal's form. They deliberately seek out races in which the horse will look bad, even though its condition actually may be improving. When it finally is ready to win, the crowd may not recognize this in sufficient numbers to make the horse a favorite. It therefore pays gratifying odds, bailing the horseman out of his financial difficulties for the time being.

Fortunately, competent handicappers can usually tell when a horse's condition is improving. The result charts and past-performance records contain all the necessary information. Thus, the modern betting coup, in which the stable and its friends bet thousands of dollars, most often finds the horse romping in at modest odds. Members of the paying audience who happen to be good handicappers frequently get in on the coup, and help bring the odds down, by recognizing omens in the past-performance records.

The Cost of the Hobby

There is such a thing as a professional horseplayer. Unless he lives across the street from the track and has a tax-free pass to the place, he must include transportation and admission among his costs of doing business. The hobbyist is well advised to do the same thing. Few players can buy their racing paper, get to the track, pay their way in, eat some lunch, and get home on less than $10.

If he goes to the track twenty times a year, the player's expenses, without betting, are at least $200. I do not regard this as exorbitant. Twenty decent dinners and movies cost as much. Twenty baseball games can also cost as much, depending on the location of the ballpark.

One of the pleasures of handicapping is the opportunity to recover the cost of the pastime. There is no need to be grim about it. In fact, being too grim spoils the fun. Yet there she sits, a $200 outlay for twenty afternoons at the track. How do we get it back?

Man O' War sets world record for mile in 1920 Withers.   UPI PHOTO

We do *not* get it back with $2 bets. If the player has reached the stage of earning about 20 cents on every dollar he bets, he is likely to make not more than sixty bets in the twenty days. At $2 a bet, the sixty bets are an investment of $120. His profit will be about $24, not enough to pay expenses.

Bets of $20 are far more sensible.

Yet not everyone can afford to bet $20 on a horse.

There would seem to be a contradiction here.

The contradiction is resolved by betting *not one penny* on horses until the results of numerous paper bets demonstrate reasonable handicapping ability. It is as unintelligent to waste money in $2 bets as in $20 bets. Readers of this book will do themselves a great favor by risking no money on its teachings until a series of dry runs has shown that the lessons work.

After achieving that plateau, the player should make the transition to actual betting. But he should bet no money that will be missed after it is lost. Perhaps he will make bets of $2 or $5. If he is a talented handicapper with exceptional self-control, he may discover that he does as well with real money in the hurly-burly of the track as he did on paper at home. If he is less exceptional, it may take a while before he becomes accustomed to the difference between dry run and actual battle.

When his results finally warrant confidence, the player should begin betting in units of not less than $20, which would require investment capital of at least $400. If he does not have the $400, he should wait until he has saved it.

If it costs him $20 a day to go to the track, he may have to make bets of $30 or $40 to retrieve his "overhead."

It's fun to do it. And, depending on the individual personality, well worth the effort.

4 The Mystery of Breeding

THOROUGHBREDS are a separate, registered breed of horse, as distinctive in purpose and appearance as Percherons, Clydesdales or Appaloosas.

The breed originated in England, where racing has been an aristocratic pastime for more than 2,000 years. Late in the seventeenth century, during the reign of Charles II, numerous Oriental stallions were imported to invigorate the tired blood of native British stock. Efforts to obtain prize Eastern specimens continued into the next century. Some of the imports were outstanding. Three of the stallions were so good that their descendants now monopolize the backstretch stalls and breeding barns of the world.

Although it is barely two centuries since the genetic superiority of the three imported stallions became evident in British racing, every single one of today's hundreds of thousands of Thoroughbreds descends in tail male (from sire to paternal grandsire and so on through the male line) from one of the three.

Their names were the Darley Arabian, the Byerly Turk and the Godolphin Barb. The Arabian, foaled in Syria, was held to be one of the foremost specimens of his breed ever seen in England. The Turk had been a military charger. The Godolphin was reputed to have been found in Paris, pulling a water cart. His ancestry was unknown, but he looked like the Moroccan (Barbary Coast) type known as a Barb.

The Darley Arabian's great-great-grandson, Eclipse, foaled in 1764, was probably the greatest runner of his century. All other Darley Arabian lines but his have vanished. But from Eclipse come almost 90 percent of the horses that win major races in the United States.

Among those whose lineage traces to Eclipse in tail male have been Citation, Kelso, Buckpasser, Whirlaway, Alsab, Equipoise, Sysonby, Assault, Princequillo, Tom Fool, Roman Brother, Hyperion, Blenheim II, Menow, Nasrullah, Nantallah, Blue Larkspur, Sweep, Count Fleet, Sun Beau, Alibhai, Ben Or, Heliopolis, Sickle, Polynesian, Bull Lea, Teddy, Sir Gallahad III, St. Simon, Black Toney, Roman, Native

Dancer, and on and on and on. The American line originated with a horse named Domino, and has been refreshed by frequent imports from Europe, among them Ribot, Princequillo, Ambiorix, Blenheim II, Nasrullah, Alibhai, Mahmoud and Sir Gallahad III.

Descendants of the Godolphin Barb, via his 1748 grandson, Matchem, have not won nearly as many American races, but it is hard to imagine the pastime without them: Man O' War, Seabiscuit, Discovery, War Admiral, Busher, and all their popular kith and kin.

From the Byerly Turk, by way of his great-great-grandson, Herod, foaled in 1758, we have had First Fiddle, Porter's Cap, Whiskery, Royal Minstrel, The Tetrarch, Epinard. The line accounts for the male ancestry of barely 3 percent of American stakes winners, but portions of its blood are found in many more than that. Cross breeding is unavoidable. Kelso, for example, descends in tail male from Eclipse, but his maternal granddam, Maidoduntreath, was a Man O' War mare, from Matchem.

As one might imagine, efforts to breed horses to go farther and faster began on a trial-and-error basis. To a large extent, the work is still largely a matter of by-guess-and-by-gosh. Scientific eugenics are standard in the breeding of cattle, hogs and poultry, but not in the breeding of Thoroughbreds. One reason is that Thoroughbreds are not cattle. They are not something to eat. Their value is not measurable in poundage, but in speed, courage and endurance. Accordingly, a breeder's mistakes and triumphs may not come into clear focus for years—when the foals have grown and raced and ended their careers and begun to produce tested runners or proven washouts of their own.

None of this necessarily rules out scientific study and experimentation, but the keenly competitive, high-pressure economics of racing and breeding are serious obstacles. If given an opportunity, a scientist might be able to argue that a mating of Stud "A" and Mare "B" could produce a promising foal. But the breeder knows that Stud "C" is more fashionable. The progeny of "C" is worth far more on the market. He therefore goes to "C." If the mating turns out poorly and the foal shows little promise, it can always be unloaded at yearling sales, and often for a fancy price, thanks to its glamorous pedigree. So many races are run every day at so many tracks that it is possible to make good money selling horses that would not have been allowed on a track thirty years ago. Moreover, such horses finally win a race or two, after they are entered against animals of their own feeble ability.

Sire vs. Dam

Thoroughbred breeding is so remote from science that completely contradictory theories are practiced without arousing more than mild

Colonel E. R. Bradley
ASSOCIATED PRESS PHOTO

controversy. Colonel E. R. Bradley used to declaim that 65 percent of a Thoroughbred's quality came from the dam. John E. Madden, breeder of five Derby winners, thought that the *sire* contributed 75 percent of the quality.

The chances are that both were wrong. Does a human being inherit his intelligence from his father or his mother? Obviously, from both. Horses, like all other living creatures, abide by Mendel's Law.

One of the few qualified persons ever to study Thoroughbred breeding was Dr. Dewey G. Steele, Professor of Genetics at the University of Kentucky. He wrote:

"Pedigrees must be judged primarily on the basis of ancestors in the first and second generation, and individuals beyond the third generation may for all practical purposes be ignored.

"There is no evidence that the tail-female line or any other line exercises a hereditary influence greater than would be expected on a purely chance basis."

Old Colonel Bradley, believing that the "class is in the dam," sought classy dams and got a percentage of classy horses. John Madden, looking at things the other way, used classy sires and got a percentage of classy horses. Why not?

The Unscience of Breeding

Breeders no longer are quite so innocent of genetic rules as they used to be. They formerly tended to evaluate horses in Mayflower terms,

Mares and new foals at a California stock farm.　　　　UPI PHOTO

poring over pedigrees to see how many champions appeared on remote branches of the family tree. Bitter experience finally taught them that the best index to an animal's possible class was the class of its parents and grandparents, as demonstrated on the track and in the breeding stall. It made no sense to cherish a man solely because one of his ancestors had been an archduke. The same was true of a horse.

To add a touch of stamina to a line that seemed short of that quality, breeders used to look for "doses" of staying power several generations back, and breed their stock accordingly. Sometimes it worked, more often it did not. Some of them persist in a variation of this, looking for "nicks"—previously successful combinations of bloodlines that might be repeated with equal success.

The simple arithmetic of genetics frustrates most maneuvers of that kind. Any single ancestor five generations removed was, after all, but one of thirty-two great-great-great-grandparents. The hereditary influence of such an ancestor is modified, for good or ill, by the contributions of the sixty-one other recent ancestors whose blood combines in the new foal.

Nowadays, the best breeders try to mate the classiest possible stallion with the classiest possible mare. They get satisfactory results if they define class properly and avoid neutralizing it by matings in which undesirable, but subdued, traits of both parents become intensified. An interesting case is the recurrent mating of Nantallah and Rough Shod II. Their offspring, Ridan, Lt. Stevens and Moccasin, have won well over $1 million among them. On the other hand, they all suffer from faulty ankles. The ankles are not bad enough to prevent the winning of major stakes races in this generation, but it will be interesting to see what kind of animals the three hotshots produce at stud.

In general, today's expensive, fashionably bred yearling is the offspring of parents and grandparents that have been producing topnotch runners. The cheap, unfashionably bred one is from parents and grandparents that were below the first flight as runners and have done nothing to redeem themselves in the boudoir. But Nature runs a lottery. Every now and then, an expensive yearling proves to be a throwback to the worst of its ancestors. And, every season, several runners of unpromising pedigree turn out to be reincarnations of great-great-grandpa, the champ.

One of the most extreme examples of this kind of thing became noticeable on October 3, 1960, when a highly unfashionable two-year-old colt named Carry Back caught Globemaster in the stretch of the seven-furlong Cowdin Stakes at Belmont Park and won by a length and a half, going away. He paid $14.60.

The opinion makers of racing were unimpressed. Carry Back's sire was Saggy, who had beaten Citation at six furlongs in the mud on a day in 1948 when the great horse was out of condition. Saggy had done nothing else to distinguish himself as a racer and had begotten no outstanding foals in several years of trying. Carry Back's dam was a $150 mare, Joppy. The breeder, Jack A. Price, served also as trainer. Nobody had nominated him for any known Hall of Fame.

A few days after the Cowdin, Carry Back was left at the post and lost the Champagne Stakes. The very notion of Price getting anything much with this beast was so unacceptable that Carry Back paid $18.40 when he sauntered to an easy victory in the Garden State Stakes on October 29. For romping the mile and a sixteenth over a sloppy track, he earned $172,782. All of a sudden the game had a Cinderella horse.

In 1961, Carry Back won seven races, including the Kentucky Derby and Preakness. He earned more purse money that year—$556,874— than any other Thoroughbred and was everyone's choice as champion three-year-old.

Experts who studied Carry Back's pedigree were unable to find any excuse for his championship stamina, speed and soundness. The sire's dam, Chantress, was by the celebrated Hyperion but had such dreadful-looking feet that her owners, the Greentree Stud (Whitney), had unloaded her. The paternal grandsire, Swing and Sway, another Greentree cull, had won some purses without reminding anyone of his daddy, Equipoise. And Equipoise, while a good runner, had suffered from hoof trouble and had been transmitting it to his get. Another blemish in Carry Back's pedigree was the maternal grandsire, Star Blen, which had shown a touch of speed but not a trace of stamina.

By any standards, Carry Back was a freak. He inherited none of the shortcomings to which his immediate ancestry should have condemned him. He was the accidental reincarnation of distinguished forebears. But all Thoroughbreds, even the worst, have distinguished forebears. Nature is fickle. "Breed the best to the best and hope for the best," shrug horsemen.

It would be silly to suggest that any scientist could have foreseen a Derby winner by Saggy out of Joppy. Science ain't all that wise. But, under present, non-scientific auspices, surprises are bred with almost comic frequency. One must assume that the horsemen are running several laps behind Nature. They hope for the best, but are not necessarily able to recognize it when it arrives.

Thousands of examples come to mind. Here are a few notable ones. The capable Sunny Jim Fitzsimmons sold mighty Seabiscuit for $7,500 to C. S. Howard, for whom the colt earned over $400,000 and became 1938 horse of the year. Alsab, two-year-old champion in 1941 and three-year-old champion in 1942, was a $700 purchase. Stymie, eventually to become handicap champion of 1945, was so hard to handle that Max Hirsch, a great trainer, entered him in a $1,500 claiming race. Hirsch Jacobs claimed the rogue and made $918,485 with him.

Ballydam had run in $1,500 claimers. Celestial Blue was a cheap mare. Their coupling yielded a foal that went for $5,000 in the yearling sales. It was Bally Ache, Preakness winner which shared 1960 horse-of-the-year honors with Kelso, earned $758,522, and was sold to a syndicate for $1.25 million.

A nonentity named Sickletoy sired only two foals that ever got to the races. One of them was out of Ariel's Image, which had broken down in a $2,000 claiming race before being sent to the breeding farm. The foal was Sickle's Image, female handicap champion of 1960 and winner of more than $400,000.

During 1965 Prince Saim sold for $4,500, earned $194,172. Our Michael, a $12,000 bargain, earned $188,620 during that year. Spring Double, which cost $7,000, had a $176,130 year in 1965.

Fancy prices have been paid for animals that never earned anything back. In 1964, Mrs. Velma Morrison bought One Bold Bid for $170,000. The animal promptly became a hospital case and did not get to the races in 1965. Swapson, bought for $130,000 by John M. Olin in 1961, won a grand total of $21,245. Bold Legend cost David Shaer $94,000 in 1964, and was not seen on any racetrack during 1965. Penowa Farms paid $85,000 for Lemso, which never raced. Golden Gorse, an $83,000 filly, earned $745 during her career. Pericles, whose purchase by William G. Helis for $66,000 was the sensation of 1943, finally won $5,200.

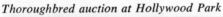

Most Expensive Yearlings in History

At the annual Keeneland, Kentucky, yearling sales in July, 1967, former jockey Johnny Longden, acting as agent for Frank McMahon, paid $250,000 for a colt by Raise A Native out of Gay Hostess, an unraced mare. This was the highest price ever paid for a yearling. A year earlier, McMahon paid $200,000 for Bold Discovery, a yearling by Bold Ruler out of La Dauphine, and Charles W. Engelhard, the mining tycoon who owns Cragwood Stable, paid $177,000 for Many Happy Returns, a yearling filly by Sailor out of Levee. The filly won zero in 1967.

Thoroughbred auction at Hollywood Park   UPI PHOTO

Training Beats Breeding

Anybody who pays big money for a yearling Thoroughbred does so on expert advice. The horse's breeding seems to warrant the investment. Similarly, not much is thought of the potentialities of a horse sold for small change or entered in a cheap claiming race. And then the surprises begin. Jack Price, operator of Carry Back, used to argue that the reason cheap horses run cheap is that they are treated cheap. He said that there was no surprise about Carry Back. The dam and foal had been treated properly.

Price was not suggesting that good handling can make a silk purse of a sow's you-know. He was just trying to remind everyone that he was a good handler. In so doing he raised a point often overlooked by the pedigree-conscious: Breeding determines the horse's potential, but training and the luck of the game determine whether the horse will have a chance to achieve its potential.

With luck, a good trainer can get more from a mediocre horse than a lesser trainer can from a potential champion. Buckpasser, by Tom Fool out of Busanda, by War Admiral, was a potential champion on paper. Bill Winfrey, who developed him, and Eddie Neloy, who guided him to greatness, provided the nurture without which Nature goes awry. Hundreds of trainers could have ruined Buckpasser, and probably would have. The list of potential Triple Crown contenders sabotaged by stupid, greedy mismanagement in their two- or three-year-old seasons would fill this chapter.

Whether making his own mistakes, or doing what his employer demands, the trainer is vital to the career of the horse. So vital that breeding eventually becomes secondary. All Thoroughbreds descend from champions, as we have seen. The humble parents of a Carry Back or Bally Ache may not have been so humble, after all. Their inability to do much as racers may have been a matter of ill fortune or misdirection.

As a two-year-old, Stymie was frantic. He would resist going to the post. He would break tardily from the gate, losing all chance at the very beginning of his races. When Hirsch Jacobs, one of the greatest connoisseurs of Thoroughbred quality in the history of racing, bought Stymie for $1,500, he treated him like a million-dollar horse. He correctly assumed that the poor thing was afraid of people. He spent hours with Stymie, calming him down. He worked the horse by leading him on a rope instead of saddling him with exercise boys. In due course, Stymie acquired the composure that was his birthright and went on to greatness.

H. Allen Jerkens, one of the younger generation of trainers, won

Stymie (second from left) *pours it on in home turn of 1947 International Gold Cup at Belmont Park. Assault* (far left) *finished third. Natchez* (on rail) *was second.*

lucrative races with Misty Day, after Sunny Jim Fitzsimmons had given up on the animal. Jerkens claimed War Command for $8,000 and six months later won the $25,000 Display Handicap with him. He claimed Admiral Vee for $7,500 and the colt went on to win seven major handicaps and upward of $300,000.

To be fair about it, similar tales could be told about all other leading trainers. All have been able to find the magic formula with horses that have defied the best efforts of other trainers. And all have had failures to match such successes. The purpose at this time is not to compare trainers with each other. We shall do that in the chapter reserved for that pastime. For now, it is important to agree that the horse that runs nowhere for Trainer "A" is the same horse that breaks track records for Trainer "B." His pedigree has not changed.

Moreover, if he is a fractious horse, the kind that exhausts itself in the paddock before getting onto the track, little purpose is served by saying, "He got that from the male line. All Nasrullahs have the tendency." It is impossible to deny that temperamental differences are discernible among the various strains of Thoroughbred, just as size and weight differences and hoof differences and color differences are. But a more essential truth is that any Thoroughbred, regardless of pedigree, can develop a ruinous disposition unless handled intelligently. And a companion truth is that 99.9 percent of every thousand horses with good pedigrees are susceptible to intelligent handling. Some rogues are born, but most rogues are made. Horses that loaf or sulk or hate the starting gate or refuse to run on the rail or stop as soon as they reach the lead or quit when whipped were born with the potential to develop evil traits of that sort. But to their handlers must go full blame for the intensification and perpetuation of the traits.

Where does that leave the racing fan? How can he use a knowledge of breeding in his efforts to pick winning horses? Here are some useful facts to bear in mind:

1. The wise player is aware of the by-guess-and-by-gosh character of Thoroughbred breeding, the haphazard results achieved by breeders, and the variable influences of trainers on their horses. He therefore refers to pedigrees only in special situations where past-performance records are too brief to tell a persuasive story.

2. These special situations are (a) maiden-special-weights and allowance races for lightly raced two-year-olds and (b) the same kinds of races for lightly raced three-year-olds.

3. Pedigrees are absolutely useless in handicapping claiming races. In such races the physically deficient or badly mismanaged offspring of champions are regularly defeated by better conditioned animals of equal or lesser lineage. A claiming race must be handicapped *exclusively* in terms of past performances.

4. Pedigrees also are untrustworthy guides to the route-running ability of Thoroughbreds. Although a Tom Fool colt might logically be expected to defeat an Olympia colt the first time they race at 1¼ mile, too many other factors are at work to permit a reliable selection on the sole grounds of breeding. The 1965 champion handicap mare, Old Hat, had a sprinter's pedigree, and none too classy a one, but won at distances up to 1⅛ mile.

OPPOSITE: *Carry Back* (far left) *outgames Crozier* (second from left) *to win 1961 Florida Derby. Johnny Sellers rode the "Cinderella Horse." Bill Hartack was on Crozier.*   UPI PHOTO

Carry Back, the lowborn aristocrat, struts onto the running surface at Aqueduct, with Johnny Sellers up.

UPI PHOTO

When the most promising new two-year-olds race each other at five and five and a half furlongs in the spring and summer, it often is possible to pick winners by handicapping their parents. After the youngsters have been to the post a time or two or three, their past-performance records usually tell more than can be guessed from their breeding. But, with first-time starters in maiden-special-weights and allowance races, or with other entrants in such races that have been out too sparingly to offer a clear picture, the player looks for the following:

1. A sire listed among the nation's leaders.
2. A maternal grandsire listed among the nation's leaders.
3. A leading breeder.
4. A leading trainer.

Leading Sires

During 1967, the following stallions were the most reliable sires in the United States. Among their offspring were the animals that won the most money in the best races. Certain sires whose get won as much or more money than the get of sires on this list are not included. The list contains only sires whose offspring won a satisfactory percentage of their starts. Handicappers who check a runner's pedigree against this list and the accompanying list of leading broodmare sires will have useful information about the potential class of lightly raced three-year-olds entered in maiden-special-weights or allowance races at major tracks.

BOLD RULER [*champion sire for five consecutive years*]

HAIL TO REASON	BAGDAD
SWORD DANCER	FIRST LANDING
ROUGH'N TUMBLE	BARBIZON
AMERIGO	ENDEAVOR II
NASHUA	NEARCTIC
ROUND TABLE	WARFARE
INTENTIONALLY	NADIR
GALLANT MAN	NEEDLES
JESTER	TULYAR
FLEET NASRULLAH	ROYAL SERENADE
TOM FOOL	ONE COUNT
MY HOST	NATIVE DANCER

Leading Juvenile Sires

During 1967, two-year-olds sired by the horses on this list won the biggest juvenile stakes races and also entered the winner's circle with relatively high consistency. Good handicappers will enjoy spotting a new two-year-old sired by one of these stallions, preferably out of a broodmare whose sire appears on the list of leading broodmare sires.

BOLD RULER [*tops*]

SIR GAYLORD	NOHOLME II
NASHUA	SENSITIVE
PETARE	TURN-TO
T. V. LARK	HAIL TO REASON
NEVER BEND	RAISE A NATIVE
FLEET NASRULLAH	POACHING
NEARCTIC	NATIVE DANCER
ETERNAL BIM	AMBEHAVING
ROUND TABLE	ROMAN LINE

Leading Broodmare Sires

A two-year-old whose dam was sired by one of the following stallions has at least a potential class advantage over a competitor of lesser pedigree.

PRINCEQUILLO [*tops*]

WAR ADMIRAL	STYMIE
NASRULLAH	EIGHT THIRTY
COUNT FLEET	SHUT OUT
ROMAN	SPY SONG
MAHMOUD	BLUE SWORDS
AMBIORIX	BIMELECH
BULL LEA	BETTER SELF
POLYNESIAN	DOUBLE JAY
HELIOPOLIS	WAR RELIC
HYPERION	DEVIL DIVER
ALIBHAI	OLYMPIA
SUN AGAIN	MY BABU

Leading Breeders

The following breeders produce the best stock. They were selected for this list because they breed horses that not only win a lot of purse money, but win with reasonable consistency.

BIEBER-JACOBS STABLE

WHEATLEY STABLE

OGDEN PHIPPS

EDWARD P. TAYLOR

KING RANCH

E. K. THOMAS

CLAIBORNE FARM

OCALA STUD FARMS

C. V. WHITNEY

MRS. EDITH BANCROFT

ELMENDORF FARM

ERDENHEIM FARMS

MEADOW STUD

DANADA FARM

GREENTREE STUD

E. B. JOHNSTON

JOHN W. GALBREATH

HARBOR VIEW FARMS

CALUMET FARM

PAUL MELLON

HOBEAU FARM

FRED BWAMAZON

HARRY F. GUGGENHEIM

LESLIE COMBS, II

J. K. HOUSSELS

MRS. M. E. TIPPETT

Anyone who had bet on Buckpasser in his first three races during 1965 would have done so on the foregoing grounds. His sire Tom Fool was not yet notable as a sire of winning two-year-olds, but was among the nation's overall leaders in the begat department. The maternal grandsire, War Admiral, had long been a sire of outstanding brood-mares. Ogden Phipps was perennially a top breeder. Bill Winfrey was an outstanding trainer. Buckpasser lost his first race, won the next two. Net profit on three $5 bets: $10.

Breeding Procedures

The breeding season runs from mid-February to the end of May. Breeders try to get the job done as early as possible, so that the foals will arrive at the beginning of the following year. Under the rules of racing, every foal becomes a yearling on the New Year's Day after his birth, and has a birthday every New Year's thereafter. A horse foaled in late spring or summer is at a disadvantage as a two-, three- and four-year-old, having to run against more mature animals. Northern Dancer, the fine little Canadian horse, overcame that disadvantage. Foaled on

May 27, 1961, he was not yet three years old when he won the 1964 Kentucky Derby.

A broodmare is ready for breeding about a week and a half after dropping a foal. The mare's tail is bound up and she goes to the stall of an unfortunate stallion known in the trade as a "teaser." His job is to make sure that the mare is ready for breeding. If she is not in season yet, the valuable stud with whom she is to mate is spared the frustration of an unsuccessful attempt.

If she proves to be ready, she is hauled away from the eager teaser and led to the big shot's stall. There she is held in position with leg straps. After the stallion is finished, the mare returns to her foal. Three weeks later she is brought back to the teaser. If she is now in foal, she will be indifferent to his advances. If she displays interest it means that the previous "cover" or "service" did not work, and she returns to the court of her mate for another attempt.

Breeding for Mud and Grass

Years ago, when muddy tracks were more common than they now are, handicappers and horsemen could often tell by an animal's pedigree whether it would run well in the heavy gumbo. Reigh Count, a great performer on off-tracks, transmitted the talent to Count Fleet and his other progeny, some of whom relayed it to their own. Man o' War, Petee-Wrack, Challedon and Sailor were other good mudders which begat good mudders. Yet every muddy racing day found horses winning in spite of pedigrees that offered no indication of such ability.

Modern tracks are well drained and contain a great deal of sand. Most of them rarely stay muddy for long. The sandiest and best-drained ones, like Aqueduct, are at their slowest when drying out and labeled "good." When covered with water and called "sloppy" they often are faster than when the tote board says "Track Fast."

Some tracks do get muddy, of course. Those that don't become really gooey nevertheless acquire what horsemen call a "holding" quality while drying out after a rain. When the track is "muddy" or "slow" or "good" or otherwise sticky enough to hold back the horses, the player can be fairly certain that animals that have run badly over similar surfaces in the past will run badly again.

A sore-legged creature that has been having trouble on hard, fast tracks sometimes runs in (wins surprisingly) on a softer footing. Horses with small hooves also seem to move ahead by several lengths on a holding track. Questions of this kind are best settled by looking at the past-performance records and examining the animals in the walking ring. The pedigree is an unreliable guide.

Leon Rasmussen, whose penetrating articles about breeding are a regular feature of *The Morning Telegraph* and *Racing Form,* writes, "Several years ago I indulged in some research on the winners of off-track races throughout the United States. Hundreds of races were studied and the breeding of the winners duly recorded. When I was all through with my analysis, no definite pattern had exposed itself. That is, no particular male line manifested itself, and neither did any particular stallion."

The current trend toward grass racing has raised new theories about pedigrees. Round Table, an exceptionally good runner on turf courses, has sons and daughters of similar disposition, though few of them boast his high class. Inasmuch as most European races are run on the grass, and outstanding European stallions are constantly being imported by American breeders, one might assume that any horse with an imported parent or grandparent would have a better-than-ordinary chance on the turf. Not necessarily. For one thing, every Thoroughbred alive has nothing but European ancestors, some more recently imported than others. The handicapper is right back where he started.

It is generally agreed that a horse with ability on holding tracks does nicely on turf, and that sore-footed animals also improve on the grass. And that the best bet on the grass is a horse that has already run good races on the infield course. Once again, the past-performance record takes precedence over pedigree.

Run-of-the-Mill Breeders

With dozens of tracks demanding seventy or eighty ambulatory Thoroughbreds with which to fill nine races a day, the quality of the breed has declined seriously. There are not that many good horses to go around, nor are purses high enough to pay for them. Accordingly, the woods are full of industrialized breeding establishments, the produce of which have nondescript pedigrees, misshapen limbs, and no more class than is needed to stagger three quarters of a mile. In bygone days, animals as disadvantaged as all this never got to the track. They could not compete with real racehorses. But they now are found in profusion— even at major tracks, where the horse shortage is as severe as anywhere else.

Unable to infuse any real class into this stock, the breeders concentrate on speed. Sometimes a mare from a family that has been showing more staying power than speed is mated with a stud from a line of front runners. All too often, in the words of Charles Hatton, the *Telegraph* and *Form* expert, the result is a horse that "has the speed of the stayer and the stamina of the sprinter." Errors of that kind also crop up in fancier breeding establishments.

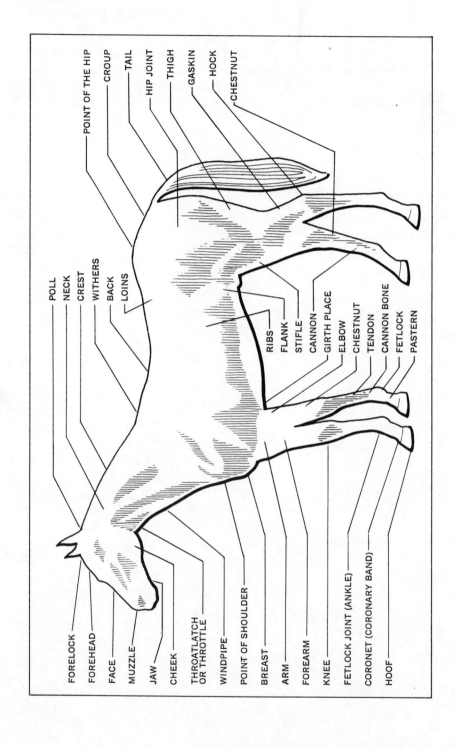

POLL
NECK
CREST
WITHERS
BACK
LOINS
POINT OF THE HIP
CROUP
TAIL
HIP JOINT
THIGH
GASKIN
HOCK
CHESTNUT

RIBS
FLANK
STIFLE
CANNON
GIRTH PLACE
ELBOW
CHESTNUT
TENDON
CANNON BONE
FETLOCK
PASTERN

FORELOCK
FOREHEAD
FACE
MUZZLE
JAW
CHEEK
THROATLATCH
OR THROTTLE
WINDPIPE
POINT OF SHOULDER
BREAST
ARM
FOREARM
KNEE
FETLOCK JOINT (ANKLE)
CORONET (CORONARY BAND)
HOOF

5 Thoroughbred Conformation

WHEN BUYING A YEARLING or trying to decide whether to get rid of one, horsemen attach major importance to the animal's physical appearance. The pedigree may be splendid, but if the conformation departs from normal in any major respect, horsemen turn thumbs down.

Yet the test of the Thoroughbred is performance on the racetrack. Every year, horses with dubious pedigrees or unfortunate conformation, or both, finish first in important races. The saying goes that any horse looks good in the winner's circle. Another saying is that there is no such thing as a perfect-looking horse. By the time a horse is two or three and has been to the post a dozen times, earlier judgments of his looks are subject to drastic revision.

Kelso, horse of the year five times in succession, and biggest earner in the history of the sport (almost $2 million), was castrated as a yearling because he was a runt. The theory was that undersized geldings grow more satisfactorily than undersized colts. Sometimes they do. Kelso became a full-sized horse. But Roman Brother, another gelded runt, remained small, ran off with almost $1 million in purses and succeeded Kelso as horse of the year in 1965. Nobody will ever know whether Kelso would have been a great racer if he had not been gelded. All that can be known is that he would now be available for breeding purposes.

No horse in history ever looked better in the winner's circle than Kelso, and he has the bankroll to prove it. But his hocks stuck out farther than is proper. He seemed susceptible to sore stifles. Also, his hooves were delicate. With less discerning care than that of Carl Hanford, his trainer, he might never have won a dollar. His hooves might have cracked if he had been shod less carefully.

Roman Brother had a crooked knee, his pasterns were somewhat too long, and he had hoof troubles. In fact these difficulties finally made it impossible for him to withstand training and he had to be retired. With $1 million.

Buckpasser's knees aroused criticism. Cracked hooves kept him out of races worth hundreds of thousands of dollars. Bold Lad's near (left) foreknee never looked too good to the experts. Gun Bow's hooves were a constant headache for his handlers. The great two-year-old, Hail to Reason, had a curby (suspiciously swollen) hock, which did not prevent him from running like one of the best of all time. His racing career ended accidentally, when he broke a sesamoid (a small bone above the fetlock). Tom Rolfe was faulted for prominent hocks and cannon bones longer than the ideal. Truly, the perfect horse is never seen.

Conformation is important to the racing fan for several reasons:

1. It is fun to appraise the physique of unraced two-year-olds when they come to the paddock and walking ring.

2. It occasionally is possible to pick the winner of a maiden-special-weights race on grounds of conformation—especially when the best-looking horse in the walking ring has a fine pedigree and hails from a leading barn.

3. If you don't know the difference between a hock and a pastern you won't know what horsemen are talking about. You therefore will get less than your money's worth from your racing papers and your days at the track.

Feet and Ankles

Horsemen begin their inspection of a Thoroughbred at the ground and work their way up. They are quite choosy about hooves, and it makes sense. The Thoroughbred weighs in the neighborhood of half a ton. When traveling at full speed—about forty miles an hour—the entire weight lands on one hoof at a time. If the hoof is too narrow, the foot has to absorb too many pounds of impact per square inch of surface. On today's hard, fast tracks, this is more than the bony structure can bear. Narrow-footed horses go lame more rapidly than horses with wider hooves. They are more susceptible to tendon troubles in the knee region, more susceptible to broken ankle bones and cracked hooves.

Hoofprints are important. If a horse is slightly pigeon-toed he may be a perfectly good runner. But if he toes in considerably, or toes out more than a bit, horsemen downgrade him. The best legs are those with hooves that point straight ahead, leaving hoofprints almost exactly parallel to each other.

As much attention is paid to pasterns as to feet. The pastern should slope at an angle of 45 degrees from fetlock to hoof. If it is more upright than that, it is less springy than it should be. It transmits concussion to the fetlock and knee, which eventually go bad. On the other hand, a

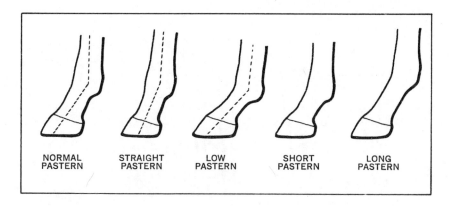

NORMAL PASTERN   STRAIGHT PASTERN   LOW PASTERN   SHORT PASTERN   LONG PASTERN

pastern with too low a slope flexes more than it should. Such a horse "runs down"—scrapes its fetlocks on the ground while running, and strains tendons and ligaments as well. Furthermore, short pasterns are preferred to long ones. Horses with long pasterns on the forelegs tend to cut their own elbows with their hooves while running. Also, the long pasterns exert undesirable strain on tendons.

On the hind pasterns, a lower slope is accepted. The hind legs provide the horse's forward propulsion and are subjected to less concussion than the forelegs, the vaulting poles of the horse's stride. Therefore, the tendon troubles attributable to faulty pasterns are found often in front and rarely in the rear.

Cannon, Knee and Hock

Horsemen like to see short, sturdy cannon bones, for a longer upper leg and longer stride. Some animals have incredibly fragile-looking cannons. Their legs immediately below the knee are so slender that they look, in the language of the trade, "tied-in." Horses with forelegs of that kind are highly susceptible to permanently disabling tendon troubles. The tendons that run down the bone from behind the knee are displaced to begin with and cannot stand the strain of racing.

The knees of the Thoroughbred are located in his forelegs only. The corresponding joint in the hind leg is called the hock. The knee contains seven or eight bones (the number varies from horse to horse and seems to make no difference). These bones help to disperse the concussion of running. Accordingly, Nature intends the normal knee to be situated plumb below the horse's elbow. In other words, straight up and down.

Horses whose forelegs bend somewhat backward at the knee are

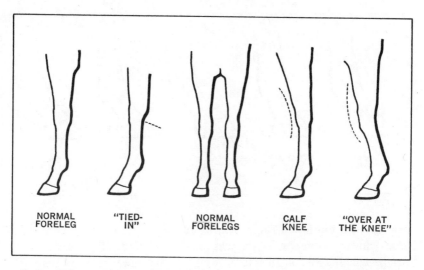

called calf-kneed or "back at the knee." They are not good candidates for long careers. Their tendons suffer, just as if they had straight pasterns. Horses whose knees protrude forward are called "over at the knee." Many topnotch runners suffer from this blemish. In fact, not many horsemen regard it as a flaw at all, unless it occurs in extreme form.

Horsemen prefer Thoroughbreds whose hind legs drop almost straight down from the hocks. If the hoof is noticeably forward of the hock, the animal is charged with a sickle hock. Pronounced cases lead to curby hocks, swellings of the tendon that often end in serious lameness. Also,

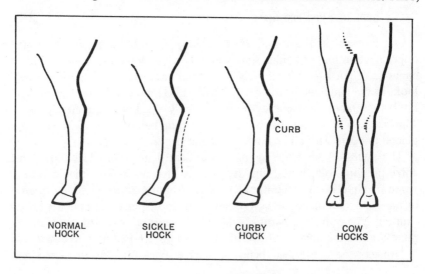

it is agreed by one and all that an animal with normal hocks can stride forward more easily, covering extra ground in each jump. However, so many other factors affect the performance of a Thoroughbred (including human factors) that a mild case of sickle hocks is not necessarily calamitous. Kelso did all right on imperfect rear legs, and so have hundreds of other stakes winners.

Cow hocks are another matter. The horse looks knock-kneed from the rear. When he runs, his hooves fly in odd directions, which is no way to get to the finish line in a hurry. Horses with this structural defect can be counted on to develop tendon trouble. Also, they "interfere"— banging their legs together in midair or hitting and cutting one leg with the hoof of the other.

Bandy-legged horses are almost as unpopular. Their hocks bow outward, and the rear hooves are pigeon-toed. The leverage for strong forward propulsion is lacking, the gait is unrhythmical and, as if that were not enough, the animals are odds-on to cut themselves with their own hooves while trying to run.

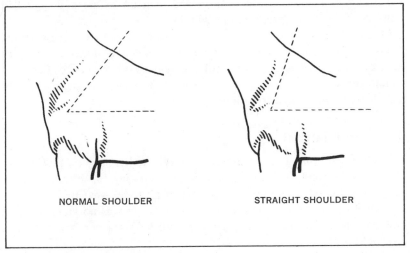

NORMAL SHOULDER   STRAIGHT SHOULDER

Shoulders, Hips and Barrel

Long, sloping shoulders are attributes of the horse that runs fast and far. They are associated with short cannons, long forearms and a consequently long, easy, powerful stride. Horses with short, straight shoulders often have short, straight pasterns—the "stilty" look that means a cramped stride.

The chest should be deep, the ribs well-sprung rather than straight and flat. Conformation of that kind suggests plenty of lung capacity and stamina. The withers should be fairly prominent, indicating the long spinal muscles of the good strider. The muscles of the loin should also be evident. They tie the horse's rear to his front, creating the "close-coupled" appearance of well-coordinated runners. If "light over the kidney" or "wasp-waisted"—slender-loined and slack in the coupling— a horse has trouble transmitting power from rear to front.

Broad, muscular, rounded (but not fat) hindquarters and close coupling are signs of speed. Narrower rumps and rangy, loose coupling suggest weakness.

Head and Neck

Short-necked horses usually lack balance and stamina. Their strides are too short, and they seldom can be counted on for anything more than a burst of early speed.

Horsemen want the neck to be relatively long and limber, with a slight convexity from withers to poll. The horse with a concave neck, which curves down from the withers and then up to the poll, is called a ewe-neck. He is not pretty but he runs as well as any other horse.

Much attention is paid to the head, ears and facial expression of the young Thoroughbred. A broad, open forehead and large, clear, dark hazel eyes are taken as signs of kindly, manageable intelligence. Ears that seldom move are a warning of sluggishness. But ears constantly twitching bespeak a nervous disposition.

Size and Weight

It is said that a good big horse can always beat a good little horse. On the other hand, little horses are forever beating big horses. Round Table, the second leading money winner of all time, was small. So were Roman Brother and Northern Dancer. Tom Rolfe was no giant. Gallant Fox was good and big at 1,100 pounds. Northern Dancer was good and little at 900.

The height of the horse is measured from the withers in "hands"— units of four inches each. A big horse is 16 or 17 hands high, a little horse about 15. If the measurement is 15 hands, 2 inches, it is given as 15.2, or "fifteen-two."

Horsemen work themselves into lathers about the relative merits of big and little horses. Handicappers keep calm. They are guided by past performances and what they see in the paddock just before the race begins.

In trying to differentiate one new two-year-old from another, it seldom pays to prefer the big horse to the smaller. A compact, well-knit juvenile usually learns how to run in a straight line more easily than a bigger, more awkward specimen. The big ones tend to need extra racing and extra training before they settle into winning form. On the other hand, if someone like Eddie Neloy or Bert Mulholland (George D. Widener's trainer) sends out a big youngster for its first start in mid-summer, the player can be sure that most of the green ungainliness has already been ironed out and the horse is ready.

Possibly because they are a bit more nimble, small horses sometimes seem to have an extra edge in races on grass or in mud. They are especially good at picking their way through the traffic jams on the turn for home, finding holes that larger, floundering animals cannot always take advantage of.

None of this constitutes a recommendation to bet on horses because of their stature. The intent is simply to reinforce the observation that the little horse is the best bet in the race if its record is best.

The only other things worth knowing about the size and shape of Thoroughbreds is that blocky animals with bunchy muscles are usually the better sprinters, while horses with staying power seem to be somewhat more lithe, with longer muscles.

Measuring a Thoroughbred for identification purposes at Hialeah Park.

UPI PHOTO

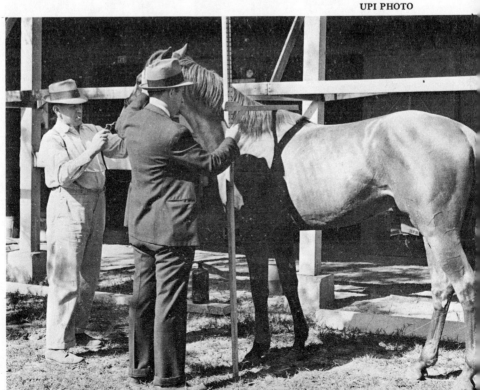

Color and Markings

The official colors:

1. BAY. About half of all Thoroughbreds have the brownish body and the black "points" (black mane, tail and lower legs) that classify them as bay. The body color may be anything from a yellowish tan to a deep, reddish mahogany or a dark brown.

2. DARK BAY OR BROWN. If the hairs on muzzle or flank are tan or brown, the horse is in this category.

3. CHESTNUT. The bodies vary from a dark liver to reddish gold, copper and light yellows. Mane and tail are brown or flaxen, never black —although a few black hairs may be present.

4. BLACK. Sometimes these are unmistakably black. Occasionally they look dark brown, but are distinguishable by the fine black hairs on the muzzle.

5. GRAY. A mixture of white and black hairs.

6. ROAN. A mixture of black, white and yellow hairs, or black, white and red.

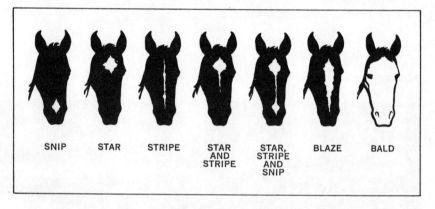

SNIP   STAR   STRIPE   STAR AND STRIPE   STAR, STRIPE AND SNIP   BLAZE   BALD

Because the patches known as "markings" are always white, they never are referred to by color.

A *snip* is a small patch of bare skin or white hairs on lip or nose.

A *star* is a small patch of white on the forehead.

A *stripe* is a narrow mark running down the face to the nose or lower.

A *blaze* is a larger patch. When it covers the entire face, the horse is called white-faced or bald-faced.

Markings also are found on the heels, the coronet of the hoof, the pasterns, ankles (half-ankle or full-ankle), and above, where they are known as socks, half-stockings or stockings. Many horsemen distrust the bone structure of horses with white legs, ankles or pasterns.

6 Handicapping Theories

SEVERAL YEARS AGO an animal named Embarrassed won the opening race on an Aqueduct program and paid more than $20. A jubilant lady in the queue outside the mutuel cashier's window explained to all within earshot that she had been dreadfully embarrassed that morning. Something to do with a shoulder strap breaking and her slip landing in a heap at her feet. As soon as she got the paper and saw that Embarrassed was running she knew she had a winner.

A man ahead of me on the line shook his head wryly. "She's some handicapper," he grinned. On impulse, I asked how he had come to play the horse.

"Easy," he said. "It was the only one in the race that ever did three quarters of a mile in less than one-ten."

Months earlier, Embarrassed had covered the first three quarters of a one-mile race in something like 1.09⅘. At lot of water had gone under the bridge since then, of course. The man evidently was a speed handicapper of some kind. He had not noticed, or had not cared, that Embarrassed's previous good clocking at three quarters of a mile had been achieved on the long straightaway which speeds up the early stages of all mile races at Aqueduct. He had seen the raw time figures and become content. Questions of pace, class, weight, condition, and the like had troubled him not. And Embarrassed, the 10 or 11 to 1 shot, had rewarded his hasty judgment. If he could make one successful guess like that in every ten attempts, he could end any season with a profit. And if my aunt were constructed differently, she'd be my uncle.

An orator on the adjoining payoff line was jubilant about the jockey. "Give me Errico every time on a horse like this!" he yelled. Scamp Errico, an able rider of front-running horses, had mounted few winners in recent years. He had suffered several injuries and was out of fashion among the trainers. Anybody who bet on him "every time" would deserve an award for marathon optimism.

"Gee!" exulted a youngster to his companion on the line. "This is some system!" He was waving a booklet. "Bang-bang-bang!" he cried. "Half a minute and you've got a longshot!"

Bang-bang-bang. The miracle system. Half a minute and you've got a longshot. Half a season and you've got an eviction notice.

I returned to the cashier's window a couple of more times that afternoon. The hunch-playing lady, the speed theorist, Errico's loyal fan and the proprietor of the thirty-second longshot system were nowhere to be seen. But some familiar faces were. Faces become familiar at the track. Especially when you see them almost every time you cash a ticket. They are the faces of expert handicappers: Speed handicappers, pace handicappers, class-consistency handicappers, and handicappers whose methods fit no particular label.

On the rare occasions when these people discuss handicapping theory with each other, they discover large areas of disagreement. And yet they have a great deal in common.

First and most prominent is their repeated presence in the payoff line. Ability to win bets is, after all, what identifies them as expert. No other credential counts.

Secondly, they are all "spot players." None attempts to bet on every race. Some go for days on end without betting at all. Many come to the track only when the racing paper's past-performance pages promise a few betting opportunities. Few bet on more than three or four races a day. It goes without saying that they bet only on races that strike them as especially favorable opportunities.

They arrive at these decisions by divergent routes. Some analyze every horse in every race, looking for animals that stand out from the crowd. Others don't bother with all that toil. They regard certain kinds of races and certain kinds of horses as less predictable than others. So they refuse to bet on two-year-olds. Or on females. Or on stakes or handicaps or allowance races. Or they shun maiden races. Or races on the turf course.

Some attach deep importance to handicapping angles, distinct from handicapping fundamentals. For example, some never play a horse that won or finished in the money in its last race. Others go to the opposite extreme, playing no horse *unless* it won its last race. Some bet only on consistent geldings that won—or did not win—their last races.

Some try to get on the side of the percentages by confining their speculation to favorites whose records can withstand severe scrutiny. Others turn a profit by looking for races in which the favorite is overrated by the crowd and a longer-priced horse has an outstandingly good chance.

Some play no horses that seem to be moving up in class. Others avoid horses moving down in class. Some give little time to a study of class as such, believing that the true quality of a horse is revealed in its

The English Derby at Epsom Downs.   UPI PHOTO

ability to set or overcome a fast early pace and get to the finish wire in good time.

Some play no horse running today's distance for the first time. Others disdain such conservatism, making their selections on the basis of numbers contained in speed charts.

Some mistrust any horse running with substantially more weight than it has been able to carry to victory in the past. Others adjust their speed ratings to reflect pounds added or deducted from the horse's most recent imposts. Some pay no attention whatever to weight, unless it is especially high and the race especially long.

Some give extra credit to horses from favored barns or with leading jockeys. Others insist that the horse is the thing. They ignore trainer and jockey alike.

You Can't Win 'em All

How contradictory can they get? How can methods so diverse produce long-term winnings in a game as difficult as this?

Answer: Nine races a day make a varied menu. During the height of the season on any major racing circuit, there is seldom a day in which an expert handicapper is unable to find one or more betting opportunities.

Moreover, the differences among successful handicapping methods are more apparent than real. In his own way, each expert takes heed of the fundamentals of the game. The winning player who emphasizes class and consistency may never look at a speed or pace chart, but he is careful to estimate how today's race will be run and whether its pace will suit the style of his horse. And the successful pace handicapper attends to class with numerical formulas which embody the relationship of class to early and late speed. At the same time, he hesitates to give a horse full credit for a fast race run in suspiciously cheap company.

The man who bets only on a horse that won its last race can win money by applying any handicapping method that encompasses the fundamentals of distance, form, class, age, sex, consistency, weight, speed, pace, jockey. So can the man who *refuses* to bet on horses that won their last races. Obviously, neither player encounters as many betting opportunities as he would if his method were less specialized. But both may own the unimpeachable certificate of the expert—the notebook-ledger that shows a long-range profit. The one who favors last-out winners to repeat probably wins a higher percentage of his bets. But his opposite number very likely gets higher mutuel prices.

The player who specializes in bets on claiming races for older horses misses wagering opportunities available to someone with a more varied approach. Yet he may end each season with a higher rate of profit, depending on how well he knows his specialty and how intelligently he manages his money. He might increase his enjoyment and enlarge his profits if he were to learn how to handicap allowance races, and races for two-year-olds, and certain maiden races. But he may not feel like it. He may be getting all the action he wants.

Prescription for Success

We have now reconfirmed a previously emphasized truth: Handicapping is a highly personal pastime. For the 99.9 percent of readers who have not yet found a suitably comfortable and successful method, or want to improve the performance of a method that is not quite in the black, some general statements will be useful:

1. The fewest bets, the highest percentage of winners, and the highest rate of profit await the player who has the time and patience to apply a method that embraces all handicapping fundamentals in full detail.

2. To the degree that standards relax and one or another fundamental is slighted, the number of bets increases and the percentage of winners decreases. But the median or average mutuel price tends to rise

Silky Sullivan, one of the most popular come-from-behind horses in history, trails the field in the 1958 Kentucky Derby. His fans expected him to overtake everybody in the stretch, but he never got under way.   UPI PHOTO

and the rate of profit may decline only slightly, if at all. This explains why some players are forever trying to simplify their own procedures. Some manage to do it quite successfully. In fact, readers who do not care for full-dress handicapping may be able to use this book's teachings to develop their own collections of spot-play systems. A player equipped with an arsenal of five or six such selection methods can "handicap" an entire program in a few minutes, find himself two or three plays a day, and do about as well as the average burner of midnight oil.

3. Rate of profit is important, but it is not everything. In fifteen days at the track, a conservative player might make thirty bets and a less conservative one might make sixty. If the conservative player bets $20 on each horse and realizes profit at the rate of 25 cents per dollar, he makes $150. If the less conservative player also makes $20 bets and his profits are 15 cents on the dollar, he nets $180.

I have prepared the following twelve chapters with such possibilities in mind. Each of the chapters deals with one or more of the fundamentals of handicapping, fully explaining the relations of each to all others. Conservative methods of using each factor are made plain. Less conservative methods—and their possible consequences—also are explained.

7 Finding the Beatable Race

MOST RACES are truly run. The best horse usually gets there first. Next week one of the losers might be in better form and beat him. But not today. Whether he won by a nose or a city block, his victory established certain truths:

1. He was in good enough condition to demonstrate his superiority over today's field.

2. The distance of the race suited him.

3. The weights suited him. (He did not carry high enough weight nor did any other entrant carry low enough weight to alter the outcome.)

4. The pace of the race was comfortable for him. (If he is a front-running type, nothing else was able to keep up with him in the early stages and he had plenty of energy left for the homestretch. If he prefers to run behind the early pace, he either outclassed the field decisively or was helped by the presence of two or more front-runners, which ran each other into the ground, clearing his path to the wire.)

5. His jockey was equal to the demands of the situation.

6. He was not outclassed. (If there were classier animals in the race they lacked the condition to prove it, or were unsuited to the distance or the weights or the pace, or were ridden by jockeys unable to get the best from them.)

It is easy to handicap a winner after the race is over. I have done it myself hundreds of times, wondering how I could have failed to notice *before* the race what suddenly became so obvious afterward. The process of retracing one's steps in hope of diagnosing error is good exercise for the beginner. It encourages careful habits.

The grandstands at any racetrack are cluttered with people who know a great deal about the game but manage to defeat themselves with sloppy handicapping. Experts are careful. They have to be. The percentages provide no margin for careless error. Just as in poker or bridge, a single thoughtless move can convert profit to loss. Knowing this, the expert makes sure that he has a complete profile on every contending horse in any race on which he bets. He knows precisely why he thinks his own choice has an unusually good chance to win. He knows exactly which animals promise to challenge his choice at each stage of the running. When his horse loses—as it does more than half the time—he may re-handicap the field to see if he has made a boo-boo, but he seldom finds one. You never hear an expert say: "I shoulda had the winner but I didn't notice that fast workout he ran the other day." If an expert's choice loses, the reason is usually one or more of the following:

1. Its condition was not as good as expected.
2. Some other horse was in surprisingly good condition.
3. The surprisingly good or bad condition of another horse affected the pace of the race, depriving the expert's choice of its predicted advantage.
4. The rider failed to exploit his opportunities, or lost unnecessary ground on the turns, or ran the animal into switches, or was victimized by bad racing luck.

The Expert's Main Problem

That list is worth analyzing. It indicates that the expert's main difficulty is his effort to assess the current condition of horses. Matters like class, weight and distance were not listed because the real expert rarely makes the kind of error that misleads him into selecting an outclassed or overweighted horse, or a horse unsuited to the distance of the race. As we shall see, there is no excuse for *anyone,* expert or beginner, to be misled in that way.

Observation of one simple rule will place the reader in position to save himself from outclassed, overweighted or outdistanced horses. And it will give him the best possible chance to determine the current condition and the pace preferences of other horses. The rule:

Avoid playing any race in which the relative abilities of the horses are not clearly evident.

Among all reasons why the great majority of players lose, none is more basic than their violation of that rule. They insist on finding a bet in every race. They treat racing as if it were a roulette wheel. One of eight or ten horses has to win, so they take a flyer. They want action. They waste their money on races in which the past-performance records offer inadequate information about the entrants' class or condition or their distance and weight and pace preferences.

Experts call such races unplayable. A more precise term would be "unbeatable."

I have heard losers dispute this. "The favorite wins one out of three, whether it's a claiming race or a turf race or a race for first-time starters," they argue. "This means that one race is like another. No matter what kind of race it is and no matter how hot a handicapper you are, you wind up making a guess. If you don't have a clear picture of class or form or pace, you can find angles to handicap from. Everybody else is in the same boat. Every race is a chance to win. And a chance to lose."

Right. But some races offer a better chance to win, which is why experts concentrate on them.

It is impossible to deny that favorites win unplayable-unbeatable races as frequently as they win any other kind. It also is impossible to deny that an undiscriminating player of favorites winds up 8 or 9 percent behind the game. But the object of the game is to reduce losses to the vanishing point and make inroads into the black. This can only be done by avoiding unbeatable races and looking for beatable ones.

Here are the guideposts.

Seasons and Cycles

Aqueduct opens New York's marathon racing season in mid-March. New Jersey starts in April. Illinois begins in May. The Florida and Maryland seasons open in November, and Southern California in December.

During the first weeks of those and all other racing seasons, handicapping is more difficult than usual. Every race includes horses whose present abilities are obscure. Some have not run in months. Will they benefit from the rest and win at the first asking? Or will they need several races before rounding into form? Some have traveled thousands of miles in vans or planes. Will they need a race or two before recovering from the ordeal and becoming acclimated? Or will the long journeys agree with them?

Most of the jockeys are familiar enough to the fans, but some are newcomers. Weeks must pass before anyone can know whether the new rider is as good as his New England or Illinois record suggests, and whether he does well with all kinds of horses or is less versatile than he might be.

And then there is the problem of weather. The beginning of all racing seasons, except those in Florida and California, is notorious for changeable weather. The mercury fluctuates wildly, affecting horses and humans in unpredictable ways.

For all these reasons, conservative players refrain from betting until their racing circuits have been in operation for three or four weeks. After the animals have had a couple of races over the track, a handicapper is liberated from the impossible job of trying to compare apples and pears. He can rate horses on the basis of what they have done lately in competition with each other at this track or on a nearby sister track. He no longer need guess whether the Illinois horse has withstood its journey better than the California horse, or whether the local horse has returned from its vacation in shape to beat the other two. He still does a good deal of guessing, of course. But it is informed guessing.

And after the season is a month or so old, the weather settles down. The very best weather is summer (or the winter equivalent found in Florida and Southern California). Horses react kindly to the warmth. The track is usually dry and fast. The owners send out their best stock in quest of purses. With a higher proportion of authentically good horses in action, the handicapper finds a higher proportion of authentically good bets.

When It Rains

Many successful players refuse to go to the track unless the weather is pleasant and they know that the running surface is dry. But patient, adaptable handicappers can find lucrative opportunities on off-tracks, just as they do on fast ones.

Several times in every season, the Weather Bureau touts everyone onto a loser. "Fair and warmer," the forecast says. But the morning sun gives way to clouds and the rain begins to fall at noon. By post-time for the first race the running surface is a mess. What to do? Some players go home. Others hunt for spots.

Official information about the condition of the track is posted on the tote board. Not infrequently, the board will pronounce the track "fast" even though everyone can see puddles gathering on it. The tote board is not exactly fibbing. It is doing the best it can. The distinction between a fast track and its immediate inferior, a "good" track, is a matter of judgment. Smart players are wary. They know that horses sometimes run seconds slower than expected and suffer serious losses of stamina on an officially "fast" but damp track.

The sandy, scientifically drained running surfaces at most modern racing plants turn from "fast" to "good" to "sloppy" in a heavy rain. Unless the rain is exceptionally heavy, the track does not even get muddy. Sun and drainage soon combine to upgrade it from "sloppy" to "slow" to "good" to "fast" in a single afternoon. Even if the surface gets actually muddy, the drying process seldom lingers at the stage known as "heavy," when the surface is as gooey as wet cement and horses' hooves sound like suction cups. Aqueduct dries from muddy to fast in a few hours of sunshine. The sequence is usually "muddy," "slow," "good," "fast."

Here is what the various terms mean, and what the handicapper does about them.

Fast: Dry. So dry that the maintenance crew waters it between races, to hold the dust down. The great majority of races are run on fast tracks. Hence, most horses are at their best on such tracks and have little experience on others. Time figures recorded on a fast track stand up quite reliably whenever the same horses run again under the same conditions on the same ground.

Information about the running styles, preferred distances, weight-bearing abilities and class limitations of most horses is based on fast-track performances. The information stands up, as long as today's race is also on a fast track. Therefore, the most conservative, most reliable handicapping is that which refuses to speculate about races held on any but a fast track. In fact, if the tote-board sign says "Track Fast" and the puddles are beginning to form, the ultra-conservative handicapper makes no bets. At any minute the sign may change from "Fast" to "Good" or "Sloppy." Regardless of what the sign says, the weather has already dampened the track sufficiently to alter the complexion of the race.

Sloppy: The track is covered with large puddles. The rain is still coming down or has ended recently. The drying process has scarcely begun. When modern, sandy tracks are sloppy, the horses run every bit as rapidly as when the surface is dry. Many players proceed with their handicapping as if the track were fast. This is a mistake. It is a mistake because front-running horses have an even better chance on a sloppy track (of the sandy sort) than on a fast track. They seem to hold their speed longer. Their come-from-behind rivals have more difficulty catching them.

It is agreed that the texture of a sloppy track favors the front-runner mainly because his position at the head of the stampede spares him the discomfort of having mud and slop kicked in his face. The horses behind him are obliged to run through a barrage of guck. Few of them appreciate it. It affects their spirit and saps their stamina. Many of them sulk or quit outright.

Therefore, when the handicapper's study shows that the best horse in the race is a front-runner, and that no other front-runner in the race has the speed to stay with him, the horse usually becomes a better bet on a sloppy track. If the horse's most formidable competitor is one that likes to come from off the pace but has done nothing in previous efforts on sloppy tracks, the front-runner becomes an even better bet.

The exception would be a front-runner that simply dislikes slop. A few of them do, and their records often show it.

A more difficult case arises when the best horse in the race is a come-from-out-of-it type. If it has already won in the slop by coming on in the stretch and overtaking the leaders, it may be a rugged sort. The player with access to old result charts would look up the animal's good race in the slop and see if the chart explains how it won. Perhaps it won because two front-runners perished in the stretch and it was the only other living thing in the vicinity of the finish wire. But if the horse ran with authentic gameness, or if today's front-runners seem likely to wear each other out—which can happen in the slop as easily as on a fast track—the player has found a good bet.

Lacking such evidence in results charts, the wise player remains skeptical about the winning chances of the come-from-behinder, even though it may have won in slop before. Unless the animal has a pronounced edge in all departments, and has never showed the slightest inclination to quit in the stretch, it may be wiser to pass the race. On the other hand, if it has won *more than one race* in the slop, it can be certified as a slop runner deserving of support.

As the reader can see, decisions of this kind depend on numerous variables. When in doubt, the expert abstains. It hurts to pass up a winner, but it costs no money. To pass up a loser saves money, and is gratifying in that respect.

Good: While getting drenched, the track passes from "fast" to "sloppy" via "good." While drying out it progresses from "slow" to "fast" with a stopover at "good." A peculiarity of sandy tracks is that "good" refers to conditions not nearly as good as the innocent bystander might think. At Aqueduct, a so-called good track contains less moisture than a "slow" one and more than a "fast" one, but it often works havoc on the figures of an unsuspecting player. In the old days, a "good" track was only a bit slower than "fast," and had no marked effect on the running styles of most horses. But when the sandy track is on the slow side of "good" it holds horses back. Front-runners run out of gas sooner. Races are won by animals that come from off the pace to score victories that would not be likely on a fast track.

The safest approach to the modern track in a situation of this kind is to bet no horse unless it figured to win on a fast track and either has a clear edge in class or is the determined type that can be rated a few lengths behind the leaders before opening up in the stretch. If it has won in the past on "good," "slow" or "muddy" tracks, it becomes a better risk.

To repeat for emphasis, a pace-setting animal is a dubious choice on a holding track unless it is figured to romp on a fast track, has a decided class edge, and has won on off-tracks in the past.

Slow: Very much the same standards apply to this moister surface. It is slow because it holds. It retards the animals. Front-runners have more difficulty.

Rogelio Olguin rides sadly back to the judges' stand after losing in the mud at Caliente.

JOHN GREENSMITH

Muddy: This kind of footing is wetter than anything but a sloppy track. And it is gummy. The clods that fly from the front-runner's heels adhere to the rearward horses and jockeys like beauty-parlor facials. Hooves slip and slide. Horses become frightened of their unsure purchase on the ground. They sometimes quit running and look for the barn.

The only horse to bet in a race of this kind is one that not only should win if the track were fast but has already proved that it can win in mud. If it does not shape up as the best horse in the race, its previous victory in mud is no evidence that it will win today. Yet, if the mudder is the second- or third-best horse in the race, and the better two have already demonstrated a reluctance to run in mud, you may have something.

As often as not, the winner of a mud race turns out to be a sore-kneed varmint that never raced in mud before but appreciates the cool comfort of the stuff so much that it runs in at huge odds. I repeat, the nearest thing to a safe bet in mud, as on any off-track, is the horse with the double edge—the potential superiority on normal footing *plus* proven ability to cope with today's goo.

Heavy: A surface of this kind is rare at modern tracks. It occurs after a long siege of rain, when enough moisture has evaporated to leave the soil with a consistency comparable to the soft, damp clay used in nursery schools. A heavy track is slower than any other kind. The best hope of the player who tries to handicap races on such a surface is to take the best horse (provided it is not a front-runner), but *only* if it has won on heavy tracks in the past. If he cashes one bet in four he will be extremely lucky. The other three races will be won by a variety of animals, including some that never have done well on off-tracks and others that have never taken the lead in their lives but suddenly move up and set all the pace today.

Bitter experience helps form the attitudes of most players toward rainfall and its consequences. If the past few pages seem to offer hope of success on days when the track is off, and the reader is emboldened to brave the elements instead of staying home, I urge caution. Like anything else in handicapping, wet-track predictions should be tested on paper before actual money travels from the wallet to the mutuel clerk.

The remainder of this chapter deals with the various types of Thoroughbred races, differentiating the less playable from the more so. Here again, a veteran racegoer may find nuggets that seem to promise him success with kinds of races that previously have defied his best efforts. I urge once more that he proceed with care. If, for example, he has always avoided races for two-year-olds, having succumbed to the widespread superstition that young horses are unreliable, he should hesitate before deciding that the information in this chapter equips him to bet on a two-year-old. While hesitating, he should see what other chapters of this book can add to his understanding of two-year-olds. And he then should confine his activity to mental bets or paper bets until he has satisfied himself that he can beat such races.

We begin our review with claiming races. They not only are the most numerous races at most tracks, but offer the highest proportion of betting opportunities.

Claiming Races for Older Horses

Without claiming races there would be no racing at all. Owners would avoid the hazards of fair competition. Instead, they would enter their better animals in races against the sixth- and twelfth-raters that occupy most stalls at most tracks. The third-class horse might be unable to win a major race from one end of the year to the other, but would go undefeated in races against his inferiors. This would leave little or no purse money for the owners of cheap horses. The game would perish.

The claiming race changes all that. When he enters his animal in a race for $5,000 claiming horses, the owner literally puts it up for sale at that price. Any other owner can file a claim before the race and lead the beast away after the running. The original owner collects the horse's share of the purse, if it earned any, but he loses the horse at a fair price.

That is, he loses the horse at a fair price if it is a $5,000 horse. If it were a $10,000 horse, in a race for cheaper ones, the owner would get the purse and collect a large bet at odds of 1 to 10, but the horse would be bought by another barn at less than its true value.

Owners sell nothing at cut rates. Not on purpose. Which is why a $5,000 claiming race always matches horses whose value—a reflection of present class and soundness and estimated future earning capacity— is not much higher than $5,000. Their value may, in fact, be a good deal lower. At major tracks, claiming prices usually range from $3,000 to $20,000. Claiming races for $25,000 and $30,000 stock are seen occasionally. Once in a great while, good horses run against each other under conditions exposing them to claim for as much as $50,000.

The sophisticated racegoer likes to open his racing paper and find a $5,000 claiming race at six furlongs for three-year-olds, or for three-year-olds and up. He knows that the race may provide his best bet of the day. That is not all he knows. He knows that the reason these horses are running at a claiming price is that they are unfit to run in better company. Some of them showed championship promise as yearlings or two-year-olds, but suffered injury from which they recovered only traces of their ability. Others may be jaded or partly crippled from too much training and racing, and may be on their way down the scale. Next year they'll be running at minor tracks, with $1,500 price tags. Others may be reliable enough animals in their present price bracket. Still others may be reliable animals in a lower price bracket, but over their heads today.

There may be ten horses in the race, and members of the crowd may bet many thousands of dollars on each, but the handicapper usually finds that not more than three or four have a reasonably good chance to win. The rest are short of condition, short of class, running at the wrong distance, or facing animals that figure to cut out the wrong kind of pace for them. Or maybe their jockeys are outclassed.

The trainers of mature claiming horses manipulate the animals like puppets, darkening their form by entering them in races they can't win and then springing them for the money in races that suit them. Expert handicappers know all this, and how to recognize what's afoot. Strangely enough, although these claiming races lack real quality, the winner often turns out to be a horse with a slight edge in class—provided, of course, that its physical condition allows it to demonstrate that inherent superiority. Where no significant class difference exists, the animal in best condition can be counted on to win, assuming that the distance and weights and pace and jockey suit him.

In the urgent effort to subsidize as many stables as possible by giving even the poorest three- and four-year-old and older horses a chance to win, the tracks are unable to rely solely on the class distinctions implied by claiming prices. Identical price tags notwithstanding, a group of $3,000 or $8,000 or $12,000 Thoroughbreds includes widely diversified talents. The tracks compensate for some of these differences by scheduling races at varying distances. But even this is not enough. The track must plan races for the least capable members of any claiming-price group and other races for the better.

In ascending order of quality, the more familiar of these claiming races are:

1. For maiden fillies. A race for four-year-olds of this description is inferior to one that includes three-year-olds or is exclusively for those younger animals.

2. For maiden colts and geldings, or for both sexes. Again, the presence of three-year-olds suggests a better race.

3. For female non-winners of two races at any time. Once more, three-year-olds are generally the best animals in the category.

4. For male non-winners of two, or for both sexes. Three-year-olds are usually of higher quality than their elders.

5. For three-year-old non-winners of one or two or more races since a specified date. The larger the number of permissible previous victories and the more recent the date, the better the competition. Also, a race for males or both sexes is superior to one restricted to females.

6. For three-year-olds and up or four-year-olds and up, with other conditions as in the paragraph above. Among horses of proven winning

ability, such as these, four- and five-year-olds usually enjoy clear superiority over three-year-olds of identical claiming price. This is especially true during the first half of the year and in longer races.

7. Open to all in the claiming bracket, aged three, or three and up, or four and up. The best $7,500 animals on the grounds might be ineligible for certain of the races described in Paragraph 6, having won too often and too recently, but can get into this kind of gallop.

The racing secretaries, who plan track programs, resort to many ingenious variations on the foregoing themes. By the end of any representative season, winning opportunities will have been programmed for all but the very sorriest stock. Any trainer who doesn't find a spot for every animal in his barn has only himself—or them—to blame.

Although this is not the place for a discussion of the weight factor, it should be pointed out that the conditions of claiming races grant weight concessions to horses that have won fewer than a specified number of races within a specified time. Additional weight advantages sometimes are given to animals entered to be claimed at less than the maximum price. For instance, a race might be programmed for horses entered to be claimed for $4,500, $5,000 and $5,500. The ones entered at the lower prices would be allowed to carry three or five or seven pounds less than those entered at $5,500.

Older Claiming Maidens

Maiden claiming races for horses aged three or more are the saddest exhibitions on any card. Most of the entrants have had several opportunities as two-year-olds and have failed. They have done no better at age three. And some have reached four without a single win. The expert almost invariably writes off the four-year-old as hopeless in a maiden claimer. If it has lived this long without winning, there can be little expectation that it will win today.

Among three-year-old maidens entered to be claimed, the majority are equally hopeless. They have shown neither speed, stamina nor spirit. One that has been getting into the money frequently may attract the business of the crowd but is not necessarily a good bet. He very likely is a sucker horse, a chronic loser. His previous experiences have conditioned him to run as fast as is necessary to stay among the leaders, but he hates—and that's the word—to get out front, where he can't see any other horses. So he loses and loses and loses, although he often finishes second or third.

I have never known an expert who approached the maiden claiming

Snow racing at Sportsman's Park   UPI PHOTO

Native Diver (nearest rail) *equals world record for seven furlongs, beating Viking Spirit in 1965 Los Angeles Handicap at Hollywood Park.*   UPI PHOTO

race for older horses with any expectation of finding a good bet. Some do not bother to handicap such races at all. Others may bet on a three-year-old in a high-priced maiden claimer (about $10,000), if the animal has not yet proved itself a dud. For example, if it has had only a race or two or three in its previous career, has run at least one of them recently without disgrace, has been working out frequently and at respectable speed, and, above all, is from a leading barn, it may be superior to its rivals today. Perhaps the animal's previous race was a maiden-special-weights event, for the most valued non-winners in the place. If it did fairly well in that race and meets other standards, the maiden claiming race may be its dish of tea.

Or perhaps its last was a spirited race against $7,500 maidens and its surprised owner has decided to boost the ante. If the horse is the only thing in the field that looks like a horse, it may be a bet.

Claiming events for non-winners of two races are designed for animals only one step removed from the maiden category. These creatures often are no better than maidens. They prove it by never winning another race at a major track. The best of them is the lightly raced, well-trained three-year-old that wins a maiden race decisively. It has demonstrated an authentic edge in class over non-winners in this price range. The chances are excellent that it retains the advantage when facing non-winners-of-two in the same price bracket.

Another good bet is the occasional animal whose lone victory occurred not in a maiden claimer but in a straight claimer (a race for previous winners). A look at the result chart usually reveals that the race was for non-winners-of-two, but the horse deserves extra credit, especially if it showed any real speed.

Still another possibility is the horse that won a maiden-special-weights race, or has been finishing close to the winners in straight claimers of a value higher than today's. Example: a three-year-old that has been beating half or more of its field when racing against four- and five-year-old winners in a similar price range.

In trying to evaluate races for *female* maidens or non-winners of two races, the criteria remain the same. Certainly, any female that has shown the slightest spark of ability in a recent race against *males* can be assumed to have an extra something going for her when pitted against unpromising females.

Bread and Butter

Straight claiming races for $3,000 to $7,500 horses with multiple victories are the bread and butter of the expert player. The fluctuations of the form cycle, the maneuvering of trainers, and the relative unsoundness of much of the stock make it possible for the player to toss out most of the entrants as probable losers. The real contenders are quite easy to find. But things become stickier when claiming prices exceed $8,000. These higher-priced animals earn their substantial valuations by winning with fair consistency, or at least by indicating that they could do so if entered in suitable races. They are sounder animals and hold their winning form somewhat longer. Thus, a field of $10,000 Thoroughbreds often perplexes the handicapper with four or five animals that have done well enough in fairly fast company—and have done it recently enough—to qualify as contenders. The player's problem may be additionally complicated by the presence of horses dropping down to the claiming ranks after facing superior competition in allowance races.

A race of this kind, in which the handicapper is unable to separate the leading contenders, is every bit as unplayable-unbeatable as a race in which the present capabilities of the horses are unknown or in which no horse has demonstrated enough reliability to deserve a bet.

It is a grievous pain in the neck to spend time handicapping a race and end with two or three or four horses so evenly matched that decision seems impractical. Yet fortune sometimes smiles. One of the horses may be scratched. In the paddock and walking ring, two of the remaining contenders may seem grossly out of sorts. All of a sudden the fourth horse is an outstanding bet. More often than not he pays excellent odds, the crowd having pushed a good deal of its money onto the other prominent contenders.

Claiming races are the staple fare of the expert handicapper. I know none who avoids playing them. I know some who seldom play any other kind.

Races for Good Two-Year-Olds

Let it be asserted at the outset that the better two-year-olds at major tracks are among the most reliable Thoroughbreds anywhere. The prejudice of many players against two-year-olds is unwarranted. Anyone who knows what to look for in juvenile races can profit without nearly the expenditure of time and sweat that other kinds of handicapping demand.

The well-bred two-year-old that reacts well to training is handled like a potential champion. Its first run for money is against other highly regarded juvenile maidens at five or five and a half furlongs under uniform weights prescribed by the racing secretary of the track. Early in the season, most of the entrants in one of these maiden-special-weights

Official photo that established Tom Fool as winner of the 1953 Suburban Handicap. Royal Vale was second.   UPI PHOTO

affairs are likely to be first-time starters. One or more may be by Bold Ruler and trained by Neloy or Mulholland or Lucien Laurin, or other first-rate conditioners who specialize in winning with two-year-olds in the first attempt. What can the player do when confronted by so many attractive unknown quantities? Sit on his hands and wait.

As the season progresses, maiden-special-weights races crop up in which all but one or two of the horses have been to the post a time or three. A high-bred swifty from a good barn is entered. His past performances show that he has been trying, has been missing narrowly but improving, and has been doing it all in excellent time. Frequently, he is the only animal of his description in the race. He is as good a bet as one ever finds.

The two-year-old may even be a good bet in its very first race. If all other entrants have had a few racing opportunities without demonstrating ability, the well-bred, well-trained youngster making its first start may well go to the post as a solid favorite.

Many players lose money on these sprints for potentially superior two-year-old maidens by overlooking an ancient tradition of the game. This tradition regards the form of a maiden as "the property of its owner."

The horse can be sent out *not* to win but to acquire experience in actual competition. Inasmuch as the trainers do not notify the public of their intentions in that regard, a lot of money is wasted at the windows.

Before anyone calls the cops to report corruption, I should point out that no decent barn wants to lose any race. Yet no decent barn will permit a jockey to punish a green but expensive two-year-old in an effort to win. If it cannot win on its own raw talent and courage, it is allowed to lose. Treatment of that sort may be unkind to players, but is good for horses.

To avoid being entrapped into betting on a two-year-old maiden whose connections are not ready to shoot the works, the smart player simply reserves his support for animals that (1) have already tried to win and look like winners today or (2) regardless of prior performance or lack of it, seem to have a clear edge in quality over the zeros in today's field. The handicapping is done mainly in terms of speed, by means to be described in a later chapter. Other basic considerations are breeding, the identity of trainer and jockey, and the swiftness of recent workouts. Class, weight and pace usually are irrelevant in these five-furlong sprints.

Winners of the maiden-special dashes proceed to allowance races, stepping-stones to the lucrative juvenile stakes. If the allowance race is at five or five and a half furlongs, and all entrants have already competed at the distance, the race can be analyzed entirely in terms of speed, with the usual edge to the best barns. If the distance is new to some of the horses, the race is harder to beat. It may even be unplayable, as we shall see in the next chapter.

At distances of six furlongs and up, under allowance or stakes conditions, the player often finds himself with too many sound, evenly matched two-year-olds to choose among. Stickouts like Native Dancer turn up too infrequently to make the player's life simple. But when one does, the juvenile stakes are a joy. A Native Dancer, Citation, Graustark, Moccasin, Bold Lad, Hail to Reason or Buckpasser pays miserly odds. But who cares? Animals of that kind figure to win big. Any race is playable in which a horse not only figures much the best but, in the manner of two-year-old champions, can be counted on to give it all he's got. The young champ loses now and then, but not often enough to throw the player's accounts out of joint.

Cheap Two-Year-Olds

Races for inferior two-year-olds are an entirely different matter. When a maiden juvenile is entered to be claimed, his proprietors announce, in effect, that he is a washout. They are so sure of his unsoundness or lack of innate talent that they do not even bother to protect him from sale. The races in which he runs are invariably the slowest at any track, and are not cheering to the eye.

Some players put their money on the supposed class of a glamorously bred two-year-old when it runs in company of this kind. But if the poor thing's breeding meant anything, it would be winning allowance races, not 'seeking its first win in the company of culls. Once in a great while, the player finds an entrant that has run faster in maiden-special-weights company than any of its competitors have run in their maiden claiming races. Unless the horse displayed that speed recently and has been working out at short, regular intervals, it can be assumed that it has deteriorated and will not equal the previous clocking today. The player who speculates on more than one of every five or six maiden claimers for two-year-olds is guilty of waste.

Straight claimers for two-year-olds are as playable as other claiming events, but not early in the season. In late summer and fall, after the young horses have run often enough to sort themselves out a bit, the player approaches their claiming races with confidence. In spring, all he really knows about a field of two-year-old claimers is that the entrants have been good enough to win in the past but that something serious accounts for their inability to win in better company. A physical or temperamental flaw of that kind may not prevent the animal from going on to a long, honorable career. Indeed, it may move right out of the claiming ranks and become a stakes winner, like hundreds of underrated Thoroughbreds in the past. But the youngster's failings may be more serious. They may prevent him from ever repeating the swift previous victory that explains why the crowd has made him the favorite in today's race. In short, two-year-old claimers are among the least consistent of horses during the early months of the year, and deserve mistrust for that reason.

Although the horse with the fastest previous race at the distance is the likeliest contender in any two-year-old claiming sprint, the player is well advised to pass the race unless the horse has been active recently and has shown that it can *consistently* cover the ground in substantially faster time than any of its competitors. Even so, it may lose out to a beast that has been performing indifferently in allowance company but runs faster today than it has ever run before. These are tough races. I doubt that anyone beats them.

Allowance Races for Older Horses

The conditions of the allowance race resemble those of the claiming race, except that the horses are not for sale. Eligibility and weight allowances are prescribed in conditions written by the racing secretary.

As in claiming races, the conditions usually tend to bar horses that are too good for the field, having won too many purses above a minimum value, or having won too often or too recently. On the other hand, the conditions permit a trainer to enter a horse that has not a prayer of winning, but needs the work.

Most players know that allowance races are designed to provide earnings for horses too good to be lost *via* the claiming route, but not good enough to beat stakes and handicap stars. But most players do not know that allowance races come in almost as many varieties as claiming races. To regard one allowance race as equal in quality to another is to invite losses. To search out those qualitative differences is to open the way to remarkable betting opportunities.

Let us suppose that two three-year-olds seem to be outstanding contenders in an allowance race. Each finished a fast-closing second in its previous start, after running close to the pace all the way. The past-performance records show that both horses have been entered in nothing but allowance races all year, and have been running successfully enough to inspire confidence.

Are they too closely matched? Not a bit of it. The player motivated to dig through the result charts discovers that the last race of Horse "A" was for three-year-olds that had not earned a purse as high as $3,000 on as many as three occasions in the previous six months. "A" was eligible for the race because his earnings had exceeded $3,000 in only two of his five victories. The horse that defeated him in the race was a three-year-old with similar credentials.

The result charts show that "B" has been facing animals of a different order. His last race was for three-year-olds and up. The purse was fatter than the purse in "A's" race. And the conditions of eligibility had permitted entry by several previous winners of handicap and stakes races. In running second, "B" outfooted several high-class animals, older than he. A couple of his earlier victories had been against horses so good that they would not have been allowed into "A's" last race, and would not be allowed into today's race, either.

"B's" trainer has found a soft spot. For a change the horse is running against animals of his own age. They have never demonstrated that they can keep up with the kind of stock "B" has been beating. The player who consults the result charts has found a bonanza. Indeed, if "A" happens to have run his last couple of races in faster time than "B" and if the rider of "A" is the "hot" jockey on the grounds and if, as may be expected, a significant number of newspaper selectors and tip sheets pick "A," the player will collect a robust mutuel after "B" waltzes home in front.

In our chapter on class, means of differentiating one allowance race from another will be presented. Meanwhile, it suffices to say that the occasional racegoer, and others who rely on past-performance records, probably will find many allowance races unplayable. But the player who uses result charts will find them a delightful source of extra revenue.

I do not mean to discourage the casual fan from trying to handicap allowance races. At many tracks, certain allowance fields are composed entirely of animals that have been running in claiming races. The past-performance records give accurate clues to their relative class. In other instances, the past performances of one entrant mark him as the choice. His consistency, his prior earnings, his pace figures, his form cycle, and the identity of his trainer all suggest him as a likely winner. He may not pay much, but you don't have to collect result charts to get the money.

Maiden-Specials for Older Horses

Many a well-bred horse goes through its entire two-year-old season without a single victory. Even after it has lost six or eight times, its owners refuse to enter it in claiming races. Perhaps they think that it may finally come to hand. Or they hope to use it for breeding purposes some day and don't want to lose it. Or the owner's wife loves its limpid hazel eyes and refuses to part with it in any circumstances.

All of a sudden January 1 arrives and the horse is a three-year-old maiden. Indeed, some otherwise successful barns harbor four-year-old maidens, still running in maiden-specials. The tracks are careful to arrange racing opportunities for the creatures. Needless to say, the majority are incurable losers. Some would have serious difficulty winning a $3,000 claimer at a minor track.

But the player misses some excellent bets if he skips past these maiden-specials without a glance at the past-performance records. Most of the four-year-olds are hopeless and can be ignored. But some of the threes *do* come to hand. They put together a couple of brisk races and some bright workouts and proceed to win like winners.

As a general rule of thumb, the likelihood that such an animal will wake up and win becomes smaller as his number of races increases. The fewer races in his record, the better his chances. The best plays of all are horses that did not start at age two, probably because they were late foals and their handlers decided not to overtax them. If they come from leading barns, this is likely to be the explanation. Occasionally, one of these three-year-old first-starters not only wins his race, but deserves betting support by the smart player. If his breeding is promising, his trainer outstanding, his workouts good, his rivals nondescript, and if he looks fit in the paddock, he's worth a chance.

More often, these good three-year-old maidens need a race or two before cracking down. They usually signal readiness by running more competently in their second outing than in their first.

It makes no sense to bypass maiden-specials for older horses. A highly satisfactory percentage of winners can be found in them by anyone who knows what to look for.

Turf Races

Most races on grass are hazardous for the player. Some are not. The ones that merit attention are composed entirely of horses whose ability—or inability—to run on grass has already been demonstrated. The handicapping process is then similar to any other. But where several members ·of the field have never run on the turf before, trouble lurks. A horse can be a bum on the dirt and a champ on the turf. It is not possible to know what to expect of him until he has tried the softer surface.

An exceptionally keen student of Thoroughbred class and form may spot an occasional horse as the likely winner of a turf race even when it has not raced on grass before. On June 2, 1966, for example, the sixth race at Aqueduct was an allowance affair at a mile and one sixteenth on the grass. The field was limited to horses aged three or more that had not won more than one race of allowance grade or better. The favorite was Fairlane, an experienced, four-year-old turf campaigner which had won a similar race at the same track in October, 1965. This had been the animal's only victory in its last thirteen races. Its most recent race had taken place three months earlier in Florida. It had finished third (at odds of almost 30 to 1), an accomplishment which apparently accounted for the vigor with which the Aqueduct crowd was betting.

The field seemed lacking in class—the quality of perseverance and consistency most important in good turf racing. Many of the entrants had done quite well in claiming races on the turf course, but could scarcely qualify as sound bets in an allowance race. One well-backed animal was Stands to Reason, a nominee for the Belmont Stakes. He had never raced on grass and, despite his eligibility for the most taxing of the three-year-old Triple Crown classics, had displayed little quality.

The only entrant that had not already proved itself mediocre was a three-year-old owned by Cragwood Stable (Engelhard) and trained by Mackenzie Miller. The colt had lost all eight of its starts as a two-year-old, but had run in some choice maiden-specials, finishing not too far

6th Race Aqueduct

TURF COURSE
1 1-16 MILES
AQUEDUCT
Start Finish

1 1-16 MILES (Turf). (Errcountess, June 28, 1963, 1.41⅕, 5, 121.) Allowances. Purse $6,500. 3-year-olds and upward which have never won two races other than maiden, claiming, optional or starter. Weights, 3-year-olds 114 lbs., older 123 lbs. Non-winners of a race other than maiden or claiming at a mile or over at any time allowed 3 lbs.

Stands to Reason

Dk. b. or br. g (1963–Ky), by Hail to Reason—My Toni, by Grand Admiral **114** 1966 6 0 0 1 $900 / 1965 18 2 7 3 $25,554

Harbor View Farm B. Parke (Harbor View Farm)

24May66–8Aqu fst 1 .46⅖1.10⅖1.35⅘ Allowance 1 3 43½ 65¼ 55½ 55½ HGustines b 110 17.00 83–20 King's Jest 1101 Imam 1111½ Double Happy 1133 Had no excuses 8
4May66–6Aqu fst 1⅛ .47⅗1.12⅘1.51⅕ Allowance 2 5 56½ 65 610 611 HGustines b 110 3.80 69–20 Deck Hand 1133 Paoluccio 1234 Vail Pass 1202½ Not a factor 8
23Apr66–5Aqu fst 6f .23 .46 1.10 Allowance 5 7 77 64½ 45 46¾ MVenezia b 108 4.70 86–14 Michigan Avenue 1143 Deck Hand 1143 BwanaPeacha119¾ Wide 8
16Apr66–5Aqu fst 7f .23 .45⅘1.22⅘ Allowance 1 5 54½ 53½ 44 35 MYcaza b 117 3.70 87–14 d–Aforethought1142½ Mr.Right1222½ Stands toReason117½ Wide 6
5Feb66–6Hia fst 7f .23⅗ .47 1.25⅕ Allowance 1 6 64½ 96 1113 1110 JLRotz b 118 9.10 73–23 Rom O'nello 115no Good Land 112¾ •Native Pitt 1151 No factor 11
22Jan66–6Hia fst 7f .23 .45⅕1.24 Allowance 1 9 65 66½ 610 610 JLRotz b 118 6.30 79–25 Stupendous 1185 B. Golden 1092½ Holly Man 1142 No factor 12
20Nov65–8GS fst 1 1/16 .45⅗1.10⅕1.42⅘ GardenSt 7 11 1114 1011 108½ 107¾ WShoemaker b 122 6.80 83–15 Prince Saim 122nk Gunflint 1222½ Amberoid 122nk Not a factor 12
10Nov65–8GS fst 1 70 .46⅕1.11⅘1.42 Allowance 5 8 83½ 21 1h 11 WShoemaker b 112 *1.70 84–18 Stands to Reason 1121 Prince Saim 1145 Defiant Son 113nk Driving 14
30Oct65–5Aqu fst 1 .45⅖1.10⅕1.37⅗ Allowance 5 3 53½ 59 58½ 21½ WShoemaker 115 *1.70 78–21 Odd Dancer 1191½ Stands to Reason 115nk Imam 1222 Fast finish 11
20Oct65–6Aqu fst 1 .45⅕1.09⅘1.35⅘ Allowance 5 11 1013 1015 79½ 210 WShoemaker 115 3.40 79–18 Stupendous 11710 Stands to Reason 1152 Odd Dancer 122½ Wide 12
6Oct65–7Aqu fst 7f .22⅕ .44⅘1.23⅗ Cowdin 3 9 109½ 1014 105¾ 910 HGustines 114 36.00 78–22 Advocator 114h Fathers Image 116¾ Our Michael 1241 Sluggish 12
28Sep65–6Aqu fst 7f .22⅘ .45⅗1.24 Allowance 1 3 62½ 53¾ 43½ 32 WBlum 115 2.40 84–17 Arabian Spy 1152 Stupendous 117h Stands to Reason 1151 Gaining 14
Nominated for Belmont Stakes. LATEST WORKOUTS Jun 1 Bel t.c. 3f fm .36 h May 21 Bel m.t. 5f gd 1.02⅕ b May 18 Bel m.t. 4f fst .51⅕ b

*Fairlane

Dk. b. or br. c (1962), by Tamerlane—Rising Fair, by Fair Trial **118**5 1966 4 0 0 1 $1,100 / 1965 9 1 4 1 $9,235

Mrs. L. J. Beecher P. G. Johnson (R. P. H. Elwes) (Ire.)

3Mar66–9Hia fm 1 1/16 Ⓣ 1.42⅘ Allowance 4 3 21 2h 2h 3nk LLoughry5 108 28.60 91–13 WesternWarrior113nk CarryForward II 115h Fairlane1081¾ Sharp 10
11Feb66–8Hia fm*1 1/16 Ⓣ 1.42 Allowance 5 6 68 710 58 49½ RTurcotte 113 *1.70 91– 5 Happy Gondolier 1132½ Cleareye1132½ RicketyDick1134½ Forced back 12
29Jan66–8Hia fm 1 1/16 Ⓣ 1.42⅗ PalmBe'hH 3 7 78 76½ 51½ 75 LLoughry 110 16.40f 87– 8 First Family 1152¼ MundenPoint116h WesternWarrior116no Tired 13
29Jan66—The Palm Beach Handicap, run in two divisions, 8th and 9th races.
21Jan66–7Hia fm 5½f Ⓣ 1.04⅕ Allowance 4 11 1113 1113 99 73½ LLoughry5 115 19.90 93– 5 Blue for Boys 114nk Hill Chance 114¾ Rare Pet 1141 No speed 12
17Nov65–8Pim fm 1 1/16 TC 1.12⅘1.45⅕ Allowance 2 3 42¾ 2h 1h 2h EBelville5 114 3.20e 89–11 Shady Living 118h Fairlane 114½ Nashua Plume 1182 Failed to last 10
6Nov65–8Aqu hd 1 1/16 TC 1.43⅘ Allowance 7 1 1½ 11 21 21½ LLoughry5 112 7.20 85–13 Tom Cat 1181½ Fairlane 112½ Austral II 1162 Showed game effort 7
30Oct65–8Aqu hd 1 1/16 TC 1.43⅕ Allowance 6 3 36 32½ 21 1h LLoughry5 107 19.60 90–10 Fairlane 107h Shee-Gwee 1153½ Lucky Flight 115½ Just Up 7
21Oct65–6Aqu fst 6f .23 .47⅖1.13 Md Sp Wt 6 3 32 2h 2½ 23 RUssery 121 *1.20 75–12 Human Dignity 1213 Fairlane 1212 Samarta 118nk 2d best, sore 7
24Sep65–1Aqu fst 7f .22⅗ .45⅘1.25⅗ Md Sp Wt 7 1 33 3½ 24 43 RTurcotte b 120 6.70 75–20 Never Pry 1191 Claim Jr. 1131 Arpino 1201 Well up, tired 8
17Sep65–1Aqu fst 6f .22⅘ .46⅘1.12⅘ Md Sp Wt 5 3 43½ 31½ 41¾ 61¾ WBlum 120 4.70 77–19 Mount Noble 115½ Trentina 117½ Marching Orders 120h Weakened 9
LATEST WORKOUTS May 27 Aqu 5f fst 1.00⅘ h May 17 Aqu 5f fst 1.05 b May 11 Aqu 4f fst .50 b Apr 27 Aqu 4f fst .50⅘ b

*Unimak

Ch. h (1961), by Unico—Parapet, by Black Peter **120** 1966 6 0 0 1 $750 / 1965 6 1 1 0 $2,034

N. Yacono L. S. Barrera (Haras La Guatana) (Arg.)

16May66–8Aqu fm 1⅛ Ⓣ 1.49⅗ Allowance 4 4 43 43 98½ 1012 CFarmer 120 52.80 75–13 Mourmelon 1151½ Mimado II 120nk Fast Start 116nk Speed, stopped 10
19Mar66–5Aqu fst 1 .46⅖1.11⅖1.37⅕ Clm 17500 6 2 43½ 816 816 821 EBelmonte 116 24.00 61–22 Rocky Ford 113¾ Rebellious 1164 Much More 116h Brief foot 8
10Mar66–8SA fm 1⅛ Ⓣ 1.10⅖1.48⅕ Allowance 8 2 23 1½ 1h 53½ FAlvarez 114 31.20 88– 8 Mustard Plaster 1141½ Royal Gunner 120½ Old Mose 1201½ Weakened 8
26Feb66–9SA fm 1⅛ Ⓣ 1.10⅖1.48⅘ Clm 10000 5 2 41½ 43 22 31 EBelmonte 115 30.80 88– 8 Cover Wave 1161 Twyneth Teg 112no Unimak 115h In close late 10
4Feb66–8SA fst 1 1/16 .46 1.10⅗1.42⅘ Allowance 6 2 33½ 1112 1117 1117 FAlvarez 114 84.10 72–13 Old Mose 1192 Prosaic One 1181 Gallant Rogue 1192 Gave way 12
26Jan66–7SA fm 1⅛ Ⓣ 1.10⅘1.48⅘ Allowance 8 2 64 75½ 1011 1012 HGustines 116 73.80 77–11 Tudor Fame 115¾ Honored Sir 120h Old Mose 1151 Early foot, tired 12
30Dec65–6SA gd 6f .22⅗ .46⅗1.12 Allowance 1 9 77¾ 1012 1015 1015 MYcaza 115 10.30 67–18 El Adem 1091 My Searcher 119nk Buonarroti 116h Never close 10
9Jly 65–San Isidro (Arg.) fm*7f 1.24⅕ tc Premio Snow Bluff(SpWt) 12 CDominguez 126 5.15 —— Unimak 1262 Repicadl 1262½ Marianito 118 Well up, led final 1/16ths 11
13Jun65–San Isidro (Arg.) fm*7f 1.23⅕ tc Premio Vernet (Spec'lWt) 22½ CDominguez 124 10.00 —— Tiburon 1232½ Unimak 124½ Resoplo 123 Clear lead entering stretch 16
27Mar65–Palermo (Arg.) fst*1 1.37⅗ Premio Sellada (Spec'lWt) Unp RLZapata 123 2.80 —— Brindisi 1231 Pichin 123h Yane Choncan 123 Dropped far off pace 11
LATEST WORKOUTS May 30 Bel tr.t. 5f sl 1.07⅖ b May 20 Bel m.t. 3f sly .36⅖ hg May 10 Bel tr.t. 3f fst .39 h Apr 23 Bel tr.t. 5f fst 1.03⅖ h

Vail Pass ×

B. c (1962), by Hill Prince—Vermiglia, by Owen Tudor
A. J. Giordano S. J. Smith (Meadow Stud, Inc.) **120**

1966	11	2	1	4	$9,625
1965	25	1	6	6	$14,725

25May66-8Aqu	fst 1⅛ .46⅕ 1.10⅗ 1.49⅗	Allowance	1	5	36½	34½	56½	613	LAdams	b 120	25.10	75-13	Highest Honors 113½ Buffle 1123½ Bushfighter 1132½	Tired	7
18May66-8Aqu	fst 1⅛ .46⅖ 1.13⅗ 1.51⅖	Allowance	4	4	34½	55	43	35½	LAdams	b 120	7.30	73-15	Fast Count 1131½ Bushfighter 1134 Vail Pass 1202½	Good try	6
13May66-9Aqu	fst 1 .46⅖ 1.11⅗ 1.38	Clm 16000	3	5	45½	33	23	32	LAdams	b 115	7.40	76-22	Selected Shorts 1131½ Rocky Ford 122½ Vail Pass 115¾	No rally	9
4May66-6Aqu	fst 1⅛ .47⅖ 1.12⅘ 1.51⅕	Allowance	1	4	35	42	35	37	LAdams	b 120	14.00	73-20	Deck Hand 1133 Paoluccio 1234 Vail Pass 1202½	Evenly in drive	8
25Apr66-5Aqu	my 7f .23 .46⅖ 1.24	Cl c-12500	6	1	21½	2h	1½	11½	BBaeza	b 119	*1.90	86-23	Vail Pass 1191½ Tajante 117no Rebel Light 119¾	Going away	6
18Apr66-6Aqu	fst 6f .22⅕ .45 1.10⅗	Clm 15000	6	5	66½	79¾	65½	53¾	BBaeza	b 119	5.70	86-17	Bargain Counter 1131½ What County 117½ Tajante 1171½	No factor	8
15Mar66-6Aqu	fst 6f .23⅗ .47⅗ 1.13	Clm 20000	5	5	57½	611	78	79¼	WBlum	b 121	6.30	69-30	Linear B. 1211½ Beau Ampere 114h Africanus 114no	Far off pace	7
1Mar66-5Hia	fst 7f .23⅕ .46⅖ 1.24⅘	Allowance	8	2	55	33	11	14	BBaeza	b 115	*0.70	85-15	Vail Pass 1154 Jim Dooley 112h Spinsome 110¾	Well in hand	8
23Feb66-5Hia	gd 7f .23 .45⅖ 1.23⅗	Clm 16000	6	7	54½	43½	2½	2½	JLRotz	b 116	*3.00	90-12	Heronslea 115½ Vail Pass 1162 Casque 109½	Showed game try	10
15Feb66-7Hia	fst 6f .22⅗ .45⅘ 1.10⅘	Clm 16000	9	6	53½	32	4½	3nk	JLRotz	b 116	8.90	90-16	Rebel Light 112h Beau Ampere 116h Vail Pass 1161½	Just missed	12

LATEST WORKOUTS Jun 1 Bel t.c. 3f fm .37 b May 12 Bel m.t. 4f fst .53⅖ b May 10 Bel tr.t. 4f fst .52⅖ b May 3 Bel m.t. 4f fst .50 b

Sea Castle

B. g (1963-Va), by Summer Tan—Coral Bell, by Khaled
Rokeby Stable E. Burch (P. Mellon) **114**

1966	10	2	3	1	$10,500
1965	3	M	0	0	——

25May66-8Aqu	fst 1⅛ .46⅕ 1.10⅗ 1.49⅗	Allowance	7	7	714	715	67½	46½	ORosado5	b 108	33.70	81-13	Highest Honors 113½ Buffle 1123½ Bushfighter 1132½	Late foot	7
4May66-6Aqu	fst 1⅛ .47⅖ 1.12⅘ 1.51⅕	Allowance	5	7	78½	54	59	511	KKnapp	b 113	4.10	69-20	Deck Hand 1133 Paoluccio 1234 Vail Pass 1202½	Raced wide	8
27Apr66-6Aqu	fst 1⅛ .48⅘ 1.13 1.51⅗	Allowance	4	5	42	2h	11½	2nk	KKnapp	b 113	*1.50	79-18	Hail the King 115nk Sea Castle 1133 Enfant Terrible 1203	Missed	6
13Apr66-6Aqu	fst 1⅛ .48⅖ 1.13⅕ 1.50⅗	Allowance	5	7	63½	73½	2h	34	KKnapp	b 112	3.90	79-16	Throne Room 113no Your Prince 1234 Sea Castle 1122½	Wide	8
4Apr66-8Aqu	fst 1⅛ .48⅕ 1.12⅘ 1.52	Allowance	4	2	1h	1½	13	12	KKnapp	b 111	*2.30	76-19	Sea Castle 1112 Tequillo 1064 Lash Back 111no	Speed to spare	7
24Mar66-6Aqu	fst 1⅛ .49⅖ 1.14 1.54⅕	Md Sp Wt	2	2	11½	12	16	18	KKnapp	b 122	*2.40	65-25	Sea Castle 1228 Prince Timmy 1223 Ronnie's Rebel 122¾	In hand	7
22Feb66-4Hia	sly 1⅛ .47⅕ 1.11⅘ 1.50⅗	Md Sp Wt	5	3	23	24	23	24½	RTurcotte	b 117	*1.40	77-13	Glenrose 1174½ Sea Castle 11712 Thirty Grand 1174	Second best	8
15Feb66-5Hia	fst 1⅛ .47 1.12⅗ 1.53	Md Sp Wt	0	7	58	44	3½	21½	RTurcotte	b 118	3.70	68-16	Ameri Pilot 1181½ Sea Castle 1182½ Jet Derby 1185	Forced wide	11
1Feb66-5Hia	fst 1⅛ .48 1.13⅕ 1.54⅗	Clm 15000	4	7	77	65¾	64¾	53	RTurcotte	b 114	11.00	59-23	LashBack1141 FrancisT.Hunter107½ PointedRemark1141½	No mishap	8
24Jan66-4Hia	fst 6f .22⅗ .46⅘ 1.13	Clm 9000	7	12	1211	1013	1111	54	RTurcotte	b 112	11.90	75-24	Buddys Choice 1161 Alhambra Pal 1133 RicoRed116no	Stride late	12

LATEST WORKOUTS Jun 1 Bel t.c. 3f fm .37 b May 24 Bel m.t. 3f fst .38 b May 19 Bel m.t. 3f fst .36⅗ b Apr 21 Bel m.t. 3f fst .38 b

Henbaj

B. g (1961), by Jabneh—Cosmetic, by Cosmic Bomb
Sallupe Stable G. Seabo (Mrs. L. d'A Carpenter) **120**

1966	7	3	1	0	$7,725
1965	19	0	1	4	$4,215

16May66-8Aqu	fm 1⅛ Ⓣ 1.49⅗	Allowance	6	6	76	74½	88	89½	MVenezia	120	8.20	78-13	Mourmelon 1151½ Mimado II 120nk Fast Start 116nk	Never close	10
27Apr66-7GP	fm 1 1/16 Ⓣ 1.10⅘ 1.43⅕	Clm 12500	1	4	44½	21½	2h	12½	CFarmer	118	8.00	88-17	Henbaj 1182½ Brant 1162 Aquanotte 1181½	Under brisk drive	6
19Apr66-9GP	fm 1 Ⓣ .47⅖ 1.37⅕	Clm 8500	1	4	45	32	11½	13	JSellers	116	4.00	88-13	Henbaj 1163 Solar Stance 116½ Single G. 1124	Under mild drive	9
4Apr66-9GP	fm 1 Ⓣ .46⅘ 1.37⅗	Clm 8500	2	6	73½	54¾	52¾	41½	CStone	114	2.40	84-13	Zippenpedium 113½ Dandy Intent 114¾ Guapote 114nk	Rallied	7
17Mar66-6GP	fm 1 1/16 Ⓣ 1.13⅗ 1.46⅘	Clm 7500	2	4	61½	43½	2½	2no	CStone	118	6.30	70-28	Ibetu 112no Henbaj 118no Bent Spur 114¾	Sharp try, just missed	12
11Mar66-10GP	fm 1 1/16 Ⓣ 1.12⅘ 1.44⅘	Clm 6750	11	4	43½	1h	11½	1no	CStone	116	6.60	80-18	Henbaj 116no Southern Light 1122¼ Egeo 109nk	Under pressure	11
19Jan66-10Hia	fst 1⅛ .47⅘ 1.12⅘ 1.52⅗	Clm 9500	2	8	812	1012	1015	1115	GMineau5	109	53.80	57-22	Bent Spur 1121 Noble Land 1165 Bud Wallace 114nk	No speed	12
28Dec65-10TrP	fst 1 1/16 .46⅘ 1.12⅕ 1.44⅕	Cl c-6250	9	6	56½	66¾	66½	65	EMBelville5	110	9.80	76-16	Cheneau 1142 Ruperto 117no Golden Grain 1192	Never close	9
13Dec65-8Pim	sly 1 1/16 .47⅗ 1.12⅘ 1.45⅘	Allowance	1	7	107¾	1017	97¼	916	DFrench	110	15.50	70-17	Vouloir 1105 Mebs Last 1141 Michael P. G. 116no	Showed nothing	10
3Dec65-8Pim	fm 1 1/16 TC 1.12⅕ 1.45	Allowance	8	8	912	810	710	43	CBaltazar	112	♦8.20	87-10	White Bear Lake 1202 Tabare 1121 Faint Saint 115h	Rallied	11

3Dec65—♦Dead heat.

LATEST WORKOUTS May 31 Bel tr.t. 3f fst .39 b May 28 Bel m.t. 5f sly 1.05 b May 24 Bel tr.t. 4f fst .51⅖ h May 15 Bel tr.t. 3f fst .38 h

Assagai X

Dk. b. or br. c (1963-Ky), by Warfare—Primary II, by Petition
Cragwood Stable M. Miller (R. F. Scully)
111
1966 3 2 0 0 $5,850
1965 8 M 2 1 $2,730

25May66-8Aqu fst 1⅛ .46⅕1.10⅗1.49⅗ Allowance 5 3 46½ 56½ 46 59 WBlum 113 11.10 79-13 Highest Honors 113½ Buffle 1123½ Bushfighter 1132½ No mishap 7
7May66-6Aqu fst 6f .22 .45⅗1.11⅖ Allowance 6 6 87¼ 65½ 52¾ 1nk WBlum 113 6.30e 86-17 Assagai 113nk Pitch Man 106h Dey Sovereign 113nk Up in time 11
13Apr66-5Kee sly 6f .22⅖ .46⅗1.12⅖ Md Sp Wt 4 3 3½ 1½ 13 12 LAdams 122 3.80 81-18 Assagai 1222 Puppeteer 1177 Dominar 1222 Under pressure 10
27Nov65-4Aqu sly 1 .46⅗1.12⅕1.39 Md Sp Wt 10 3 3nk 1½ 11½ 2¾ MVenezia 122 4.20e 72-25 Highest Honors 122¾ Assagai 1223½ Prospect Street 117½ 2nd best 11
20Nov65-1Aqu fst 1 .46⅘1.12⅖1.40⅕ Md Sp Wt 5 3 41½ 32 23 44¾ WBlum b 122 4.00 62-20 Tequillo 1171½ Squadron E. 1222½ Paddyland 122¾ Speed, tired 10
13Nov65-3Aqu fst 1 .47⅖1.13 1.39⅕ Md Sp Wt 8 5 62¼ 63 44 31¾ MVenezia b 122 5.90 70-22 Earldom 122¾ Mask of Play 1221 Assagai 1221 Finished fast 9
6Nov65-4Aqu fst 1 .46⅗1.11⅗1.37⅘ Md Sp Wt 5 8 76½ 62¾ 51¾ 42¾ JSellers b 122 10.20 76-17 Poker 122no Earldom 1222 Ameri Pilot 122¾ Only mild late rally 12
2Nov65-4Aqu fst 6f .23⅕ .46⅘1.12 Md Sp Wt 3 8 78½ 711 511 28 WBlum b 122 7.20 75-18 Nashwood 1228 Assagai 1221 Exhibitionist 122½ Closed well 14
26Oct65-5Aqu fst 6f .22⅗ .45⅘1.13 Md Sp Wt 7 9 109¾1016101511 15 WBlum b 122 3.00 63-18 Draeh's Folly 122nk Nashwood 1226 Pilot Major 122½ Bore out 14
19Oct65-1Aqu fst 6f .22⅗ .46⅗1.12⅗ Md Sp Wt 8 9 86¼ 85¾ 55 43 WBlum 122 4.70 77-18 Clarinetist 122nk Space Citation 122¾ Draeh's Folly 1222 Wide 10
12Jly 65-4Aqu fst 5½f.22⅗ .46 1.04⅗ Md Sp Wt 5 7 78½ 69 56 55¾ WBoland 122 48.90 84-10 Amberoid 1221 Draeh's Folly 1221 Bobillard 1223 No mishap 12
LATEST WORKOUTS May 30 Bel t.c. 5f fm 1.03⅗ b May 24 Bel m.t. 4f fst .49 b May 20 Bel m.t. 1m sly 1.44 b May 16 Bel m.t. 5f fst 1.03 b

Talk Big

B. g (1962), by Speak Up—Ascona, by Rosemont
G. Farraro J. E. Rich (Dr.-Mrs. F. P. Miller)
120
1966 4 2 1 0 $5,585
1965 24 0 4 4 $7,390

11May66-2Aqu fst 6f .22⅘ .47 1.12⅘ Clm 6000 6 6 62½ 53½ 4nk 22½ AValenzuela b 113 19.70 76-19 Arranger 1122½ Talk Big 113½ Martial Owens 1162½ Good effort 7
30Apr66-9Aqu my 1 3/16 .48⅘1.14⅗2.03⅘ Hcp 3500s 2 5 31½ 32 712 721 HGustines b 109 11.60 41-20 Black Joy 124f Fighting Phantom 1162½ Gonna 1111 Tired 8
18Apr66-2Aqu fst 1 .45⅘1.11⅕1.38⅖ Cl c-4000 5 2 13 13 14 1½ WBlum b 117 2.80 76-17 Talk Big 117½ Artist Town 1152½ Glass House 1151 Hard drive 7
9Apr66-2Aqu fst 7f .23⅗ .47⅕1.26⅖ Clm 3500 1 6 2½ 2h 2h 1h WBlum b 113 5.90 74-18 Talk Big 113h Prince Easy Mon 1242½ Cornish Lad 1155 Just up 10
3Sep65-9Dmr fm*7½f TC .46⅕1.31⅗ Clm 5000 7 2 33½ 33 22 97 EBurns 114 *2.20 82-10 King Jay 112nk Ruths Acres 1141 Laddy Peggy 1141 Tired 9
25Aug65-4Dmr fm*7½f TC .46⅖1.32 Clm 6250 4 5 513 512 52 52 MYanez 114 6.70 85-17 Klack Klickety 109h Consultation 115¾ Green Orchid 119h Well up 9
21Aug65-4Dmr fst 6f .22⅗ .46 1.10⅗ Clm 6250 6 6 33½ 42½ 54½ 53½ WHartack 116 5.40 83-12 Khaledheir 117½ Joela 1122 Keepanion 112½ Even effort 8
14Aug65-3Dmr fst 6f .22⅖ .45⅖1.10⅕ Clm 6250 1 7 63¾ 43½ 44½ 34½ WHartack 116 *2.10 83-13 Khaledheir 1143½ I'm Special 1141 Talk Big 116½ Rallied 8
7Aug65-2Dmr fst 6f .22⅕ .45⅘1.10⅖ Clm 6250 4 5 76½ 63¾ 31½ 22 EBurns 114 6.40 85-11 Kings Lad 1142 Talk Big 114¾ Green Orchid 1171½ Rallied 9
31Jly 65-3Dmr fst 6f .22⅗ .46⅕1.10⅗ Clm 6250 2 6 64½ 53¾ 44½ 35½ BJennings 114 3.50 81-14 Flashey Luke 1174½ Green Orchid 119¾ Talk Big 114¾ Evenly 7
LATEST WORKOUTS Jun 1 Bel t.c. 3f fm .37 b May 27 Bel t.c. 1m fm 1.44⅗ b May 21 Bel m.t. 1m gd 1.46⅗ b May 18 Bel m.t. 3f fst .37 b

Nashwood

B. c (1963-Ky), by Nashua—Querida, by Alibhai
Adele L. Rand W. W. Stephens (L. Combs 2d, J. W. Hanes-Walmac Farm)
109[5]
1966 12 1 0 0 $4,150
1965 10 1 1 1 $3,990

28May66-8Aqu sly 1 .45⅕1.10⅕1.37⅗ Allowance 5 1 15 16 15 1h ORosado5 106 16.30 80-18 Nashwood 106h Best Irish 1142 Ameri Pilot 113½ Tiring, lasted 7
7May66-6Aqu fst 6f .22 .45⅗1.11⅖ Allowance 1 8 45½ 99½ 75¾ 89 BFeliciano 110 37.10 77-17 Assagai 113nk Pitch Man 106h Dey Sovereign 113nk Not a factor 11
26Apr66-5Aqu fst 7f .22⅘ .45⅗1.23⅖ Clm 16000 1 4 1½ 1½ 42½ 67½ BFeliciano 112 35.60 81-18 LightningStorm1191½ IndianFighter1191½ HollyMan1161½ Used up 9
19Apr66-5Aqu fst 6f .22⅘ .46 1.10⅗ Clm 19000 2 6 64½ 73¾ 64¾ 66 BFeliciano 114 23.60 84-17 Beaustone 114h Pitch Man 116nk Indian Fighter 117nk No mishap 7
12Apr66-8Aqu fst 1⅛ .46⅘1.11⅗1.51⅘ Allowance 3 2 2h 2½ 811 821 WShoemaker 109 12.40 56-19 Neparoo 109½ Highest Honors 1123 Ameri Pilot 1124 Tired 9
8Apr66-6Aqu fst 6f .23 .47⅕1.12⅕ Allowance 10 6 95¾107¼118¾117 EGuerin 116 48.10 75-19 Cool Oasis 116no Bushfighter 116h Unintentionally 1142½ No threat 12
10Mar66-9GP fm 1 1/16 Ⓣ 1.10⅗1.42⅗ Allowance 7 2 22 2½ 36 44½ JSellers 113 18.50 87-13 Crown Land 119nk Minstrel Moud 1173½ Greek Jab 113½ Tired 12
2Mar66-2Hia fst 6f .22⅕ .45⅖1.11⅕ Allowance 8 6 63½119¾1114 87 RUssery b 116 32.20 81-13 Notice Me 116nk d-Sky Duke 116h Devil's Tattoo 116h No factor 12
21Feb66-7Hia fm*1 1/16 Ⓣ 1.44⅗ Allowance 6 3 33 23 33 811 BBaeza b 115 20.50 77 9 HappyHighway1101½ ShannonPower1151½ AmeriPilot1161 Wide 12
4Feb66-7Hia fst 1⅛ .47 1.13 1.53⅕ Allowance 4 2 12 12 33 613 BBaeza b 116 13.90 56-25 Nashaweena 1161½ Bright Monarch 1165 Neparoo 1161½ Bumped 11
31Jan66-9Hia fst 7f .23⅕ .46⅖1.24⅖ Allowance 9 1 2½ 21½ 610 815 DBrumfield 114 66.10 72-21 Poker 1143 Abe's Hope 1182 Old Bag 1143 Forced pace, stopped 9
LATEST WORKOUTS May 24 Bel tr.t. 5f fst 1.08 b May 18 Bel tr.t. 5f fst 1.03 h May 13 Bel tr.t. 4f fst .49⅗ h Apr 4 Bel m.t. 5f fst 1.03 b

Results of 6th Race Aqueduct—June 2, 1966

SIXTH RACE 1 1-16 MILES (turf). (Errcountess, June 28, 1963, 1:41½, 5, 121.)
Aqu 27715 Fisherman Purse. Allowances. Purse $6,500. 3-year-olds and upward which have never
June 2. 1966 won two races other than maiden, claiming, optional or starter. 3-year-olds, 114 lbs.;
older, 123 lbs. Non-winners of a race other than maiden or claiming at a mile or over
at any time allowed 3 lbs.

Value to winner $4,225; second, $1,300; third, $650; fourth, $325. Mutuel Pool, $327,004.

Index	Horses	Eq't A Wt	PP	St	¼	½	¾	Str	Fin	Jockeys	Owners	Odds to $1
27588Aqu5	—Assagai	3 113	8	5	23	25	24	12	12½	W Blum	Cragwood Stable	12.30
27588Aqu4	—Sea Castle	b 3 114	5	9	91	92	51	43	25	K Knapp	Rokeby Stable	8.20
27516Aqu8	—Henbaj	5 120	6	7	82	6½	75	51	3½	B Baeza	Mrs D H Carter	5.50
27615Aqu1	—Nashwood	3 109	10	6	14	15	12	22	44	O Rosado5	Adele L Rand	20.30
27588Aqu6	—Vail Pass	b 4 120	4	3	41	3h	32	3½	51	L Adams	A J Giordano	14.10
26830Hia3	—Fairlane	4 118	2	2	6½	5h	6½	74	6¼	L Loughry5	Mrs L J Beecher	1.70
27579Aqu5	—St'ds to R'son	b 3 114	1	10	10	10	92	86	7no	H Gustines	Harbor View Farm	4.70
27577Aqu4	—Bwana Peacha	5 120	7	4	32	44	42	6½	810	R Turcotte	P Fuller	7.70
27474Aqu2	—Talk Big	b 4 120	9	8	7½	8h	10	9h	9h	M Venezia	G Ferraro	39.50
27516Aqu10	—Unimak	5 120	3	1	51	71	8½	92	10	E Belmonte	N Yacono	18.20

Time, 1:41¾ (crosswind in backstretch). Track firm.

$2 Mutuel Prices: 8-ASSAGAI 26.60 12.00 8.00
5-SEA CASTLE 9.80 5.40
6-HENBAJ 4.80

OFF AT 4:10 EASTERN DAYLIGHT TIME. Start good. Won easily.

Dk. b. or br. c, by Warfare—Primary II, by Petition. Trainer, Mac K. Miller, Bred by R. F. Scully (Ky.).
IN GATE—4:10. OFF AT 4:10 EASTERN DAYLIGHT TIME. Start good. Won easily.
ASSAGAI, forwardly placed and saving ground until near the stretch, took command from NASHWOOD
before reaching the furlong pole and retained a clear advantage without the need of urging. SEA CASTLE, far
back until the last three-eighths, moved between horses in the upper stretch and finished fast. HENBAJ, outrun
for three-quarters, was unable to threaten the leaders when set down through the stretch. NASHWOOD went
to the front early, drifted out at the initial turn but established a long lead and tired before entering the
stretch. VAIL PASS weakened during the last eighth. FAIRLANE, never dangerous after the start, had no
mishap. STANDS TO REASON began slowly and disliked the turf course. BWAMA PEACHA stopped after
showing early speed. TALK BIG showed nothing. UNIMAK was finished early.
Scratched—Fleet Musketeer, Annette's Ark, Night Show, Resolute King.
Overweight—Assagai, 2 pounds.

Courtesy of The Morning Telegraph

behind good juveniles such as Amberoid (ultimate winner of the 1966 Belmont), Highest Honors, Tequillo and Poker. In one race it had beaten Exhibitionist for place money.

After the winter's rest that carefully nurtured young horses deserve, the colt returned to action at Keeneland in April, winning a maiden-special on a sloppy track. Then to Aqueduct in May for victory over some fair allowance horses. Later that month—only eight days before today's grass race—it had finished fifth behind Highest Honors, Buffle and Bushfighter in a brisk but not especially taxing effort at a mile and an eighth. The horse had never competed on grass, but had worked nicely on it only three days ago. Was it worth a bet?

"Of course," said the ace handicapper sitting with me. "He's the only thing in the race with a hint of class. Maybe he has a lot of it. Maybe he has less than I think. But you have to admit that he hasn't made a bum of himself yet, compared with these others."

The colt won by three lengths, paying $26.60. Name: Assagai. In a few months, Assagai was everybody's champion grass horse of the year, beating all American comers of all ages and almost capturing the Washington, D.C., International, in which he ran against the world's best.

Turf races are immensely popular with horsemen and audiences alike. They provide the horsemen with opportunities for stouthearted animals whose feet hurt too much on dirt but are comfortable on sod. They provide the players with a colorful spectacle and solid longshots like Assagai. Solid, because the more obvious aspects of their dirt-track records fail to conceal the inherent class and courage that win on the grass.

Stakes and Handicaps

Purists will be offended because I lump all handicap races and all the great stakes under one heading. I do so because I think that these aristocratic races offer relatively few betting opportunities. They are delightful to watch, of course. They bring together the best horses in the country, or the best horses at the particular track—animals so well matched that prediction is extra hazardous. In the year of a Tom Fool, a Buckpasser, a Kelso, a Count Fleet or a Citation, it is possible to make out nicely on some of the more important events. But most of the other name races simply are too close to bother with.

Overnight handicaps are not much better for the player. In these, top allowance-grade horses compete under handicap conditions—with the weights assigned by the racing secretary according to his evaluation of the entrants' recent performances. As might be expected, the problem is whether the class horse is in good enough condition to win at the particular weights and under the stress of the pace at which the procession is likely to go. Sometimes there is no way of telling whether one of the horses actually *does* have a class advantage. These are tough nuts to crack, and playing the favorite is no way out: it wins a third of the time but the player ends on the losing side of the ledger. Unless, of course, he plays odds-on favorites to place—risking dollars to win nickels.

Starter Handicaps

These are fascinating races. Eligibility is limited to horses that have started at a specified claiming price at some time during their careers, or during a fixed period of time. Weights are assigned by the racing secretary according to his estimate of the horses' abilities. Or the race might be called a "starter allowance," with weights prescribed according to number or value of recent victories.

In no other form of Thoroughbred racing do the maneuverings of trainers become more noticeable than in these regattas. The race may be limited to animals that have run in $3,500 claiming company, yet the field is sure to include several that usually bear price tags as high as $7,500, their $3,500 days long behind them. In fact, trainers have been known to enter $7,500 horses in $3,500 claiming races for no other reason than to make them eligible for subsequent starter handicaps and starter allowance races. (At some tracks, horses cannot be claimed on the first day of the season, enabling a barn to drop an expensive horse into a cheap race and qualify it for later starter handicaps without fear of losing it.)

Certain horses seem unable to win anything but these starter races. They lose when they run in straight claimers for lower purses, but they perk up when the bigger money is on the line. At Aqueduct, many insiders with a nose for large mutuel prices take it as a rule of thumb that the best bet in a starter handicap is the horse that has won such a race in the past, regardless of how poorly he may have been doing in his most recent outings. It is a fact that such horses jump up and win these races—often winning two or three a season without accomplishing much in any other kind of race. Their success can be taken as evidence that their trainers know how to get them ready for a spot without advertising the readiness in the past-performance records.

Optional Claimers

In these races an animal may be entered to be claimed or not, depending on the preference of its management. If it wins when *not* entered to be claimed it is penalized by being declared ineligible for another optional race of the same grade at the same meeting, except if entered to be claimed. Also, the horse's eligibility for future allowance races is affected: The track usually credits its victory as having taken place in an allowance race! But if it *is* entered to be claimed in the optional affair that it wins, it is charged only with a victory in a claiming race.

By and large, these optional races are more difficult to handicap than straight claimers, but are not always as obscure as allowance races. To a player who uses result charts, they pose no special difficulty beyond that of riffling through the charts to see what the past-performance record actually represents. Sometimes the past-performance records suffice, the class of the animals being apparent in the claiming prices and results of their recent efforts.

Jump Races

Hurdle races are run over low obstacles. Steeplechase races involve higher fences and water hazards. Both types are extremely dangerous for the horses and their riders and far too unpredictable for betting purposes. They are great fun to watch (except when some poor rider gets thrown onto his skull), but are absolute booby traps for the players. The reason should be obvious—the best horse in the race might meet with interference from a fallen horse, or might fall itself. Flat racing is tough enough. Jumps present the handicapper with an extra unknown factor. Only an incurable gambler risks important amounts of money in such circumstances.

Over the brush in a steeplechase race.   **UPI PHOTO**

Roll Up Your Sleeves

So much for playable-beatable races. Now for a detailed review of the methods whereby experts play them and beat them. In the next eleven chapters we shall explore matters such as distance, current condition, class, age, sex, consistency, weight, speed, pace, the trainer, the rider, special handicapping angles, the paddock and post parade.

The chapters deal with these factors not in order of importance but in a sequence likely to be most convenient for the reader. Indeed, it is impossible to say which handicapping factor is most important of all. Importance varies according to the particular race and the particular horse. But no factor stands alone. Each affects the others, and must be considered with the others in mind.

8 The Distance Factor

THE LATE Robert Saunders Dowst achieved prominence in the late thirties when his articles in *Esquire* and other magazines of mass circulation explained some of the rudiments of handicapping to the natives. Dowst enjoyed his fame but found that it had its price. Within a couple of years after he revealed to the general public that any dodo could make big money by betting on highly consistent horses, the system stopped winning.

It stopped winning mainly because the horses were yielding lower mutuel prices than ever. Dowst's grateful followers had not only been betting the boodle but spreading the word. Another reason why the system stopped winning was that a slightly lower percentage of the consistent horses was finishing first. As if their trainers were rebelling against the low odds and waiting for more lucrative opportunities.

Dowst himself denied, and rightly so, that any important number of trainers were deliberately stiffing the best, most consistent horses in racing rather than win at low odds. He mused that maybe the game was changing a little. It certainly was. His system had become public property when the sport was in transition to its present assembly-line state. The practice of racing Thoroughbreds into shape, long resisted by conscientious horsemen, was becoming more commonplace. Hence, an animal's record of consistency (an unusually high percentage of winning or in-the-money starts) could no longer be taken as absolute evidence that the creature was in condition to vie for the marbles every time it went to the post. The kind of horse that might have won a third of its starts in 1935 was unlikely to win more than a quarter of them in 1941, its handlers having discovered the boons and benefits of letting it get some of its training exercise in actual competition. While losing, that is.

From time to time during the years that have elapsed since Dowst's mild embarrassment, I have heard racetrackers cite his system as evidence that it doesn't pay to share the goodies of the game with members of the public. All that happens is that the odds go down, they say. And then, when the odds go down, the horsemen change their methods and the handicapping system or angle or theory becomes obsolete.

Could be. But I doubt it. I especially doubt it as far as the substance of the present chapter is concerned. What is revealed herein about the problem of a Thoroughbred's suitability to the distance of its race is unknown to most players of the game and neglected by many of the few who know it. If hundreds of thousands of players suddenly become aware of it, and begin betting accordingly, and boasting of the results, certain winning horses unquestionably will pay lower odds than before. But the game will not change as a result. The suitability of a Thoroughbred to the distance of its race is a product of heredity and cannot be turned on or off like a spigot.

The Law of the Yardstick

Most published material on the art of picking winners urges the reader to avoid betting on sprinters in route races and routers in sprints. The sprint is defined as a race of seven furlongs or less. All other distances are regarded as routes.

To classify an animal as a sprinter or a router, the player usually examines its record to see the kind of races in which it competes most often. More sophisticated analysts look for the kind of races in which it has won or finished close. Few players carry the investigation further. Which is a primary reason for the dismal regularity with which they lose.

Distance is a crucial factor in the training and racing of horses. Confronted with the problem of finding races that his livestock can win, the professional horseman takes pains to learn the *exact* distances best suited to their individual physiques, running styles and temperaments. The wise handicapper is no less painstaking about the distance preferences of the horses on which he bets.

The winning range of most horses is severely limited. If its trainer points at a four-year-old and declares that it can win at any distance in any company, you should remove your hat: You are in the presence of an all-time great Thoroughbred. The $7,000 gelding that beats its own kind every now and then at six furlongs may never be better than second best against the same company at seven furlongs. The slightly sturdier horse able to win at a mile and a sixteenth may lack the zip to beat a similar field at a mile, even though the half-furlong difference between the two races is only a matter of 110 yards. The run-of-the-mill Thoroughbred that steps out of its own distance category and wins is either the beneficiary of freakish good luck or enjoys a pronounced class advantage over the animals it beats at the new distance.

Several years ago, one of the world's foremost authorities on Thoroughbred racing and breeding, Peter Burrell, director of Britain's National Stud, summarized the facts:

"Races are run at all distances from five furlongs to two and a half miles, requiring different types of horse, the sprinter being as different from the stayer as a dairy cow from a beef cow.

"So high is the standard required today at each distance that the individual horse has become specialized for that particular distance, and we must regard the horse which is top class at all distances as something of a freak . . .

"It is not difficult to breed sprinters, but it is an undisputed fact that the more speed one breeds into a horse the less distance he stays, and with the stayers—also a type that breeds true—one can breed them to stay further, but they then begin to lack the turn of speed so essential to the final dash to the winning post.

"Our task would be much simpler if all two-year-old races were run at five to six furlongs and all races for older horses at a mile. After two hundred and fifty years we might and should have produced a definite type. Instead of which, we struggle to produce a sprinter with more stamina, a stayer with more speed, and in between find our classic horse —bred for more and more speed—failing to go the distance."

Because all that has been true for generations, its meaning has been incorporated into a maxim well known on the backstretch of any Thoroughbred track: "Every horse's best distance can be measured with a yardstick."

The player who accepts that truth and puts it to work for him has launched himself toward success at the races. *He stops betting on horses entered at unsuitable distances.* And he clears the air for himself in numerous other ways. Knowledge of the distance factor is essential to any workable understanding of other vital matters such as pace, current condition and the maneuverings of trainers.

How Trainers Use Distance

If you open any copy of *The Morning Telegraph* or *Racing Form* it will take you only a few seconds to find a six-furlong horse. Chances are that its only victories have been at that exact distance. Several weeks ago, let us say, it won when entered to be claimed for $5,000. Seven days later, it ran against $6,000 claimers at the same distance and lost, tiring in the stretch. It probably was slightly outclassed, and may also have lost its keen edge in the exertion of winning its previous race. Ten days later it was back in another $5,000 claimer at its favorite distance and finished a well-beaten fifth. Clearly, it had gone off form.

The trainer rested it for almost a month and brought it back against $6,000 stock at the usual distance. It led to the half-mile call, pooped out and staggered home seventh. Today it again is entered for $6,000, but in a mile race. What goes on?

The animal has run the mile before and has never had a thing left in the stretch. It has never even finished in the money at seven furlongs. Why is the trainer bothering to enter it at a mile today?

Two reasons. First and foremost, the brief layoff seems to have refreshed the horse. It showed a nice lick of early speed in its last race. It may soon be able to win, especially if it runs against its own kind—$5,000 horses—at its own distance. The trainer evidently believes that it needs another tune-up, a "tightener." To make that tightener a mile race may help the horse's condition by requiring it to gallop farther than it likes. Which brings us to the second reason for entering it at the unsuitable distance.

The trainer does not expect to win today's race and has no intention of taxing the horse with an all-out try. Obviously, he would be pleased if the horse took an early lead and managed to hold it all the way to the finish wire. Pleased? Astonished! But he would strangle the jockey with his bare hands if the boy whipped the horse into a state of exhaustion just to finish third or fourth. The trainer's principal interest is to prepare for a race scheduled to take place five or six days from now—a $5,000 claimer at three quarters of a mile. If the beast finishes seventh today, as expected, and loses the predictable six or eight lengths in the final stages, many members of the crowd will refuse to bet on it next week. The odds will be better. The trainer and his employer, the owner, will like that.

The trainer could have entered the horse in a six-furlong scamper on today's program. The race could have been an effective tightener. But the horse might have come close to winning. Its improving form would have been too apparent. When it went for the marbles next week, the odds would be anemic. The trainer and owner would not like that.

What I am getting at here is that the player who bets on a horse entered at an unsuitable distance must assume not only that the horse will violate its own nature and win, but that the trainer will violate *his* nature and go for broke. That is too much to assume.

In virtually every race, most of the entrants have negligible chances to win. Of these all-but-certain losers, some are entered at an uncomfortable distance. Their trainers are darkening their form while doing what they can to improve it. Stayers are encouraged to develop early speed by chasing fleet sprinters out of the starting gate. Sprinters develop needed stamina by chugging behind stayers in the final stages of route races.

How, then, do experts tell if a horse is entered at a suitable distance? Let's see.

The Right Distance

The conservative handicapper is more likely to win than his reckless companion. But it is possible to become too conservative. For example, it is possible to exaggerate the importance of the distance factor beyond all reasonable limits, refusing to bet on any horse that has not already *won* at today's exact distance. Certainly, if a horse has won several times at the distance, its qualifications in this department can be taken for granted. But to eliminate a horse only because it has never won at the distance may be costly.

To illustrate, let us compare the recent races of two animals entered in a $5,000 claimer at seven furlongs.

Horse "A"

6f	23⅕	46⅗	1.11⅘	Clm 5000	4	8	7^5	6^5	5^4	3^4
6f	22⅘	46⅕	1.11⅗	Clm 5000	2	9	8^7	8^6	5^4	3^3
7f	23⅗	46⅘	1.25	Clm 5000	3	6	5^7	4^4	2^2	$1^{1/2}$

Horse "B"

6f	22⅖	45⅖	1.10⅘	Allowance	3	4	4^2	5^3	6^4	7^5
6f	22⅘	46	1.11⅖	Clm 6500	1	1	1^2	1^4	1^3	1^{11}
7f	23	46⅕	1.24⅕	Clm 7000	3	1	1^3	$1^{1/2}$	1no	4^3

Horse "B" is plainly the faster, classier animal. To discard it from consideration because it failed to carry its speed all the way in its only seven-furlong attempt would be a grave mistake. It set the pace in that race but was hooked at the quarter pole by another $7,000 horse (the result chart may show that the other horse was actually an $8,000 or $9,000 one), and continued gamely into the stretch before fading. In a six-furlong race, "B" would be odds-on against "A" on grounds of class, speed, pace, whatever. Its loss to allowance horses can undoubtedly be forgiven.

As to "A," it plainly qualifies for today's distance. Six furlongs apparently is too little ground for it, but it seems able to lumber into contention during the stretch run of a seven-furlong event. At least, it can do that when opposing $5,000 horses incapable of "B's" speed. If "B" is in shape today it should win in a walk over "A."

Problems of this kind are most perplexing early in the year, especially in races for three-year-olds. Many of them have not raced often enough to be ruled out on grounds of inability to win at the distance. The handicapper needs to develop criteria other than previous victories at the distance—unless he wants sorrow.

Later in the year, or in races for four-year-olds and older, the problem subsides. Unless the race is for what my friend Howard Rowe calls "giraffes," several entrants will already have won at the distance. And among the others that have run the distance without winning, several will have covered the ground swiftly enough, and against sufficiently good opposition, to qualify as contenders.

Make Your Own Guidelines

If a horse has already won a race of today's distance, its eligibility as a contender can be accepted. Other questions about its chances can be deferred until the player is ready to consider matters such as form, class, age, sex, consistency, weight, speed, pace.

Many handicappers work that way, one step at a time, systematizing their methods to avoid confusion. Others prefer to take larger bites. If the horse has won or run close-up in a race of today's distance, these players ask additional questions:

1. **Against what kind of animals did the horse do it?**
2. **When did he do it?**
3. **How authoritatively did he do it?**

In attending to such questions, the player recognizes the interrelationships between distance and class, form and pace. He disposes immediately of chores that otherwise would have to be performed later. He gets the job done more quickly.

The reader's own approach will depend mainly on his personal tastes and partly on how much experience he has had with past-performance records. As long as he understands and applies the principles set forth in these pages, his eventual method will be as good as any other.

Before deciding *how* to analyze the distance factor, the reader might want to consider whether to dispose of it at the very beginning of his handicapping procedure.

Should Distance Come First?

The Compleat Horseplayer and *Ainslie's Jockey Book* recommend a selection method in which the distance factor is handled before the other fundamentals. Excellent results may also be attained by starting with current condition, class, consistency, speed or pace. Since the fundamentals of handicapping are intertwined, the player who deals with one of them must at least touch on some of the others at the same time. Furthermore, no matter where the handicapping process starts, it ends by covering the same ground.

Mrs. Richard C. DuPont goes to the winners' circle with her wonderful Kelso and a happy Arcaro after the 1960 Jockey Club Gold Cup. WIDE WORLD PHOTOS

Bold Ruler, a good middle-distance runner, beats General Duke in the 1957 Flamingo Stakes at Hialeah. Eddie Arcaro looks over his shoulder while hand-riding the colt that later became one of the great sires of modern times.
UPI PHOTO

I prefer to take up distance before all other factors because I have found that it saves time. Using fairly simple standards to determine horses' suitability to the distance of today's race, the player often is able to eliminate as many as half of the entrants. This sharply reduces the remaining work. To be sure, similar savings of time are achieved by starting with the factor of current condition. Many experts manage to attend to condition and distance with one sweep of the eye, having been in the game long enough to develop that kind of ease.

For readers who are not already set in their handicapping ways, I should like to propose that they plan to dispose of distance first. However, I shall describe the various methods in such a way that the reader may choose the ones he prefers, and fit them into any sequence he likes.

The Conservative Approach

Some experts refuse to bet on a slow or inconsistent horse, even when it seems to have a clear edge over the other nonentities in its race. These conservatives reason that it is bootless to try to pick the least unreliable animal in an unreliable field. In this same spirit, they bypass a race unless some entrant has already run the exact distance in respectable fashion.

What's more, they never bet that any horse, however good it may be, will be able to do something today that it has not tried to do in the past. They refuse, in other words, to risk their money on a horse running at an unfamiliar distance.

They have a point. They avoid many a loser that way. They also steer themselves off many a winner. More relaxed players do quite nicely with carefully selected bets on cheap races, horses that have never raced before, and horses running at new distances.

Which approach is best? A quick answer would be fraudulent. It all depends on the psyche and talent of the individual player. Those unwilling or unable to dig deeply and imaginatively into the records are best advised to work the conservative side of the street. This might also be the best plan for beginners. As experience accumulates, greater flexibility becomes possible and profitable.

Whether the expert be conservative or not, his study of the distance factor is the very keystone of the work he does on races for two-year-olds. The following review of the best approaches to that problem shows how some players win by playing relatively few such races, and how others win while playing many more.

Two-Year-Olds and Distance

The most cautious approach to the distance factor in juvenile races is this:

1. Consider no two-year-old for play unless (a) it and each of its rivals has already raced at today's distance and (b) the horse has managed to run within two seconds of the track record for the distance.

That rule restricts play to certain high-class allowance and stakes races and a very occasional maiden-special-weights affair. It bypasses the hazards of guessing how youngsters will perform at five and a half furlongs if they have never tried to race farther than five. It protects the player from the first-time starters that sometimes upset the dope and win at long prices. It forbids bets on other, more highly touted debutantes that go to the post as favorites and lose.

The rule requiring a previous speed rating of 90 or better (no worse than two seconds slower than the track record for the distance) guarantees that the player will risk money only on the best two-year-olds around.

A reader attracted to that method will bet on few two-year-olds and seldom will collect a large mutuel payoff. If the remainder of his handicapping procedure is in keeping with his approach to the distance factor, he will hit a high percentage of winners. But he will pass race after race in which other smart, slightly less cautious players find excellent wagers.

To increase his betting opportunities without exposing himself to accusations of recklessness, he might amend his procedure slightly:

2. After making sure that all horses in the race for two-year-olds have already run at today's exact distance, consider only those that have earned a speed rating of 85 or better at the distance.

He now will be able to play additional maiden and allowance sprints. But he will continue to detour races in which some of the horses are strangers to the distance.

A somewhat less conservative outlook permits many experts to cash a satisfactory percentage of bets on juvenile races in which some of the horses have not yet tried the distance:

3. Consider no two-year-old for play unless it has earned a speed rating of at least 87 at today's exact distance.

Observe that nothing is said about whether other horses in the race have run the distance. Yet the method is quite safe. At most tracks, any two-year-old that has traveled today's distance rapidly enough to earn a speed rating of 87 (2⅗ seconds short of the track record) is talented enough to be conceded an excellent chance against first-time starters or other animals which have never tackled the distance before. The horse not only is swift but has undoubtedly profited from the experience of testing its speed in an earlier race at the distance.

If the horse with the previous figure of 87 or better is being asked to face a well-publicized first-time starter from a leading barn and sired by a Bold Ruler, the cautious player may choose to pass the race, depending on his assessment of other factors.

A player who wants to cash in on some of the plausible betting opportunities presented by first-starters and other animals that have never tried today's distance must be prepared for more than occasional losses. If he is essentially a careful type, he may find the following approach comfortable:

4. A well-bred first-time starter from a leading barn qualifies for consideration if (a) it has been working out frequently and rapidly, (b) it is to be ridden by a leading jockey, and (c) none of its rivals has been able to earn a speed rating of 80 or better at today's distance.

In this case the player establishes that none of the horses that has tried the distance is any great shakes at it. The trainer of the high-priced newcomer seems to have found an ideal spot for its debut. Circumstances of this kind arise quite frequently in maiden-special-weights races. The first-starter usually goes to the post as favorite when facing animals that have shown no real speed. The favoritism is deserved.

5. A juvenile that has raced before but has not raced at today's distance qualifies for consideration if (a) no other animal in the race has demonstrated high-class speed at the distance and (b) the horse's races at a distance not more than half a furlong shorter than today's have indicated real ability.

This is not as elaborate as it may sound. If a two-year-old has never traveled six furlongs in competition, one would hesitate to back it against a competitor that has already shown authentic talent at the distance by earning a speed rating of 88 or thereabouts. But if no such speedster is in the race, the horse may be worth a closer look. If it ran at least as fast at five and a half furlongs as any other horse in today's race, it becomes quite interesting. And it qualifies for the most serious consideration if its record shows that it was able to stay fairly close to the pace of the shorter races before *gaining ground in the homestretch*. Whether it won or lost the races, it looks very much like an animal that will be comfortable at the extra sixteenth of a mile. If its own speed ratings at the shorter distance were genuinely high, it may be a splendid risk today.

Why Use Speed Ratings?

The use of speed ratings to determine a Thoroughbred's aptitude for the distance of its race is standard practice, even among many experts who deride speed handicapping and rely mainly on analyses of class and form. The alternative to handling the distance factor in terms of speed ratings is to require the horse's record to show that, regardless of time or speed, the candidate has managed to finish reasonably close to the winner in a race contested over today's distance by a field whose class was not seriously inferior to today's.

In handicapping races for two-year-olds, it is immensely difficult to solve the distance problem *except* by means of speed ratings or actual clockings. Anyone who tries to figure out the class of a maiden-special race for two-year-olds has nothing to go on except the time in which it was run. The same is true of a juvenile allowance race. All that is known about the horses is that they are previous winners of maiden-specials or allowance affairs. The fastest are best. By the end of the season, the slower ones will be running in claimers.

And what about the distance factor in juvenile claiming races? Suppose the player is the less conservative kind who bets on some of the slower two-year-olds and wins at it? How does he do it?

6. In any two-year-old race, if none of the entrants has run the distance rapidly enough to earn a speed rating of 80 or higher, consider betting on any animal that has earned a rating at least 2 points higher than that of any of its rivals.

Every day during the spring and summer, maiden-specials, maiden claimers and straight claimers for two-year-olds are won by horses whose best previous speed ratings have been in the 70's. It is possible to get a satisfactory percentage of winners in these slower races by confining one's action to entrants that have shown slightly more speed than their opponents. Naturally, the player has to be a shrewd analyst of current condition, trainers, jockeys, and—as the season progresses—class. But the distance factor can be attended to by means of speed ratings.

The reader who surveys the foregoing information will find in it all he needs for his study of the distance factor in juvenile races. He can tighten or loosen any of the requirements, according to his own preferences and the results he achieves. During the early part of the year, before the youngsters are stretched out to six furlongs and beyond, he will find that his solution of the distance problem is almost all he needs to do about handicapping the race. In these short sprints for two-year-olds, time—speed—is all-important. And time, of course, is what the player uses to decide whether any two-year-old is qualified to run the distance of its race.

Races for older horses are something else entirely. Class distinctions, current condition, weight and pace now become more important. Many experts refuse to look at speed ratings on older horses, even in connection with the distance factor. Others find the ratings convenient indicators of whether a horse can get today's distance in reasonably good time, quite apart from the effects of class, condition, pace and weight. Still others, as we shall see later, do *all* their handicapping in terms of speed.

Older Horses and Distance

In trying to decide whether an animal aged three or more is suited to the distance of his race, the most cautious players of the game often operate on the following line:

1. A horse qualifies if (a) it has won a race of this exact distance, or has finished close to the winner in respectable time and (b) the race took place this season.

Many practitioners of this theory add the further condition that the horse's good race should have been against animals not greatly inferior to those it faces today. In that way they manage to lop off obviously outclassed horses. I mention this merely to suggest that it can be done, but I ask the reader to go through the chapter on class before deciding whether he wants to keep his distance and class studies separated or not.

The phrase "close to the winner," as used in the above rule, usually means a finish not more than three lengths behind. Some experts prefer a finish within two lengths. Others, anxious to qualify more horses on the distance factor, ask only that the animal has run fourth or better. Still others want the horse to have come very close to winning in a cheaper race, but are lenient about its finishing position in a race of higher quality.

As to the term, "respectable time," the following speed ratings can be accepted as adequate, subject to slight variations which arise from unique conditions at the individual track:

90—Sprints for animals of handicap and stakes quality. (In weighing the distance factor in terms of speed, a sprint should be defined as any race run around no more than one turn. At some major tracks, this will include distances up to and including a mile. At others, where there is no mile chute at the head of the backstretch, the longest race run around one turn may be at six and a half or seven furlongs.)

88—High-grade allowance sprints.

85—Handicaps and stakes run around two turns. (If a race is at a mile and an eighth or longer, most experts disregard speed ratings entirely. They evaluate the horse's suitability in terms of the class and stamina it displayed in previous efforts at such distances.) ·

80—High-grade allowance routes, lesser allowance sprints and sprints for claimers valued above $4,000.

78—Cheap claiming sprints ($4,000 or less).

73—Route races for better claimers.

69—Route races for claimers valued at $4,000 or less.

A player who tosses out all horses that fail to meet those requirements is well on his way to sharing the success enjoyed by arch-conservative handicappers. He passes race after race. He frequently tosses out the eventual winner of an apparently playable race, but is so strict about other fundamentals of handicapping that he often saves his neck by eliminating the losers at later stages of the work, and passing the race altogether. If some losers qualify on the distance factor, they fail to meet his rigid requirements as to class, condition, consistency, weights, running styles, trainers or jockeys. He may get less action than he might, and far less than most players want, but a handicapper of this kind gets his kicks from winning. Action means nothing to him.

The main flaw in his handling of the distance problem is its requirement that the horse's qualifying race be a recent one. To be sure, a good race last year is no guarantee that a horse will repeat the performance this year. Injuries, illness and overwork make many of last year's $10,000 horses into $3,500 ones by May of this year. But problems of that kind can be surmounted by a player who wants to catch some of the winners that the more cautious player misses. For example:

2. A horse qualifies at today's distance if (a) it has ever finished as close as fourth, or within two lengths of a winner, in a race of today's exact distance at a major track, and (b) it has earned a respectable speed rating at the distance at some time within the past year at a major track, and (c) its record indicates that it may still be able to run well at the distance.

When handicapping horses aged four or more, the requirement of a mere close-up finish at the distance is terribly lenient. Any fully mature horse that cannot meet that requirement is undoubtedly entered at the wrong distance. For that matter, many mature horses that satisfy the rule are also at the wrong distance: a router sometimes produces sufficient steam in the stretch to finish close to the winner of a six-furlong race. But he is still a router, and hardly an ideal choice in a sprint. However, the two additional parts of the rule tend to weed out such duds. So, for that matter, does the common sense of the player. If he sees that most of the races and all of the victories listed in the past-performance record of a mature horse were at distances more than a furlong longer or shorter than today's race, he can be reasonably sure that the horse is out of its element today.

The loose requirement of a close-up finish is most helpful in handicapping lightly raced three-year-olds. Every season, scores of races are won at handsome odds by improving three-year-olds which have never won at the distance before. Their victories occur not only in claiming races but in allowance events for some of the snazzier young horses in the business. Part of the trick of catching these up-and-comers is to give them credit for even a mediocre previous race at the distance.

The notion that a horse can qualify for further attention if it logged good time at the distance within the past year could be dangerous, but need not be. For example, if the horse has declined very much in class since that ancient race, or if it has been running badly or infrequently since the race, the player has good reason to suspect that it has gone sour. He therefore would disqualify it on grounds of form or class, either at this stage of the handicapping or later.

But the idea pays off at the mutuel windows in the late spring and early summer. At that time of year, a rigidly cautious player often discards an animal for failure to show a good recent race at the distance— even though it is perfectly ready to win today. It may be a nice little miler that has been campaigning at tracks where mile events are not programmed. Or it may have been resting for the winter. Its races this year may all have been at distances other than the mile. But if the horse's form has been improving (regardless of whether it has been winning or not), the trainer may be ready to crack down today.

If the approach embodied in this three-part rule is followed alertly, it can be counted on to qualify the ultimate winners of most playable races, and to disqualify a high proportion of the losers. It therefore clears the decks for concentrated study of the genuine contenders.

Older Horses at New Distances

At the beginning of each season and, to a lesser extent, throughout the remainder of the racing year, one encounters races in which three-year-olds attempt to run an altogether new distance. The safest approach is to bypass the race. Alternatively, one can handle the distance factor by methods similar to those employed in evaluating two-year-old races. Preference would go to horses with the best previous records and/or the most successful trainers and/or recent performances suggesting that the new distance might be comfortable for them.

Distance and Speed Charts

As readers of my earlier books are aware, I advocate pace handicapping, in the sense that I recommend inclusion of pace analysis in the player's methods. Some dyed-in-the-wool enthusiasts of pace and speed charts pay no attention to the distance factor, relying on the charted numbers to compensate for all unknowns. But others, whether they favor pace analyses or speed-weight formulas, may be interested in trying to profit from the distance factor. That is, they may want to experiment with the kind of pace handicapping or speed handicapping that applies pace or speed figures only to horses judged suitable to the distance of today's race.

To work in that fashion with pace or speed charts, it is highly advisable to use races that the horse has run at today's exact distance either on today's track or at a sister track on the same circuit. While some players profess to be able to make profits by pace-rating races run at different tracks, I have yet to see any evidence to support the claim.

Accordingly, the reader who contemplates trying a realistic form of pace handicapping (or some down-to-earth version of speed handicapping), should know now that he will be unable to work effectively with horses that have not run reasonably good races at today's exact distance on today's circuit. In my opinion, the races bypassed for lack of such information are more than compensated for by a higher percentage of winning selections.

Naturally, more on speed and pace handicapping will appear in the appropriate chapters.

Sprinters in Route Races

Once in a while, a horse that has never run farther than six furlongs leads from wire to wire in a race at a mile and an eighth. A carefully observant player can sometimes foresee the possibility. It arises most often in route races among animals with no inclination to go to the front in the early stages. If the sprinter is the kind that has been taking the lead in its own shorter races and tiring in the stretch, if not earlier,

Count Turf and Conn McCreary fool them all, winning the 1951 Kentucky Derby. UPI PHOTO

Lee Town, a sprinter, leads the 1962 Kentucky Derby at the first turn. The distance was too much for him and he finished far back. UPI PHOTO

it probably lacks the stamina to maintain the long, early lead it will enjoy today. But if it is the type that usually is fourth or fifth or sixth at the half-mile call in sprints and seldom quits in the stretch, it may be an excellent bet against today's plodders. Accustomed as it is to a much faster early pace than is characteristic in route races, it will undoubtedly take the lead immediately. If the jockey is good at rating horses to conserve their strength, and if the horse does not drop dead of surprise at being out in front so soon, it may last to the wire. The player should not discard it on grounds that it fails to satisfy his distance requirements. Not, that is, unless he is sure that something else in the field has enough foot to catch the sprinter in the late stages.

Routers in Sprint Races

Every spring, last year's stakes and handicap champions begin tuning up for the season's big money races. For many of them, the process includes entry in an allowance race at six furlongs. They usually lose. They lose because they are out for exercise and because they are unsuited to such short distances. Unless the confirmed distance runner entered in a sprint has shown pronounced early speed in its own good races, and unless its opponents in the tune-up are dismally inferior sprinters, the race is not worth a risk.

Among Thoroughbreds of less than championship quality, very much the same facts apply. An animal that wins at a mile and an eighth is odds-on to be out only for conditioning purposes any time it goes to the post in a sprint.

9 The Condition Factor

OF ALL HANDICAPPING PROBLEMS, none is more challenging than the riddle of condition—the form or fitness or sharpness or readiness of Thoroughbreds. In a representative field of nine horses, three or four may be in such dull form that even a novice can see the signs in their records. But the other entrants are likely to be a puzzlement.

Is the class horse in good enough shape to stand off its sharper, cheaper rivals? Can last week's victor do it again, or did the winning effort blunt its edge? Should one expect improvement from the animal that has been running closer and closer to the pace, or is it past the peak of its form cycle? Can Trainer Doe's gelding return from its six-week layoff and get the job done on workouts alone? Will the speed horse from Santa Anita show its California form in this, its first Maryland race?

The process of attempting to answer such questions is indispensable to success at the track. Knowledge of form prevents the astute player from betting on certain false favorites whose recent good races fool the rest of the crowd. The same knowledge enables him to back animals that win at long prices after apparently poor recent races. Yet, no matter how astute he may be, the subtle complications of the condition factor continue to challenge his best efforts. For every bet he loses through racing luck or a misjudged ride or an error in evaluating the class of a horse, he can expect to lose two because of surprises in the form department.

Most of these surprises derive from the very nature of the Thoroughbred. Contrary to the wishes of every loser, horses are not machines. They are highly sensitive beings, very much alive. Each is an individual, responsive in its own special way to changes in the weather, delays in feeding or watering, the moods of its handlers, the tensions of other horses, the commotion of the racetrack audience, the discomfort of an aching joint or muscle, the sight, sound or impact of the whip.

A horse's record may proclaim him the class of his field and sharp as a knife. He may breeze through his last pre-race workout in smashing time, without drawing a deep breath. He may eat everything in sight.

His coat may shine with the deep gloss of health. But he may take it into his head not to race. His reluctance may be so evident in the paddock and walking ring that sophisticated players immediately cancel any plans they may have had to bet on him. Or his mood may sour when he steps on a sandwich wrapper while trotting to the post, or when one of the assistant starters grabs him too unceremoniously, or when an adjoining horse brushes or bumps him.

Or he may go to the post as spry as can be, and run his race, and be beaten to the wire by a crippled old hide whose chronic disabilities vanish for a minute or two in the warmth of the afternoon and the heat of competition.

Hidden Form

Other reversals of form are more apparent than real. They have less to do with the nature of the Thoroughbred than with the nature of man. From time immemorial, most trainers have regarded it as their sacred duty to conceal or obscure the improving form of a horse. In the old days, when the sport was unsupervised, the object was exclusively to fool everybody and collect big odds. Nowadays, when racing is relatively well policed and detailed past-performance records are published for all to see, trainers have more trouble fooling the experts, but most of them continue to try. Moreover, the game has developed in such a way as to perpetuate the ancient practice of darkening a horse's form.

The demand for horseflesh with which to fill nine races a day is so urgent that only the most aristocratic and/or affluent stables are allowed to condition their animals carefully. All the others are expected to race the livestock as often as possible. This means entering unready horses. Or, as the saying goes, "racing a horse into shape."

The trainer does not live who has not been called into the racing secretary's office for a favor. "I need to fill the fourth race day after tomorrow," goes the request. "How about helping me and putting your filly in there?"

Stable space is hard to get. The uncooperative barn may find itself without house room at next year's meeting. So the typical response from the trainer is, "Sure! Glad to oblige! Any time!"

A less typical answer: "She isn't ready for a race. Needs a few more workouts. But if you say so, I'll enter her and let her work out in public!"

A veteran trainer comments, "Of course we darken a horse's form. How can we help it? How can a horse fail to look bad when it's not in condition to look good? Two or three bad races and it begins to improve, which is when you have to start worrying. You've paid four, five, six grand for the horse and nursed the soreness out of it and you're just beginning to run it into good condition and—bam!—some guy claims it away from you before it's paid for all the time and effort and fees and food you've invested. You've got to try to protect yourself against that, while waiting for it to get in shape to steal a purse.

"If the horse has a pretty fair reputation around the track, you have no choice but to run it over its head—at the wrong distances and at higher claiming prices than anyone in his right mind would pay. And you put stumblebum riders up, who can't handle the horse. And it loses so bad that a lot of people begin to believe you when you cry that something is wrong with it.

"Like as not, the horse is your main meal ticket," he continues. "When it wins, you want it to win at a price. The best way to build the price is to enter it against cheap ones of its own class *before* it is ready to win. Every time you do that, you take an awful chance on having it claimed. But let's say you have the guts to try. You tell the boy not to punish the horse because you've got a better spot picked out for later on. So he lets it pretty much alone and it finishes like sixth. Sure as God made little green mushmelons, half the wise guys in the park notice that the horse picked up five lengths in the backstretch before running into a blind switch on the turn. When next week comes, the horse goes off at 5 to 1 instead of the 20 you've been looking for. Don't let anyone tell you that this is an easy business."

Efforts to inflate the mutuel odds by hiding a horse's improving condition are attributed mainly to smaller stables. But, as I have indicated before, all but the most exclusive barns race their animals into shape. This practice, and the maneuvering whereby trainers seek to protect their cheaper stock from claims, are chiefly responsible for the ostensibly poor form of actually fit and ready horses.

A bad ride by a jockey carrying out the deliberately misleading orders of the trainer sometimes contributes to the build-up, making the horse look worse than it is. But aside from occasional manipulations in daily-double races at smaller tracks, no trainer in possession of his sanity knowingly defeats one of his horses when he thinks it ready to win. If it can't win, he may prefer it to lose badly. But if it can win, he strikes while the iron is hot, placing the horse in exactly the right company, at exactly the proper distance, with the best rider available. In other words, stables go all-out to win with any horse that has a chance. They go all-out because they know how briefly most horses retain top form. To enter a ready horse in the wrong kind of race is to risk never winning at all.

All this being so, the crucial task of the player is to penetrate the darkness and locate the signs of improvement tucked away in the past-performance records. At the same time, he seeks out equally significant signs of deteriorating condition among horses thought by others to be in the best of shape.

Schools of Thought

The condition factor is so strategic that many successful players devote most of their attention to it, giving only a lick and a promise to matters such as distance, class, weight, pace and jockey. It is possible to win this way, if the player really understands form and is not downright careless about horses which, good condition or not, are severely outclassed or outdistanced or overweighted, or are likely to suffer from an unfavorable pace or an inadequate ride.

A player who begins his examination of a field of Thoroughbreds by applying the distance and condition factors often finds himself with only two or three qualified contenders when the time comes to proceed to the next phase of his work. This makes life easier.

Other players, especially those who cherish class and consistency, pay no great attention to the condition factor, beyond making sure that the horses they like are not positively out of shape. They often are able to attend to this with a swift glance at the record. If they know what to encompass in the glance, they may be able to survive.

But nobody can ignore the condition factor and come close to winning this game. The more you know about Thoroughbred form and the more attention you give it, the more reliable your selections become.

The Form Cycle

Some horses hold their form for a relatively long time. Others seldom run two really good races in succession. In general, the animals capable of contending for four or five purses in a row are the better ones on the grounds, the ones able to withstand repeated hard efforts. Accordingly, they tend to be males rather than females, and younger rather than older.

Here are typical running lines to demonstrate the form cycle of a cheap, seven-year-old claimer. I have omitted the post position, which is irrelevant to the present discussion. The first column represents the horse's running position at the start of each race:

$$8 \quad 9^4 \quad 9^5 \quad 9^8 \quad 9^8$$
$$3 \quad 4^3 \quad 4^2 \quad 4^3 \quad 6^4$$
$$4 \quad 3^3 \quad 2\frac{1}{2} \quad 1\frac{1}{2} \quad 1^2$$
$$4 \quad 4^5 \quad 4^4 \quad 3^2 \quad 2\frac{1}{2}$$
$$5 \quad 4^2 \quad 5^2 \quad 6^3 \quad 7^5$$
$$8 \quad 9^3 \quad 9^4 \quad 9^7 \quad 9^{10}$$

The horse won its third race back and the effort knocked it off form. The improvement which foreshadowed that victory came rather suddenly in the fifth race back, when the horse picked up its feet well enough to stay fairly close to the early pace. In its next race it improved again and gained ground in the stretch. An alert player would have noticed that improvement and would have been careful to consider the animal in its subsequent race, unless it was obviously outclassed or entered at the wrong distance, whereupon the player would have considered it in the race after that. Unless horses of this quality are absolute washouts without a victory in them, they make their winning effort within a race or two of showing improved form. And, unless dropped sharply in class, they seldom run well after winning or finishing close up.

Good horses are always in the money or close to it. If properly managed they hold the winning sharpness for weeks:

$$4 \quad 3^2 \quad 4^2 \quad 4^3 \quad 4^4$$
$$3 \quad 3^3 \quad 2^2 \quad 2^2 \quad 2^3$$
$$2 \quad 2^1 \quad 2\frac{1}{2} \quad 2\frac{1}{2} \quad 1^{no}$$
$$2 \quad 2\frac{1}{2} \quad 1^2 \quad 1^3 \quad 1^4$$
$$2 \quad 1\frac{1}{2} \quad 1^1 \quad 1^1 \quad 1^2$$
$$4 \quad 3^2 \quad 2^2 \quad 2^1 \quad 2\frac{1}{2}$$
$$5 \quad 4^5 \quad 4^4 \quad 4^4 \quad 3^3$$

In its sixth race back, this horse showed that it had approached its best shape. It won three races in succession and now seems to have gone off its feed. It probably will be rested for a month or six weeks and, assuming no injury, will return to the head end of the parade after a preparatory race or two.

Standards of Form

In studying the past-performance records for clues to current condition, the player concerns himself with the following information:

1. **The dates and whereabouts of the animal's most recent races and workouts.**
2. **The probable effects of this activity on the animal's form.**
3. **Individual variations in the normal form cycle.**

Effective form analysis requires a series of decisions, some negative and others positive. In the negative vein, the player discards animals whose records fail to meet his minimum standards. For example, a horse that has been inactive recently might be discarded for that reason alone, regardless of how promising its last race might have seemed at the time. Another horse, recently active, might be discarded because its last race was inexcusably bad, or because the race was too good and unlikely to be repeated!

The records of animals that measure up to the negative standards are then scrutinized for positive indications of winning form. In that phase of the work, the player pits his knowledge against the wiles of the trainer, who may have been trying to conceal or obscure improvement.

Having completed his paper work, the expert reserves decision until he has seen the horses in the paddock and walking ring. Here he often finds that the animal that looked best on paper is wretched in the flesh. The player's detective work at the paddock will occupy a later chapter. For the present, we deal with his studies of past performances.

Recent Action

Every now and then someone breaks into print with the revelation that two thirds of all races are won by horses whose most recent starts occurred within two weeks of the winning effort. Or that a third of all races are won by horses that have had a race within the preceding seven days.

Innumerable systems are based on such statistics. But the facts are that the figures are not nearly so pregnant with meaning as they may seem. For instance, there is no reason why two thirds of all races should not be won by horses that have raced within two weeks: *At least two thirds of all horses that go to the post have had a race within two weeks!* And, while horses that return to the races within a week of their latest start win a third of all races, *at least a third of all starters have had a race within the previous seven days!*

Because of the large number of two-week and one-week horses that race every day, the probability of cashing a bet on either type of horse (without considering any other factor) is something like one in nine. Mathematically, the natural odds against victory by any random one-week or two-week horse are in the neighborhood of 8 to 1. Which are the exact natural odds against any random horse in any typical field of nine horses! In other words, the player has to know more about a horse than that it has been to the post within a week or two.

I make that assertion not to stage a display of statistical wizardry, but to emphasize a truth that recurs frequently in these pages and is, indeed, the most important truth in handicapping: No handicapping factor stands alone. The date of the last race is often important. But only when related to other vital matters.

At a recent New Jersey meeting, the largest single category of winners was the group of 25 horses which won after layoffs of a month or more. Horses in the next largest group—22—had raced exactly five days before their winning efforts! At a recent California meeting, 11 percent of the races went to horses that had not run in thirty days or more. Another 11 percent were won by horses that had run exactly seven days earlier.

The player must concern himself with the dates of the horse's most recent races. But he must bear in mind that a horse that has not run in a month may often be in good enough trim to defeat something else that ran six days ago.

Recent Action in Claimers

My own experience has taught me to be extremely wary of any *claiming* horse that has not had at least one race or one workout within twelve days of its race. In *The Compleat Horseplayer* and *Ainslie's Jockey Book,* I suggested that the horse not only should have had a race or workout within twelve days, but should have had two races or two workouts, or one of each, within seventeen.

Those requirements are lenient. They work effectively only if the player attends to all other aspects of his handicapping with intelligent care. For example, a horse that had not raced in two and a half weeks and had not worked out in nine days would qualify under that method. Yet if it were entered in a $5,000 claimer today, the wise player might hesitate to endorse its condition by comparison with that of an entrant which showed two races and a couple of workouts in the same seventeen-day period. Why has the first animal been totally inactive for nine days? The player would take a long, close look at it in the walking ring.

In analyzing claiming races, the safest approach to the problem of recent action hews fairly close to the following guidelines:

1. Any horse with two races in the past two or two and a half weeks need not have worked out during that period, although a workout would be a positive sign of fitness.

2. Any horse that has been working out at four- or five-day intervals, has had a race within the past week or two, and another race within the previous week or two, is probably in acceptable shape, quite apart from its winning chances at today's distance and pace and class and weights.

3. A horse that was out of action for more than three weeks prior to its last race is discarded unless the last race was quite recent, and was a good performance (see page 164–170), and the animal has been working out steadily.

4. Any horse that has not raced in two weeks or more and has not

worked out in the meantime is discarded on grounds of probable disability.

5. Any horse that has not raced in three weeks or more, but has been working out, is eliminated unless (a) it is an unusually consistent animal that wins at least one race in every five attempts and manages to be in the money about half the time, or (b) its record shows victories after layoffs of similar duration in the past, or (c) it seems to have a distinct class advantage, or (d) it comes from a leading barn and will carry a leading rider.

To recapitulate, the custom of racing horses into condition is so widespread, especially with cheaper stock, that the player should mistrust any claiming animal that has not been racing and working out frequently and recently. The presumption must always be that soreness or other disability has prevented work.

By and large, the more rigid you become about demanding recent action by claiming horses, the less you need perspire over the remainder of the handicapping, and the less sure you need be of your diagnostic powers at the paddock and walking ring. For an extreme example, it is entirely possible to stay even with the game by playing no claimer that has not had a race within a week—provided one is prepared to apply other simple handicapping rules with equal inflexibility and is willing to pass up a considerable number of races.

With the development of experience and the facile ability to relate form to class, the player becomes more relaxed about recent action (in appropriate cases, that is) and catches some fat mutuel prices that might formerly have been beyond his grasp.

Recent Action and Better Horses

Allowance, handicap and stakes horses need not race so often to maintain their sharpness. But they seldom are acceptable choices unless they have worked out frequently, recently and with respectable clockings (see page 160). What's more, if the field in an allowance race is composed entirely of authentic allowance horses, the one that has raced well within the last week or two is usually a far better risk than one that has not been to the post for three or four weeks. The most conspicuous exception would be a sparsely raced three-year-old trained by a Bert Mulholland, Frank Whiteley, Johnny Nerud, Eddie Neloy or similar top-drawer horseman whose animals invariably have a touch of class and usually go to the well only when ready to fill the bucket.

Another prominent exception is a handicap star returning from vacation for a tune-up in allowance company. If the horse's workouts suggest an effort to win today's race, the player must treat the animal with respect, even if it has not raced in months.

The Workout Secret

Like physicians, art critics and losing horseplayers, professional horsemen manage to disagree on a monstrous variety of subjects. In moments of candor, however, the more experienced and competent among them tend to agree that a horse should be at its very best after a freshening layoff from actual competition, followed by a program of workouts.

Once in a great while, the truth of this theory is demonstrated in a claiming race. An honest old animal benefits so much from a lengthy rest that it wins at first asking and pays a mint. It rarely is possible to tell when one of these miracles is going to happen. The assumption must be that the horse will need two or three or more races before recovering its old form. An equally valid assumption is that it has gone bad and will never recover its old form. Once in a while, however, the player notices unusual signs in the workout line of a claiming animal about to return from a long rest:

1. **Frequent workouts, including at least one of real speed.**
2. **Long workouts.**

The claimer returning from a layoff is usually sent to the post after only two or three slow works. If it is a sprinter, two of the workouts are likely to be at four furlongs. The third may be at three. But if it has worked four times in the past two or three weeks and has run one or two of the exercise gallops in close to racing speed, it merits attention. And if one of its works was at the distance of today's race, or longer, the player has a problem: He must decide whether to bet on this impressively fresh animal or pass the race altogether.

Sometimes a horse of this kind runs a grand race but lacks the stamina to carry its speed all the way, because it is still short of top condition. But no less often, the workouts mean what they say. The horse is in remarkable shape for its kind. It wins. The safest procedure for the conservative player is to abstain from betting on the race. A more adventurous type might go for the freshened animal, but only if everything else in the race looked awful.

The reader no doubt noticed that I called frequent, fast, long workouts "unusual signs." In the record of a claiming horse, that is. Cheapsters rarely are asked for speed in their workouts: They do not have the speed to spare. They need it for their races. In fact, whenever a claimer of medium or lower grade ($6,000 or less) shows a swift workout since its last race, the player is entitled to believe that it may be in extraordinarily fine fettle. But, regardless of clockings, the simple presence of a claiming horse on the training track every four or five days between races is ample evidence of physical fitness.

The phrase, "workouts every four or five days" recurs throughout this book and so does the synonymous expression, "frequent workouts." To avoid misunderstanding, I should emphasize that a lapse of six or seven days between an animal's race and its next race or workout is entirely normal. But, when workouts begin, they should almost always recur at regular, short intervals terminated, of course, by the creature's next race. In light of this, the player should wonder about the readiness of a horse that has not raced in three weeks and whose record shows only two workouts during that period. If the latest of the workouts was more than four days ago, doubts should enlarge. Mind you, I say "doubts." Some horses win decisively after going for nine or ten days without a race or workout. Moreover, their victories are predictable on grounds of class, consistency, trainer, jockey, pace and—as far as current condition is concerned—the kind of running the horse did nine or ten days ago.

If I seem to be complicating the reader's existence with these somewhat contradictory interruptions of his train of thought, I apologize. The point, I suppose, is that this is a game in which flexible thinking based on general principles gets more mileage than rigid formulas do. The reader who absorbs the principles of this chapter, and the general guidelines that delineate those principles, will discover sooner rather than later that he is able to modify the guidelines to suit the unique problems presented by the individual race and the individual horse. While he will accept recent races and workouts as a good sign in the record of any apparently improving horse entered in a claimer, he will be disinclined to eliminate a relatively classy, consistent horse from consideration in the same race merely because it has been idle for a few days. He will, in sum, relate the factor of condition to that of class, and in due course to those of weights and pace. If he is rigid to that extent— remembering and using the interrelationships among the fundamental factors of handicapping—he will find it necessary to be rigid about little else.

I am sure that all this will become satisfactorily apparent as the reader proceeds through the book.

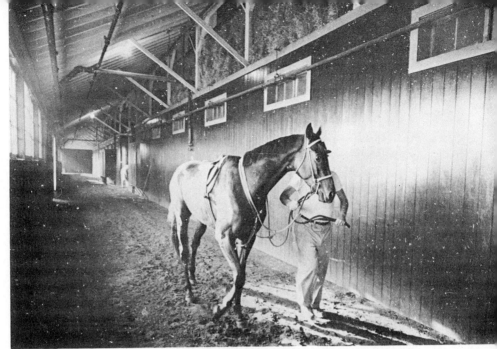

Carry Back cools out under the shed at Belmont Park.   **UPI PHOTO**

Back to the barn at Belmont after a late winter workout on the training track.
UPI PHOTO

Workouts by Better Horses

Higher-grade animals that have not raced in recent weeks can be credited with acceptable condition only if they have been working out frequently and show one or two genuinely impressive morning trials. If an allowance or handicap runner produced good speed in a workout seven or eight or nine mornings ago, did not disgrace itself in another gallop four or five days ago, and romped through a final blowout yesterday, it deserves respect. Its last race may have been three or four weeks ago, but the player can be quite sure that the horse is sharp.

Here are standards useful in evaluating the workouts of better-grade horses, including two-year-olds. Obviously, whenever a claiming racer's works approach these standards, he bears watching:

1. At most tracks, a workout is more than satisfactory if the horse breezes (b) (runs entirely without urging) at a rate of approximately 12 seconds for each eighth of a mile. A workout of .36 b for three furlongs or .48 b for four or 1.00 b for five is a definite sign of life. So is 1.13 b for six furlongs, 1.27 b for seven and 1.42 b for the mile. To determine whether your own track is slower or faster than this, check through a few of the workout columns in your racing paper, and alter your par figures accordingly.

2. If a breezing work of .48 is acceptable, so is .47 h—the symbol for "handily." In such an effort, the exercise boy gives what the trade calls a "hand ride," rolling his knuckles along the horse's neck in the familiar pumping motion, which encourages speed. Thus, if two horses do five furlongs in 1.00, but one of them does it breezing and the other handily, the breezer gets the applause. Persons who enjoy arithmetic usually allow a one-second difference between breezes and hand rides in workouts of five furlongs or less. A second and a couple of fifths is more like it at six or seven furlongs. And three seconds is not too much at a mile or more.

3. Another second of credit is given for a workout that begins in the starting gate (g) rather than from the customary running start. Hence .47 hg is as good as .47 b.

4. If the horses work out on a training track (tr.t.) as well as on the main track (m.t.), the workout lines show it. Training tracks are usually deeper and slower, to help the animals develop stamina. Which is why tr.t. .48 h is as good as m.t. .48 b.

5. A longer workout is always more significant than a shorter. It is especially significant if the horse has been away from the races for a while. After a layoff of more than a month, works of three or four furlongs are not too promising for a horse scheduled to race against animals of its own class. But if the race is at six furlongs and the horse spun off six or seven furlongs in good time within the last week or ten days, and has breezed another three or four furlongs in the past 48 hours, one can be reasonably sure that it is ready to try today. Similarly, if today's race is over a distance of ground, the laid-off animal should show a workout or two of at least a mile, and in respectable time.

6. A highly useful way to evaluate workouts is to watch the daily summaries published by the racing papers. An animal whose exercises are impressive enough to earn comment in the bold-face type at the bottom of those columns is usually worth keeping in mind. So is any cheaper horse whose workout was within a few fifths of a second of the better animal's time on the same morning. An advantage of this method is that it compares horses with each other, rather than with par timings. Daily variations in the speed of the track can alter workout figures considerably—especially on damp mornings.

7. In the record of any horse, especially one that has been racing and working out frequently, a nice breezing effort on the day before the race is a highly reassuring sign of fitness.

Misleading Workouts

A seldom-mentioned aspect of workouts is that they, too, may help a trainer in his hallowed effort to darken his animal's form. Among the techniques:

1. Using a heavy exercise boy, or boosting the horse's burden with lead weights in the saddle pad. If the animal totes thirty pounds or more above the weight it will carry in the race, slow time is a certainty. But the weights carried in workouts are never reported.

2. Wrapping heavy bandages on the horse's legs. Tinfoil beneath a few layers of flannel and gauze used to be a favorite. The weight slows the horse's stride, worsens its time, builds its mutuel price and develops its physique even more effectively than a heavy exercise boy can.

3. Exercising the horse late in the morning. By that time the track has been chewed up thoroughly by hooves, slowing it considerably.

4. Ordering the boy to keep the animal in the middle of the track until it has completed the turn into the homestretch. This deliberate loss of ground adds seconds to the workout time. It does not fool the official clockers, but the past-performance records have no room to explain why the workout was so slow.

5. Ordering the boy to keep as tight a hold as possible, converting a breezing work into a strangling one, a second or two slower.

6. Exercising the horse at night when the official clockers are not around. This seldom is permitted at major racing centers, but remains a favorite tactic on certain smaller circuits.

7. Working the horse not at the track itself but on a nearby private oval, away from prying eyes. This happens too seldom to be important. But it happens. If a trainer begins winning with horses whose records show neither recent races nor workouts, you may discover that, yes, he happens to have a workout strip behind his restaurant.

8. Disguising a horse so that the clockers will not recognize it. This is done by dressing the animal in blinkers and saddlecloth of a color never associated with its stable, or putting a strange exercise boy aboard, or wrapping its legs in bandages (which it has never worn and does not need). Some trainers go so far as to give a wrong name to the clockers when they inquire. Again, practices of this kind are extremely rare in major racing.

The Form of Two-Year-Olds

During the first months of the New York season, Lucien Laurin, who has a lovely training farm in North Carolina, wins a few maiden-special-weights races with well-schooled juveniles that have never raced before. The same trick is routine—spring, summer and fall—for Bert Mulholland, Max Hirsch, Eddie Neloy, and Clyde Troutt. The very presence on the entry list of a two-year-old from one of these barns is enough to give pause to any knowledgeable player.

If the player approaches the distance factor in juvenile races along the lines described in the previous chapter, he can assume that any of the logical contenders is in condition, provided it has had a recent race and has been working out briskly at four- or five-day intervals. If it has not raced recently, or has never raced at all, the workouts not only should be frequent but one or more of them should be nice and fast— and the longer the better. A two-year-old in good condition runs as fast as it can at every opportunity. Which is why the speed of recent races or—when real speed is missing in the field—the speed of recent workouts is just about all the player needs to make his selection.

Horses for Courses

I hope it is agreed by now that the winning player prefers a horse that has been running and working out with regularity. And that he appreciates it if a horse of that description shows a fast, long workout. And that he hesitates to discard a horse that has been away from the races for a month or so if it is a higher-grade animal and has been working in something close to actual racing speed, preferably at distances longer than the customary three or four furlongs.

In process of noticing how frequently and how recently a horse has been racing and working out, the smart player takes care to see where all this activity has taken place. An allowance animal that ran nicely last week at Hawthorne might be credited with excellent condition if entered today at the same track. It would be a dubious bet if shipped to Bowie.

Many horses withstand long trips remarkably well. But an enormous majority require a race or two before becoming fully acclimated to a new track. Horses that recover quickly from the stress of travel and the tension caused by new surroundings are known as "good shippers." They sometimes manage to win their first race at the new oval without so much as a workout there. But only sometimes. Not often.

A rule honored with unswerving devotion by most experts is this:

1. Unless a horse outclasses its field and has worked out impressively at today's track, its last race must have taken place here or at a sister track on the same circuit.

A Buckpasser can amble into Chicago, work out a couple of times and break the world's record. And every year some European or South American horse wins the Washington, D.C., International at Laurel, outclassing America's best turf runners in spite of its long journey and its lack of local action. Similarly, Howard (Buddy) Jacobson manages to win with his New York claimers in their first attempts at Bowie or Laurel or Rockingham or Suffolk. And Frank Whiteley can train a Damascus in Maryland, yet win with it in New York. Again, the reason is an edge in class.

"Horses for courses," say veterans of the backstretch, nodding their heads sagely. Undoubtedly some horses run better at some tracks than at others. A speed horse does better on the pasteboard surfaces of California than on the sandy, holding tracks of the East. A come-from-behind animal does all right at Bowie or Suffolk and is lucky to reach third money at Golden Gate Fields. But the real meaning of "horses for courses" is that all horses, regardless of running style, are creatures of habit. Until they have become accustomed to a new track, they run below their best form.

Players who care to pursue this line of reasoning will profit from some additional ideas:

2. Unless it is entered at a substantially lower claiming price than usual, discard any claiming horse whose last race was at a track of lower class than today's. The only exception would be a local horse returning from a one- or two-race excursion out of town.

3. Throw out any front-running horse in its first start over a track that favors come-from-behinders. The hotshot from Santa Anita is a virtual cinch to perish in its first start at Churchill Downs or Bowie.

4. Throw out any come-from-behind horse in its first start over a track that favors front-runners. The only unvarying exception would be a Buckpasser, an exception to everything, anyhow.

5. In choosing between two animals that have run their most recent races at today's track or on today's circuit, give preference to the one that has been working out at today's track. Horses stabled at Hialeah win races there from rivals stabled at Gulfstream. When the action moves to Gulfstream, the horses that regard the Annandale plant as home begin beating steeds that have to be vanned from Hialeah. At Aqueduct, the most successful stables are invariably ones with stalls on the premises, rather than at nearby Belmont. Horses that work out at Aqueduct sleep there and win there.

Danger Signals

Some of the most popular selection systems are based on the concept of "last-out-in-the-money." The player eliminates any horse that did not finish first, second or third in its last race. If two or more qualify, he bets on the one with the most recent race.

To the extent that such systems take cognizance of class, pace and distance, they are not too bad. Their inescapable weakness is the uncritical assumption that a good race last week foreshadows a good race today. Life is not that simple.

A probable reason that favorites win no more than one race in three is that the crowds tend to make their bets on the basis of "last-out-in-the-money." Failing to appreciate that an animal's good recent effort may have overtaxed its powers, they make it the favorite. But it no longer is in condition to win. The player who recognizes certain signals in the past-performance lines is able to avoid a good many of these false favorites and false second choices. If he finds another bettable horse in the race, he has a good chance to collect a robust mutuel.

Here comes some ideas which should enable any player to avoid such sucker horses:

1. Throw out any horse that bled, ran sore, or finished lame in its last race. The *Telegraph* past-performance records give that information. *Racing Form* readers must dig up the result charts. Sore-legged animals win every day, but rarely after a race in which the disability was noticeable enough to draw comment. The term "bled" refers to the rupture of blood vessels in the nose or throat under the strain of racing. The flow of blood hampers the animal's breathing. A horse that bled in its last race may not bleed again today, but is unlikely to have recovered from the experience sufficiently to win today.

2. Throw out any horse that lugged in or bore out in its last race. A horse unable to run in a straight line is either badly schooled or ouchy. If it has borne in or lugged out before, it can be discarded without a second thought—unless it seems to enjoy enormous class or speed advantages over the rest of its field, at which point the smart operator resolves to pass the race rather than play roulette.

3. Throw out any horse that is stepping up in class after a race it won while losing ground in a driving stretch run. A horse that has trouble beating its own kind is a poor risk if it tries to tackle superior stock in its next effort. Among cheaper claiming racers, in fact, the exertion of lasting to the finish wire against a gaining rival is usually enough to guarantee that the horse will lose its next start even if it does not go up in class. On the other hand, a horse that merely lopes to the wire, winning easily or handily, can be forgiven if something else gained on it during the stretch. *Racing Form* readers without result charts can safely assume that the horse was engaged in a driving finish if its winning margin was two lengths or less.

4. Throw out any four-year-old or older horse that engaged in driving finishes in each of its last two races. Win or lose, a hard drive knocks the average horse off form. Two drives in succession are murder. Notable exceptions to this rule are handicap and stakes racers from leading barns, better-grade two-year-olds, lightly raced three-year-old fillies of high quality, and three-year-old colts and geldings of almost any grade. Three-year-old males often come to life in the summer, putting together a series of three or more good races against increasingly tough competition.

If the player likes a four-year-old in a claiming race and wonders whether it can do well today after two successive taxing efforts, its past-performance record may show whether it has ever been able to run well in such circumstances before. In the absence of result charts or *Telegraph* comment lines, the player can assume that the horse was involved in a driving finish if it won by two lengths or less, or finished within a length or less of the winner. If it was similarly situated at the pre-stretch call or stretch call, the drive was that much more prolonged and intense.

So much money is wasted in bets on false favorites of this particular kind that I shall offer an actual example, in hope of making the point more firmly. On July 1, 1966, the ninth race at Aqueduct was at a mile and an eighth for $6,000 to $6,500 animals. The favorite at even money was Hy-Nat, a wonderfully consistent eight-year-old that had won $15,000 in its ten starts during the year, winning five of them and finishing out of the money only twice. Note that the pre-stretch, stretch and final calls of its last two races looked like this:

$$4^2 \quad 2^{1\frac{1}{2}} \quad 2^{1\frac{1}{2}}$$
$$2^{1\frac{1}{2}} \quad 1^h \quad 1^{no}$$

The old gelding was a victim of overwork. It was lucky to finish third. The official chart reported that it "was unable to gain when put to pressure." The winner of the race, and by all means the logical choice at a generous 7 to 2 was Tobir, which had whipped a similar field with great authority on May 14. In its next race, on May 27, it had made no special effort. It was claimed out of that race by the astute Buddy Jacobson, who had rested it until today, except for breezing works on June 25 and 28. Jacobson, a genius at winning with recently claimed, rested animals, entered Tobir for $6,000—$500 less than he had paid for the creature. Obviously, he intended to win the purse and was confident he could do so. At the lower claiming price, and with Ernest Cardone, the nation's finest apprentice rider, Tobir had to run under only 111 pounds—seven pounds less than he had carried to victory six weeks earlier. The $9 mutuel was in the nature of a gift from Hy-Nat's supporters to those who had sense enough to avoid the horse. Note the lack of workouts in Hy-Nat's recent record!

5. Throw out any horse aged four or older whose best effort at today's distance occurred in its last race, unless the horse is a male that demonstrated reserve speed in that race. The simplest way to check this wrinkle is to see whether the horse ran the distance more rapidly in its last race than in any previous try. If so, the presumption must be that the horse ran

July 1, 1966

9th Race Aqueduct

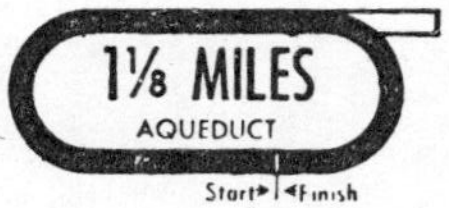

1 1-8 MILES (Sinatra, December 7, 1964, 1.47⅕, 5, 111.)

Claiming. Purse $4,700. 3-year-olds and upward. Weights, 3-year-olds 116 lbs., older 123 lbs. Claiming price, $6,500. 2 lbs. allowed for each $250 to $6,000. Non-winners of two races at a mile and a furlong or over since March 12 allowed 3 lbs., such a race since then, 5 lbs. (Races where entered for $5,000 or less not considered.)

With Promise × $6,250

Gr. g (1962), by Promised Land—In Love With, by Ace Admiral
H. Fiol H. Fiol (A. B. Karsner) **116**
1966 7 1 0 2 $3,760
1965 9 1 1 1 $2,775

21Jun66-5Aqu fst 7f .23⅗ .47⅕1.25⅗ Cl c-5000 11 2 42 87¼1013 1118 MVenezia b 121 *2.60 60–24 William E. 110¾ Bobandit 1161½ New Recruit 119½ Stumbled start 12
8Jun66-9Aqu fst 1⅛.47⅕1.11⅘1.51⅗ Clm 9000 1 2 24 48 714 717 LLoughry5 b 111 3.10 61–12 SelectedShorts123¾ Eagle'sScream1201 GetCrackin'1132½ Tired 7
2Jun66-9Aqu fst 1⅛.47⅘1.12⅘1.52 Clm 8500 1 3 41½ 32 21 31½ ECardone7 b 113 3.90 74–15 GetCrackin' 118no Aberrant 1161½ WithPromise 1132½ Loose band'ge 8
26May66-8Aqu fst 1 .46⅖1.11⅗1.37⅕ Clm 8500 1 1 1h 11 1h 1no LLoughry5 b 111 32.30 82–19 With Promise 111no Get Crackin' 116h Tan Guapo 1144 Driving 8
19May66-2Aqu sly 7f .22⅗ .45⅗1.24⅘ Cl c-6500 6 2 32 55½ 49½ 515 WBoland b 117 4.30 67–17 Tan Guapo 117½ Koh-I-Noor 11710 C. U. Later 1164 Tired steadily 6
16Apr66-5Mid fm*6f Ⓣ 1.15 Allowance 5 5 52¾ 55½ 87¼ 66 WMoore b 163 ——e —— Win's Star 1431 In the Prime 139½ Big Tulyar 155½ Had no mishap 15
5Jan66-2CT fst 1 1/16.48⅗1.14⅖1.47⅗ Allowance 7 5 42½ 21 2h 3h FDRivera b 114 *1.30 82–20 Maysie Daisy 113h Easy Amber 106no With Promise 1148 Gamely 10
29Dec65-3CT fst 1 1/16.49 1.14⅘1.47⅘ Allowance 4 2 21½ 31½ 1½ 2¾ FDRivera b 116 5.70 80–23 Drafted 116¾ With Promise 1165 Thirty Pieces 1143½ Sharp 8
9Dec65-7Pim hd 1 1/16 TC 1.13⅖1.46⅕ Clm 7500 7 6 4nk 72¾ 97¾ 916 EMcIvor b 121 30.20 68–13 Tosinisbad 1212 Willogate 1161½ Curator 1143 Failed to stay 12
22Nov65-5Pim my 6f .24⅕ .48⅖1.14⅘ Md 7500 3 4 1h 11½ 11½ 12½ ENelson b 120 *2.40 76–24 With Promise 1202½ Taxled 1221½ Glorious Gay 112¾ Easily 11
17Nov65-3Pim fst 6f .24 .48⅖1.14⅖ Md Sp Wt 4 5 73½ 88 810 813 CRogers b 118 31.10 65–29 Fine Kettle 1185 Jove 118½ Hill Indian 115h Showed nothing 11
LATEST WORKOUTS Jun 29 Bel m.t. 4f fst .49 h May 24 Aqu 3f fst .37 b May 18 Bel m.t. 3f fst .36⅖ h May 13 Bel m.t. 6f fst 1.15 h

No Kidding * $6,500

B. g (1962), by Nilo—Crown Note, by Royal Gem II
W. C. Pitfield L. C. Cavalaris, Jr. (D. J. Thomson) **113⁵**
1966 8 2 0 0 $3,380
1965 22 6 2 2 $10,750

18Jun66-9Aqu fst 1⅛.48 1.12⅘1.52⅘ Hcp 5000s 2 5 710 711 69½ 57¾ RUssery 115 7.50 64–19 Gypsy Baron 119½ Mid Montana 1091 Steve's Vow 1106 No threat 7
9Jun66 7WO sf 1 Ⓣ .48⅗1.43⅕ Allowance 5 8 99½1016 715 716 RGrubb10 106 13.40 41–43 Marvina's Tusc 1115 Baranof 1203 So Good 116¾ Always far back 10
3Jun66-7Grd fst 1 .47 1.11⅗1.38⅘ Allowance 7 7 711 78¾ 76¼ 65 RGrubb10 104 3.90 85–19 Top Victory 114½ So Good 1143½ Blue Sol 114½ Showed very little 7
24May66-6Grd fst 1 .46⅘1.11⅕1.38⅘ Clm 9000 5 5 47½ 36½ 35 1h RGrubb10 112 8.10 87–19 No Kidding 112h Park Heights 116¾ Reap the Wind 1221½ Up in time 5
13May66-8Grd sl 1 .49⅗1.15⅕1.42⅗ Clm 9000 5 6 64½ 32¾ 34 1¼ PMaxwell 116 19.35 68–30 No Kidding 1161¼ Johns Champ 111h Park Heights 1167¾ Ridden out 8
4May66-5FE fst 1 70.46⅕1.11⅗1.42⅕ Cl c-6500 2 3 25 36 59½ 512 GNedeau 117 3.10 86–15 So Good 117½ Main Count 1127 Scadadle 117nk Early speed, tired 5
16Apr66-7FE fst 6f .22⅖ .45⅘1.11⅕ Clm 6500 8 7 58½ 57¾ 68½ 65¾ GNedeau b 116 13.70 87–10 Reap the Wind 116h Little Red 1141 Duby Cat 1082¼ Showed even try 8
7Apr66-6FE sl 5f .23⅗ .48 1.01 Clm 6500 2 4 44½ 45 55½ 54¾ GNedeau 116 23.30 78–18 My Marion 115½ Little Red 1141 Get Some More 122½ Raced evenly 7
24Nov65-7Grd sly 1 .47⅗1.14⅕1.43 Clm 6500 4 3 610 59¼ 54½ 2h JFitzsimm'ns b 116 11.05 66–39 Fast Jay 116h No Kidding 1162¾ Ice Cold 117¾ Strong late effort 7
LATEST WORKOUTS Jun 30 Bel tr.t. 3f fst .38 b Jun 23 Bel m.t. 3f fst .36⅘ b Jun 17 Bel m.t. 3f fst .36⅖ h

Victaray $6,500

Ch. c (1962), by Nicaray—Clay Queen, by Hail Victory
J. C. Lawrence J. C. Lawrence (J. R. Luker) **113⁵**
1966 15 1 3 0 $6,020
1965 14 3 0 1 $6,369

24Jun66-9Aqu fst 1⅛.47⅘1.13⅘1.54 Cl c-5000 4 7 75½ 62¾ 31 11½ DHidalgo5 113 7.80 66–21 Victaray 1131½ Inhand 1122½ Egocentrical 118¾ Going away 7
17Jun66-9Aqu fst 1⅛.48⅖1.13⅕1.53 Clm 6000 5 3 32½ 62½ 56½ 48½ LLoughry5 109 10.30 62–22 Brother Bones 120½ Hy-Nat 1116 Atlantic 1162 Brief speed 10
10Jun66-9Aqu fst 1⅛.47⅖1.12⅘1.52⅗ Clm 6000 4 5 512 55 57¼ 48 EBelmonte 116 5.20 65–16 Old Bailey 11203 Duke'sLiberty1202½ BrotherBones1132½ Checked 7
3Jun66-9Aqu fst 1⅛.48 1.13⅕1.52⅖ Clm 6000 3 3 34 22 1½ 2nk EBelmonte 116 7.80 74–16 Duke's Liberty 118nk Victaray 1163 Del Coronado 115½ Game try 7
27May66-9Aqu fst 1⅛.48⅗1.13⅗1.52⅗ Clm 6500 6 3 46½ 63¼ 65½ 67¾ DHidalgo5 111 12.10 65–18 Aberrant 1142 Street Fair 1162½ Egocentrical 1053 Tired 9
20May66-9Aqu gd 1⅛.47⅖1.13 1.54⅗ Clm 6000 5 5 514 68 53½ 2½ DHidalgo5 107 37.80 62–18 Safety Zone 119½ Victaray 107½ Atlantic 1142 Was gaining rapidly 7
11May66-8Aqu fst 1 .46⅕1.11⅖1.39⅕ Cl c-4000 1 4 52 56½ 65½ 85¼ GMineau5 b 110 8.00 67–19 Tablin 112½ Artist Town 1151 Never Wrong 1151 No mishap 12
26Apr66-9Aqu fst 1⅛.48⅖1.12⅗1.52⅕ Clm 5000 5 2 32 43 45½ 611 GMineau5 b 111 7.40 64–18 Hy-Nat 1172 Rough Divot 1225 Duke's Liberty 116nk Tired 8
15Apr66-9Aqu fst 1⅛.47⅘1.12⅗1.52 Clm 6500 5 1 12 11 54 58½ GMineau5 b 111 11.40 67–15 Ruperto 109h Latin Artist 1152½ Hy-Nat 1133 Used setting pace 7
9Apr66-4Aqu fst 7f .23 .46⅕1.24⅘ Clm 7500 4 7 75¾ 74½ 67 69 MSorrentino b 113 28.20 73–18 SafetyZone1171 From the Top1081 Hail the Admiral1206 Sluggish st. 7
30Mar66-9Aqu fst 1⅛.49 1.13⅗1.52⅖ Clm 6500 5 6 75¾ 78¾ 815 719 MSorrentino b 116 9.00 55–20 Safety Zone 1145½ Hy-Nat 113nk Mi Rey 1162 Dropped far back 8
LATEST WORKOUTS May 18 Bel tr.t. 4f fst .51 h May 9 Bel tr.t. 4f fst .51⅘ h May 4 Bel m.t. 6f fst 1.18 b

Tobir * $6,000

Ch. g (1958), by Tenerani—Merry Game, by Big Game
N. Hellman   H. Jacobson

1115 1966 11 3 3 1 $10,370
      1965 26 0 5 4 $8,210

Hy-Nat * $6,250

B. g (1958), by Bimelech—Orage, by Pilate
Mrs. W. A. Kelley   W. A. Kelley

116 1966 10 5 2 0 $15,090
     1965 32 6 6 0 $27,785

(North Cliff Farm)

Latin Artist $6,500

Ch. h (1960), by Tenerani—Nenuphar, by Jacovelli
J. T. Jacovelli   N. J. Jacovelli

118 1966 8 1 3 $4,980
     1965 16 2 0 $9,45

(Bell-Gardiner)   by Blue Peter

***Dongo** **$6,000** Dk. b. or br. h (1961), by Fez—Dogaresa, by Madara **107⁷**
Leejim Stable W. R. Corbellini (Haras La Divisa) (Chile)

1966	11	0	0	0	—
1965	9	2	1	3	$1,658

25Jun66-2Aqu	fst 6f	.22⅖	.46	1.12⅕	Clm	6000	5	6	$3^{1\frac12}$	$6^{5\frac14}$	8^9	9^{15}	HWoodhouse	b 115	25.10	67-17	Rio Coreo 115¾ Gay Orchid 117 1½ Jay Roger 114¹	Brief foot, tired	9
18Jun66-3Aqu	fst 6f	.23	.46⅘	1.12⅘	Clm	6250	7	4	$9^{5\frac14}$	10^{12}	$10^{6\frac34}$	$9^{8\frac34}$	ORosado5	114	25.50	70-19	Sleepy Native 112½ Gay Orchid 117¾ Jay Roger 114nk	In close	10
16May66-5Aqu	fst 6f	.22⅖	.45⅖	1.10⅘	Clm	8500	1	5	6^6	7^8	6^8	9^{21}	JRuane	117	31.00	68-19	Solid Mike 113 3½ Misurata 117¾ Safety Zone 117¾	Far back	9
4May66-8Aqu	fst 6f	.23	.47	1.12⅘	Clm	13000	4	4	$6^{2\frac12}$	7^5	7^{11}	7^{18}	DHidalgo5	108	27.90	61-20	Supreme Count 117³ Tajante 115¹ Bargain Counter 120no	Far back	7
28Apr66-6Aqu	my 7f	.23	.46⅕	1.25	Clm	15000	4	2	2^3	3^6	$4^{5\frac12}$	$5^{8\frac34}$	DHidalgo5	108	27.80	72-24	Upset Victory 117 3½ Terminator 120¹ Blue Dale 112¾	Early speed	8
23Apr66-6Aqu	fst 6f	.22⅕	.45⅖	1.10⅕	Allowance		4	5	$7^{6\frac34}$	7^{10}	7^{17}	7^{17}	ORosado5	112	84.00	75-14	Understudy 117h Hi-Hasty 117¹ Black Mountain 112¹	No speed	8
4Apr66-5Aqu	fst 6f	.22	.45	1.10⅗	Clm	16500	5	2	$3^{2\frac12}$	4^8	7^{21}	7^{27}	JRuane	b 115	25.40	63-19	Terminator 115 3½ MixedUpKid 115½ BargainCounter 110³	Wide	7
26Mar66-6Aqu	fst 7f	.22⅗	.45⅖	1.24⅖	Allowance		4	2	2^h	$2^{\frac12}$	7^{14}	7^{18}	JRuane	b 117	32.20	66-19	Chinatowner 114no Rocky Ford 112² Ikeya 117no	Speed, stopped	7
10Feb66-8Hia	fst 7f	.23	.46	1.23⅘	Allowance		5	3	3^1	$6^{9\frac12}$	Eased		JRuane	b 113	68.90	——	Sunstruck 113 4½ Bonetero 113no Nassau Hall 113 2½	Loose equipm'nt	7
22Jan66-7Hia	fm 1 1/16 Ⓣ			1.42⅕	Allowance		8	5	6^9	10^{19}	12^{37}	12^{41}	GMunsell	113	72.50	53- 9	Point du Jour 116 2¾ Brave Lad 122h Ampose 116⁴	Dropped far back	12
1Jan66-7TrP	fst 6f	.22	.44⅗	1.09⅖	Allowance		5	6	6^7	6^{10}	8^{18}	8^{22}	GMunsell	b 116	39.10	73-13	Rorque 115½ Ask Gus 118 3½ Vertex Record 118no	Never a contender	8

LATEST WORKOUTS Jun 23 Aqu 3f fst .37⅗ b Jun 19 Aqu 4f fst .51⅘ b Jun 14 Aqu 4f fst .51⅖ b

Results of 9th Race Aqueduct—July 1, 1966

NINTH RACE **Aqu - 28009** July 1, 1966

1 1-8 MILES (Sinatra, December 7, 1964, 1.47⅕, 5, 111.)
Claiming. Purse $4,700. 3-year-olds and upward. Weights, 3-year-olds 116 lbs., older 123 lbs. Claiming price, $6,500. 2 lbs. allowed for each $250 to $6,000. Non-winners of two races at a mile and a furlong or over since March 12 allowed 3 lbs., such a race since then, 5 lbs. (Races where entered for $5,000 or less not considered.)

Value to winner $3,055, second $940, third $470, fourth $235. Mutuel pool $288,223. (Minus show pool $48.29.)

Index	Horse	Eqt	A	Wt	PP	St	¼	½	¾	Str	Fin	Jockey	Cl'g Pr	Owner	Odds $1
27607Aqu5	—Tobir		8	111	3	6	6	5^1	3^1	$2^{\frac12}$	$1^{\frac34}$	E Cardone5	6000	N Hellman	3.50
27844Aqu5	—No Kidding		4	113	1	4	1^h	$1^{1\frac12}$	1^4	$1^{1\frac12}$	2^3	D Hidalgo5	6500	W C Pittfield	4.30
27835Aqu2	—Hy-Nat	b	8	116	4	3	3^4	3^5	2^3	3^3	3^1	B Baeza	6250	Mrs W A Kelley	1.00
27889Aqu1	—Ⓓ Victaray		4	118	2	1	4^2	4^h	4^h	4^3	4^6	O Rosado†	6500	J C Lawrence	Ⓓ-7.60
27607Aqu9	—Latin Artist		6	118	5	5	5^4	6	5^{10}	5	5	R Turcotte	6500	J T Iacovelli	8.10
27891Aqu9	—Dongo	b	5	107	6	2	2^2	2^4	6	Eased up		D Ch'mb'in7	6000	Leejim Stable	17.40

Ⓓ Disqualified and placed last.
†Five pounds apprentice allowance waived.

Time .24⅕, .48, 1.13⅕, 1.39⅖, 1.52⅘ (with wind in backstretch). Track fast.

$2 Mutuel Prices:

4-TOBIR	9.00	4.60	2.40
2-NO KIDDING		6.00	2.60
5-HY-NAT			2.20

Ch. g, by Tenarani—Merry Game, by Big Game. Trainer H. Jacobson. Bred by M. Ritzenberg (Eng.).

IN GATE AT 5.30. OFF AT 5.30 EASTERN DAYLIGHT TIME. Start good. Won driving.

TOBIR, outrun early, moved into contention racing wide leaving the three-furlong pole and continuing wide during the stretch run and was along in time to wear down NO KIDDING. The latter made all the pace came slightly wide turning into the stretch and was unable to repulse the winner in the final sixteenth. HY-NAT was unable to gain when put to pressure. VICTARAY came out ad interfered with LATIN ARTIST at the half mile pole then lacked a rally. LATIN ARTIST had to check sharply leaving the half mile pole. Jockey Ron Turcotte's claim of foul was allowed and VICTARAY was placed last. DONGO dropped out of contention after five furlongs and was eased when hopelessly beaten.

Scratched—27858Aqu11 With Promise.
No Kidding was claimed by N. Hellman, trainer A. A. Scotti.

Courtesy of The Morning Telegraph

as fast as possible and will not be able to duplicate the effort today. If the previous rapid effort took place on another track, check pages 255–258 in this book to see whether the track is slower or faster than today's. For instance, if the times are approximately equal, but the earlier race was on a slower track, the more recent effort probably was the less taxing of the two and the horse may be all right.

As to the concept of "reserve energy," if the horse won easily or handily, or, as may happen once in a great while, covered the ground without any great exertion in the kind of race known by the chartmakers as an "even effort," it can be accepted as a possibility today. Also, it can be credited with plenty of reserve juice if it won after staying close to the pace, arriving at the stretch call first or second or within a length of the leader, and gained thereafter. Like one of the following, which are the best kind of races. I call them big wins:

$$3 \quad 3 \quad 3^4 \quad 2^1 \quad 1^1 \quad 1^2$$
$$1 \quad 2 \quad 1^1 \quad 2^{1/2} \quad 2^{1/2} \quad 1^{1/2}$$

6. Throw out any claimer whose last race was a big win more than two weeks ago. A horse able to win that powerfully is at the top of its form. The trainer naturally tries to get it another opportunity, before it loses its edge. If more than two weeks elapse, the player should suspect that something has gone awry with the horse. Exceptions can be made for animals that have been working steadily while awaiting today's race. But if the horse has had little or no public exercise, the player had better plan to look for signs of distress in the paddock and walking ring.

Before proceeding to our next array of negative signs, it might be a good idea to review the circumstances in which smart players overlook or excuse a poor last race, no matter how bad it may have seemed.

The Airtight Alibi

Because the conditioning process finds horses entered in races they cannot win, it is important not to be misled by their dismal performances in such races. Like the trainer who shoots the works after darkening his horse's form, the expert player dearly loves a situation in which his choice's last race looked so bad that today's odds increase. The handicapper who knows when to disregard a horse's latest race is destined for repeated happiness.

A bad race in the wrong company is, indeed, not a bad race at all. If anything, it suggests to the player that things are working out exactly as he and the maneuvering trainer might wish.

Here is now a list of the circumstances in which a poor effort is forgivable. Overlook a horse's last race if:

1. It was on an off-track of a kind that the horse has never negotiated successfully in the past.

2. The horse was entered at the wrong distance.

3. The horse ran against animals of a higher class than it has been able to challenge successfully in its most recent seven or eight efforts.

4. The horse carried substantially more weight than is good for it. (Some Thoroughbreds cannot win under more than 115 pounds and look dreadful with 119 or more. Others, able to win with 117 or 118, die with 121 or 122. If a claimer ran poorly with 119 or more, check its record to see if the high weight constitutes an alibi.)

5. The race was the horse's first in a month or more.

6. The race was the horse's first since arriving on this circuit from another part of the country.

7. The horse showed high early speed before tiring or even stopping or quitting. This often is more than just an alibi for a poor finish. It may be a positive sign of approaching form, and of a trainer's imminent readiness to lower the boom. The past-performance line shows that the animal led or ran within a length or so of the early pace (usually to the pre-stretch call) before conking out. Unless the animal is a chronic quitter that does this sort of thing in almost every outing, the player should be delighted to forgive the eighth-place finish. Dollars to doughnuts, if the horse is well placed today it will show early speed again, and carry it farther.

All those solid alibis derive from peculiarities of the modern conditioning process. Other good excuses are more usually attributable to racing misfortune. The expert tosses out the last race if:

8. The jockey had never finished first or second with the horse, is not a national or local leader, and, for today's race, has been replaced by a more successful boy.

9. The jockey lost his whip, or a stirrup broke, or a bandage came undone, or some other mishap fouled the tack.

10. The jockey rode weakly or unintelligently enough to attract comment in the result chart.

11. Other horses prevented the animal from running its race. The chart or *Telegraph* trouble line might say "Blocked," "Impeded," "Roughed," "Rough trip," "Forced to check," "Shuffled back," "In close," "Close quarters," or "Forced wide." Or it might say "Wide" or

Veterinarian William Reed checks Proud Clarion's underpinnings at Belmont Park.

"Ran wide," indicating a bad ride or interference rather than the affliction of bearing out.

12. The horse got off to a poor start, but seldom has that kind of trouble.

Inexcusable Performances

Assuming that the horse ran in its own class range and at its best distance and had no excuse for its last performance, it can be eliminated on grounds of poor condition if:

1. It failed to beat about half its field—finishing fifth or worse in a field of seven, sixth or worse in a field of eight or nine, seventh or worse in a field of ten or more—and earned a speed rating at least 5 points below the ones recorded in its better local races.

2. It failed to gain on the leader at any call in the race and finished out of the money more than six lengths behind. (Some players use this kind of standard in preference to the first. Others use both in sequence.)

3. It lost more than two and a half lengths between the stretch call and the finish.

4. It got off to a poor start, and poor starts have been one of its problems.

5. It earned an uncomplimentary chart comment such as "Dull," "No speed," or "Showed nothing."

Signs of Improvement

"Accentuate the positive, eliminate the negative," wrote Johnny Mercer in a song that was popular during the Stone Age. Numerous horseplayers take the advice literally. They look for horses whose most recent races gave notice of better things to come. They ignore other horses.

In my opinion, a little more work than that pays dividends. A player who follows a sequence similar to the one in this chapter achieves a considerable edge by discarding horses that figure to be out of contention today. He then decides what to do about the remaining horses. If he is really hipped on the condition factor, he can toss out any of the surviving contenders that fail to check out on the positive angles described below. But if he cares to consider some advice from an old hand, he may refrain from crossing off such horses until he has evaluated them in terms of class, pace and other fundamentals. My reasons for

Kelso and the farrier.   UPI PHOTO

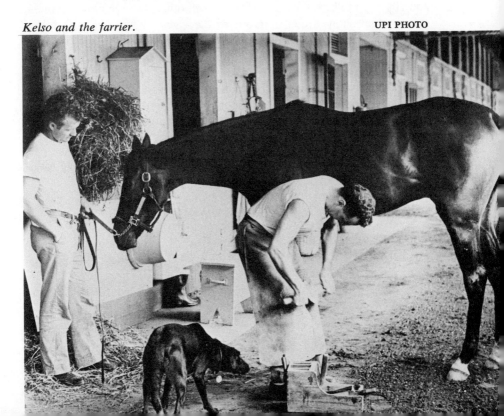

suggesting this are readily understandable: A horse that has been sufficiently active and has earned no black marks in its recent performances may well be in good enough shape to win today, even if its last race or two were unspectacular. For one thing, the horse might have run an alibi race last time out and this in itself might be a sign that the trainer's gears are meshing. Even without the evidence of an alibi its trainer might be a master at concealing improvement from the public, whereupon the player would live to regret eliminating the animal.

Players not already committed to a different way of doing things really should see if their winning percentage does not increase when they accept as contenders any animals that qualify on the distance factor and show none of the signs of unreadiness reviewed earlier. A player who does not care to excuse a bad last race on grounds of one of the alibis discussed earlier should then look for negative signs in the horse's next-to-last race. If the race took place in the past three weeks and was a good one, the player had better not eliminate the horse.

In setting forth the following methods of spotting improvement or other signs of current readiness in the past-performance records, I recommend that the player regard them as plus factors. A horse may show none of these angles in his record, but may be the class of the race and win in a walk. Where these factors are especially useful is in separating contenders that (1) qualify on distance, class, pace, etc., (2) have checked out successfully against the negative standards of condition, and (3) need to be differentiated from each other. In such circumstances, a horse that showed one or more of the signs of improvement would ordinarily be the better bet (see Chapter 16). Another use of the signs of improvement is as a homing device for lovers of longshots. As everyone knows, many players hate to handicap, but enjoy a longshot more than anything. If they check out a field of horses against the following series of improvement angles and bet on the longest-priced horse whose record contains one or more of the angles, they can count on an entertaining run for their money.

A horse that has not been eliminated for any of the reasons reviewed earlier can be expected to run a good race today if it:

1. Won its last race easily or handily.
2. Won its last race in big-win style (see page 170).
3. Lost its last race but gained at least two lengths in the stretch, earning favorable comment such as "Rallied," "Gaining," "Game try," "Sharp try," or "Good effort."
4. Lost ground in the middle stages but gained in the stretch. A horse

may lose ground to the leader while hunting for racing room, but if it is in a running mood, it often demonstrates that fitness by recovering the lost ground and more:

6   6 4^2 4^4 4^3 3^1

5. Showed high early speed (see page 171).

6. Ran within the past week.

7. Ran in the money in its first effort after a long layoff or a long trip.

8. Steps down in class today after a race in which it ran well enough to earn a comment like "Evenly" or better.

9. Steps down in class today to a level at which it has never been beaten by more than half a length.

10. Ran the final quarter of its last race in 24 seconds or less. (The famous Colonel E. R. Bradley invented this one. He found that any horse able to cover the last two furlongs that rapidly was an especially good bet next time out. To calculate a horse's final-quarter speed in a six-furlong race, subtract the race's official half-mile clocking from its official final time. For every length the animal gained on the leader from the half to the finish, deduct one fifth of a second. If the horse lost ground, add a fifth for every length it lost. The only other kind of race in which this calculation is possible for most fans is the mile, wherein the three-quarter-mile and final clockings are used.)

11. Ran closer to the early pace than in its previous race or two.

12. Was closer at the stretch call than in its previous race or two.

13. Finished closer to the winner and earned a higher speed rating than in its previous race or two.

14. Gained three or more lengths between the first and second call, or between any other two calls in the race.

15. Is a front-running type that carried its speed farther than in its previous race or two, even though it tired toward the end.

16. Ran an even race, in second or third position all the way, earning a substantially higher speed rating than in its previous race or two.

17. Has earned increasingly high speed ratings in its past three races, even though out of the money in its latest.

As the reader has noticed, many of these positive signs are infinitesimal. Most players overlook all but the more obvious of them. The handicapper sophisticated enough to understand that even slight improvement is often a prelude to major improvement can expect to make extra money by exploiting the above list, along with similar subtleties that will appear in later chapters.

10 The Class Factor

THEY CLAIM that the ebullient president of Tropical Park, Saul Silberman, decided one day to make a splendid and unusual gesture of goodwill toward his paying customers. He would go to the grandstand with sheaves of currency and give it all away. For free.

It turned out to be quite an experience. When Silberman offered greenbacks to strangers, many not only refused the gift but behaved as if he were trying in some way to take advantage of them.

I can understand that. Racing is a weird game. A proportion of its clients become so accustomed to calamity that they cannot recognize good fortune when they see it face to face. This self-defeating turn of mind reflects itself in their betting. Let me illustrate.

Class Bonanzas

The nearest thing to a cinch at any track is a sharply conditioned horse of substantial class, when entered at a suitable distance against inferior animals. Did I say racing was weird? Racing is astonishing. One of its most astonishing features is the frequency with which betting opportunities of this kind occur. At the height of the season on major circuits, the discerning player finds at least two such bonanzas every week.

What makes them bonanzas is that the best horse usually wins and almost invariably pays longer odds than it should. Even at Aqueduct, where a relentlessly shrewd crowd sometimes makes odds-on choices of animals that might pay 4 to 1 elsewhere, the kind of near-cinch I have in mind often pays 3 to 2, when it ought to be 4 to 5.

Allowance races provide the happiest hunting. An example was the sixth at Aqueduct on July 1, 1966. It was at six furlongs, offering a $6,000 purse to fillies and mares aged three and up that had never won two races other than maiden or claiming. All eight entrants were three-year-olds, of which three had run in stakes competition at age two. Lucky Eagle, 5 to 2 on this particular day, had led to the eighth pole in the Adirondack Stakes at Saratoga the previous August, but had stopped, finishing eleventh. She later had won an allowance at Garden

State and then lost decisively in a better allowance at Aqueduct. Trainer Woody Stephens had rested her for the winter and brought her back in an Aqueduct allowance on June 17, just two weeks ago. She led to the half, continued gamely to the eighth pole and tired. In preparation for today's race, Stephens had given her two smart workouts, including one of five furlongs in .59⅗, handily.

Lyvette, 7 to 2 today, had finished second to Native Street as a long-shot in the Astoria Stakes at Aqueduct almost a year ago. Later she was beaten more severely by the same filly at Monmouth Park, ran fifth in a seven-horse field behind Moccasin in the Spinaway at Saratoga, and was a surprising second (at 74 to 1) to Moccasin in the Matron at Aqueduct. Trainer Nick Combest had given her the winter vacation that better young horses usually get. Her first effort of 1966 had been in the same race as Lucky Eagle, whom she challenged for the lead and pickled in the stretch before running out of wind.

The third former stakes competitor in the race was C. V. Whitney's Silver Bright, which had won the Lassie at Arlington Park at 13 to 1 on a sloppy track in September, had lost a subsequent allowance affair at Garden State when forced to check, and had looked dull and unready in her 1966 debut in the race with Lyvette and Lucky Eagle.

Which of these three fillies shaped up as top class in the race on July 1? None. As nearly as one could tell from the past-performance records, Lucky Eagle was a speed horse with insufficient quality to withstand challenge from fillies of better than allowance grade. Lyvette, a gamester, had lost ground in the stretch run of every six-furlong race she had attempted. Perhaps she was still short of top condition in her most recent race and would show more leg today, but a far safer presumption was that she lacked the intrinsic class to beat good fillies. As to the Whitney horse, Silver Bright, it was conceivable that trainer Ivor Balding was bringing her along slowly in this year's campaign. Perhaps her dismal race two weeks ago was not representative of what she finally might accomplish. Until she showed more, however, nobody could reasonably credit her with real class.

Of the five other demoiselles in today's race, four had failed to demonstrate high quality, although each had been given numerous chances. If these four, and the three fillies described earlier, were the only contestants, the race would have shaped up as a typical allowance scrimmage on a typical summer Friday. But the eighth filly in the race altered the picture entirely.

Belle de Nuit, by Warfare out of the Eight Thirty mare, Evening Belle, was owned by Mrs. George D. Widener and trained by the redoubtable

6th Race Aqueduct

6 FURLONGS
AQUEDUCT
Start
Finish

6 FURLONGS. (Near Man, July 17, 1963, 1.08⅗, 3, 112.)
Allowances. Purse $6,000. Fillies and mares. 3-year-olds and upward which have not won two races other than maiden or claiming. Weights, 3-year-olds 116 lbs. ,older 123 lbs. Non-winners of a race other than maiden or claiming since May 31 allowed 3 lbs., such a race since April 20, 5 lbs., such a race since March 12, 7 lbs.

Scarlet Carpet

B. f (1962), by Cosmic Bomb—Red Carpet, by Roman **116** 1966 8 1 0 0 $4,875
C. B. Lyman, Jr. A. R. White (Mr.-Mrs. C. B. Lyman, Jr.) 1965 21 0 1 4 $3,090

17Jun66-6Aqu fst 6f .22⅘ .46⅕1.12 f- Allow 5 3 6³¾ 8⁸½ 9¹³ 9¹⁶ LLoughry5 b 115 97.90 67-22 College Boards 120no Chavalon 115¹ Lyvette 114h No threat 10
30Mar66-7Bow fst 6f .22⅘ .45⅗1.11⅕ f- Allow 2 8 8⁸¾ 8¹⁴ 8¹⁶ 8¹⁵ RMcCurdy b 121 38.30 76-17 SummerScandal116²¼ SharonMarket116³ Ironshire116no Trailed 8
22Mar66-7Aqu fst 6f .22⅗ .45⅗1.11⅖ f- Allow 7 3 7¹³ 7¹⁸ 7¹⁷ 7¹⁹ ACordero b 123 59.10 67-21 Winnie 116² Wine and Song 120h Candy Stripes 116³ Trailed 8
15Mar66-7Aqu fst 6f .23⅗ .48⅕1.13⅖ f- Allow 4 4 6³½ 6⁸½ 6¹³ 6¹⁴ ORosado5 b 118 13.40 62-30 Save Up 116⁴ Adorable 118h Bright Sister 111¹ No factor 6
16Feb66-8Pim my 6f .23⅘ .48 1.14 f- Allow 4 8 9⁵½10¹⁸10¹³ 9¹⁹ GPatterson b 122 12.20 61-34 Cease Lass 115⁷ A Clear Spin 108no Lucy Bean 114no Far back 10
4Feb66-7Bow fst 6f .22⅗ .45⅗1.11⅗ f- Allow 6 2 2² 3¹ 3² 1¾ RMcCurdy b 114 10.40 89-17 Scarlet Carpet 114¾ Miss Cotton 109³ Mary Alan 116¾ Hard drive 6
21Jan66-7Bow fst 7f .23⅕ .46 1.24⅖ Allowance 3 3 2¹½ 5⁶ 8⁶¾10⁹½ RMcCurdy b 109 103.00 81-21 Frosty Ore 121¹ Consecrate 115¹¼ Silver Monarch 122no Tired 11
14Jan66-8Bow fst 6f .22⅘ .45⅖1.12⅘ f- Allow 3 8 6³¾ 6⁴½10⁷¾ 8⁸¼ BThornburg b 113 11.80 77-22 Well Heeled 117²½ Roz 113¾ Brzina 115¾ Early foot, tired 12
18Dec65-4Pim fst 1 1/16 .48 1.13 1.47⅖ Allowance 8 2 4⁴½ 9¹² 9¹⁵ 9¹¹ RMcCurdy b 113 15.40 62-22 •Reluctant Angel 113³ •War Alert 116³ Foolish 114³ Tired 11
13Dec65-8Pim gd 6f .24 .47⅘1.13⅖ f- Allow 5 2 1h 1h 1h 2nk RMcCurdy b 112 47.80 83-24 Teekon 112nk Scarlet Carpet 112¹ Well Heeled 112²½ Just failed 8
6Dec65-8Aqu fst 7f .23 .47 1.25⅘ Allowance 2 2 3¹½ 4²½ 5⁹ 4¹¹ ACordero b 110 26.70 66-22 Tom Poker 118³ R. Anniversary 113¹ Thirty Pieces 113⁷ Steadied 6
LATEST WORKOUTS Jun 29 Bel m.t. 4f fst .49⅖ h Jun 24 Bel m.t. 4f fst .48⅗ h Jun 14 Bel m.t. 4f fst .49⅕ h Jun 9 Bel m.t. 6f fst 1.14⅗ h

Lyvette *

Dk. b. or br. f (1963-Ky), by To Market—Clinker, by Coaltown **111** 1966 1 0 0 1 $600
Birchfield Farm N. Combest (W. L. Jones, Jr.) 1965 9 2 3 0 $37,436

17Jun66-6Aqu fst 6f .22⅘ .46⅕1.12 f- Allow 9 2 2¹ 2h 1h 3¹ JCombest 114 5.90 82-22 College Boards 120no Chavalon 115¹ Lyvette 114h Weakened 10
3Nov65-6Aqu fst 6f .22⅘ .46 1.11⅕ f- Allow 4 9 8⁴ 7⁶ 9¹⁴ 9¹⁵ JCombest 116 5.20 72-15 Around the Roses119¹½ChosenPeople114¹BeSuspicious116no No sp'd 9
11Sep65-7Aqu fst 6f .22⅗ .46⅘1.11⅗ f-Matron 12 4 7²¾ 7⁴ 3⁴½ 2⁶ JCombest 119 74.40 79-20 Moccasin 119⁶ Lyvette 119² Shimmering Gold 119¹ Second best 12
25Aug65-7Sar fst 6f .22 .45⅕1.11 f-Spinaway 1 2 4⁴½ 4³½ 2⁴ 5⁷ JCombest 119 25.80 86-10 Moccasin 119³½ Swift Lady 119no Forefoot 119h Mild bid, tired 7
10Aug65-7Sar fst 5½f .22⅘ .46⅖1.05 Allowance 8 4 5³ 3¹ 1³ 1⁴ JCombest 119 3.40 92- 9 Lyvette 119⁴ One Night Stand 122¹ Defiant Son 117nk Easily 9
31Jly 65-8Mth fst 6f .21⅗ .45 1.10⅖ f-Sorority 9 6 4⁴ 4⁵ 5⁷½ 8¹⁵ JCombest 119 11.20 75-17 NativeStreet119⁶ ShimmeringGold114⁷ LovelyGypsy119¾ Fell back 15
14Jly 65-7Aqu fst 5½f .21⅗ .44⅘1.04⅕ f-Astoria 3 2 3² 4²½ 2³ 2²½ JCombest 117 28.00 89-16 Native Street 117²½ Lyvette 117¹ Lady Pitt 117¹ Went well 10
28Jun65-6Aqu fst 5½f .22⅖ .45⅘1.04⅕ f- Allow 5 4 3¹½ 2² 2² 2⁵ JCombest 119 2.30 87-16 Stealaway 114⁵ Lyvette 119⁶ Spearfish 119¹½ Easily best of others 6
11Jun65-4Aqu fst 5½f .22⅕ .46⅕1.06 f-MdSpWt 12 2 1h 1h 1³ 1⁴ JCombest 119 4.65 83-18 Lyvette 119⁴ Spearfish 119¹ d-Fizzy 119no Ridden out at end 12
3Jun65-4Aqu my 5f .23 .47⅕1.00 f-MdSpWt 5 4 4³ 5⁶ 5⁴ 4¾ JCombest 119 43.55 84-24 Swinging Mood 119no Be Suspicious119¾ Our Spinney119nk Greenly 10
LATEST WORKOUTS Jun 28 Aqu 4f fst .50 b Jun 24 Aqu 5f fst 1.03⅕ b Jun 15 Aqu 4f fst .47⅗ h Jun 11 Aqu 7f fst 1.29⅖ h

Lucky Eagle

Dk. b. or br. f (1963-Ky), by Bald Eagle—Lucky Mistake, by Olympia **104⁵** 1966 1 0 0 0 $300
Lucille E. Stephens W. C. Stephens (Mrs. L. E. Stephens) 1965 7 2 0 1 $5,680

17Jun66-6Aqu fst 6f .22⅘ .46⅕1.12 f- Allow 6 1 1¹ 1h 2h 4¹ PAnderson 115 5.70 82-22 College Boards 120no Chavalon 115¹ Lyvette 114h Used up 10
3Nov65-6Aqu fst 6f .22⅘ .46 1.11⅕ f- Allow 8 3 3² 5²½ 4³½ 6³½ MSorrentino 119 17.00 83-15 Around the Roses119¹½ChosenPeople114¹BeSuspicious116no Tired 9
26Oct65-7GS fst 6f .22⅗ .45⅗1.11⅘ f- Allow 7 6 4nk 1h 1h 1²½ MSorrentino 117 *1.60 85-17 Lucky Eagle 117²½ Reel Irish 114² Royalene 116¹½ Ridden out 8
18Oct65-6Aqu fst 6f .22⅖ .45⅘1.11⅕ f- Allow 1 5 1h 2h 4²½ 6¹⁰ MYcaza 116 4.50 77-19 Around the Roses 116³ Indian Sunlite 114¹ Boiseana 113⁵ Tired 13
11Sep65-4Aqu fst 6f .22⅗ .46 1.11⅖ f- Allow 3 3 2½ 2³ 2⁵ 3⁸¾ MSorrentino 119 2.60 77-20 Priceless Gem 114⁸ Ameri Belle 114¾ Lucky Eagle 119⁵ Tired 7
18Aug65-7Sar gd 6f .22⅕ .45⅘1.11⅗ f-Ad'rack 1 7 1¹½ 1¹½ 1½ 11¹¹ WBoland 114 20.10 79-13 Lady Dulcinea 114nk Lovely Gypsy 120¹½ Prides Profile 123² Tired 14
6Aug65-3Sar fst 5½f .22⅕ .45⅘1.05⅗ f-MdSpWt 5 1 1³ 1² 1³ 1³½ WBoland 119 *2.40 89-13 Lucky Eagle 119³½ High Bluff 119no Squeeze 119⁶ Speed to spare 12
17Jun65-3Aqu fst 5f .22⅗ .46⅖ .58⅘ f-MdSpWt 10 5 2h 2h 2¹½ 5⁷ MSorrentino 119 *2.25 84-15 Spearfish 119³½ Ultra Quest 119¾ Ogirema 112² Well up, no rally 10
LATEST WORKOUTS Jun 28 Bel m.t. 4f fst .47⅗ h Jun 23 Bel m.t. 5f fst .59⅘ h Jun 14 Bel m.t. 3f fst .36 b Jun 9 Bel m.t. 6f fst 1.12⅗ h

Silver Bright ×

Ro. f (1963–Ky), by Barbizon—Silver Fog, by Mahmoud
C. V. Whitney I. G. Balding (C. V. Whitney) **113**
1966 1 0 0 0 ——
1965 5 2 1 0 $123,745

17Jun66-6Aqu fst 6f .22⅘ .46⅕1.12 f- Allow 2 4 32½ 45 79¼ 813 JLRotz b 113 4.60e 70-22 College Boards 120no Chavalon 1151 Lyvette 114h Tired 10
19Oct65-5GS fst 6f .22⅖ .46 1.13⅗ f- Allow 3 2 43 31 43 41¾ SHernandez b 119 *0.70 84-18 Cloud High 1191 Royalene 112¾ Caxambas 116h Forced to check 7
4Sep65-8AP sly 6½f.23 .46⅕1.18⅕ f-Lassie 9 1 21½ 2½ 11 13¼ JNichols b 119 13.30 85-19 Silver Bright 1193¼ Ole Liz 1192 Prides Profile 1191¾ Driving 10
18Aug65-8AP my 6f .22 .46 1.12⅖ LassieTr'l 7 1 22 22 22 23½ HMoreno b 112 29.50 77-24 Ole Liz 1123½ Silver Bright 1122½ Native Street 119½ Raced wide 9
12Aug65-4AP fst 6f .21⅕ .45⅗1.11⅘ f-MdSpWt 1 7 11½ 12 13 13¼ JNichols b 115 13.50 84-12 Silver Bright 1153¼ Maywatt 1153¼ Hon's Gal 1153½ Easy score 12
10Jun65-3Hol fst 5f .22⅕ .46 .58⅘ f-MdSpWt 11 4 106½107¾1214 98¾ JLeonard 116 13.20 80-19 Babyville 116nk Turn True Blue1162 WindyKate116h Showed nothing 12
LATEST WORKOUTS Jun 27 Bel t.c. 7f fm 1.27 h Jun 22 Bel tr.t. 5f fst 1.04 b Jun 16 Bel tr.t. 3f fst .37⅖ h Jun 14 Bel m.t. 5f fst 1.03⅘ b

Apasionadamente

Blk. f (1963–Ky), by Beau Max—Apasionada, by War Admiral
King Ranch Max Hirsch (King Ranch) **1117**
1966 7 0 0 1 $550
1965 7 1 0 1 $3,360

9Jun66-7Aqu fm 1 1/16 Ⓣ 1.43⅕ f- Allow 2 7 67 44½ 33 65½ JJMartin7 104 12.30 85-10 We Try Harder 1131 Ogirema 111½ Darlin Phyllis 1152½ Wide 10
6Jun66-7Aqu fm 1 1/16 Ⓣ 1.43⅗ f- Allow 6 8 817 88¼ 67¼ 712 ECardone7 100 47.50 76-12 Mount Regina 118nk Gallarush 1112 Treachery 1165 No speed 9
27May66-6Aqu fst 6f .22⅕ .45⅖1.11⅖ f- Allow 6 7 129¼1211 52½ 65½ JLRotz 113 7.30 80-18 Fatal Step 103h Sweety Kid 1142½ Darlin Phyllis 116¾ Tired 13
9May66-6Aqu gd 6f .23 .47 1.12⅗ f- Allow 8 2 69½ 68½ 52 31½ KKnapp 111 3.50e 78-25 Tutasi 105no Fatal Step 1071½ Apasionadamente 111½ Rallied 8
29Apr66-6Aqu my 6f .22⅗ .46 1.11 Allowance 2 5 31½ 52½ 5¾ 74¾ HWoodhouse 109 27.60 83-16 There Goes Sam 1131½ Dion 121no Woodford 115no Tired 8
20Apr66-6Aqu fst 6f .22⅘ .46⅕1.11⅕ f- Allow 4 3 42½ 32 34 66 MYcaza 116 13.80 81-16 Blooming Hills 116½ First Query 109nk Darlin Phyllis 1144 Tired 6
4Apr66-6Aqu fst 6f .22⅘ .46⅗1.11⅘ f- Allow 7 2 45½ 45 56½ 510 MYcaza 118 7.30 74-19 Home Lass 118nk First Query 1136 Fatal Step 1183 Raced wide 7
25Nov65-4Aqu gd 6f .22⅗ .47⅕1.14⅖ f-MdSpWt 6 4 53 2h 11 11¾ MYcaza 119 *2.60 71-26 Apasionad'ente1191¾ FederalPrincess114½ Gem'sRew'd1191½ Driving 12
19Nov65-6Aqu fst 7f .23 .47 1.25⅘ f-MdSpWt 11 4 43 45 1118 1123 BBaeza 119 6.90 54-26 Evening Off 119no Gentle Rain 1193½ Miss Proctor 1192½ Stopped 11
15Oct65-4Aqu fst 6f .22⅖ .45⅘1.12⅗ f-MdSpWt 4 8 86¼ 77¾ 55 45½ JLRotz 119 8.50 74-23 Miss Foxcroft 1194 Chinook 114½ Tribal Chant 1191 No mishap 11
24Sep65-5Aqu fst 6f .22⅗ .46⅗1.12⅕ f-MdSpWt 5 9 94½ 74¼ 73½ 77 RTurcotte 119 6.20 75-20 Yankeenesian 109¾ Rose Court 1195 Happy Kitten 119½ No mishap 13
17Sep65-5Aqu fst 6f .22⅘ .46⅗1.11⅗ f-MdSpWt 14 10 53½ 51¾ 32 36 RTurcotte 119 21.90 79-19 Chosen People 1196 Politely 119no Apasionadamente 119¾ Good try 14
LATEST WORKOUTS Jun 28 Bel m.t. 3f fst .35 h Jun 26 Bel m.t. 4f fst .51 b Jun 25 Bel m.t. 3f fst .37⅖ b Jun 21 Bel m.t. 6f fst 1.15 h

River Lady

B. f (1963–Ky), by Prince John—Nile Lily, by Roman
Cain Hoy Stable R. Laurin (H. F. Guggenheim) **113**
1966 3 0 0 1 $900
1965 8 2 0 2 $7,565

17Jun66-6Aqu fst 6f .22⅘ .46⅕1.12 f- Allow 4 5 76¾ 66½ 56½ 65 MYcaza 114 *3.00 78-22 College Boards 120no Chavalon 1151 Lyvette 114h Dull 10
25May66-6Aqu fst 6f .22⅘ .46 1.11⅕ f- Allow 3 4 42½ 12 12 3h MYcaza b 113 *2.30 87-13 Royalo 120no Roman Correl 107no River Lady 113½ Failed to last 7
18May66-5Aqu fst 6f .23 .46⅖1.11⅖ f- Allow 3 2 2½ 1½ 2h 44¼ MYcaza b 114 3.80 82-15 LadyDulcinea113½ WeTryHarder1143½ BloomingHills113nk Weak'n'd 6
3Nov65-6Aqu fst 6f .22⅘ .46 1.11⅕ f- Allow 2 1 74 65 75 74¼ WShoemaker b 119 7.30 83-15 Around the Roses1191½ChosenPeople1141BeSuspicious116no No exc. 9
20Oct65-4Aqu fst 7f .23 .47 1.24⅘ f- Allow 1 5 32 2½ 14 18 MYcaza b 119 4.00 82-18 River Lady 1198 Zatullah 113nk Scairt 116½ Easily the best 8
21Sep65-7Aqu fst 6f .21⅕ .45 1.09⅘ f- Allow 10 4 86¼ 77¼ 512 918 JCombest b 115 11.00e 76-18 Priceless Gem 1168 Lady Diplomat 1192 Lady Pitt 1164 No factor 12
10Sep65-5Aqu fst 6f .22⅗ .46⅖1.12⅕ f-MdSpWt 11 3 94¾ 54½ 23 13½ MYcaza b 119 3.00 82-19 River Lady 1193½ First Feather 1195 Our Spinney 1194 Mild drive 14
27Aug65-5Sar fst 5½f.22⅖ .46⅕1.06 f-MdSpWt 8 1 2½ 21 21 31¾ MYcaza b 119 *1.50 85-14 Well in Hand 119¾ Tutasi 1191 River Lady 1192½ Pressed pace, tired 12
20Aug65-4Sar gd 5½f.22⅗ .46⅕1.05⅗ f-MdSpWt 7 3 31½ 21 21 31½ BBaeza b 119 2.80 89-12 For Joy 119nk Fizzy 1191 River Lady 1194 Held on willingly 9
6Aug65-4Sar fst 5½f.22⅕ .46 1.04⅖ f-MdSpWt 5 4 32 21½ 37 416 WBoland b 119 8.30 79-13 Moccasin 1198 Lady Dulcinea 1196 Ultra Quest 1192 Wide 12
24Jun65-3Aqu fst 5f .23 .46⅗ .59⅕ f-MdSpWt 2 5 52 44½ 45 43 MYcaza b 119 6.15 86-19 Zatullah 119¾ Home Lass 119¾ Thirty Lima 1191½ Even effort 10
LATEST WORKOUTS Jun 24 Bel m.t. 3f fst .38 b Jun 15 Bel m.t. 4f fst .48 b Jun 10 Bel m.t. 4f fst .49 b Jun 4 Bel tr.t. 4f fst .51 h

Fatal Step

Ch. f (1963–Ky), by Flaneur II—Nature Walk, by Discovery
Mrs. G. Smith R. L. Dotter (Mrs. G. Smith) **113**
1966 7 1 1 2 $5,675
1965 8 1 2 2 $4,732

17Jun66-6Aqu fst 6f .22⅘ .46⅕1.12 f- Allow 1 8 910 912 810 54 ECardone7 b 107 8.40 79-22 College Boards 120no Chavalon 1151 Lyvette 114h Rallied 10
27May66-6Aqu fst 6f .22⅕ .45⅖1.11⅖ f- Allow 13 9 53¼ 43¼ 3½ 1h ECardone7 b 103 5.50 86-18 Fatal Step 103h Sweety Kid 1142½ Darlin Phyllis 116¾ Driving 13
9May66-6Aqu gd 6f .23 .47 1.12⅗ f- Allow 1 6 44½ 55½ 21 2no GMineau5 b 107 14.00 80-25 Tutasi 105no Fatal Step 1071½ Apasionadamente 111½ Nosed 8
27Apr66-4Aqu fst 6f .23 .46⅗1.11⅘ f- 12500 2 6 31½ 32 21½ 3½ JLRotz b 116 2.70 83-18 HangingGardens115nk Yankeenesian116nk FatalStep1162½ Good try 7
15Apr66-8Aqu fst 1 .45⅗1.10 1.36⅗ f- Allow 2 3 33 43½ 43 89½ JLRotz b 114 16.80 75-15 Dorian League 1101½ Roz 1201½ Tomeen 1103 Tired badly str. 8
4Apr66-6Aqu fst 6f .22⅘ .46⅗1.11⅘ f- Allow 2 3 23 23 31½ 36¼ JLRotz b 118 11.60 78-19 Home Lass 118nk First Query 1136 Fatal Step 1183 Bid, tired 7
21Mar66-6Aqu fst 6f .22⅖ .46 1.13⅕ f- Allow 1 2 33 33½ 32½ 64 JLRotz b 114 27.40 73-22 Rifle Ruby 114nk First Query 1091½ Darlin Phyliss 116½ Weakened 8
16Nov65-7Aqu fst 6f .22 .45 1.10⅘ f- Allow 7 5 52½ 44½ 57½ 612 DPierce b 114 10.80 77-21 Zatullah 1123 Miss Puzzle 1144 Chosen People 1111 Tired 7
12Nov65-3Aqu fst 6f .22⅘ .46⅗1.13⅕ f- 15000 5 3 31½ 33½ 32½ 21½ DPierce 116 3.40 75-21 Ji'ie Potatoes 1121½ Fatal Step 116½ Royal Tantrum 1165 Gamely 7
20Oct65-4Aqu fst 6f .22⅘ .46⅗1.13 f- 12500 2 1 1h 1h 2h 2nk DPierce 118 12.90 78-18 Farmer's Waltz 118nk Fatal Step 1181½ Kisco Babe 108no Swerved 11
20Oct65-4Aqu fst 7f .23 .47 1.24⅘ f- Allow 5 6 75¾ 75½ 56½ 512 DPierce 114 25.70 70-18 River Lady 1198 Zatullah 113nk Scairt 116½ Never a factor 8
LATEST WORKOUTS Jun 27 Bel m.t. 5f fst 1.02⅗ b Jun 24 Bel m.t. 4f fst .52 b Jun 16 Bel m.t. 3f fst .37⅕ b Jun 12 Bel m.t. 5f fst 1.01⅖ h

Results of 6th Race Aqueduct—July 1, 1966

SIXTH RACE
Aqu - 28006
July 1, 1966

6 FURLONGS. (Near Man, July 17, 1963, 1.08⅗, 3, 112.) Allowances. Purse $6,000. Fillies and mares. 3-year-olds and upward which have not won two races other than maiden or claiming. Weights, 3-year-olds 116 lbs. ,older 123 lbs. Non-winners of a race other than maiden or claiming since May 31 allowed 3 lbs., such a race since April 20, 5 lbs., such a race since March 12, 7 lbs.
Value to winner $3,900, second $1,200, third $600, fourth $300. Mutuel pool $317,652.

Index	Horse	Eqt	A	Wt	PP	St	¼	½	Str	Fin	Jockey	Owner	Odds $1
27796Aqu^{1}	Belle de Nuit		3	116	5	3	2^h	2^3	1^2	1^6	J Ruane	Mrs G D Widener	1.70
27832Aqu^{4}	Lucky Eagle		3	104	3	2	1^2	1^1	2^5	2^6	E Cardone^5	Lucille E Stephens	2.40
27832Aqu^{6}	River Lady	b	3	114	7	1	6^8	3^h	$3^{\frac{1}{2}}$	3^h	M Ycaza	Cain Hoy Stable	8.00
27770Aqu^{6}	Apasionad'm'nte		3	106	6	6	5^1	5^1	4^2	$4\frac{1}{2}$	D Ch'mb'lin^7	King Ranch	35.00
27832Aqu^{5}	Fatal Step	b	3	113	8	8	8	6^3	6^3	$5^{2\frac{1}{2}}$	K Knapp	Mrs G S Smith	14.30
27832Aqu^{3}	Lyvette		3	113	2	4	$3\frac{1}{2}$	4^3	5^3	6^8	J Combest	Birchfield Farms	3.80
27832Aqu^{8}	Silver Bright	b	3	113	4	5	$4\frac{1}{2}$	7^1	7^6	7^4	J L Rotz	C V Whitney	9.10
27832Aqu^{9}	Scarlet Carpet	b	4	116	1	7	7^1	8	8	8	A Cordero	C B Layman	68.10

Time .22⅘, .45⅕, 1.09⅘ (with wind in backstretch). Track fast.

$2 Mutuel Prices:			
5-BELLE DE NUIT	5.40	2.80	2.20
3-LUCKY EAGLE		3.20	2.60
7-RIVER LADY			3.60

Gr. f, by Warfare—Evening Belle, by Eight Thirty. Trainer W. F. Mulholland. Bred by Mrs. G. D. Widener (Ky).

IN GATE AT 4.02. OFF AT 4.02 EASTERN DAYLIGHT TIME. Start good. Won easily.

BELLE DE NUIT, off alertly, followed the pace in hand moved quickly to take command in upper stretch and drew off rapidly while her rider flashed his whip alongside her head. LUCKY EAGLE cut out a swift pace and while no match for the winner easily bested the others. RIVER LADY outgamed APASIONADAMENTE for the minor award. FATAL STEP passed tired horses. LYVETTE and SILVER BRIGHT were unable to keep up. SCARLET CARPET appeared overmatched.

Overweights—Lyvette 2 pounds, Apasionadamente 2, River Lady 1. Corrected weight—Apasionadamente 7104 pounds.

Courtesy of The Morning Telegraph

Bert Mulholland. She had not raced at all as a two-year-old, which would be a sign of disability in a cheap horse but is a proclamation of careful nurture in a Mulholland horse. In her premiere on June 2, a six-furlong affair for maiden fillies, she had broken last in the nine-girl field. But she collared the leader within a quarter mile, dropped back a half length midway in the running, took the lead by a head at the eighth pole and increased it to a neck at the wire in a driving finish. If Johnny Ruane had been able to get her out of the gate more quickly, the race undoubtedly would have been easier for her.

On June 13, she made her second start, this time in allowance company at six furlongs. Once again she was slowest of all to leave the gate, but had the class to overcome that deficit. In the first quarter mile she ate up enough ground to come within a length and a half of the leader. At the half-mile call she was only three quarters of a length behind. She took the lead on the turn, extended it to two lengths at the eighth pole, and then began to tire. She won by a scant nose, all-out.

It seemed clear enough that this filly would have grave problems in races against top-quality stock if she continued to loiter at the starting gate. But she was not facing such competition today. She had already shown more than a touch of class in overtaking all lesser animals to which she had given head starts. Finally, and most important, her trainer was a rare bird. Bert Mulholland would withdraw Belle de Nuit from competition and send her back to school unless he was sure that her laggard behavior at the gate was only a passing phase.

What about the speed of Belle de Nuit? She had won her maiden effort in 1.11⅕. Two other fillies in today's race had equaled that figure on this track. They had done it, furthermore, after overcoming much faster early pace clockings than had challenged the class of Belle de Nuit. What should the player do?

Go the class horse. Every time. The class horse does not care about the early pace figures or final times of lesser horses. Class rises to the occasion. When a young, lightly raced Thoroughbred has class of a higher, more reliable order than that of its adversaries, many of the axioms of conventional handicapping can be shelved.

Although the smart player rarely expects an older, shopworn animal to do something today that it has never been able to do in the past, he looks for improvement in a younger animal. If a fresh, well-bred young horse from a Grade A barn has done the few things ever asked of it, the player can expect it to improve and improve and improve.

Some readers may argue that Belle de Nuit had never run in stakes races. Could she reasonably be credited with higher class than her competition simply because they had done little in stakes? I offer a repetitious answer: If the lightly raced animal from a good barn has done everything asked of it, the player will most often be right if he credits it with an edge in class when it is entered in an allowance race against animals that have been tried and found wanting.

Quite naturally, if more than one horse of this description is entered in the race, the player is in an altogether different situation. Like as not, the records are too sparse to permit differentiation between the two animals, and the player passes the race.

Even among horses of low class, similar betting opportunities arise with far greater frequency than most players realize. In allowance races for young horses, the expert looks greedily for the one with a hint of real class, as illustrated above. And in cheap races, if he finds a horse that merely enjoys a relative *edge* in class, and if he is satisfied that it likes the distance and is in shape to run, he holds his hat under the slot and waits for the jackpot. This is especially true of longer races, in which stamina and courage are usually decisive. In sprints for cheaper stock, the slight class superiority of one horse is sometimes nullified by other factors, such as pace.

The ninth at Laurel on December 12, 1966, offered an entertaining example of how even a cheap race may be dominated by an animal with a slight class advantage. The purse was $3,500, the claiming price $4,000, the distance a mile and an eighth, four-year-olds and up. The favorite, Atlantic, had won a $7,500 claimer over the same distance at Aqueduct

December 12, 1966

9th Race Laurel

TURF COURSE
1⅛ MILES
LAUREL
Start
Finish

Ab't 1 1-8 Miles (Turf). (Bull Market, Oct. 30, 1964, 1.51⅕, 4, 119.)
Claiming. Purse $3,500. 4-year-olds and upward. Weights, 122 lbs. Non-winners of three races since Oct. 15 allowed 3 lbs., of two races, 6 lbs., of a race, 9 lbs. Claiming price $4,000.

Cannelton — $4,000 — 116

Dk. b. g (1962), by Stella Aurata—Puffball, by Bimelech
Mrs. W. C. Wright — M. H. Dixon, Sr. — (D. F. Stewart)

1966	17	1	2	1	$1,625
1965	18	M	4	4	$3,585

6Dec66-7Lrl	fst 6f	.23⅖ .47⅘1.13	Clm	6000	8	10	63¼	76¾	98¼	96½	JBrocklebank	b 117	57.20	80-16	HurryUpPorter111nkWorldReport1171Fight'gPhant'm114nk	Far b'ck 12
26Nov66-9Lrl	fm 1⅛ (T)	1.50	Clm	7500	7	1	2h	22	23	89	SBrooks	b 119	61.10	78-11	Red Dog 1171¾ Footprint 108¾ The Gent 1151½	Speed to stretch 12
5Nov66-2Mtp	fst 1	1.37	Allowance		2	1	1½	1½	11	1¾	EDeveau	b 141	——e	——	Cannelton 141¾ War Union II 1423 Edinburgh II 1431	Hard drive 11
29Oct66-1FH	fm*1 (T)	1.39	Allowance		2	6	69¾	421	411	312	EDeveau	b 144	——	——	d-Glen Arm 1498 Mr. Pat 1523½ Cannelton 1441	Mild rally 8
29Oct--Placed second through disqualification.																
15Oct66-3Med	fm*1 (T)	1.48⅘	Allowance		14	1	2no	2½	2nk	2½	EDeveau	b 143	——	——	Little Falcon 146½ Cannelton 1433 Pardor 147¾	Good effort 15
11Aug66-4Atl	fst 6f	.22⅖ .46 1.11⅗	Md Sp Wt		8	8	75¾	67¾	68½	614	BThornburg	b 121	32.30	70-23	Call Me Fritz 1172 Wheels Up 1171½ Readership 1173	No factor 9
29Jly66-4Del	sf 1 (T)	1.41⅖	Md Sp Wt		4	8	915	921	823	821	BThornburg	b 122	15.10	47-30	Chai Cha-Na 1141½ Arvan 1225 At the Helm 1149	Never a factor 9
22Jly66-4Del	hd 1 (T)	1.38⅗	Md Sp Wt		6	3	44	69½	611	612	BThornburg	b 121	8.00	70-18	Royal Trumpeter 1146 Chai Cha-Na 1142 River Spot 1081	Tired 10
13Jly66-3Del	fst 6f	.22⅘ .46⅕1.11⅘	Md Sp Wt		5	8	88	67	56½	56	BThornburg	b 122	8.20	80-12	Grove Hill 114½ Noble Don 1143½ Little Fleet 114no	Began slowly 8
6Jly66-5Del	fst 6f	.22⅖ .45⅗1.11⅗	Md Sp Wt		4	6	66½	711	57¼	46	RKimball	b 122	12.40	81-14	Lillington 1143½ Noble Don 114h Grove Hill 1142½	Saved ground 9
29Jun66-6Del	fm 1 (T)	1.38⅘	Md Sp Wt		1	3	43	62½	62	64½	RKimball	b 122	11.20	77-15	Lucid 1141½ Lillington 1141 Brandon Hill 114¾	No real threat 11

LATEST WORKOUTS Dec 6 Lrl 4f fst .49 b — Dec 1 Lrl 4f gd .50 b — Nov 18 Lrl t.c. 6f fm 1.16⅖ b — Nov 11 Lrl 4f fst .51 b

Securus — $4,000 — 116

Ch. g (1962), by Sure Welcome—Dagnabbit, by Son Altesse
T. J. Stable — C. E. Linton — (Mr.-Mrs. A. Stabler)

1966	20	1	1	0	$1,488
1965	5	M	0	0	$65

22Nov66-7CT	fst 7f	.24⅘ .50⅕1.30⅘	Clm	2500	5	2	22	23	68	616	JKratz5	b 115	24.40	53-38	Watcina 1202½ Taydall 120¾ Mal Perdedor 1171½	Early foot, tired 8
16Nov66-1Lrl	fst 6f	.23⅕ .47 1.13⅗	Clm	3000	10	8	87½	1020	1115	1113	RAdams	b 119	97.60	71-14	Attribute 1131 Nail Down 1141½ Forewarned 1131½	No speed 12
9Nov66-9CT	fst 4½f	.22⅗ .47⅖ .54	Allowance		3	6		77	86½	912	JKratz5	b 117	28.20	79-10	Vibrissa 1092½ Chilly Should 1161½ Frosty Gold 1171½	No speed 10
21Oct66-6Mar	fst 6½f	.23⅗ .48⅗1.22	Clm	3000	8	6	62¾	53½	41	78¼	RAdams	b 115	44.20	——	Warwolf 1161½ Walnut Bill 1192 Polyvox 119¾	Mild bid, tired 10
15Oct66-1Mar	fst 6½f	.23⅗ .48⅗1.22⅗	Md	2500	5	2	1½	14	13	11	RAdams	b 120	16.90	——	Securus 1201 Brown Bag 117¾ Grace W. C. 1144	Was under pressure 10
11Oct66-2Mar	fst 6½f	.24⅕ .49⅕1.23⅘	Md	2500	9	4	52½	21½	52¾	54¾	EMcIvor	b 120	26.90	——	Cornish Rock 1171½ Grace W. C. 114¾ Combustion Hill 1091	Tired 10
17Sep66-2Fai	fm*7f (T)	1.28⅘	Allowance		13	4	2nk	21½	23	919	WHearfield3	b 139	13.20f	——	Idea Fija 1322 Law Partner 1483½ Shadowbox 1354	Stopped 13
10Sep66-1Fai	hd*7f (T)	1.31⅕	Md Sp Wt		8	7	52¾	32	32½	57½	EHairfield	b 148	12.70	——	Dreyfus 141½ Maracock 1412½ Carlomine 138h	Well up, tired 9
22Aug66-1Tim	fst 5½f	.23⅘ .49⅗1.12⅗	Clm	1500	7	10	813	712	616	714	CRiston	b 117	15.20	63-22	Heavy Sea 1183½ Double Drums 1133 Rastap 1133½	Poor start 10
10Aug66-2ShD	fst 5½f	.23⅗ .48 1.08⅘	Clm	1250	1	4	43	34½	36	46¾	BHewitt	b 114	54.50	78-21	LadyTarantula1144½StrutMissLizie1151¾BeatItBuster114½	No mis'p 9
26Jly66-2CT	fst 6½f	.23⅗ .48⅘1.22⅘	Clm	1250	6	10	88¼	78	64¾	69¼	CFRiston	b 118	25.40	66-23	Brownygret 113¾ Nyrop 118h Little Band 1082½	No threat 10
12Jly66-4CT	fst 6½f	.24⅕ .47⅘1.21⅘	Clm	1250	1	8	54½	47½	612	716	CFRiston	b 118	14.50	64-23	Nebulous Norah 1137 Little Band 1081½ Dirty Face 1143	Tired 10

Prince Devil × — $4,000 — 116

B g (1957), by Princequillo—Barlow, by Devil Diver
J. P. Harris — J. P. Harris — (Claiborne Farm)

1966	24	4	2	1	$9,706
1965	10	3	1	2	$4,874

6Dec66-2Lrl	fst 1 3/16	.49 1.14⅘2.00⅘	Clm	3000	12	10	104½	511	611	617	TLee	b 110	11.50	75-16	Demagogo 1142½ Vicious 1167 Communicate 113¾	No response 12
1Dec66-9Lrl	fm*1½ (T)	1.17⅖2.39⅘	Clm	4000	7	11	99	810	55	76½	TLee	b 112	14.10	——	Metamora 114½ Admiral Zip 1121½ Mike Canron 1171	Never close 12
14Nov66-9Lrl	fm*1⅛ (T)	1.54⅘	Clm	5500	3	5	55½	74¾	65½	64¾	TLee	b 111	78.80	77-13	Henbaj 115h Frosted Prince 1152½ Jalico 1171	Never a threat 11
5Nov66-3Lrl	fst 1 3/16	.48⅗1.14⅖2.02	Clm	3750	1	7	712	713	818	816	JKratz5	b 113	15.20	70-14	Absent Son 1092½ Scarlet Stone 117nk Admiral Zip 114½	No speed 9
22Oct66-9Mar	fst 1 1/16	.48⅘1.15⅖1.50⅖	Clm	2500	9	9	89¼	56½	31½	11	JKratz5	b 110	*1.60	——	Prince Devil 1101 Lord Put Put 121nk Dulcie Way 104no	In time 9
15Oct66-9Mar	fst 170	.49 1.15⅖1.46⅘	Clm	3000	9	5	53½	52½	51¾	54¼	MAMar'ccio7	b 110	*2.40	——	Happy Mick 1191 Vicious 116nk Torino 1172½	Well up, tired 10
8Oct66-5Mar	fst 1 1/16	.49 1.16⅕1.50⅗	Clm	3500	1	3	32	42½	56½	55½	MAMarin'io7	b 107	*1.20	——	Park Bench 109nk Torino 114h Rimbaud 1144	In close 6
21Sep66-7Hag	my 1	.47⅘1.15⅖1.41⅗	Allowance		6	6	610	512	516	514	MAMarin'cio7	b 114	3.10	78-14	Uptick 116h Aprendiz 1127 Baltimore Buddy 115nk	Disliked mud 6
7Sep66-8Tim	fst 1	.48⅕1.15⅕1.41⅖	Allowance		3	7	716	815	819	816	FCampion7	b 109	49.10	71-27	Jig on Deck 119nk Benedict C. 113h Tudor Mistress 1132	Far back 8
1Sep66-7Tim	fst 1	.48⅗1.15⅕1.42⅕	Clm	5000	1	6	510	411	34½	1nk	FCampion7	b 110	10.30	83-23	Prince Devil 110nk Saxony King 1143 Surge Ahead 114½	Driving 7
25Aug66-7Tim	fst 1	.49⅖1.16⅗1.43⅕	Clm	4000	5	5	69½	48½	46½	47	FCampion7	b 109	5.20	71-23	Wakely Terrace 109no Saxony King 1123 Scampabout 1114	No f'ctor 6
17Aug66-7Tim	fst 1	.49 1.15⅖1.41⅖	Allowance		6	10	1014	916	613	412	FCampion7	b 115	25.20	75-23	Jig on Deck 1228 Turbo Lee 1151 Evening Flirt 1103	No threat 10

***Eiffel II *** $4,000 B. h (1961), by Eppi d'Or VIII—Deyanira, by Davistan (Haras El Chircal) (Arg.) P. Fisichella H. Jacobson **116** 1966 9 1 2 1 $4,995 1965 15 3 3 0 $12,350

6Dec66-9Aqu fst 1⅛.48⅗1.14⅕1.53⅘ Clm 3500 7 2 21 11 15 14 ECardone5 111 3.80 67-26 Eiffel II 1114 Start Dancing 1135 Te 120½ Under brisk urging 10
1Nov66-9Aqu fst 1⅛.48⅖1.14 1.53 Cl c-4000 2 5 56½ 54½ 46½ 412 RNeira 116 8.90 59-19 Golden Mike 1138 Punisher 1152½ El Gordo 1161½ No mishap 12
8Oct66-9Atl fst 1 1/16.47⅕1.13 1.46⅗ Clm 6500 3 8 814 811 88¾ 49 RNeira 115 12.20 65-23 Amberjack 1212½ Absent Son 1172½ Brumby 1154 Passed tired ones 8
9Sep66-7Atl fm*1 1/16 Ⓣ 1.48⅕ Clm 6500 3 7 79½ 44½ 32½ 21 HBlock 116 12.00 83-15 Amberjack 1181 Eiffel II 116¾ Maggie Fast Step 116no Gamely 8
19Aug66-9Atl fm*1 1/16 Ⓣ 1.46⅖ Clm 7500 2 10 1013 1014 711 813 RNeira 116 22.40 62-15 Hellenic Ro:·l 1182 Will Reward 1164 Dummy 1161½ No speed 10
13Jly 66-9Mth hd 1 1/16 Ⓣ 1.45⅗ Clm 8500 2 7 78½ 77¼ 85¼ 77¼ RNeira 113 15.00 81-12 Hessian 1151½ Ajewel 117¾ Syncope 1152 Never a contender 8
30Jun66-9Mth fm 1 1/16 Ⓣ 1.45⅘ Clm 7250 1 4 42½ 32½ 2½ 23 RNeira 114 16.40 83-14 Tan Guapo 1143 Eiffel II 114¾ Bayard Park 114nk Held on gamely 10
15Jun66-9Mth fst 1 1/16.47⅕1.12⅖1.45⅕ Clm 8500 9 6 714 914 99¾ 913 RNeira 113 47.70 66-16 Knobs 1131 Bud Wallace 1192½ Intact 114¾ Was never close 10
7Mar66-6GP fm 1 1/16 Ⓣ 1.12⅖1.44 Clm 7500 6 6 63½ 44 34 35¾ RNeira 116 14.90 78-12 Conjunto 1121¾ Mister Lumpus 1164 Eiffel II 1161½ Held evenly 12
20Nov65-9Pim fm 1 1/16 TC 1.13 1.45 Clm 9000 9 9 117½ 1114 1010 99¼ RNeira 114 33.90 81- 6 Office Sweeney 117nk Ali Baba II 121no Triumvirate 1242¾ No sp'd 12
1Nov65-7Lrl fst 7f .23⅕ .46⅘1.23⅘ Clm 10000 3 6 54¼ 66½ 512 511 RNeira 116 11.40 90- 9 Consecrate 1161½ Prince Hara 1161½ Two Wise 1135 Fell back 7
23Sep65-9Atl hd*1 1/16 TC 1.46⅗ Clm 11000 5 11 1114 1116 1012 1014 HBlock 116 31.70 78- 5 Mr. Steu 1161½ Ajewel 116no Solar Stance 114¾ Never in contention 11

LATEST WORKOUTS Dec 5 Aqu 3f fst .36 h

Mystarfire × $4,000 Dk. b. or br. g (1961), by Fireagain—Ray Star, by Good Goods (M. J. Eglin) R. E. Porter G. M. Whitehair **122** 1966 35 8 1 2 $7,939 1965 16 1 5 1 $2,505

3Dec66-7CT fst 6½f.23⅗ .47⅕1.20⅗ Clm 2500 4 3 3nk 4¾ 72½ 88¼ SSmall b 120 4.60 78-17 Silent Sun 120½ Triple Dip 1142 Torino 114¾ Early factor, tired 9
26Nov66-8CT fst 6½f.24⅖ .49⅕1.24⅗ Clm 2500 4 2 11½ 13 13 13½ SSmall b 120 3.00 65-39 Mystarfire 1203½ Triple Dip 1142¾ Monkton Devil 1131¼ Handily 10
18Nov66-9CT fst 6½f.24⅖ .48⅘1.23⅕ Clm 2500 5 4 21½ 21½ 43 49¾ SSmall b 120 5.10 63-34 Dancing Light 120no Belsabar 120¾ Top Down 1179 Speed, tired 8
11Nov66-7CT fst 6½f.23⅘ .48⅕1.22⅖ Clm 2500 7 1 1h 12 12 12 SSmall b 120 5.40 77-27 Mystarfire 1202 Manford 115nk Mongoose Jr. 1202 Brisk drive 10
5Nov66-2Lrl fst 6f .23⅗ .48⅕1.13⅖ Clm 3500 11 4 21½ 68½ 1015 1014 TDePalo b 117 32.10 71-14 Tony's Pat 114¾ Attribute 1142½ Uncle Buzz 1141 Brief foot 12
22Oct66-7CT fst 6½f.24 .48 1.21⅘ Clm 2500 5 2 11 11½ 11½ 32¼ SSmall b 122 12.90 78-25 Gingerman 122¾ In Hock 1221½ Mystarfire 1222 Couldn't last 9
14Oct66-9CT fst 7f .24⅕ .48⅘1.30⅕ Clm 2500 5 1 2h 21 21 54 SSmall b 120 10.30 68-31 Gingerman 1203 Shorco 120nk Mal Perdedor 120h Speed, tired 6
10Oct66-8Mar fst 6f .24⅘ .48⅘1.15⅗ Clm 2500 1 1 1h 54 510 58 CRogers 122 8.70 —— Vinherst 1192 Black Tyrone 1175½ Ducolay 116½ Tired 9
30Sep66-7Hag fst 5½f.23⅖ .47⅖1.08 Clm 2500 5 8 89 55 43½ 43¼ SSmall b 123 *1.60 86-14 Lulu Page 1161½ Another Goldie 1171 Miss Flexible 1171 St'mbl'd st. 8
26Sep66-6ShD fst 5½f.23 .47⅗1.07⅕ Clm 2000 3 2 11 11½ 11½ 11¾ SSmall b 121 *1.70 91-16 Mystarfire 1211¾ Newton 1212¾ Champion Lady 112¾ Driving 8
16Sep66-7ShD fst 5½f.23⅗ .47⅗1.08 Clm 1600 2 2 11½ 13 13 13 SSmall b 120 *1.10 87-16 Mystarfire 1203 Jeb Star 1141½ Viley Boy 1161 Handily 9
2Sep66-7ShD fst 5½f.22⅗ .47 1.07 Clm 2000 1 4 31½ 44 43 46¼ SSmall b 120 2.00 86-17 Shorco 1203 Dante Day 120¾ Bellverine 1172½ Speed, tired 7

LATEST WORKOUTS Oct 31 CT 3f fst .39⅖ b

***Atlantic** $4,000 Ch. h (1960), by Speechmaker—Atletica, by Avestruz (Haras General Lavalle) (Arg.) E. P. Jenks E. P. Jenks **113** 1966 17 5 0 5 $18,645 1965 16 2 4 1 $10,474

(Raced in Venezuela as Atlantic II)

8Oct66-9Aqu fst 1⅛.47⅘1.13⅕1.52 Hcp 5000s 1 7 75 72¾ 44½ 45 JLRotz 118 5.80 71-17 Ruperto 121h Aerie 1142½ Hy-Nat 1132½ No late response 10
23Sep66-9Aqu sl 1⅛.47⅘1.12⅘1.53⅗ Cl c-6250 6 6 55 33 31½ 12½ JLRotz 121 2.10 68-26 Atlantic 1212½ Main Count 1102 Never Wrong 1161 Easily 6
17Sep66-9Aqu fst 1 3/16.47⅖1.12⅖1.59 Hcp 3500s 5 5 512 59½ 57¼ 48½ JLRotz 119 2.90 75-18 Hy-Nat 113h Ruperto 1222½ Aberrant 1236 Had no mishap 8
10Sep66-9Aqu fst 1⅛.47⅕1.12⅗1.53⅕ Hcp 5000s 9 10 1013 56 44½ 34½ JLRotz 119 6.60 65-23 Nike Site 1121½ Flannel 1093 Atlantic 119nk Found stride late 10
3Sep66-9Aqu fst 1 3/16.48 1.13⅕1.59⅘ Hcp 3500s 4 5 514 511 48 47¾ MYcaza 122 5.70 72-22 Hessian 1195 Nike Site 1142½ Aberrant 125nk Not a factor 7
6Aug66-9Sar fst 1⅛.47⅗1.12⅘1.53⅖ Hcp 3500s 7 7 712 65 52 1¾ JLRotz 120 *1.40 78-12 Atlantic 120¾ Kalonji 1122½ Express Stop 110½ Strong handling 8
30Jly 66-9Aqu fst 1⅛.48⅘1.13⅗1.52⅖ Hcp 5000s 6 4 44 41½ 41½ 31½ CErrico 115 7.50 72-22 Count Moore 111½ Ruperto 1201 Atlantic 115½ Held on willingly 9
20Jly 66-9Aqu fst 1⅛.48 1.13⅕1.52⅕ Clm 7500 7 6 411 38 2½ 12½ BBaeza 116 2.90 75-23 Atlantic 1162½ No Kidding 118¾ Tobir 111½ Was ridden out 7
9Jly 66-8Aqu fst 1 3/16.48⅗1.13 1.59⅗ Hcp 3500s 3 4 57½ 57 76½ 711 MYcaza 122 *1.70 70-19 Ruperto 1162½ Duke's Liberty 1195 Filisteo II 1101 Dull try 9

LATEST WORKOUTS Dec 5 Bel tr.t. 4f fst .50⅘ h Nov 6 Bel tr.t. 3f sly .40 b Oct 20 Bel tr.t. 4f sly .48⅘ h

Leo M. $4,000 Br. g (1962), by Master Boing—Leora M., by Hadagal
Mrs. D. Sukundo M. Holubeshen (J. Hill) **113** 1966 16 0 0 3 $1,257 / 1965 17 1 3 2 $4,605

5Dec66-9Lrl fst 1⅛ .47⅗ 1.14⅕ 1.53⅕ Clm 6000 3 8 1213 926 921 EMcIvor b 113 18.60 60-17 Red Erik 1116 Bayard Park 1133 Fabison 1181½ Fell back early 12
24Nov66-4Lrl fst 6f .23⅕ .47⅗ 1.13 Clm 7000 9 10 107½ 811 1012 1012 EMcIvor b 112 47.40 75-17 Budco 1222½ Portfolio 1191½ Al Getz 1151½ Never close 10
31Oct66-8Det fst 170 .46⅗ 1.11⅗ 1.43⅘ Clm 5000 5 3 37 35 36½ 32½ DHolmes b 111 5.90 81-22 Tedrol 1141½ Norcat 1141 Leo M. 111nk Showed even try 9
25Oct66-8Det fst 6f .22⅖ .45⅗ 1.11⅘ Allowance 8 9 1110 911 87½ 75½ DGargan b 121 5.20 75-20 Anniversary 1132 Make Your Own 1151 Fort Greenhow 113½ No speed 11
17Oct66-7Det gd 6f .22⅕ .45⅗ 1.12 Allowance 9 8 97½ 85½ 84¾ 86½ DHolmes b 122 *2.40 73-26 Laurentian Way1161 Sandy's Friend1161½ Angelic Star1163 Wide 9
5Oct66-8Det fst 6f .22⅕ .45⅖ 1.10⅘ Allowance 2 5 31½ 4nk 3½ 33½ DHolmes b 121 6.30 82-20 Meetabody 1182 Clown's Image 1151½ Leo M. 121¾ No mishap 7
28Sep66-6Det fst 6f .22⅕ .45⅘ 1.10⅘ Allowance 5 6 44 46½ 37 36½ DHolmes b 122 8.90 79-15 Halvek 1183½ John Day 1183 Leo M. 1225 Showed an even try 8
15Sep66-6Det fst 6f .22⅘ .45⅘ 1.11⅘ Allowance 5 9 96 97¼ 713 67 BWalt b 122 14.10 74-18 Jet Crusader 1181 Sandy'sFriend115no Clown'sImage1151½ Broke sl. 9
8Sep66-8Det fst 6f .22⅗ .45⅕ 1.10⅗ Allowance 11 2 105½ 1211 1115 1018 WCox b 122 8.40 69-19 Tenor 118h Court Rule 1184 Jet Crusader 1186 Raced far back 12
LATEST WORKOUTS Dec 1 Pim 1m fst 1.46⅗ b Nov 14 Pim 4f fst .50⅕ b

Ash's Dream $4,000 Br. g (1961), by Weatherman—Sweet Bobby, by Double Scotch
J. P Hyde T. Johnston (A. R. Clatterbuck) **113** 1966 21 1 1 1 $2,734 / 1965 25 3 4 2 $8,135

6Dec66-2Lrl fst 1 1/16 .49 1.14⅘ 2.00⅘ Clm 3000 6 1 1h 411 814 719 JBrocklebank b 116 38.70 73-16 Demagogo 1142½ Vicious 1167 Communicate 113¾ Speed, tired 12
22Nov66-4Lrl fst 1⅛ .48 1.14⅗ 1.54⅘ Clm 3000 12 2 2½ 23 412 412 JBrockleb'nk b 116 114.20 61-20 Newton II 1166 Pat's Toughie 1143 Vicious 1163 Used in pace 12
15Nov66-2Lrl fst 1⅛ .48⅖ 1.15 1.55⅖ Clm 3000 5 3 36½ 57 610 59½ JBrockleb'nk b 116 97.50 60-21 The Rock 1146 Admirals Image 109no Briarcliff Boy 1092 Tired 12
29Oct66-2Lrl fst 1⅛ .48⅖ 1.14⅗ 1.56⅖ Clm 3500 2 6 812 1220 1118 1117 DJohnstonJr b 113 62.40 48-16 Park Bench 109nk Torino 114h Rimbaud 1144 Far back 6
8Oct66-5Mar fst 1 1/16 .49 1.16⅕ 1.50⅗ Clm 3500 6 5 68½ 68½ 613 69½ FKratz b 114 14.00 —— Scarlet Stone 110nk Happy Mick 118nk Brumby 122¾ No speed 12
30Sep66-4ShD hy 1 1/16 .50⅘ 1.18⅘ 1.55⅖ Clm 2500 1 6 66½ 31 1½ 14 DJohnstonJr b 114 5.40 46-45 Ash's Dream 1144 Party Wire 1181½ Little Barnwell 115nk Driving 6
23Sep66-8ShD gd 1 1/16 .48⅖ 1.15⅖ 1.49⅗ Clm 2500 1 2 22 11 2½ 45¾ DJohnstonJr b 115 11.30 69-22 Medium Done 1153 War Dice 1152 Bit of War 118¾ Used 8
3Sep66-6Tim fst 1 .49⅖ 1.16⅕ 1.42⅖ Clm 3500 4 8 813 917 917 920 RMikkonen b 114 31.10 62-23 Torino 114h Walnut Bill 1172 Fabulous Lee 1141 No speed 9
24Aug66-6Tim fst 7f .24⅗ .49⅘ 1.29⅖ Clm 3500 8 7 811 89 816 717 RWitmer b 116 22.10 67-20 Rinlag 116no Torino 11614 Black Tyrone 116¾ Never close 8
6Aug66-8ShD fst 1 1/16 .47⅗ 1.13⅘ 1.48⅕ Allowance 8 5 89¼ 813 812 814 MO'Rourke b 115 24.10 68-16 Prince Devil 109nk Jezibel A. 1142 My New Frontier 114h Trailed 8
30Jly 66-1Del fst 6f .22⅗ .47 1.13⅖ Clm 3000 1 10 88¼ 914 97½ 97 AValenzuela b 115 13.80 71-15 Sputnitsa 111¾ Black Tyrone 115¾ Nail Down 118no Broke slowly 12
23Jly 66-2Del fst 6f .22⅖ .46⅕ 1.12⅗ Clm 3250 5 5 118¾ 1219 1011 1011 WJPassm're b 115 21.50 71-14 Mr. Bernie 1131 Nail Down 118½ Torino 1151 Raced far back 12
14Jly 66-2Del fst 6f .22⅘ .46 1.12⅖ Clm 3500 12 3 75¾ 611 59½ 46½ JVasquez b 120 7.20 77-12 Broad Run 1202 Indian Rock 120¾ Knight Pride 1133½ Wide late 12
LATEST WORKOUTS Nov 19 Bow 4f fst .50 b Nov 5 Bow 5f fst 1.04⅕ b Oct 27 Bow 5f fst 1.04⅖ b Oct 22 Bow 4f fst .50⅗ b

Horses Shown Below Are on the "Also Eligible" List and Are Not Listed in Order of Post Positions.

***Chicoco** $4,000 Ch. g (1959), by Latido—Chilpa, by Frigio
Irene Comber H. Steward Mitchell (Haras El Heurton) (Chile) **119** 1966 16 3 0 5 $8,305 / 1965 6 1 0 0 $710

22Nov66-4Lrl fst 1⅛ .48 1.14⅗ 1.54⅘ Cl c-3000 7 6 916 69 615 613 ENelson b 122 *2.20 60-20 Newton II 1166 Pat's Toughie 1143 Vicious 1163 Dull effort 12
10Nov66-9Lrl gd 1 3/16 .49 1.15⅖ 2.01⅘ Clm 3000 3 4 43 21½ 13 11½ ENelson b 119 *3.50 87-14 Chicoco 1191½ Blue Nahar 1132½ Knight-King 1061 Safe margin 11
2Nov66-1Lrl fst 1⅛ .48⅗ 1.15⅖ 1.55⅗ Clm 3000 7 3 35 31½ 1h 11½ ENelson b 113 11.50 69-21 Chicoco 1131½ The Rock 1133 Blue Nahar 1135 Drew out 12
8Oct66-2Atl fst 1⅛ .48 1.13⅕ 1.55⅕ Clm 3000 11 11 1222 1021 812 69 ENelson b 113 5.50 53-23 Newton II 113¾ Arrow King 113½ Mapache II 113¾ No threat 12
18Aug66-9Atl fm*1½ Ⓣ 2.36⅕ Clm 4500 6 7 611 712 717 827 ENelson b 116 12.10 68-5 Valenciano II 1221½ Metamora 1131½ Grey Ruler 1193 No speed 8
11Aug66-9Atl fm 1½ Ⓣ 2.32 Clm 4000 3 8 712 56½ 47 45¼ ENelson b 110 15.30 78-19 Valenciano II 1211½ Stone the Crows 114h Disuelto 1134 Hung 9
30Jly 66-2Del fst 1 1/16 .47⅘ 1.13 1.45⅘ Clm 3500 8 9 915 913 57½ 36 ENelson b 116 4.90 74-15 Majority Leader 1191 Long Sunset 1165 Chicoco 1162 Rallied 9
25Jly 66-9Del fst 1 1/16 .48 1.13 1.45⅘ Clm 3250 8 9 711 45½ 35 33½ ENelson b 117 *2.90 76-13 Majority Leader 1201½ To Eternity 1152 Chicoco 1171½ Rallied 9
14Jly 66-6Del hd 1⅜ Ⓣ 2.20⅕ Clm 3500 5 9 924 611 49½ 511 ENelson b 115 4.30 50-33 Hap's Bomber 1154½ Mapache II 1153 Far Call 1051 Broke slowly 9
8Jly 66-8Del my 1½ .49⅕ 1.15⅖ 2.37 Hcp 4000s 3 7 721 519 524 534 ENelson b 114 4.70 36-25 The Contest Man 11812 Big Bridge 112½ Bar Gossip 1199 No speed 7
LATEST WORKOUTS Oct 23 Lrl 6f fst 1.19⅗ b

Sept Erin **$4,000** B. g (1961), by Sea O Erin—Sept Isle, by Blenheim II **116** 1966 19 1 2 4 $4,500
Mrs. D. Gaudet E. D. Gaudet (J. S. Evans) 1965 18 3 1 4 $7,535

1Dec66-1Lrl	gd 7f	.23⅕ .47⅕ 1.27⅖	Clm	3000	7	2	10^{6}	$7^{2\frac34}$	$4^{2\frac14}$	1^{2}	WChambers	b 113	30.10	82–18	Sept Erin 113^{2} Black Tyrone 113^{nk} Jimzbarb $113^{\frac34}$	Driving	12
15Nov66-2Lrl	fst 1⅛	.48⅖ 1.15 1.55⅗	Clm	3000	11	9	10^{13}	11^{13}	9^{14}	11^{16}	TLattarullo	b 114	14.50	54–21	The Rock 114^{6} Admirals Image 109no Briarcliff Boy 109^{2}	No speed	12
8Nov66-2Lrl	fst 6f	.23⅗ .48 1.13⅘	Clm	3000	11	11	11^{11}	12^{18}	10^{15}	9^{12}	TLattarullo	b 114	8.30	71–16	Rejected Blues $116^{1\frac14}$ Second Mortgage 113^{nk} Billy Bert 109^{2}	No sp'd	12
13Oct66-2Haw	sf 7f Ⓣ	.48⅗ 1.30⅗	Clm	3500	3	10	10^{20}	10^{14}	5^{4}	$2^{1\frac14}$	TLattarulo	b 116	18.50	61–37	Burquin $122^{1\frac14}$ Sept Erin 116^{2} Encantador 118^{3}	Rallied	10
7Oct66-4Haw	fst $1\frac{1}{16}$	.47⅗ 1.11⅘ 1.44⅕	Clm	4000	1	4	$4^{6\frac12}$	$4^{6\frac12}$	$5^{3\frac34}$	$6^{8\frac12}$	TLattarulo	b 116	17.10	77– 8	Sand Trap 113no Teachers Apple 115^{1} True Doctor 115^{3}	No mishap	9
28Sep66-9Haw	fst $1\frac{1}{16}$	.48 1.12⅕ 1.45⅕	Clm	4000	4	5	$5^{2\frac12}$	4^{2}	5^{4}	6^{10}	LSpraker	b 116	18.50	71–13	Little Gemmy 116^{h} Boy About Town 120^{h} Mad Rock $114^{2\frac12}$	Tired	8
20Sep66-4Haw	fst 6½f	.22⅗ .46⅕ 1.18⅕	Clm	4000	12	4	12^{13}	11^{13}	$7^{5\frac12}$	$5^{4\frac34}$	FKastel[5]	b 111	58.70	79–12	Nemrac $122^{1\frac12}$ Jack P. F. $116^{2\frac12}$ Windy Weather 113^{h}	Late foot	12
5Aug66-6Det	fst 1 70	.47⅗ 1.12⅗ 1.43	Clm	c2500	1	1	$4^{2\frac12}$	$1^{1\frac12}$	$1^{1\frac12}$	$4^{3\frac34}$	LSnyder	b 114	*1.90	84–20	ChargingFast $114^{1\frac12}$ FairyGodMother 113^{2} BlueTattoo 112^{nk}	Weakened	8
28Jly66-9HP	sl $1\frac{1}{16}$	.46 1.16⅕ 1.50	Clm	c2500	8	6	6^{11}	4^{3}	$3^{4\frac12}$	3^{6}	TBarrow	b 114	*2.20	58–33	Blue Tassle 122^{4} Just Fine 109^{2} Sept Erin 114^{2}	Mild late gain	8

LATEST WORKOUTS Nov 29 Lrl 4f sly .53 b Oct 31 Lrl 5f fst 1.04⅖ b Oct 25 Lrl 5f fst 1.04⅖ b

Results of 9th Race Laurel—December 12, 1966

(Run on main course. Originally carded to be run on turf course.)

NINTH RACE **1 1-8 MILES. (First Landing, April 9, 1960, 1.49⅖, 4, 124.)**
Lrl - 29590 Claiming. Purse $3,500. 4-year-olds and upward. Weights, 122 lbs. Non-winners of three races since Oct. 15 allowed 3 lbs., of two races, 6 lbs., of a race, 9 lbs. Claiming price $4,000.
December 12, 1966
Value to winner $2,775, second $700, third $350, fourth $175. Mutuel pool $101,474.

Index	Horse	Eqt A Wt	PP	St	¼	½	¾	Str	Fin	Jockey	Cl'g Pr	Owner	Odds $1
29545Aqu[1]	—Eiffel II	5 116	4	7	5^{5}	$2^{1\frac12}$	1^{10}	1^{12}	1^{14}	J Culmone	4000	P Fisichella	2.70
29538Lrl[7]	—Ash's Dream	b 5 114	8	1	1^{3}	$1^{1\frac12}$	$2^{1\frac12}$	2^{h}	2no	P Kallai	4000	J P Hyde	23.50
29538Lrl[6]	—Prince Devil	b 9 116	3	9	7^{h}	6^{1}	4^{4}	3^{2}	3^{2}	T Lee	4000	J P Harris	16.20
29501Lrl[1]	—Sept Erin	b 5 116	10	10	10	10	$6^{\frac12}$	4^{2}	$4^{1\frac12}$	W Chambers	4000	Dean Gaudet	5.40
29536Lrl[9]	—Leo M	b 4 113	7	4	8^{5}	7^{h}	7^{h}	6^{5}	5^{4}	E McIvor	4000	Daisy Sukundo	16.40
29543Lrl[9]	—Cannelton	b 4 116	1	5	$2^{1\frac12}$	3^{3}	3^{3}	5^{h}	6^{2}	W J Passm'e	4000	Mrs W C Wright	4.90
28963Aqu[4]	—Atlantic	6 113	6	8	9^{h}	9^{3}	9^{15}	$8^{\frac12}$	7^{3}	R Stovall	4000	E P Jenks	2.20
29339Lrl[6]	—Chicoco	b 7 119	9	3	$6^{\frac12}$	8^{1}	8^{3}	9	$8^{1\frac12}$	C Rogers	4000	Irene E Comber	14.00
29379CT[6]	—Securus	b 4 116	2	2	3^{h}	4^{2}	5^{2}	7^{h}	9	R Adams	4000	T J Stable	157.20
29526CT[8]	—Mystarfire	b 5 122	5	6	4^{2}	5^{2}	10	Outdist'ced		T Depalo	4000	R Porter	54.40

Time .23⅕, .47⅘, 1.13⅗, 1.40⅕, 1.53⅘. Track good.

$2 Mutuel Prices:			
4–EIFFEL II	7.40	4.60	3.40
8–ASH'S DREAM		12.80	6.40
3–PRINCE DEVIL			6.20

B. h, by Eppi d'Or VIII—Deyanira, by Davistan. Trainer H. Jacobson. Bred by Haras El Chircal (Arg.).

IN GATE AT 4.17. OFF AT 4.17 EASTERN STANDARD TIME. Start good. Won easily.

EIFFEL II moved around the tiring ASH'S DREAM to take command leaving the backstretch, was whipped into a commanding lead in upper stretch and won easily. ASH'S DREAM went to the front at once, saved ground, could not stay with EIFFEL II and outduelled PRINCE DEVIL for the place. The latter finished evenly. SEPT ERIN was never a factor. CANNELTON was never in contention. ATLANTIC was always outrun. MYSTARFIRE was not persevered with when hopelessly outdistanced.

Scratched—29554Lrl[6] Ducolay, 29536Lrl[12] Congratulations, 29509Lrl[4] Holy Mackerel, 29391Lrl[5] Chalkey II, 29373Lrl[5] Larsa, 29509Lrl[5] Dadivoso. Overweight—Ash's Dream 1 pound.

Atlantic was claimed by W. E. Walker Jr., trainer T. Bromley.

Courtesy of The Morning Telegraph

in July, had taken a starter handicap at Saratoga in August, and had won again at Aqueduct in September, when entered for $6,250. It had won five of its seventeen starts during 1966, earning $18,645. The notion of $4,000 Maryland horses trying to keep up with an Atlantic was so ludicrous that the crowd sent the six-year-old off at 2 to 1. The crowd was sadly in error. Atlantic had not raced in more than two months and had been working out only once a month. It obviously had gone bad and would not be worth a plugged nickel in any company until it showed signs of life.

Only two other horses in the field of ten had ever showed affinity for the distance. One of them, Chicoco, seemed able to beat $3,000 stock on the Maryland circuit when in shape. But Thoroughbred class barriers are such that a seven-year-old, $3,000 animal must be in extraordinary condition, and extraordinarily lucky, to hold its own in $4,000 company. Chicoco, unfortunately, had looked dreadful against other $3,000 claimers in its last race, three weeks ago, and had not even worked out since. Toss out Chicoco.

The remaining candidate, a five-year-old gelding named Eiffel II, had been claimed by Buddy Jacobson for $4,000 at Aqueduct on November 1. In its eight 1966 races up to and including that date, it had been entered for prices as high as $8,500. It had not won, but had been in the money three times. In a typical Jacobson rehabilitation project, Eiffel II was rested and coddled for more than a month. No less typically, the trainer then shot the works. He entered the gelding for $3,500—less than the purchase price. The track was Aqueduct, the date December 6, less than a week before the Laurel race that concerns us. Eiffel II won that first race under the Jacobson banner by four lengths.

In doing so, it beat animals of a higher grade than it would face in the $4,000 Laurel field. The claiming price was lower, to be sure, but the purse was higher, the class of the meeting was higher, and the quality of the competition better.

Under Joe Culmone, one of the nation's most able and consistent riders, Eiffel II galloped nonchalantly for the first half-mile of the Laurel race. The brief canter was good enough to put him in second position, only a length or so behind a longshot called Ash's Dream. Culmone then depressed the accelerator slightly and Eiffel II left everybody else for dead. At the three-quarter-mile call he was ten lengths in front, moving easily. He won by fourteen and paid $7.40, as the chart shows.

Leading Money Winners of All Time

As of Dec. 31, 1967, the following horses were the biggest earners in the history of the sport.

KELSO	$1,977,896
ROUND TABLE	1,749,869
BUCKPASSER	1,462,014
NASHUA	1,288,565
CARRY BACK	1,241,165
CITATION	1,085,760
NATIVE DIVER	1,026,500
SWOON'S SON	970,605
ROMAN BROTHER	943,473
STYMIE	918,485
T.V. LARK	902,194
SWAPS	848,900
DAMASCUS	843,806
SWORD DANCER . . . ,. .	829,610
CANDY SPOTS	824,718

What Class Is

Thoroughbred class, or quality, is easy to recognize and hard to define. From Eclipse to Buckpasser, the horses of highest class—the champions—have been the ones whose physical soundness, speed, stamina and competitive willingness enabled them to beat everything in sight. They won under serious weight disadvantages. They won on off-tracks. They won by narrow margins after overcoming serious lack of running room in the stretch. And sometimes they won by exhausting their opponents in the first three quarters of a mile and romping home all alone, a city block in front.

Many of the horses they whipped were every bit as sound. Some were speedier. Some had no less stamina and as much courage. But the champions combined those traits in maximum quantity. And, lest we forget, they were trained well enough to remain sound and consistent in race after race. Not many trainers can make a champion of a potential champion. Indeed, nine out of every ten trainers can be relied on to ruin any potential champion they handle. Competence is as rare a quality in this field as in any other.

THE BEST OF THE BEST—THOROUGHBRED CHAMPIONS SINCE 1937*

	Two-year-old Male	Two-year-old Filly	Best Two-year-old	Three-year-old Male	Three-year-old Filly	Best Three-year-old	Handicap Horse	Handicap Mare	Turf Horse	Steeplechase Horse	Horse of the Year
1937	Menow	—	Menow	War Admiral	—	War Admiral	Seabiscuit	—	—	Jungle King	WAR ADMIRAL
1938	El Chico	Inscoelda	El Chico	Stagehand	—	Stagehand	Seabiscuit	Marica	—	—	SEABISCUIT
1939	Bimelech	Now What	Bimelech	Challedon	Unerring	Challedon	Kayak II.	Lady Maryland	—	—	CHALLEDON
1940	Our Boots	Level Best	Our Boots	Bimelech	—	Bimelech	Challedon	War Plumage	—	—	CHALLEDON
1941	Alsab	Petrify	Alsab	Whirlaway	Painted Veil	Whirlaway	Mioland	Fairy Chant	—	Speculate	WHIRLAWAY
1942	Count Fleet	Askmenow	Count Fleet	Alsab	Vagrancy	Alsab	Whirlaway	Vagrancy	—	Elkridge	WHIRLAWAY
1943	Platter	Durazna	Platter	Count Fleet	Stefanita	Count Fleet	Market Wise Devil Diver	Mar-Kell	—	Brother Jones	COUNT FLEET
1944	Pavot	Busher	Pavot	By Jimminy	Twilight Tear	Twilight Tear	Devil Diver	Twilight Tear	—	Rouge Dragon	TWILIGHT TEAR
1945	Star Pilot	Beaugay	Beaugay	Fighting Step	Busher	Busher	Stymie	Busher	—	Mercator	BUSHER
1946	Double Jay	First Flight	First Flight	Assault	Bridal Flower	Assault	Armed	Gallorette	—	Elkridge	ASSAULT
1947	Citation	Bewitch	Citation	Phalanx	But Why Not	Phalanx	Armed	But Why Not	—	War Battle	ARMED
1948	Blue Peter	Myrtle Charm	Blue Peter	Citation	Miss Request	Citation	Citation	Conniver	—	American Way	CITATION
1949	Hill Prince	Bed o' Roses	Hill Prince	Capot	Two Lea Wistful	Capot	Coaltown	Bewitch	—	Trough Hill	CAPOT
1950	Battlefield	Aunt Jinny	Battlefield	Hill Prince	Next Move	Hill Prince	Noor	Two Lea	—	Oedipus	HILL PRINCE
1951	Tom Fool	Rose Jet	Tom Fool	Counterpoint	Kiss Me Kate	Counterpoint	Hill Prince	Bed o' Roses	—	Oedipus	COUNTERPOINT
1952	Native Dancer	Sweet Patootie	Native Dancer	One Count	Real Delight	One Count	Crafty Admiral	Real Delight	—	Jam	ONE COUNT
1953	Porterhouse	Evening Out	Porterhouse	Native Dancer	Grecian Queen	Native Dancer	Tom Fool	Sickle's Image	Iceberg II.	The Mast	TOM FOOL

THE BEST OF THE BEST—THOROUGHBRED CHAMPIONS SINCE 1937* (continued)

	Two-year-old Male	Two-year-old Filly	Best Two-year-old	Three-year-old Male	Three-year-old Filly	Best Three-year-old	Handicap Horse	Handicap Mare	Turf Horse	Steeplechase Horse	Horse of the Year
1954	Nashua	High Voltage	Nashua	High Gun	Parlo	High Gun	Native Dancer	Parlo	Stan	King Commander	NATIVE DANCER
1955	Needles	Doubledogdare	Needles	Nashua	Misty Morn	Nashua	High Gun	Misty Morn	St. Vincent	Neji	NASHUA
1956	Barbizon	Leallah	Barbizon	Needles	Doubledogdare	Needles	Swaps	Blue Sparkler	Career Boy	Shipboard	SWAPS
1957	Nadir	Idun	Idun	Bold Ruler	Bayou	Bold Ruler	Dedicate	Pucker Up	Round Table	Neji	BOLD RULER
1958	First Landing	Quill	First Landing	Tim Tam	Idun	Tim Tam	Round Table	Bornastar	Round Table	Neji	ROUND TABLE
1959	Warfare	My Dear Girl	Warfare	Sword Dancer	Royal Native	Sword Dancer	Sword Dancer	Tempted	Round Table	Ancestor	SWORD DANCER
1960	Hail to Reason	Bowl of Flowers	Hail to Reason	Kelso	Berlo	Kelso	Bald Eagle	Royal Native	—	Benguala	KELSO
1961	Crimson Satan	Cicada	Crimson Satan	Carry Back	Bowl of Flowers	Carry Back	Kelso	Airmans Guide	T. V. Lark	Peal	KELSO
1962	Never Bend	Smart Deb	Never Bend	Jaipur	Cicada	Jaipur	Kelso	Primonetta	—	Barnabys Bluff	KELSO
1963	Hurry to Market	Tosmah	Hurry to Market	Chateaugay	Lamb Chop	Chateaugay	Kelso	Cicada	Mongo	Amber Diver	KELSO
1964	Bold Lad	Queen Empress	Bold Lad	Northern Dancer	Tosmah	Northern Dancer	Kelso	Tosmah	—	Bon Nouvel	KELSO
1965	Buckpasser	Moccasin	Buckpasser	Tom Rolfe	What a Treat	Tom Rolfe	Roman Brother	Old Hat	Parka	Bon Nouvel	ROMAN BROTHER
1966	Successor	Regal Gleam	Successor	Buckpasser	Lady Pitt	Buckpasser	Buckpasser	Open Fire	Assagai	Mako	BUCKPASSER
1967	Vitriolic	Queen of the Stage	Vitriolic	Damascus	Furl Sail	Damascus	Damascus	Straight Deal	Fort Marcy	Quick Pitch	DAMASCUS

* As voted by the staffs of *The Morning Telegraph* and *Racing Form.*

Class and Speed

One of the hallmarks of superior class is speed. But it is speed of a special kind. Most good horses (professional horsemen seldom say "great") set speed records only when pressed by an able, ambitious rival. Otherwise, they run just hard enough to win. Their failure to break watches during the early stages of their three-year-old seasons—when they are big and strong enough to do so—is terribly misleading to race-track crowds. Large numbers of customers, impressed by the speedy past performances of relatively undistinguished three-year-olds, make the mistake of backing them against classier animals whose own clockings have been slower.

An illustration is in order. The sixth at Aqueduct on November 3, 1966, was a seven-furlong allowance race for three-year-olds and up that had never won two races other than maiden or claiming. Nothing in the race looked like an imminent national champion, but class distinctions are as important among second- or third- or tenth-rate stock as among the champs. The co-favorite at slightly less than 5 to 2 in this particular sprint was a nicely bred three-year-old, Second Venture, which had been in the money in each of its four starts, winning two of them. In its only effort at seven furlongs, it had run within half a length of an excellent early pace of .45⅕ to the half-mile, tiring in the stretch and finishing third, four and a half lengths behind a winner clocked in 1.23⅗. In its most recent start, exactly a week before, it had set a pace of .46⅖ to the half in a six-furlong allowance race and had lost by a nose in 1.11⅖, after swerving under its apprentice rider. The superb John L. Rotz would be up today.

The other co-favorite, Sermon, was not only well bred but a product of the spectacularly successful Claiborne Farm. Its owner was the renowned William Haggin Perry. The trainer was Jim Maloney, one of the nation's leaders. These credentials spell class. The colt had made its only two-year-old start at Saratoga in August, 1965, coming on strong at the end of a losing race at five and a half furlongs. Its potential class had made it the betting favorite in that maiden affair. It returned to the wars in September, 1966, at Aqueduct, again in a maiden-special, again as the favorite. Again it lost while gaining in the stretch, this time at six furlongs.

It broke its maiden in October, again as favorite, winning by eleven

6th Race Aqueduct

7 FURLONGS. (Chute). (Rose Net, Sept. 17, 1962, 1.21⅕, 6, 114.)
Allowances. Purse $6,000. 3-year-olds and upward which have never won two races other than maiden or claiming. Weights 3-year-olds 122 lbs., older 124 lbs. Non-winners of a race other than maiden or claiming since October 1 allowed 3 lbs., of such a race since August 27, 5 lbs., of such a race since July 30, 7 lbs.

Fence Rider

Ch. g (1963-Ky), by Middleground—Friponne, by Shut Out — King Ranch — Max Hirsch — (King Ranch) — **115**
1966 14 2 1 1 $8,035
1965 1 M 0 0 —

27Oct66-7Aqu fst 1⅛ .48⅘ 1.13⅕ 1.51 Allowance 1 5 55½ 44 23 42¾ JRuane b 112 2.80e 78-20 Bol 'n Jac 1152½ Without Warning 112no Naturalist 116nk Tired 7
20Oct66-6Aqu sl 7f .23⅖ .46⅗ 1.25 Allowance 5 9 109¼ 1015 89 65½ DHidalgo b 112 31.0 76-3 Glenrose 1162½ Prince Graff 115nk Lord Byron 1181 Began slowly 10
29Sep66-4Aqu fst 7f .22⅘ .45⅘ 1.23⅖ Allowance 5 5 66 66¾ 64½ 55¾ JLRotz b 115 23.80 83-18 End Man 1131½ Mountainside 120nk Golden Buttons 1132½ No factor 6
16Jly66-6Aqu fst 7f .22⅕ .45⅕ 1.23⅗ Allowance 6 9 88¾ 77¼ 78 79¼ WBoland b 117 10.30 79-18 Woodford 112½ Vail Pass 1124 Second Venture 1171 Never close 9
30Jun66-6Mth fst 1 1/16 .48 1.12⅖ 1.45⅘ Allowance 3 3 31½ 1h 11½ 1nk SBoulmetis b 117 3.20 76-18 Fence Rider 117nk Ready All 1171¼ Ridgid 1154 Narrowly best 8
20Jun66-6Aqu hd 1⅛ Ⓣ 1.52⅖ Allowance 2 7 77½ 76 55½ 56¼ JLRotz b 114 7.50 67-27 Prince Rico 1151 Tartan Dance 1113½ Gourmand 1111 No factor 8
31May66-5Aqu fst 1⅛ .48⅘ 1.13⅗ 1.52⅖ Md Sp Wt 7 6 66 41½ 1½ 1½ JLRotz b 113 5.30 74-22 Fence Rider 113½ Intangible 114h Poker Table 113nk Driving 8
25May66-3GS fst 170 .47⅕ 1.11⅘ 1.42⅕ Md Sp Wt 3 6 5¾ 24 24 23¾ SBoulmetis b 115 2.90 79-16 Gallant Flash 1153¾ Fence Rider 1156 Black River 1151½ Gamely 7
12May66-3Aqu fst 1⅛ .48⅘ 1.13⅗ 1.53⅘ Md Sp Wt 4 3 23 21½ 3½ 44 JLRotz b 113 4.40 63-20 Densaland 113no Intangible 113½ Poker Table 1133½ Broke whip 7
LATEST WORKOUTS Oct 31 Bel m.t. 6f fst 1.15 h Oct 24 Bel m.t. 6f fst 1.14⅘ h Oct 17 Bel t.c. 6f fm 1.16 b Oct 15 Bel m.t. 7f fst 1.30 h

Absolute Power ×

B. c (1963-Ky), by Bold Ruler—Who Dini, by Hypnotist II — High Tide Stable — L. S. Barrera — (E. G. Burke) — **115**
1966 7 1 1 0 $5,350
1965 3 1 0 0 $2,750

27Oct66-5Aqu fst 6f .23 .46⅗ 1.11⅖ Allowance 1 4 1h 4¾ 54½ 57½ EBelmonte 112 27.90 78-20 Lord Byron 118no Second Venture 1113½ Tom Poker 1101½ Swerved 7
1Mar66-7SA fst 1 1/16 .45⅕ 1.10⅕ 1.43⅖ Allowance 2 2 34½ 45 710 715 EBelmonte 118 6.40 71-17 Vague Image 116h Triple Tux 1163½ Keen Kutter 1162¼ Early foot 7
19Feb66-3SA fst 1 1/16 .47⅕ 1.11⅕ 1.41⅘ Allowance 5 1 1½ 2½ 26 210 EBelmonte 120 16.20 84-7 Boldnesian 11810 Absolute Power 1206 Mejor 1181½ 2nd best 10
15Feb66-7SA fst 1 1/16 .46⅖ 1.10⅘ 1.42⅗ Allowance 2 4 21 31½ 66½ 77¾ MYanez 113 2.00e 82-12 Understanding 113¾ Fleet Shoe 115½ Wingover 1172 Lost ground 7
5Feb66-3SA fst 1 1/16 .46 1.11 1.45 Allowance 5 2 21 21½ 1½ 11 EBelmonte 115 5.50 78-12 Absolute Power 1151 Plimenek 1151 Go It Alone 115nk Driving 12
13Jan66-4SA fst 6f .22⅖ .45⅕ 1.10⅖ Allowance 1 7 32 54½ 66½ 66¼ EBelmonte 116 7.70 84-13 Vague Image 118nk Royal Step 1185 Perfect Prince 116¾ Tired 11
5Jan66-6SA fst 6½f .22⅕ .45⅖ 1.17 LosFeliz 1 7 3½ 2½ 68 78½ EBelmonte 122 8.50 81-12 Brand Royal 1222 Twins Orbit 122¾ Golden Buttons 122¾ Tired 10
5Jan66—The Los Feliz Stakes run in two divisions, 6th and 8th races.
29Dec65 4SA sly 6f .22⅖ .46 1.11⅖ Md Sp Wt 1 7 31 11 1½ 1nk EBelmonte 118 16.30 85-19 Absolute Power 118nk Fact Seeker 1185½ Dominar 1181½ Driving 12
LATEST WORKOUTS Oct 21 Bel m.t. 5f fst 1.00⅘ hg Oct 13 Bel tr.t. 5f fst 1.02⅖ b Oct 8 Bel tr.t. 5f fst 1.05 b Oct 4 Bel tr.t. 4f fst .48⅗ h

Second Venture

Ch. c (1963-Ky), by Porterhouse—Blue Robe, by Shut Out — H. S. Nichols — E. Jackson — (Mr. R. W. P. Johnston) — **115**
1966 4 2 1 1 $8,205
1965 0 M 0 0 —

27Oct66-5Aqu fst 6f .23 .46⅗ 1.11⅖ Allowance 6 2 31 1h 11 2no JJMartin7 111 6.90 86-20 Lord Byron 118no Second Venture 1113½ Tom Poker 1101½ Swerved 7
16Jly66-6Aqu fst 7f .22⅕ .45⅕ 1.23⅗ Allowance 4 5 2h 2½ 2½ 34½ WBlum 117 *0.90 83-18 Woodford 112½ Vail Pass 1124 Second Venture 1171 No excuse 9
7Jly66-6Aqu fst 6f .22⅕ .45⅘ 1.11⅖ Allowance 3 7 21 21½ 2h 1h WBlum 117 *1.10 86-15 Second Venture 117h Rego 110½ Happy Noble 112¾ Lost whip, up 7
29Jun66-1Aqu fst 6f .22⅘ .46⅗ 1.11⅖ Md Sp Wt 2 4 2h 1h 1½ 14 WBlum 115 3.00 86-17 SecondVenture 1154 Age of Reason 115h NightCloud 115h Handily 8
LATEST WORKOUTS Nov 2 Bel tr.t. 3f fst .35⅕ h Oct 22 Bel m.t. 5f gd 1.01 b Oct 15 Bel tr.t. 5f fst 1.02 b Sep 9 Bel tr.t. 5f fst 1.07 b

Sermon

Ch. c (1963-Ky), by Nadir—Edified, by Jacopo — W. H. Perry — J. W. Maloney — (Claiborne Farm) — **122**
1966 4 2 1 0 $7,405
1965 1 M 0 0 $210

26Oct66-8Aqu fst 6f .22⅘ .46⅕ 1.10⅘ Allowance 7 2 42½ 32½ 1h 1h EBelmonte b 121 4.40 89-19 Sermon 121h Counsellor 113¾ It's Blitz 1074 Strong urging 10
17Oct66-6Aqu fst 7f .23 .46⅖ 1.24⅗ Allowance 4 3 3nk 1h 3½ 2½ EBelmonte b 121 *1.60 82-19 Hurry Khal 115½ Sermon 121h As You Like 1212½ Held on gamely 7
6Oct66-5Aqu fst 6f .23⅖ .47⅕ 1.12⅖ Md Sp Wt 1 3 11 15 18 111 EBelmonte b 121 *1.60 81-24 Sermon 12111 Vocalist 121½ Birdsofafeather 1214 Won easily 10
29Sep66-1Aqu fst 6f .23⅕ .47 1.12⅖ Md Sp Wt 7 7 74½ 89½ 68¾ 54 BBaeza b 120 *1.30 77-18 Emerald Lake115h Soldier'sStory120½ Birdsofafeather1203½ No exc. 10
14Aug65-1Sar fst 5½f .22⅗ .46⅕ 1.05⅗ Md Sp Wt 12 8 4¾ 53¾ 53½ 42¼ LAdams b 122 *1.70 87-6 Total Talent 1221 Gig 1221 Royal Step 122nk Going well at end 12
LATEST WORKOUTS Oct 31 Bel tr.t. 5f fst 1.01⅗ h Oct 25 Bel tr.t. 3f fst .37⅖ b Oct 22 Bel tr.t. 4f fst .50 b Oct 14 Bel tr.t. 4f fst .50⅖ b

Red Beach ×

B. c (1962), by First Landing—Recite, by Citation
Saddle Rock Farm J. P. Conway (H. B. Phipps) **117**

1966	6	0	1	0	$1,000
1965	12	1	3	0	$7,100

20Oct66-6Aqu	sl	7f	.23⅖	.46⅗1.25	Allowance	9	5	5^{4}	3^{3}	$6^{6\frac12}$	$8^{9\frac14}$	HWoodhouse	b 115	21.80	72–23	Glenrose 116$^{2\frac12}$ Prince Graff 115^{nk} Lord Byron 118^{1}	Early factor	10
11Oct66-8Aqu	fst	6f	.22⅗	.46⅕1.11⅗	Allowance	8	3	3^{1}	8^{6}	8^{15}	8^{15}	HWoodhouse	b 115	7.70	70–21	Yucatan 118^{nk} Tom Poker 110^{2} Stands to Reason 112^{h}	Stopped	8
18Feb66-6Hia	fst	7f	.23	.45⅖1.23⅗	Allowance	3	3	1^{1}	$1^{\frac12}$	1^{2}	2^{1}	EGuerin	b 115	4.50	90–19	Full of Fun 108^{1} Red Beach 115$^{3\frac12}$ Yucatan 108^{1}	Drifted out	8
8Feb66-9Hia	fst	7f	.23	.45⅖1.23⅕	Allowance	4	3	2^{h}	2^{2}	3^{4}	6^{9}	EGuerin	b 116	17.90	84–13	Sky Wonder 116^{1} Tronado 113^{7} Dogeola 113^{h}	Hard used early	8
26Jan66-7Hia	sly	7f	.23⅖	.46⅕1.25	Allowance	5	6	4^{4}	6^{12}	9^{13}	$8^{8\frac34}$	EGuerin	b 116	15.30	75–17	d–GrandMarais 109$^{\frac34}$ Comprehensive 114^{nk} HurricaneTim 114$^{\frac12}$	Tired	11
12Jan66-8TrP	fst	6f	.22⅕	.45⅖1.09⅕	Allowance	2	8	$7^{6\frac14}$	$8^{9\frac14}$	8^{16}	8^{13}	DBrumfield	b 119	2.40	83–14	Judge Morris 119no Admiral Clove 109$^{2\frac12}$ Hill Chance 109^{h}	Bore out	8
30Dec65-9TrP	fst	6f	.22	.44⅗1.09⅖	Allowance	6	4	$2^{\frac12}$	2^{3}	$3^{6\frac12}$	$7^{8\frac12}$	DBrumfield	b 115	5.40	86–17	I'm Rusty 110$^{4\frac12}$ Red Redeemer 113$^{\frac34}$ Hill Chance 108$^{\frac12}$	Tired	11
21Aug65-5Sar	fst	7f	.22⅘	.45⅗1.23⅘	Allowance	8	3	$5^{3\frac34}$	2^{2}	2^{2}	$3^{2\frac12}$	SHernandez	119	3.40	88– 9	d–Timurid 117$^{\frac12}$ Tudor Manor 112^{2} Red Beach 119^{5}	Taken up sharply	9
21Aug65—Placed second through disqualification.																		
13Aug65-5Sar	fst	1⅛	.47⅘	1.12⅕1.50⅘	Allowance	2	2	3^{2}	2^{1}	1^{2}	1^{8}	SHernandez	112	4.30	91– 9	Red Beach 112^{8} Alackaday 112no Known Quantity 115^{h}	Easily	8

LATEST WORKOUTS Nov 2 Bel m.t. 3f fst .37⅘ b Oct 27 Bel tr.t. 4f fst .52 b Oct 8 Bel m.t. 5f fst 1.00⅕ h Oct 4 Bel m.t. 1m fst 1.41⅗ b

Tom Poker

B. h (1961), by Tom Fool—Miss Stripes, by Big Game
Hobeau Farm H. A. Jerkens (Shawnee Farm) **112^{5}**

1966	3	0	1	1	$1,850
1965	11	2	1	3	$8,680

27Oct66-5Aqu	fst	6f	.23	.46⅖1.11⅖	Allowance	2	3	2^{h}	2^{h}	3^{2}	$3^{3\frac12}$	ECardone5	b 110	*0.60	82–20	Lord Byron 118no Second Venture 111$^{3\frac12}$ Tom Poker 110$^{1\frac12}$	No exc.	7
20Oct66-6Aqu	sl	7f	.23⅖	.46⅗1.25	Allowance	1	4	$2^{\frac12}$	$5^{4\frac12}$	Bolted		WBoland	b 115	*1.10	——	Glenrose 116$^{2\frac12}$ Prince Graff 115^{nk} Lord Byron 118^{1}	Rein broke	10
11Oct66-8Aqu	fst	6f	.22⅗	.46⅕1.11⅗	Allowance	1	2	2^{h}	2^{1}	1^{h}	2^{nk}	ECardone5	b 110	6.70	85–21	Yucatan 118^{nk} Tom Poker 110^{2} Stands to Reason 112^{h}	Gamely	8
11Dec65-6Aqu	fst	7f	.23⅕	46⅕1.24⅗	Allowance	5	4	$6^{4\frac14}$	$5^{3\frac34}$	$4^{2\frac12}$	$3^{2\frac34}$	WBoland	b 124	3.50	80–26	Twin Teddy 124$^{\frac34}$ Yucatan 112^{2} Tom Poker 124$^{2\frac12}$	Wide, mild bid	9
6Dec65-8Aqu	fst	7f	.23	.47 1.25⅘	Allowance	3	4	4^{3}	$3^{\frac12}$	1^{3}	1^{3}	WBoland	b 118	2.10	77–22	Tom Poker 118^{3} R. Anniversary 113^{1} Thirty Pieces 113^{7}	Easily	6
25Nov65-8Aqu	gd	7f	.23	.46⅕1.25⅗	Allowance	2	3	$3^{4\frac12}$	3^{8}	4^{10}	$5^{6\frac12}$	WBoland	117	5.70	71–26	Round Table Pet 115$^{\frac12}$ El Premiere 110^{4} GreatDepths122^{2}	Weakened	8
29Oct65-4Aqu	fst	6f	.22⅘	.45⅖1.11	Allowance	2	4	5^{11}	3^{11}	3^{11}	3^{11}	SHernandez	119	5.50	77–18	Brooklyn Bridge 121^{8} Mount Noble 113$^{2\frac12}$ Tom Poker 119$^{2\frac12}$	No mis'p	6
19Oct65-8Aqu	fst	6f	.22⅗	.45⅕1.12	Allowance	2	1	$8^{7\frac12}$	8^{6}	$5^{\frac34}$	4^{2}	JLRotz	121	5.10	81–18	Twin Teddy 117no Great Depths 115no Vail Pass 115^{2}	In close	9

LATEST WORKOUTS Nov 1 Bel m.t. 3f fst .39⅘ b Oct 25 Bel tr.t. 4f fst .51 b Oct 19 Bel tr.t. 4f sly .53 b Oct 10 Bel tr.t. 4f fst .50⅗ b

Results of 6th Race Aqueduct—November 3, 1966

SIXTH RACE
Aqu - 29224
November 3, 1966

7 FURLONGS. (Chute). (Rose Net, Sept. 17, 1962, 1.21⅕, 6, 114.)
Allowances. Purse $6,000. 3-year-olds and upward which have never won two races other than maiden or claiming. Weights 3-year-olds 122 lbs., older 124 lbs. Non-winners of a race other than maiden or claiming since October 1 allowed 3 lbs., of such a race since August 27, 5 lbs., of such a race since July 30, 7 lbs.
Value to winner $3,900, second $1,200, third $600, fourth $300. Mutuel pool $271,281.

Index	Horse	Eqt	A	Wt	PP	St	¼	½	Str	Fin	Jockey	Owner	Odds $1
29097Aqu1	—Sermon	b	3	122	4	2	$1^{\frac12}$	2^{3}	1^{3}	$1^{\frac34}$	E Belmonte	W H Perry	2.40
29103Aqu3	—Tom Poker		5	112	6	1	$3^{\frac12}$	3^{h}	$3^{\frac12}$	2^{3}	E Cardone5	Hobeau Farm	2.80
29050Aqu8	—Red Beach	b	4	117	5	3	2^{1}	1^{h}	$2^{\frac12}$	3no	H Woodh'use	Saddle Rock Farm	14.80
29105Aqu4	—Fence Rider	b	3	115	1	6	6	5^{h}	5^{3}	$4^{1\frac12}$	W Blum	King Ranch	10.20
29103Aqu2	—Second Venture		3	115	3	4	$4^{\frac12}$	4^{2}	4^{3}	$5^{2\frac12}$	J L Rotz	H S Nichols	2.40
29103Aqu5	—Absolute Power		3	115	2	5	5^{2}	6	6	6	B Baeza	High Tide Stable	4.20

Time .23, .45⅘, 1.10⅘, 1.23⅘ (with wind in backstretch). Track sloppy.

$2 Mutuel Prices:			
4–SERMON	6.80	3.20	2.60
6–TOM POKER		3.60	3.20
5–RED BEACH			5.60

Ch. c, by Nadir—Edified, by Jacopo. Trainer J. W. Maloney. Bred by Claiborne Farm (Ky.).

IN GATE AT 2.59. OFF AT 2.59½ EASTERN STANDARD TIME. Start good. Won driving.

SERMON sent along inside to make the pace under good rating, shook off RED BEACH to draw clear in upper stretch and was fully extended to hold TOM POKER safe. The latter, never far back, raced wide throughout and was slowly getting to winner. RED BEACH weakened after duelling for lead to upper stretch. FENCE RIDER was forced to steady when caught in close quarters leaving backstretch. SECOND VENTURE failed to seriously threaten. ABSOLUTE POWER was outrun.

lengths at six furlongs, after Eddie Belmonte hustled it into an early lead. Its next was a seven-furlong allowance affair. It lost in a game effort, after leading at the half-mile in .46⅖—more than a second slower than Second Venture's early speed in a similar race. And the final clocking of the race was 1.24⅗, a full second slower than the Second Venture race. On October 26, Sermon ran in a six-furlong allowance and won by a head in the excellent time of 1.10⅘.

Plainly, the horse had more than a smidgeon of class and was beginning to get its sea legs. Why would anyone pick a Second Venture over an animal of this kind? True, Second Venture had run more swiftly at seven furlongs. But Sermon had run more determinedly, and under 121 pounds. And had followed that effort by traveling six furlongs in faster time than Second Venture ever had.

Knowing how horseplayers think, I believe that many of them preferred Second Venture because (1) he looked like a speed horse, a grabber of the early lead, (2) he had run the half-mile in considerably faster time than Sermon, (3) he might have been short of condition in his last race, having been away for three months, and (4) he might benefit enough from a ride by Rotz to show all his speed today.

Those who recognized the signs of class in Sermon's record collected a $6.80 mutuel. Second Venture was no factor in this race against able older horses. But young Sermon took an early lead and held it. Pressed by the four-year-old Red Beach and the five-year-old Tom Poker, he ran the half in .45⅘, the three quarters in 1.10⅗ and the full distance in 1.23⅖—better time than Second Venture had ever traveled.

The example shows how a young horse of superior class exceeds its best previous clockings when the occasion demands. It demonstrates—as the Belle de Nuit race did—that the identity of owner, trainer and breeder are excellent tip-offs to superior class in a lightly raced young Thoroughbred, as is the determined manner in which it has contested its few races. Determination and class go together. The classy horse may tire in the stretch, but it does not quit.

Cheap Horses Know It

The ability of better horses to turn on the speed when they need to is noticeable at every level of Thoroughbred class. In the pell-mell two-year-old sprints at five and five and a half furlongs, the better juveniles log excellent speed ratings, because the races are run lickety-split, little pace strategy is employed, and the distances are short enough to permit a speedy animal of little class to reach the wire without dropping dead. Therefore, the better horse must run swiftly, too.

After the races are stretched to six furlongs, and especially after the animals have turned three, the horse with the fastest previous time at the distance is no longer a copper-riveted certainty to be the one with the fastest potential at the distance. When it faces a genuinely superior Thoroughbred, it invariably loses in slower time than it has recorded in the past.

Horsemen are so accustomed to this phenomenon that they seldom even discuss it. A $5,000 horse able to get the half-mile in .45 and the six furlongs in 1.10 when racing with utmost courage against its own kind, has not a prayer of equaling those figures against an allowance runner which may never have done better than .45⅘ and 1.10⅖.

Invariably and inevitably, the class horse prevails. Whether on the backstretch, on the turn, or in the homestretch, the better horse makes a run, easily overtakes the speedster, keeps pace with it for several strides and pulls ahead with little effort. During those few moments, the cheaper horse gets the message. It acknowledges its own inferiority and gives up. The better horse wins, perhaps in 1.10⅘. It will not run the three quarters in the 1.09⅕ of which it is capable until challenged by an animal more nearly its match.

It is unnecessary to become mystical about the ease with which a class horse trounces its inferiors, the authority with which it bullies them into running more slowly than usual, the "knowledge" they seem to display in promptly accepting defeat by a superior. Students of animal intelligence and animal psychology would not be surprised by this, and would find nothing mystical in it. Every known species of bird, fish and mammal has it own social order in which physical superiority wins privileges.

Thoroughbred horses, whose function in life is to run, evidently establish their own social order in the process of running. How? Horsemen agree that animals of higher class possess greater reservoirs of racing energy. They can turn on the speed at will, or whenever the rider asks for it. And they can maintain the speed for as long as may be necessary to demonstrate the prowess that discourages a lesser rival. In most cases, it does not take long. The inferior horse hoists the white flag. Whereupon the good horse relaxes into a less taxing stride and ambles home as he pleases.

This curious physical and psychological dominance of higher-quality Thoroughbreds over lower is misinterpreted by many players and more than a few horsemen. Having noticed that the good horse beats the cheap one in slower time than the cheapie has run in the past, they conclude that time is irrelevant to the handicapping of races. They overlook the fact that the speed potential of most horses is thoroughly tested long before the end of the three-year-old season. Except for out-and-out

The Triple Crown

Only eight three-year-olds have managed to win the celebrated Triple Crown of American Racing—the Kentucky Derby, the Preakness Stakes and the Belmont Stakes:

1919—Sir Barton	1941—Whirlaway
1930—Gallant Fox	1943—Count Fleet
1935—Omaha	1946—Assault
1937—War Admiral	1948—Citation

The following horses won two of the three great races: Man O' War (1920), Pillory (1922), Zev (1923), Twenty Grand (1931), Burgoo King (1932), Johnstown (1939), Bimelech (1940), Shut Out (1942), Pensive (1944), Capot (1949), Middleground (1950), Native Dancer (1953), Nashua (1955), Needles (1956), Tim Tam (1958), Carry Back (1961), Chateaugay (1963), Northern Dancer (1964), Kauai King (1966), Damascus (1967).

---

champions, virtually all horses aged four or more have shown repeatedly what they can do in the speed department when subjected to the *extremely accurate test of races against their own kind*. In such races they run as fast as they can.

Because that is so, and because races among seasoned animals of roughly equal quality are a majority of all races run in this country, one of the most reliable ways of determining subtle differences in class is by means of time figures and pace analyses. (See Chapter 13.)

Class and Form

We agree, then, that a horse of higher class is physically and temperamentally superior to one of lesser class. If he is a handicap star, he has proved it by starring in handicaps. If he is a $5,000 animal, he can walk away from $4,000 ones. It does not matter how sharp their condition may be, if his own is good. But, no matter how keen his edge, he cannot beat well-conditioned $6,500 stock.

Class and physical condition are closely related. A horse may drop down the scale to $4,000 before it wins a race. If it is still young, it may suddenly iron out its own kinks, get its legs under it and turn hot. Or a new, perceptive trainer may repair the aches and pains or correct the bad habits, as Hirsch Jacobs did in promoting Stymie from a $1,500 claiming race to a national championship.

Rarely does a horse spend an entire career at one class level. Rather, it moves up and down the scale. For most, the peak of class is attained during the three-year-old season. And then injury, overwork and unintelligent handling begin to take effect. Anyone who qualifies as an experienced racing fan has seen more than one former Kentucky Derby contestant struggling to win part of a purse in $3,500 claimers. At every bull ring in the land, animals of former high class pit their arthritic limbs and stout hearts against beasts that would not have been allowed in the same yard with them a few years earlier.

Quite apart from the pathos of such cases, they demonstrate that the effective class of a horse is related to its current condition. It does no good to ask what kind of fields the horse has beaten. One needs to know what kind it has beaten lately.

Schools of Thought

The dedicated class handicapper looks for the top-quality animal in the race, employing any of several standards and techniques which we shall examine shortly. If he thinks the horse is in shape, he plays it. Otherwise, he goes to the one that rates second or third or fourth on his scale of class values.

His opposite number, the fervent speed handicapper, regards speed ratings as expressions of class, and rarely looks further.

Some class handicappers are as keen on arithmetic as any speed-chart fancier. They assign each contending horse a class rating, usually $\frac{1}{10}$ or $\frac{1}{100}$ of its supposedly true claiming price or class value. They modify the figure by adding or subtracting other homemade numbers in which they try to embody the probable significance of average earnings, consistency, weights, recent form, the winning averages of rider and trainer, and whatever other angles appeal to them.

Players less inclined toward paper work may also concentrate on the class horses in the race, eliminating all but the final choice on the basis of current condition, distance, weight, pace, jockey or whatever.

In my own play, I attend to distance and form eliminations first. I then check the survivors to see if any is clearly outclassed and can be discarded for that reason. By the same token, if one of them is obviously the class of the field, and nothing about the jockey or weight assignments or probable pace seems likely to undermine its class superiority, I regard the handicapping process as completed, pending the routine visit to the walking ring. There is, of course, good reason to do a more thorough handicapping job than that on the other contenders, outclassed though they may be. They are, after all, in shape and suited to the distance. If the class horse is scratched, it's nice to know which of the others might become a good bet.

Certain astute speed handicappers depart from their rigid speed-weight formulas sufficiently to credit a horse for a good recent performance in superior company. I think that some of them do very well at the mutuel windows, having broadened their methods to that extent.

I doubt that anyone who does *not* pay due deference to the class factor can win money at the races. On the other hand, abundant rewards await the player willing to probe beneath the surface of the past-performance records to obtain a really accurate notion of each contender's current class. To adopt any of the procedures that involve such digging is to gain an unbeatable advantage over the rest of the crowd.

Basic Principles

Thousands of racegoers make the costly assumption that a horse which has run against higher-class animals than it meets today is a classier horse. Such reasoning is never valid unless:

1. **The horse won or ran close to the winner in the higher class.**
2. **Nothing has happened in the meantime to indicate that the horse has gone bad.**
3. **The horse is in good enough condition today to demonstrate whatever class advantage it might have.**

The first point is basic. Few horses begin their careers in $5,000 claiming races. They descend to that level because they are unable to earn their keep in better company. Until each has found a class in which it can win, or give promise of winning, the experienced horseman assumes, quite properly, that its true class is probably lower.

The horse that never wins but sometimes gets into the money at a given level is usually conceded a good chance of improving when entered against cheaper stock. This is especially true if it has shown pace-setting tendencies or willingness in the stretch. A fairly widespread and entirely valid concept holds that any animal able to finish within three lengths of a winner may be expected to come out on top in the same company at a later date, and should have a class advantage if entered with cheaper animals while still in condition.

In any list of entries at any track, the player finds horses whose records suggest that they have defeated better fields than challenge them today. A horse is entered at $5,000 today, but has won here at $8,000.

Should the player credit it with an edge in class? Not too quickly. In assessing the class of claiming animals that have been racing steadily, without long layoffs, it usually is hazardous to consider any performance that occurred more than three months ago. In fact, the safest procedure is to find the *latest* victory or in-the-money effort and base the class evaluation on it. If the horse won with great authority, or ran close in excellent time, the player should be fairly confident of its ability to hold its own against another field of the same or even slightly higher class. Provided, of course, that it is in shape.

If a claiming horse's record shows an absence from racing of six weeks or more at any time since its good performance in the higher class, the player has stronger reason than ever to suspect that it no longer is able to cut the mustard with better animals. Unless its most recent performances have been powerful enough to indicate that it is as good as it used to be, it should be credited with class no higher than that of the horses it lately has been beating or running close to.

Among bettors who try to do their own handicapping, the customary approach to the class factor is quite simple: The player accepts at face value the class notations in past-performance records. But, as we have already seen on several occasions in this chapter, significant qualitative differences often exist among horses entered at the same price, or in allowance races.

The Purse Is the Thing

The better the field, the higher the purse. At your track, allowance races may offer purses as low as $4,000 and as high as $12,000, with numerous gradations between. Some of the better claiming races will be run for purses higher than those awarded in lower-grade allowance races. And cheaper handicaps may sometimes pay no more than better allowances.

For the professional horseman, the purse is the thing. Regardless of whether he is a betting man, his business is the winning of purses, as large and numerous as possible. Toward this end, he watches the racing secretary's condition book like a vulture. Far beyond the ken of an innocent public, that book often provides soft spots which permit the trainer to drop his horse in class without seeming to. The horse that chases allowance animals without success in races for $7,500 purses can be run into shape and given a soft touch in an allowance that offers only $6,000. The public does not realize that the horse is moving down the class ladder to steal the money. It often wins the race at good odds.

Purse and Age

The size of the purse being so helpful an index to the overall quality of almost any field of horses, the player profits who pays due heed. Let us say that each of two three-year-olds has run nicely on the local track within the past couple of weeks, when entered to be claimed for $6,500. The past-performance records show that much. But they do not show that one of the races was for a purse of $4,700 and the other for $5,000. The $5,000 one was a better race. If today's is another $4,700 purse, the horse that ran well in the $5,000 race is stepping down in class.

The size of previous purses becomes especially useful knowledge in cases where the past-performance lines are even more misleading than in the above example. Let us say that one of the three-year-olds of supposed $6,500 quality won its last race narrowly and the other lost narrowly and that both seem to be in condition. If the loser was beaten in contention for a $4,700 purse and the winner prevailed with a $5,000 purse at stake, a real class distinction may exist. Or, if the situation is reversed, the horse that lost narrowly in the better field may often be excused for the defeat, all other factors being equal.

To show the possibilities of this kind of analysis, I shall refer to a 1966 Aqueduct condition book. I find a race at a mile, with a purse of $5,000, for three-year-olds and upward, entered to be claimed for $6,500, $6,750 and $7,000. The claiming price of each entrant is selected by its brain trust, depending on whether they want weight concessions of two to four pounds in exchange for lowering the horse's price and increasing the risk of sale. The only horses barred from the race are those that have won two races at a mile or longer in the past month, when entered to be claimed for more than $6,000. This opens the door to most of the best $6,500 to $7,000 milers in the barns, while permitting trainers of lesser ones to try their luck or darken their form, or both.

Five days after this race, the Aqueduct condition book schedules another mile event for animals that have not won two races at that distance or longer in a month. But this time the purse is $4,700. And this time horses older than three are barred. And the claiming prices range from $6,000 to $6,500.

It can be seen that a three-year-old that wins the first of those two races, when entered to be claimed for $6,500, achieves more than a three-year-old victor entered at the same price against the weaker, less valuable stock eligible for the second of the races. Yet the past-performance lines in each horse's record may look identical. Certainly, the lines will not convey that the one victory was far more substantial than the other.

The player who jots down the size of the purse in every race run on his local circuit compiles a valuable record. Having narrowed a field to the animals that qualify as to distance and condition, he sometimes can separate these contenders in terms of class simply by checking the purses of their best races.

In making these discoveries about the true values of past races, the player goes a far distance toward thwarting the efforts of trainers to conceal or obscure the readiness of their horses. When the trainer drops his steed into the right company, the size of the purse will make the maneuver evident to an alert player.

The work not only is simple, but the information is readily obtainable. Most daily newspapers publish racing entries and results which include the dollar value of each purse.

The Golden Notebook

The player who saves the *Telegraph* or *Form* result charts of all races run on his local circuit not only has the purse values at hand, but the special conditions of each race, plus revealing comments about the performance of each horse. His deliberations about class and form are sure to become far more rewarding than in the past.

A somewhat more efficient procedure is to transcribe the purse value and main eligibility conditions of each race into a notebook. This takes a few minutes, but saves time later.

The main reason to go to any part of this trouble is that it puts the player in the way of extra windfalls. The conditions of entry in claiming and allowance races are often quite complicated. Just as identical claiming prices may hide fields of widely diverse quality, so may identical purses. If I seem now to be contradicting what I said earlier about the significance of purse sizes, I plead guilty. There are times when the conditions are written in such a way, and the equine population at a track is assorted in such a way, that races with identical purses may be races of different class. The player who watches for such occurrences is leagues ahead of the one who relies entirely on the notations in past-performance lines.

For example, an allowance race might offer a $7,500 purse to three-year-olds that have not won two races of $2,925 in four months. (Translation: Two races in which the winner's share was $2,925. At most tracks, the winner gets 65 percent of the total purse, the runner-up earns 20 percent, the show horse 10 and the fourth horse 5. In allowance conditions, "races of $2,925" are races run for purses of $4,500.)

In offering a purse of $7,500 to animals that have not won twice when competing for far less money in recent races, the racing secretary invites trainers to move some of their three-year-olds ahead in class. He also opens the door to better stock, such as one of last year's juvenile stakes winners in its first or second conditioning start of the season. Or a lightly raced animal whose only victories in a brief career may have occurred in a maiden race and in an allowance of today's value or better!

Another allowance race might offer an identical purse, but confine eligibility to horses that have won a somewhat larger number of recent races, or races of higher purse value. And it might admit older horses along with the three-year-olds.

The player who wants to unearth the opportunities buried in such conditions must know the kind of races in which the contenders have been competing. He can make the check by referring to his file of result charts, or he can consult his notebook. It might look like this:

1. 4200-MSW3up
2. 3700-f3500-4up-NW2 mile 8/1
3. 5500-10.5-12.5-3up
4. 5000-fAlw-2s-NW2
5. 7500-Alw-3up-NW3 of 2925 12/7

Any similar shorthand will do. The above notations say that the purse in the first race on this particular day was $4,200, under maiden-special-weights conditions, for horses aged three and up.

The second was a claimer for $3,500 females, aged four and up, which had not won two races of a mile since August 1. The purse was $3,700.

The third was a $5,500 purse for three and older, entered to be claimed at $10,500 to $12,500.

The fourth offered $5,000 under allowance conditions to two-year-old fillies that had never won two races of any kind.

The fifth was a $7,500 allowance purse for threes and older that had not won $2,925 three times since December 7.

It is not necessary to include distances in such notes, since that information appears in the past-performance records which the notes are designed to supplement.

Absolutely the most de luxe notebooks are the kind maintained by players so enamored of the game that they handicap every race every day. Rather than depend entirely on purse sizes and eligibility conditions for their evaluation of the quality of a horse's past performances, they jot down the age, sex and class of the horses that finish first, second or third in each race. In the right hands, notes of this kind are like a telescope into the future.

Let us pretend that we are trying to get a line on Horse "A," a five-year-old. The past-performance record shows that its last outing was a strong victory when entered at $6,000. The conditions of the race accommodated four-year-olds and up, at claiming prices of $6,000 to $7,000. So far so good. It was not simply a $6,000 race, as one might conclude from the past-performance record. But it was not simply a $7,000 race, as one might conclude from the conditions.

The player who keeps handicap figures on every race finds in his notebook that "A" beat a four-year-old rated at $5,500, and that the show horse had been a five-year-old rated at $5,000. "A's" own rating prior to that race had been $6,000. If there were any legitimate $7,000 animals in the race they were not in condition to demonstrate that superior class. "A's" rating remains $6,000. If one of its opponents in today's field ran third in a good effort last week, behind horses rated at $8,000 and $8,500, the opponent might be a good bet at splendid odds today.

Decisions about class ratings are often tricky. Some note-keepers work entirely in terms of purse value, rather than claiming price. For example, if yesterday's purse was $5,000 and the winner went into the race with a rating of $4,400, based on previous accomplishments, the player would not increase the rating to $5,000 unless the animal whipped horses that (1) had such ratings and (2) ran well enough to justify them. Thus, the relationship between class and condition is kept in view.

By the same reasoning, if each of the first three finishers went into the race with $5,000 ratings, the winner would retain that rating. The second and third horses would be reevaluated on the basis of their performances. If it was a close finish, and the two horses ran extremely well, they might remain at $5,000. If they were beaten decisively, or ran in such a way as to suggest a decline in condition, their ratings would be decreased. One man I know operates on the basis of 50 points a length, assuming a truly run race: If "A" and "B" both rated at 5,000 and "A" beats "B" by a length, gaining in the stretch, "A" might emerge from the race with a rating of 5,050, and "B" with 5,000. If "A" won by the length only because "B" tired, "A" might retain 5,000 and "B" get 4,950.

Working on the basis of claiming prices rather than purse figures, I have had good results by giving full value to a victory or a finish within

Class in action. Damascus wins the 1967 Preakness from In Reality and Proud Clarion. UPI PHOTO

Kelso romps home in the 1963 Woodward Stakes at Aqueduct. Never Bend, three lengths back, got there before Crimson Satan. UPI PHOTO

one length, deducting $500 for a second-place finish or a finish within two lengths, and $1,000 for show. Hence, if the first three finishers went into the race with ratings of 3,700, 3,300 and 3,600, respectively, the winner would retain its original rating (unless it were a young, improving horse that had won most decisively and powerfully). The second finisher might be promoted to 3,700 for running only a jump behind, and the third finisher would end with anything between 2,700 and 3,700, depending on how well it ran, and where the race fit into its own form cycle.

Although this kind of method allows the player to operate at the very nub of the class-condition problem, it requires more attention and is more complicated than the casual hobbyist may like to be bothered with. I include it only because some of the more enthusiastic players in the audience might enjoy a fling at it someday. It works with special efficiency in handicapping allowance races, especially the kind that find high-priced claimers all mixed up with handicap animals.

Needless to say, if any horse suffers interference serious enough to affect the outcome of a race, the player must make due allowances in assigning his post-race class ratings.

Track Class

Two months ago, the horse won a couple of allowance races at Shenandoah Downs and here it is in a $3,500 claimer at Aqueduct, facing the cheapest stock on the New York circuit. Does the West Virginia horse have an advantage in class? Almost certainly not. Its victories occurred in allowance races for purses of less than half the amounts for which $3,500 New York horses compete.

Experienced players usually discount the chances of any animal entered in a race at a major-league track until it runs well in a race at such a track. The Shenandoah Downs horse travels but a few miles to Laurel or Bowie, but the Maryland ovals are worlds removed from West Virginia, as far as class is concerned. Similarly, a Laurel animal would deserve little support in its first effort at Saratoga, unless it had been beating the best available stock at the Maryland plant, came from a leading barn and was fracturing the clocker's watches in its workouts.

The class differences between major tracks and minor ones, and the differences between one major track and another, are entirely matters of purse money. A $4,000 claiming animal competes for $4,000 purses at Hollywood Park. Why would anyone take it to Turf Paradise and enter it for $5,000 to get the winner's end of a $1,300 purse?

California or New York?

The best stables take the best horses where the most money is to be won. For that reason, the best index to the class of a track is the amount of money it pays out in purses. The player need not wonder whether the New England horse has been beating animals as good as those it faces today in Delaware. He simply consults *Racing Form* chart books, and checks the purses. In the absence of those useful books, he consults the *American Racing Manual* to see its latest tabulation of average purses paid by each track.

Averages, as I went to some length to point out in an earlier chapter, can be deceptive. A track that pays out six-figure purses in a couple of two-year-old stakes races has less money to spend on claiming purses, even though its average may be quite high. But, by and large, the class of tracks can be judged in terms of average purses.

The main exception to all this is California. Or, if you happen to be a Californian, the main exception is New York. The major California tracks pay substantially larger purses than New York does. This has been going on for years. Yet no serious student of Thoroughbred racing believes that a $5,000 California claimer outclasses a New York animal of identical price—the Californian's greater average earnings notwithstanding.

The truth is that California racing is quite different from the New York brand. Its purses are higher, but its major-league season is far shorter, a disadvantage that makes Eastern stables hesitant about shipping their animals all that distance. The Easterners can stay at home, or in the vicinity, and amass higher total earnings by the end of the long New York season, even though the average purse is somewhat leaner.

The class superiority of the New York circuit is enhanced still further by the texture of its racing surfaces. It takes class to maintain speed over a distance of ground at Aqueduct and Saratoga. At Santa Anita and Hollywood, the tracks are fast as lightning, and a mediocre horse can carry its swift further. Finally, with so many of the nation's top owners and trainers gathered in New York, the best riders also congregate there. Johnny Longden, idol of the West Coast, was never more than ordinary in New York. Bill Shoemaker, one of the greatest of all time, has never had the automatic success in New York that he enjoys in California.

I go into all this not for reasons of Eastern pride, which I lack in any case, but to warn the reader against being overimpressed by the earnings records of California horses that invade the East.

Track Class: What They Paid in Purses, 1966

The official "daily average purse distribution" statistics of most tracks are inflated by inclusion of the enormous purses paid in a handful of stakes races. The tracks need the $50,000 and occasional $100,000 races to attract big stables and get extra publicity. But the money spent in that way comes from somewhere: specifically, from the total sums available for claiming and allowance purses. The more $150,000 races a track offers, the less it can pay to the winners of less glamorous races.

The most accurate available index to track class is the range of typical purses it offers, day in and day out. Rather than publish the misleading official average-purse figures, I have adjusted them downward, to compensate for the sums each track spent on outsized stakes races. Note, however, that the column headed "Total Paid to Horsemen" includes *all* purses, less the amounts paid by horsemen themselves in nominating fees.

	Total Paid to Horsemen	Racing Days	Average Adjusted Purse
Hollywood Park	$4,377,800	55	$8,600
Santa Anita	4,244,900	55	8,100
Saratoga	1,655,275	24	7,440
Aqueduct	9,822,306	160	6,500
Belmont (Aqueduct)	3,535,700	60	6,220
Hialeah	2,484,500	40	6,220
Washington (Arlington)	2,284,900	37	5,780
Arlington Park	1,924,900	36	5,560
Balmoral (Arlington)	1,442,200	30	5,330
Bowie	2,510,700	51	5,220
Hawthorne	1,647,150	35	5,000
Laurel	2,255,650	47	5,000
Monmouth Park	2,590,220	56	5,000
Garden State Park	2,645,150	56	4,890
Pimlico	2,456,950	52	4,890
Sportsman's Park*	2,210,600	49	4,890
Gulfstream Park	2,087,800	46	4,670
Delaware Park	2,208,450	55	4,330
Atlantic City	2,112,400	56	4,000
Del Mar	1,480,900	42	3,890
Churchill Downs	1,597,700	44	3,780
Keeneland	1,118,875	32	3,780
Tropical Park	1,492,700	45	3,670
Detroit	2,744,600	83	3,600
Rockingham Park	1,954,800	54	3,560

* ⅝-mile track.

Having made that point, I also warn against crediting a New York horse with an advantage when it makes its debut in California. The class superiority of either animal is likely to be canceled by the strain of its long journey, and unfamiliarity with the new climate and the new racing strip.

Purses in Claiming Races

To give the reader a notion of the large spectrum of equine quality that may be concealed by the class notations in a past-performance record, here is a list of representative tracks and the purses they offer for the cheapest claiming races on their programs:

Track	Lowest Claiming Price	Purse
Aqueduct	$3,500	$4,000
Arlington	3,000	3,000
Bowie (winter)	3,000	3,300
Caliente	1,000	1,600
Charles Town	1,500	1,200
Churchill Downs	2,500	2,800
Delaware	3,000	3,000
Fair Grounds	2,000	2,000
Florida Downs	1,500	1,500
Garden State	3,500	3,500
Golden Gate	2,000	2,000
Gulfstream	3,500	3,000
Hialeah	3,500	3,500
Hollywood	4,000	4,000
Lincoln Downs	1,500	1,500
Monmouth Park	3,500	3,500
Oaklawn Park	2,000	2,300
Pimlico (winter)	3,000	3,300
Santa Anita	3,500	4,000
Suffolk Downs	2,000	2,000
Tropical Park	3,500	2,700

In each claiming bracket, purses increase with the distance of the race. At New York and California tracks, a route race for $4,000 animals, aged four and up, sometimes carries a purse as much as $500 higher than the one offered for a sprint among three-year-olds of the same claiming price.

Players who evaluate class entirely on the basis of the past-performance lines are advised not to try to assign class ratings to out-of-town horses, unless they come from circuits of higher class than today's.

In such circumstances, they can be granted a class advantage against any field in which the claiming price is not more than $500 higher than the prices at which they have been entered in their own victorious races.

Horses moving to a better circuit from a lesser one win so seldom in their first two or three outings that the player is better off waiting for them to demonstrate their local class level in actual competition.

Consistency

An honest, relatively sound campaigner is likely to be a factor in the running of every race that finds it entered at the right distance against animals of its own quality. Modern conditioning methods are such that a consistent animal's only severe losses occur when it is entered at the wrong distance, or on wet footing, or over its head, or after a long trip or a long layoff. This applies whether the horse be a handicap champion or a $5,000 meal ticket.

In every price bracket, some horses are sounder and more reliable than others. Many are so unreliable that they never win and rarely run in the money. Having failed to establish class of any kind, they warrant betting support by nobody. But what of the creature that has won only once in its last fourteen attempts yet seems properly placed today?

It may be a winner. It may beat off a horse that has won 20 percent of its own races, and has run somewhere in the money half the time. Inconsistent horses beat consistent ones every day.

Some of the worst sucker bets at all tracks are "consistent" horses that run second, third or fourth in race after race after race, yet almost never win. Another sucker bet is the truly consistent animal that finally runs one race too many and comes out of it incapable of another good race for weeks.

The key to a workable knowledge of consistency is that it means little unless the animal is in good condition and properly placed as to class and distance. And notwithstanding a record of inconsistency, a horse is a threat if entered today at a class and distance which have found it a winner on every similar occasion listed in its record. As far as the record shows, that horse is admirably consistent when in today's company.

Many old-time players refuse to consider an animal that has been unable to win at least one of every five of its starts—the traditional yardstick of Thoroughbred consistency. Some also demand that the horse have finished in the money at least half the time. They count its wins, places and shows, and compare them with its total starts this year, or this year and last.

An even more conservative approach makes additional requirements. Even if its overall record is one of consistency, the horse must show at least one victory in its last two or three races, and two or three victories and/or three to five in-the-money finishes in the published past-performance lines that represent its ten or twelve most recent races. Some players go still further, demanding four in-the-money finishes in the last five races, or not less than four victories in the list of itemized past-performance lines.

Anyone who adheres to such principles of consistency and applies other simple rules involving distance, recent action, basic class and pace can expect to catch a high percentage of winners. Most of the horses turned up by a method of that kind run at short prices, but the player loses very little money betting on them, and may even be a winner in the long run.

Between two horses whose most recent good races were against authentic $7,500 stock, the smart player would naturally tend to favor the one that had been in the money with substantially greater consistency than its rival. And if the more consistent horse had been displaying that enviable quality in its latest races, the proposition would become even more inviting.

But what do you do when confronted by two horses, each entered for $7,500, if one has run at a price that high only once in its career and the other has run at a price that *low* only once in its career? And what if both races at that level were good performances within the last ten days? And what if the horse that stepped up at $7,500 and ran well was a truly consistent animal at lower claiming prices, whereas the other had been quite inconsistent when entered at $8,500 and $10,000, winning only two races of its last fifteen?

Some players automatically go to the consistent horse. Others automatically go to the "class" horse—the one with victories at a higher claiming price. On any given day, either or both players may be entirely wrong. Assuming both animals are in condition to run their best, the pace of the race may be such as to prevent either from winning. Because pace is so often a determining factor in situations of this kind, I advise the reader to be chary about eliminating relatively inconsistent horses or, at the other extreme, backing them simply because they have won at higher prices in the past.

To my way of thinking, downright inconsistent horses should be eliminated on grounds of class. Horses of middling consistency should be retained—unless obviously outclassed by a truly superior animal, as in the examples on pages 176-186.

For anyone who cares to undertake a comprehensive brand of handicapping, moving from distance to form to class to weight to pace to trainer to jockey to special angles and finally the paddock, I recommend the following standards of consistency:

1. Accept as a potential contender any horse with at least one victory in seven to thirteen starts or two victories in fourteen or more starts this year. If it has had fewer than seven races this year, make the computation on the basis of its races this year and last.

2. Accept any horse, regardless of consistency, if it finished in the money or within a length of the winner in its last race, or had an excuse.

3. Accept any horse, regardless of consistency, that steps down in claiming price at least $1,000 to a level at which it has been able to win or run within a length of a winner at today's distance.

These rules are, of course, useless in handicapping maiden races. They also do not apply to two-year-olds. In handicapping older, more experienced claiming horses, they have the great virtue of allowing the player to prepare himself for the upsets that are standard at all tracks— the "surprise" victories by horses that have seldom won but, regardless of prior inconsistency, happen to be well suited to today's race. Handled this way, consistency is not overlooked. On the contrary, the player may find that the only advantages of one horse over its main rival is a more consistent record, plus its superior jockey, plus its superior barn. In a contest of that sort, consistency becomes a plus factor of great significance.

Average Earnings

Because races of higher class pay larger purses, a quick means of separating two horses in point of class is to consult their earnings records. If both have made ten starts and have run in the money five times, the one that has earned $6,500 has obviously done so in more demanding races than the one whose earnings total only $4,400.

Some players are so confident of the earnings tabulations published with the past-performance records that they incorporate the figures into their methods. Thus if the above two horses are rated at 50—meaning that each has won or run close when entered for $5,000—the player might add 7 to the rating of the horse that has won $6,500, and add 4 to the rating of the horse that has won $4,400.

Other players go to the bother of adding the total earnings of the entire field for this year and last. They then divide the total by the number of entrants. All horses whose earnings are below the average are discarded. Horses with earnings above the average are looked upon as the class. I have no idea whether this works or not. I can think of numerous circumstances in which it would not, especially in better claiming races and allowance races at major tracks. Yet, if the player who went in for these calculations were a good judge of form and carried his class studies beyond the arithmetical stage, he might have a fighting chance.

The late Les Conklin once published a book-length system *Payday at the Races,** which defined consistency among claiming animals as the ability to earn money at the rate of $500 a start. Fifteen years have passed, but the figure continues to stand up. Confining his bets to geldings in medium-priced claiming races and betting only on those that have run recently and have either averaged $500 a start or won their last races while gaining in the stretch, an acquaintance of mine is several thousands dollars ahead of his bookmaker, and extends the lead by a few hundred dollars a year.

The earnings table is perhaps most useful when the casual racegoer tries to make head or tail of allowance races and handicaps. Not knowing one horse from another, he can be confident of the class superiority of any entrant that *not only has won and finished in the money consistently* but has managed to amass higher earnings than its other consistent rivals. The higher earnings mean that the horse has been running for larger purses, and doing it effectively.

Age

A properly handled Thoroughbred achieves the pinnacle of its speed and endurance in the late summer of its four-year-old season and does not necessarily lose these fundamental attributes of racing class until age six or seven. Unfortunately, most Thoroughbreds are not properly handled. Many are so badly abused that they begin to deteriorate at three.

Because of this, one finds three-year-olds winning races of a mile and longer in the spring and summer of the year against older animals that should leave them many lengths behind. If the feat is performed by a Buckpasser or Tom Fool, it should surprise nobody. But when it happens in ordinary races, experts have every right to gnash their teeth.

Four- and five-year-olds are supposed to outclass the threes, especially at distances in excess of seven furlongs. They usually do. Which is one of the chief reasons why the expert player keeps an eye on purse values or on the eligibility conditions of races. The three-year-old that has been losing by narrow margins to older horses does considerably

* (Citadel Press, New York, 1953.)

better against animals of its own age. The five-year-old that has been victimizing threes may be unequal to more mature competitors.

On the other hand, many claiming racers are so badly off by the age of four or five that a relatively sound three-year-old handles them with no difficulty.

Here are some tested rules that help experienced players to cope with the age problem:

1. No horse aged four or older is likely to win a handicap or stakes race unless it usually runs in such company and either has won or finished in the money when so entered.

2. No three-year-old is a good candidate in a handicap or stakes race against older horses unless it has already beaten such a field, or has been running with exceptional power against its own kind, suggesting a clear edge in intrinsic class and condition.

3. No three-year-old is a good bet against older horses in allowance or claiming races during the first eight months of the year unless it has a noticeable advantage in class. In the fall it remains a dubious bet if any older horse is not only in condition but seems superior as to class.

4. In maiden races and races for non-winners of two races, three-year olds are almost invariably better prospects than the older, chronic losers they meet in such fields.

Sex

With rare exception, female Thoroughbreds have less strength and stamina than males. They retain winning condition for briefer periods, and seldom are able to win the second of two successive driving finishes. They need jockeying of intelligence and sensitivity, because they react badly to punishment. Also, their sexual cycle affects their form.

For these reasons, no filly (a female aged four or less) or mare (a female aged five or more) is a good bet against males unless it enjoys a pronounced edge in class.

In *The Compleat Horseplayer* I disclosed a gimmick that I had found helpful in comparing the class of female and male horses: Deduct 20 percent from the claiming price at which a female beats other females, to determine the kind of geldings, colts (whole males, aged four or less) and entire horses (aged five or more) against which she might have a chance. In short, victory in an f-6,000 is rated at $4,800—not quite good enough to beat a $5,000 colt or gelding.

Among males, geldings usually are regarded as the most reliable claiming racers. Having been castrated, they have nothing in mind but racing. Indeed, they often are easier to train and ride than colts.

Some useful ideas embodying the class distinctions between male and female Thoroughbreds:

1. No female is a likely contender against males unless it has already beaten males of today's value at today's distance or longer, or has run close to males of higher value, or has beaten females when entered at a price substantially (25 percent) higher than today's top claiming price.

2. No female is a likely contender against males if the top claiming price listed in today's conditions is $500 or more above the price for which the female was entered in her last race. If that last race was an f-claimer, reduce its value by 20 percent before making the comparison. An occasional exception to this rule is the filly that scored a powerful win over males in its last race, finishing first by a comfortable margin after gaining in the stretch.

3. No female can be expected to win today against males or females if it is stepping up in class after a race in which it engaged in a driving finish and failed to gain ground during the stretch run.

Rises in Class

Vigorous three-year-olds often improve tremendously. The horse that beat $4,000 claimers at 15 to 1 in June may continue to win, despite boosts in class, and may be a 7 to 5 favorite when it goes to the post against $10,000 animals in August.

Older horses also climb the class ladder, but less often and less spectacularly. Unless a horse ran an exceedingly promising race in its last try, it probably has no business stepping up in claiming price today. The most frequent reason for running it in superior company is that the trainer is trying to work it into condition and wants to protect it from a claim while doing so. If the horse not only is out of its class but is entered at an unsuitable distance, the trainer's motives become that much more apparent.

But the player needs to wrinkle his brow over a rise in class by a horse that won, ran close or showed signs of important improvement in its latest effort. Ability to perceive those signs of improvement (see Chapter 9), when combined with a solid understanding of the class factor, enables a good player to catch winners at nice prices. Racetrack crowds sometimes bet on a horse that moves up in class, but are unlikely to do so unless its most recent race was an obviously strong performance. As the reader now knows, some signs of improvement are by no means obvious.

As in other aspects of handicapping, it is possible to become too mechanical about rises in class, and miss wonderful betting opportunities. The animal that ran well in its last race, entered for $7,500, may not be stepping up in class at all today, even though its price has been raised to $9,000. A notebook-keeper or a collector of result charts would see at a glance that the horse defeated animals every bit as good as those it meets this afternoon. In other circumstances, a horse that remained at $7,500 today might be facing better stock, and might even be tossed out on grounds of inability to handle the assignment.

Step-ups in class are a serious handicapping problem only to the player who depends entirely on past-performance records and must guess the actual quality of the races described in the record. Such players will find some helpful ideas in the remainder of this section.

Class Ratings without Charts

A horse that was entered for $3,500 in its last start, and runs today in a race for animals priced at $3,500 to $4,000, may be stepping up slightly in class, or may be running under precisely the same eligibility conditions as last time. The best way to solve the problem is to assign the horse the most accurate possible class rating, based on its best recent race or races, and see how it compares in that department with other leading contenders. Later, an accurate pace rating will help to settle the question.

By and large, if today's top claiming price is *within the range of the entered prices at which the horse has run well in the past,* the apparent step-up need arouse no anxiety. (I take it for granted that the player is careful to judge the horse's basic class in terms of recent races or, in exceptional cases, good recent performances that strongly suggest an ability to match the high quality of races run last season.)

A concept of claiming-price ranges is extremely important to the player who depends on the class notations in past-performance records. For example, a confirmed $2,000 horse seldom wins in $2,500 company, except after moving to a lesser track. Other difficult step-ups in entered claiming prices:

$2,500 to $3,000	$5,500 to $6,750
$3,000 to $3,500	$6,000 to $7,250
$3,500 to $4,250	$6,500 to $7,750
$4,000 to $4,750	$7,500 to $8,750
$4,500 to $5,250	$8,500 to $10,250
$5,000 to $6,250	$10,000 to $12,500

A horse that runs the overpowering kind of race described on page 170 and earns the accolade of a big win can, however, be conceded a good chance to step up as much as 50 percent in price, when his entered price in that good race is compared with the top claiming price stated in the conditions of today's.

Indeed, when dealing with a three-year-old coming off a big win, it makes a good deal of sense to credit it with class no lower than the bottom price in today's eligibility conditions. Horses of that kind should never be underrated, and should be allowed to make huge jumps in class. They can do it. They often are the best bet of the day, week and month.

Here, for persons who depend exclusively on past-performance records, are additional ideas about step-ups in class, supplementing other notions set forth on pages 210-214:

1. To be acceptable as a contender in an allowance race, a horse whose last start was in a claimer should (a) have won an allowance race on this circuit or one of equal class, or (b) should be facing other non-winners of such allowance races, and (c) should not be asked to beat another contender that has run in the money in a handicap race within the last three months.

2. No female may step from a claiming race to an allowance race, or from an allowance to a handicap, unless today's race is for females and no other entrant has ever been able to finish in the money when entered in a race of today's class. An obvious exception is the female stakes winner that tuned up for today's effort by running in an allowance race.

3. A female running against other females may seem to be stepping up in class after a race in which it was entered against males at a lower price. But it may actually be an excellent prospect whose trainer has maneuvered it into a concealed soft spot. For example, if it ran well against males last week, when entered to be claimed for $7,000, it is actually dropping in class if entered against $8,000 fillies and mares today (see page 212).

Drops in Class

A horse rarely drops very much in class unless something is wrong, and the barn has lost hope of winning any money with it at its customary price level. Yet races are won every day by animals entered at lower prices than those listed in their most recent past performances. These are not usually authentic class drops. They merely are proper placements of well-conditioned horses, restoring them to the proper class after running them into shape against better stock.

A player who considers the factors of distance and form before concerning himself with class can save a lot of effort. A horse out of shape is a horse out of shape: it may be dropping in class by $2,500 today, but if it is not in condition to run its current best, nobody should hazard a bet on it.

Assuming that the player restricts his attention to animals entered at suitable distances, and in sufficiently good form to qualify as contenders, the following ideas about class drops will prove useful:

1. The horse should improve today if the highest claiming price allowed in the race is lower than the price at which it was entered in its last race.

2. The horse may improve if it stepped down in price for its last race and is entered today at the same price, especially if it ran at the wrong distance in its last race, or will have a better rider today.

3. The horse should improve if it went up in claiming price for its last race and is entered today at a price lower than in its next-to-last. For example, if it is entered at $4,000 today, it might have been entered for $5,000 in its last race, and $4,500 in the race before.

4. A female should improve if it ran against males in its last race and is entered at a lower claiming price today in a race for females. This is a significant reduction in class.

5. A horse should improve today if it is running at a price lower than any listed in its past performances. An allowance horse is invariably a threat when entered in a claiming race for the first time.

6. A horse should be conceded a chance in a claiming race if it has won an allowance race on a major circuit within the last three months.

7. A horse should improve today if it is entered at a price lower than the price at which it was claimed, especially if it was claimed within the past two months and has had not more than three races in that time— all of them losses at a higher claiming price.

The Class of Two-Year-Olds

Until the juveniles are asked to run three quarters of a mile and beyond, nobody has more than a hazy idea of their real class. In the shorter dashes, the two-year-old that has demonstrated its ability to cover the ground in the shortest time is the best bet. He may beat a youngster that goes on to stakes victories at more representative distances. And he may end as a $3,000 claimer himself. Forget it. He remains the best bet today, because speed is all that counts today.

For the same reason, an apparent drop in class from a maiden-special-weights to a maiden claimer, or from one claimer to another of less value is unimportant among two-year-olds entered at distances of less than six furlongs.

Later in the year, when most two-year-olds are running at six and seven furlongs, things change. The player welcomes the presence in a high-priced claimer of a youngster that has run middling well in an allowance race of today's distance. If all other things are equal, the former allowance runner may have a decisive edge in class.

Likewise, the speediest two-year-old in the field is a good bet in any juvenile allowance or stakes race at less than six furlongs, even if its only victory was in a maiden race. But when the distances are stretched out a bit, and the ready stamina of superior class becomes operational, no juvenile should be considered in a stakes unless it has proved its mettle in allowance company.

Class in Handicaps and Stakes

The fields in handicap and stakes events for horses aged three or older are normally so closely matched that victory goes to the animal in best condition—a superiority which may be impossible to foresee in the past-performance lines. On other occasions, especially at secondary tracks, the player may note the presence of a horse that has been doing most of its running in the very best company on the very best circuits and has the earnings to prove it. If its rider is one of the nation's best and its barn is also one of the leaders, the horse probably has a class advantage. The player then checks the weights, the condition factor, and the probable pace, and often as not finds himself with a nice bet.

Class in Starter Races

One of the neatest ways to separate the sheep from the goats in the tricky starter handicap and starter allowance races that complicate the programs at some tracks is to keep records of purse sizes. These races often are run at longer distances, which demand superior endurance and determination. An animal that has displayed those qualities while running for higher purses is very likely a good bet in starter races at a mile or beyond.

11 The Weight Factor

TO DIFFERENTIATE THEMSELVES from mere horseplayers, racing fans who analyze the past performances of Thoroughbreds like to call themselves handicappers. It is an impressive term, well deserved. Technically and traditionally, however, a handicapper is a racing official, not a customer. His job is to heighten the sporting aspects of the game—and make life more difficult for its players—by attempting to equalize the winning chances of horses. He does this by saddling better horses with relatively heavy weights, allowing inferior horses to carry relatively light weights.

The procedure is at least four centuries old. It originated in common sense: A horse with less weight on its back retains more energy for the stretch run. Whenever a longshot carrying 110 pounds noses out a favorite carrying 123, there is little room for doubt that the favorite could have reversed the order of finish under a lighter burden.

In contests among well-conditioned Thoroughbreds of approximately equal quality, with first-rate riders aboard, the only measurable, tangible, fully predictable advantage is lighter weight. During the actual race, this advantage may be insufficient, of course. Horses carrying heavier loads may prove to be in sharper condition, or better suited to the pace, or unapproachably superior in class, or better ridden. Professional horsemen know all this very well. It is their duty to avoid or minimize whatever disadvantages they can. So they look for spots in which their horses will be required to carry the lightest possible weights. In some circumstances, they try to augment that advantage by employing apprentice jockeys, reducing weight by the additional three, five, seven or ten pounds allowed as bonuses to trainers who risk the services of inexperienced riders.

When the late Ben Jones trained for the mighty Calumet Farms, he kept his horses out of countless rich races in which they would have been freighted with a few more pounds than he liked. His son and successor, H. A. "Jimmy" Jones, allowed the great Citation to carry as much as 130 pounds only four times. The horse lost all four of the races and never won with more than 128 throughout its career. As far as the Joneses were concerned, track handicappers had but one goal in life—to beat Calumet with high weights.

At the bottom of racing's totem pole, Trainer Joe Blow maneuvers for months with an arthritic nag until he finds a cheap race in which the poor thing must carry only 109 pounds. He fires the gun. The horse wins in a walk. Joe Blow feels like a genius. His horse might have whipped the identical field under 119 pounds, but don't try to argue that with Blow. He wants the largest possible bulge in the weights. In a game of perilous uncertainty, weight is something of which he can be sure. Only a fool, says Blow, would think that 109 pounds ain't ten pounds less weight than 119.

The commonsensical belief that a horse is best off with least weight on its back has become a kind of springboard. From it, horsemen, track officials and vast numbers of paying customers dive headlong into error and confusion. "Weight," they say, "brings 'em all together." By this they mean that a competent racing secretary-handicapper can assign weights of such exquisite accuracy that all entrants in a race will have almost exactly equal chances to win. Nonsense.

Condition, class, distance, pace and jockey are factors of such fundamental importance that weight differentials seldom obscure them. Of the 54 races run every week at a major track, the outcome of one or two may be attributable to the effects of weight. In the other 52, weight is one factor among many, and not decisive.

The Scale of Weights

The tabulation on page 220 is the most honored of all the weight formulas. It derives from rulings propounded in the middle of the last century by Admiral John Francis Rous, who was unchallenged czar of British racing. The old salt knew something about Thoroughbreds and a great deal about human beings. His scale put the damper on certain larcenies by using weights to neutralize the natural advantages of older horses over younger, and males over females, at various distances and at various times of year.

It is quite a good scale. It is so good that it virtually eliminates weight as a prime factor in weight-for-age stakes races. When both horses are weighted according to the scale, victory in a contest between a three-year-old and a four-year-old invariably goes to the animal that rates best on the distance, condition, class, pace and jockey factors. To observe that this probably would remain true if the scale's weight differentials were lowered or increased by a pound or two does not belittle the admiral's accomplishment.

When assigning weights for handicaps, or in writing conditions for allowance and claiming races, track officials employ the scale's guidelines, but seldom its exact poundages. For example, the conditions of a

Jockey Club Scale of Weights

(a) The following weights are carried when the weights are not stated in the conditions of the race.

Distance	Age	Jan.	Feb.	Mar.	April	May	June	July	Aug.	Sept.	Oct.	Nov.	Dec.
Half Mile	Two years	x	x	x	x	x	x	x	105	108	111	114	114
	Three years	117	117	119	119	121	123	125	126	127	128	129	129
	Four years	130	130	130	130	130	130	130	130	130	130	130	130
	Five years & up	130	130	130	130	130	130	130	130	130	130	130	130
Six Furlongs	Two years	x	x	x	x	x	x	x	102	105	108	111	111
	Three years	114	114	117	117	119	121	123	125	126	127	128	128
	Four years	129	129	130	130	130	130	130	130	130	130	130	130
	Five years & up	130	130	130	130	130	130	130	130	130	130	130	130
One Mile	Two years	x	x	x	x	x	x	x	x	96	99	102	102
	Three years	107	107	111	111	113	115	117	119	121	122	123	123
	Four years	127	127	128	128	127	126	126	126	126	126	126	126
	Five years & up	128	128	128	128	127	126	126	126	126	126	126	126
One and a Quarter Miles	Two years	x	x	x	x	x	x	x	x	x	x	x	x
	Three years	101	101	107	107	111	113	116	118	120	121	122	122
	Four years	125	125	127	127	127	126	126	126	126	126	126	126
	Five years & up	127	127	127	127	127	126	126	126	126	126	126	126
One and a Half Miles	Two years	x	x	x	x	x	x	x	x	x	x	x	x
	Three years	98	98	104	104	108	111	114	117	119	121	122	122
	Four years	124	124	126	126	126	126	126	126	126	126	126	126
	Five years & up	126	126	126	126	126	126	126	126	126	126	126	126
Two Miles	Three years	96	96	102	102	106	109	112	114	117	119	120	120
	Four years	124	124	126	126	126	126	126	125	125	124	124	124
	Five years & up	126	126	126	126	126	126	126	125	125	124	124	124

(b) In races of intermediate lengths, the weights for the shorter distance are carried.

(c) In races exclusively for three-year-olds or four-year-olds, the weight is 126 lbs., and in races exclusively for two-year-olds, it is 122 lbs.

(d) In all races except handicaps and races where the conditions expressly state to the contrary, the scale of weights is less, by the following: for fillies two years old, 3 lbs.; for mares three years old and upward, 5 lbs. before September 1, and 3 lbs. thereafter.

(e) Welterweights are 28 lbs. added to the weight for age.

(f) In all overnight races except handicaps, not more than six pounds may be deducted from the scale of weights for age, except for allowances, but in no case shall the total allowances of any type reduce the lowest weight below 101 lbs., except that this minimum weight need not apply to two-year-olds or three-year-olds when racing with older horses.

(g) In all handicaps which close more than 72 hours prior to the race the top weight shall not be less than 126 lbs., except that in handicaps for fillies and mares, the top weight shall not be less than 126 lbs. less the sex allowance at the time the race is run; and scale weight for fillies and mares or three-year-olds may be used for open handicaps as minimum top weight in place of 126 lbs.

(h) In all overnight handicaps and in all claiming handicaps, the top weight shall not be less than 122 lbs.

(i) In all overnight races for two-year-olds, for three-year-olds, or for four-year-olds and upward the minimum weight shall be 112 pounds, subject to sex and apprentice allowances. This rule shall not apply to handicaps, nor to races for three-year-olds and upward.

typical allowance race at six furlongs in April stipulate basic weights of 113 pounds for three-year-olds and 126 for older horses. Non-winners of a certain number of races, or of races of a specified value, get lighter imposts than these. But the deductions are made from the basic weights, acording to the age of each horse. The purpose of using 113 and 126 instead of the official scale's 117 and 130 is to make the proposition more attractive to trainers. It allows mediocre older horses to run under weights they are able to carry.

There can be no doubt that the differentials suggested by the official scale of weights are highly useful in the management of the sport. They bestow rules and standards on an area where chaos and chicanery might otherwise prevail. But there is no magic in them. They are far from precise in their effects on Thoroughbred performance. They do not begin to nullify class and condition—nor are they intended to.

Some horsemen complain that the scale is considerably off base in its treatment of four-year-olds during the early months of the year. They argue, with considerable justice, that it is unfair to require these young horses to run at equal weights with older, stronger animals in March, April, May and June.

The complaint would be worth acting on if significant numbers of races found horses running under weights at all close to the basic age differentials prescribed by the official scale. But factors like class, consistency and form are *also* embodied in the eligibility conditions of races. By the time weight concessions have been granted for failures to win, or for entry at slightly lower claiming prices, or for lower earnings, the extra poundage which a trainer might regard as unfair to his four-year-old has been compensated.

Handicappers' Weight Formulas

Because weights are precisely measurable, are an integral part of the eligibility conditions of every race, and are much on the mind of every horseman, efforts have been made to develop formulas expressing the effects of poundage on running time. One set of formulas is widely accepted among racing secretaries, newspaper selectors, trainers and players, many of whom concede it the authority of Holy Writ:

1. **Four extra pounds of weight slows a horse by one fifth of a second, or one full length, in a sprint.**
2. **Three extra pounds have the same effect at a mile.**
3. **Two extra pounds have the same effect at a mile and an eighth.**
4. **One extra pound has the same effect at a mile and a quarter.**

It may be so. But nobody can prove it. Horses are living beings whose fitness and mood improve or deteriorate from day to day according to the fluctuations of the individual form cycle. Condition, class, pace and jockey invariably are so decisive in the running of a race that the effects of small differences in weight become less exact than the formulas pretend.

Horse "A" loses by a neck under 115 pounds this week. Next week, under 110, the creature runs the same distance in the same time, losing by five lengths. Or runs slower and wins. Horse "B" does three quarters in 1.11⅗ under 112 pounds this week, losing to a classier animal. Next week, with 119, he beats his own kind in 1.11 flat. Someone who pays close attention to the weight formula at the expense of other factors condemns himself to grief.

Where the weight formula is more useful is in the work of racing secretaries. Like the official scale of weights, the formula has the virtue of being orderly. It is as good an aid as any in the process of deciding how many pounds to assign to each horse entered in a handicap race. Traditionally, and justly, the horse that has been winning the biggest races is burdened with higher and higher weight in each succeeding effort. The horses that have been chasing him get less and less. When one of them finally beats him, weight may be to blame—especially if he has been required to carry genuinely high weight. More often, however, his handlers refuse to run him under really heavy imposts. He loses simply because he has reached the downcurve of his form cycle, and something else not only has rounded into shape but is able to demonstrate it under a low impost.

Weight in Handicap Races

The handicap race is the supreme test of the theory that "weight brings 'em all together." Here the racing secretary has comparatively free rein. The only limitation on his experiments is the reluctance of certain barns to accept high weights. He sometimes solves the problem by assigning their champion horses the minimum top weight allowable under the rules of racing, and lightens the weights on all other entrants as much as necessary to provide a reasonable handicap.

If his calculations result in a close finish, he not only is good at his work, but lucky. Weight does not bring 'em all together. Not even in handicaps.

I have just reviewed the charts of the 100 richest handicap races run in the United States during 1965. They dispel for all time the theory that weight differentials come close to equalizing the chances of horses whose class, condition, jockeys and pace and distance preferences are unequal.

If the theory were valid, horses carrying the highest weights in each handicap field would win no more races than horses carrying the lowest weight. But here is what actually happened in 100 races:

1. **Horses carrying the lowest weight in their fields won only two of the 100 races and finished in the money in only 18.**
2. **Horses carrying the highest weight in their fields won 32 of the races and finished in the money in 59.**
3. **Horses carrying the highest weight finished last in only seven of the races.**
4. **Horses carrying the lowest weight finished last in 26 of the races.**

These statistics indicate most strongly that the weight concessions given to inferior horses and the weight penalties imposed on better horses do not cancel the more fundamental factors of class, condition, pace and jockey.

That an indeterminate number of the high-weighted losers might have done better with lower weights is undeniable. Yet, of 18 horses high-weighted at 126 pounds, only six ran out of the money and six won. Of five high-weighted at 127, one ran out of the money and one won—the others finishing second or third, of course. Of three horses high-weighted at 130, one won and the other two ran in the money. Of three high-weighted at 131, two ran out of the money. Affectionately, the only horse weighted with as much as 137 pounds in handicap competition during the year, won her race.

Handsome Boy, 116 pounds, defeats the mighty Buckpasser, who carried 136, in the 1967 Brooklyn Handicap at Aqueduct.   UPI PHOTO

A perhaps more convincing indicator of the failure of weight to "bring 'em all together" is the margin of victory that separates the typical handicap winner from the horses that pursue him. Of the 100 leading handicaps during 1965, only 36 were won by a margin of half a length or less. And in only 26 of the races was the last horse to cross the finish line as close as 15 lengths to the winner! The usual gap was about 30 lengths, weights notwithstanding!

When Weight Counts

As the results of handicap races demonstrate, large weight concessions rarely make winners of outclassed or unfit horses. The principle stands up in all kinds of races, including the cheapest claimers.

For this reason, the expert turns his attention to weight only after deciding which horses are in decent form, are not outclassed, are suited to the distance and, therefore, qualify as contenders. At this point, the following ideas become helpful:

1. Weight usually is no factor in two-year-old races at less than six furlongs. If the fastest animal gets in with as many as five pounds less than its leading rivals and is being handled by a good rider, the bet becomes more inviting. But weight spreads large enough to neutralize superior speed are unheard of in these short dashes.

2. Three-year-old and older horses, and two-year-olds entered at distances of six furlongs and beyond, vary in their weight-carrying ability. If well-placed as to class, distance, condition and pace, and if assigned a weight no higher than it has carried in previous strong performances, a horse can be backed confidently, regardless of any weight concessions to other entrants. But if the horse has never run well at today's distance when carrying as much weight as it is assigned today, it probably is a bad bet. This is especially true of front-running horses with a tendency to tire in the stretch. It is almost equally true of one-run horses that win only by coming from far off the pace.

3. If today's weight is higher than the horse has ever carried in the past, but if the assigned weight is below 120 pounds, the player checks to see how the horse has fared with three or four pounds less. Is it the kind of cheapie that seems comfortable only with 114 and below? Does it die in the final stages whenever it has 116 or more? If it seems a fairly courageous runner, and qualifies on other counts, it usually can be conceded ability to carry four or five pounds more than it has ever won with in the past—provided today's race is a sprint. At longer distances, three pounds is an equally safe assumption.

Quick Pitch shows that weight is not everything by carrying 172 pounds to victory over the jumps at Aqueduct in 1967. **UPI PHOTO**

The mighty Citation, shown winning the 1948 Kentucky Derby, never won a race when carrying more than 128 pounds. **UPI PHOTO**

4. For most horses, 120 pounds is the beginning of difficulty at any distance. Except for young, sharp animals of allowance quality or better, no horse should be granted ability to carry 120 or more unless (a) it has already done so with aplomb in a race of today's distance or longer, or (b) it has run a powerful, reasonably recent race at the distance or longer, under 118 or more.

5. In races at a mile or longer, weights in excess of 120 pounds become most burdensome. A horse entered in a race of that kind under such an impost can be backed with confidence only if (a) it has demonstrated its ability to tote the load, (b) it is in superb form and does not come to the race off a recent tough effort under similar high poundage, and (c) no other fit animal of equal class has a weight advantage of five pounds or more.

6. In races at a mile or more, it pays to keep an eye peeled for weight shifts. Assuming that Horse "A" had a five-pound advantage when it beat "B" by a nose last week, "B" deserves consideration if the advantage is canceled or reversed today.

7. At any distance, weight in excess of 120 pounds becomes additionally unfortunate if the track is muddy or slow or heavy, and other contenders have lighter burdens.

8. A horse running with less weight than it carried in its last race should be viewed with extra respect when it qualifies on the distance, form and class factors. Trainers being poundage-conscious, today's weight shift, however slight, may represent opportunity to the barn.

9. If the track announcer reports that a horse will carry two pounds or more in excess of the weight prescribed in the conditions of the race, the horse is probably out for exercise. Being weight-watchers, horsemen want every pound of advantage they can scrounge, and do not ordinarily accept the services of an overweight jockey on a day when the horse has a good chance to win.

10. If the track announcer says that the horse will carry one pound of overweight, the player has reason to suspect the physical fitness of the rider. Presumably the horse has a good chance—or the player would be paying no attention to it. Presumably the rider has tried to make the low weight to which the horse is entitled. If he has failed by a pound, he may be woozy-headed from dehydration. Has he been winning many races lately? If he has been in a slump, his weight problem may be the answer. The horse should be viewed with extreme caution.

11. If a trainer waives an apprentice weight allowance in order to put a leading rider on his horse, the bettor should perk up and take notice.

On the other hand, if the trainer has switched from a hot apprentice to a run-of-the-mill boy who never has won with the horse, the player should beware.

12. Except in dealing with races over a distance of ground among extremely well-matched horses of superior class, it is a waste of time to worry about weight shifts or weight advantages of less than three pounds. A pound or two does not make that much difference, but other factors do.

13. When in doubt as to the weight-bearing ability of your leading contender, pass the race.

12 The Speed Factor

HORSEMEN AGREE that most Thoroughbreds are unable to maintain full speed for more than three-eighths of a mile. When three-furlong baby races were a standard feature of January and February programs, the player who put his money on the previously demonstrated speed could expect to be right seven or eight times out of ten.

As distances lengthen, the ability of horses to run full tilt does not. Courage, endurance, nimbleness and responsiveness to the rider come into play. Day in and day out, relatively slow horses defeat faster ones by running more efficiently and with greater determination.

In racing parlance, a "speed horse" is the kind that leaves the starting barrier swiftly and contends for the lead at once. It performs best when allowed to set the early pace without serious challenge, running well within its limits and consuming its fuel gradually enough to have some left at the end. Its past-performance record is full of one's and two's—at least at the early calls of its races.

Players who understand the peculiarities of Thoroughbred speed, and the role played by speed horses, pay a great deal of attention to early pace. They are known as pace handicappers. We shall get to them in the next chapter. In preparation, we now discuss the outlook and methods of their country cousins— the large, loyal, somewhat mystical cult of speed handicappers.

The Theory of Speed

Theories of speed handicapping derive from an undeniable fact: The winning horse is the one that gets to the finish wire in the shortest time. The faster he gets there, the better he is, the speed handicappers say. The ultimate demonstration of class and condition, they assert, is the time it takes the horse to run the race. Accordingly, they concentrate on final time—the minutes, seconds and fractions of seconds that measure the interval between start and finish. Everything else is secondary.

I sometimes think that speed handicappers have more fun than anybody. For them, the game is an arithmetical pastime. Its subtleties, contradictions and intangibles are digested in speed charts, supplemented by formulas for calculating the significance of weight, beaten lengths and variable track conditions. The charts and formulas award each horse a number. The one with the best number becomes the choice.

This approach is most popular, and understandably so, wherever the racing favors pace-setting speed horses. For example, speed handicappers flourish at bull-ring tracks, which feature short sprints around sharp turns. The horse with the fastest final time at these minor ovals is usually a comparatively sound front-runner. Given reasonable readiness, an even break in the weights, and an inside post position today, he can be expected to break on top, save ground by monopolizing the rail on the turns, and lead from wire to wire. The speed handicapper will cash tickets, having been tipped off by his charts.

For another example, many of the top public selectors and high-rolling punters in Southern California are expert speed handicappers. The running surfaces at Del Mar, Hollywood Park and Santa Anita are exceptionally fast. At distances up to seven furlongs, sharply conditioned front-runners tire much less noticeably than on the deeper, holding tracks of the conservative East. Early pace has comparatively slight effect on the outcome of such California races. The horses require less sophisticated jockeying. The animal with the fastest previous final time, or the fastest recent final time, may still be in form, a good bet.

At tracks like Aqueduct, Saratoga and Bowie, which have long home-stretches and deeper footing, early pace is a primary factor. Come-from-out-of-it horses have a good chance to win, if the pace is favorable to them. Previous final times are, therefore, an uncertain guide. The player needs more information than that. Speed handicapping is disdained. Howard Rowe, a New Yorker, once quipped in *American Turf Monthly,* "Very few speed handicappers are lolling in loot . . . In fact, one of them we know is rarely permitted out of the attic, and steadfastly maintains that he is Martin Van Buren."

This chapter and the next will supply ample basis for decision as to whether speed handicapping should be embraced, ignored, or perhaps adapted in part to the reader's own methods. For now, it might be a good idea to list situations in which the use of final time is uncontroversial. A handicapper of any persuasion should find final time useful for the following purposes:

1. As an indicator of a horse's suitability to a particular distance (see pages 142-144).

2. As an indicator of improving or deteriorating form (see pages 172 and 175).

3. As the most reliable means of handicapping short sprints for two-year-olds (see pages 140-142).

4. As an occasional indicator of class (see pages 190-191).

How Speed Handicappers Work

Speed handicappers deal in numbers. Beginning with the final time of a previous race, they use their charts and formulas to produce a numerical rating which embodies that time figure and modifies it to compensate for beaten lengths, today's assigned weight, the relative slowness or speed of the track on which the race was run, and, perhaps, the manner in which the horse ran.

Some speed handicappers attend to the form factor by refusing to consider any animal that has not been to the post in ten days or two weeks, or whatever other standard of late action inspires them with confidence. They then consider only the horse's latest race. Or, if the race was unimpressive for some excusable reason, they use the next previous one. Other speed handicappers, after invoking a standard of late action, look for the fastest race in the animal's entire record, and base their figures on its final time.

Many speed handicappers pay no attention whatever to the distance factor. Their charts purport to show how quickly a horse should cover any distance, given its final time at any other. More realistic types believe that a horse should be rated only on the basis of a race not more than a furlong shorter or longer than today's. Relatively few use the distance factor as rigorously as this book recommends in Chapter 8. In truth, California tracks are so kindly to a pace-setting horse that it is not at all unreasonable to expect a winner at six furlongs to hold his speed for seven. This happens in the East less often, and should rarely be expected there unless the horse is the type that gains authoritatively in the stretch of the shorter race.

Most speed handicappers trouble themselves not at all with class. Final time, they say, is a reflection of class, just as it is of everything else that goes into the making of a winner. Rather than split hairs about class and condition, worrying whether the one will outfoot the other, they throw the whole thing into their arithmetical meat-grinder and accept the figures that emerge from the other end.

Lest anyone think I am being unfair, let me hasten to acknowledge that good speed handicappers hold their own with any other kind. What makes the good ones successful, of course, is that they regard their charts and formulas as conveniences, rather than as gospel. By whatever route they follow to their final speed ratings, they are careful to attend to the fundamentals of handicapping. Their results are sometimes down-right astonishing, as when the guy in the seat next to you at Del Mar shows you that his handicap figures predicted the exact order of finish in an eight-horse race.

As to the ability of less thoughtful speed handicappers to survive at the track, all I can say is that their comparative success demonstrates that any orderly procedure—even a somewhat irrational one—gives the player of this game a fair chance to overcome a large part of the 17 per-cent loss that befalls random guessers and stabbers.

Speed and Class

In Chapter 10 I observed that horses usually generate maximum speed and fastest final times when challenged by animals of equal class. But a $7,500 horse may defeat a $5,000 one in time that would not tax the abilities of a $3,500 one.

Although class differences explain the outcome of a substantial frac-tion of races, and occasionally cause untypically slow final times, an orderly pattern exists. All responsible studies of the final times of races show that races of higher purse value tend to be run more quickly than races of lower value.

I once riffled through an entire season of Aqueduct result charts and found that the average $5,000 claiming race on a fast track at six fur-longs was run in about 1.11⅘. The average $10,000 claimer was about two fifths of a second faster. The average allowance race was almost a second faster than the $10,000 claimer. Averages being unreliable, I took due note of the *range* of final times in each category. As might have been expected, some $5,000 claimers were faster than some $10,000 ones. But the majority clustered around 1.11⅘, whereas the majority of the better claimers were about two ticks swifter.

If a large preponderance of $10,000 races were exactly two or three fifths more rapid than an equal preponderance of $5,000 races, it might be reasonable to credit any horse with superior class on the simple evi-dence that it has run two or three fifths faster than its rival. This, of course, is not always reasonable, but it is what speed handicappers do, whether they spell it out in such terms or not. Moreover, their weight computations sometimes involve numbers large enough to cancel what-ever genuine class differences may have been reflected in their original speed ratings. On my desk is an assortment of speed charts and speed-weight formulas that allow the unwary player to rate a $3,500 horse above a $7,000 one, simply ignoring the class factor, and trusting the clock and the weights.

Am I saying that some speed handicappers bet their money on out-classed horses? I most certainly am. At half-mile tracks, of course, speed and current sharpness are the main determinants of victory, and class is often nonexistent, or close to it. In California, class is most definitely a factor, but is perhaps not so formidable at sprint distances as it is in the East.

At distances of a mile and beyond, by the way, the best speed handi-cappers suspend their arithmetical operations sufficiently to take heed of class, stamina and pace, which are fundamental factors in the outcome of longer races. In this respect, their methods vary in no essential par-ticular from the methods of more conventional handicappers.

U. S. Speed Records

Distance	Time	Horse, Age, Weight	Track	Date
3f	.33½	Atoka (6) 105	Butte, Mont.	9/7/06
3½f	.39	Deep Sun (7) 120	ShD*	7/11/59
4f	.45	Beau Madison (2) 120	TuP	3/30/67
4f	.45	Another Nell (2) 113	Spt	5/8/67
4½f	.50⅖	Kathryn's Doll (2) 111	TuP	4/9/67
5f	.55⅖	Zip Pocket (3) 122	TuP	4/22/67
5½f	1.01⅗	Zip Pocket (3) 129	TuP	11/19/67
6f	1.07⅖	Zip Pocket (2) 120	TuP	12/4/66
6½f	1.14⅖	Sandy Fleet (4) 122	Lga	8/14/66
7f	1.20	El Drag (4) 115	Hol	5/21/55
		Native Diver (6) 126	Hol	5/22/65
7½f	1.29	Aurecolt (3) 122	CD	11/12/57
1m	1.32⅗	Buckpasser (3) 125	AP	6/25/66
1m70y	1.38⅘	Drill Site (5) 115	GS	10/12/64
1¹⁄₁₆	1.39	Swaps (4) 130	Hol	6/23/56
1⅛	1.46⅖	Bug Brush (4) 113	SA	2/14/59
		Colorado King (5) 119	Hol	7/4/64
1³⁄₁₆	1.52⅗	Fleet Bird (4) 123	GG	10/24/53
1¼	1.58⅕	Noor (5) 127	GG	6/24/50
1⅜	2.14⅕	Man o' War (3) 126	Bel	6/12/20
1½	2.26⅕	Going Abroad (4) 116	Aqu	10/12/64
1⅝	2.38⅕	Swaps (4) 130	Hol	7/25/56
1¾	2.52⅘	Noor (5) 117	SA	3/4/50
1⅞	3.13⅘	Pharawell (5) 119	GP	4/8/47
2m	3.19⅕	Kelso (7) 124	Aqu	10/31/64
2¼	3.47	Fenelon (4) 119	Bel	10/4/41
2½	4.14⅗	Miss Grillo (6) 118	Pim	11/12/48
2¾	4.48⅗	Shot Put (4) 126	Was	8/14/40

* Abbreviations of track names explained on page 461.

U.S. Turf-Race Records

Distance	Time	Horse, Age, Weight	Track	Date
5f	.57⅖	Sikkim (4) 122	LrL	11/21/67
5½f	1.02⅗	Isaduchess (4) 109	Atl	8/13/65
6f	1.09⅖	Benedicto (4) 112	Was	6/17/59
		Benedicto (4) 119	Was	6/26/59
7f	1.21⅗	Dead Ahead (3) 114	Bel	10/20/62
7½f	1.31⅖	Star Duke (5) 112	RD	8/30/65
1m	1.34	Portsmouth (3) 116	Lrl	10/30/65
1m70y	1.40⅕	Oink (7) 116	AP	5/23/64
		Conte Jondo II (5) 118	AP	8/1/64
1¹⁄₁₆	1.39⅘	Pretense (4) 128	Hol	6/17/67
1⅛	1.46⅗	Geechee Lou (5) 112	SA	1/2/61
		Kelso (7) 118	Sar	8/27/64
1³⁄₁₆	1.53⅖	Round Table (5) 132	AP	8/22/59
1¼	1.53⅖	Round Table (5) 132	SA†	1/24/59
1⅜	2.12⅖	Cool Prince (5) 114	Del	7/3/65
1½	2.23⅘	Kelso (7) 126	Lrl	11/11/64
1⅝	2.38⅗	Quick Pitch (4) 117	Sar	8/28/64
1¾	2.58⅖	Roborante (8) 126	RD	9/3/66
1⅞	3.11⅘	El Moro (8) 116	Del	7/22/63
2m	3.25⅖	Penaway (5) 118	AP	7/24/53

* Abbreviations of track names explained on page 461.
† Downhill turf course.

How Many Lengths Per Second?

Races are timed in fifths of seconds. Traditionally, a Thoroughbred is thought to cover its own length in a fifth of a second. Most speed handicappers use that equation in calculating a losing horse's final time. If the beast finished four lengths behind a winner clocked in 1.12, its own time is recorded as 1.12⅘.

Like so many other widely accepted traditions of this unbelievable game, the one-fifth-per-second theory is utterly wrong. Its only virtue is convenience. It allows the player to think in terms of fifths. Five lengths per second. The horse beaten six lengths is one and one-fifth second behind the winner. And so forth. Very convenient.

But horses happen to drive across the finish line more rapidly than that. At the finish of a sprint, good horses travel at a rate close to seven lengths per second. In longer races, or among cheaper horses, or for any horse—winner or loser—that may be tiring and shortening its stride at the finish, the rate is about six lengths per second. The animal that moves as slowly as five lengths per second—one fifth per length—is the horse that is only loping, having dropped out of contention.

In case anyone cares to check this out, let him understand that a length is between eight and nine feet. Horsemen prefer nine, but eight is closer to the fact. To travel at the rate of five lengths per second, a nine-foot horse must slow down to 14.6 seconds per furlong (660 feet). Milk wagons move faster than that. No matter how long the distance, or how cheap the competition, the contending animals cross the finish line much more rapidly. And the finish line is, of course, where the final time is recorded and the speed handicapper does his work.

On the assumption that anyone who wants to tinker with speed handicapping should have better charts and formulas than are generally available, I have composed some especially for this book. They permit the player to crank out speed ratings which respect actuality. They are based on the notion that a horse travels across the finish line at a rate of about six lengths per second. This is not accurate in all cases, of course, but is 20 percent closer to reality than the conventional one-length-per-fifth theory.

Speed Charts

All speed charts embody the principle of parallel time. By grace of a logic that collapses under the slightest scrutiny, they show that a horse that travels six furlongs in a final time of such-and-so should go a mile and a quarter in so-and-so. Charts differ from each other by as much as two seconds in their separate versions of this phenomenon. I shouldn't wonder. No power on earth can predict how fast any horse will run in competition at a new distance.

I urge the reader not to use this book's speed charts in that way. Today's horses should be rated off races at today's distance. To stretch a point, they can be rated off races not more than a furlong longer or shorter than today's.

The experienced speed handicapper will note with some surprise that the charts award 12 points for each fifth of a second of running time. Most charts are laid out in intervals of 5, 10, 50 or 100 points, depending on preference. The reason for designing the present charts in units of twelve is mathematical. With 60 points allowed for each full second of running time, it becomes easy to work out a formula for beaten lengths. If a full second of running time is equal to 60 points, and a horse covers six lengths in a second, it can be seen that one length—equal to a sixth of a second—is worth 10 points. No complicated arithmetic is required. The formula is clearly presented with the charts.

To those who hope to use the charts for best effect, I make the following suggestions:

1. Eliminate all outdistanced, outclassed, and out-of-form horses by applying standards set forth earlier in this book.

2. Rate each surviving contender off the winner's final time in its most recent good race, but do not be afraid to use a race run last season at this track, as explained on page 145.

3. If tempted to rate the horse off a race run at another track, adjust its rating by using the track-speed compensation method described below.

4. Use the beaten-lengths and weight-shift formulas to arrive at a final rating.

5. Test the method on paper for weeks before risking a dime on it. In fact, if your natural habitat is the East Coast, read the next chapter, on pace, before deciding whether to bother with speed handicapping at all.

Track-Speed Adjustments

Players who want to try speed ratings based on races at tracks other than their own must compensate for the differences in speed between the two racing surfaces. Because the footing changes from day to day at all tracks, accuracy is impossible. However, useful compensations can be made by referring to the monthly tabulations in which *Turf and Sport Digest* publishes the best times of recent races at all distances at all leading ovals.

If the best time at *your* track turns out to be *slower* than the best time recorded over the same distance at the out-of-town track, *the rating for the out-of-town race must be lowered.* For example, if the difference is two fifths of a second, the rating for the out-of-town race would be lowered by 24 points. Or, *if the out-of-town track is slower than your own by a full second,* the rating for the race would be *increased* by 60 points —12 points per fifth.

No effort is made to supply a table of comparative track speeds in this book because such information becomes obsolete within weeks.

Daily Speed Variants

The sun shines bright. The track is fast. A detachment of $8,000 animals races a mile in 1.39⅗, breaking no records. A week later, sun still shining, track still fast, the same field runs the same distance in 1.37⅗. Why?

Any number of reasons. Fluctuations in the form cycle, for instance. Horses that pressed the pace last week may drop out of contention sooner this week, giving the winner an easier time. Or a rider's strategy may misfire. Attempting to reserve his stretch-running mount until the last possible moment, he finds himself without racing room at the quarter pole. By the time he navigates to an opening, the horse has thrown in the towel. It declines to run another yard, and allows the early leader to stagger home alone.

Speed handicappers pay little heed to such nuances in the actual running of a race, but are alert as hawks to variations in final time. While

Speed Chart for Races with One Turn

Half *Mile	Basic Rating	5f	5½f	6f	6½f	7f	1m
.43	500	—	—	1.08	1.14—2	1.20—2	1.33
—1	488	.56	1.02	—1	—3	—3	—1
—2	476	—1	—2	—2	—4	—4	—2
—3	464	—2	—2	—3	1.15	1.21	—3
—4	452	—3	—3	—4	—1	—1	—4
.44	440	—4	—4	1.09	—2	—2	1.34
—1	428	.57	1.03	—1	—3	—3	—1
—2	416	—1	—1	—2	—4	—4	—2
—3	404	—2	—2	—3	1.16	1.22	—3
—4	392	—3	—3	—4	—1	—1	—4
.45	380	—4	—4	1.10	—2	—2	1.35
—1	368	.58	1.04	—1	—3	—3	—1
—2	356	—1	—1	—2	—4	—4	—2
—3	344	—2	—2	—3	1.17	1.23	—3
—4	332	—3	—3	—4	—1	—1	—4
.46	320	—4	—4	1.11	—2	—2	1.36
—1	308	.59	1.05	—1	—3	—3	—1
—2	296	—1	—1	—2	—4	—4	—2
—3	284	—2	—2	—3	1.18	1.24	—3
—4	272	—3	—3	—4	—1	—1	—4
.47	260	—4	—4	1.12	—2	—2	1.37
—1	248	1.00	1.06	—1	—3	—3	—1
—2	236	—1	—1	—2	—4	—4	—2
—3	224	—2	—2	—3	1.19	1.25	—3
—4	212	—3	—3	—4	—1	—1	—4
.48	200	—4	—4	1.13	—2	—2	1.38
—1	188	1.01	1.07	—1	—3	—3	—1
—2	176	—1	—1	—2	—4	—4	—2
—3	164	—2	—2	—3	1.20	1.26	—3
—4	152	—3	—3	—4	—1	—1	—4
.49	140	—4	—4	1.14	—2	—2	1.39
—1	128	1.02	1.08	—1	—3	—3	—1
—2	116	—1	—1	—2	—4	—4	—2
—3	104	—2	—2	—3	1.21	1.27	—3
—4	92	—3	—3	—4	—1	—1	—4
.50	80	—4	—4	1.15	—2	—2	1.40
—1	68	1.03	1.09	—1	—3	—3	—1
—2	56	—1	—1	—2	—4	—4	—2
—3	44	—2	—2	—3	1.22	1.28	—3
—4	32	—3	—3	—4	—1	—1	—4
.51	20	—4	—4	1.16	—2	—2	1.41

Adjustments

If the horse **lost**, reduce the basic rating of its race by 10 points for every beaten length; 5 points per half-length; 3 points per quarter-length or neck.

If the horse won easily, increase its basic rating by 10 points; 5 points if it won handily; 3 points if it won ridden out. If it won driving and is running in a higher class today, treat any lengths it lost in the stretch as beaten lengths, and lower its basic rating.

Reduce the horse's rating by 3 points a pound if it is to carry more weight today than in the rated race. If it is to carry less weight, increase the rating by 3 points a pound.

* For use in pace handicapping. See page 259.

Speed Chart for Races with Two Turns

Basic Rating	1m	1-70	1 1/16	1 1/8	1 3/16	1 1/4
572	1.33—1	—	1.39—4	1.46—3	1.53—1	1.59—2
560	—2	—	1.40	—4	—2	—3
548	—3	—	—1	1.47	—3	—4
536	—4	1.39	—2	—1	—4	2.00
524	1.34	—1	—3	—2	1.54	—1
512	—1	—2	—4	—3	—1	—2
500	—2	—3	1.41	—4	—2	—3
488	—3	—4	—1	1.48	—3	—4
476	—4	1.40	—2	—1	—4	2.01
464	1.35	—1	—3	—2	1.55	—1
452	—1	—2	—4	—3	—1	—2
440	—2	—3	1.42	—4	—2	—3
428	—3	—4	—1	1.49	—3	—4
416	—4	1.41	—2	—1	—4	2.02
404	1.36	—1	—3	—2	1.56	—1
392	—1	—2	—4	—3	—1	—2
380	—2	—3	1.43	—4	—2	—3
368	—3	—4	—1	1.50	—3	—4
356	—4	1.42	—2	—1	—4	2.03
344	1.37	—1	—3	—2	1.57	—1
332	—1	—2	—4	—3	—1	—2
320	—2	—3	1.44	—4	—2	—3
308	—3	—4	—1	1.51	—3	—4
296	—4	1.43	—2	—1	—4	2.04
284	1.38	—1	—3	—2	1.58	—1
272	—1	—2	—4	—3	—1	—2
260	—2	—3	1.45	—4	—2	—3
248	—3	—4	—1	1.52	—3	—4
236	—4	1.44	—2	—1	—4	2.05
224	1.39	—1	—3	—2	1.59	—1
212	—1	—2	—4	—3	—1	—2
200	—2	—3	1.46	—4	—2	—3
188	—3	—4	—1	1.53	—3	—4
176	—4	1.45	—2	—1	—4	2.06
164	1.40	—1	—3	—2	2.00	—1
152	—1	—2	—4	—3	—1	—2
140	—2	—3	1.47	—4	—2	—3
128	—3	—4	—1	1.54	—3	—4
116	—4	1.46	—2	—1	—4	2.07
104	1.41	—1	—3	—2	2.01	—1
92	—1	—2	—4	—3	—1	—2
80	—2	—3	1.48	—4	—2	—3
68	—3	—4	—1	1.55	—3	—4
56	—4	1.47	—2	—1	—4	2.08
44	1.42	—1	—3	—2	2.02	—1
32	—1	—2	—4	—3	—1	—2
20	—2	—3	1.49	—4	—2	—3

Adjustments

If the horse **lost,** reduce the basic rating of its race by 10 points for every beaten length; 5 points per half-length; 3 points per quarter-length or neck.

If the horse won easily, increase its basic rating by 10 points; 5 points if it won handily; 3 points if it won ridden out. If it won driving and is running in a higher class today, treat any lengths it lost in the stretch as beaten lengths, and lower its basic rating.

If the horse is to carry more weight than in the rated race, lower the rating by 4 points a pound if today's race is shorter than 1 1/8; 6 points a pound if today's is 1 1/8 or 1 3/16; 12 points a pound if today's race is 1 1/4 miles.

overlooking the effects of running style and racing strategy on their figures, they make careful adjustments for the effects of weather and the changing texture of the racing surface. The effort of calculating these daily track-speed variants is vital to their success. It protects them from crediting an undeserved edge in speed to some nag whose apparently swift final time was a result of lightning-fast footing rather than any great swift of its own. It protects them from assuming that a horse with slow final time is off its feed—if the track was slower than usual on the day the horse ran. And, most important, by making allowances for these external influences, the process helps the speed fanciers to recognize the horse whose recent speed at the distance has actually been fastest. This, of course, is the goal of speed handicapping.

It is forgivable to complain, as I do, that pace or class may annul an advantage in speed. But it would be idiotic to pretend that an expert speed handicapper who knows how to calculate track variants cannot stay ahead of the game. The horse with the best previous final time at the distance (after adjustments for weights and variants) wins often enough.

Daily variations in track speed result from combinations of the following circumstances:

1. Moisture on or near the surface of the racing strip. Even when labeled "fast," a track may be considerably slower than usual. On other days, it may be faster than usual.

2. When the maintenance crew harrows the surface, it becomes deeper than usual, producing slower final times.

3. After the track is rolled, the hard-packed surface permits greater speed.

4. As the season advances, hooves exert an effect similar to that of motor-driven rollers, compressing the surface. Faster clockings result.

5. High winds slow or accelerate horses, just as they affect anything else that moves.

6. The intense humidity of midsummer depletes the stamina and jangles the nerves of Thoroughbreds, affecting their running time.

Calculating the Variant

The most familiar method of computing daily track variants is to compare the final time of each race with the track record for the distance. Simple arithmetic then discloses the *average* number of fifths by which a day's races fell short of the records. Thus, if *The Morning Telegraph* past-performance line contains the figure 82-14, the player knows that the horse ran $18\frac{4}{5}$ slower than the track record ($82 + 18 = 100$) on a day when the average winner ran $2\frac{4}{5}$ seconds behind the record ($14\frac{4}{5} = 2\frac{4}{5}$). Many players add the 82 and the 14, crediting the horse with a 96. Naturally, they prefer horses that rate at 101 or better, believing that a sign of sharpness is the ability to come closer to the track record than the day's average winner did.

The difficulty of the published variants is that they rise and fall not only with changes in the holding properties of the racing strip but with variations in the quality of the day's racing. All other things being reasonably equal, the official track variant is higher on a Tuesday than on a Saturday. The Saturday average is affected by races among top-grade animals able to run closer to record times than Tuesday horses do. Accordingly, a player might tend to underrate the performance of a $3,500 horse that earns a perfectly nice 80 on a Saturday, when the track variant is only 12. By the same token, he tends to overrate the performance of a good allowance horse that logs an unremarkable 88 on a Tuesday, when the track variant is 22.

To avoid the inevitable penalties of using track variants that fail to differentiate the effects of moisture or harrowing on final time from the effects of low-grade racing, conscientious speed handicappers calculate their own track variants. They make adjustments for the distance of each race and the quality of its field. In no area of handicapping are players more resourceful, or their formulas more complicated.

There is no easy way to do it well. The simplest of the genuinely useful methods begins with a session in the library. Go through last season's charts of the results at your track. Ignore all occasions on which the track was labeled anything but fast. Write down the *distance, purse or class, and final time* of every race except grass and jump races. Record two-year-old and maiden races separately.

If you use purse sizes to separate your class categories at a big-league track, it is a good idea to peg them at $500 intervals up to about $7,000. From that amount to $12,000, the categories can be $1,000 apart. Above $12,000, a $6,000 spread is all right, ending with a top class of $25,000 or over.

In using claiming-price brackets, a typical breakdown in top-flight racing would be $3,500 or below; $4,000-$4,500; $5,000-$6,000; $6,500-$7,500; $8,000-$9,500; $10,000-$12,000; $12,500-$15,000; over $15,000 plus allowance races with a purse value of $8,000 or less; better allowance races; handicaps; stakes. The top claiming price stated in the conditions of each race would determine the class of the race.

The next step is to determine the most typical running time in each class-distance category. To do this, you should begin with the categories in which you have jotted down at least five examples each. In some you may have ten or more. Start with those. For example, if you have a dozen figures for $5,000 claiming races at six furlongs, and most of the figures are between 1.11$\frac{4}{5}$ and 1.12$\frac{2}{5}$, you know immediately that the usual time for such a race at your track is 1.12 or 1.12$\frac{1}{5}$. The occasional 1.13$\frac{4}{5}$ or 1.11 is untypical and should not affect your reckoning.

After you scan the most crowded class-distance categories and assign typical final times to each, a pattern should become clear. At each dis-

Buckpasser sets a new world record for the mile—1.32⅘—in winning the 1966 Arlington Classic. Creme de la Creme was second. **UPI PHOTO**

tance, the times should improve as class increases. Do not accept any sample that makes the usual final time in one class grouping faster than the time in the next higher grouping. Chances are 100 to 1 that the sample is too small. Do not be afraid to raise or lower the figures in any category by a fifth to make them logical. Example: You might find that the time for $4,500 animals is 1.11, and is no higher for $6,000 ones, but that the $7,500 class rates at 1.10⅘. Simply make the $6,000 figure 1.10⅘.

Very well. You emerge from the library with a splitting headache and a page of invaluable figures—typical times for each distance and each class of horse at your home track. After making one simple adjustment, you will be ready to approximate the inherent speed of the racing strip on every day of the next meeting. The adjustment consists of increasing the typical final-time figure in each class-distance category by two full seconds, converting them from typical times to par times. The sole reason for doing this is to guarantee that the final times of most races will be faster than par. If par were closer to reality, some races would be slower and some faster, requiring complicated arithmetic later on.

Here is how to use the par figures to work up your daily track variant:

1. At the end of each racing day, note the number of fifths of a second by which the final time of each race failed to equal par in its class-distance category (almost always, the time will be faster than par).

2. After the nine figures are written down, divide them into two lists —one for races around one turn, the other for races around two turns.

3. Add the numbers on each list. Then divide each sum by the number of items on its list. The resultant averages are the day's track variant for distance races and the day's variant for sprints.

4. Adjust the official final time of each sprint race by adding the daily sprint variant. Add the daily route variant to the final time of each route race. Enter the adjusted times in a notebook.

5. When computing speed ratings, use the adjusted times instead of the official times.

The only problem likely to arise with this method—aside from that of remembering to keep the records up to date—occurs on days when the track has only one route race on its program. If the difference between the final time of that race and par for its class-distance category is within two or three fifths of the day's sprint variant, you are probably home free. If in doubt, check back to see what the route variant has been on other days when the sprint variant was the same as today's, and be guided accordingly.

–An excellent, time-saving substitute for all the labor of computing par times and daily variants is supplied by an ingenious slide rule called Amer-Var. It is printed on the back of another gadget, Ray Taulbot's Pace Calculator, with which it sells for $20 at *American Turf Monthly*. Although its class-distance figures are compromises which may be out of kilter to some extent at certain distances on some tracks, Amer-Var comes close enough to get the job done more than adequately.

Handicapping Two-Year-Old Dashes

Whether one uses daily variants or not, the best way to handicap two-year-old races at five and a half furlongs or less is to pick the animal that has run the distance most swiftly in the past. I am aware that I have said this repeatedly in earlier chapters, but I think an example belongs in a chapter on speed.

In the fifth at Monmouth Park on July 8, 1966, the favorite was Jean-Pierre, trained by the formidable Frank Bonsal. The colt had shown determination, but little early foot, in three five-furlong races at Dela-

Start of a six-furlong race at Aqueduct, where early speed often lasts to the finish wire.   NEW YORK RACING ASSN.

5th Monmouth

Start
5½ FURLONGS
MONMOUTH PARK
Finish

5 1-2 FURLONGS. (I'm For More, June 9, 1961, 1.03⅘, 2, 112.)
Maidens. Special weight. Purse $3,500. Colts and geldings. 2-year-olds. Weight 118 lbs. (Sapling nominees preferred.)

Broker John

Dk. b. or br. c (1964–Va), by Bagdad—Treasure Trove II, by Nearco — **118** — 1966 4 M 1 0 $1,120

G. Ring — J. W. Garth — (J. A. Radney)

1Jly 66-5Mth fst 5½f .22⅕ .45⅗1.05⅖ Md Sp Wt 1 4 55½ 512 47½ 28 GPatterson 118 4.50 82–15 In Reality 1188 Broker John 118½ Fiddler's Green 118¾ Rallied 12

3Jun66-3Mth fst 5½f .22⅖ .46⅖1.05⅖ Md Sp Wt 2 6 33 34 45½ 45 SBoulmetis 118 11.60 85–15 Gallant Moment 1182 Rhiwin 1181 All At Sea 1182 Even effort 12

26May66-2GS sly 5f .22⅘ .47 .59⅖ Md Sp Wt 2 4 22 35½ 48 413 SBoulmetis 117 4.50 79–24 Futura Bold 1173 All At Sea 1174½ Martial Eagle 1175 Gave way 8

13May66-4GS fst 5f .22⅗ .46⅘ .59 Md Sp Wt 3 5 61¼ 86¼ 67 67¾ SBoulmetis 117 9.10 86–17 Royal Malabar 1172½ Columnist 1171¼ Bucks County 117no No threat 11

LATEST WORKOUTS Jun 28 Mth 4f fst .49⅕ b — Jun 10 Mth 3f fst .37 b — Jun 2 Mth 3f fst .38 b — May 23 GS 4f sl .49⅗ b

Cord of Wood

Dk. b. or br. c (1964–Fla.), by Correlation—Woodcate, by Case Ace — **118** — 1966 2 M 0 1 $350

R. Metcalf — R. Metcalf — (J. C. Dudley-B. M. Heath)

16Jun66-3Mth fst 5f .22⅗ .46⅘ .59⅗ Md 10000 1 4 53 68½ 67½ 58¼ JVelasquez 118 3.90 84–17 Stick Up 1184½ Lexingtonian 1181½ That Guy 1072 No mishap 12

9Jun66-1Mth fst 5½f .22⅘ .47⅕1.07⅖ Md 10000 3 9 67¼ 67¼ 52½ 32½ JVelasquez 118 8.20 77–17 Big Hat 1182 Tank Tiger 118½ Cord of Wood 1183 Mild late bid 12

LATEST WORKOUTS Jun 30 Mth 4f fst .49 b — Jun 26 Mth 5f fst 1.02 b — Jun 22 Mth 5f fst 1.03 bg — Jun 14 Mth 3f gd .37⅖ b

Pointsman

B. rig (1964–Fla), by Bolivar II—Aquamarine, by Star Pilot — **118** — 1966 7 M 1 0 $850

P. Bongarzone — P. Bongarzone — (Cavanaugh-Associates, Inc.)

1Jly 66-5Mth fst 5½f .22⅕ .45⅗1.05⅖ Md Sp Wt 12 10 1114 816 612 610 BPearl 118 7.80 80–15 In Reality 1188 Broker John 118½ Fiddler's Green 118¾ No factor 12

23Jun66-4Mth fst 5f .22⅗ .47 1.00⅗ Md Sp Wt 4 11 116 99¼ 67 2nk BPearl 118 15.80 87–14 King Gordius 118nk Pointsman 1181 Mount Pelion 118¾ Sharp 12

10Jun66-5Mth fst 5½f .23⅖ .48 1.07⅕ Md Sp Wt 7 7 66½ 88 55½ 55½ SHernandez 118 25.80 75–21 All At Sea 1181½ Columnist 1181¼ Stockpile 118nk Never close 12

18May66-3GS sly 5f .23 .47⅖1.00⅗ Md Sp Wt 1 7 78 611 69½ 65¾ RMcCurdy 117 26.50 80–19 Forward Charge 1171½ Dollar Moore 117¾ Rhiwin 117½ No factor 8

7May66-3GS fst 5f .22 .45⅘ .58⅘ Md Sp Wt 1 11 1212 1217 914 79¼ RMcCurdy 117 34.70 89–10 Bold Point1171½ Milady's Man117no Royal Malabar1172½ Sluggish 12

22Apr66-3GP fst 5f .23⅕ .47⅘1.01⅖ Md Sp Wt 5 7 78¼ 53¼ 43½ 43½ TBarrow 120 44.40 77–23 d-Fastpack 120h Thread 117no Your It 1173½ Raced evenly in drive 9

11Apr66-3GP fst 5f .22⅘ .47⅖1.00⅖ Md Sp Wt 11 11 109 1010 97½ 911 MSolomone 119 80.10 75–21 Mr. Purpose119½ Fastpack 1191 d-Commodore Cobh 1191 No speed 12

LATEST WORKOUTS Jun 29 Mth 4f fst .50 b — May 28 GS 3f sly .36⅗ b — May 16 GS 3f fst .36 b

Mafioso

Ch c (1964–Mass), by Backbone—In Content, by Greek Song — **118** — 1966 0 M 0 0 —

Mrs. R. Pollara — L. Murray — (Dr. L. Pollara)

LATEST WORKOUTS Jly 6 Mth 3f fst .38 b — Jly 1 Mth 6f fst 1.16 bg — Jun 27 Mth 4f fst .49⅘ b — Jun 22 Mth 5f fst 1.04 bg

Jean-Pierre

Ch. c (1964–Ky), by Prince John—Evilone, by Tom Fool — **118** — 1966 3 M 1 1 $1,050

T. S. Nichols — F. A. Bonsal — (T. S. Nichols)

13Jun66-4Del fst 5f .22⅗ .48⅕1.00⅕ Md Sp Wt 5 6 79¼ 67 61¾ 22½ TLee 120 3.30 85–18 Bridge Hand 1202½ Jean-Pierre 1203 Tudor House 1201¾ Wide 7

7Jun66-5Del fst 5f .23⅗ .47⅕1.00 Md Sp Wt 1 10 97¼ 97¼ 76¼ 34¾ TLee 120 10.50 84–17 Godfather 1204 Bridge Hand 120¾ Jean-Pierre 120¾ Rallied 11

17May66-3Pim fst 5f .23 .47 .59⅘ Md Sp Wt 7 11 1118 1115 1014 1012 JGiovanni 120 *1.00e 83–16 Kar-Stan 117nk Mr.Albemarle 1204 China Bay 1203 No factor 11

LATEST WORKOUTS Jly 4 Del 5f fst 1.02⅖ b — Jun 27 Del 4f fst .49 b — Jun 21 Del 5f fst 1.02⅖ b — Jun 12 Del 3f fst .36⅘ b

Fuel King

B. c (1964–Fla), by Bolinas Boy—Oil Show, by Ponder — **118** — 1966 0 M 0 0 —

A.-J. Pepino — J. Pepino — (Farnsworth Farm)

LATEST WORKOUTS Jly 7 Mth 3f fst .36⅕ hg — Jly 3 Mth 5f fst 1.02 b — Jun 27 Mth 5f fst 1.01⅗ hg — Jun 22 Mth 5f fst 1.03⅗ b

Marais

Ch. c (1964—NJ), by Decathlon—Sly Sheila, by Crafty Admiral — **118** — 1966 1 M 0 0 —

Acorn Farm — A. J. Zolman — (Acorn Farm)

23Jun66-4Mth fst 5f .22⅗ .47 1.00⅗ Md Sp Wt 6 12 Outdistanced RMcCurdy 118 40.40 — King Gordius 118nk Pointsman 1181 Mount Pelion 118¾ Far back 12

LATEST WORKOUTS Jly 7 Mth 3f fst .36⅗ b — Jun 17 Mth 5f fst 1.04 bg

Panajoy B. c (1964–Ky), by Panacean—Gadilla, by Arctic Prince 118 1966 1 M 0 0 —
Hi'l-N-Dale Farm F. J. Baker (Mrs. R. Winer)
25Jun66-1Mth fst 5f .22⅗ .46⅗ .59⅖ Md Sp Wt 3 5 65¾ 611 69¾ 59¼ RMcCurdy 118 33.80 84–13 Lord Robert 118no By the Numbers 1186 Rupin 1181½ No factor 11
LATEST WORKOUTS Jun 30 Mth 3f fst .37 b

Winslow Homer Dk. b. or br. c (1964–Va). by Sailor—Blade of Grass, by Nasrullah 118 1966 2 M 0 0 —
Rokeby Stable E. Burch (P. Mellon)
1Jly 66-5Aqu fst 5½f.22⅖ .46⅖1.05⅗ Md Sp Wt 10 9 64 78¼ 811 67¾ KKnapp b 122 13.40 77–19 Top Bid 122o Gay Lord Flynn 122¾ Seance 117nk Never a threat 12
17Jun66-5Aqu fst 5½f.22⅕ .46 1.05⅗ Md Sp Wt 8 8 910 1118 1017 916 ACordero 122 5.40 69–22 Favorable Turn 12212 Lift Off 122no Top Bid 122no Raced greenly 12
LATEST WORKOUTS Jun 30 Bel m.t. 3f fst .36 h Jun 27 Bel m.t. 5f fst 1.00⅕ hg Jun 22 Bel m.t. 3f fst .37⅕ b Jun 14 Bel m.t. 5f fst 1.00 hg

That Guy B. c (1964–Ky), by Charlie's Song—Happy Birthday, by Jamestown 118 1966 1 M 0 1 $350
P. D. De Paul C. L. Robbins (Mereworth Farm)
16Jun66-3Mth fst 5f .22⅗ .46⅘ .59⅗ Md 9000 10 3 42 31½ 21½ 36 CMcPeek7 b 107 17.90 86–17 Stick Up 1184½ Lexingtonian 1181½ That Guy 1072 Faltered stretch 12
LATEST WORKOUTS Jly 3 Mth 5f fst 1.00⅗ h Jun 29 Mth 3f fst .37 b Jun 25 Mth 6f fst 1.15 h Jun 21 Mth 3f fst .37 b

Results of 5th Race Monmouth—July 8th, 1966

FIFTH RACE 3 1-2 FURLONGS. (I'm For More, June 9, 1961, 1.03⅘, 2, 112.)
Mth - 28059 Maidens. Special weight. Purse $3,500. Colts and geldings. 2-year-olds. Weight 118 lbs. (Sapling nominees preferred.)
July 8, 1966

Value to winner $2,275, second $700, third $350, fourth $175. Mutuel pool $188,689.

Index	Horse	Eqt	A	Wt	PP	St	¼	½	Str	Fin	Jockey	Owner	Odds $1
28005Mth2	—Broker John		2	118	1	2	3h	32	1h	1h	G Patterson	G Ring	3.90
28005Mth6	—Pointsman		2	118	3	6	53	2½	21	23	J Velasquez	P Bongazone	7.00
28005Aqu6	—WinslowHomer	b	2	118	8	8	71	83	41	3h	D Brumf'ld	Rokeby Stable	3.10
27802Mth5	—Cord of Wood	b	2	118	2	5	41	4½	31	4nk	B Phelps	R Metcalf	13.90
27794Del2	—Jean-Pierre		2	118	5	4	8½	7h	53	56	C Baltazar	T S Nichols	2.80
27857Mth	—Marais		2	118	7	7	62	51	61	61	K Korte	Acorn Farm	52.40
	—Fuel King		2	118	6	9	9	9	71	71	R McCurdy	A-J Pepino	9.00
	—Mafioso		2	118	4	3	22	62	81	83	R Br'ussard	Mrs Rose Pollara	19.30
27802Mth3	—That Guy	b	2	118	9	1	11	11	9	9	H Block	P DePaul	8.80

Time .22⅗, .47, .59⅘, 1.06⅗. Track fast.

$2 Mutuel Prices:

1-BROKER JOHN	9.80	5.00	3.40
3-POINTSMAN		6.60	4.20
8-WINSLOW HOMER			3.80

Dk. b. or br. g, by Bagdad—Treasure Trove II, by Nearco. Trainer J. W. Garth. Bred by J. A. Radney (Va.).

IN GATE AT 359. OFF AT 3.59½ EASTERN DAYLIGHT TIME. Start good. Won driving.

BROKER JOHN unhurried while within striking distance of the early pacemakers responded to urging entering the home lane and outgamed POINTSMAN in the concluding strides. POINTSMAN worked his way up gradually to engage the leaders dueled with BROKER JOHN through the home lane but was not quite enough. WINSLOW HOMER, rallied in the late stages after lacking early foot. CORD OF WOOD turned in a fair effort. JEAN-PIERRE lacked the necessary speed. MARAIS was outrun. FUEL KING raced greenly. MAFIOSO showed nothing. THAT GUY set the pace for a half-mile then wilted.

Scratched—27872Mth5 Panajoy.

Courtesy of The Morning Telegraph

ware and Pimlico. It had never raced at Monmouth and had not worked out there.

The second favorite was a Sailor colt, Winslow Homer, trained by Elliott Burch. The youngster had shown nothing in two Aqueduct tries, although a couple of its Belmont workouts had been good. If anyone was willing to assume that today's company would be less formidable than Winslow Homer had been facing in New York, he would also have to assume that the colt was itself superior, would wake up, show some early speed, and get there in time on a strange track.

The third favorite, and logical choice, was Broker John, which had shown a good, even turn of speed at the distance on June 3, and had come back only a week ago to run a strong final quarter after being shuffled back in the early stages. Nothing else in the field had come close to Broker John's 1.06⅗ (or if you prefer six lengths per second—1.06⅙) on this or any other track. Horses of this type are reliable bets.

A dedicated speed handicapper would have been delighted by the result of the July 6th race. Broker John won in exactly 1.06⅗.

Final Warnings

At its best, conventional speed handicapping works fairly well. But any careful player can do better *without* entangling himself in the rigamarole of numerical charts and weight formulas. At its worst, speed handicapping seduces the player into suspending his thought processes. Under the spell, he allows numerical tabulations to substitute for alert study of the temperament, physical condition, class, distance preference and pace aptitude of the horse.

I think it significant that Eastern players have always found Southern California—heartland of the speed handicappers—the softest touch in the game of racing. Easterners pick no higher percentage of winners than usual when they invade Hollywood Park, Santa Anita or Del Mar, but the mutuel prices are out of this world. The local talent, using speed-weight-beaten-length formulas, or taking advice from persons who do, seem hypnotized by the horse with the fastest, most recent race. Someone who pays closer attention than that to the fundamentals of handicapping gets excellent prices on other horses after recoiling in horror from the overworked, wilted specimens on which Californians blow the bundle. Time and again, the West Coast crowd overlooks an improving horse on grounds that it has not been getting to the wire as rapidly as the favorite. Or is picking up a few pounds.

So much for speed handicapping. Now to a more substantial undertaking—pace.

13 The Pace Factor

ASK ANY COMPETENT TRAINER of Thoroughbreds what strategy he would employ with a ready miler on a day when it meets its own kind at its favorite distance. He replies with a shrug: "How do the other horses run? How does my horse run?"

Racing strategy is entirely a matter of pace, which is determined mainly by the running styles of the contestants and partly by class, condition, distance and weights. After a horse wins a truly run race, the trainer knows that his strategy was correct. The player with the negotiable mutuel ticket knows that his own handicapping was correct. And they both know that, in the particular circumstances of the particular race, the class, condition, distance preferences, weights and running styles of the other horses were advantageous to the winner. In other words, he was a ready Thoroughbred, well placed.

Because pace is the very crux of the trainer's pre-race calculations, it should occupy no lesser position in the mind of the player. No matter what school of handicapping thought may claim his loyalty, his results improve as soon as he budgets a few minutes of intelligent attention for a study of pace.

This applies with special emphasis to speed handicappers, whose arithmetic takes place on the outskirts of pace handicapping. The mutuel machines are invariably kinder to the speed fancier who makes no bet unless reasonably sure that the pace of the race will help his choice to run back to its best previous clockings.

Pace wins the race. Sprint races are won or lost in the first half-mile. Longer races are won or lost in the first three-quarters. This remains true whether the ultimate winner be a front-runner which leads all the way, or a stretch-runner which steams out of the pack to win in the last jump. The pace analyst looks for the horse able to set or overcome the fastest probable early pace without tiring too badly in the homestretch. It is as starkly simple as that.

How Pace Works

In the last chapter I observed that Thoroughbreds are able to produce top speed for ·about three furlongs. The rider's problem is to consume this energy efficiently. His ability to do so is limited by the physique and temperament of his mount, which govern its racing style.

The cheap front-runner has only one way of going—lickety-split from the gate and decelerating from exhaustion in the last quarter-mile.

Better front-runners can be rated on the lead, restrained just enough to avoid premature fatigue while staying in front.

The familiar "one-run" horse allows itself to be rated behind the pace and then expends its strength in a single burst—losing if the jockey lets it run too soon, or if he waits too long, or cannot find racing room, or if the leader simply ran too fast and too far.

A really useful horse of rare versatility may be able to lead from wire to wire in some races, or run slightly behind the early pace in others, allowing the rider to adapt to the demands of the situation.

The rider is limited not only by his mount's style, but by the effect on the horse of the way its opponents run. The most fortunate front-runner on a program is the one whose trainer has managed to enter it in a field which includes no other front-runner of equal class, condition and intrinsic speed. Unless the horse is the hopelessly rank sort that shoots its load in the first half-mile and then loses interest, the jockey can expect to win. He wins by rating the beast, allowing it to run just quickly enough to stay in front, but slowly enough to have plenty left in the stretch. But even a rank quitter can win once in a while, when its early lead is too great for the plodders to overcome.

Any front-runner encounters trouble when opposed by another front-runner or two of equal or superior class. In such contests of early speed, the outclassed horse gives way two or three seconds after it is challenged. The other two, if equally matched, usually cook each other before the eighth pole is reached, and the winner is something that has run slightly behind the pace, awaiting its turn. Or, in some sprints and most longer races of this kind, the winner may be an animal that was many lengths off the early pace but improved its position on the hometurn until within striking distance at the eighth pole.

In any truly run race, let it be remembered, superior class tells the tale. A horse with a decided class advantage wins if it is in shape to do so, no matter whether it is a front-runner or a stretch-runner. If a front-runner, it pickles all the other front-runners and has enough left to win.

If it prefers to run behind the early pace, it turns on the engine in the stretch and leaves everything else behind, like a Buckpasser or Kelso.

Without a pronounced edge in class, the stretch-gainer wins its race pretty much by default, long before the final turn for home. It wins by staying sufficiently close to the early leaders and waiting for them to beat each other. Quite often, they have no choice. Should one of them slow down in the early running, in an attempt to conserve strength, its front-running rival would invariably do the same. When both slow down too noticeably, the shrewd rider of an off-pace horse smells the rat, speeds up, takes the lead ahead of schedule and holds it to the wire. Eddie Arcaro used to do that sort of thing at every opportunity.

The Right Track

Most Thoroughbreds being prisoners of their own running styles, breeders and owners select their stock with an eye to exploiting the differences. Speed horses are found in greatest profusion at tracks that favor early speed. Horses with more stamina are in demand where the finishing kick has a better chance at the gravy. The front-runner has a slight extra advantage at relatively fast tracks with relatively short homestretches. Such plants include Bay Meadows, Del Mar, Detroit, Garden State, Golden Gate Fields, Hollywood, Longacres, Rockingham Park, Santa Anita, Tropical Park and Turf Paradise. The thin top cushions and springy foundations of most such strips enable pace-setting horses to hold their speed for longer distances. The short homestretches allow come-from-behinders minimum time and space in which to uncoil and catch up.

At the opposite extreme are tracks with deeper, slower, more holding surfaces and longer homestretches. Horses that come on at the end have an advantage at Beulah Park, Bowie, Churchill Downs, Fair Grounds, Hawthorne, Laurel, Pimlico, Saratoga and Suffolk Downs.

No great advantage is enjoyed by any specific type of horse at Aqueduct, Arlington Park, Delaware Park, Gulfstream, Hialeah, Monmouth Park or Keeneland, where footing and contours are well balanced. When such tracks are on the fast side, front-runners rule the roost. When the footing slows down a bit, the stretch-runners improve.

The Illusion of Stretch Speed

Because the rider who falls too far behind the early pace invites everyone else to run away from him and hide, the fast start has become a fundamental of the sport. Precious speed is spent in the rush from the gate and the duel for favorable position at the head of the line, and/or on the rail, and/or on the dry center of the strip, or wherever the riders want to be.

The finish being a product of what took place earlier, practically all races are run more rapidly in the beginning than at the end. Most players are unaware of this. But it is crucial to an understanding of pace and of jockeying.

The front-runners in a typical six-furlong sprint at Aqueduct cover the first quarter-mile in less than 23 seconds. They require at least 25 seconds to run the final quarter. Whenever a horse runs the last quarter in .24 it rates headlines.

The sensational sight of a Thoroughbred coming on strong to pass four or five others in the stretch is mostly optical illusion. It obviously is running faster than the others. But it may actually be slowing down: It passes its rivals because they are "backing up"—decelerating more rapidly. Whether slowing down or not, the stretch-gainer in no circumstances runs as rapidly as it did in earlier stages of the race. If it manages to win, its victory is attributable not only to its class, condition and rider, but to the inability of earlier leaders to keep going.

The optical illusion deserves further comment. A come-from-behind type that wins in 1.11⅗ very possibly ran the first quarter in .23⅗, the second in .23⅗ and the last in .24⅖. This is what the racing brotherhood knows as an "even race." The horse holds its stride comfortably all the way to the stretch and loses relatively little motor power when it gets there. To the crowd in the stand the horse may seem to be flying, but it is not. Good riders run such races on good horses. Riders like Bill Shoemaker, Braulio Baeza, Manuel Ycaza, Laffit Pincay, Jr., Bill Boland, Avelino Gomez, Howard Grant, John L. Rotz, Milo Valenzuela and other masters of pace do it frequently. A speed-minded, whip-conscious public chews its fingernails and unburdens itself of oaths when such a horse loses by a nose, wondering why the boy did not let it run sooner. But pace is tyrannical. Energy expended earlier is unavailable later. When Shoemaker wins or loses by a nose, it is an odds-on bet that a whoop-de-doo rider would have lost by lengths, having wasted the horse prematurely.

Varieties of Pace Handicapping

The public confuses pace with speed. Some persons who call themselves pace handicappers are no such thing. They are speed handicappers. Rather than study the records for a clue as to the possible pace of the race, they use ordinary speed charts and deal entirely with final time. Some of the charts are known as "average pace" charts, on the assumption that the horse with the best final time has covered each yard of ground at the swiftest average pace. This is beyond refute: As final time improves the horse can be said to run the distance at a faster rate, or pace. But this is word-mongering. "Average pace" is merely a different way of expressing final time. It has nothing to do with the running style of any Thoroughbred, and is no help whatever to a player who cares to figure out how today's race may be run.

Confusion about the meanings of speed (or final time) and pace may explain why Damon Runyon pinned the label, "Speed Boys," on the brilliant pace handicapper Jule Fink and his colleagues. Fink specialized, and still does, in cashing large bets on speed horses. But he bets them only after analyzing the pace and satisfying himself that the speed horse has a bettable chance of remaining in one piece all the way.

Many practitioners of pace handicapping concentrate their attention on the two, three or four horses in the race that seem to deserve the highest pace ratings. By whatever methods they assign such ratings, they single out the best of the lot and ignore everything else. For some reason, they usually rate the horses indiscriminately, on the basis of races run anywhere, in any year, at any distance. Their choice, more often than not, is the highest-rated animal whose recent record suggests that the trainer may be trying. They hit enormous mutuel prices. But their indifference to distance, current class and the fine points of form produces a lamentably high percentage of losers.

A somewhat more rational group tosses out entrants that have not raced in the last week or two, accepts the rest as contenders, and pace rates them. Again, little attention is given to class or distance. Speed or pace charts (which are one and the same thing) are used to compare a race at Fair Grounds with one at Suffolk Downs, or a race at Hawthorne with one at Tropical Park. These players also get high prices, but enough losers to condemn them to the scrambler category. The high prices they get are by no means accidental, of course. Any horse that has ever run well enough to deserve a superior pace rating is a threat to jump up and win whenever it gets into shape.

In my view, the most profitable pace handicapping consists of analyzing the running styles of all sharply conditioned horses that are suited to the distance and are neither outclassed nor overweighted. A means of computing numerical pace ratings is often desirable. I shall explain how to do it later. For now, please believe that the key to pace handicapping is to waste no time on animals whose records disqualify them as logical contenders. Pace analysis then becomes a prime means of differentiating one contender from the others.

Analyzing Pace

Let us examine the fractional times and running lines of the best races of two horses.

"A:" $22\frac{2}{5}$ $45\frac{3}{5}$ $1.10\frac{2}{5}$ 4   2 1^2 $1\frac{1}{2}$ $1\frac{1}{2}$ 1no
"B:" $22\frac{2}{5}$ $45\frac{1}{5}$ $1.10\frac{3}{5}$ 5   4 4^3 3^1 $2\frac{1}{2}$ 1^2

Given no important difference in the weights, a conventional speed handicapper or "average pace" handicapper would regard Horse "A" as better by a fifth of a second, or one full length. It broke swiftly, was well in front after a quarter-mile, led at the half in $.45\frac{3}{5}$ and held its lead to the finish, although closely pressed all the way. Horse "B" was not too far off the pace in the early stages (a fact that most speed handicappers and other arithmeticians might overlook), but took a full fifth longer to get home. The believers in charts would go to "A" by a large majority, and would be wrong.

A pace analyst would prefer "B" and would be right. His object, as described earlier, would be to find the animal able to set or overcome the fastest early pace and hold its lick to the end. "B" overcame a half-mile pace of $.45\frac{1}{5}$ and had so much left at the end that it won going away. Its own time to the half-mile was faster than "A's," about $.45\frac{2}{5}$ (figuring six or seven lengths per second). The power of its subsequent performance suggests that it would have enough juice for a stout stretch run even after chasing a pace-setter that did the half in .45 or $.44\frac{4}{5}$. An early pace of that kind would wreck "A." Indeed, it is possible that "B" might pickle "A" shortly after they leave the half-mile pole, and might beat the poor thing by ten lengths. The only kind of front-runner with a reasonable chance against a well-conditioned "B" would be one able to finish comfortably in $1.10\frac{2}{5}$ or better after reaching the half in .45 or better.

For an example of another kind, try this:

"C:" 23   45 $1.23\frac{4}{5}$ 5   2 2^1 2^1 1^1 1^2
"D:" 23 $45\frac{3}{5}$ $1.23\frac{2}{5}$ 3   5 5^5 4^4 3^2 2^1

This time the speed handicapper picks the off-pace horse because its final time is better. But the on-pace horse happens to be the superior risk. "C" was able to run the half in less than $.45\frac{1}{5}$, yet retained enough energy to pull ahead and draw out in the stretch. If his only problem today is "D," he can throttle all the way back to .46 or more, which will make him unbeatable in the stretch. Worse, if "D" tries to stay close to

ASK THE FARE
FAVORABLE TURN
CELTIC AIR
IN REALITY
REASON TO HAIL
GREAT POWER
CLARION
DAMASCUS
MISTY CLOUD
BARBS DELIGHT

14

Proud Clarion and Damascus make their runs at the pace setters at the quarter pole in the 1967 Preakness. Proud Clarion had more stamina that day and scored a smashing victory.   UPI PHOTO

Two front-runners exhaust each other in a typical speed duel at the old Jamaica track.   UPI PHOTO

"C" in the early stages, so as to be in striking range later, he will have less left at the end than he did in his best race. The record shows that "D's" ability to win in 1.23⅗ depends on a relatively slow early pace and the presence of one or two tiring front-runners. But "C" was able to outclass the leader in his own race, and could probably have done 1.23⅗ if pressed through the last eighth of a mile.

Pace-Class Ratings

Numerical ratings help the player to expose fine differences between sharply conditioned contenders. Where one horse enjoys a slight class superiority over another, or seems to, it also may earn a higher pace rating. The two numbers, one for class and the other for pace, confirm the original impression. Or, if the horse with the higher class rating emerges with an inferior pace rating, the player realizes that the contenders are closely matched and seeks other ways to separate them. I would guess that for every player able to encompass such variables without use of pencil and paper, at least five will find that the time spent in working up formal pace-class ratings saves a good deal of confusion and perplexity.

Two principles should be borne in mind:

1. Numerical ratings supplement but do not replace analysis of the running styles, inherent quality, and present form of the horses.

2. Numerical pace ratings seldom are reliable in races longer than 1¹⁄₁₆ miles. As distances stretch out, fractional and final clockings become more than ever a product of conflicting styles, with courage, stamina and readiness contributing much more to the outcome than can possibly be summarized in a numerical formula. The route race goes to the swift *only* when the early pace favors its speed. Far more often than in sprints, races over longer distances find animals with low pace or speed ratings romping ahead of others which have run several seconds faster on other occasions.

Basis of the Class Rating

Means of assigning class ratings to Thoroughbreds were suggested in Chapter 9. For purposes of the present discussion, I shall assume that the player attempts to determine the highest grade of competition in which the individual contender is not outgunned. Most often, the information is found in the past-performance record. Examining the running lines of the animal's best race or races during the present phase of its career, the player should be able to approximate its current class. The most convenient rating method awards the horse a figure of approximately ¹⁄₁₀₀ of the claiming price at which it ran its best race. For instance, if it won at $7,500, its rating would be 75. If its victory or close-up finish was at $3,250, the rating would be 33.

As usual, possession of result charts permits more precise work. The horse that won when entered at $6,500 would deserve a rating of 75 if the result chart revealed that it defeated $7,500 animals in that race.

An alternate method, and a thoroughly good one, is to use the purse values of the races. This is particularly helpful in attempting to rate allowance and handicap runners.

Basis of the Pace Rating

To obtain a numerical expression of the fastest pace that a contender can set or overcome, the player looks for the race with the fastest fractional and final times in which it won or finished close to the winner. At distances up to seven furlongs, the player jots down the half-mile and final time of the race, and the final time of the horse itself. When races at a mile or longer are involved, the three-quarter-mile time and final times are used.

Before taking up the techniques that convert these time figures into ratings, we had better give a minute to the large question of choosing the right race for the purpose.

Some pace handicappers, as noted earlier, do not hesitate to use obsolete races run at irrelevant distances on distant tracks under virtually unknown conditions. They crank the figures through parallel time charts and wait for the money to engulf them. I do not recommend such practices. The race should have been at today's distance. It should have occurred recently enough to indicate that the horse is still able to run that well (see pages 144-145).

Finally, and of the utmost importance, the race should have taken place at the present track or on the present circuit, on a day when the footing was fast.

To compare a race run at today's track with one that occurred a few weeks ago at a sister track on the same circuit, the player must be carefully patient. The tracks may differ considerably, as Saratoga differs from Aqueduct, or Hialeah from Tropical Park. Yet the player can learn the principal differences. For example, all alert New York players know why the courageous front-runner with an inside post position has an edge on a fast or sloppy track in a mile and one eighth race at Aqueduct. The distance to the first turn is only 330 feet. The horse gets out fast, captures the rail position and, before anything else can run with it, the turn has arrived and the horse is saving ground. At Saratoga, the first turn is only 344 feet away from the start of such a race, but the track usually is slightly deeper than Aqueduct's, with a greater tendency to tire front-running animals in the final stages.

Similarly, the New Yorker knows that *mile* races are run from a backstretch chute at Aqueduct, and the horses go around only one turn. But at Saratoga the mile chute discharges the horses onto the clubhouse turn, requiring them to make a half-turn onto the backstretch. This adds a good four fifths of a second to the three-quarter-mile time in a mile race at Saratoga, quite apart from the relative slowness of the track surface during some seasons.

I do not deny that a California player who puts his mind to it can learn as much about Saratoga and Aqueduct as is known by all but the most inexpert New Yorkers. Will he also take the next step and keep daily track-speed variants so that he may be able to make sense of all time figures in the past-performance records of all horses? I seriously doubt it.

Yet, the player who knows a bit about his own circuit, and refuses to attempt numerical ratings of fractional and final times run elsewhere, need not necessarily compile daily variants. They are useful, but one can live without them. The observant player is helped, for example, by the fact that the same horses run at all tracks on the circuit. In handicapping at Monmouth Park, the player takes no great risk if he uses a Garden State race for pace-rating purposes. Chances are the animal ran in that race against some of the stock it faces today. If the race was exceptionally fast or slow, the player knows it from previous experience. A check of the past-performance line or the day's result charts may show that the race was slow because the track was slow, or because some animal led all the way, without much challenge. Likewise, if the track was unusually fast, the published track variant will be lower than usual, and the day's result charts will show that ordinary horses were busting watches all afternoon. He could hardly make the same interpretations of a race run at Arlington Park. Not unless he were a full-time professional.

Let it be assumed, therefore, that the prudent player confines his pace *ratings* to races run on his own circuit. This need not prevent pace *analysis*—assessing the class and running style of an out-of-town horse and deciding how it will affect the pace of today's race.

A player studying a $4,000 claiming race at Rockingham Park might notice that one of the entrants is a New York horse which led all the way in winning a race of similar value at Aqueduct earlier in the season.

How Leading Tracks Differ (1967)

AQUEDUCT (1⅛-mile oval)

Relatively fast surface, stays fast when sloppy. Homestretch: 1,156 feet, gives off-pace horses a good chance when early pace favorable or track slower than usual. Distance from judges' stand to first turn only 330 feet, helping front-runners with inside post positions in 1⅛-mile races. Mile and 7-furlong races start from backstretch chute.

ARLINGTON PARK (1⅛)

Lightning-fast strip slows when wet. Homestretch: 1,029 feet, long enough for sharp late-gaining horses. 1⅛-mile races start only 375 feet from first turn. Mile and 7-furlong backstretch chutes.

ATLANTIC CITY (1⅛)

Rather fast strip, slower when sloppy, but front-runners usually do well. Short homestretch: 947 feet. 1⅛-mile races start 370 feet from clubhouse turn. 1⅛-mile races have good start of 700 feet. 7-furlong backstretch chute.

BELMONT PARK (1½)

The running surface at this glamorous new plant is expected to resemble that of its neighboring sister, Aqueduct.

BOWIE (1)

Relatively slow strip, slower when sloppy. Stretch-runners favored by surface and 1,150-foot homestretch. No mile or 1⅛16-mile races run. 1⅛-milers go 960 feet to first turn. 6- and 7-furlong backstretch chutes, 1¼-mile chute at head of homestretch.

CHURCHILL DOWNS (1)

Fairly deep strip, but not bad when wet. Long homestretch: 1,235 feet. 1⅛16-mile races go 444 feet to first turn. Mile chute on backstretch.

DELAWARE PARK (1)

Fairly deep strip, slower when sloppy. Homestretch: 995 feet, long enough for off-pace horses against tiring front-runners. Mile-and-70-yard races go 535 feet to turn. 6-furlong backstretch, 1¼-mile homestretch chutes.

DEL MAR (1)

Exceptionally fast, slower when wet. Homestretch: 832 feet, giving extra edge to pace-setters. Mile races run 488 feet to first turn. 6-furlong backstretch and 1¼-mile homestretch chutes.

DETROIT (1)

Fast, holds speed well when sloppy. Homestretch: 990 feet. Mile races go only 330 feet to first turn. 6-furlong backstretch and 1¼-mile homestretch chutes.

GARDEN STATE (1)

Fairly fast track, slows when sloppy. Homestretch only 960 feet. 1¹⁄₁₆-mile races go 660 feet to first turn. 6-furlong backstretch and 1¼-mile homestretch chutes.

GOLDEN GATE FIELDS (1)

Exceptionally fast, slower when wet. Homestretch: 1,000 feet but front-runners do well on the hard surface. Mile races start 383 feet from first turn. 6-furlong backstretch and 1¼-mile homestretch chutes.

GULFSTREAM PARK (1)

Fairly fast track, holds speed well when sloppy. Homestretch: 952 feet. 1¹⁄₁₆-mile races start 645 feet from first turn. 7-furlong backstretch chute and, for baby races, 3-furlong homestretch chute.

HAWTHORNE (1)

Fairly fast track, slows when sloppy. Long homestretch: 1,290 feet. 1¹⁄₁₆-mile races start 514 feet from first turn. 6½-furlong chute.

HIALEAH PARK (1⅛)

Relatively fast track, holds speed when sloppy. Homestretch: 1,075 feet. 1¹⁄₁₆-mile races start 655 feet from first turn. 7-furlong backstretch chute and 3-furlong nursery course on homestretch for baby races.

HOLLYWOOD PARK (1)

Exceptionally fast, slows when wet. Short homestretch: 988 feet. Mile races start only 330 feet from first turn. 7-furlong backstretch and 1¼-mile homestretch chute.

KEENELAND (1⅟₁₆)

Relatively fast, slower when wet. Long homestretch: 1,174 feet. 1⅟₁₆-mile races start only 146 feet from first turn. 4½-furlong Headley Course chute onto last turn, 7-furlong chute on backstretch.

LAUREL (1⅛)

Slow track, slower when wet. Homestretch: 1,014 feet, helping off-pace horses. 1⅟₁₆-mile races start only 150 feet from first turn. Mile chute issues onto far end of first turn, near backstretch. Also, 7-furlong backstretch and 1⅜-mile homestretch chutes.

MONMOUTH PARK (1)

Fast track, holds speed quite well when sloppy. Homestretch: 985 feet. Mile races start 440 feet from first turn. 6-furlong backstretch and 1¼-mile homestretch chutes.

PIMLICO (1)

Slow track, slower when wet. Long homestretch: 1,152 feet. 1⅟₁₆-mile races start 492 feet from first turn. 6-furlong backstretch and 1¼-mile homestretch chutes.

SANTA ANITA PARK (1)

Fast track, slower when wet. Homestretch: 990 feet, giving well-placed stretch-runners a fighting chance. 1⅛-mile races start 990 feet from first turn. 6- and 7-furlong backstretch and 3-furlong and 1¼-mile homestretch chutes.

SARATOGA (1⅛)

Rather deep track, but holds speed well when sloppy. Long homestretch, 1,156 feet. 1⅛-mile races start only 344 feet from first turn. Mile chute opens onto midpoint of first turn. 7-furlong backstretch chute.

SUFFOLK DOWNS (1)

Very fast track, slower when sloppy. Homestretch: 1,030, good for off-pace horses. 6-furlong backstretch and 1¼-mile homestretch chutes.

TROPICAL PARK (1)

Unusually fast, slower when wet. Extremely short homestretch, 716 feet, favors front-runners. 1⅟₁₆-mile races start 696 feet from first turn. 6-furlong backstretch and 1¼-mile (approx.) homestretch chutes.

Perhaps the horse also has showed its heels to $5,000 New York stock before tiring in the late stages. Perhaps it ran a nice, even race at an unsuitable distance in its Rockingham debut last week and has been working out frequently. To attempt pace ratings in such a situation would be difficult, for reasons that might as well be repeated: Normal pace at Aqueduct is much different than at Rockingham. The differences are compounded by unknown differences in the quality and running styles of the horses that run at each of the two tracks. But the Rockingham player need not bother with pace ratings. Staring him in the face is an animal that figures to outclass today's competition and run in front from wire to wire, making its own pace.

Class standouts of that kind occur often enough to reward the player who perceives them. On the typical day, however, class is less obvious. The player probably wants to go beyond running style. He wants to see whether subtle but decisive class differentiations can be unearthed through pace ratings.

Computing Pace Ratings

Today's race is a six-furlong affair with a top claiming price of $5,500. Nine entrants have been eliminated for failure to measure up in terms of distance, form, class, sex or consistency. Each of the remaining three horses has run good recent races in $5,000 company and poor races when entered at $6,000. Each therefore earns a class rating of 50.

The best recent race of each at today's track and today's distance is broken into its components:

```
"A:"  .45    1.10  —beaten by 2 lengths
"B:"  .44⅘   1.10⅗—beaten by a nose
"C:"  .45⅘   1.11⅕—won ridden out
```

The simplest method of comparing these performances makes the traditional assumption that one length equals a fifth of a second. The final time of each horse works out as follows:

```
"A:"  1.10⅖
"B:"  1.10⅗
"C:"  1.11⅕
```

Having calculated these individual final times, the player now uses numbers to rate the fractional times of the three races, the final times of the three races, and the final times of the three horses. In each instance, he awards 10 points to the fastest time and deducts a point for each fifth of a second by which other times are slower. Here is how it would work in the present example:

```
"A:"   9 + 10 + 10 = 29
"B:"  10 +  7 +  9 = 26
"C:"   5 +  4 +  6 = 15
```

"B" earned 10 points in the first column, because its race was run in .44⅗ to the half-mile. It got only 7 points in the second column, because the 1.10⅗ final time of its race was three ticks slower than the "A" race. Similarly, "B" gets a 9 in the last column because its own running time in the race was a fifth of a second slower than the final time of "A," who looks like the best bet, at least for now.

A player who cares to undertake a bit more work will be able to make finer distinctions by using the speed charts on pages 236 and 237.

Again, the fractional and final times of the three races are rated. However, instead of using the approximate final times of the horses, beaten-length adjustments are made, as prescribed on the speed charts themselves. The ratings would look like this:

```
"A:"   380 + 380 + 360 = 1120
"B:"   392 + 344 + 344 = 1080
"C:"   332 + 308 + 311 =  951
```

The 311 given to "C" in the third column is the 308 which the chart awards for a final time of 1.11⅕, plus 3 points for a victory, ridden out.

The advantage of the speed-chart method lies in its somewhat more precise six-lengths-per-second formula (as explained on page 233) and its award of bonuses depending on the manner in which a horse won its race.

In using the chart to pace rate races of a mile or more, the three-quarter-mile fractions are awarded whatever number of points the chart would give them if they were final times.

Having computed the pace-rating figures, the player must decide how to interpret them. Before getting into that, he might be interested in reading about some elaborate methods of developing pace-rating figures —methods used by certain successful professionals.

The Pace Handicapper's Notebook

Pace handicappers who keep track of daily speed variants, purse sizes and other such information usually compute a pace rating for every race, every day.

To do this, they use speed charts such as the ones on pages 236-237.

They may even rate quarter-mile clockings, which is extra work but helps clarify things to the maximum. (For work with the charts in this book, a quarter-mile time of 22 would be worth 440—or any other figure the reader prefers, just so he allows 12 points per fifth-second.)

If the track-variant formula announces that the day's racing at a mile was four ticks slower than par, the handicapper raises the official fractional and final clockings in proportion. Those clockings, in case anyone has forgotten, give the time of the race (sprint) at the quarter, the half, the three quarters and the finish. If the player believes, as is most likely, that the track was slower than usual because of dampness, he distributes the four fifths of a second evenly. He increases the official quarter-mile time by a fifth. He adds another fifth to the next quarter-mile—meaning that he increases the half-mile time by an aggregate of two fifths. He adds three fifths to the three-quarter-mile time, and the full four fifths to the final time.

Speed handicappers, being unconcerned with pace, get this part of their work done by slapping the variant onto the final time alone. But the pace handicapper is plagued by the knowledge that *final time is a result of pace*. If the track was four fifths off par, it did not suddenly slow down at the finish wire. Its slowness was operational throughout the race. For that reason, the pace handicapper parcels out his track variant in a realistic way: The entire variant is applied to the final time, and proportionate shares of it are added to or subtracted from fractional times.

If the chart of the race shows that the horses were assisted by a tail wind in the backstretch, or retarded by a head wind, the player may decide to use a larger share of the variant on the early fractions. For that matter, even if the pace handicapper ignores daily variants, he can make profitable allowance for winds by checking result charts and recognizing that the animal that ran the half in .46 against an Aqueduct head wind is at no great disadvantage against one that bettered .45 with a tail wind.

Be that as it may, the pace handicapper's notebook contains a pace rating for every race, compounded of fractional times and variants. Using this book's speed chart, plus columns for the quarter-mile and half-mile calls, the player produces a string of numbers like 254, 268, 280, 268, representing the point value of the fractional and final times. He adds them, getting a total of 1070 for the race. Later, when time comes to give a pace rating to an animal that ran in the race, he awards it the full 1070 if it won, and deducts points at the rate of 10 per length if it lost.

Needless to say, the more simple methods presented earlier can also be extended to include the quarter-mile time in sprints and the quarter and mile times in longer races. I do not think it necessary, however.

At this point I might mention that some players otherwise drawn to pace handicapping but afraid of arithmetic can get the advantages of the one without the discomfort of the other. Ray Taulbot's Pace Calculator is a handy device, sold in combination with the Amer-Var track variant gadget by *American Turf Monthly*. Constructed like a slide rule, it does its own arithmetic, turning out pace-rating figures in terms of the five-lengths-per-second concept.

The only trouble with the Pace Calculator is that it uses *Telegraph* or *Form* speed ratings instead of the final times of the horses. No harm comes of this as long as the player rates only performances that occurred at his own track. If he attempts to use races run elsewhere—even races run at another track on the same circuit—he is well advised to ignore the official speed ratings. They can throw his figures off by many lengths, being based on records set when track conditions may have been vastly different at the out-of-town track than they now are at the local one.

For example, the track record for six furlongs at Atlantic City is 1.08⅗, but the fastest time run there during 1966 was 1.09⅖, suggesting a slower strip. The record at Monmouth Park is also 1.08⅗, but the fastest time there during 1966 was only a fifth slower. A horse that ran 1.11⅖ at Atlantic City would get an official speed rating of 85, but, in light of existing conditions, would deserve at least an 89. A horse that ran in 1.11⅖ at Monmouth would get an 85 and deserve it. To get best results with the Pace Calculator, the player should consider doing at least a little arithmetic. He should compute the horse's actual final time and subtract the best recent time at the distance, as published in *Turf and Sport Digest*. He then should subtract the answer in fifths of a second from 100. The result is a more accurate speed rating. What is more, if the prevailing final times at the local track vary by more than a fifth or two from the recent best times over the same distance at a sister track, the player should be prepared to adjust not only the final but the fractional times by suitable amounts. Otherwise his pace ratings may be far out of phase and, for all practical purposes, not much good.

Interpretation of Ratings

In handicapping the second race at Aqueduct on July 9, 1966, it was possible to eliminate several of the entrants before getting down to the nitty-gritty of pace.

Gay Orchid (the second favorite) was coming off three exceedingly

2d Race Aqueduct

6 FURLONGS AQUEDUCT

6 FURLONGS. (Near Man, July 17, 1963, 1.08⅗, 3, 112.) Claiming. Purse $4,200. 3-year-olds and upward. Weights 3-year-olds 117 lbs., older 123 lbs. Non-winners of two races since April 20 allowed 3 lbs., of a race since then, 6 lbs. Claiming price $6,500. 2 lbs. allowed for each $250 to $6,000. (Races when entered to be claimed for $5,000 or less not considered.)

Gay Orchid $6,000

Br. g (1959), by Oil Capitol—Gay Fairy, by Fairy Manhurst
Mrs. E. S. Lipari   J. Lipari   (W. duPont, Jr.)   108⁵   1966 15   2   6   1 $11,145
                                                                       1965 18   2   0   2 $7,515

2Jly 66-4Aqu	fst 6f .22⅖ .46⅖1.11⅖ Clm	1 5	5²⅖ 4²⅖ 3¹ 2²⅖	ACordero	2.80	82-15 Escobar II 119³⅓ Gay Orchid 115ᵘ⁰ Jay Roger 114ʰ Second best 10
25Jun65-2Aqu	fst 6f .22⅖ .46 1.12⅖ Clm	6 8	8⁵⅖ 7⁵⅓ 4⁵ 2³	ACordero	*2.20	81-17 Rio Coreo 115¾ Gay Orchid 11711 Jay Roger 1141 Belated rally, wide 9
12Jun63-3Aqu	fst 6f .23 .46¾1.12⅖ Clm	6 10	5¹³ 3¹ 2ʰ 2½	HWoodhouse	*2.60	78-19 Sleepy Native 112½ Gay Orchid 117¼ Jay Roger¹114ⁿᵏ Gamely 10
10Jun55-1Aqu	fst 6f .22⅖ .46 1.11⅖ Clm	1 5	4² 4⁴ 6²⁴ 4²½	HWoodhouse	*1.60	81-16 King Salmon 119½ Oribi 114½ Garb¹au 119½ Had no excuses 11
2½May66-4Aqu	fst 6f .22⅖ .45⅖1.11½ Clm	1 5	4² 2⁴ 2³ 1⁵	HWoodhouse	5.20	87-15 Gay Orchid 121⁵ Charge Hill 119¹½ Oribi117½ Drew out easily 7
14May56-3Aqu	fst 1⅛ .47¾s1.13 1.52⅖ Clm	6 1	1 5¹½ 6¹¹ 6²¹	JLRotz	5.20	51-13 Tobir 118¹ Vilcapugio 115² Atom Smasher¹15¹ Fell back early 7
4May56-2Aqu	fst 7f .23⅖ .46³⅖1.25⅖ Clm	8 2	5³ 5⁵¼ 4⁴½ 3⁶	ACordero	6.30	71-20 Royal Victory 117ⁿᵒ Knobs 1176 Gay Orchid 117ⁿᵏ Fair effort 7
27Apr66-2Aqu	fst 7f .23 .46³⅖1.25¹⅖ Clm	7 4	4⅜ 1ʰ 1¼ 53	ACordero	*0.90e	77-18 From theTop108⅓ d–TanGuapo121½ Arranger1171 Tired in drive 10

LATEST WORKOUTS   Jly 8 Mth 3f fst .37 b

Lost Lad X $6,500

Ch. c (1962), by Olympian King—Absent Scholar, by Sir Gallahad III
or Rhodes Scholar   N. Manzi   (Mr.–Mrs. L. R. Shaw)   112⁵   1966 21   0   1   0 $²om
D. B. Schmeck   1965 28   0   5   5 $16,407

30Jun66-5Mth	fst 6f .22⅘ .45⅘1.10¾ Clm	5 5	3¹ 53² 45² ADeSpirito	b 115	19.30	82-18 Third Flyer 1C33 Rhdiom 115¾ Mister Snow Man 1172 No rally 8
24Nov65-9Aqu	my 1 .47⅖s1.12¼s1.39⅘ Clm	5 2	9⅜ 811 814 815 JLRotz	b 115	14.60	54-24 No Snakes 116⅓ Do No Evil 113ⁿᵏ Hail the King 1162½ No fac1or 9
17Nov65-5GS	my 6f .23⅖ .47½s1.13⅖ Cl c	7 6	7⁷ 5⁹¾ 46½ 44½ FLovato	b 114	*1.70	72-27 Court of Law 1143 Babs' Brother 112⅓ Big Manassa 114¼ Dull try 7
10Nov65-2GS	fst 6f .23 .46³⅖1.12³⅖ Clm	1 8	75 9⁵¾ 6⁴¾ 5⁵½ FLovato	b 118	⁴5.60	79-18 Overture 120ⁿᵏ Court of Law 1141 Wild Toss1151½ Some late foot 11
10Nov65—	Dead heat.					
3Nov65-6GS	fst 6f .22⅖ .46 1.11³⅘ Clm	5 5	512 59⅛ 33 24 FLovato	114	5.00	82-21 Boulder M. 1164 Lost Lad 1141¾ Zipperpedium 1131½ Good effort 8
26Oct65-5GS	fst 6f .22⅘ .46 1.11½ Clm	9 1	91¹ 96¼ 67 47 FLovato	120	9.50	82-17 Overture 11431 Boulder M. 1181¼ Mr. Inside 1142½ Passed tired ones 9
19Oct65-4GS	fst 6f .22⅖ .46 1.11½ Clm	8 7	76¼ 5¹½ 53 32 FLovato	114	⁴1.30	85-18 Highly Esteemed 112ʰ Overture 1132 Lost Lad 1141½ Closed well 8
28Jul65-2Atl	fst 7f .23 .46³⅖1.26³⅖ Clm	4 8	72½ 42½ 1¼ 1ʰ FLovato	114	9.60	70-29 Lost Lad 114ʰ Our Mink 1135 Slapstick 1181½ Under brisk drive 10

LATEST WORKOUTS   Jly 8 Mth 3f fst .37 b

Jay Roger $6,000

B. c (1962), by Jet Master—Chickdale, by Jacobs
Estelle S. Swirbul   E. Jacobs   (Mrs.   E. S. Swirbul)   106⁷   1966 13   1   0   3 $2,535
                                                                        1965   5   1   1   0 $3,900

2Jly 66-4Aqu	fst 6f .22⅖ .46⅖1.11⅖ Clm	8 2	4½ 2ʰ 3³½ ECardone⁵	b 114	9.00	82-15 Escobar II 119³⅓ Gay Orchid 115ⁿᵒ Jay Roger 114ʰ Weakened str. 10
25Jun65-2Aqu	fst 6f .22⅖ .46 1.12⅖ Clm	7 1	1¹ 12 12 3³¼ ECardone⁵	b 114	6.00	80-17 Rio Coreo 115¾ Gay Orchid 11711 Jay Roger 1141 Clear lead, weak'd 9
18Jun66-3Aqu	fst 6f .23 .46³⅖1.12⅖ Clm	2 2	3ⁿᵏ 2¼ 3½ 6⁴½ ECardone⁵	b 110	5.30	78-19 Sleepy Native 112½ Gay Orchid 117¼ Jay Roger 114ⁿᵏ Faltered 10
10Jun66-1Aqu	fst 6f .22⅖ .46 1.11⅖ Clm	2 3	1ʰ 1ʰ 6⁴¼ 6⁴½ ECardone⁷	b 117	2.90	79-16 King Salmon 119½ Oribi 114½ Garbeau 119½ Used setting pace 11
7May66-2Aqu	fst 6f .23 .46³⅖1.23³⅖ Clm	3 3	1⁵ 13 13 12½ MYcaza	b 117	2.90	80-17 Jay Roger 117⁵½ Prince Easy Mon 1173 Te 117¼ Under mild urging 8
19Mar66-4Aqu	fst 6f .22⅖ .45⅖1.11⅖ Clm	2 1	1¹ 23 3⁹ 818 JLRotz	b 117	4.10	66-22 Solid Mike 1176 Jovial Twist 112²¼ Arranger 177²¼ Used up 8
14Mar66-4Aqu	fst 6f .22⅖ .45⅖1.11⅖ Clm	10 10	3³½ 11151119 JLRotz	b 117	17.70	71-21 Abuso 115ⁿᵏ Misurata 1171½ MixedUpKid121ⁿᵏ Early foot, tired 12
1Mar66-6Hia	fst 6f .22⅖ .45⅖1.11 Clm	10 10	8¹² 712 712 55 JLRotz	b 114	12.00	84-15 Garwol 116²¼ Bargain Counter 116¼ Cimanyd 116¼ Stride late 12
17Feb66-9Hia	fst 7f .23⅖ .46 1.23⅖ Clm	3 6	52²10⁹ 12¹⁹12¹⁸ JLRotz	b 114	31.30	74-16 Comprehensive 116ʰ Garden King 115¹¼ Rebellious 116ʰ Tired 12
7Feb66-6Hia	fst 6f .22 .44⅖1.10³⅖ Clm	9 2	22¼ 2⅖ 8⁵ JLRotz	b 116	45.20	85-15 Rebellious 114¼ Joe Jolly 118¼ Bully Heart 116¼ Tired 12
1Feb66-9Hia	fst 6f .22½ .45½1.10¾ Allowance	4 2	2¼ 23 ⁵9 815 MVenezia	b 113	56.90	76-23 Brooklyn Bridge 1133 Space Song 113¼ Sky Wonder 1085 Tired 8
28Jan66-9Hia	fst 6f .22⅖ .45⅖1.11³⅖ Allowance	5 5	21 2ʰ 33 810 MVenezia	b 119	105.20	77-22 Dark King 1132 Canal 108³¼ Superado 119¼ Tired badly in drive 9

LATEST WORKOUTS   Jly 7 Aqu 3f fst .38 b

Brimer Pass × $6,250 B. g (1962), by Hannibal—Glossette, by Isolater 118 1966 17 2 2 6 $11,560
A. T. Cordero A. T. Cordero (E. K. Thomas) 1965 18 2 4 4 $10,335

22Jun66–4Aqu fst 7f .22⅗ .45⅗1.24⅖ Clm 7500 2 6 1h 1½ 4¾ 44¾ BBaeza b 121 *1.20 79–20 Brother Bones 124¾ Del Coronado 1141 Sleepy Native 1193 Tired 7
18Jun66–4Aqu fst 1 .45⅕1.10⅖1.37⅗ Clm 7500 2 1 16 14 1½ 33½ ACordero b 118 6.50 76–19 Rhyton 1153½ Tan Guapo 118h Brimer Pass 1184 Long lead, tired 7
11Jun66–4Aqu fst 6f .23 .46⅕1.10⅘ Clm 9500 9 9 51¾ 43¼ 74¾1012 JLRotz b 122 3.60 77–15 New Leader 1195½ Barwood 115h Local Talent 124no Fell back 10
30May66–3Aqu fst 7f .22⅘ .45⅖1.24 Clm 12500 3 3 3nk 11 32 35¾ ACordero b 124 9.20 80–13 Tajante 1145 Rebel Light 119¾ Brimer Pass 124h Bore out 7
23May66–5Aqu fst 6f .22⅘ .45⅖1.11⅕ Clm 12500 4 6 47 511 512 59 ACordero b 124 11.00 78–20 Joe Jolly 1171½ Solid Mike 1131½ Mixed Up Kid 121no Pore out 7
11May66–4Aqu fst 6f .22⅗ .45⅘1.11⅘ Cl c-10000 2 3 22 23 24 36 GMineau5 b 116 1.70 78–19 Tajante 1174 Inflexible 1152 Brimer Pass 1165 No mishap 6
30Apr66–5Aqu my 6f .23 .46⅕1.11⅕ Clm 10000 5 1 12 12 12 12½ GMineau5 b 114 *1.30 87–20 BrimerPass1142½ Listen to Reason1193 Artist'sAward1173 Easily 6
16Apr66–3Aqu fst 6f .23 .45⅘1.11 Clm 10000 3 6 21½ 21½ 34¾ 32 RUssery b 121 *2.40 86–14 Two Stelle 1142 Safety Zone 113no Brimer Pass 1214 No excuse 7
11Apr66–9Aqu fst 7f .22⅗ .45⅗1.24⅖ Clm 12500 4 5 53½ 23 33 33½ RUssery b 119 5.10 80–22 The Clown 1193½ Listen to Reason 113no Brimer Pass 119nk Gamely 9
2Apr66–4Aqu fst 6f .22⅘ .46⅘1.12⅖ Clm 10000 7 8 53¾ 42 1h 1½ RUssery b 119 2.90 81–21 Brimer Pass 119½ Misurata 119h Shook 1142 Under strong handling 9
26Mar66–3Aqu fst 6f .22⅗ .45⅗1.11⅖ Clm 10000 3 4 44½ 33 23 22½ MVenezia b 119 6.10 83–19 Abuso 1192½ Brimer Pass 1193 Two Stelle 1194 Drifted out late 6
18Mar65–8Aqu fst 6f .22⅘ .46⅕1.12 Clm 13000 5 6 57½ 56 66 56¼ MVenezia b 113 16.40 77–22 Off the Top 1172 Terminator 1171½ Casque 119¾ Had no mishap 8
LATEST WORKOUTS May 20 Bel tr.t. 3f .39 h

Chris-Top $6,000 Ch. g (1962), by Nashua—Zumani, by Persian Gulf 113 1966 5 M 0 1 $835
G. H. Bostwick G. H. Bostwick (C. J. Devine) 1965 2 M 0 0 $175

1Jly 66–1Aqu fst 1 .46 1.11 1.38 Md 6500 5 1 1½ 13 12 36 WBlum b 119 3.00 72–19 Stowe 1062½ Arpino 1233½ Chris-Top 119½ Used setting pace 10
25Jun66–2Aqu fst 6f .22⅖ .46 1.12⅕ Clm 6000 2 2 21 22 22 67 EGuerin b 115 2.90 75–17 Rio Coreo 115¾ Gay Orchid 1171½ Jay Roger 1141 Used forcing pace 9
14Jun66–1Aqu fst 1⅛.48⅖1.13 1.51 Md Sp Wt 4 1 1½ 1h 25 415 MVenezia 123 13.60 66–19 Cherimoya 1028 Intangible 1145 Isokeha 1142 Used up early 10
8Jun66–1Aqu fst 6f .22⅕ .45⅗1.11⅕ Md Sp Wt 1 5 64¾ 45 36 47½ MVenezia 124 24.00 79–12 Farmer's Son 1151 Smooth Seas 1155½ Right Reason 1151 Evenly 14
28May66–5Pur sf*1⅛ Ⓣ 2.09⅗ Allowance 1 3 56¼ 516 48½ 411 PBiger 144 3.80 Mako 1488 March King 1571½ Combined Operation 1531 No factor 6
16Aug65–5Atl fst 6f .22⅗ .45⅖1.12⅗ Md Sp Wt 3 12 61¾ 99 11131011 SBrooks b 116 *2.60 68–21 Cuetip 1164 Make or Break 112nk Holli Dawn 111¾ Broke very poorly 12
4Aug65–4Mth fst 6f .22⅕ .45⅘1.13 Md Sp Wt 3 4 13 11½ 11½ 41¾ SBrooks b 117 4.50 75–22 Olympia Dear 1171¼ Keisling 112nk Beau Imperial 117nk Weakened 8
20Jun64–3Aqu fst 5½f.22⅗ .46⅕1.05⅘ Md Sp Wt 2 2 1½ 53 56½ 611 MYcaza b 122 *1.75 73–15 Pass the Word 1221 Upset Victory 1222 Altiplano 122½ Greenly 9
26May64–4Aqu fst 5f .22⅗ .46⅘ .59⅘ Md Sp Wt 8 5 2h 2½ 79 89¾ MYcaza b 122 3.00 76–16 India Ink 1221 Bold Lad 122¾ Egocentrical 1222 Early speed, tired 10
LATEST WORKOUTS Jly 6 Bel m.t. 4f fst .50 b Jun 30 Bel mt. 3f fst .36 h Jun 23 Bel m.t. 4f fst .47⅗ h Jun 20 Bel m.t. 4f fst .52 b

King Salmon ✱ $6,000 Ch. c (1962), by King Hairan—Sea Blossom, by War Admiral 119 1966 14 3 2 1 $10,635
A. R. Codispoti P. J. Horn, Jr. (Patrina Corp.) 1965 10 0 1 1 $2,000

28Jun66–2Aqu fst 7f .22⅗ .45⅘1.24⅖ Clm 7000 2 10 108¾118½ 84 95¾ HGustines 120 11.10 78–19 Koh-i-Noor 114½ Navy Heroine 115½ Moral Suasion 119½ No threat 12
16Jun66–4Aqu fst 6f .22⅖ .46 1.12 Clm 6750 7 5 59 56½ 3½ 1nk RUssery 122 2.80 83–21 King Salmon 122nk Escobar II 1195 Arranger 117¾ Hard drive 7
10Jun66–1Aqu fst 6f .22⅖ .46 1.11⅘ Clm 6500 5 7 52½ 54¾ 4¾ 11½ RUssery 119 6.90 84–16 King Salmon 1191½ Oribi 114½ Garbeau 119½ Was going away 11
28May66–2Aqu sly 7f .22⅘ .46⅕1.25⅘ Cl c-5000 1 2 24 24 31½ 31¾ BBaeza 118 *1.50 75–18 Charge Hill 115nk Rio Coreo 1211½ King Salmon 1182½ Bore out 7
20May66–9Aqu gd 1⅛.47⅖1.13 1.54⅗ Clm 6500 7 1 15 13 2½ 73¼ MYcaza 116 4.40 60–18 Safety Zone 119½ Victaray 107½ Atlantic 1142 Used in pace 7
14May66–2Aqu fst 7f .23 .46⅖1.24⅖ Clm 5000 1 4 12 11 13 17 BBaeza 117 *2.50 84–13 King Salmon 1177 Hindoo II 1173½ William E. 108no Easy score 9
27Apr66–2Aqu fst 7f .23 .46⅗1.25⅕ Clm 6500 4 5 1h 41 75 814 WBlum 117 7.10 66–18 From the Top 103¾ d–TanGuapo121½ Arranger1171 Early sp'd, tired 10
20Apr66–8Aqu fst 7f .22⅘ .46⅖1.24⅗ Clm 6500 1 4 13 12 13 21½ WBlum 117 3.70 81–16 Tan Guapo 1151½ KingSalmon 117¾ Egocentrical 110no Couldn't last 7
14Apr66–5Aqu fst 7f .22⅘ .45⅘1.24⅖ Clm 6500 4 2 1½ 1h 21 43 EBelmonte 117 4.30 81–17 Gay Orchid 1152½ Garbeau 117no Aberrant 113½ Weakened in drive 8
9Apr66–8Aqu fst 6f .22⅘ .46⅖1.11⅗ Cl c-5800 4 7 79½ 65½ 36½ 28 WBlum b 117 4.20 77–18 Solid Mike 1198 King Salmon 117¾ Make Sense 1123 Second best 9
29Mar66–5Aqu fst 6f .22⅖ .46⅘1.13 Clm 6500 2 4 63½ 73¾ 67 65¾ LAdams b 117 8.30 72–25 Big Party 1152 Gay Orchid 112½ Gypsy Baron 117¾ No mishap 9
22Mar66–6Aqu fst 6f .22⅘ .46 1.11⅗ Clm 8500 2 3 1½ 1h 33 98¼ LAdams b 117 12.10 77–21 Abuso 1245 C. U. Later 108nk King Pooley 121½ Used early pace 9
LATEST WORKOUTS Jly 6 Bel tr.t. 5f fst 1.03⅖ b Jly 2 Bel tr.t. 4f fst .49⅖ h Jun 23 Bel tr.t. 4f fst .50 h Jun 7 Bel tr.t. 4f fst .50⅖ h

Jovial Twist — $6,000

B. c (1962), by Jovial Jove—Lofty Gal, by Nirgal — **1067**
N. Krohn S. Cardile (J. H. Glass Corp.)

1966	8	0	2	0 $1,500
1964	16	4	2	5 $9,130

2Jly 66–4Aqu	fst 6f	.22⅗	.46⅖1.11⅖	Clm	5750	2	6	1½	1h	41½	55½	DHidalgo5	b 110	18.20	80–15	Escobar II 1193½ Gay Orchid 115no Jay Roger 114h	Used early	10
20Jun66–2Aqu	fst 6f	.22⅖	.46⅕1.13	Cl	c–3500	2	2	13	11½	11½	2no	EGuerin	b 117	*3.00	78–21	Tudor Court 112no Jovial Twist 1171 The Jouster 1173	Gamely	7
21Apr66–2Aqu	fst 6f	.22⅖	.45⅖1.10⅗	Cl	c–4500	4	1	11	21½	26	719	WBoland	b 117	2.90	71–13	Royal Victory 1108 Col. Mengel 117h Te 117½	Early speed, stopped	7
14Apr66–5Aqu	fst 7f	.22⅘	.45⅘1.24⅖	Clm	6250	1	3	55½	89½	810	813	WBoland	b 115	31.30	71–17	Gay Orchid 1152½ Garbeau 117no Aberrant 113½	Dropped far back	8
6Apr66–5Aqu	fst 7f	.22⅗	.45⅖1.25⅕	Clm	6250	11	1	76¾	77¾	1113	128¾	WLester	b 115	72.10	71–16	Big Party 117no Del Coronado 1191 Hopeful Gus 112no	Wide late	12
29Mar66–5Aqu	fst 6f	.22⅖	.46⅘1.13	Clm	6500	4	3	3½	43	711	916	WLester	b 117	25.50	62–25	Big Party 1152 Gay Orchid 112½ Gypsy Baron 117¾	Brief foot	9
19Mar66–4Aqu	fst 6f	.22⅖	.45⅘1.11⅘	Cl	c–5000	7	1	34	36	26	26	ORosado5	b 112	5.10	78–22	Solid Mike 1176 Jovial Twist 1122½ Arranger 1172½	Second best	8
16Feb66–1Hia	fst 6f	.21⅘	.45 1.10⅘	Cl	c–5500	8	4	22	22	66	98½	WZakoor	b 116	18.30	81–17	Below Deck 1161 Gay Orchid 1112¼ Shook II 1161½	Early factor	12
9Oct64–4Haw	gd 6½f	.23	.46⅖1.19⅕	Clm	9000	2	2	2h	2h	3½	31½	RBroussard	b 117	2.10	76–21	MyMarion 112no RosyPlum 1161½ JovialTwist 1172½	Sharp effort	9
2Oct64–3Haw	fst 6f	.22⅖	.47⅘1.11⅕	Clm	10000	8	3	43½	22	24	47	LSpraker	b 121	3.40	84–14	Flying Scotsman 1126 Threescore 1191 Fleet Mama 116no	Tired	11
5Sep64–1AP	fst 6f	.21⅘	.45⅖1.11⅕	Clm	12500	2	3	23	2½	22½	26	LSpraker	b 115	4.20	81–13	Speedy Lady 1086 Jovial Twist 115nk Title Judge 116½	Gamely	9
22Aug64–3AP	fst 6f	.22⅖	.45⅕1.12⅕	Clm	12500	2	3	42	42	32½	3nk	LSpraker	b 118	4.40	82–18	Babu's On 118no TitleJudge115nk JovialTwist118¾	Missed, sharp try	9

LATEST WORKOUTS Jly 8 Bel m.t. 3f fst .35⅗ h Jun 18 Bel m.t. 4f fst .48 h Jun 15 Bel m.t. 5f fst 1.04 b Jun 11 Bel m.t. 5f fst 1.01⅗ h

Coatee — $6,000

Dk. b. or br. g (1962), by Besomer--Formal Note, by With Pleasure — **113**
Franlyn Stable W. J. Pascuma (C. MacLeod, Jr.)

1966	5	1	0	0 $2,600
1965	14	2	1	0 $6,835

2Jly 66–4Aqu	fst 6f	.22⅗	.46⅖1.11⅖	Clm	6250	10	10	913	1013	1012	913	RFerraro	b 119	4.00e	73–15	Escobar II 1193½ Gay Orchid 115no Jay Roger 114h	Dull effort	10
11Jun66–2Aqu	fst 6f	.22⅘	.46 1.12⅕	Clm	5000	6	5	34	2½	11	11	RFerraro	b 119	15.00	82–15	Coatee 1191 Measure 114¾ Templado 1192½	Under brisk drive	10
28May66–4Aqu	fst 7f	.22⅘	.46⅕1.24⅖	Clm	6250	10	5	77½	810	88	611	RFerraro	b 115	48.40	73–19	Martial Owens 1215 Knobs 117¾ Rough Divot 117¾	Far back	10
7May66–4Aqu	fst 6f	.22⅖	.46⅖1.13	Cl	c–5000	9	9	54¼	44	54½	84½	AValenzuela	b 117	10.00	73–17	Rio Coreo 117½ Empey Rullah 117h Charge Hill 119¾	No rally	11
27Apr66–2Aqu	fst 7f	.23	.46⅗1.25⅕	Clm	6500	8	3	2h	2h	99	914	AValenzuela	b 117	27.50	66–18	From the Top 108¾ d–TanGuapo121½ Arranger1171	Speed, stopped	10
17Nov65–9Aqu	fst 6f	.23	.47 1.12⅗	Clm	6500	5	5	76½	86½	1018	1017	JRuane	b 119	36.80	63–27	Trial Balloon 1192½ Decade 113½ Inflexible 1173	Far back	11
10Nov65–3Aqu	fst 6f	.22⅗	.46⅖1.12⅗	Clm	6500	7	2	43½	64¾	117¼	1110	HWoodhouse	b 119	10.80	70–20	Gay Orchid 1141½ Inflexible 117nk New Leader 119no	Fell back	11
27Oct65–2Aqu	fst 7f	.22⅘	.47 1.25⅕	Clm	7500	5	14	1413	1414	1421	1420	WBlum	b 118	13.70	55–23	Silly II 1171½ Yucatan 114nk Nick J. G. 1153	Far back throughout	14
22Sep65–8Aqu	fst 7f	.22⅘	.45⅘1.25	Clm	10000	4	4	31	21	61¾	67	ENelson	b 116	4.20	74–17	Missile Step 1142½ Grey Spot 116½ James B. W 116½	Bid, tired	9
13Sep65–2Aqu	fst 6f	.22⅗	.46⅕1.11⅖	Clm	7500	6	1	11	11	2h	1h	WBlum	b 117	8.80	86–21	Coatee 117h On Holiday 1138 Make Sense 114¾	Came again driving	7
4Sep65–3Aqu	fst 6f	.23	.47 1.12⅗	Clm	6500		1	11	11	13	1¾	WMahorney	b 116	9.20	80–20	Coatee 116¾ Oribi 116¾ Phantom Cottage 1162	Strong urging	9

LATEST WORKOUTS Jly 8 Bel m.t. 3f fst .35⅕ hg Jun 10 Bel m.t. 3f fst .37⅗ b Jun 5 Bel m.t. 6f fst 1.15⅗ h May 22 Bel m.t. 5f sly 1.06 b

*Rio Coreo * — $6,000

Blk. h (1959), by Espace Vital—Raquelita, by Corn Belt — **116**
E. Dolce L. S. Barrera (Haras Curiche) (Chile)

1966	19	3	1	1 $10,320
1965	25	1	1	1 $4,890

2Jly 66–4Aqu	fst 6f	.22⅗	.46⅖1.11⅖	Clm	5750	4	8	75½	77½	53	43½	EBelmonte	120	9.60	82–15	Escobar II 1193½ Gay Orchid 115no Jay Roger 114h	No threat	10
25Jun66–2Aqu	fst 6f	.22⅖	.46 1.12⅕	Clm	6000	3	3	75	35	33	1¾	EBelmonte	115	12.80	82–17	Rio Coreo 115¾ Gay Orchid 1171½ Jay Roger 1141	Under brisk drive	9
18Jun66–3Aqu	fst 6f	.23	.46⅘1.12⅘	Clm	5750	8	5	63¼	54½	41¾	41½	EBelmonte	115	17.50	77–19	Sleepy Native 112½ Gay Orchid 117¾ Jay Roger 114nk	Hung	10
10Jun66–1Aqu	fst 6f	.22⅖	.46 1.11⅘	Clm	6000	4	11	118	1110	106½	95	EBelmonte	115	20.30	78–16	King Salmon 1191½ Oribi 114½ Garbeau 119½	Raced far back	11
28May66–2Aqu	sly 7f	.22⅘	.46⅕1.25⅘	Clm	5000	6	3	38	34½	21½	2nk	EBelmonte	121	9.40	77–18	Charge Hill 115nk Rio Coreo 1211½ King Salmon 1182½	Bore in	7
14May66–2Aqu	fst 7f	.23	.46⅖1.24⅖	Clm	5000	8	6	93¾	761	58	411	KKnapp	124	9.00	73–13	King Salmon 1177 Hindoo II 1173½ William E. 108no	Wide turn	9
7May66–4Aqu	fst 6f	.22⅖	.46⅖1.13	Clm	4000	7	10	109¼	810	64¾	1½	RUssery	117	18.00	78–17	Rio Coreo 117½ Empey Rullah 117h Charge Hill 119¾	Hard drive	11
28Apr66–2Aqu	my 1	.47⅕	1.13⅕1.40⅖	Clm	4000	2	2	1½	1h	2h	53½	RUssery	117	*2.80	62–24	Sir Pep 110¾ Espartaco II 114¾ All Chant 112no	Used in lead	8
23Apr66–2Aqu	fst 7f	.22⅘	.45⅗1.25	Clm	5000	2	6	65¾	68¼	55½	45¾	RUssery	119	5.60	75–14	Arranger 119nk New Recruit 117½ March's Ott 1202	Evenly late	8
15Apr66–1Aqu	fst 6f	.22⅕	.45⅖1.11⅗	Clm	4500	7	2	57½	49	48	37	RUssery	117	5.90	78–14	Charge Hill 1122 March's Ott 1175 Rio Coreo 1173	Raced wide	7
29Mar66–8Aqu	fst 7f	.22⅗	.45⅖1.24⅘	Clm	6250	6	7	79½	711	611	612	RUssery	115	9.00	70–21	Inflexible 117½ Gay Orchid 1123½ Gregg's Pal 1172½	No factor	9
16Mar66–2Aqu	fst 6f	.23	.47⅖1.14⅕	Clm	4500	3	6	69	67	35	11½	RUssery	117	*2.70	72–25	Rio Coreo 1171½ Taj Mahal 121nk Oh What Fun 1172	Under brisk dr	10

LATEST WORKOUTS June 6 Bel m.t. 4f fst .49⅖ h

Results of 2nd Race Aqueduct—July 9, 1966

SECOND RACE   6 FURLONGS. (Near Man, July 17, 1963, 1.08⅗, 3, 112.)

Aqu - 28065

July 9, 1966

Claiming. Purse $4,200. 3-year-olds and upward. Weights 3-year-olds 117 lbs., older 123 lbs. Non-winners of two races since April 20 allowed 3 lbs., of a race since then, 6 lbs. Claiming price $6,500. 2 lbs. allowed for each $250 to $6,000. (Races when entered to be claimed for $5,000 or less not considered.)

Value to winner $2,730, second $840, third $420, fourth $210. Mutuel pool $363,056.

Index	Horse	Eqt A Wt	PP	St	¼	½	Str	Fin	Jockey	Cl'g Pr	Owner	Odds $1
27909Aqu9	King Salmon	4 119	6	8	7½	6¹	5²	1¾	W Blum	6000	A R Codispoti	4.30
28013Aqu5	Jovial Twist	b 4 106	7	2	4¹½	44	2½	2no	D Chamb'lin7	6000	N Krohn	29.30
28013Aqu3	Jay Roger	b 4 106	3	4	1¹	1h	1½	3²	J J Martin7	6000	Estelle S Swirlbul	9.90
28013Aqu9	Coatee	b 4 113	8	5	3h	2½	4½	4no	R Ferraro	6000	Franklyn Stable	21.90
27866Aqu4	Brimer Pass	b 4 118	4	3	2¹	3h	3h	5h	E Belmonte	6250	A T Cordero	3.00
28013Aqu4	Rio Coreo	7 116	9	9	9	8²	6½	6¾	M Ycaza	6000	E Dolce	6.20
28013Aqu2	Gay Orchid	b 7 108	1	7	8³	7½	7²	74	D Hidalgo5	6000	Mrs E S Lipari	3.70
28001Aqu3	Chris-Top	b 4 113	5	2	5²	5h	8²	8¹	L Loughry	6000	G H Bostwick	10.90
27912Mth4	Lost Lad	b 4 112	2	6	6½	9	9	9	E Cardone5	6500	D B Schmeck	5.90

Time .22⅖, .45⅗, 1.11⅘ (with wind in backstretch). Track fast.

$2 Mutuel Prices:

6-KING SALMON	10.60	5.60	4.60
7-JOVIAL TWIST		22.40	13.40
3-JAY ROGER			6.40

Ch. c, by King Hairan—Sea Blossom, by War Admiral. Trainer P. J. Horn Jr. Bred by Patrina Corp.

IN GATE AT 2.02. OFF AT 2.02 EASTERN DAYLIGHT TIME. Start good. Won driving.

KING SALMON closed with good speed through the stretch to collar the tiring leaders and prove slightly best. JOVIAL TWIST finished well along the inside. JAY ROGER tired slightly in the final sixteenth. COATEE arced wide. BRIMER PASS was unable to keep up under urging. RIO COREO was slow to respond. GAY ORCHID was never a factor. CHRIS-TOP and LOST LAD were outrun.

Chris-Top was claimed by Hollylor, trainer D. McCoy.

Courtesy of The Morning Telegraph

tough races in succession—too much to ask of a seven-year-old. Lost Lad, a New Jersey horse, had raced but once all year, and had not even had a workout in New York. Jay Roger had been perishing in the stretch of every race since stepping up from $3,500 company. It seemed in condition to run its best today, but there was no reason to expect that its best would be good enough—especially not against front-runners like Brimer Pass and Jovial Twist.

Brimer Pass, the favorite, was moving down after six successive failures. It had not worked out since its last race two and a half weeks ago. Something obviously was wrong. Chris-Top, a maiden, was clearly out of its class. Jovial Twist seemed able to generate early foot, but its inability to hold together after doing so was hard to overlook. Coatee had run miserably in its latest outing and had shown nothing in any of its 1966 attempts to compete with $6,000 horses.

The only animals that shaped up as possible contenders for a bet were King Salmon and Rio Coreo. Both were off-pace runners, which promised to be an advantage in this particular field. King Salmon's best race looked like this:

.46 1.11⅘ Won going away

Rio Coreo's:

.46 1.12⅕ Won driving

Inasmuch as both were mature animals, unlikely to have unsuspected extra swift up their sleeves, it could be presumed that King Salmon's best was superior to Rio Coreo's. In this connection, it was not insignificant that King Salmon had a superior consistency and money-earning record and had fared better in good company than Rio Coreo had. The King's last race, when entered for $7,000, was no rap. After an unaccountably slow departure from the gate, the colt had made up a good deal of ground. Its ninth-place finish, less than six lengths behind Koh-I-Noor, was scarcely a disgrace. Nor could the observant player fail to deduce that the race was a nice workout for the horse, after the tough ones it had run in its previous two starts.

The player who wanted to go all the way with numerical ratings would put King Salmon four fifths ahead of Rio Coreo on the pace scale —meaning 4 or 20 or 40 or 400 or 48 points better, depending on the number of points he used for each fifth of fractional times. He also would give King Salmon a markedly superior class rating—68 for the June 16 race. The best class rating for Rio Coreo would be 60. King Salmon stands out on class, and its class is verified by the superior pace rating.

The reader should take a minute to notice that if Gay Orchid had not been eliminated on the condition factor, it would have earned a considerably better pace rating than King Salmon. The gelding's May 21 race was better at every call than King Salmon's best race. King Salmon's victory at a $10.60 mutuel can be accepted as evidence that it pays to consider only horses that seem to be in ready condition.

But how, you may ask, does one handle the situation in which one horse has a higher pace rating than a horse of apparently superior class?

The following rules help resolve such situations:

1. In allowance races involving lightly raced three-year-olds from good barns, always go to the class and forget pace. If class evaluations are too difficult, pass the race.

2. In choosing among seasoned horses whose class levels are evident, discard any whose class and pace ratings are each 10 points lower than those of any other contender. (If you use the six-lengths-per-second method, discard any horse whose rated class is $1,000 lower and whose pace rating is 120 points lower.)

3. Discard all females whose pace and class ratings are no better than those of all male contenders.

4. Before August, do the same with three-year-olds running against older horses. After August, accept any three-year-old whose combined pace and class ratings are each as high as any in the race.

5. Discard all horses aged eight or more whose pace and class ratings are not superior to those of all other contenders.

6. After checking its condition in the paddock and walking ring (see Chapter 17), prepare to bet on any remaining contender that (a) rates among the top three on pace and on pace plus class and (b) is either the only front-runner among the contenders, or (c) has a front-running style and usually gets to the half (sprints) or three quarters (routes) a tick or two more rapidly than anything else in the field.

7. After confirming its good condition in the paddock and walking ring, be prepared to bet on any horse that rates among the top three contenders on pace and class if (a) it usually runs slightly off the early pace and (b) will race today against two or more highly rated front-runners.

8. If none of the foregoing procedures has turned up a bet, differentiate the surviving contenders by means of the handicapping fine points discussed in Chapter 16.

Pace in Long Races

At races beyond a mile and one sixteenth, the safest procedure is to hunt for the animal that has already demonstrated suitability to the route, is in condition and, if you are lucky, has an edge in class. More often than not, a record of coming on in the stretch is a reassuring sign, especially if the late gains have taken place recently and the animal is otherwise in good trim. Should a couple of fast-breaking front-runners be in the field, the come-from-behinder looks even better. There seldom is any occasion to resort to arithmetical pace ratings in races of this kind.

If the track, like so many, presents route races in which the horses run only about 100 yards before reaching the first turn, it pays to keep an eye peeled for front-runners with inside post positions. Moreover, if the field includes two front-runners of which one is not in particularly sharp condition and will break from an outside post position, possibilities remain bright for the horse with the inside post.

Once in a while an especially sharp player spots a sprinter in one of these longer races. If the horse is the only speed in the field, it may be a lucrative bet. The player must be careful that it is not being entered at the longer distance for purposes of exercise. It should have genuine speed to begin with, and no prospect of competition for the early lead. Even if it has had difficulty holding the lead in shorter races, it may open up an enormous margin against the heavy-footed routers it faces today.

An example occurred in the ninth at Aqueduct on July 8, 1966. The only authentic speed horse in the field was Main Count, which had been failing in the stretch in sprints but had once won at a mile and one sixteenth at Fort Erie. A couple of other entrants had shown inclination to vie for the lead in races of today's distance but had never been able to hold it. And had never shown anything approaching Main Count's early foot.

The horse had been claimed for $5,000 in its last race, nine days earlier. Was the trainer putting it in this route today simply to build its stamina? Possibly. But he had given it a mile work only two days ago, suggesting a serious try today. Was Main Count a good bet? I would say so. Especially in view of the nondescript credentials of the rest of the field. Old Bailey II looked like a possible threat, but not at the weight. Inflexible might turn out to have a class edge, but had been descending the class ladder without finding a comfortable level, and had not shown much appetite for the distance. Under Osvaldo Rosado, a good judge of pace who had been aboard the horse in better company, Main Count had to be conceded a good chance, especially at the price.

I include this example not to undermine anything I said earlier about the distance factor in Thoroughbred racing, but to show that a player alert to all possibilities is better off than one who lives by the book— including this book.

Pace in Two-Year-Old Races

I have said repeatedly that final time is the main criterion in handicapping juvenile dashes. But there are occasions when contenders seem equally matched in that respect. A pace analysis may help to separate them.

In the sixth at Aqueduct on July 12, 1966, Mopolina, Up And At 'Em and Gay Gobha seemed to be the speed of the race. But, by any standard, Gay Gobha looked able to command the pace of the race. If, as seemed probable, its most recent performance was a signal of improvement, the filly looked capable of leading to the half in .46 and two or three ticks, with plenty in reserve for a finish of 1.05⅗ or perhaps a fifth slower. Up And At 'Em, after failing at Suffolk, had won easily over maiden claimers in New York, and might actually be better than her management originally thought. But the presence of a raw apprentice on a relatively slow-starting horse did not augur well. As to Mopolina, her scant

9th Race Aqueduct

1⅛ MILES
AQUEDUCT
Start▸|◂Finish

1 1-8 MILES (Sinatra, December 7, 1964, 1.47⅕, 5, 111.)
Claiming. Purse $4,700. 3-year-olds and upward which have never won two races at a mile or over since April 20. Weights, 3-year-olds 116 lbs., older 123 lbs. Non-winners of a race at a mile and a furlong or over since May 31 allowed 3 lbs., of such a race since April 20, 5 lbs. Claiming price, $6,500. 2 lbs. allowed for each $250 to $6,000. (Races when entered to be claimed for $5,000 or less not considered.)

Del Coronado

$6,500 B. g (1961), by The Pie King—El Panell, by Bric A Bac
N. Hellman A. A. Scotti (B. W. Martin–L. Welk) 113^5
1966 21 1 2 5 $7,810
1965 33 2 3 5 $7,641

28Jun66–2Aqu fst 7f .22⅗ .45⅘1.24⅖ Clm 7500 4 8 86¼ 84¼ 74 62½ RTurcotte b 119 7.80 81–19 Koh–I–Noor 114½ Navy Heroine 115½ Moral Suasion 119½ No mishap 12
22Jun66–4Aqu fst 7f .22⅗ .45⅗1.24⅖ Clm 7500 6 3 53¾ 53 51¼ 2¾ ECardone5 b 114 9.80 83–20 Brother Bones 124¾ Del Coronado 1141 Sleepy Native 1193 Sharp 7
3Jun66–9Aqu fst 1⅛.48 1.13⅕1.52⅖ Clm 6500 5 1 13 12 2½ 33¼ LLoughry5 b 115 8.50 71–16 Duke's Liberty 118nk Victaray 1163 Del Coronado 115½ Tired 7
26May66–8Aqu fst 1 .46⅖1.11⅗1.37⅕ Clm 8500 6 5 61¾ 62¼ 74¾ 711 BBaeza b 116 7.00 71–19 With Promise 111no Get Crackin' 116h Tan Guapo 1144 Tired 8
19May66–9Aqu sly 1⅛.48⅖1.13⅖1.52⅗ Clm 10500 2 2 fog 712 726 ECardone7 b 105 22.90 47–17 Dodgertown 114¾ Dark Alloy 1164 Enfant Terrible 1194 Far back 7
14May66–8Aqu fst 1 .46⅕1.11⅖1.37⅗ Clm 10000 1 1 1½ 2½ 43 75 ECardone7 b 109 22.30 75–13 From the Top 1072½ Listen to Reason 1161 Cab Stan 114½ Tired 9
5May66–9Aqu fst 1⅛.47⅗1.11⅘1.52⅘ Clm 10500 4 3 45 45¼ 35 38 ECardone7 b 105 9.50 64–20 SelectedShorts1168 FleetMusketeer122no DelCoronado1052¼ Hung 7
13Apr66–9Aqu fst 1⅛.47⅘1.13⅕1.52 Cl c–8250 7 2 2h 2h 43½ 68½ WBlum b 114 3.40 67–16 Fleet Musketeer 1162 Aerie 114½ Mi Rey 114½ Well up, tired 9
6Apr66–5Aqu fst 7f .22⅗ .45⅖1.25⅕ Cl c–6500 7 8 43¼ 34½ 33½ 2no MYcaza b 119 5.50 80–16 Big Party 117no Del Coronado 1191 Hopeful Gus 112no Just missed 12
29Mar66–8Aqu fst 1 .46 1.12 1.39⅖ Clm 8500 6 4 36½ 25 25 37½ ACordero b 116 5.80 63–25 King Pooley 1113½ Local Talent 1164 Del Coronado 1162½ Evenly 7
22Mar66–6Aqu fst 6f .22⅘ .46 1.11⅗ Clm 8250 7 7 63½ 65¾ 56 66¼ RUssery h 115 9.70 82–21 Abuso 1245 C. U. Later 108nk King Pooley 121½ Had no mishap 9

LATEST WORKOUTS Jun 18 Bel m.t. 4f fst .48 hg Jun 13 Bel tr.t. 3f fst .39 b Jun 2 Bel tr.t. 5f fst 1.08 b

Latin Artist

$6,500 Ch. h (1960), by Tenerani—Nenuphar, by Blue Peter
J. T. Jacovelli N. J. Jacovelli (Bell–Gardiner) 118
1966 9 1 1 3 $5,215
1965 16 2 0 0 $9,145

1Jly 66–9Aqu fst 1⅛.48 1.13⅕1.52⅘ Clm 6500 5 5 612 58 58 511 RTurcotte 118 8.10 61–19 Tobir 111¾ No Kidding 1133 Hy–Nat 1161 Checked in early going 6
1Jly 66—Placed fourth through disqualification.
27May66–9Aqu fst 1⅛.48⅗1.13⅗1.52⅗ Cl c–6000 8 8 89 42 96¼ 912 MVenezia 112 7.40 61–18 Aberrant 1142 Street Fair 1162½ Egocentrical 1053 Stopped 9
29Apr66–9Aqu my 1⅛.48⅘1.13⅕1.52⅖ Clm 6250 6 3 33½ 58 510 612 RUssery 115 *1.60 62–16 Ski Dancer 1111 Go Overboard 1143 Ruperto 1143 Brief speed 6
22Apr66–9Aqu fst 1⅛.48⅕1.12⅘1.51⅘ Clm 6250 2 2 3½ 41½ 1h 3nk RUssery b 115 *1.70 77–14 Street Fair 116nk Nick J. G. 112h Latin Artist 1155 No excuse 6
15Apr66–9Aqu fst 1⅛.47⅘1.12⅗1.52 Clm 6250 7 4 55 55 2h 2h RUssery 115 4.20 76–15 Ruperto 109h Latin Artist 1152½ Hy–Nat 1133 Late lead, missed 7
5Apr66–9Aqu fst 1⅛.47⅕1.12⅗1.54 Clm 5000 3 8 814 65 11 11½ RUssery 116 *1.90e 66–23 Latin Artist 1161½ Escatimo 1155 Last Not Least 1114 Brisk drive 9
29Mar66–9Aqu fst 1⅛.47⅖1.13⅖1.54⅘ Clm 5000 5 7 913 76¼ 43½ 32¾ WBlum 116 *2.70 59–25 Rough Divot 1141¾ Go Overboard 1161½ Latin Artist 1161½ Rallied 9
22Mar66–9Aqu fst 1⅛.48⅖1.14 1.53⅗ Clm 5000 6 8 815 812 412 37½ ORosado5 111 3.90e 60–21 Hy–Nat 1166 Wateau II 1141½ Latin Artist 1114 Best stride late 9
24Jan66–8Bow fst 1 1/16.48⅖1.13 1.45⅘ Clm 7500 6 11 1214 1114 916 922 AValenzuela 115 19.60 62–18 Absent Son 1136 Expresivo 1137 Battle Order 114¾ No speed 12
18Dec65–7Pim fst 1 1/16.47⅘1.13 1.47⅖ Cl c–7500 1 10 1014 1015 96¼ 76¾ CRogers 121 5.20e 66–22 Honey Doc 1132 Pajaro Bravo 1121 Curator 1131 No factor 10

LATEST WORKOUTS Jun 24 Bel t.c. 7f fm 1.03 h Jun 17 Bel t.c. 4f fm .50 b Jun 13 Bel t.c. 7f fm 1.32 b May 25 Aqu 4f fst .53 b

Inflexible *

$6,500 B. g (1961), by Jutland—Manchette, by Johnstown
Mrs. L. Dalsemer A. A. Fiore (J. E. Hughes) 118
1966 15 1 3 2 $7,575
1965 32 3 5 4 $14,310

28Jun66–2Aqu fst 7f .22⅗ .45⅘1.24⅖ Clm 7500 6 11 1111 107½ 106½ 85½ EBelmonte †19 8.60 78–19 Koh–I–Noor 114½ Navy Heroine 115½ Moral Suasion 119½ No threat 12
15Jun66–9Aqu fst 1⅛.48⅘1.14 1.53⅗ Clm 9000 2 4 42½ 2½ 3nk 51½ ACordero 116 5.40 66–16 Listen to Reason 116½ Formal Johnny 113h Wyoming 102¾ Tired 6
11Jun66–4Aqu fst 6f .23 .46⅕1.10⅘ Clm 9000 3 6 84¼ 75½ 44 66¼ EBelmonte 115 6.40 83–15 New Leader 1195½ Barwood 115h Local Talent 124no No rally 10
1Jun66–6Aqu fst 7f .23⅕ .47 1.25 Clm 8500 1 6 32 41½ 32 2no ACordero 115 6.60 81–19 Local Talent 119no Inflexible 1152 Koh–I–Noor 1191½ Sharp try 7
21May66–8Aqu fst 7f .23⅗ .46⅗1.24⅕ Clm 9500 8 5 73¼ 54¾ 89 88¼ HWoodhouse 115 10.20 77–15 Cab Stan 114¾ Rhyton 114nk Rebel Light 117¾ Never a threat 9
11May66–4Aqu fst 6f .22⅗ .45⅘1.11⅘ Clm 9500 5 4 48 39 36 24 EBelmonte 115 13.60 80–19 Tajante 1174 Inflexible 1152 Brimer Pass 1165 Second best 6
30Apr66–5Aqu my 6f .23 .46⅕1.11⅕ Clm 9500 3 3 34 44½ 45 48½ ACordero 115 6.60 78–20 BrimerPass1142½ Listen toR'son1193 Artist'sAw'rd1173 Lost b'nd'ge 6
23Apr66–3Aqu fst 6f .22⅖ .45⅗1.10⅘ Cl c–7500 7 6 86½ 65 710 78¼ MYcaza 117 3.90 81–14 Big Party 1151½ Solid Mike 1132½ Cambio 1131 Not a factor 8
16Apr66–3Aqu fst 6f .23 .45⅘1.11 Clm 10000 7 5 64¾ 53½ 58 56 EBelmonte 118 10.90 82–14 Two Stelle 1142 Safety Zone 113no Brimer Pass 1214 No mishap 7
9Apr66–9Aqu fst 1⅛.47⅗1.12⅗1.52⅕ Hcp 5000s 1 1 12 2h 31 44¼ EBelmonte 115 3.70 71–18 Gypsy Baron 113h Burned Up 1204 Mr. Elwood W. 113h Used early 10
2Apr66–8Aqu fst 1 .47⅖1.13 1.39 Allowance 4 3 42½ 32 56½ 512 EBelmonte 116 11.60 61–21 Rocky Ford 116nk Portfolio 1162 Linear B. 1185 Dropped far back 6
26Mar66–9Aqu fst 1⅛.48⅕1.13 1.54⅖ Hcp 5000s 7 3 31 2½ 11½ 2no EBelmonte 115 3.60 64–19 Nike Site 111no Inflexible 115½ Humorismo 1133 Just missed 7

LATEST WORKOUTS Jun 23 Bel m.t. 4f fst .49⅕ b Jun 8 Bel tr.t. 3f fst .37⅕ h May 18 Bel tr.t. 4f fst .52 h May 7 Bel tr.t. 4f fst .51⅗ h

Fultonville $6,250 Ch. g (1962), by Intent—Athena II, by Marsyas II **116** 1966 12 2 0 2 $8.345
W. Lorenz S. R. Shapoff (Sanford Stud Farms) 1965 13 2 2 0 $7,970
28Jun66-2Aqu fst 7f .22⅗ .45⅘1.24⅖ Clm 7500 11 1 5⁵ 7⁴¼11⁷½11⁸¾ JRuane 119 37.40 76–19 Koh-I-Noor 114½ Navy Heroine 115½ Moral Suasion 119¾ No threat 12
1Jun65-6Aqu fst 7f .23⅕ .47 1.25 Clm 8500 5 1 7⁶½ 6⁴ 5⁷½ 6¹⁰ LLoughry5 110 6.80 71–19 Local Talent 119no Inflexible 115² Koh-I-Noor 119¹½ No factor 7
26May66-8Aqu fst 1 .46⅖1.11⅗1.37⅕ Clm 8000 8 2 2h 4¹½ 4³ 4⁴ ECardone7 107 5.00 78–19 With Promise 111no Get Crackin' 116h Tan Guapo 114⁴ Tired 8
14May66-8Aqu fst 1 .46⅕1.11⅗1.37⅗ Clm 9500 2 6 5³½ 7⁴ 9¹¹ 8⁸ JRuane 114 18.70 72–13 From the Top 107²½ Listen to Reason 116¹ Cab Stan 114½ Tired 9
4May66-9Aqu fst 1⅛.48⅕1.13⅘1.52⅘ Clm 8500 3 1 2³ 2h 3¹½ 3³½ JRuane 116 9.10 68–20 From the Top 107² Hail the Admiral 118¹½ Fultonville 116h Good try 6
6Apr66-9Aqu fst 1⅛.47⅕1.11⅘1.51⅕ Clm 9500 3 2 2⁴ 2³ 3⁸ 5¹² JRuane 115 7.90 68–16 King Pooley 110⁴ King Trece 117⁵ Aerie 110nk Early speed 6
21Mar66-9Aqu fst 1⅛.48⅕1.13⅕1.53 Clm 10000 5 3 4⁴½ 4⁶ 4¹² 5¹² JRuane 116 5.30 59–22 Fieroval 116¾ Old Bailey II 114⁸ Ram's Horn 116³ Bore out 7
14Mar66-8Aqu fst 1 .46 1.11 1.37⅘ Clm 11500 11 3 3²½ 6¹¹ 5¹² 6¹³ JRuane 114 15.70 66–21 Rocky Ford 114² SelectedShorts116¹ EnfantTerrible114⁴ Weakened 12
19Feb66-9Pim gd 1 1/16.47⅕1.13⅗1.47⅗ Clm 10000 6 5 5⁵½ 2¹½ 1h 1¹½ PIGrimm 116 7.80 72–30 Fultonville 116¹½ Arctic Swirl 116¾ Ungersmon 113³½ Drew out 8
12Feb66-9Bow fst 1 1/16.48⅘1.13⅘1.47⅖ Clm 11000 3 4 3½ 6³¼ 7⁶ 7⁶ PIGrimm 116 6.20 70–18 Southern War 113¹ Blue Nahar 113nk Frosted Prince 113² Tired 10
22Jan66-6Bow fst 1 1/16.48⅘1.14⅕1.48⅖ Clm 9500 5 3 3½ 2¹ 3²½ 3¾ PIGrimm 115 4.30 70–19 Grandioso 117h Plane to Spain 117¾ Fultonville 115¹ Came again 12
LATEST WORKOUTS Jun 23 Bel tr.t. 4f fst .50⅘ h Jun 18 Bel m.t. 5f fst 1.02 h May 21 Bel m.t. 6f gd 1.17⅖ b May 11 Bel tr.t. 4f fst .51⅗ h

Main Count $6,250 B. h (1961), by Count of Honor—Humane, by Broadside **116** 1966 13 1 5 1 $5,490
B. W. Steinberg M. Cohn (L. B. Combs) 1965 19 4 1 2 $10,957
29Jun66-2Aqu fst 7f .22⅘ .45⅗1.24⅘ Cl c-5000 7 1 1½ 1h 2h 2³ DHidalgo5 b 116 *2.40 79–17 Swift Stream 119³ Main Count 116³ New Recruit 119¹½ Gamely 8
23May66-4Grd fst 7f .22⅘ .47 1.26⅗ Clm 6500 3 2 1¹ 2h 3¹ 4⁵ BWerry5 b 109 *2.15 85–15 TryBrandy 116¾ Ky.Quill 119² RubberStamped 114²¼ Speed, no exc. 8
14May66-8Grd gd 7f .24 .48⅖1.28 Clm 6500 4 2 1¹½ 1¹ 1½ 2¾ BWerry5 b 110 *1.55 81–24 Ky. Quill 112¾ Main Count 110¹ Rubber Stamped 115h Held willingly 7
4May66-5FE fst 170.46⅕1.11⅗1.42⅕ Clm 6500 3 2 1⁵ 1²½ 2h 2½ BWerry5 b 112 3.65 97–15 So Good 117½ Main Count 112⁷ Scadadle 117nk Held on stubbornly 5
30Apr66-8FE gd 1 1/16.47⅗1.12⅘1.47 Clm 5000 1 1 1⁵ 1⁵ 1²½ 1nk BWerry5 b 111 4.45 78–19 MainCount 111nk SafetyMan111nk QuestSpeaker113¹⁰ Tiring,lasted 7
23Apr66-6FE my 170.45⅘1.11⅘1.42⅗ Clm 6500 2 1 1½ 2²½ 5¹² 6¹³ BWerry5 b 111 4.50 83– 6 Reap the Wind 119½ BrassLace 119¹½ FastJay 116⁸ Away fast, tired 8
11Apr66-7FE sl 5½f.23⅖ .47⅘1.07⅕ Clm 9000 4 3 2½ 5⁵½ 5⁸¾ 5⁹½ BWerry5 b 111 3.75 77–20 Lebon M. L. 116³½ Buttermilk Pike 111¹ Winisteo 113¹½ In close 6
23Mar66-2Aqu fst 1 .47 1.12⅕1.38⅖ Clm 7000 1 1 1¹ 1³ 2¹ 2² ORosado5 b 108 4.90 74–25 Blacks Charge 120² Main Count 108² Renege 112⁴ Weakened late 7
14Mar66-4Aqu fst 6f .22⅘ .46⅖1.12⅖ Clm 6250 2 7 7⁵ 7¹¹ 9⁹ 8⁷ ORosado5 b 110 26.70 74–21 C. U. Later 109¾ Solid Mike 113nk Inflexible 117h Never close 13
19Feb66-2Hia sly 7f .23⅕ .46⅖1.24⅘ Clm 6500 10 1 1½ 1² 2² 2⁴½ RTurcotte b 120 *2.50 80–17 Safety Zone 114⁴½ Main Count 120²½ Remove Cause 116² Wide 11
LATEST WORKOUTS Jly 6 Bel tr.t. 1m fst 1.48 b

Metamora $6,500 Br. g (1962), by Stella Aurata—Pardee, by Hawley **118** 1966 10 0 0 0 ——
Shady Acres Farm J. W. Smith (Mrs. A. J. Leonard) 1965 30 3 5 6 $14,850
18Jun66-4Aqu fst 1 .45⅕1.10⅖1.37⅗ Clm 7500 7 2 2⁶ 7¹² 7¹⁸ 7²⁰ GLanoway b 118 33.00 60–19 Rhyton 115³½ Tan Guapo 118h Brimer Pass 118⁴ Early sp'd, stopped 7
1Jun65-6Aqu fst 7f .23⅕ .47 1.25 Clm 9500 4 7 6⁵ 7⁴½ 7⁸½ 7¹¹ GLanoway b 119 26.50 70–19 Local Talent 119no Inflexible 115² Koh-I-Noor 119¹½ No factor 7
23May66-5Aqu fst 6f .22⅘ .45⅖1.11⅕ Clm 12500 3 7 7¹¹ 7¹⁹ 7¹⁹ 7¹⁶ GLanoway b 117 47.60 71–20 Joe Jolly 117¹½ Solid Mike 113¹½ Mixed Up Kid 121no Trailed field 7
9Apr66-6GP fm 1 1/16 Ⓣ 1.11 1.43 Clm 12500 9 6 7⁷½ 4²½ 6⁴¼ 6⁶ FToro 116 4.50 83–16 Scambio 122¹ Brant 120²½ Officer Sweeney 116h Mild bid, tired 10
2Apr66-6GP fm 1 Ⓣ .47⅖1.37⅗ Clm 15000 1 6 6³½ 6⁴½ 6⁴½ 6³¾ SBrooks b 116 15.00 82–16 Chancero116no Two Up112h Dynamic Jack116½ In close backstretch 10
5Mar66-5GP fst 6f .23 .46⅖1.11 Clm 17000 5 8 8⁴½ 10⁶¼ 7⁶½ 8¹¹ SBrooks b 114 33.90 78–15 Casque112² BigJudge114²Ramflow109¾ Never in contention 10
11Feb66-8Hia fm*1 1/16 Ⓣ 1.42 Allowance 6 4 3³ 3⁴ 3⁴ 6¹¹ GMineau5 b 108 81.90 90– 5 Happy Gondolier 113²½ Cleareye113²½ RicketyDick113⁴½ No rally 12
5Feb66-9Hia fst 7f .23 .46 1.24⅖ Allowance 3 10 9⁸¼10¹¹12¹⁵12¹⁹ GMineau5 b 108 322.90 68–23 Irvkup 116¹½ Swoonaway 113nk Battle Star 113¹½ Far back 12
26Jan66-7Hia sly 7f .23⅖ .46⅕1.25 Allowance 2 9 7⁶ 8¹³ 8¹¹10¹¹ GMineau5 b 109 22.10 73–17 d-GrandMarais109¾Comprehensive114nkHurricaneTim114¾ No fact. 11
13Jan66-10Hia fm 1 1/16 Ⓣ 1.42⅖ Clm 27500 8 3 5⁴½ 7⁶ 4⁴½ 6⁷½ GMineau5 b 109 55.10 85– 8 RepublicanWay 114³ ChiefGeronimo 116nk Tarpon 112³½ Fell back 11
24Dec65-8TrP fst 170.46 1.10⅘1.42 Allowance 1 8 7⁶½ 5⁴¼ 5²¾ 5² BThornburg b 116 12.50 85–12 Chief Geronimo 114½ Rhyton 119½ Linear B. 119h No threat 12
LATEST WORKOUTS Jly 5 Bel m.t. 5f fst 1.01⅖ bg Jun 29 Bel m.t. 5f fst 1.03 b Jun 17 Bel m.t. 3f fst .36⅗ h Jun 14 Bel m.t. 1m fst 1.46 b

***Mi Rey** $6.500 B. h (1959). by Monterey—Factually, by His Eminence II 118 1966 8 0 1 2 $2,485
Mrs. S. Westfal R. B. Murray (Haras Tarapaca) (Chile) 1965 27 4 1 5 $17,050
28Jun66-2Aqu fst 7f .22⅗ .45⅘1.24⅖ Clm 7500 5 12 12121212128 107¾ JLRotz b 119 13.20 76-19 Koh-i-Noor 114½ Navy Heroine 115½ Moral Suasion 119½ No threat 12
20Jun66-4Aqu fst 6f .22⅘ .46 1.12⅕ Clm 8500 7 5 711 78½ 57 43¼ JLRotz b 115 19.60 79-21 Local Talent 114¾ Hail the Admiral 1151½ Bulco 1191 Rallied 7
20Apr66-9Aqu fst 1⅛.47⅘1.13 1.51⅗ Clm 8500 2 5 57 54 54 46¼ JLRotz b 114 5.00 73-16 Aerie 111no Renege 1146 Local Talent 114nk Lacked late rally 7
13Apr66-9Aqu fst 1⅛.47⅘1.13⅕1.52 Clm 8250 3 6 65¼ 73¾ 74¼ 32½ HGustines b 114 11.50 73-16 Fleet Musketeer 1162 Aerie 114½ Mi Rey 114½ Found stride late 9
30Mar66-9Aqu fst 1⅛.49 1.13⅗1.52⅖ Cl c-6500 6 8 87¼ 810 510 35¾ RUssery b 116 3.00 68-20 Safety Zone 1145½ Hy-Nat 113nk Mi Rey 1162 Best stride late 8
23Mar66-2Aqu fst 1 .47 1.12⅕1.38⅖ Clm 7500 2 3 52¾ 510 58¼ 48 GMineau5 b 112 *1.50e 68-25 Blacks Charge 1202 Main Count 1082 Renege 1124 Close quarters 7
17Feb66-10Hia fst 1⅛.47⅗1.12⅕1.51⅕ Clm 9000 4 9 811 78 57½ 53¼ RUssery b 115 7.90 76-16 No Snakes 118no Follow Thru 1123 Golden Bugles 116nk Rallied 10
11Feb66-5Hia fst 7f .23⅕ .46 1.24 Clm 7750 8 8 87¾ 88¼ 35 29 GMineau5 b 109 8.30 80-18 Mixed Up Kid 1229 MiRey109nk SomaliBird112nk Best of others 12
28Dec65-7TrP fst 1$\frac{1}{16}$.46⅘1.11⅘1.44⅕ Clm 8500 9 6 79½ 88¾ 710 79¼ LLoughry5 b 110 3.60 72-16 Everullah 1101 Indian Tint 113nk Fighting Phantom 1082 No factor 10
LATEST WORKOUTS Jun 16 Bel m.t. 4f fst .49⅕ h Jun 12 Bel m.t. 4f fst .52 b Jun 8 Bel m.t. 3f fst .38 b

Victaray $6,250 Ch. c (1962), by Nicaray—Clay Queen, by Hail Victory 116 1966 16 1 3 0 $6,020
J. C. Lawrence J. C. Lawrence (J. R. Luker) 1965 14 3 0 1 $6,369
1Jly 66-9Aqu fst 1⅛.48 1.13⅘1.52⅘ Clm 6500 2 4 411 48 45 44¾ ORosado 118 d-7.60 67-19 Tobir 111¾ No Kidding 1133 Hy-Nat 1161 Bore out early 6
1Jly 66—d-Disqualified and placed last.
24Jun66-9Aqu fst 1⅛.47⅘1.13⅘1.54 Cl c-5000 4 7 75½ 62¾ 31 11½ DHidalgo5 113 7.80 66-21 Victaray 1131½ Inhand 1122½ Egocentrical 118¾ Going away 7
17Jun66-9Aqu fst 1⅛.48⅖1.13⅕1.53 Clm 6000 5 3 32½ 62½ 56½ 48½ LLoughry5 109 10.30 62-22 Brother Bones 120½ Hy-Nat 1116 Atlantic 1162 Brief speed 10
10Jun66-9Aqu fst 1⅛.47⅖1.12⅘1.52⅗ Clm 6000 4 5 512 55 57¼ 48 EBelmonte 116 5.20 65-16 Old Bailey II1203 Duke'sLiberty1202½ BrotherBones1132½ Checked 7
3Jun66-9Aqu fst 1⅛.48 1.13⅕1.52⅖ Clm 6000 3 3 34 22 1½ 2nk EBelmonte 116 7.80 74-16 Duke's Liberty 118nk Victaray 1163 Del Coronado 115½ Game try 7
27May66-9Aqu fst 1⅛.48⅗1.13⅗1.52⅗ Clm 6500 6 3 46½ 63¼ 65½ 67¾ DHidalgo5 111 12.10 65-18 Aberrant 1142 Street Fair 1162½ Egocentrical 1053 Tired 9
20May66-9Aqu gd 1⅛.47⅖1.13 1.54⅗ Clm 6000 5 5 514 68 53½ 2½ DHidalgo5 107 37.80 62-18 Safety Zone 119½ Victaray 107½ Atlantic 1142 Was gaining rapidly 7
11May66-8Aqu fst 1 .46⅕1.11⅖1.39⅕ Cl c-4000 1 4 52 56½ 65½ 85¼ GMineau5 b 110 8.00 67-19 Tablin 112½ Artist Town 1151 Never Wrong 1151 No mishap 12
26Apr66-9Aqu fst 1⅛.48⅖1.12⅗1.52⅕ Clm 5000 5 2 32 43 45½ 611 GMineau5 b 111 7.40 64-18 Hy-Nat 1172 Rough Divot 1225 Duke's Liberty 116nk Tired 8
15Apr66-9Aqu fst 1⅛.47⅘1.12⅗1.52 Clm 6500 5 1 12 11 54 58½ GMineau5 b 111 11.40 67-15 Ruperto 109h Latin Artist 1152½ Hy-Nat 1133 Used setting pace 7
9Apr66-4Aqu fst 7f .23 .46⅕1.24⅘ Clm 7500 4 7 75¾ 74½ 67 69 MSorrentino b 113 28.20 73-18 SafetyZone1171 From the Top1081 Hail the Admiral1206 Sluggish st. 7
30Mar66-9Aqu fst 1⅛.49 1.13⅗1.52⅖ Clm 6500 5 6 75¾ 78¾ 815 719 MSorrentino b 116 9.00 55-20 Safety Zone 1145½ Hy-Nat 113nk Mi Rey 1162 Dropped far back 8
LATEST WORKOUTS May 18 Bel tr.t. 4f fst .51 h May 9 Bel tr.t. 4f fst .51⅘ h

***Old Bailey II *** $6,500 Dk. b h (1958), by Welsh Honey—Orange, by Carnaval 123 1966 14 1 2 1 $5,955
Grandview Stable T. A. Ecklund (Haras El Bosque) (Chile) 1965 26 3 3 2 $15,260
28Jun66-9Mth fm*1$\frac{1}{16}$ Ⓣ 1.48⅖ Clm 6500 7 8 87½ 55½ 38 36 SBoulmetis b 119 4.90 86-7 Hessian 1162 Vilcapugio 1174 Old Bailey II 1194 Rallied 10
15Jun66-9Aqu fst 1⅛.48⅘1.14 1.53⅗ Clm 8500 3 5 65½ 52¾ 66½ 67½ KKnapp b 114 3.30 60-16 Listen to Reason 116½ Formal Johnny 113h Wyoming 102¾ No mishap 6
10Jun66-9Aqu fst 1⅛.47⅖1.12⅘1.52⅗ Clm 6500 6 4 46½ 12 14 13 KKnapp b 120 7.10 73-16 Old Bailey II 1203 Duke's Liberty 1202½ Brother Bones 1132½ Driving 7
2Jun66-9Aqu fst 1⅛.47⅘1.12⅘1.52 Clm 7500 8 8 85 88 76½ 78 KKnapp b 116 28.30 68-15 Get Crackin' 118no Aberrant 1161½ With Promise 1132½ No speed 8
26May66-8Aqu fst 1 .46⅖1.11⅗1.37⅕ Clm 8500 7 4 41 89¼ 89¾ 814 RTurcotte b 116 13.90 68-19 With Promise 111no Get Crackin' 116h Tan Guapo 1144 Tired 8
11May66-9Aqu fst 1⅛.48⅖1.12⅗1.53 Clm 8000 5 7 68½ 510 714 714 KKnapp b 116 6.40 57-19 SkiDancer105nkSparklingEarth1088Egocentrical 1051 No speed 8
4May66-9Aqu fst 1⅛.42⅕1.13⅘1.52⅘ Clm 8500 6 5 511 52¾ 43½ 43½ RTurcotte b 116 5.50 68-20 From the Top 1072 Hail the Admiral 1181½ Fultonville 116h No mis'p 6
13Apr66-9Aqu fst 1⅛.47⅘1.13⅕1.52 Clm 8500 6 9 89½ 94¾ 64½ 53½ BBaeza b 116 6.40 72-16 Fleet Musketeer 1162 Aerie 114½ Mi Rey 114½ Never a factor 9
6Apr66-9Aqu fst 1⅛.47⅕1.11⅘1.51⅕ Clm 9500 4 3 49½ 58 510 612 MYcaza b 115 2.20 68-16 King Pooley 110o King Trece 1175 Aerie 110nk Raced wide 6
21Mar66-9Aqu fst 1⅛.48⅕1.13⅕1.53 Clm 9500 2 4 34½ 2½ 21½ 2¾ BBaeza b 114 *1.50 70-22 Fieroval 116¾ Old Bailey II 1148 Ram's Horn 1163 Drifted out 7
15Mar66-9Aqu fst 1⅛.48⅘1.15 1.54⅖ Clm 8500 6 4 47½ 33 21½ 21 BBaeza b 116 5.30 63-30 Concession 1111 Old Bailey II 11610 Golden Mike 1071 Game try 6
LATEST WORKOUTS Jly 7 Aqu 3f fst .37 b Jun 27 Aqu 3f fst .36 b Jun 23 Aqu 3f fst .36 b

Results of 9th Race Aqueduct—July 8, 1966

NINTH RACE

Aqu - 28063

July 8, 1966

1 1-8 MILES (Sinatra, December 7, 1964, 1.47⅕, 5, 111.)
Claiming. Purse $4,700. 3-year-olds and upward which have never won two races at a mile or over since April 20. Weights, 3-year-olds 116 lbs., older 123 lbs. Non-winners of a race at a mile and a furlong or over since May 31 allowed 3 lbs., of such a race since April 20, 5 lbs. Claiming price, $6,500. 2 lbs. allowed for each $250 to $6,000. (Races when entered to be claimed for $5,000 or less not considered.)

Value to winner $3,055, second $940, third $470, fourth $235. Mutuel pool $293,329.

Index	Horse	Eqt A Wt PP St	¼	½	¾	Str	Fin	Jockey	Cl'g Pr	Owner	Odds $1
27918Aqu2—Main Count		b 5 116 5 1	1^2	1^4	1^5	1^5	$12\frac{1}{2}$	O Rosado	6250	B W Steinberg	6.30
28009Aqu4—Latin Artist		6 118 2 2	4^1	$61\frac{1}{2}$	6^3	2^2	2^6	R Turcotte	6500	J T Iacovelli	9.20
27909Aqu6—Del Coronado		b 5 113 1 6	$6\frac{1}{2}$	7^6	7^8	6^2	$3\frac{1}{2}$	E Cardone5	6500	N Hellman	1.50
27909Aqu8—Inflexible		5 118 3 5	5^3	4h	3h	4^2	$4\frac{3}{4}$	E Belmonte	6500	Mrs L Dalsemer	3.70
27909Aqu11—Fultonville		4 116 4 3	2h	2^1	2^4	3h	5^1	J Ruane	6250	W Lorenz	16.20
27898Mth3—Old Bailey II		b 8 123 7 7	7^6	$5\frac{1}{2}$	$5\frac{1}{2}$	7^6	6nk	K Knapp	6500	Grandview Stable	6.00
27839Aqu7—Metamora		4 118 6 4	3^3	3^5	4^1	$5\frac{1}{2}$	7^8	G Lanoway	6500	D E Taylor	38.60
27909Aqu10—Mi Rey		b 7 118 8 8	8	8	8	8	8	R Ferraro	6500	Mrs S Westfal	7.20

Time .24⅗, .48⅖, 1.13, 1.39⅗, 1.53⅗ (with wind in backstretch). Track fast.

$2 Mutuel Prices:

5-MAIN COUNT	14.60	9.60	4.80
2-LATIN ARTIST		9.80	4.80
1-DEL CORONADO			2.80

B. h, by Count of Honor—Humane, by Broadside. Trainer M. Cohn. Bred by L. B. Combs.
IN GATE AT 5.29. OFF AT 5.29 EASTERN DAYLIGHT TIME. Start good. Won driving.
MAIN COUNT opened up a lengthy lead at once and under clever rating prevailed. LATIN ARTIST rallied to pass tired horses. DEL CORONADO was never a serious contender. INFLEXIBLE saved ground but was unable to threaten. FULTONVILLE tired chasing the pacemaker. OLD BAILEY II was wide. METAMORA was finished early. MI REY showed little.
Inflexible was claimed by Alice Hill, trainer E. L. Cotton.
Scratched--28009Aqu Victary.

Courtesy of The Morning Telegraph

record suggested that she would be in hot water unless something else was able to cook Gay Gobha's goose during the early stages. Mopolina had shown no great speed after running three lengths behind the early pace in her last race. She had remained three lengths behind all the way.

I would hesitate to use numerical pace ratings in a situation like this, where none of the entrants has been around long enough to do its very best.

Pace and Post Position

We have already considered the advantage of an inside post position to a fast-breaking front-runner when the first turn is only a few hops from the starting gate. Logically enough, an outside post position is a serious disadvantage to such a horse in a race of that kind, unless it is the class of its field.

Needing to get out front in a hurry so that it can run with maximum ease at the slowest possible pace over the shortest possible distance, the front-runner needs extra class and stamina to overcome the handicap of the outside post. Lacking those qualities, but imprisoned by its running style, it may defeat itself in the effort to get to the rail, in front, before reaching the first turn. Or, if the rider does not try to get to the

6th Race Aqueduct

5½ FURLONGS AQUEDUCT (Start / Finish)

5 1-2 FURLONGS. (Raise a Native, July 17, 1963, 1.02⅗, 2, 124.) Allowances. Purse $5,500. Fillies. 2-year-olds which have never won two races. Weight, 119 lbs. Non-winners of a race since May 31, allowed 3 lbs., of a race since Apr. 20, 5 lbs., maidens, 7 lbs.

Lady Ebony

Blk. f (1964–Ky), by Tudor Minstrel—Prize Day, by Royal Charger — D. E. Taylor — J. W. Smith — (L. Combs 2d) — 114^{5} — 1966 3 1 1 0 $3,530

30Jun66–3Mth fst 5½f .22⅘ .46⅕ 1.05⅘ f– Allow 7 2 4^{1} 5^{2}¾ 3^{3} 2^{6} GLanoway 116 *1.80 82–18 Hot Streak 116^{6} Lady Ebony 116^{1}½ Behaving Bess 101^{1} Wide turn 7

22Jun66–7Aqu fst 5½f .22 .45⅗ 1.05⅕ f–Stallion 3 5 5^{4} 4^{4}½ 7^{9} 9^{15} GLanoway 119 9.80 72–20 Lady Brilliance 114^{8} Intriguing 119½ Gateway Clipper 119^{h} Tired 9

8Jun66–5Aqu fst 5f .22⅕ .46 .59 f–MdSpWt 4 2 1^{1}½ 1^{2} 1^{2} 1^{3}½ GLanoway 119 25.10 90–12 Lady Ebony 119^{3}½ Treacherous 119^{5} Angcourt 119^{1} Easily 10

LATEST WORKOUTS Jly 10 Bel m.t. 4f fst .49⅕ b — Jun 29 Bel m.t. 4f fst .49⅕ b — Jun 21 Bel m.t. 3f fst .37 b — Jun 18 Bel m.t. 6f fst 1.17 b

Statosphere

Ch. f (1964–Tex), by Zenith—Airosa, by Heliopolis — King Ranch — Max Hirsch — (King Ranch) — 112 — 1966 0 M 0 0 —

LATEST WORKOUTS Jly 10 Bel m.t. 6f fst 1.18⅖ b — Jly 6 Bel m.t. 3f fst .36⅗ bg — Jly 3 Bel m.t. 6f fst 1.15 h — Jun 27 Bel m.t. 3f fst .38⅘ bg

Gay Gobha

Dk. b. or br. f (1964–Va.), by Besomer—Iarrtas, by Alquest — Mrs. C. MacLeod — C. MacLeod, Jr. — (C. MacLeod, Jr.) — 119 — 1966 3 1 1 1 $3,990

6Jly 66–6Aqu fst 5½f .22⅘ .46⅘ 1.06⅕ f–MdSpWt 7 3 2½ 1½ 1^{1} 1^{2}½ HWoodhouse 119 *1.00 82–20 Gay Gobha 119^{2}½ Needles Lady 119^{4} Imanative 119^{2} Mild drive 9

29Jun66–5Aqu fst 5½f .22⅘ .46⅕ 1.05⅘ f–MdSpWt 6 6 5^{2}¾ 5^{3}½ 2^{1} 2^{1}½ HWoodhouse 119 3.80 82–17 Vanilla 119^{1}½ Gay Gobha 119^{6} Henrietta 119no Wide on turn 12

22Jun66–5Aqu fst 5½f .22⅗ .46⅗ 1.06⅗ f–MdSpWt 3 10 9^{9}½ 8^{7}½ 7^{6} 3^{2} BFeliciano 119 5.00e 78–20 Green Glade 119^{1} Sorche 119^{1} Gay Gobha 119^{2}½ In close, rallied 12

LATEST WORKOUTS Jly 5 Bel m.t. 3f fst .37⅗ b — Jun 28 Bel m.t. 3f fst .38 b — Jun 18 Bel m.t. 5f fst 1.01⅖ h — Jun 15 Bel m.t. 5f fst 1.02⅖ h

Off Target

Dk. b. or br. f (1964–Fla), by Jet Ace—Jet Wave, by Ace Destroyer — A. B. Crain — A. B. Crain — (T. M. Daniel) — 119 — 1966 8 1 2 0 $2,190

24Jun66–4Cka fst 5f .23 .46⅗ 1.01⅕ Allowance 4 4 6^{5} 7^{8} 3^{6} 2½ WEdler b 114 30.80 82–18 Worldly Step 118½ Off Target 114^{nk} Hanaka 121^{1} Strong late effort 9

17Jun66–8Cka fst 5f .23⅖ .47 1.00 Allowance 5 7 7^{5}¾ 8^{9}½ 8^{12} 7^{12} REYoung b 116 8.70 77–16 Worldly Step 111^{7} Beamingly 119^{1} MendyJoan 114^{2} Showed nothing 9

10May66–3Suf sl 4½f .23⅗ .49⅕ .55⅘ f–MdSpWt 2 3 4^{3}¼ 3^{2}½ 1^{1}½ WSoirez b 118 12.30 80–20 Off Target 118^{1}½ Lynn Bradley 118^{2}½ Freds Girl 118^{1}½ Drew out 8

4Apr66–3GP fst 5f .23⅕ .48 1.02 f–MdSpWt 4 3 5^{1}¾ 6^{6} 9^{14} 9^{10} DDeRoin b 119 4.80 68–22 Jen–Jen's Story 119^{2}½ Sincere 119^{1}½ Rocks Reel 119½ In close 12

16Mar66–4FD fst 4½f .23⅘ .49⅕ .55⅕ Md Sp Wt 1 1 2^{h} 2^{h} 2^{1}½ CJGilbert b 115 6.40 88–10 MagicBud 113^{1}½ OffTarget 115^{4} WhiteMark 115^{1}½ Made sharp try 9

4Mar66–3FD fst 4½f .23⅗ .49⅗ .57⅗ f–MdSpWt 9 5 4^{4} 4^{6} 4^{2}½ PBrandt 118 12.40 75–22 Miss Batfish 118^{1}½ Speedy O'Shay 113½ Lotta Miss 118½ Evenly 10

11Feb66–3FD fst 3f .24 .35⅕ Md Sp Wt 9 9 7^{6}¾ 6^{5}¼ PBrandt b 115 38.70 87– 3 Laffin Mango 118^{3} Speedy O'Shay 110^{1} Gideon Kay 118^{nk} No factor 10

14Jan66–4FD fst 3f .23⅗ .34⅘ Md Sp Wt 3 10 5^{7} 6^{11} NCartwright 115 6.00 83– 6 Quillostar 118^{2} Fox Star 118^{4} Miss Batfish 115^{4} No factor 10

LATEST WORKOUTS Jly 11 Bel m.t. 3f fst .39 b

Best Secret

Dk. b. or br. f (1964–Fla), by Clandestine—Liked Best, by Fighting Frank — Kamejab Farm — A. A. Fiore — (West Wind Ranch) — 119 — 1966 2 1 0 0 $2,275

22Jun66–7Aqu fst 5½f .22 .45⅗ 1.05⅕ f–Stallion 5 3 4^{3} 6^{6} 9^{12} 8^{14} HWoodhouse 114 44.30 73–20 Lady Brilliance 114^{8} Intriguing 119½ Gateway Clipper 119^{h} Tired 9

7Jun66–5Aqu fst 5f .23⅕ .47 .59⅖ f–Md 7500 8 5 3^{2}½ 1^{h} 1^{1} 1^{3} ACordero 119 4.30 88–17 Best Secret 119^{3} My Ego 119^{2}½ Fuss Fuss 115^{5} Easily 10

LATEST WORKOUTS Jly 10 Bel m.t. 3f fst .36 h — Jun 30 Bel m.t. 4f fst .50 b — Jun 20 Bel m.t. 4f fst .49⅕ b — Jun 16 Bel m.t. 4f fst .47⅗ h

Up And At 'Em

B. f (1964–Fla), by Hilarious—Auratum, by Blue Swords — Hobeau Farm — H. A. Jerkens — (E. K. Heubeck) — 109^{10} — 1966 2 1 0 0 $2,600

5Jly 66–4Aqu fst 5½f .22⅘ .46⅘ 1.06 f–Md 12500 6 1 4^{3} 4^{3}½ 2^{h} 1^{2}½ ECardone^{5} b 116 *2.40 83–20 Up And At 'Em 116^{2}½ Greek Song's Get 119^{5} Nursemaid 121^{2}½ Easily 10

24Jun66–5Suf fst 5f .23 .47 .59⅘ f–MdSpWt 7 8 10^{6}½ 11^{16} 10^{10} 6^{6}¾ WMayorga 118 7.90 85–15 Fragrantly 118^{4} English Jane 118¾ Dora Mia 118no No factor 12

LATEST WORKOUTS Jly 9 Bel tr.t. 4f fst .53 b — Jly 2 Bel tr.t. 5f fst 1.02⅗ b — Jun 28 Bel m.t. 3f fst .38⅘ bg — Jun 22 Bel m.t. 5f fst 1.03⅕ b

Mopolina

B. f (1964–Fla), by Bolinas Boy—Mop Squeezer, by Parnassus — A. Muller — J. Lipari — (A. Muller) — 114 — 1966 2 1 1 0 $3,375

28Jun66–6Aqu fst 5½f .22⅗ .46⅗ 1.05⅗ f– Allow 9 7 4^{2}½ 3^{3} 2^{3} 2^{3} BBaeza 114 ● 6.90 82–19 Snap Alive 119^{3} Mopolina 114^{3}½ Gala Honors 119¾ Went well 10

25Feb66–3Hia fst 3f .22⅕ .33⅕ f–MdSpWt 13 9 4^{1}½ 1^{2} BBaeza 117 *1.40 96– 4 Mopolina 117^{2} Trolley Car 117^{3} Ethical 117½ Scored easily 14

LATEST WORKOUTS Jly 9 Bel tr.t. 3f fst .35 h — Jly 6 Bel tr.t. 5f fst 1.04⅗ b — Jun 25 Bel tr.t. 4f fst .50⅗ h — Jun 21 Bel m.t. 5f fst 1.02⅕ hg

Results of 6th Race Aqueduct—July 12, 1966

SIXTH RACE **5 1-2 FURLONGS. (Raise a Native, July 17, 1963, 1.02⅗, 2, 124.)**
Aqu - 28087 Allowances. Purse $5,500. Fillies. 2-year-olds which have never won two races. Weight, 119 lbs. Non-winners of a race since May 31, allowed 3 lbs., of a race since Apr. 20, 5 lbs., maidens, 7 lbs.
July 12, 1966

Value to winner $3,575, second $1,100, third $550, fourth $275. Mutuel pool $263,653.

Index	Horse	Eqt	A	Wt	PP	St	¼	½	Str	Fin	Jockey	Owner	Odds $1
28042Aqu1	—Gay Gobha		2	119	3	4	2²	2²	1¹	1¾	H Woodho'e	Mrs C MacLeod	4.30
27913Aqu2	—Mopolina		2	114	7	2	3¹	3¹½	3²	2½	B Baeza	A Muller	.80
27869Aqu8	—Best Secret		2	119	5	1	1h	1h	2½	3nk	E Belmonte	Kamejab Farm	21.20
28031Aqu1	—Up and At 'Em	b	2	109	6	6	5½	5³	4¹	4⁴	A Logue'o10	Hobeau Farm	5.10
27910Mth2	—Lady Ebony		2	114	1	3	4³	4²	5⁶	5⁶	E Cardone5	D E Taylor	4.30
27857Cka2	—Off Target	b	2	119	4	5	6⁵	6⁴	6⁴	6⁵	L Adams	A B Crain	32.30
	—Statosphere		2	115	2	7	7	7	7	7	E Guerin	King Ranch	24.70

Time .22⅖, .46, .58⅘ 1.05⅗ (with wind in backstretch). Track fast.

$2 Mutuel Prices:			
3-GAY GOBHA	10.60	3.20	2.60
7-MOPOLINA		2.40	2.20
5-BEST SECRET			3.80

Dk. b. or br. f by Besomer—Iarrtas by Alquest. Trainer C. MacLeod Jr. Bred by C. MacLeod, Jr. (Va).
IN GATE AT 3.57. OFF AT 3.57 EASTERN DAYLIGHT TIME. Start good. Won driving.

GAY GOBHA took command from BEST SECRET in the upper stretch and was hard ridden to retain a safe margin over MOPOLINA. The latter raced evenly for a half mile and finished strongly. BEST SECRET faltered when challenged by GAY GOBHA. UP AND AT 'EM drifted out entering the stretch but swerved during the drive and could not better her position. LADY EBONY had no mishap. OFF TARGET and STATOSPHERE showed nothing.

Overweight—Statosphere 3 pounds.

Courtesy of The Morning Telegraph

rail that soon, the mount must cover extra ground on the turn and may lose that way.

In circumstances of that sort, a stretch-running type with a more favorable post position is often a better bet. When ridden by a good postboy able to get it out in a hurry and find a good position in the pack, it is able to lay slightly off the pace and, with ordinary luck, find the room it needs to pass the fatigued front-runner in the stretch.

Races with a long, straight run to the first turn are quite different for the jockey and the player. The front-runner is at no serious disadvantage in any post position. Even if it breaks from the extreme outside, its rider has plenty of time. He may ease over to the rail at any point before the first turn occurs, losing little ground and expending practically no extra energy in the process.

The slow-breaking horse with an inside post position is in grave trouble, however. Unable to get out of the gate as fast as many of the others, it often is pinched back as they fight their way toward the rail. To its difficulty in gathering stride and momentum is added the exertion of staying out of trouble and, finally, the problem of trailing everyone around the turn and, as the stretch arrives, finding—as often as not—that the only way home is on the outside of the pack, covering extra ground.

An added complication, for front-runner and off-pace horse alike, is the condition of the running surface. On muddy days, the deepest, most difficult running is often along the rail. The speed horse, which usually needs to save as much ground as possible, can now do so only at the risk of tiring itself in the deep gumbo. The competition now becomes a struggle for room in mid-track. The stretch-runner with a touch of stamina and class sometimes manages to come on along the rail at the end, deep footing or not.

Perhaps the most important fact about post positions, apart from the special situations we have just reviewed, is that they usually are of no significance in handicapping. A player who bet on post positions instead of horses should end each year with a loss of exactly 17 cents on the wagered dollar! Why? Because no post position has a long-range advantage over any other. Horses win with equal frequency from each stall in the starting gate. Playing post positions is therefore like picking horses at random by stabbing the program with a hatpin.

14 The Stable Factor

DURING 1966, Thoroughbred tracks in the United States, Canada and Mexico disbursed over $125 million in purses to more than 22,000 owners of racing stables.

If the money had been divided equally, which it was not, the average owner would have won about $5,600—enough to keep a one-horse stable out of the red at a minor track.

Averages, as I keep saying, are deceptive. In a typical year, 10,000 stables (a good 45 percent of all owners) win less than $1,000 each! The top hundred stables (less than ½ percent), usually win 20 percent of the purse money. In 1966, thirty stables (hardly more than 1/10 of 1 percent) raked in over $14 million—more than 11 percent of North American purses!

Eliminating the top hundred and the bottom 10,000 owners, one finds that the "average earnings" of the remaining 12,000 stables were $8,000 during 1966. This was not quite enough to maintain a one-horse stable at a major track, and not nearly enough to pay the way of the multiple-horse stables that occupy most backstretch barns.

Modern racing is founded on the willingness of 98 percent of owners to lose money. Most can afford to. If they could not afford to, they would quit the game. Indeed, there is reason to believe that a certain few would quit if they ever accidentally began to *make* money. Their chief interest in racing is as a tax gimmick.

Socialites and Pros

Owners come in all shapes, sizes, sexes and ages, from all walks of life. Those who form the political backbone of the big-time sport and supply it with most of its famous glamor are persons of inherited wealth. The breeding and racing of Thoroughbreds is a traditional avocation of their families. They share dominance of the pastime with a few millionaires of more recent vintage and a scattering of professional horse-men who rose to the top the hard way and now own important stables. In 1966, when the Phipps-Wheatley interests won purses of almost $2.5 million, it was interesting to find that the runner-up on the owners' earn-ings list was a professional horseman, Marion H. Van Berg. He won $847,794. His 277 victories were an all-time record. In 1967 this veteran won 268 times, leading all owners for the eighth successive year.

Diverse though owners may be, they fall into two categories. The smaller (by far) is composed of those with sufficient sense and taste to leave horsemanship to horsemen. Their paragons are the Phippses, of course, and Mr. and Mrs. George D. Widener, aristocrats of the Eastern sport. The Wideners allow their trainers, Bert Mulholland and Sylvester Veitch, to run the barns and pick the spots. A more numerous group includes owners whose desire for prominence exceeds their interest in horseflesh. If certain trainers behave like con artists and seem to know as much about soft soap as they do about the care and schooling of Thoroughbreds, it is from years of coping with bubble-headed employers.

Many owners want the trainer to pretend that they know something about horses. They crave to make strategy. They sulk if the trainer fails to adorn each horse with a popular rider. They want to know why the trainer spends so much money on straw. They get sore if the trainer doesn't tip them off to a longshot once in a while. They fume if they don't win stakes races and get on television. They make general nui-sances of themselves. But they pay bills.

One of the most celebrated owners of modern times was Elizabeth (Arden) Graham, the cosmetics queen who owned Maine Chance Farms. During her thirty-five years in the sport, she employed at least sixty-five trainers. Some of the most competent horsemen of the era were unable to achieve lasting rapport with the lady. For examples, Eddie Neloy, Clarence Buxton, Eddie Holton, H. Guy Bedwell, George Odom, Frank Christmas, Tom Barry, Mose Shapoff, Ivan and Monte Parke, Ben Stutts, W. O. Hicks, Frank Merrill, Jr., Casey Hayes, Willie Molter, Randy Sechrest, Al Scotti and George Poole.

The player needs to know something about owners. He especially needs to know the names of the most successful ones. Generally, he will pay much more attention to the doings of trainers, who are the most decisive influences in the life of a Thoroughbred. But trainers move from owner to owner, their fortunes rising or falling according to the kind of livestock the owner provides. And year after year the same owners appear on the list of leading money winners. It pays to know who is who.

Leading Owners

To qualify for a player's alert respect, a stable should not only win a lot of money but should win more than 15 percent of the races it enters. The following owners have established their ability to meet these standards, and are likely to merit attention for years.

WHEATLEY STABLE ⎫
OGDEN PHIPPS ⎬ Tops. In 1966, earned $2,455,365
OGDEN M. PHIPPS ⎭ among them.

MARION H. VAN BERG	HOLIDAY STABLE
HOBEAU FARM	ROKEBY STABLE
HARBOR VIEW FARM .	HARRY GORDON
MRS. ETHEL D. JACOBS	BILL BEASLEY
PATRICE JACOBS	ADA L. RICE
T. ALIE GRISSOM	CLAIBORNE FARM
C. V. WHITNEY	W. HAGGIN PERRY
G. D. WIDENER	EVERETT LOWRANCE
GREENTREE STABLE	MEADOW STABLE
FRED W. HOOPER	HARVEY PELTIER
POWHATAN	FRANK M. McMAHON
BWAMAZON FARM	NEIL HELLMAN
TARTAN STABLE	F. and H. N. SELTZER
PETE MAXWELL	

Man vs. Horse

Horsemen sometimes convey the impression that the sport would be more to their liking if a way could be found to eliminate the horses.

Eddie Arcaro once complained that three out of four horses don't want to win their races. Other riders say that unwillingness is even more prevalent than that. Throughout the industry, a standard conversational theme is the perverse, mulish, erratic contrariness of these animals.

After centuries of selective breeding, racing apparently remains alien to the essential nature of the Thoroughbred. Despite training routines intended to bring any fairly sound horse into some kind of racing trim, the breed continues to balk.

Exactly what is wrong?

Human stupidity and greed, intensified by the economics of a highly precarious business.

Owners of Champions

When owned by Warren Wright, the late baking-powder tycoon, Calumet Farm was the leading Thoroughbred racing stable in the United States. No fewer than thirteen national champions raced under its colors. They were, A Glitter, Armed, Barbizon, Bewitch, Citation, Coaltown, Mar-Kell, Real Delight, Tim Tam, Twilight Tear, Two Lea, Whirlaway and Wistful.

Other owners of several champions have been:

A. G. Vanderbilt: Bed o' Roses, Discovery, Native Dancer, Next Move, Now What, Petrify and Social Outcast.

Wheatley Stable: Bold Ruler, Castle Forbes, High Voltage, Misty Morn, Bold Lad, Queen Empress, Successor.

C. V. Whitney: Bug Brush, Career Boy, Counterpoint, First Flight, Phalanx, Silver Spoon.

George D. Widener: Battlefield, Jaipur, Platter, Seven Thirty, Stefanita, What A Treat.

Greentree Stable: Capot, Devil Diver, Jungle King, Malicious, Tom Fool.

Maine Chance Farm: Beaugay, Jewel's Reward, Myrtle Charm, Rose Jet, Star Pilot.

Meadow Stable: Cicada, First Landing, Hill Prince, Sir Gaylord.

Claiborne Farm: Bayou, Doubledogdare, Moccasin, Nadir.

C. S. Howard: Kayak II, Mioland, Noor, Seabiscuit.

Responsible racing journals are replete with articles on the techniques of breaking and schooling yearlings, maintaining equine health, and preparing a horse for its race. Regardless of disagreements on technical matters, virtually all the articles play variations on a single theme: A Thoroughbred treated with rough impatience is unlikely to amount to much.

If kindness, patience and intelligence were dominant characteristics of the racing industry, such articles would be unnecessary. But they are necessary. Anyone can prove it to himself by wandering around the barns of a morning, or keeping his eyes and ears open at the paddock in the afternoon.

Many trainers, stablehands, exercise boys and jockeys truly love and understand horses. Many more do not. The heart of the misunderstanding seems to be the unwarranted assumption that modern racing is a natural activity for horses and that the animals, though mentally dim,

Noms de Course

The player ought to know that he is talking about John Hay Whitney when he says, "Greentree Stable." Here are some of America's most important racing stables, and the names of the persons who own them.

Audley Farms (James F. Edwards)
Barclay Stable (John McShain)
Bohemia Stable (Mrs. Richard C. DuPont)
Briardale Farm (Anthony Imbesi)
Brookfield Farm (Harry Z. Isaacs)
Bwamazon Farm (Millard Waldheim)
Cain Hoy Stable (Harry F. Guggenheim)
Calumet Farm (Mrs. Lucille P. Markey)
Charles Offset Horse Farm (Charles Friedfertig)
Christiana Stables (Jane duPont Lunger)
Claiborne Farm (A. B. Hancock, Jr.)
Cragwood Stables (Charles W. Engelhard)
Dane Hill Acres (E. B. Seedhouse)
Darby Dan Farm (John W. Galbreath)
Edgehill Farm (Leonard Fruchtman)
El Peco Ranch (George A. Pope, Jr.)
Ford Stables (Michael J. Ford)
Fourth Estate Stable (John S. Knight)

should adopt a more human attitude toward their work and be grateful for the opportunity to participate. When the bland manageableness that passes for equine gratitude is withheld, and sulkiness or rebelliousness sets in, the tendency of the human being is to react with resentment of his own. In due course, there arises the peculiarly negative, self-defeating, quite widespread feeling that the meal-ticket, the horse, is an infernal nuisance, a necessary evil.

The truth is that racing is no more natural for horses than the hundred-yard dash is for men. To engage successfully in activities of that kind, a horse (or man) must be carefully schooled and tended. To survive any great number of races or training workouts without breaking down, the muscles, joints, heart and lungs of horse or man must be trained for undue stress. The difference, of course, is that a human footracer can discuss his pain. And he can make choices.

Foxcatcher Farms (John E. duPont)
Gedney Farms (Harry P. Albert)
Gem State Stables (Mrs. H. W. Morrison)
Golden Triangle Stables (Thomas A. Eazor)
Gray Willow Farm (Ace Fessenden)
Greentree Stable (John Hay Whitney)
Harbor View Farm (Louis E. Wolfson)
Hobeau Farm (Jack J. Dreyfus)
Holiday Stable (Charles F. Parker)
Jaclyn Stable (Leon Levy)
Jacnot Stable (Jack Hogan)
Jumping Brook Farm (Stella Colt)
King Ranch (Robert J. Kleberg, Jr.)
Llangolen Farm (Liz Whitney Tippett)
Meadow Stable (Christopher T. Chenery)
Murray Stable (Matthew J. Murray, Jr.)
North Star Ranch (Stanley E. Hubbard)
Powhatan (Raymond R. Guest)
Rokeby Stables (Paul Mellon)
Tartan Stable (William L. McKnight)
Warner Stable (Albert Warner)
Wheatley Stable (Gladys Phipps)
Willow Downs Farm (Saul Wagman)
Windfields Farms (Edward P. Taylor)

But horses cannot. They are entirely dependent on man. Like other domesticated animals such as the dog, they thrive or wilt according to the treatment they get from humans. A well-nurtured Thoroughbred tolerates the hullabaloo of the track, the repeated exhaustion of training and racing, the sometimes frightening ministrations of handlers, blacksmiths and veterinarians. He is willing to race. He sometimes even seems to like it. When he is retired he may act, like an Exterminator or Kelso, as if he missed the excitement, and may perk up considerably when brought back to a track to parade in front of the stands.

But the unwilling Thoroughbred is a different specimen. He fears noise, or people, or some particular handler, or his knee hurts after repeated concussion of hoof on racing strip, or his lungs are congested, or he was soured on the whole game by unpleasant early experiences. Sometimes he can be whipped into cooperating and running a good race.

More often, the punishment frightens him into losing his stride. Or he retaliates in the only ways he knows, which are to sulk or swerve or duck or stop.

As the Hirsch Jacobs' experience with Stymie illustrates, and as has been shown in many other cases of the same kind, a trainer with time, skill and motivation may sometimes undo the previous experiences or present afflictions that cause unwillingness in a Thoroughbred. Unfortunately, the tempo and pressures of the business make most such speculative experiments uneconomical. The horse is a commodity on which a quick return is craved. Either it delivers or it goes elsewhere. The need for the quick dollar, earned from minimum investment, affects what happens to most Thoroughbreds from the moment of birth. Financial pressures influence the behavior of trainers, grooms, exercise boys and stablehands— all but a lucky few trainers and their backstretch help.

While most owners fully expect to lose money, each wants to win every purse he can—and some specialize in nagging about it. The goal of the average trainer and his staff is to keep the owner quiet—if not happy—by providing maximum action. Moreover, backstretch incomes are tied to purse revenues. The trainer gets 10 percent. Bonuses go to everyone else, including the humblest swipe.

Under those pressures for quick returns, and with the track's racing secretary screaming for horses with which to fill out his programs, it is perhaps no wonder that comparatively sound animals are grievously overworked. And that they continue to race even after overwork begins to take its toll. And that they finally break down forever. And that the year never passes without half a dozen good three-year-olds going permanently bad before they ever get to Churchill Downs. And that many three-year-old champions poop out at four or five. And that a topnotch six-year-old is a rarity.

You can argue until you turn blue that a horse might last longer and earn a great deal more money if raced more sparingly, prepared more carefully for each race. The trainer answers with a grimace, "Horses make no money standing in their stalls or browsing in pastures. I'm not Johnny Nerud, Jack Gaver, Bert Mulholland or Frank Whiteley. I'm not working for Mr. McKnight, Mr. Whitney, Mr. Widener or Mr. Guest. I've got payrolls to meet and my owners are breathing down my back. Horse either gets up and does it or I go rustle me another horse."

Scores of trainers—possibly hundreds—do the very best that can be done for their animals, on the sound theory that proper care will be repaid at the finish wire some afternoon. Their ability to function this wisely depends not only on their own competence but on the **dispositions** of their employers—the owners—and on the quality of their stable help. Good stablehands are hard to find nowadays. The others tend to give as little time and care as possible to a horse, thereby helping to worsen whatever quirk or ailment may be preventing it from winning. I have seen the trainers of world-famous stables seethe in helpless rage at the barbarically stupid impatience with which exercise boys and grooms handle frightened animals. "I'll fire that bum as soon as I can find another," is a familiar refrain in the front offices of racing barns.

How Horses Learn

All scientific studies of horses reveal them to be less intelligent, in the human sense, than apes, dolphins, elephants, pigs or dogs. But they are keenly sensitive to their surroundings and to the experiences they undergo at human hands. And they have memories that would do credit to any elephant. It is easier for them to learn than to forget what they have learned. A bad habit implanted by a misused whip, an ill-advised shout or cuff, or an accidental collision, may persist for years.

It is unlikely that any horse actually understands the difference between winning and losing. Yet horses obviously do what they can to avoid or resist discomfort. There seems no doubt that they do best when taught their trade with a minimum of fear and pain, and when convinced by repeated experience that the rewards of good performance are worth the considerable effort.

It all begins with the yearlings. Patient, gentle treatment being costly, because it consumes the time of expensive personnel, an appalling number of Thoroughbreds are ruined at this, the earliest stage of their careers.

The process known as "breaking" is meant to accustom the young horse to the feel of the rider and his tack. It is a hideously frightening experience for the yearling, unless the handlers take their time. All writings on the subject (and trade journals are at it constantly), emphasize that human violence during the breaking period often spoils the disposition of a horse, leaving it dispirited or fractious.

Damage at that stage is compounded for many horses by impatience and carelessness during their first months of drill on the training track. They must learn to run straight, and to respond to the rider's voice, hands and reins, and to change leads on the turns, and to break from a standing start at the gate. It is a tricky business in which, once again, the future abilities of the animal may be impaired by unintelligent handling.

Yet the pressures are to school 'em as fast as possible (to save money)

The late Sunny Jim Fitzsimmons, one of the most successful trainers of all time, with his great Nashua.

UPI PHOTO

and get 'em to the races as early in the two-year-old season as possible (to get the money back). Thousands never make it to actual competition, having broken down from running too fast too early in their lives.

Horses do not grow a complete set of adult teeth until they are five! One of the chief reasons why young horses break down is that their immaturely soft bones give way under the concussion of running full tilt over hard surfaces. Incredibly, some veterinarians assert that the problem is worsened and disaster assured by ill-fitting shoes, which throw the animals off balance when they run.

Among horses that finally get to the races, few are without quirks of temperament or running style. Horsemen ascribe many of these idiosyncrasies to equine family traits. But candid ones agree that proper handling from the very start of schooling could minimize the effects of these inherited characteristics and, above all, could prevent development of other bad habits.

When the jockey grumbles that he always has to whip a particular horse to get some run from it in the early stages of a race, he refers in most cases to an animal whose earliest handlers taught it, altogether unintentionally, to behave that way. Horses that panic in the paddock or do not like to run on the rail, or between horses, or behind horses, or in front of horses, or on the turns, or that quit when whipped, or refuse to run unless whipped, are victims of their early conditioning. Horses whose tongues must be tied down with straps are, most often,

Mares and foals at Dickey Stables in the Florida Green Grass country.

horses whose first handlers did not know how to break them to the bit.

One of the best-known facts about Thoroughbreds is that their first experiences in competition often have a decisive effect on their later performances. A horse whose trainer is careful to give it an easy first race or two has a much better chance of going on to better things than a horse that almost expires of exhaustion in its first outings. Even better at the beginning is an easy *winning* race. The horse that loses its first races in all-out efforts may take months to recover from the experience. It usually behaves as if it is *supposed* to chase the others, not beat them.

In 1961, *The Thoroughbred Record* provoked considerable debate with a series of articles by the veteran horseman Colonel Phil T. Chinn Among other statements uncomplimentary to modern racing, Chinn declared that the bucked shins, osselets and other arthritic ailments that afflict today's overworked two- and three-year-old horses were virtually unknown in his era. Horses were not subjected to premature strain when he was a lad. When they turned sore, he said, they were rested. And rest was more beneficial to bones and joints worn and torn by overstrain than the modern practice of cauterizing damaged tissue with a red-hot iron.

During the ensuing uproar, *The Thoroughbred Record* polled horsemen for their opinions. Three out of five agreed that the modern Thoroughbred is less sound than its ancestor of thirty years ago. Those who agreed tended to blame today's harder tracks, the demand for more speed, the failure to rest modern horses during the winter, and the strain of breaking from the stationary starting gate.

Some of the comments were enlightening.

Sam Sechrest said, "It's not a question of soundness. If horses were given more time as two-year-olds and at the time of breaking, and not started so soon, I don't believe there would be so many bucked shins and osselets."

Max Hirsch: "Horses not raised with common sense."

Robert L. Dotter: "Asking for too much speed from horses that have not finished growing."

Stephen Di Mauro: "Bad exercise boys—snatching, twisting and turning horses too sharply. Same for hot walkers. All in all, careless help."

John H. C. Forbes: "Thirty years ago there was time to rest a horse."

R. H. McLellan: "Starting juveniles at the start of the year and racing the majority of them too often thereafter."

W. C. Freeman: "Too many sprint races which force a trainer to rush his young horses before they have achieved their growth."

Dale Landers: "Racing and breaking colts too young."

Other articles in authoritative trade periodicals have deplored abuses visited on horses that survive the rigors of premature racing. Writer after writer pleads with horsemen to give ailing or jaded Thoroughbreds the rest they need. But rest takes time. And time is money. From stakes winners to $1,000 derelicts, lack of rest is a prime factor in the development of disability.

Veterinarians agree, and many have written, that a horse with cold symptoms should be rested. In recent years, outbreaks of what horsemen call "cough"—actually influenza—have caused alarm throughout racing. The proper treatment includes rest—an absolute termination of training and racing. But the lung capacities of innumerable Thoroughbreds have been impaired permanently by the strain of racing while infected with flu.

"I know, I know," says a top trainer. "I'm as sad as you are that the sport is not as gracious as it was when lords and their ladies sat under parasols and watched Arabian chargers run around their pastures for side bets. But this thing is bigger than all of us. It's just a reflection of changes that have taken place in every area of life. If you want to get indignant about the industrialization of the Thoroughbred, be my guest. But while you're at it, you might consider the industrialization of everything else. When was the last time you saw a piece of homemade bread, or milk fresh from a cow, or a new-laid egg, or an automobile that looked like the guy who made it cared about his work? You go get indignant about horses. Me, my main worry is whether I can get my horses onto the track for their exercise tomorrow morning before the strip is shut down for rolling. And whether I can talk some snot of an exercise boy into taking my filly around the track twice before he runs off to pick up another few bucks working some other guy's horse. And whether tomorrow's shipment of feed will have mold in it like the last one. And whether the damned accountant will get the stable's books in order for the next damned tax examination."

All of this has a good deal to do with the handicapping of horse races. The player is better off when he realizes that most trainers are not more competent than most haberdashers or auto mechanics and are under no greater compulsion to be. That realization surely clears the air for the player and inspires greater respect for the feats of those very few trainers who manage somehow to surmount all obstacles, winning far more than their share of races every season. These are the trainers the smart player favors. They have better horses and/or induce more racing readiness and willingness in their stock than other trainers do. Between two evenly matched contenders—one trained by a national or local leader and the other by a scrambler—the expert player grants an advantage to the horse from the more successful barn.

Trainers to Watch

A Bert Mulholland, Frank Whiteley, Jr., or Johnny Nerud handles nothing but good horses, or potentially good horses, and races them only when he believes they are ready for a genuine effort. Such horsemen operate that way because they prefer to, and because they are fortunate enough to be employed by owners willing to be patient. Other trainers may be every bit as knowing but have less to work with. Handling the discards of better barns, or struggling with stock spoiled by others, they hang on by their fingernails and wait for luck to smile.

In the past decade a younger generation of trainers has earned prominence. Smart go-getters like Buddy Jacobson, Al Scotti, Allen Jerkens and Lou Cavalaris, Jr. have shown repeatedly that it is possible to reverse and upgrade the fortunes of a Thoroughbred by treating it more sensibly than its previous operators did.

There may be no accomplishment in modern sport to equal that of Jacobson. He has few high-class animals, yet manages to achieve a higher percentage of winners in big-league racing than most of the glamor stables do. He repairs cripples, places them properly, and wins time after time. In the process, he demonstrates that many losing Thoroughbreds and any number of losing barns could prosper with better management.

The most publicized trainer of this era is, of course, Eddie Neloy, who began his career as a stable·boy. There is nothing he has not done around a barn. For years he ran all kinds of horses, including cheap ones, and became recognized as a trainer able to get a great deal from ordinary animals. He was a sharpie at claiming apparently indifferent horses, nursing them into trim, and moving them up in class. After establishing himself at the top with Gun Bow, a champion, he took over for the Phipps interests. And promptly set an all-time earnings record for a year of racing—almost $2.5 million in 1966, when his horses won an incredible 33 percent of their starts.

Neloy says that he can think of seven or eight trainers who are better than he is. It is probably a fair estimate: Some people think nobody is as good as Neloy, others might name twenty or thirty horsemen as his equals. Such debates are fun, but pointless. To the player, the proof occurs at the mutuel cashier's window.

Here is how to do it:

1. Never bet on the trainer alone. The best seldom win more than one race in every four or five attempts.

2. If the horse seems to be a leading contender in its race and is being handled by a reliable trainer, it deserves extra favor. Indeed, it is rarely a mistake to differentiate closely matched horses on such grounds. Successful trainers get that way by beating the unsuccessful ones.

3. A contending horse deserves special consideration if its trainer meets one of the following standards:

   a. Mention on the published daily list of leading trainers at the current meeting, with a winning average of at least 17 percent.

   b. Mention on the list of consistent trainers that appears on the facing page. The list should be revised and updated by consulting The American Racing Manual each year. From the player's point of view, a high percentage of victories is more important than high total earnings.

The suggestion that a winning average of 17 percent be the timberline between reliably consistent trainers and their rivals is based on the knowledge that the most reliable trainers manage in the long run to win a race in every four or five attempts. A trainer capable of such a winning average can be regarded as off his feed or in bad luck if he falls much below 17. But, unless he loses his good horses, he will improve his average before long. This is why the list on the next two pages should be used in conjunction with the current list of local leaders, and should be updated annually.

Buddy Jacobson   *Frank Whiteley, Jr.*   *Eddie Neloy*

THE CONSISTENT ONES

Most of the best and some of the best-connected trainers in the U.S. and Canada are listed here. They win consistently.

EDDIE ANSPACH	EDDIE HOLTON
VINCE ARTHUR	BOB IRWIN*
GEORGE M. BAKER	BUDDY JACOBSON
LAZ BARRERA	L. W. JENNINGS
TOM BARRY	ALLEN JERKENS
WARREN BEASLEY	H. H. JOLLEY*
BERNIE BOND	FARRELL JONES
J. BOWES BOND	WALTER A. KELLEY
ELLIOTT BURCH	ED KELLY
L. R. CARNO	LUCIEN LAURIN
DEL CARROLL	ROGER LAURIN
LOU CAVALARIS, JR.	BUD LEPMAN
JIM CONWAY	M. LIPTON*
WILLIE CORBELLINI	MILT LONGERBEAM
W. A. CROLL, JR.	JIM MALONEY
JACK DEATRICH*	W. MASTRANGELO*
GROVER DELP	D. C. MAXWELL*
DOUG DODSON	PETE MAXWELL
J. J. DOUGHERTY	FRANK H. MERRILL, JR.
FLOYD DUNCAN	RAY METCALF
DAVE ERB	JEROME C. MEYER
HENRY FORREST	BUSTER MILLERICK
MIKE FREEMAN	H. D. MONTGOMERY*
JACK GAVER	FRANK L. MOORE
TOMMY GULLO	PETE MOSCONI
EVERETT HAMMOND*	BERT MULHOLLAND
GEORGE HANDY	EDDIE NELOY
DICK HAZELTON	EDDIE NELSON
ROBERT HILTON*	JOHNNY NERUD

* Active on minor tracks

Jim Maloney

Charlie Robbins

Elliott Burch

LEFTY NICKERSON
C. C. NORMAN
S. B. OTT
IVAN PARKE
JOE H. PIERCE, JR.
W. L. PROCTOR
W. J. RESSEGUET, JR.
CHARLIE ROBBINS
SLIM ROLES
DAVE SCHNEIDER
AL SCOTTI
RANDY SECHREST
DEWEY SMITH

ANDY SMITHERS
WOODY STEPHENS
NOBLE THREEWITT
CLYDE TROUTT
CLYDE TURK
JACK VAN BERG*
SYLVESTER E. VEITCH
SHERRILL WARD
A. H. WARNER
FRANK Y. WHITELEY, JR.
CHARLIE WHITTINGHAM
ARNOLD WINICK

Who's Who

It helps to know how leading trainers work their wonders. The following brief sketches offer useful insights into the methods employed by many of the nation's best.

EDDIE NELOY—Even if the Phipps-Wheatley luck diminishes, Neloy will remain one of the game's biggest talents. An enthusiastic, freewheeling bettor, he can always go back to winning with longshots in claiming and allowance races, meanwhile maintaining the respectable winning percentage of which he is capable. As of now, and for the foreseeable future, his first-starting two-year-olds are usually ready to run, and no horse can become two-year-old, three-year-old or handicap champion without beating Neloy's candidate for the honor.

W. F. "BERT" MULHOLLAND—Sharing the carefully pruned Widener string with Sylvester E. Veitch, this spry veteran makes unbelievably good use of his infrequent excursions to the saddling enclosure. In 1966, his charges started only 70 times, but won 24 of the races for a dazzling

* Active on minor tracks

Bert Mulholland   Eddie Anspach   Bud Lepman   Lou Cavalaris, Jr.

percentage of 34. During the previous year he was right 26 percent of the time. He never sends an unready animal to the post. His first-starters are excellent risks. He does his best work on his home grounds, New York.

FRANK Y. WHITELEY, JR.—A younger, Maryland version of Mulholland, he keeps nothing but the likeliest prospects in his Powhatan stalls, and is a contender for the prize every time he goes, and wherever he goes. In 1966, he won 32 percent of his starts. In other hands, the plucky little Tom Rolfe might never have been a stakes winner, much less a champion.

DEWEY SMITH—Trainer for the busy stable of T. Alie Grissom, this shrewd operator manages to win one start in four with ordinary horses at New Orleans, Hazel Park, Keeneland and Detroit. Most of the time he is in head-to-head combat with the stable of Marion H. Van Berg, winningest owner in the country for seven consecutive years. Any secondary track that gives stall space to the Grissom and Van Berg stock can expect them to monopolize the purses.

BOB IRWIN and JACK VAN BERG—They handle the duties for Jack's father, winning one of every five, and competing with such as Lou Cavalaris, Buddy Jacobson, Dewey Smith and Arnold Winick for national leadership in the win department. They claim with wholesale frequency, and win with the horses they claim.

BUDDY JACOBSON—Because he wears no man's collar and runs his public stable in his own way, this young genius occasionally has fewer horses than his talents suggest that he should. But he won the national championship three times and is always close. Wins with claimed horses at the first asking and can repeat with a stepped-up claimer once he gets it in shape. Is invariably a cinch to win about 20 percent of his starts.

LOU CAVALARIS, JR.—More than holds his own in New York and really knocks 'em kicking in his native Canada, where he usually boosts his overall winning average to 25 or better. May be Jacobson's equal in rehabilitating cripples. Goes for the money in first start with a newly claimed horse.

RAY METCALF—Always among the New Jersey leaders and a smart apple with a claiming racer. Gets fillies ready by racing them against

Charlie Whittingham   *Farrell Jones*   *Allen Jerkens*   *Jack Gaver*

males, and sharpens males by running them against better. Occasionally has a nice two-year-old and enjoys winning its second or third race.

ARNOLD WINICK—Saddles all kinds from handicap stars to cheapies, and is always among the national leaders in total victories and winning percentage. At home in Illinois, Jersey and Florida. Does well with first-starters, South American imports, horses dropping in class. Believes in workouts the day before the victory.

CHARLIE WHITTINGHAM—Good all-around maneuverer, handles Mrs. Cloyce Tippett's Llangolen Farm cavalry in California. Celebrated for ability to win routes with young horses at first asking. Sometimes tips his hand with a fast workout. Is good for at least one win in every five tries.

BUSTER MILLERICK—Californian perennially contends for national leadership in total earnings, winning percentage and total races won. Excellent results with first-starters, horses returning from layoffs. If horse shows good works, it's a sign Millerick has it on edge. Is good at keeping it there. His charges often put together two wins in succession.

NOBLE THREEWITT—Doesn't earn purses like those grabbed by Whittingham and Millerick, but is always in the running for California supremacy in terms of total victories. Winning percentage a reliable 20. Not afraid to lower a claiming price drastically if he thinks there's a purse to be had. Equally unafraid to push a horse up the claiming scale, and often gets a price with it. Other horsemen respect his way with fillies, some of whom run in at good odds.

FARRELL JONES—Always among the California leaders, does wonderfully at Santa Anita with first-starters, repeaters. Multiple recent workouts a good sign. Has a knack with grass runners.

ALLEN JERKENS—Former steeplechase rider is one of the most popular trainers in New York, where hundreds bet on him instead of his horses. Good for a 20 percent average, does a fine job with claimed horses and tries for the purse every time. When he drops one into a claimer from an allowance race, it's often an excellent bet, as its form in its next-to-last effort usually reveals.

WOODY STEPHENS—Florida, New York and Illinois players should watch out for this Kentuckian with two-year-olds, grass horses, step-ups.

Johnny Nerud   *Lucien Laurin*   *Randy Sechrest*

Once took a claimer named Blue Man and won the Preakness with it. Hasn't had much publicity in recent years but gets his share of big purses, and wins one in five starts.

GROVER DELP—Known as Buddy. Cuts an impressive figure in Maryland and New Jersey, with good winning average. Shrewd with claimed horses. Takes two or three weeks to work them out and spruce them up, and wins in first attempt remarkably often. When he drops a horse in class, he usually knows just where to place it.

JACK GAVER—Trainer of the intermittently formidable Greentree troop, Gaver is an expert with a really good horse (as witness Capot, Devil Diver and Tom Fool) and is always there or thereabouts with a well-bred juvenile in its first outing.

EDDIE NELSON—The New York fans don't know who he is (he never gets publicity), but he is as sharp a horseman as any in the East, and won 22 percent in 1966. Has been associated from time to time with betting stables, and is always a threat to win at a price.

JOE H. PIERCE, JR.—Son of the celebrated "Slim" Pierce seems ready to fill the shoes. Consistent winner with all sorts of stock in Illinois, Florida. Wins after drops in class. Bad last race no sign horse won't improve: look at the previous race. If it was a good one, respect the horse.

JOHNNY NERUD—One of the best, and has carte blanche from his employer, William L. McKnight of Tartan Stable (named after the emblem of Scotch Tape, McKnight's firm). His winners repeat. His first-starters win. During phases of his career that find him claiming horses, he does it brilliantly.

FRANK H. MERRILL, JR.—Always high on the national list of trainers with most victories, and often hits a high average, even though he starts upward of a thousand times a year. Has campaigned everywhere, especially including his homeland, Canada, and is a reliable winner in Illinois, Florida, New York, wherever. Wins with horses that he drops in class. Patient with his juveniles, which do better after a few conditioning races.

W. C. FREEMAN—Alfred Vanderbilt's trainer, called "Mike," is one

Lefty Nickerson   *Hirsch Jacobs*   *Tommy Gullo*   *Max Hirsch*

of the most remarkable young operatives in New York. Wins more than his share of races in which his horses go off as favorites, and also bobs up with several enormous longshots every season. Knows how to ship a horse, does well with first-starters, claims. Yet his overall winning percentage is below par. Moral: Watch him when his horse is a longshot, or the favorite!

LUCIEN LAURIN—An absolute ace with first-starters, he springs a few at Aqueduct every year. Also good with rested animals in their first or second appearance after the vacation.

PETE MOSCONI—New Yorker may be tops at claiming. Works wonders with these buys. Won the Dwyer Handicap with Staunchness, a $25,000 claim. Won the Firenze with Clear Road, a former claimer. Won over $200,000 with Hot Dust and Cedar Key, which he had claimed. Comes close to winning one in every five attempts, year after year.

RANDY SECHREST—This patient veteran stood New York on its ear during early months of 1967 season. Hits with horses in second race after a claim, or in second try after a rest.

VICTOR "LEFTY" NICKERSON—A solid, consistent winner in New York's fast company, Nickerson is especially good at finding out what ails a loser, fixing it, and moving the creature up the ladder for repeated purses. Good man with favorites.

HIRSCH JACOBS—One of the immortals of the sport, this New Yorker wins more consistently in California than on his home grounds, where he operates a huge string. One of several trainers who never bet, he employs many maneuvers usually associated with betting stables, such as cracking down with a three-year-old against its equals after getting it trounced by older horses. Also moves nicely with fillies, dropping them into cheap races for both sexes, after they lose to classy females. When he puts an allowance racer into claiming company, it usually is extremely well-placed and ready to go.

TOMMY GULLO—A trainer of claiming stock has to be a good handicapper. Nobody on the New York circuit is better at it than Gullo. His horses are invariably well situated, and he occasionally gets magnificent

Laz Barrera   *Al Scotti*   *Phil Johnson*   *Willie Corbellini*

prices with them. His claims are legendary. Most of them win soon, and repeat soon again at higher claiming prices than he paid.

MAX HIRSCH—The old-timer is still to be reckoned with, especially when the public likes his horse. Half his favorites win. Likes weight off, and takes advantage of it.

LAZ BARRERA—One of the most respected trainers on the California and New York wheels, Laz was in less than his best form during 1966, but was expected to be back around the 20 percent mark before long. He knows the business. Given a sound horse, can race it into shape and win part of the purse time after time.

FRANK "PANCHO" MARTIN—The Cuban bon vivant grosses a quarter of a million a year in New York purse money and can do anything with a horse—if it can do anything. Works wonders with cripples, rested horses, grass runners.

AL SCOTTI—Former jockey seems on verge of becoming one of the very top trainers in New York. Scored in better than one of every four attempts during 1966. Does not hesitate to drop a horse drastically to get a purse. Has earned wide respect as an expert claimer and refurbisher of other people's stock.

WILLIE CORBELLINI—One of the youngest of the New York go-getters, this shrewd operator pressed Allen Jerkens for leadership at the Aqueduct meetings in 1967. A specialist in high-priced claimers and an excellent judge of the other guy's horse, he has a loyal, close-knit following of big bettors who see to it that his ready horses run at low odds. Indeed, when a Corbellini horse goes at 3 to 1 or less, the New York fan can be sure that the trainer and his friends are confident.

SCOTTY SCHULHOFER—Former steeplechase rider is earning respect in the big-time for his patient tutelage of grass horses and routers. Likely to improve with age.

MICKEY WALSH—An excellent horseman from Ireland, who handles topnotch jumpers as well as runners on the flat. Should never be underestimated in a jump race.

PHIL G. JOHNSON—A good example of the truism that a trainer can't win without livestock, Peegee does marvels in New York with far less four-legged help than he deserves. Any season now, his ability to exploit an improving horse or steal purses with a deteriorating one will get him the troop he needs for a 20 percent winning average.

OTHERS—The ups and downs of winning averages notwithstanding, New England players are advised not only to respect the abilities of the men whose names appear on the foregoing lists but to keep alert to the talents of Tony Cataldi, Bill Hinphy, Charlie Heaverly, Dick Gottsman and Phil Utman. In California, Warren Stute, Charlie Comiskey and the strong-minded Mish Tenney are always in contention. In Kentucky, Doug Davis, Jr., is a cinch to win a lot of juvenile races. T. J. Baker, J. P. McCormick, W. H. Foales, Eddie Yowell, H. Paley and Ed Weymouth are always to be reckoned with in the New Jersey-Delaware area. Hal Bishop's midwestern average would be much higher if he started fewer horses, and he wins more races per year than most trainers. In New York, the backstretch is cluttered wtih individuals capable of high consistency. Among them are Kay Jensen, Eddie O'Brien, Everett King, Warren Pascuma, Mario Padovani, Charlie Reynolds.

Trainers of Champions

Of trainers now or recently active in the sport, the following have handled the most national champions:

W. C. "BILL" WINFREY: Bed o' Roses, Buckpasser, Castle Forbes, Native Dancer, Next Move, Social Outcast, Bold Lad, Queen Empress.

W. F. "BERT" MULHOLLAND: Battlefield, Evening Out, Jaipur, Platter, Seven Thirty, Stefanita.

JIM CONWAY: Chateaugay, Grecian Queen, Miss Request, Primonetta, Pucker Up.

SYLVESTER E. VEITCH: Career Boy, Counterpoint, First Flight, Phalanx, What A Treat.

J. H. "CASEY" HAYES: Cicada, First Landing, Hill Prince, Sir Gaylord.

They Win with Favorites

Among the services offered to New York fans by the State Racing Commission is a yearly statistical review of the work done by owners, trainers and riders. One of the most valuable features is the report on how trainers fare when their horses are favorites. Obviously, a trainer who wins less than a third of the time with favorites is woefully unlucky, or attracts undeserved betting support, or mismanages his animals.

Here is a list of New York trainers whose favorites win at better than an average rate. If you like the horse, and it is the favorite, and one of the men on this list is the trainer, you have a good bet.

	Percentage of Winning Favorites	
	1966	1965
Ivor G. Balding	38	50
Elliott Burch	59	50
Lou Cavalaris, Jr.	46	41
W. C. Freeman	53	26
Jack Gaver	53	48
Max Hirsch	50	54
Hirsch Jacobs	38	39
Buddy Jacobson	34	46
Allen Jerkens	45	49
Roger Laurin	33	42
Frank Martin	34	36
Bert Mulholland	64	53
Eddie Neloy	49	36
Burley Parke	43	41
Woody Stephens	37	45
Sherrill Ward	50	50

All photographs in this chapter are courtesy of the NEW YORK RACING ASSN. (PAUL SCHAFER) *except for those of Lou Cavalaris, Jr.* (MICHAEL BURNS) *and Bud Lepman* (TURFOTOS).

15 The Jockey Factor

EXCEPT FOR five or six professional golfers who amass small fortunes in television fees and advertising testimonials, the richest athletes on earth are American jockeys. A really good one takes home not less than $100,000 a year for a decade or two, if he keeps his weight down, his nose clean and his mind on his work.

By tradition, the victorious rider gets 10 percent of the purse. Many owners sweeten this bonus with other gifts, such as the proceeds of a large bet on the horse. As pin money, the big-league jock also earns $50 for winning, $40 for finishing second, $30 if third, and $25 for fourth or worse. The fee for winning is usually regarded as part of the 10 percent bonus, although no rule forbids an owner to pay both.

This sounds like a splendid career for any little fellow who likes horses. It certainly is, in the same sense that a top executive position with General Motors is a splendid career for anyone who likes cars. The trouble is that a man can be wild about cars and spend his career in the grease pit of a filling station. And a little fellow who likes horses may become a jockey without ever making big pay at it.

Success as a race rider requires more than small size and large desire. Talent is essential. Luck helps. An ingratiating personality does no harm. The top riders have those qualities in abundance. Most do not, which is why there are so few top riders.

Many jockeys are untalented to begin with. Others, fearful of injury, fail to exercise what little talent they may have. It is not at all unusual to see races in which one or more of the riders do nothing but cling to the reins and wave the whip.

According to the Jockeys' Guild, about half of all active riders earn $5,000 a year or less. Recent editions of *The American Racing Manual* spell this out. An amazingly small group of riders dominates the profession. They own the winner's circle, lock, stock and bonus. They are so much more successful than their colleagues that there simply is no comparison.

About 2,000 men have riding licenses. In the course of a year, fewer than 1,400 of them ride in actual races. Of those who do, almost half get 100 or fewer mounts, compared with the 1,000 to 1,800 assignments obtained by successful jockeys.

Of the 1,400 who ever get to the post during a year, 500 win not a single race. More than half the races are won by perhaps 200 riders—the middle and upper classes of the profession. Each of these goes to the post at least 500 times a year, either because the trainers vie for his services or because they regard him as the least of the available evils and give him the try.

And now we reach the heart of the matter. An elite group of less than four dozen riders—hardly more than 2 percent of the profession—wins more than 9,500 races a year. Members of this tiny elite win one race in every five! Moreover, they win about $42 million in purses for their employers—fully a third of the purse money paid at all tracks!

To see what this means at the local level, let us consider New York, where earning possibilities are highest, competition keenest, and the quality of riding by far the best. Of 171 men licensed to ride at Aqueduct and Saratoga during 1966, *exactly seven won more than half the races!* Ernest Cardone, Braulio Baeza, Bob Ussery, John L. Rotz, Walter Blum, Angel Cordero and Ron Turcotte—4 percent of the local jockey population—captured 1,100 of the 2,022 races! Cardone, Baeza, Ussery, Rotz, Blum, Turcotte and Eddie Belmonte took more than half of the $16 million in purses paid by the New York tracks!

Betting on Jockeys

Awareness of the enormous statistical edge enjoyed by a handful of leading riders leads some players to center their handicapping on the jockey rather than the horse. If the handicapping is fairly competent, taking due account of the horse, the player who refuses to bet on any but a top rider has an excellent chance to get by. Unfortunately, such players usually ignore the horse. They "follow" individual jockeys, often betting according to the formulas supplied by progressive betting systems. As pointed out on page 49, this leads straight to ruination. Any jockey inevitably encounters streaks of from twenty to fifty consecutive losers.

Neither does the player do himself a favor by going to the opposite extreme. "The horse is the thing," some say. "All I do is look for the live horse in the past performances. I let the trainer pick the jockey." Bad logic. The actual "liveness" of a horse often is revealed in the identity of its rider.

Players are right in supposing that most trainers know which riders to put on their horses. But most jockeys and their agents know something, too. They know which horses are the likeliest contenders. Successful riders have their pick of the best mounts. The presence on a horse of an obscure or relatively ungifted rider is frequently a sign that the trainer is marking time, or that the horse is less ready than its record implies.

In any case, the probability of victory by a leading rider is so disproportionately high that it should not be overlooked. The past performances of the jockey should always be evaluated, as part of the evaluation of the horse.

The Importance of the Ride

In 1966, Avelino Gomez led all North American riders with 318 victories in 996 attempts. His winning average of .321 was a new record among champions in the races-won department, surpassing the .301 achieved by Bill Shoemaker in 1954. Gomez has long been one of the finest reinsmen in the world, an extraordinarily consistent winner wherever he rides. It so happens, however, that he prefers to ride in Canada and Mexico. He has his choice of mounts in those places. He rides very few stiffs.

If he were to return to New York, pickings would be less easy. Other outstanding jockeys would compete with him for the best mounts. He would get fewer winners.

The point of this is that no rider can make a winner of a non-contender, except by accident. To be a consistent winner, the jockey must get the mounts. And even the most consistent winner loses about eight of every ten races in which he rides. Most of the losses are simply part of the form cycle. It's a nice horse, but it won't win for another two or three weeks, and the leading rider is content to stay with it in the meantime, so that he may cash in later.

Other losses find the topnotcher on some downright rotten animals. Contractual commitments, the politics of the business, or the wish to do a friend a favor often result in Braulio Baeza or Bill Shoemaker going postward on a hopeless hulk. Because the Shoe or Baeza has the mount, the odds drop. But the chances of victory remain as slim as they would be if Joe Nobody were aboard.

Where good jockeys come into their own is on fit, well-placed horses. As their riding records illustrate, they bring something extra to the assignment. They win the big ones and the close ones. The trainer able to induce one of them to ride his animal knows in his heart that he has done everything possible for victory. The owner loves him for it. And if the horse loses, the owner blames the horse and consoles the trainer. Trainers would rather be consoled than blamed.

Does the second- or third-best horse in the race win because its rider is the best in the race? It happens somewhere every day. And it happens everywhere several times a week. The frequency with which it happens depends, of course, on the class of the track. In a field of nine horses at the height of the Aqueduct season, one usually finds that each of the three or four logical contenders is being ridden by a first-rate jockey. Yet there are occasions when this is not so, and the player is able to make his choice on grounds that one or two of the contenders are carrying outgunned boys.

Buddy Jacobson maintains that New York riders are so evenly matched that none of them can move a horse more than a neck farther than any of a couple dozen others. Races are won, however, by necks and heads and noses. Cordero, Baeza, Shoemaker, Ussery, Rotz, Ycaza and Blum do it often enough in New York to warrant the eagerness with which trainers seek their services. Yet, if the best horse in the race is ridden by Larry Adams, Hedley Woodhouse, Johnny Ruane or Ben Feliciano, no knowledgeable player would refrain from betting on that account. These four riders had a combined winning average of less than 8 percent in their New York appearances during 1966, but are widely respected in the sport and can be regarded as hindrances to no Thoroughbred. They won far fewer races than the local leaders, whose averages ran from Cordero's 12 percent to Baeza's 22. Yet they accounted for more than $1 million in purses. Ruane was good enough to ride the Bert Mulholland string. Adams was accepted as peerless with sensitive fillies. Feliciano rode Amberoid and other Lucien Laurin horses. Woodhouse got 719 riding assignments.

What is the New York player to do? If so many of the riders there are better than their records indicate, how is he to tell one from another?

He should do exactly what he would do at any other track, where the distinctions among riders are often easier to recognize. He should bear in mind that the most successful riders are those most sought after by trainers. They get the best mounts. They get more good mounts—and the statistics prove it—than are assigned to riders who may be equally good but are less successful. Therefore, the player bears the percentages in mind. He scrutinizes the field in terms of distance, condition, class, weights, pace, barns. At some point—whether sooner or later depends entirely on his preference—he eliminates horses to which non-winning riders are assigned. A leading rider should never be dismissed, of course.

Bill Shoemaker   *Eddie Arcaro*   *Bill Hartack*

But a good rider with unimpressive winning statistics can often be ruled out. A bit later I shall present some ways of making these decisions.

Riding Ability Defined

The ideal rider has an instinctive sense of the needs, capacities and peculiarities of his mount. Developed through years of experience in the barns, on the training tracks and in money competition, this sensitivity enables him to get extra effort from any kind of horse, with or without helpful instructions from the trainer.

The ideal rider is an expert judge of pace. He can tell whether the early going is too slow or too fast for his horse, and he adjusts the animal's stride accordingly. Unless the horse is unmanageably rank, he runs it as slowly as possible before the final turn for home, giving it the breather it needs for that last burst of effort.

The ideal rider is a master strategist. He takes the trouble to learn all about changes in the footing, so that he can navigate his horse over the fastest part of the track. If the rail is the place to be, he will be there, even if behind horses. His knowledge of his own mount, and of its rivals, and of the other riders, usually enables him to find daylight and come through at the end, still on the rail.

The ideal rider has extraordinarily quick reflexes and remarkable powers of anticipation. In the split second that he recognizes the development of a potential traffic jam, he steers his horse away from the trouble. In the split second that a hole begins to open in front of him, he takes advantage of it.

The ideal rider is unswervingly courageous. His confidence is unshaken by the dreadful spills that he and all other jockeys suffer from time to time. He takes calculated risks. He goes through holes from which battle-weary jockeys back off. Yet he is not reckless. He knows when to take up or go wide rather than risk harm to himself, his horse and the others in the race.

| *Angel Cordero* | *Bob Ussery* | *Braulio Baeza* |

Leading Riders of All Time

As of January 1, 1967, the following men had won more races than any other riders in the history of American racing. Eight of them—Shoemaker, Brooks, Hartack, Gomez, Ussery, Baird, Blum and Culmone—continued to ride during 1967.

	Victories	Total Purses
JOHNNY LONGDEN	6,026	$24,665,800
BILL SHOEMAKER	5,495	37,460,295
EDDIE ARCARO	4,779	30,039,543
STEVE BROOKS	4,387	17,814,333
TED ATKINSON	3,795	17,449,360
RALPH NEVES	3,771	13,781,114
BILL HARTACK	3,679	21,668,898
AVELINO GOMEZ	3,290	7,551,326
JOHNNY ADAMS	3,270	9,741,889
BOBBY USSERY	2,953	16,821,217
ROBERT LEE BAIRD	2,794	8,213,798
SAM BOULMETIS	2,783	15,425,935
WALTER BLUM	2,674	13,980,225
HOWARD CRAIG	2,669	4,970,353
JOE CULMONE	2,542	10,212,037

The ideal rider is alert at the gate. He keeps his horse on its toes in readiness for the start. He gets out of there as quickly as the horse can manage it, to achieve the all-important racing position that enables him to save ground later.

The ideal rider has unlimited competitive spirit. As long as his mount has a chance, he refuses to give up. He continues trying until the race is over. This, combined with his knowledge of pace and strategy, makes him what the trade calls a "strong" rider—a strong finisher. If he wasted his mounts in the early going, they would have nothing left at the end, and his finishes would be less strong.

The ideal rider uses the whip no more than necessary. He gets all he can by exploiting the pace of the race, and by distributing his weight evenly on the withers (which is comfortable for the animal), and by using voice, reins, legs and, above all, hands. He rolls his hands on the horse's neck, in rhythm with its stride, urging it forward. When he whips, the emphasis means something to the horse, and it usually reacts by lengthening stride.

The ideal rider spares his horse in other ways. He is able to win by a neck when less capable jockeys might need the security of a three-length lead. Similarly, if the horse is clearly beaten, he does not bother to whip it in a spurious display of determination. He eases it, saving it for next time.

The ideal rider has no weight problems. Without having to resort to the self-denial, the steam baths and the deliberate heaving after meals which make ashen, wasted, weakened, prematurely old men of other jockeys, he rides at full strength. A well-nourished, clear-headed rider is an asset to a horse. A starved rider is likely to conk out at any time.

The ideal rider brings absolute concentration to the job. Like any other athlete, he does whatever is necessary to remain in decent physical and mental condition. His private life is an orderly one that helps, rather than disrupts, his frame of mind. If he boozes or wenches, the recreation is never excessive enough to harm his performance and generate disfavor among trainers. If he gambles, he does it according to the rules, betting only on his own mounts, through their owners. He does not become so immersed in the gambling aspects of the game that his "investments" distract him from his riding.

Among riders now active, many come close to these ideal standards. Braulio Baeza and Bill Shoemaker are closest. In fact, many trainers call Baeza the perfect rider. A complaint about Shoemaker is that he is not quite robust enough to get the best from a heavy-headed or willful horse such as Native Dancer or Kelso. Baeza seems able to handle anything. A third rider of outstanding skill is Bill Hartack, who set an all-time record of 417 winners in 1955, and another of $3,060,501 in total purse winnings in 1957. Hartack won with an incredible 25 percent of 1,702 mounts in '55 and with 28 percent of 1,238 in '57. He still ranks among the leading money-winners in the game, despite an abrasively independent personality, which has estranged him from agents, trainers, newspaper reporters and racing officials. Were he a less militant soul, or a con artist, he undoubtedly would be challenging Baeza, Shoemaker, and Velasquez for national leadership every year. His abilities remain undimmed, but he gets fewer good mounts than he should.

Riders for Courses

During 1966, Bill Shoemaker accepted 246 mounts in New York. He won on 37 of them, for a batting average of .150. Outside New York —mainly in California—he won 194 times in 791 attempts, for an average of .245. This made his overall statistic a nifty .213.

It is no disgrace to score with only 15 percent of one's mounts on the New York circuit. But Shoemaker always does better than that elsewhere. He is one of the rare riders able to win at least once in every five races—the brand of consistency most significant to players. But he cannot win that often if he does not get the horses. The reason he has fewer good horses to ride in New York is simple enough: Trainers tend to stay with topnotch boys who they know will remain available for the entire season. If rider Doe is good enough to be among the six or seven leaders at Aqueduct, he is good enough for any horse—even though he may lack the virtuoso qualities of a Shoemaker. Rather than antagonize Doe and Doe's noisy agent, by using Shoemaker during the champ's irregular trips East, the trainer stays with the local rider, and Shoemaker has to take the leavings.

Earlie Fires, leading apprentice rider of 1965, when he scored in 19 percent of his starts, invaded New York in 1966 and made a splendid impression. But he won only 8 percent of the time, as contrasted with the 15 percent he was able to log during the same year in less rugged company elsewhere.

Sammy Boulmetis and Jimmy Stout, heroes of New Jersey racing and thorough pros in their own right, could never get much in New York. Nor could Johnny Longden, the wizened godling of the West Coast. On the other hand, Laffit Pincay, Jr., a 1966 sensation in Illinois, was no less sensational in New York, and proceeded to maintain the level when he wintered in California.

Generally speaking, a rider who has distinguished himself sufficiently to earn national ranking is a fair bet to win on any track—provided his horse qualifies for support. However, he *usually is a much better bet on his home circuit or on some lesser circuit*. To take an extreme, hypothetical case, if he breaks records in Arizona, he must prove himself all over again before meriting support in New Jersey. But if he is Baeza, he rates as tops anywhere.

Among the first things the expert does in handicapping a field of horses is check the current jockey standings at the track. He carefully notes the names of the two or three top riders, and any others whose listings show that they have been winning at least 16 or 17 percent of their starts. These are the boys who are getting the live horses. And who are justifying the trainers' confidence.

In conjunction with this, the player refers to national listings. Good ones appear below and on pages 307 and 308.

The Reliable Riders

The following jockeys win an unusually high percentage of their starts. The presence of one of them on a likely looking horse means that the animal has an especially good chance to win.

BRAULIO BAEZA	JERRY LAMBERT
CARLOS BARRERA*	BILL MAHORNEY
CONCEPCION BARRIA*	MIKE MANGANELLO
ANGEL CORDERO	ALVARO PINEDA
JOE CULMONE	LAFFIT PINCAY, JR.
JESSE DAVIDSON*	JOHN L. ROTZ
PAUL FREY*	JOHN SELLERS
BOB GALLIMORE*	BILL SHOEMAKER
CARL GAMBARDELLA*	LARRY SNYDER*
AVELINO GOMEZ	BOB USSERY
EMEDE HINOJOSA*	JACINTO VASQUEZ
LENNY KNOWLES*	JORGE VELASQUEZ

Apprentice Jockeys

The chronic shortage of first-rate riders impels horsemen to beat the bushes for promising new talent. To encourage the search and expedite the development of newcomers to the trade, trainers are allowed weight concessions for any horse on which they seat an apprentice jock.

If the apprentice wins a race or two in fairly authoritative style, he usually gets more work than his skills warrant. He rides and wins, while full-fledged journeymen sit in idleness and grumble about the politics of the game.

Politics has something to do with it. The notorious eagerness of many owners to see fashionable riders aboard their horses combines with the weight allowance to make the "hot" apprentice an attractive proposition to certain trainers.

* Active on minor tracks

The Money Riders

Many of the following riders earn more than $1 million a year for their employers. Others on the list come close, or have been in the million-dollar club in the past, or threaten to join it soon. Their winning percentages fluctuate, because some of them ride every horse in sight, and others have difficulty in obtaining suitable mounts. When assigned a leading contender, these riders yield points to few in the game. They are special threats in allowance, handicap and stakes races.

LARRY ADAMS	BILL HARTACK
CHUCK BALTAZAR	KENNY KNAPP
EDDIE BELMONTE	FRANK LOVATO
WALTER BLUM	LEROY MOYERS
BILL BOLAND	JIM NICHOLS
RAY BROUSSARD	JOHNNY RUANE
DON BRUMFIELD	RON TURCOTTE
EARLIE FIRES	MILO VALENZUELA
HELIODORO GUSTINES	MANUEL YCAZA

Of course, apprentices often lose on horses that might win with better jockeying. But this is not always a negative factor from the trainer's point of view. A player who takes ten minutes to study any random issue of *Telegraph* or *Form* will notice that some horses seem to lose when the apprentice is up, and win only with a leading rider. The function of the apprentice in such cases is to give an unready horse a brisk workout in actual competition under light weight. If the horse accidentally wins, so much the better. Certain stables specialize in manipulations of that kind, and attentive players have no trouble recognizing the signs in the records.

A more wholesome, widespread and significant reason for the popularity of apprentices is their eagerness. They ride the cheapest race as if it were the Kentucky Derby. When the eagerness occurs in combination with genuine ability—as sometimes happens—the trainer of a cheap horse often prefers the apprentice to an older hand. The boy may be green, but his spirit is beyond doubt. It frequently enables him to finish ahead of more experienced riders whose own competitiveness has been dulled by prosperity. Apprentices rarely get mounts in important races, and seldom win when they do. But they have an extra something going for them in lesser races.

Ernie Cardone   *Howard Grant*

Underrated Riders

In the riding profession, last year's hero is this year's bum. The riders on this list have had their moments as heroes and remain capable of becoming national leaders at any time. None of them harms the chances of a well-placed horse.

ERNEST CARDONE	GARTH PATTERSON
BEN FELICIANO	BILLY PHELPS
HOWARD GRANT	DON PIERCE
PHIL GRIMM	OSVALDO ROSADO
MARTINEZ HEATH	NICK SHUK
MICHAEL HOLE	CALVIN STONE
BOBBY JENNINGS	FERNANDO TORO
TOMMY LEE	NOEL TURCOTTE
JOE LOPEZ	MIKE VENEZIA
CARLOS MARQUEZ	HEDLEY WOODHOUSE
ELDON NELSON	

In recent years Ernest Cardone, Bill Mahorney and Earlie Fires have each been an authentically hot apprentice. After losing the weight allowance (see Rules of Racing, pages 392-415), each has continued to get good mounts and win numerous races. The transition from bug-boy to journeyman is usually more difficult than that. Most leading apprentices disappear from prominence as soon as the rules require them to ride at equal weights against polished jockeys. Trainers no longer assign them the live horses. The boy who could do nothing wrong suddenly becomes an also-ran.

As might be expected, apprentices do their best work on horses that require the least jockeying. To win a six-furlong sprint on a sharply conditioned pace-setter, the boy need only get out of the gate in a hurry and remain in the saddle for an additional minute and eleven seconds or so. A more experienced rider might use the animal's energies more

Jockeys on Favorites

A jockey should win with at least a third of the favorites he rides. Here, thanks to the New York State Racing Commission, is a list of New York riders who usually do that well, or better.

	Percentage of Winning Favorites	
	1966	*1965*
LARRY ADAMS	41	30
BRAULIO BAEZA	37	39
ERNIE CARDONE	36	—
HELIODORO GUSTINES	50	32
DAVID HIDALGO	36	31
KENNY KNAPP	51	—
GARY MINEAU	43	34
LAFFIT PINCAY, JR.	40	—
JOHNNY RUANE	43	41
BILL SHOEMAKER	38	26
RON TURCOTTE	35	39
BOB USSERY	36	44
MIKE VENEZIA	43	38
HEDLEY WOODHOUSE	37	34
MANUEL YCAZA	35	34

efficiently, but horsemen often prefer the five- or seven-pound weight concession for a sprinter of that type.

Cardone, Mahorney and Fires were remarkable for their precocious ability to win at all distances on horses that required rating off the pace. Ordinarily, off-pace horses are poor risks when ridden by apprentices. At sprint distances, the kid has too little time to recover from his mistakes or solve the problems presented by traffic jams. At longer distances, he is worse off: his sense of pace is not yet trustworthy. Also, the extra turn of the track presents additional headaches for which the best cure is experience.

Accordingly, expert players bet on an apprentice jockey only if his mount is a front-running sprinter or, in rare cases, if the boy has shown that he can win at the distance with the particular come-from-behinder.

Match the Rider to the Horse

An approach to the jockey factor becomes sensible as soon as it embraces a key reality: the high percentage of races won by the leading riders. The player who favors leading riders directs himself toward live horses.

Yet the player must reckon with the fact that other riders also win races. And that some of those less prominent riders are uniquely suited to certain horses which refuse to run for more successful jockeys.

Here is a good way to handle the jockey problem:

1. Accept as a contender any ready, well-placed horse ridden by a journeyman jockey who (a) is a national leader or (b) is a leader in the current standings at the track or (c) has won at least 16 percent of his races at the meeting or (d) has won with the horse in the past.

2. Eliminate any horse ridden by an apprentice jockey unless (a) it is a front-running type entered in a race around not more than one turn or (b) the boy has won with the horse in the past or (c) the boy rates among the most successful riders at the current meeting and has been winning at least 16 percent of his starts.

3. Play no apprentice in route races unless he has demonstrated in the past that he can handle assignments of that kind.

Needless to say, these suggestions are valid only as part of a comprehensive approach to handicapping.

The most convenient and productive time to analyze the rider's qualifications is at the end of the handicapping process, after the more fundamental questions of distance, condition, class, weight, and pace have been attended to. It makes no sense to eliminate a horse on the jockey factor until then. The penalty for doing so is exacted on the afternoon of the race, when the trainer switches from the unsuccessful jockey to Baeza: If the player has not checked the horse for distance, class, etc., he has no idea whether the switch to Baeza is as meaningful as it might seem.

Who's Who

LARRY ADAMS (Born 1936. Rides at 112 pounds)—At his best is the equal of any rider in the business. Though his performances have been erratic in recent years, he always manages to win about $1 million

Larry Adams   *Eddie Belmonte*   *Walter Blum*

in purses. Finishes first with more than his quota of longshots at New York, because his overall consistency is too low to attract an automatic following at the windows. Without peer on fillies and tender-mouthed horses.

PETE ANDERSON (1931—115)—Long an acute sufferer from weight problems and a seeming desire to knock the other guy over the fence, this New York veteran is effective on the grass and in routes.

BRAULIO BAEZA (1940—112)—Like all truly great riders, the Panamanian belongs to the sit-still school, reserving his big move for the strategic moment. Calm and cool, he wins some by noses that he could win by lengths, but he wins and wins, and has yet to meet the horse he cannot ride effectively. His purse winnings of $2,951,022 in 1966 have been surpassed only by the $3,060,501 that Bill Hartack won in 1957.

ROBERT LEE BAIRD (1920—112)—Nobody rides with shorter stirrups or greater aplomb than this old-timer. Content for years to be the big frog in the small puddles of secondary tracks, he still packs enough resourcefulness and moxie to hold his own wherever he rides.

CHUCK BALTAZAR (1947—108)—A brilliant youngster, as consistent as they come. A good judge of pace, excellent at a distance, and a likely bet to be on top or thereabouts for many years.

TOMMY BARROW (1932—114)—Best remembered as the regular pilot of Hillsdale, this relatively inconsistent rider has showed flashes of ability which establish him as only a jump or two from the best. Has a real knack with headstrong animals at a route.

EDDIE BELMONTE (1943—112)—Many horsemen see the Puerto Rican as a potential great. Close to the $1-million mark, has already won some important stakes in his relatively brief career. His riding style is vigorous to the brink of actual roughness. Figures to be a leading light indefinitely—and in the fastest company.

WALTER BLUM (1934—113)—A member of the top flight ever since his first job with Hirsch Jacobs, the Brooklynite is known primarily as a postboy who holds his sprinters together with the whip. Those days

Bill Boland   *Ray Broussard*   *Don Brumfield*

are actually long behind him. He remains spectacular at the starting gate, but can now come from off the pace with the best. No prima donna, takes every mount he can get. Which explains why he rarely wins more than 15 percent of his starts.

BILL BOLAND (1932—114)—One of the strongest finishers in modern racing history, this polished veteran is no great shakes at getting out of the gate. Trainers tend to forsake him in favor of whoop-de-doo types, but there is nobody better in the stretch.

RAY BROUSSARD (1936—116)—If he weighed a few pounds less, this Louisianan would get more mounts and be a surefire bet to hit the $1-million mark. But he approaches that level and is recognized as one of the finest stretch riders in the game. A top chauffeur on the grass.

DONALD BRUMFIELD (1938—112)—A high-class journeyman, at home on anything in any company, the wry Kentuckian is not as showy as some, but gets the job done, especially in New Jersey. Good judge of pace.

ERNIE CARDONE (1944—101)—No kid ever rose as rapidly as this tiny New Yorker. With riding sense far beyond his years, he was one of the few apprentices of modern times to ride like a veteran while he still had the bug. If he retains his enthusiasm there is no telling how far he may go.

MIKE CARROZZELLA (1944—110)—Another former apprentice star, young Mike has found a niche in New England racing. Can rate a horse and is no timid soul when it comes to finding the shortest way home.

ANGEL CORDERO (1942—108)—A tremendous athlete who keeps himself in superb condition, this member of a prominent Puerto Rican racing family became a topnotcher in 1967, when he led all New York riders. A real hustler out of the gate and vigorous in the stretch, he is becoming a master of pace.

JOE CULMONE (1931—114)—No longer as busy as he was in 1950, when he rode 388 winners and tied Shoemaker for the national title,

Mike Carrozzella   *Avelino Gomez*   *Tony DeSpirito*

Culmone remains a masterful pilot on any horse that responds to careful rating.

JESSE DAVIDSON (1940—114)—Unchallenged king of the West Virginia circuit and winner of the national championship with 319 winners in 1965, this young man has been doing so well on the sharp turns at Shenandoah Downs and Charles Town that he has postponed his invasion of the big time. Some say he could make it in New York or California if he wanted to take the chance.

TONY DeSPIRITO (1935—113)—For sheer guts, DeSpirito is the peer of any rider, past or present. Has been injured more often and more severely than is good for him, but continues to ride as if there were no tomorrow. His hustling style is particularly well suited to sprinters. Regarded in jockey circles as one of the roughest competitors in the business.

HUGO DITTFACH (1936—109)—This German immigrant has an unorthodox riding style, but is a steady, consistent winner, especially in Canada and New England. Has done nicely in his few New York attempts. Likes to ride nine horses a day, if he can get the mounts—which makes his good winning average that much more impressive.

EARLIE FIRES (1947—103)—Not yet a fully matured rider, Earlie has so much will to win that he compensates for some of his mistakes. The mistakes are becoming less numerous in the hard school of Eastern racing. Everyone agrees that the kid will be one of the good ones, at all distances, for years.

LARRY GILLIGAN (1937—113)—Long dismissed as nothing but a quick man out of the gate and a waster of equine energy, Gilligan surprised in 1967 by getting assignments from Bert Mulholland, who uses nothing but the best. Won a few races by rating his mounts off the pace, and gave promise of becoming a well-rounded reinsman at last.

AVELINO GOMEZ (1928—115)—For years the Cuban has been a

Larry Gilligan   *Helidoro Gustines*   *David Hidalgo*

top-rated journeyman able to handle anything with a leg in each corner. Could win anywhere, but prefers Canada, where he rules the roost.

HOWARD GRANT (1939—117)—Regarded as washed-up in 1966, this lover of the bright lights made a sensational comeback at Tropical Park that winter, occasionally weighing out at 116, although he had formerly been unable to do better than 120. A premiere rider of the sit-still variety, he is at his best on class horses in routes. A complaint some-times heard is that he prefers to race overland rather than in the melee. With the type of horses he likes best, this is seldom a disadvantage: He brings 'em out on the turn and lifts 'em over the wire.

PHIL GRIMM (1934—112)—Likes to pick and choose, rather than ride any hay-burner offered him. Has the know-how to handle the best handicap racers as well as less glamorous stock. Most comfortable in Maryland and New Jersey.

HELIODORO GUSTINES (1940—109)—His deserved reputation as a good rider in turf races may explain why many trainers overlook him when assigning mounts for races on the main track. A good postboy and a splendid finisher in races of all distances, he is rather inconsistent.

DEAN HALL (1936—110)—As steady as they come, and a good rider of two-year-olds and fillies, this Californian deals more in pace than in flogging.

BILL HARTACK (1932—115)—If there is space to squeeze a horse through, Hartack will be there. Courageous without being a fool, he excels not only at saving ground but at starting, rating and finishing. In short, a superbly well-rounded and versatile rider.

DAVID HIDALGO (1945—105)—Under the careful tutelage of Johnny Nerud, this native of California developed into a highly promising rider on the New York circuit. Has a pronounced flair for coming off the pace, but is not yet the best postboy in captivity.

MICHAEL HOLE (1941—111)—British import fares handsomely in New England. A consistent winner, especially good with fillies and juveniles.

Paul Kallai   *Kenny Knapp*   *Darrell Madden*

PAUL KALLAI (1933—112)—Popular Hungarian refugee rides every horse to the last ounce, and is by no means incapable of winning $1 million a year. Surpassed $800,000 in 1966 and is still vigorous, ambitious, and dedicated.

KENNY KNAPP (1940—108)—After two successive years in the $1-million club, Knapp's stature in the trade seemed assured. Some New Yorkers continue to believe, however, that he has not yet proved his ability to out-think and out-hustle the nation's best. While the jury continues to deliberate, Kenny continues to win stakes races—especially outside New York.

JERRY LAMBERT (1940—114)—Famous as rider of California's celebrated Native Diver, this well-rounded journeyman could not win $1 million a year (as he does) and win between 15 and 20 percent of his starts (as he does) if Native Diver were the only thing going for him. A good postboy and a good judge of pace.

TOMMY LEE (1936—109)—Not quite in the first flight, Lee (whose forebears came from China) is a handy fellow on the Maryland circuit. Excels with hard-to-handle steeds and has streaks in which he rides like a champion.

FRANK LOVATO (1937—109)—One of the most underrated riders in the game, Lovato is a strong finisher, a fine judge of pace, an excellent turf pilot and, all-in-all, a likely bet to break loose someday soon.

DARRELL MADDEN (1923—114)—Formerly a Vanderbilt contract rider, this veteran has forsaken the big time, apparently for keeps, and has become a real craftsman. Is seldom missing from the list of leading New England riders.

ROBERT McCURDY (1941—108)—One of the few Negro jockeys, McCurdy has shown that he can win in New York, New Jersey and Maryland. A good, strong finisher with plenty of patience, his main problem seems to be that of getting mounts.

BILL MAHORNEY (1940—105)—As precocious as Earlie Fires and almost as slick as Ernie Cardone, this outstanding apprentice of the 1964

Bill Mahorney   *John L. Rotz*   *Johnny Ruane*

season was even more successful in 1965, and continued in high gear during 1966. A finished professional who can handle any assignment, he seems to have settled down on his native West Coast, after showing New York and Illinois that he could win anywhere.

ESTEBAN MEDINA (1938—113)—Always in contention on the California circuit, this hustling Mexican has not yet reached the peak of his powers. In 1965, when he was hot, he rode winners in 19 percent of his starts. May do better than that before long.

ELDON NELSON (1927—110)—When not bogged down in one of his slumps, Nelson is as classy as they come. Especially patient, has the confidence to wait long enough to get the most from one-run horses in stakes races.

JIM NICHOLS (1927—115)—Formerly one of the most popular riders of two-year-olds, the oft-injured cowboy continues to specialize in that department. His long legs help him to keep a green youngster on course.

GARTH PATTERSON (1944—108)—In recent years, this intelligent reinsman has invariably been among the New Jersey leaders. Some connoisseurs believe that he is, at least potentially, the best rider in that top-flight cavalry. Won over $800,000 in 1965, tailed off the following year, but continued to ride well.

BILLY PHELPS (1938—113)—Delaware's favorite rider has shown that he can handle any kind of horse, and that the race does not necessarily have to take place in Delaware. A good, all-around jockey.

DON PIERCE (1937—112)—Another perennial member of the $1-million-a-year group, Pierce is the subject of lively debate among clubhouse orators, some of whom don't think he's all that good. The answer is that he doesn't *look* all that good, but gets there just the same. When at his intermittent peak, is a genuinely strong boy in the stretch.

LAFFIT PINCAY, JR. (1946—110)—Latest in the apparently endless succession of brilliant Panamanian riders, this youngster is a fully rounded operative able to compete with the Baezas and Shoemakers. Patient, a

Johnny Sellers   *Ron Turcotte*   *Jacinto Vasquez*

superb strategist and judge of pace, and an unusually strong finisher, he promises to be riding and winning in top company for many years.

ALVARO PINEDA (1945—112)—He rides every race he can, and hits the $1-million mark. His astonishing 419 victories in 1967 established him at the top of the profession.

JOHN L. ROTZ (1934—112)—Narrowly missed $2 million in winnings during 1966. One of the best, most stylish riders of the era. Can ride anything.

JOHNNY RUANE (1936—109)—They used to say that he was all whoop-de-doo and no class. They may have been right several years ago, but he has changed radically. As good a handler of grass horses as there is, Ruane is fully accomplished with any other kind of beast, and needs more work to prove it to the satisfaction of one and all.

JOHNNY SELLERS (1937—113)—The gangly Sellers is at his best when off the pace. His best is good enough to keep him in the $1-million class.

BILL SHOEMAKER (1931—106)—Someday he will be tired of winning all that money all the time. Meanwhile, he rides with the enthusiasm of a teen-ager and the wile of an all-time great, which he is.

RON TURCOTTE (1941—112)—Another whip specialist who seems to be getting suaver with experience. Not as rough on his mounts as he used to be, gets plenty of work in New York and Florida, wins the $1 million for the owners, and has mastered the pace problem sufficiently to win at any distance on dirt or grass.

BOB USSERY (1935—116)—The Oklahoman is a notorious whipster with far more versatility than one might think from watching him come windmilling down the stretch. Has become a sharp assessor of pace, has few equals in getting to the rail (and staying there), and is good for more than $1.5 million in purses every year. Nobody is better on a front-running horse, but Ussery can make do with the other kind, too, as he proved with Proud Clarion in the 1967 Kentucky Derby.

Jorge Velasquez *Hedley Woodhouse* *Manuel Ycaza*

ISMAEL VALENZUELA (1934—114)—When Milo was Kelso's regular rider, the word spread (perhaps unfairly) that claiming races bored him. Kelso is gone now, but the best of the Valenzuela brothers remains in the vicinity of the $1-million-a-year class. Physically powerful, an artistic finisher, great with unruly horses and most dangerous in big races.

JACINTO VASQUEZ (1944—111)—Least publicized of the fantastic Panamanians, the steady, reliable, quick-thinking youngster wins his million a year in Delaware, New Jersey and Florida. An asset to any horse, at any distance, on any track.

JORGE VELASQUEZ (1946—108)—In 1967, this Panamanian led everybody with 437 winning races. "Owns" the New Jersey and Florida tracks. A sensational boy out of the gate, an excellent judge of pace, a good saver of ground and a fairly strong finisher, Jorge is also a remarkable analyst of track surfaces. Gives his mounts big advantages by steering them on the fastest part of the strips.

HEDLEY WOODHOUSE (1920—109)—Still without a superior at the gate or at holding a fatigued sprinter together in the stretch, Woodhouse is a staple item at Aqueduct. Rides all kinds for a deceptively low winning average. But when he's on the sharpest contender, look out.

MANUEL YCAZA (1938—115)—No longer the unbelievably reckless roughhouser who won everything in sight when he wasn't under suspension, the first of the great Panamanians now capitalizes on his mastery of pace and his gifts as a powerful finisher. Some say he lacks the competitive fire of yore, but his earnings remain above $1 million. He continues to invite disqualification far more often than he should.

RAY YORK (1932—113)—A solid citizen in California racing, York no longer crowds the nation's top earners as closely as he used to. Because his abilities seem undimmed and he is known for his ability to get there with any kind of mount, he must be conceded a chance to return to the very top.

16 The Plus Factors

YOU HAVE ELIMINATED seven of the eight horses, including the favorite in the race. The remaining animal seems admirably situated as to distance, class, weight and pace. It is in good form. Its jockey's name is Baeza. The crowd is letting it go to the post at 4 to 1. You buy a ticket.

The horse finishes second, a few jumps ahead of the favorite. The winner is a 20 to 1 shot. You turn back to the past-performance records to see if you missed anything. No. The horse had fallen on its face every time it had tried to go farther than a mile. And it had never been in the money against animals of today's caliber.

On the other hand, the horse was ridden by the only jockey who had ever won with it before. And was carrying seven fewer pounds than in its last race. And had worked out only yesterday. As they say in the trade, it had a few angles going for it.

Because racing is a game in which victory rewards the shrewd as often as it does the swift, innumerable players do their handicapping entirely in terms of angles—patterns in the past-performance record which reveal significant maneuvers by a trainer or possible improvement by the horse itself. Distance, form, class, pace and jockey are all surveyed in such figuring, but seldom in any fundamental way. The angle player hits longshots, as does anyone else who takes a cavalier attitude toward the basics of the sport. Naturally, he also suffers long droughts and generally ends by losing more money than he wins.

But angles have their place in handicapping. They are especially useful as a means of separating well-placed, legitimate contenders whose pace and class ratings are too close for easy decision.

Readers of *The Compleat Horseplayer* and *Ainslie's Jockey Book* will recall that each contained a compilation of selection angles helpful in singling out live horses. I called them "plus factors" and urged the reader to use them only *after* more fundamental analyses. I renew the advice in this chapter, with the admission that almost any of the plus factors might constitute the basis of an interesting selection system. Players drawn to the idea of mechanical systems, which require no effort beyond the application of rules, will find that Chapter 18 of the present volume contains the greatest abundance of systems ever published in one place. Before attempting to adapt any of the plus factors to system play, it might be a good idea to look through the assortment of mechanical methods in the later chapter.

In the meantime, anyone who prefers to do his own handicapping will find the following wrinkles a useful adjunct to whatever method he favors. If unable to separate two or three horses by ordinary means, see whether any of the following factors apply to one or more of the horses. Generally, a contender is a good bet if it earns four more of these credits than any other contender does.

1. Winning Favorite: A horse that goes to the post as betting favorite in its race deserves extra credit if its barn customarily wins more than a third of the races in which its horses run as favorites.

2. Consistent Stable: Whether the horse is favorite or not, it deserves credit if its trainer is among the leaders at the current meeting or is shown by *The American Racing Manual* or the daily racing program or the tabulations in this book to be exceptionally consistent.

3. Consistent Jockey: If the rider is an unusually consistent winner or a national or local leader, the horse gets credit. If the horse happens to be the betting favorite and the jockey is good on favorites, the horse gets an additional check or star or whatever symbol you prefer.

4. Favorable Jockey Shift: Credit any contender that lost its last race but is to be ridden today by a different jockey, provided the boy is a national or local leader, or has a winning percentage of at least 16 at the meeting, or has won with the horse in the past. Likewise, a shift to the hot apprentice of the meeting also deserves credit. A switch to a winning rider is almost invariably a sign of readiness, especially in a horse that qualifies as a legitimate contender on more fundamental grounds.

5. Won Last Race Easily: Such horses are among the best bets to repeat.

6. Won Last Race Handily: The difference between "handily" and "easily" is not great. An animal that wins handily usually retains enough of its form to win at the next asking, provided it is properly placed (a question that should be settled at earlier stages of the handicapping).

7. Last Race a Big Win: The most powerful kind of victory is that in which the horse leads at the stretch call, or is close to the pace, and wins going away.

8. Lost Last Race but Gained in Stretch: If the result chart or *Telegraph* past-performance line says "rallied," "just missed," or "finished fast" and the horse picked up at least two lengths in the stretch, it may do better today. Unless, of course, the effort dulled its form (which the player should have noticed in analyzing the form factor).

9. Lost Ground in Middle Stages but Gained in Stretch: A horse may be shuffled back by heavy traffic after a good start. If it at least regains the lost ground, it demonstrates the willingness and condition that win races. The past-performance line might look like this:

$$3 \quad 3 \quad 2^3 \quad 5^5 \quad 4^4 \quad 2^2$$

In seeking this angle—known to old-time punters as the "Up and Down System"—little attention need be paid to running position. Lengths behind the leader are more important, although it is nice to note that the horse managed to pass others while closing in on the leader.

10. Gained Three Lengths or More at Any Call: A burst of speed at any stage of a race is often a sign of improvement:

$$3 \quad 4 \quad 5^5 \quad 3^2 \quad 4^3 \quad 5^4$$

The horse turned it on sufficiently to gain three lengths between the quarter-mile and pre-stretch calls. Or, if it was a route race, between the half-mile and three-quarters.

11. Passed More than Half the Field: If an animal that usually breaks alertly got off to a poor start and, though losing, passed more than half the other horses in the race, it probably will improve today.

12. Ran Closer to the Early Pace than in Its Previous Two Races: An almost invariably reliable sign.

13. Was Closer at the Stretch Call than in Its Previous Two Races: Ditto.

14. Finished Closer to the Winner than in Its Previous Two Races: Ditto.

15. Is a Front-Running Type that Carried Its Speed Farther than in Either of Its Two Previous Races: More of the same.

Racegoers prefer to stand, as this Bowie crowd demonstrates. UPI PHOTO

16. Ran an Even Race, No Worse than Fifth All the Way, Earning a Higher Speed Rating than in Either of Its Previous Two: A particularly telling sign, often overlooked.

17. Has Earned Increasingly High Speed Ratings in Each of Its Last Two Races: Not necessarily as obvious a sign as it might seem, especially if horse has not been finishing in the money.

18. Has Earned Increasingly High Speed Ratings in Each of Its Last Three Races: Dynamite.

19. Displayed Early Speed: A fast start is often a better sign than a fast finish. Unless the horse is an habitual quitter (which should have been eliminated early in the handicapping), it deserves credit for leading or running close to the leader of its last race, whether it carried the speed beyond the first call or two or not.

20. Led or Ran Within Two Lengths of the Winner to the Stretch Call before Losing Ground in the Stretch Run of a Longer Race than Today's: The reference, as usual, is to the animal's last race. The horse might have won if the race had been at today's comfortable distance. The distance switch, combined as it often is with a class drop and jockey shift, is a dead giveaway that the stable is shooting.

21. Has Led from Wire to Wire in a Race at Today's Distance: The type of horse able to get out on top and stay there is an extra-good bet when in shape and properly situated. He encounters none of the problems that befall off-pace animals.

22. Last Race Easy, Previous Race Good: The last race was easy if the horse never challenged for the lead, finished fourth or worse, and earned chart comment like "No excuse," "No mishap," "Ran evenly," "Wide," or "No rally." If everything else in the record suggests a good performance today, and if the animal's next-to-last race was a good one, the chances are that its last outing was a conditioning effort—a tightener.

23. Alibi: A horse that lost because it was misplaced or because it ran into trouble is often a nice bet when properly placed in its next effort. The public often overlooks the reason for its last defeat, seeing only that it lost badly.

24. Last Race within Seven Days of Today: A horse good enough to survive close scrutiny in terms of distance, condition, class, weight, jockey and pace, deserves extra consideration if its trainer is running it within seven days of its last race. There can be little doubt that the animal is ready and that the barn is trying.

25. Last Race within Five Days of Today: Five days is so much more impressive than seven that the player can give the animal an extra star on that account.

Morning workout at Saratoga.   PAUL SCHAFER—NEW YORK RACING ASSN.

26. Second Start after Long Layoff or Long Trip: Horses usually do far better in the second effort at a new track or after a layoff.

27. Ran in Money after Long Layoff or Long Trip: If the horse ran second or third in its first attempt at the new track (or after a vacation), and did so without the all-out effort of a hard stretch drive, it almost certainly will improve today. An especially good sign is early speed that petered out in the later stages of the race. The horse was undoubtedly short of wind, and should improve today.

28. Stabled at Today's Track: Horses stabled at Belmont Park win a lower proportion of races at Aqueduct than horses that sleep at Aqueduct. The workout line in the past-performance record tells where the horse lives —a good plus factor at any track.

29. Worked Yesterday: Many trainers believe in giving the horse a breezing workout on the day before a winning effort.

30. Recent Long Workout: If the horse has been tiring in the stretch, or has been away from the races for a while, a six-furlong workout for today's sprint or a workout of a mile or more for today's route is an indication that the trainer has been building the animal's stamina. The workout should have occurred at least three days ago, to enable the horse to recover from it.

31. Three Workouts in Two Weeks: A racer that works every three to five days is in adequate physical condition and is being prepared for something.

32. Six Pounds Less Weight than in Best Race: If the trainer has found the spot in which the horse can run with considerably less weight than it carried in its best effort at the distance, he is likely to want to cash in on the opportunity. The fact that the horse qualifies as a contender suggests that the trainer knows what he's up to.

33. Five Pounds Less than in Last Race: Trainers like to get weight off. Even though the last race may have been a much different kind of affair than today's, the lighter burden remains significant.

34. Distance Switch: Today the horse is running at a suitable distance or the player would (I hope) have eliminated it. If it ran at the wrong distance last time, the effort probably was for conditioning purposes, which may pay off today.

35. Down in Class: If the top claiming price at which horses may be entered in today's race is lower than the price at which the horse was entered in its last start, today's company is probably easier pickings.

36. Steps Down after "Even" or Better Race: A horse bears watching when it drops in class after a race in which it neither exerted itself nor earned unfavorable comment. If the comment was "Even," the player can assume that the trainer had today's race in mind and was merely preparing the horse. If the comment was "Good try" or "Rallied" or something equally complimentary, the horse probably will be an odds-on favorite today.

37. Steps Down Today and Stepped Down Last Time: If the horse's recent record qualifies it as a contender, repeated drops in class may not be the woeful signs that they are in the case of a worn-out animal. They may only mean that the barn is desperate for a purse and a bet.

38. Stepped Down Last Time, Runs in Same Class Again: The trainer evidently thinks that the horse has found its best level. Since the horse is plainly one of the leading contenders in the race, the trainer may be right. If the check mark is added to others earned on the bases of distance switches, weight shifts, jockey switches and the like, the player may be in on a betting coup.

39. Up One Notch Last Time, Down Two Today: Good manipulators get nice prices with this one. For example, the horse might be entered for $5,500 today and its last two races might look like this:

    Clm 6500
    Clm 6000

If the $6,000 race was fairly good and the $6,500 one pretty bad, the trainer may be wound up for a killing. Racetrack crowds seldom penetrate the past-performance records deeply enough to notice maneuvers of this kind. They see that the horse is dropping $1,000 in price after a bad race. They do not notice that it also is dropping $500 in price after a previous, but recent, good race. Naturally, the good race should have taken place within two or three weeks.

40. Drops from Claimer to f-Claimer without Face-Value Drop: A filly or mare entered in a race for $5,000 females is dropping in class and will have a better chance than she did if her last race was for $5,000 animals of both sexes.

41. Drops from Claimer to f-Claimer with Apparent Value Rise: A filly that ran in a Clm 5000 last week is not stepping up in class if today's is an f-6000. At most tracks, she will pay extraordinarily good odds, because the crowd will think she is being pushed up the class ladder. Review the 20 percent formula on page 212.

42. Properly Placed Three-Year-Old: A three-year-old that has been running fair races against older horses is a cinch to move ahead by several lengths when the trainer finally drops it in with its own kind. If the maneuver is combined with an apparent increase in class—a rise in claiming price of not more than $1,000—it is an especially powerful gimmick and should get a second check mark.

43. New Low Class Today: A contender deserves credit if it is meeting the cheapest field of its career.

44. Has Never Lost by More than Half a Length at This Distance against This Class or Lower: A strong indication that the trainer has found the right spot for the horse.

45. Highest Class Rating: A horse should be credited if its class rating is the highest among the leading contenders.

46. Highest Class Rating by 15 Points: A $1,500 edge in class merits an extra check mark. Or, if the player prefers to use purse values, a $200 difference is significant.

47. Has Won Allowance Race at Major Track: This is significant in handicapping claiming races.

48. Has Won Handicap Race at Major Track: This occurs in claiming races sometimes, and should get an extra check. It also is well worth noticing in allowance races.

49. Recently Claimed: The rules of racing require a recently claimed animal to be run in a higher bracket during the first month it is in the new hands.

Longshot! Musica (at left) wins a Gulfstream claiming race under Milt Dalgo, paying $77.80.   **UPI PHOTO**

Distance runners begin the clubhouse turn at Aqueduct.

NEW YORK RACING ASSN.

Exceptions occur when one meeting ends and a new one starts, whereupon the animal is let out of jail and can run at any price the trainer chooses. Horses claimed within the last month that have not yet won for the new proprietors are among the best bets a handicapper finds—provided he has already assessed distance, condition, class, weights, jockeys and pace.

50. Drops Below Price at Which It Was Claimed: Buddy Jacobson does this all the time—winning his first attempt with a newly claimed horse, and insuring the win by entering it for less than he paid. In general, if a horse qualifies as a live contender, was claimed within two or three months, and is running for the first time at a price lower than the owner paid, an all-out effort should be expected.

51. Consistency: This is one of the most powerful of plus factors, provided, of course, that the horse has adequate pace and class ratings, is in shape and likes the distance. A horse qualifies for the credit if it has won 20 percent of six or more races this year or, if less active this year, has won 20 percent of all its races this year and last. In claiming company, an earnings average of at least $500 per start is also reassuring.

52. Only Consistent Horse: If no other contender meets the consistency standards, the consistent one should get a second check mark.

53. Gelding: A gelding in shape to run its best is the most trustworthy of Thoroughbreds.

54. Entry: A contender coupled in the betting with another horse has something extra on its side. Because the contender is ready to go, the trainer undoubtedly will use the other half of the entry to make the pace easier for the contender. Therefore, if the contender is a stretch-running type, and its stablemate is a front-runner, and the contender's chief rival in the race is another front-runner, it pays to give the contender not one but two checks. The player is safe in assuming that the stablemate will run the rival pace-setter into the ground, clearing the way for the winning half of the entry.

55. Fast Final Quarter: Colonel E. R. Bradley, the professional gambler who had the Kentucky Derby in his hip pocket, used to make money backing on horses that had run the final quarter-mile of their latest races in 24 seconds or better. The angle is especially useful if the horse qualifies on other counts. To tell how fast a horse traveled the final quarter of a six-furlong race, subtract the half-mile time of the race from the final time. If the horse gained ground from the pre-stretch call to the finish, allow one fifth or one sixth of a second for each length it gained and subtract from the previous figure. Or, if the horse lost ground, add. If the horse's last race was at a mile, subtract the three-quarter-mile clocking from the final time, and then adjust the result according to the number of lengths gained or lost by the horse. It is impractical to attempt this calculation except if the race was at six furlongs or a mile. The angle is so good that it deserves not one but two check marks.

17 Paddock and Parade

WHEN OFF-TRACK BETTING finally is legalized in the United States, the customer will spend his afternoon in a neighborhood establishment similar to the branch office of a brokerage house. In air-conditioned splendor, safe from wind, rain, sun or chill, he will surrender his spending money to an electronically computerized tax collector, and will watch his horses lose on closed-circuit television.

"This," he will say, "is the life!"

A close approximation of "the life" already exists. Among the more popular facilities at modern tracks are indoor seating areas, completely walled off from any direct view of the race course. Throngs of punters congregate in these sanctuaries beneath the stands, handicapping, betting and watching four-legged shadows move across the screens of TV monitors. Legal off-track betting will be a great convenience for such folk, sparing them the ordeal of travel to and from the track on congested highways or jouncy rails. They will find everything at the state or municipal bookie parlor that they now get at the track itself.

The Thoroughbred racing industry regards off-track betting as a peril to its existence. If this is true, which I doubt, the industry has only itself to blame. As I complained in the preface to this book, the rulers of the sport are so afraid to offend morality that they fail to educate their customers in the theories and techniques of handicapping. They fail, therefore, to publicize the overwhelming advantage that accrues to the player who does his betting at the track: The horse is at the track! The player cannot see the horse in the flesh unless he makes the trip. And if he does not see the horse in the flesh he does not know what he is betting on.

The helpless innocence of Thoroughbred racing's loyal clientele is displayed most nakedly in its unawareness of the need to look closely and critically at a horse before risking good money on its chances. In a typical racing crowd of 20,000, hardly 1,000—many of them tourists—go to the paddock and walking ring to inspect the animals before the race. A much larger faction mills around beneath the stands, hoping to stumble onto a hot tip.

The paddock and walking ring are where the expert makes his final decision about the winning chances of his horse. Before going there to see the animal, and preferably before leaving home for the track, he has done his preliminary handicapping. He probably has from one to three contenders in mind. One may seem clearly superior on paper. The other one or two interest him only if the first turns out to be in unready condition.

The player therefore devotes main attention to the likeliest horse. If he approves what he sees, and regards the odds as reasonable, he makes his bet and awaits Destiny. However, if the appearance or behavior of the horse arouses mistrust, he studies the secondary contenders. At times, his observations may last throughout the ceremonies at paddock and walking ring, the parade in front of the stands, and the pre-race gallops.

Recognizing Readiness

When a good barn sends a fit horse to the races, the animal looks the part. Whether a two-year-old maiden or a five-year-old handicap champion, its class and condition are usually recognizable without the aid of a scoreboard. Its healthy coat glows like well-oiled, hand-rubbed wood. Its mane and tail are carefully groomed. Its eyes are bright, head up, ears erect and forward, muscles firm, ribs barely visible. Its stride is long, easy and free. Its nervousness, if any, resembles the wound-up tension of a human athlete eager for action.

The handsomest, soundest-looking, best-behaved, most devotedly groomed horse in the field is an extraordinarily good bet—but only if it seemed a likely winner during the paper-and-pencil phases of the handicapping. Relatively unimposing Thoroughbreds often win championships, and some of the finest-looking horses you ever saw never got beyond the allowance stage.

Kelso was unimpressive in the walking ring. There have been $4,000 horses with snazzier-looking coats. Yet the player who noted from the past-performance records that Kelso was the best horse in the race could not possibly have been put off by the great gelding's looks. Kelso did not look bad. He just looked unremarkable.

And there you have the main point of the jaunt to the saddling enclosure. You go there to see if there is any reason to refrain from betting on your choice. You hunt for negative signs.

The professional horseman and professional bettor enjoy a considerable advantage in this setting. Because they are on the scene every day, they know which few horses are able to run well even after displays of pre-race fretfulness. They know which horses are running in bandages for the first time. They know which horses customarily race with special shoes or special bits, and which are heavier or skinnier or more languid than usual.

The hobbyist or infrequent player is unable to keep abreast of such things. But if he knows what to look for and what, in general, it all means, he guarantees himself more winners, fewer losers and a higher rate of profit than can possibly be achieved by omitting the paddock visits.

Nervousness and Reluctance

Loyd (Boo) Gentry was roundly criticized because Graustark, the best-looking colt in years, broke down before getting to the 1966 Kentucky Derby. I sang in that critical chorus myself and shall never believe that the horse's ruination was unavoidable.

If Gentry offered any excuses, I did not read about them. A man with an ironic, rather cynical view of things, he kept his own counsel. He also kept his job as trainer of the high-class animals which his father, the celebrated Olin Gentry, breeds and raises for John W. Galbreath's Darby Dan Farm.

Coming into 1967, word got around that Boo might have a fresh chance at the Derby with a nice colt called Cup Race, a half-brother of Graustark. But Cup Race went the way of so many others. Injuries knocked it out of the entry box. Gentry then decided to see what might be done with a second colt, Proud Clarion.

This particular animal had suffered so severely from the sore shins that plague today's hard-worked two-year-olds that it had raced only three times during 1966 and had failed to win. A slow learner, and set back still further by the shin ailments, it also suffered from extreme nervousness. However, it showed enough promise early in the year to deserve a shot at Louisville.

On two afternoons during the week before the Derby, Gentry took the trouble to come to grips with Proud Clarion's nervousness. He paddocked the horse. That is, he brought it to the paddock amid the uproar of actual racing and saddled it, as if for actual competition.

"He shook so, his teeth rattled," said Gentry.

On each occasion, the horse did not recover its composure until safely back in the barn.

Derby Day came. Gentry again brought Proud Clarion to the paddock—this time not merely to be saddled but to run in the big race. This time the horse was quite calm. It finally had become accustomed to the

The parade from walking ring to track at Tropical Park.   UPI PHOTO

noise of the track. Proud Clarion won the Kentucky Derby at 30 to 1.

The betting favorite on that day was Damascus, trained by Frank Y. Whiteley, Jr. Like other Whiteley horses, this handsome son of Sword Dancer had been the beneficiary of patient, careful handling. It had long since overcome its natural fear of human crowds and of the special tension associated with pre-race ritual. It might get keyed up, but was not the skittish type that exhausts itself before the race starts.

Yet Damascus was nervous before the Derby. Unaccountably nervous. So nervous that certain New Yorkers who had seen the horse win the Wood Memorial at Aqueduct now changed their minds about betting on it in the big one. They suspected that something was wrong. So did Frank Whiteley.

Bill Shoemaker brought Damascus from the gate in a rush, found the horse unusually rank, but managed to snug it back slightly off the pace until the turn for home. Coming into the stretch, he located daylight, pointed Damascus at it and asked for speed. The colt started after the leader, Barbs Delight, as if able to eat it up and win by yards. And then the predictable happened. Damascus ran out of gas and was lucky to finish a well-beaten third. It had left its race in the paddock.

I do not know why Damascus was nervous on Derby Day. But I do know that 99 out of 100 noticeably nervous horses use up so much energy before the start of their races that they stop in the stretch.

Among two-year-olds and certain lightly raced threes such as Proud Clarion, the chief cause of serious nervousness is fear of a strange environment. A frequently complicating factor is dread of the discomfort which the animal has learned to associate with the sights, sounds and tugs and hauls to which it is subjected on the day of a race. Many horses seem literally to dread the prospect of the stressful dash from the starting gate or the punishing drive to the wire.

Later, after becoming adjusted—or resigned—to the demands of racing, Thoroughbreds manifest reluctance—or the nervousness it often begets—only when returning to the track from a long vacation, or when running for the first time at a strange place, or when ill or in pain or when jaded from too much work.

Here are signs of reluctance severe enough to warn the player that the horse may be out of kilter:

Fractiousness. Instead of walking cooperatively from the receiving barn to its paddock stall, the animal fights its handler. It tosses its head, swishes its tail restlessly, kicks, tries to wheel. The behavior may become more intense in the stall, or may not erupt until that point (as if the animal suddenly realized that it had not merely been out for a stroll but was actually going to be asked to race). It may try to kick down the walls of the stall. It may resist the saddle. It may try to savage its handlers with its teeth.

Later, in the parade around the ring, the horse may calm down—a good sign, if accompanied by other good signs to be described below. But if the fractiousness or unhappiness persists, the player knows that precious, unrecoverable energies are being squandered.

Note well that a horse that jogs, toe-dances and whinnies before its race should not be charged with undue nervousness unless it presents other signs of the condition. It may simply be keyed up, which is better than being uninterested.

Note also that inexperienced horses display more nervousness than seasoned animals do. Allowances must be made for this, although the really frantic juvenile seldom has anything left for its race. It is most comforting to discover that the two-year-old with the best previous clockings is also a cool cat in the walking ring.

Human Failure. The reaction of the horse's handlers to its fractiousness is frequently a dead giveaway to their estimate of the animal's prospects. When the groom or trainer displays viciousness or impatience of 'his own, he reveals that he has no more liking for the race than the horse does. If the horse had a substantial chance, the handler would do everything possible to protect his bet and his share of the purse. This, incidentally, is why stakes horses of notoriously erratic temperament, such as certain members of the Nearco-Nasrullah-Nantallah line, win even after giving their handlers fits. The thing is that they *are* stakes horses and the handlers are under orders to accept the trouble or find employment elsewhere. A fractious claiming racer seldom is treated with such deference. Once the battle starts in the paddock, little is done to improve the animal's disposition, or relieve the fears that account for the misbehavior. Not, that is, unless the horse has an excellent chance in the race and the handlers are willing to suffer injury and indignity in an attempt to salvage the situation.

Washiness. A lather of nervous sweat appears early in the paddock proceedings and the dampness spreads along the horse's neck and flanks like a stain.

In very hot weather, all healthy horses are expected to sweat. Indeed, horsemen worry about the condition of an animal that remains dry when most others are wet. But a nervous, washy horse has a particularly distressed air, no matter what the weather may be. His handlers sponge off the foam, yet he generates more. The sweatiness usually occurs in combination with other signs of nervous strain, such as rapidly flicking ears, or ears that lie flat, or a tossing head, or outright fractiousness.

Kidney Sweat. Nervousness betrays itself with an accumulation of white foam between the animal's rear legs. Occasionally, this is the only visible sign of unease. If the nervousness is not severe, the kidney sweat should diminish or disappear before the horses leave the walking ring for the track. If it becomes more profuse, the horse is probably out of sorts. On closer or more expert inspection, other signs of unreadiness may become apparent.

It is useless to speculate about the causes of any individual case of paddock distress. Whether produced by inexperience, physical discomfort or a sudden, perverse reluctance to play the game, it prevents horses from winning. The player need know no more than that. Even if the horse's record proclaims it the best runner in the race, the player who sees signs of serious reluctance or apprehensiveness had better not risk his money, unless the horse snaps out of its difficulties in short order. Or unless it is the kind of freak that always acts like a loser before it wins.

Bandages

Short bandages around fetlock and pastern are beneficial to a horse that tends to scrape its ankles on the surface of the track, a difficulty known in the trade as "running down." If the horse seems otherwise fit, these short bandages can be ignored.

Long bandages on the hind legs often are applied for much the same reason that a handball player wears a wrist strap—to give extra support. In this case, muscles and ligaments held firmly together enable the animal to propel its weight forward with greater comfort. A really sound horse requires no such artificial assistance, but hind bandages are acceptable unless the horse seems reluctant to race. In those circumstances, the bandages can be accepted as an additional sign of trouble and the horse should be tossed out.

Long bandages on the forelegs are strong signs of tendon trouble where the horse can least tolerate it. If an animal wearing these things seems ready to run, and figures to be the best in its field, the wise player passes the race. The horse might indeed win, but nobody should bet on it. Sooner or later, horses with foreleg ailments break down. Naturally, if the leading contender bobs up in front bandages and shows no liking for the day's activity, the player goes to his second choice with considerable confidence.

Soreness and Lameness

Some gallant old campaigners have legs so gnarled and knotted with wear-and-tear that it hurts to look at them. It surely hurts worse to run on them. But the horses get out there and win. Accordingly, the player should hesitate to rule out a contender whose knee is swollen or who has an alarmingly prominent tendon. Far better to assume, as racing officials do, that any horse able to get to the post is probably "racing sound" and may occasionally overcome its ouchiness and finish on top.

The trick is to recognize "racing sound" animals that are hurting too badly to stand the gaff. Most give fair warning by the unwillingness with which they surrender to saddle, rider and post parade. Others, more stoical about it, seem quite content to run, but reveal in their gaits that they are too stiff and sore to do it well. The goings-on in the paddock stall also help the player to spot such trouble.

Now that pain-killing drugs and nerve surgery are banned on major racing circuits, the law-abiding trainer of a lame or sore horse is forced to rely on bandaging, liniments and the analgesic properties of cold water. It is by no means unusual to walk into a receiving barn and find half the entrants in a claiming race standing in tubs of ice. The ice relieves discomfort by dulling the nerves that transmit pain. It also counteracts inflammation, at least briefly. To prolong its effects, trainers often wrap the sore member in a bandage soaked in the ice water. On arrival at the paddock stall, the bandage is removed. So are less significant bandages known as shipping, standing or stall bandages, which protect the legs from accidental kicks and scrapes.

It is not a particularly good idea to cross out the name of a contending horse that comes to the paddock in cold-water bandages. The soothing comfort may be all the animal needs to run in its best possible form.

Before making up his mind, the player should watch what goes on in the stall after the bandage is unwrapped. If trainer and groom fuss over the suspect joint, feeling it for signs of inflammation, one can assume that they are worried. Or if the horse shies away from the attention, the player knows that it hurts at a touch and is unlikely to run well.

After a few weeks of experience, the player can recognize horses that are stiff and sore. Their walking gait is less fluid than it might be. They favor the ouchy limb or foot, getting off it as quickly as possible in what amounts to a limp.

In the absence of an outright limp, the horse's head or hips may tell the tale. The head rises when a sore foreleg touches the ground, and then it nods to the opposite side. In the case of a painful rear leg, the opposite hip drops noticeably while walking. If the forelegs spread and seem about to straddle, as if the animal were on a skating rink, it has a sore knee or two, and will confirm the diagnosis with a mincing, choppy stride when it tries to run.

Every now and then, a horse's gait is so stilted in the walking ring that the player has no trouble deciding to bet on something else, or pass the race entirely. Perhaps more often, the player waits to see whether the animal eases out of its stiffness en route to the starting gate.

The Final Minutes

The horse that arouses expert suspicion in the walking ring generally confirms it during the post parade or the pre-race gallops. Like a child being dragged to the woodshed for punishment, it sweats, strains, has difficulty keeping its feet under it, and needs to be escorted under a tight hold by an outrider on a lead pony. Head high, eyes wild, chewing on the bit, the horse looks like the embodiment of defeat. Its occasional victory does not make a sucker of the player who refuses to bet on it. This kind of animal is not a good bet to begin with, and it proves this over the long haul by losing far more often than not.

Other unready horses do not have to be carried to the post, or held in check to prevent them from bolting to the stable. They simply run sore. The jockey sets them down for a gallop in front of the stands and they do not step out with the characteristically long stride of the Thoroughbred. Short, choppy steps, often with head unusually high or unusually low, reveal soreness. When the rider gets to the backstretch and busts the horse a couple of times with his whip, it may seem to lengthen stride and run more easily, a sign that it is working out of the trouble and may be able to run. No magic formula can be offered to help the player decide whether to bet or not. The only safe prescription is familiar enough: When in doubt, pass.

For my taste, the best bet is the horse that navigates to the starting gate under its own power, without a lead pony and without any special exercises beyond a brief gallop or two. Lead ponies have become so common in modern racing, however, that the bettor would cut his play below the reasonable minimum if he made the lack of a pre-race escort a large factor in his handicapping.

Shoes

Horseshoes come in a multitude of varieties, most of which are of absolutely no interest to the player.

In the old days, when horsemen solved their economic problems by conniving with each other to cash large bets on fixed races, deliberately poor shoeing was a favorite means of stiffing a horse. Nowadays, purses are more numerous, and big-time horsemen have little incentive to hobble a potential winner. The ancient custom of stiffing it today so that it may win at long odds next time is hard to practice in an era of overworked horses which seldom retain winning form from one race to the next. And an era of relatively vigilant policing. And of claiming races which help a trainer to darken improving form until ready to crack down at a price.

It also is an era in which some veterinarians swear that horses would last longer if greater attention were paid to their shoes. I mention this only for background. The player may deplore the incompetent handling of horses, but is powerless to act against it. As far as shoes are concerned, his role begins and ends with a glance at the official shoe-board and a close look at the feet of his horse.

He should bet money on no horse that wears steel shoes, now that aluminum ones are the mode. The aluminum weighs several ounces less than steel and, as the saying goes along shed row, "an ounce on the foot is like a pound on the back."

The player also should bet no money on a horse that wears bar shoes. These differ from the usual open-ended footwear. A bar is built across the opening. The purpose is to prevent a weak hoof from spreading and cracking under the animal's weight. Winners rarely wear these.

On tracks that tend to get gooey when wet, or on any kind of track

The windows at Garden State.   UPI PHOTO

Bobby Ussery enjoys the scent of roses and the taste of triumph on Proud Clarion after the 1967 Kentucky Derby.   UPI PHOTO

labeled muddy or heavy, the player should favor a sharp, well-placed horse whose handlers have spent the $20 necessary to equip it with stickers, or mud calks. These cleats provide extra traction.

Blinkers and Bits

The track's printed program advises the player whether a horse that has been running in blinkers will run today without them ("blinkers off") or vice-versa ("blinkers on"). The purpose of the hoods is to keep the horse running in a straight line, with his mind on his work. They prevent him from seeing what he might ordinarily shy away from or veer toward—such as other horses, or the inside rail or the grandstand. The heavy reliance of horsemen on trial-and-error is demonstrated by their experimentation with blinkers. A two-year-old that runs a couple of unaccountably erratic races when blinkered is quite likely to be sent post-ward without them in its next attempt. Sometimes the change works wonders, but don't bet on it. By and large, the change to favor is "blinkers on," when the two-year-old is from a smart barn, has never run hooded, and needs only to improve its previous clockings by a fifth or two to win a maiden race.

Bits come in as many varieties as shoes. The only interesting one is the extension, run-out bit. If the horse has been lugging in, it may go to the post with a bit that is longer on the off (right) side, enabling the rider to develop greater leverage with the reins. Similarly, a bearing-out horse benefits from an extension on the near (left) side. If the player gets to the races frequently enough to notice this change in equipment, and if the horse shapes up well with respect to class, condition, distance and the like, the mutuel ticket may be a better investment than usual.

Drugging and Stiffing

Heroin is known as "horse" because trainers used to dose race-horses with it. The dreaded opium derivative is a powerful stimulant of horses. Its effect is exactly the opposite of the lethargy associated with human addiction. Indeed, a heroin-stimulated horse may become uncontrollably wild, thereby frustrating its handlers, who had hoped only to dull its pain and shock its nervous system into condition for a winning effort.

I mention heroin because it is interesting. What is perhaps most interesting about it is that it has gone out of fashion at the tracks. More reliable, less dangerous, and far less easily detected stimulants and pain-killers are now in use.

The rules of racing forbid the administration of such chemicals. Concern for the betting public, to say nothing of concern for the well-being of the Thoroughbred, explains why official track laboratories test saliva and urine samples taken from the winners of all races. In some jurisdictions, tests are required for any horse that runs in the money. And in several, tests are run on any animal whose form is suddenly and inexplicably better or worse than expected, regardless of whether it finishes in the money or not.

Unfortunately, the intent of all this policing is more impressive than the results it achieves. For one thing, at least three of every four horses need medication of some kind to withstand training and racing. Secondly, in an age of wonder drugs, horsemen constantly stumble upon marvelous new preparations which not only help relieve pain but stimulate a horse's nervous system and, when administered in proper dosage, are exceedingly difficult to detect in saliva or urine samples.

In racetrack chemistry, as in war, the offense is always a jump or two ahead of the defense. By the time the track chemists have discovered how to detect a new drug, unscrupulous horsemen have found an even newer one.

Thus, one of racing's strongest weapons against stimulation of horses is its network of undercover intelligence agents. In plain language, spies. If these shoeflies were not padding around the barns pretending to be other than what they actually are, and if trainers and stablehands were not thoroughly conscious that Big Brother is watching, the game would be much less orderly and predictable than it is.

Every year, about one tenth of 1 percent (.001) of urine and saliva tests turn out positive. Which is to say that racetrack chemists find traces of one or another banned drug. Heads roll. But not the heads of trainers. Responsible though the trainer is supposed to be for what takes place in his stalls, the industry tends to rally behind him when traces of hop are found in one of his steeds. The crime often is blamed on a stable boy, who then vanishes. Once more, calm descends on shed row. Or the trainer, after serving a brief term of suspension, becomes more vigilant than ever. In some cases this means vigilance against hanky-panky. In other cases it means vigilance against getting caught at hanky-panky.

Nobody really knows how many horses go postward under the influence of drugs which relieve discomfort and augment the animals' natural energies. But the high degree of predictability in racing strongly suggests that the problem need alarm no player. Most races are won by horses whose records of increasing readiness are confirmed by good appearance and pleasant deportment in the paddock. If, as seems highly improbable, the victory is often a triumph of medication, the situation is potentially dangerous and deserves even more attention than it already gets behind the scenes of the sport. But, as nearly as I or anyone else can tell at present, drugs have not yet become a factor as important as distance, class, condition, pace or jockey. Nor are they likely to.

Another use of drugs is for purposes of preventing victory by the best horse in the race. It would be naive to pretend that horses never are stiffed, either by their handlers or some other bettor. Barbiturates, which turn up in twenty or thirty horses a year, are a favorite means of inducing languor and defeat. No doubt other chemicals, less easily discovered, are also in use. But stiffing—and of this you can be sure—is an extremely rare occurrence in major racing, and is by no means common in minor racing. Whatever else the boys may do, they want those purses. To stiff one horse does not assure victory to any other horse unless all the jockeys and/or trainers are in collusion. With Big Brother watching, that kind of conspiracy is riskier than it is worth. So the stiffing, when it is done, is done surreptitiously, as a gamble. If the gambles were uniformly profitable, there would be more of them and racing would be in the throes of a dreadful problem. Happily, the situation seems to be well in hand.

Tote-Board Tips

Privileged insiders, who supposedly have a better-than-fair idea about what's what before the race starts, are known enviously as the smart money. When the odds on a horse drop sharply before post-time, the crowd convulses. Hundreds stampede to the windows to join the smarties in the good thing, thereby weighing down the odds still more.

It is true that stable owners, trainers, grooms and clockers—and their relatives, friends and clients—bet thousands of dollars on a horse deemed ready to win. If the horse is unready, or is considered so, they don't bet on it. And, if they *do* bet, the odds decline.

Is it possible to tell whether smart money is on a horse? Sometimes. Is smart money smart enough to bother about? Sometimes.

In my opinion, the tote board is an interesting object but should be allowed to play no role whatever in the player's handicapping. His first problem is to find himself a horse. If he finds it, the tote board tells him whether the odds are reasonable. The better his handicapping, the less attention he need pay to the odds, of course. But if he is a neophyte, and not sure whether his horse merits a bet, low odds may well be sufficient reason to abstain.

This, of course, flies in the face of the belief that the player's handicapping is confirmed whenever his horse goes to the post at lower odds than expected. Confirmed by what? By smart money? But what about the two or three other platoons of smart money that have sunk the family jewels on two or three other horses in the same race?

The smart money is not a formally organized league of superlatively knowledgeable bettors. It does not move in a single phalanx to the mutuel windows. Any individual insider or group of insiders is as likely to be wrong about a horse as anyone else. Assuming, of course, that "anyone else" is a good handicapper.

The test of whether smart money is on a horse is whether relatively more is bet on it to win than to place or show. The insiders bet to win, because that's where profit lies. Accordingly, if bets on the horse account for a fifth or sixth of the win pool but only a seventh or eighth of the place or show pool, the player knows that certain presumably smart plungers expect big things and have backed their opinion with cash. Exception: an odds-on horse. The public often bets as heavily on such a horse to place or show as to win.

A last-minute drop in the odds on a horse may or may not reflect inside action by the stable. Occasionally, it means nothing but the infectiousness of a wild rumor. Not so many years ago, I was buttonholed by two hustlers in five minutes, each trying to tout me onto the same two-year-old. I thought it had no chance in its race, and was fascinated to see the odds drop. The horse ran out of the money at 7 to 5. A 4 to 1 shot won. That night I heard from a quite reliable source that several thousand dollars had been wagered on the winner by some smart guys who had employed a few hot-walkers to circulate through the crowd touting the other nag. This kind of thing happens quite often at smaller tracks.

At all racetracks in this country, a sharp drop in the tote-board quotation during the final minutes before post-time usually is a result of a rumor that somebody has loaded up on the horse in the win pool. The news spreads and the rush begins. For the record, let it be noted that the smart money, if it be involved at all, usually feeds its bets into the machines gradually, in an effort to elude discovery. Or, in some cases, it bets at the very start of wagering.

Now that I have done my level best to discourage the reader from allowing himself to be swayed by what he sees on the tote board, I should admit that it seldom pays to buck such betting trends in maiden races at major tracks. This is particularly true when a first-time starter goes postward at odds considerably lower than its morning-line quotation. The reason is simple enough. The only reliable dope about first-starters and lightly raced maidens is the opinion of clockers and other horsemen who have seen it in the mornings. Including, of course, its own handlers. When the slightest amount of extra cash shows up for such a horse in the win pool, the word spreads through the crowd with great rapidity and the odds plummet. I have never kept records of the results attainable through bets on such maidens, but I should not be surprised if profits await anyone who bets on them—provided that he does so only when he thinks that nothing else in the race has an obviously superior chance.

Another kind of tote action worth watching is the *lack* of change in the quotation on a medium-odds horse when the odds drop on another. Plainly, when odds drop sharply on one horse, carrying it into the even money range or thereabouts, odds should rise on everything else in the race. If one horse holds steadily in the 3 to 1 to 6 to 1 range, somebody is hurrying the money in on it. If your handicapping has already singled out that animal, it might pay you to increase your bet.

18 Seventy-seven Selected Systems

THE TYPICAL SYSTEM PLAYER stands in awe of the expert handicapper. He plucks at the cashmere sleeve and begs for secrets. The handicapper replies with the scorn that insiders reserve for outsiders. The only secret, he growls, is comprehensive knowledge of the game.

True. A system is a set of rules, a mechanical procedure, a formula. But handicapping is different. To tell one race from another and one horse from another, the handicapper makes personal evaluations of many interrelated, variable factors. No rules concise enough for practical use could possibly encompass all those variables. The handicapper's secret is his mental store of the general concepts from which rules derive. Examining a field of horses, he uses his knowledge in an orderly way—*systematically,* if you like—but he relies in the end on what he knows and believes and foresees, rather than entrusting his game to canned rules.

Because the theories and techniques of genuine handicapping have been guarded as jealously as the secrets of Voodoo, it is not surprising that racing fans pay hundreds of thousands of dollars a year for selection systems. Some of the formulas cost $100 each and arrive in plain white envelopes. Others are obtainable for pennies in the pages of *American Turf Monthly* and *Turf and Sport Digest.* I have a file drawer full of the things and have seen thousands more. Most are quite worthless, including some that sell at high prices. The best, including many published in the two major fan magazines, are substantially useful, especially in the hands of someone who knows enough about handicapping to evaluate the rules and adapt them to his own purposes.

Having gone to some pains to make a handicapper of my reader, I shall not now invite him to become a system player. Yet I have filled this chapter with the largest compilation of workable systems ever published. I have done this for several reasons. First, I believe that the analysis and dry-run testing of systems is an interesting way to enlarge one's grasp of handicapping. Secondly, I believe that a player who *knows* handicapping might well prefer to attack the mutuel machines with three or four valid spot-play systems. Knowing what he does, he is able to choose the right method for the right occasion. Sparing himself most of the labors of actual handicapping, he remains able to invoke the principles of handicapping whenever he recognizes the special situations in which system rules must be stretched or ignored.

Systems are not supposed to be played that way, of course. What makes them systems in the first place is the reassuringly inflexible set of rules which the player is required to apply unquestioningly. So be it. The systems in this chapter are composed of rules. Each is supplemented, however, with suggestions which show any fairly well-informed player how he might improve matters by using his own noodle.

How to Evaluate Systems

Systems cover a wide spectrum. Some are ingenious attempts to codify basic principles of handicapping in relatively simple form. Some apply handicapping standards to the business of locating exceptionally worthwhile favorites, or the likeliest selections of newspaper handicappers. Some are angle systems that point out a horse as playable without regard to the potentialities of the other horses in the race. Some stress class, some consistency, others current condition or speed or jockey.

Before describing this book's systems in detail, I think it important to agree on methods of evaluating them. And of evaluating other systems which the reader might encounter elsewhere or dream up himself. First, a system should contain no eccentric rules. It should be attuned to the established realities of the sport. It should make sense from a handicapping standpoint.

I have in mind hundreds of systems I have seen which advise the player to back the least consistent horse in the race, or the only maiden in the race, or the horse with the poorest recent performance, or the horse moving furthest up in class, or the horse carrying the least weight, or the horse with the apprentice rider, or the only female in the field, or the only three-year-old in a race against older. It is quite easy, but thoroughly dishonest, to "substantiate" such a system by citing longshot victories. Any attempt to make money by departing so far from the percentages of Thoroughbred racing is doomed. The player who persists in a disregard of the laws of equine nature and the principles of handicapping must end without a dime.

Given a system that seems compatible with some of the basic probabilities of the game, the player needs to find out whether its mechanical rules cover a sufficient range of circumstances to permit a profit. The only way to find out is to run a test. Test it on paper, preferably over a period long enough to permit at least 100 paper bets. For most systems and most tracks, this would mean checking through the racing papers of an entire meeting.

A less extensive test is likely to be misleading, like the brief published "workouts" that "prove" the validity of bets on the only maiden in the race, or the only horse carrying an apprentice. A profitable system might show a loss in any random series of 50 plays. A losing system might show a profit in a similar test.

Beware of the system that yields a paper profit of less than 10 percent on the hypothetically wagered dollar. This is better than losing, but is hardly sufficient profit to sustain one's enthusiasm, unless the bets are huge.

Beware especially of the system that produces fallow periods of more than seven or eight successive losses. One or two such losing streaks may be endurable in a system that yields clusters of winners. But give it some thought. Do you really want to stretch your nerves with a procedure that bails itself out with a $24 winner after nine successive losses? Adventurous though you may be when betting on paper in the privacy of your den, would you deliberately suffer nine or ten losses in a row when risking your own money?

Beware also of systems that require a large financial outlay without a proportionate return. The system that produces two plays a day and a 20 percent profit is far more suitable to most players than the kind that obliges him to bet on two or three horses in each of four or five races, and ends with a 2 percent profit. The first system lends itself to supplementation. For example, the player can use it in conjunction with another that picks a fair percentage of winners in other kinds of races. He then can make a total of three or four or five bets a day. But the second system jams him up, requires too much capital, and, no matter how nice some of its mutuels may seem, it pays too little in the end.

Shun systems full of "tie-breaking" rules which sound suspiciously as if they were added during, rather than before, the test of the system. Good systems separate qualified contenders by means of fundamental handicapping factors. For example, a system based on speed ratings and class should use distance and current condition to eliminate the less likely contenders. Tear it up if it says something like, "In case two or more horses qualify, play the one that carries the highest weight today; if still tied, play the one that was closest to the leader at the pre-stretch call of its next-to-last race." In breaking ties among horses selected by any of the systems in this chapter, always, but always, use whatever fundamentals are not covered in the system. Apply those fundamentals in this sequence: distance, current condition, sex, age, class, consistency, weight, jockey.

Beware most earnestly of the system that depends for its paper profits on a couple of boxcar mutuels. When you disregard the $76 winner does the system still show a profit? If so, it may merit further testing. If not, the system probably is a waste of time. For most temperaments, any system that throws off fewer than 25 percent winners is no use at all, the $76 bonanza notwithstanding. Far more significant than the big longshot is the price range of *most* winners produced by the system. If it hits one out of four or five, with mutuels large enough to make the difference, and if its long losing streaks are few and far between, perhaps you can tolerate it.

Finally—if I may repeat my warning against the ever-present temptation to adopt or invent eccentric rules—avoid any system that gets its longshots by making unreal requirements. For example, you may notice that the system would have caught a $96 winner if it had accepted horses idle for nineteen days instead of the prescribed fourteen. Before embracing the idea, be sure to recheck. How many losers would it *add* by extending the late-action rule? Is it a longshot system to begin with, or was the $96 thing a freak occurrence? Most urgent of all, was your test extensive enough to be meaningful?

System Principles

Most systems are silent about one or more of the fundamentals of handicapping. The great delight, of course, is to find one that shows a profit anyhow, requiring a minimum of toil. You will see several in this chapter.

Others, which perform erratically, are subject to revision. You can tighten them by supplying additional rules to cover distance or condition or weights or sex or class or consistency or jockey—reliable factors that seem most pertinent. If in doubt about the kind of rule to add, you might riffle through whatever chapter in this book covers the particular factor.

The player unwilling or unable to test a variety of spot-play systems in hope of working up a battery of the things may be equally unready to test his own handicapping with real money. He will find excellent alternatives in some of the more comprehensive systems that appear late in this chapter. After putting one or two through a dry run for several weeks, he is certain to notice certain aspects of handicapping falling into place for him. He may adopt part of the system to his own blossoming method of selection. Or he may revamp the system radically and make it entirely his own. If his changes comply with the fundamentals of the game, he will discover in due course that he has become a pretty good handicapper. Welcome to the club.

Class-Consistency Systems

Some interesting selection systems emphasize Thoroughbred class and/or consistency. Like most canned methods, they are least likely to disappoint when the following restrictions are observed:

1. No maiden races.
2. No races for two-year-olds at less than six furlongs.
3. No jump races.
4. No races on other than a fast track.
5. No females against males.
6. No horses whose best races have been run at tracks inferior to today's.
7. No horses carrying more than 120 pounds in races which find the competition less severely burdened.
8. No horses making their first starts after long trips or lengthy layoffs.

Having issued those warnings, I urge the reader to use his knowledge of handicapping to find occasions on which some of the warnings may be ignored.

SYSTEM 1

Principle: Play a horse entered for a claiming price at least $2,000 below a price tag it has carried in the past, provided it is the only such horse in the race and is regarded highly enough to go postward at odds of 15 to 1 or less.

Reasoning: Class will tell.

Comment: All minor tracks and some major ones are replete with gimpy, cut-rate horses that used to win allowance races or $15,000 claimers. However, the published past-performance records are brief. They seldom cover more than the most recent six or eight months of an active animal's career. For that reason, this system tends to point out horses that have only recently declined in market value. Such a Thoroughbred unquestionably has gone sour, but it may still have enough class to beat the cheapies it faces this afternoon.

Fantastic results have been recorded in tests of this idea. E. R. DaSilva and Dr. Roy M. Dorcus, faculty members at the University of California at Los Angeles, reported in their interesting book, *Science in Betting* (Harper, New York, 1961), that the method turned up 27 plays at a 55-day meeting at Hollywood Park. Thirteen of the bets won, at a profit of $1.50 on every wagered dollar! Somewhat more action—37 plays in 55 days—occurred at Santa Anita, with only a slight reduction in profits. At Aqueduct, a 50-day workout produced 11 plays and an 82 percent profit.

I ran through three weeks of a Delaware Park meeting and found that plays arose at the rate of three or four a week. The sample was too small for significance, but I was interested to note that four of ten selections won and that the prices were long enough to return almost exactly 100 percent of every dollar invested. To achieve this, however, certain elaborations were necessary. Like other apparently simple notions about racing, the one embodied in this system produces endless confusion unless shored up with additional rules.

Suggestions: The player should avoid maiden races, because drops in claiming price mean little in such company. Similarly, if he finds that an entrant in a straight $5,000 claimer once ran in a race for $10,000 maidens, he dare not qualify the animal on such grounds, but should confine his interest to horses that qualify on the basis of a race for previous winners. Moreover, danger lurks in the assumption that a filly entered against $6,000 males should be bet because it once ran in an f-8000. The player should take pains to adjust the value of the f-claimer (see page 212) or should pass the race entirely.

Another problem is that of the horse whose only qualification is that it ran in an allowance race or a higher bracket claimer at a minor track. Such stock should be ignored. Finally, high-priced claiming races at major tracks frequently involve animals that have run in allowance company. Unless the player is satisfied that the allowance race was substantially classier than today's claimer, he should toss out the horse or pass the race.

The player attracted to this system should run it through a full season at his own track. See what happens when its basic principle is taken literally, without regard to the previous winning status or sex of the horses, or the tracks at which they have run their apparently classier races, or the real value of the allowance races in which they have started. Also see what happens when my suggestions are applied. And see how things work out when rules affecting distance and/or recent action are added. I believe that tightening of this kind would leave the player with two or three bets a week, a high percentage of winners, an excellent rate of profit and, most important, a sound procedure likely to withstand the test of time.

SYSTEM 2

Principle: Play any horse running in a claiming race for the first time, provided it has been racing and working out regularly, was beaten by not more than five lengths in its last start, and either led or was within two lengths of the leader at some stage of the race.

Reasoning: An allowance or maiden-special competitor in good enough physical condition to race and work frequently must be conceded an excellent chance when it drops into claiming company after a race in which it showed signs of life.

Suggestions: If in doubt as to what constitutes sufficient recent action, consult Chapter 9. Or require at least one race in the past eighteen days, with workouts at the rate of one per five days for any horse that has not raced in eight days or longer. A distance rule is probably less necessary with this system than in other methods of selection: The trainer who drops a formerly promising horse into a race from which it may be claimed is likely to put it where it can do its best.

SYSTEM 3

Principle: Play a horse that led or ran within a length of the leader at one or more of the early calls of its last race and drops down today to a class at which it has won in the past.

Reasoning: Trainers do this sort of thing all the time.

Comment: This system should produce profits if supplemented with a late-action rule. A pace-setting type that tires in the late stages after showing some run is usually brought back to the races in a hurry, to exploit its apparently improving form. When dropped in with cheaper company than it has been facing, it usually holds its speed longer. The trainer probably places it at the right distance in a situation of this kind.

Suggestions: In addition to a condition rule, the player should resolve to bypass turf races. The only exception might be a horse that has won on the grass against a field exactly like today's.

SYSTEM 4

Principle: Bet any horse that was claimed in one of its last three races and is entered today at a price lower than the new owner paid for it.

Reasoning: Horsemen sometimes make dreadful claims, but not very often. If the horse has been running and working regularly and the owner now risks losing it for less than he paid, the player knows that the barn wants today's purse. Badly.

Comment: An occasional horse goes to pot during the very race from which it is claimed. Others conk out during their first days in the new barn. But a majority of the remainder give the new owners some run for the money, having been chosen on grounds of impending good form. Certain shrewd haltermen often win with the horse on the first try, even though it runs against better company than it has been meeting in the recent past. Others take a couple of races to prepare the animal for the crackdown, and do not hesitate to enter it for $500 or $1,000 less than the purchase price, to insure the best possible results. This system probably will not make money if played indiscriminately, but should be a powerful instrument for anyone who knows the habits and gimmicks of his local track's leading trainers.

Suggestions: The system is unworkable with maidens. It gains strength if the player checks the horse in the paddock, to make sure it is ready. It also improves with tight distance and condition rules, and when the jockey is among the local leaders. Addition of such rules eliminates the most spectacular longshots turned up by this system, but increases the winning percentage greatly and should bring the player onto the profit side of the ledger, where he belongs.

SYSTEM 5

Principle: Play a horse stepping down in class after a race in which it ran out of the money, provided that (1) it had stepped up in class for that race and (2) it was never worse than third at any call in its next-to-last race.

Reasoning: This combines Plus Factors 22 and 23 (see Chapter 16). They often are accompanied by as many as six or seven others, signifying an authentic "go."

Comment: Formal handicapping procedures often single out this system's horse as a contender, yet it may pay a handsome mutuel because of its apparently bad last race.

Suggestions: Distance and current-condition rules make this system a nice addition to anyone's collection of spot-play methods.

SYSTEM 6

Principle: Play a horse stepping down in class after a race in which the chart-maker's comment indicated that it ran an "even" or better race.

Reasoning: This is Plus Factor 30. A horse that did not disgrace itself in competition with better horses might move ahead a few lengths today.

Comment: Years ago, I used to finish no worse than even, and sometimes with a nice seasonal profit, using this system in races where I could find (1) no truly consistent horse with a clear edge in class and (2) none that ran powerfully enough in its last race to look like a serious threat on grounds of current form. I believe the system is most effective in races for animals aged four and older and, of course, only when more fundamental factors fail to suggest a likely play.

Suggestions: Recent action and a liking for the distance should be a routine part of this one.

SYSTEM 7

Principle: Play a horse that finished second in its last race if (1) it runs in the same company or cheaper today and (2) the winner of its last race has subsequently stepped up in class and won.

Reasoning: The horse lost to something that was much too good for the field. But it beat everything else and should be a good bet today.

Comment: This is what is called a "follow-up" system. A player who already keeps a notebook record of results, the true class of races, and the like, can turn a pretty penny with this angle. It produces not more than one or two plays a week, but the winning percentage ranges between 33 and 50, depending on how careful the player is about avoiding females against males, three-year-olds against older horses on the down slope of the form cycle, and horses that have not had sufficient recent work to deserve support.

Suggestions: If you do not maintain a notebook, the infrequent plays produced by this system may not seem worth the trouble. On the other hand, the results are most gratifying for anyone with the necessary patience. The system is particular dynamite with fillies and mares that finish second to males and seem to be stepping up in class when entered at a slightly higher price against females. As readers of Chapter 10 are aware, such a step up is really a step down. The system gets equally good results with three-year-olds that race against their own kind after running second to older horses. In any case, careful observance of the form cycle is necessary. A horse that runs second may get so tuckered out that it can't beat anything in its next effort. Check Chapter 9 and devise rules to assure bets on ready horses.

SYSTEM 8

Principle: Play a horse that has gone to the post as betting favorite in at least 40 percent of the races described in its past-performance record, provided that it (1) has earned more money this year than anything else in the field and (2) has finished in the money in at least half the races for which detailed past-performance lines are published and (3) has won no less than 25 percent of its total races this year and last.

Reasoning: A horse of established consistency and recognized class (note the frequency with which it runs as favorite) is seldom a hopeless risk.

Comment: Strangely enough, this system puts the player on cheapies as well as stakes runners. It gets surprisingly good prices at times. The crowd often discounts the chances of a vigorous young three-year-old against better stock than it has faced in the past. Odds also rise when a well-backed horse loses two or three times in succession.

Suggestions: The system is at its best when the player takes pains to avoid jaded horses. Sufficient late action and, among older horses, not too many hard recent races, should be minimum requirements. A distance rule should also be used—preferably one that demands a previous victory at today's exact distance. Two-year-olds are not covered by this system, which calls for consistency over a period of two years.

SYSTEM 9

Principle: Play a horse that has won at least 25 percent of no fewer than six races this year, or this year and last combined, provided that (1) it has run within the past ten days at this track and (2) has won at today's distance against animals of today's class.

Reasoning: An authentically consistent horse, properly placed and physically fit, is usually a real contender.

Comment: This one is typical of better systems. It saves the player the labor of handicapping the entire field, yet directs him to a horse whose record suggests ability to hold its own.

Suggestions: The results improve if the condition rule is enlarged to include negative factors like overwork. A simple pace analysis, a walk to the paddock, and avoidance of horses unlikely to do their best under today's weights will reduce the number of losing bets. Also, they will tout the player off an occasional longshot! But the long-run results should be satisfactory.

SYSTEM 10

Principle: Play a horse that has won and/or finished second at least ten times during this year and last, provided that (1) it has finished first or second in at least half its races during that period and (2) has won at least 25 percent of its total starts during that period and (3) has raced within the past eight days and (4) has won or finished second within the past two months.

Reasoning: A genuinely consistent horse that ran eight days ago should be fit enough to live up to its record today.

Comment: Even more potent than System 9, this one seldom gets more than two or three plays a week. Prices range from odds-on to $30 and better, with the majority somewhere between 2 to 1 and 5 to 2. *Turf and Sport Digest* published a full-season New York workout of a closely similar system many years ago. It hit 40 percent winners and the profit exceeded 100 percent.

Suggestions: A player would diminish losses by tightening the condition rule to avoid bets on older horses that have been raced too strenuously in their recent starts. A distance rule would reduce the action still further, but would probably push the winning percentage above the 40 mark.

SYSTEM 11

Principle: Of all entrants that ran within the past ten days and finished out of the money, play the one whose record shows a victory at today's exact distance in a field of today's class.

Reasoning: The recent losing race and the proper placement suggest an effort to win at a price.

Comment: Like so many methods of its kind, this one leads to the poorhouse unless the player fortifies it with sensible condition rules. Otherwise, its losing streaks will be more compelling than the longshots it finds.

Suggestions: With condition rules, this kind of play becomes an especially promising bet, particularly when the maneuvering trainer assigns the mount to a leading jockey.

SYSTEM 12

Principle: Play a horse that lost its last race but earned a "Form" or "Telegraph" speed rating of 95 or better.

Reasoning: It takes an exceptionally good horse to earn such a rating, win or lose. An animal of such class should win next time out if given any part of a break.

Comment: Like most systems, this one improves in the hands of a player willing to supplement mechanical rules with knowledge of the game. For example, no cut-and-dried condition formula is much help in evaluating the readiness of the stakes and allowance runners likely to qualify under this method. Yet an analysis of their fitness is most important, and so is analysis of the assigned weights. The player who uses the system in that fashion should find it helpful in big races.

Suggestions: Do not try this on turf races. Watch the opportunities it presents at secondary tracks, when big-league stakes runners are entered. Also watch it in top-grade sprints at major tracks.

SYSTEM 13

Principle: Play the horse that has won or finished closest to the front end most often in its last seven races. Add the finishing positions in those races, counting a victory as 1, a second-place finish as 2, and so on, but giving nothing worse than a 5, even if the horse finished tenth in one of its races. The horse with the lowest total is the play. If any horse has fewer than seven races, but has won any, pass the race.

Reasoning: Recent consistency is the best kind.

Comment: Surprisingly good prices await anyone who plays this mechanically, in nine races a day, breaking ties by means of distance, class and recent action, in that order.

Suggestions: Profits are possible for the player willing to convert this from a mechanical system to a simple handicapping method. The key elements to be added are class and its relationship to form. Grant high-class animals the ability to win in second-rate company after a layoff. Likewise, be lenient about demanding recent races of consistent claiming animals which have shown in the past that they can win in their own class off workouts alone. Be careful about betting females against males.

Form Systems

Thousands of systems purport to zero in on ready horses without requiring the player to ponder the numerous subtleties of the current-condition factor. To the degree that they deal in fundamentals of form and take heed of class, they do quite well.

SYSTEM 14

Principle: Bet a horse that won its last race easily, provided that the race took place not more than a week ago.

Reasoning: An easy winner is at top form. The trainer seeks a repeat victory as soon as possible.

Comment: A sound idea, except when the animal steps up to meet one or two classier animals whose own condition is sharp.

Suggestions: Worth trying if the horse is the only one of its kind in the race. In allowances, handicaps and stakes, and in top-grade claimers at major tracks, the one-week rule might be eased to ten days.

SYSTEM 15

Principle: Play a horse that won its last race by gaining in the stretch after leading or running within two lengths of the leader at the stretch call, provided the race occurred within two weeks.

Reasoning: The big win (see page 170) is the most reliable sign of powerful form. But if the horse is kept out of action for more than two weeks, one must assume that illness or injury has prevented the trainer from cashing in again.

Comment: The player who is careful about age, sex, and jockey can beat the game with this spot-play system.

Suggestions: Play no race in which more than one horse qualifies. Avoid three-year-olds against older, except in allowance sprints, or if you know that the three-year-old beat older in its big win. Also avoid females against males. Otherwise, do not worry about animals moving up in class. This kind does it and wins. Flexibility about the two-week rule also helps: If the horse has been working briskly at four- or five-day intervals, it can be allowed up to three weeks since its last race. Obviously, however, the situation is rosier if not more than a week elapses.

SYSTEM 16

Principle: Bet a horse that gained in the stretch in its last race, provided that it beat at least three horses, has average earnings of at least $500 per start, and does not step up in class.

Reasoning: Class, consistency and form.

Comment: An excellent spot-play method for claiming races in the $2,500 to $7,500 range, but only when not more than three animals qualify and no other apparently sharp entrant has superior consistency. Gets excellent prices.

Suggestions: Try combining this with Systems 13 and 14, using it when they fail to produce a play in a medium-grade claimer. A severe late-action rule is needed for best results. I would not bother with a horse unraced for more than two weeks unless it had worked out at least twice in the last eight or ten days. To break ties, discard an animal that seems less than ideally suited to the distance. If the tie persists, favor the horse stepping down in price. If still a tie, go to the one that raced most recently and/or got the most favorable chart comment.

SYSTEM 17

Principle: Play a horse that ran close to the early pace of its last race, slowing down in the later stages, provided that (1) it had not showed as much early speed in its previous two races and (2) it earned a higher speed rating in the last race than in either of the previous two.

Reasoning: Early speed is a reliable sign of improvement.

Comment: Innumerable systems derive from this idea. Their virtue is in steering the player away from obvious choices, many of which turn out to be past the peak of form.

Suggestions: Try this with horses that have raced in the past seven days or have worked out at short intervals since racing not more than two weeks ago. Concentrate on claiming races, and favor a horse entered at a class and distance which it has handled successfully in the past. In testing the system, notice whether results improve if the jockey factor is introduced. Also notice how the winning percentage increases when the probable pace of the race suits the animal's running style. Finally, see if you can steal a few hours to see what happens when these horses are played three times in succession, stopping the play sooner if the horse wins.

SYSTEM 18

Principle: Play a horse that lost its last race provided that it was first, second or third at the pre-stretch call and that (1) it had been at least two positions farther back at that call in each of its previous two races and (2) it earned a higher speed rating than in either of the two previous races.

Reasoning: Another sign of improvement, representing a sign of life in the semifinal stages of the race.

Comment: Everything said about System 17 applies here.

SYSTEM 19

Principle: Play a horse that was first, second or third at the stretch call and, while losing, earned a higher speed rating than in its previous two races.

Reasoning: Another hint of imminent victory.
Comment: See System 17.

SYSTEM 20

Principle: Play a horse that finished two positions closer to the winner and earned a higher speed rating than in its previous two races.

Reasoning: Still another sign of improvement.
Comment: See System 17.

SYSTEM 21

Principle: Play a horse that ran an even race, in second, third or fourth position (it does not matter which), at each of the four calls (ignoring the "Telegraph's" notation of the animal's position at the start). The horse should have earned a higher speed rating than in either of its previous two races.

Reasoning: Such a horse is on the verge.
Comment: See System 17.

SYSTEM 22

Principle: Play a horse that has earned increasingly high speed ratings in each of its last three races without winning, and has been increasingly close to the winner at each of the four calls in each race. Judge closeness to the winner either in terms of running position or number of lengths behind. If the horse led at any call in its third race back or its next-to-last race, it should have led at the same call in the following race.

Reasoning: The occasional animal whose record shows an overall improvement of this kind is on its way to the winner's circle.
Comment: See System 17.
Suggestions: Consider combining all these improvement-angle systems into one. A careful study of results at your own track will disclose the blend of distance, class, consistency, sex, jockey and pace rules that yields the most satisfactory profits.

SYSTEM 23

Principle: Play a horse that raced twice in the past fourteen days but did not win, provided that it has won at today's distance and class at some time in the past three months.

Reasoning: A properly placed animal fit enough to race three times in two weeks is fit enough to win, perhaps at a price.

Comment: This one gets longshots, but misleads the player toward animals that are being raced into shape and have not yet achieved it.

Suggestions: Things improve considerably if the player requires that the horse's record show a bit of improvement in either of its last two efforts. It also pays to avoid any four-year-old or older animal that lost in close, driving finishes in both of its most recent starts.

SYSTEM 24

Principle: Play a horse that has raced within two weeks, has worked out every four days since, worked out yesterday, and is dropping in claiming price.

Reasoning: Such a recent record portrays a trainer getting ready to shoot the wad with a physically able animal.

Comment: A nice system. Losing streaks are no problem if the player digs into the past-performance record instead of leaving everything to the trainer. Trainers, as we know, are not infallible.

Suggestions: Avoid allowance races and higher-bracket claimers. The system is best in medium-grade claimers and maiden claimers for three-year-olds and up. In testing, note the effects of the distance, sex, weight and jockey factors.

SYSTEM 25

Principle: Among entrants that have raced in the past seven days, finishing out of the money, play the one that has run in the highest-grade race in the last two months. Break ties by finding the qualifier that has earned the highest "Form" or "Telegraph" speed rating in the past month.

Reasoning: A race within seven days is always a good sign. Many successful players refuse to bet on any other kind of animal.

Comment: This is a longshot special, best used when other selection methods fail to produce a candidate.

Suggestions: If you want to try this as a last resort, after your other systems come up empty on a race, your chances of breaking even with it will be enhanced by giving first preference to horses that have already shown ability at the particular distance and class. The presence of a winning jockey also means a good deal on a horse of this kind.

SYSTEM 26

Principle: Play the horse that finished in the money most recently.

Reasoning: What better clue to top form than a recent good performance?

Comment: The last-out-in-the-money system may be the most popular of them all. It requires absolutely no work and tends to protect the player against serious losing streaks by directing him to animals whose trainers are trying to cash in on good form. It can be used in any kind of race.

Suggestions: The player who understands the form cycle increases the winning percentage of this system by ruling out horses whose in-the-money finishes are forecasts of deterioration rather than improvement. See pages 164-170. Distance, class, sex, consistency, weight and jockey rules each help the system, although they rob it of its extreme simplicity. I can think of no better drill in the principles of handicapping than a long workout with this system, including a study of how its results vary with the addition and modification of fundamental handicapping factors.

SYSTEM 27

Principle: Play a horse that finished in the money in its last two starts, provided that (1) it won not more than one of them, (2) was out of the money in its third race back, (3) steps up not more than $1,000 in claiming price today and (4) is the only qualifier in the race.

Reasoning: The horse demonstrated improvement in its next-to-last and either improved still more in its last or ran well enough to get some of the money. It may still have enough on the ball to win today.

Comment: Frank Bouche served this one to readers of *American Turf Monthly*. It gets good prices, encounters few long losing streaks, and locates a play or two on most racing days. Its ingenious rules cover the kind of animal that lost last time because it was stepped up in class after a victory. Also covered are the animals that won last time but which may be able to win again because they step up only $1,000 or less today. The rule against races with more than one qualifier prevents confusion. It also tends to turn up races in which the one horse, regardless of odds, is a form standout.

Suggestions: A distance rule would help the player to avoid losers that won their next-to-last, tailed off slightly in their last and are being entered today at the wrong distance for exercise. A rule requiring recent races and/or works might cancel an accidental longshot or two, but also would eliminate bets on horses that have not run in months. A rule eliminating older horses that ran to the limits of their ability in their last two races would spare the player bets on animals that should be resting instead of racing.

SYSTEM 28

Principle: By reading the official result charts, including the chartmaker's comments, note the name of any horse that finished fast in the stretch and reached the wire not more than two lengths behind the winner. Note also horses that encountered interference of some kind but showed late speed. And horses that go off at 2 to 1 or less but finish out of the money after a poor start or interference of some kind. Play each horse each time it races again until it wins, but do not play it more than four times. Compile the list from charts of all races except jumps, two-year-old and maiden races.

Reasoning: The stout stretch finish is a splendid clue to impending victory. The alibi (see pages 170-172) is a strong plus factor in cases of this kind.

Comment: The man who introduced me to Thoroughbred racing thirty-five years ago used to make a pretty penny with a follow-up system quite similar to this. In 1949, R. H. Matthews explained the present version to readers of *Turf and Sport Digest*. He published a workout covering 1,752 bets at seven tracks in a period of almost a year. The winning percentage was 23 (418 winners), and the profit was a robust 57 cents for every wagered dollar. Some of the mutuel payoffs were extraordinary —one horse paid $94.90, another $87.20, another $86.70. And so on, including dozens at 5 to 1 or better. The system beat every one of the seven meetings.

Suggestions: All this takes is patience, alertness and access to the daily result charts. Winning percentage and, I am quite sure, rate of profit would be increased by using a distance rule to avoid bets when the horse is being sent out to build its speed or stamina. In testing the method at your own track, try expanding it to include horses that show early speed and tire in the stretch. If you happen to patronize book-makers (shame on you), it pays to follow the listed horses even if they ship to out-of-town tracks.

SYSTEM 29

Principle: Play a horse that runs within four days after being scratched from a race, provided that (1) the track was fast on the day the horse was scratched

Eddie Arcaro (at right) wins the 1958 Wood Memorial on Jewel's Reward. Photo shows how narrowly horses and their riders avoid collision in the effort to get there first.   UPI PHOTO

Bill Hartack and Gen. Duke nip Eddie Arcaro and Bold Ruler at the wire in the 1957 Everglades at Hialeah.   UPI PHOTO

and (2) the horse was assigned a post position for the race from which it was scratched and (3) the horse has been racing and working out regularly.

Reasoning: The trainer scratches the horse because a better opportunity is in prospect a few days later. If he were not hoping to win with the animal, he would let it get its tightener in the earlier race and would not bother to scratch it.

Comment: A sound enough idea, limited by the inescapable fact that the wish to win and the ability to win are two different things. The post-position rule is important. Often, more entries are received than can be accommodated in a race. The extra horses are placed on an "also-eligible" list and are assigned no post positions. If one of the others is scratched, a horse is moved into the race from the also-eligible list. Therefore, a horse whose name appears on the also-eligible list may be scratched for no reason other than that the race was filled.

Suggestions: If the trainer and the horse are both consistent winners, it may be possible to work this nice little angle with no more handicapping than that. Otherwise, it will pay to make sure that the horse is properly placed as to distance, is not outclassed, has demonstrated at least a hint of improvement in its last race or two, and will enjoy the probable pace.

SYSTEM 30

Principle: Consider only horses that ran within ten days and finished out of the money. Determine the number of lengths by which each was beaten in each of its three most recent races (counting a victory as zero). Add the number of beaten lengths. Play the horse with the smallest total.

Reasoning: A horse that has been getting close to the winner, or winning itself, benefits from an easy, out-of-the-money race. If it then returns to the wars within ten days, it is in adequate physical condition. Its poor last race will inflate the mutuel price.

Comment: This is a nice angle for players sensible enough to steer away from animals that are on the downgrade.

Suggestions: Use the form factor and alibis as carefully as you can. Watch distance and class.

SYSTEM 31

Principle: Play a horse that finished fourth in its last race provided that it (1) gained at least two lengths in the stretch or (2) led or ran within a length of the leader at any call or (3) steps down at least $1,000 in claiming price.

Reasoning: The fourth-place finish, being out of the money, discourages a certain amount of public play, augmenting the odds. A horse that ran fourth after giving notice of improvement, or that steps into easier company, should never be overlooked.

Comment: Some of the best longshot systems concentrate on horses that run fourth or fifth or sixth. This one turns up winners at all sorts of prices but cannot be counted on for sustained profits without additional, protective rules.

Suggestions: As usual with systems that supposedly emphasize current condition, it pays to make sure that the horse is improving rather than deteriorating. And that it is entered in the right company at the right distance. And, of course, that the race under scrutiny took place recently enough to mean something.

SYSTEM 32

Principle: Play a horse that returned to racing after a layoff of six weeks or more and, in its first or second outing, led or ran within a half length of the leader at the first three calls (not counting the "Telegraph's" start notation), but tired in the stretch and lost.

Reasoning: The "short" horse needed that race to build its stamina and demonstrate the benefits of its freshening layoff.

Comment: A player who exercises the slightest discrimination about the pace factor should be able to make profits with this, especially at tracks that favor horses with front-running styles.

Suggestions: Make sure the horse's promising race took place within the last week or two or three. If more than a week ago, workouts are essential. It also pays to check the distance and class factors. As to pace, the player should make certain that the animal has more than enough early speed to show its heels to other front-runners that may be entered. Or else that it is the only front-runner in the field.

SYSTEM 33

Principle: Play a horse that finished out of the money but within five lengths of the winner.

Reasoning: The apparently poor finish conceals the fact that the horse was actually quite close to the winner. Good mutuels are likely.

Comment: This is a cousin of System 31. It gets enormous prices. The difficulty is that as many as four or five horses in a single field may qualify. Means of separating them are likely to become as complicated as actual handicapping, unless one decides to bet on more than one animal per race, whereupon investment costs soar.

Suggestions: It is best to demand a lot of recent action from an animal whose sole recommendation is that it finished within five lengths of the winner. Try demanding one race within eight days or a race and two workouts within two weeks. In case of a tie, favor the horse that has run within ten days or less. If still tied, try the distance factor. If still tied, go to the horse that has won the highest-class race in the past three months. If, as often happens with the kind of animals spotted by this system, none has won in three months, go to the winning jockey and finally, in desperation, to the horse that goes postward at the highest odds. When playing this system, there seldom is any sense in betting on one of its horses that goes off at less than 4 to 1. The system is meant to discover longshots and is not geared for the kind of handicapping that points out solid, relatively short-priced animals.

SYSTEM 34

Principle: Play a horse that ran out of the money in its last race, if (1) it finished not more than a length behind the second-place horse and (2) the winner of the race crossed the wire at least five lengths in front.

Reasoning: A horse that wins by five lengths or more has demonstrated unusual superiority over its field. In those circumstances, an out-of-the-money finish, a length or less behind the second-place horse, is evidence of form.

Comment: This is another longshot system that gets prices because of the failure of racing crowds to differentiate between a badly outclassed or badly conditioned horse and one that ran quite close to the leaders, even though it failed to get into the money. As usual, efforts to reduce the number of losers also reduce the number of longshots.

Suggestions: Make sure the horse is suited to today's distance, is not carrying substantially more weight than seems good for it, has been racing and working regularly, and is not stepping up in class. These grade-school rules give the system a good chance of paying off at the mutuel window, although the cherished $100 winners—and the series of fourteen consecutive losers—may be eliminated.

SYSTEM 35

Principle: Play any horse that ran as betting favorite within the past six days and finished in the money.

Reasoning: The trainer strikes while the iron is hot.

Comment: This gets a high percentage of winners, which can be increased by closer attention to the form factor.

Suggestions: Do not be afraid of a horse stepping up in class. But be careful not to risk money on overoptimistic trainers who send older horses back to the post too soon after grueling races. If the animal's last couple of races have not been the kind likely to exhaust it, its race today may well be a victory. The distance factor is unlikely to be as important as usual here, since the trainer is all-out for a win and—except in the case of an occasional incompetent—figures to place the animal properly.

SYSTEM 36

Principle: Play a horse that has been in the money in each of its last four races.

Reasoning: The horse is due.

Comment: No horse is ever "due" on these grounds alone. Furthermore, some horses, especially two- and three-year-olds, become habitual runners-up, unwilling to pass the leader. Within these limitations, the system can be used to catch a fair percentage of winners. Moreover, the prices are often not bad, possibly because the crowd tends to lose faith in horses of this type.

Suggestions: Confine play to secondary tracks, or to horses stepping down in class, or horses switched from ordinary jockeys to local or national leaders.

SYSTEM 37

Principle: Play a horse that was the favorite in its last race but lost, provided it gained in the stretch.

Reasoning: The animal wanted to run. Perhaps it was victimized by lack of racing room or a badly judged ride.

Comment: Some racegoers play every beaten favorite they can find. The advantage of this system is its usual avoidance of false favorites, the sucker horses that get the public's money after they have begun to lose their racing sharpness.

Suggestions: If the selection was entered at the wrong distance last time, expect big things today. If the last race was at the right distance, it is safest to require that the horse stay in the same class or step down a bit. Make sure that the last race was recent, or that the animal has been working out regularly. Welcome a change of riding assignments, especially if today's jockey is a leader.

Repeaters

Among the rules most familiar to system fanciers is, "Eliminate any horse that won its last race." The reason is statistical: Many horses are incapable of winning twice in succession. Yet many others win two or three or four in a row. Among the best methods of locating potential repeaters are Systems 13 and 14. Here are some other good ones.

SYSTEM 38

Principle: Play a horse that goes to the post within six days after a race in which it led at every call and won by two lengths or more.

Reasoning: The horse is hot.

Comment: Indeed it is.

Suggestions: Unless the horse gained in the stretch it is unlikely to repeat the victory in a substantially higher claiming bracket. If the top claiming price in the last race was $6,000 or less, today's should be not more than 20 percent higher. If the last race was in a higher range, the animal can step up 25 percent. An exception would be the horse that previously has won in today's class or better.

SYSTEM 39

Principle: Play a horse that won its last race "handily," "easily" or "going away" provided that (1) the race took place within ten days and (2) the horse has won at least 25 percent of its starts, finishing out of the money in fewer than half.

Reasoning: This catches good horses at the peak of their form.

Comment: Incredibly, not all the horses unearthed by this system are short-priced favorites.

Suggestions: If the horse has had ten or more races this year, it is safe to calculate its consistency on this year's record alone. Otherwise, combine this year's total with last year's. Do not attempt to use this method with two-year-olds. Somewhat bigger class rises can be permitted than in System 38. But if the animal moves from a claimer to an allowance race, do not bet on it unless it has already won in such company.

SYSTEM 40

Principle: In starter-handicap races at New York tracks, play the horse that has won such a race earlier in the season. If more than one qualify, pick the horse that has won the highest percentage of its starter-handicap efforts. If still tied, play the one that won a race of this kind most recently.

Reasoning: Each season a different group of trainers dominates the starter races in New York, winning these tough races with animals that run for Sweeney in straight claimers.

Comment: This is not strictly a repeater system. The horse probably has been doing poorly since its last romp in a starter race. The mutuel prices are excellent. This system has shown an annual profit for years.

Suggestions: Ignore everything but the horse's propensity for winning this kind of race.

Favorites

Endless profits await the player able to identify 45 percent of winning favorites *before* their races. System fanciers tinker by the hour with gimmicks designed to eliminate false favorites. Here are a few wrinkles well worth studying.

SYSTEM 41

Principle: In races with a purse value of $10,000 or less for four-year-olds and up, play the favorite if (1) it has won at least 20 percent of its races this year and (2) it has won at least 20 percent of its races this year and last and (3) its list of recent performances includes at least three wins and two places, or four wins and one place, or five wins, and (4) it finished in the money in its last start, which occurred at today's track not more than eighteen days ago and (5) it has won at today's exact distance.

Reasoning: A four-, five- or six-year-old of proved consistency and fitness is the steadiest of all Thoroughbreds. This is especially true in races of less than top quality, where the competition is less severe. The system bars races open to three-year-olds only because animals of that age frequently have not yet found their proper class level: An apparently inconsistent one might actually be the class and speed of its field. A handicapper could discern this, but the means of doing so are too complicated for inclusion in a system of this kind.

Comment: When Lawrence Lalik published this method in *American Turf Monthly,* the magazine reported that tests at Bowie, Fair Grounds and New York had produced winners in 55 to 63 percent of its selections, with profits ranging between 40 and 60 percent. Plays arise two or three times a week.

Suggestions: Females should not be backed against males. Animals that have had two hard races in succession should be avoided. Lawrence Lalik also eliminated horses that had won their three previous races and "any horses showing races at a foreign track." These two angles are worthwhile to the extent that a winner of three straight races may have overexerted itself and that a horse whose overseas races show in the past-performance list may not have done enough racing here to prove its consistency. Canadian racing is not regarded as foreign, of course.

SYSTEM 42

Principle: Play an odds-on favorite to place in any race with a purse of $10,000 or more.

Reasoning: Year in and year out, bets of this kind show a small profit.

Comment: As far as I know, this is the only kind of place or show betting on which profit is assured without resort to handicapping. The explanation is that the animals are especially good ones, less susceptible than others to sudden lapses of form. They win or finish second about two thirds of the time. The place prices are customarily wretched, but perk up a bit when the place pool is shared with backers of a longshot.

Suggestions: Unless yours is a track of authentically major caliber, you had better test this on the few races of $10,000 value that were run there last season. In my experience, odds-on favorites are most reliable at New York, California, Illinois, Maryland, New Jersey and Delaware.

SYSTEM 43

Principle: When the track is sloppy, play a front-running horse that goes to the post as favorite.

Reasoning: Front-runners have a special advantage in the slop.

Comment: This is a particularly good bet for a player equipped to do a bit of handicapping on matters like distance, class and pace.

Suggestions: If the horse happens to qualify under one of the other systems concerned with favorites, it can be supported with considerable confidence. Otherwise, the player should see whether the animal is the only apparently fit front-runner in the field. In case another seems capable of running with it, and there is doubt about the favorite's staying power in such circumstances, the next factor to examine is class. If the favorite is moving up in class and does not seem completely capable of surviving early competition for the lead, pass the race.

SYSTEM 44

Principle: Play a favorite if (1) it is male, (2) it raced not more than five days ago and (3) it won the race.

Reasoning: It may still be at peak form.

Comment: In 1956, *Turf and Sport Digest* reported a fifteen-month test, covering about 2,800 races at all major tracks. This simple system yielded a profit of 13 cents on every wagered dollar.

Suggestions: A test at your track might produce considerably higher paper profits, but less action, if play were confined to animals that won their last races easily, handily, or going away. It also would be worthwhile to see how four-year-olds and older horses did after hard stretch drives in their two latest races.

SYSTEM 45

Principle: If the favorite did not win its last race, or goes to the post at odds higher than even money, play the second choice in the betting, provided that (1) it is male and (2) it won its last race within the last five days (ten days if today's purse is $5,000 or higher).

Reasoning: The crowd's second choice wins about one race in five. This means that, in almost two races on an "average" afternoon, the crowd overestimates the favorite's winning chances by comparison with those of its second choice. This system directs the player to a kind of race in which the crowd errs rather frequently.

Comment: Jud Onatsirt, who also devised System 44, reported a six-month test of this one. It cranked out a 55 percent profit. Plays occurred at the rate of about two a week at major tracks. In combination with 44, this system is as simple and rewarding as any purely mechanical selection method I have ever seen.

Suggestions: I can think of no reason why Systems 44 and 45 should not work as effectively nowadays as they did in the 1950's. Try them on your own circuit.

Speed

Conventional speed handicapping is as mechanical as any predigested system, demanding nothing of the player but willingness to follow rules. Because those rules require a good deal of time and patience, many speed fanciers prefer to take their chances with systems which quickly single out the fastest horse in the race. Hundreds of methods are in circulation. The following are quite useful, especially in sprints. Avoid wet weather and grass races.

SYSTEM 46

Principle: Among horses whose last races were at today's track, note the three

that earned the highest "Telegraph" or "Form" speed ratings at today's exact distance within the past thirty days. Play the animal that earned the rating in a higher class and/or when carrying more weight than today's. In case of a tie, favor the horse that drops the most weight.

Reasoning: If it is still in decent shape, the horse should be able to run at least as well under today's more favorable conditions.

Comment: The effectiveness of this sort of thing depends greatly on the kind of racing programmed at the individual track. A four-week test of claiming races for three-year-olds and up should show whether the method warrants further study on your own home grounds. One of the strong merits of the system by comparison with most speed-rating methods, is that it concedes the possibility of victory by a higher-class horse over a cheaper one, even though the cheaper may show a higher speed rating.

Suggestions: There is little reason to expect help from this system in allowance or handicap or stakes races. Also, be careful of animals that have not raced or worked out with recent regularity.

SYSTEM 47

Principle: Consider any horse entered in a claiming race that earned a 90 while finishing fourth or better in one of its two most recent starts. Also note any horse that earned an 85 or better while finishing in the money in one of its two most recent starts. If more than two qualify, play the horse that won or finished closest to the winner in its good race. Break any remaining tie by playing the horse whose good race was most recent.

Reasoning: At most tracks, speed ratings of this kind are the marks of able claiming horses.

Comment: This would be best at secondary tracks, where most of the action for claiming prices is at six furlongs and the animals race frequently.

Suggestions: Addition of distance and late-action rules could make a solid winner of this one, especially if play were limited to sprints and no horse were expected to win in company more than $500 more expensive than it had beaten at some time in the past three months.

SYSTEM 48

Principle: In races no longer than six furlongs, find the highest speed rating earned by each horse when running at today's exact distance in the past month.

Add or subtract 1 point for each three pounds of difference between today's weight and the weight carried in the rated race. If the horse goes with lighter weight today, add the difference. If the horse carries more weight today, subtract the difference. Play the horse with the highest net figure.

Reasoning: Many speed handicappers do little more than this.

Comment: Dorcus and DaSilva, who gave us System 1, recorded profits of almost 50 cents on the dollar in lengthy workouts with this one at Hollywood Park and Aqueduct. Prices were not large, but more than 40 percent of the choices won.

Suggestions: In using speed to make selections in dashes for two-year-olds, there is no need to bother about weights.

SYSTEM 49

Principle: Add the running positions of each horse at the pre-stretch and stretch calls of its last two races. Play the horse with the lowest total.

Reasoning: The horse closest to the front during the middle stages of its last two races is certain to be in contention today.

Comment: Best suited to the speedy tracks of California and Illinois and some of the half-milers, which favor front-runners. Gets good mutuels sometimes.

Suggestions: Addition of simple form and distance rules ought to make this a profitable system at certain tracks.

SYSTEM 50

Principle: Among horses that finished in the money within the past week, play the one that has earned the highest speed rating in a race of today's exact distance on the present circuit during the past three months. If a tie, play the one that carried the highest weight when earning the top rating.

Reasoning: A horse that races twice in a week is physically fit and might show its previously superior speed.

Comment: The seven-day rule saves this one. A bit of attention to the class factor would help, too.

Suggestions: The system lends itself to experimentation. More detailed examination of current condition would permit play on horses other than those that have run in seven days.

SYSTEM 51

Principle: To the highest speed rating earned by each horse during the past thirty

days, add 1/100 of the claiming price for which it was entered, and add the weight it carried. Play the horse with the highest total.

Reasoning: Speed, weight and class are the bases of many successful handicapping procedures.

Comment: This one gets winners. Because it disdains distance and form, some of the winners pay high prices, but long strings of losers are a positive certainty.

Suggestions: It would be fun to see what combinations and modifications of distance, form, consistency and jockey rules might shorten the losing streaks without eliminating all the longshots.

SYSTEM 52

Principle: Play the horse that has earned the highest speed rating in the past sixty days, provided the rating was earned in a higher-class race than any in which the other horses earned their highest speed ratings during that period.

Reasoning: The class edge and the superior speed rating make a formidable combination.

Comment: This one should earn profits at most tracks, but not until condition and distance rules are added.

Suggestions: The horse should be suited to the distance and should have offered a hint of form in its last race or two. If the rider is a local or national leader or has won with the animal in the past, the bet might be well worth making.

SYSTEM 53

Principle: Among the three entrants that have earned the highest speed ratings in the past month, play the one that (1) has won at least 20 percent of its races during this year and last, (2) has had two races, or a race and two workouts, or three workouts in the last eleven days, and (3) has won at today's distance when entered at a claiming price not more than $1,000 below the price at which it is entered today.

Reasoning: This is comprehensive enough for relative safety, yet permits good mutuel prices by directing the player to animals that may have been running indifferent races at odd distances and at lower claiming prices in their most recent starts.

Comment: The heavy late action and the horse's established ability at the distance make this a more substantial method than most of its kind.

Suggestions: In case of ties, try to use the jockey factor for separation purposes.

Jockeys

Followers of jockeys learn in time that it is a good idea to pay some attention to the horses which the young men ride. Almost any of the more solid systems in this chapter will suffice. And here are a few others designed expressly for the purpose.

SYSTEM 54

Principle: Play one of the five leading jockeys at the current meeting when he rides a horse that (1) lost its last race, (2) finished in the money in at least one of its latest three attempts, (3) has won 20 percent of its starts this year and last combined, and (4) raced not more than ten days ago.

Reasoning: A fit, consistent horse that lost its last race should go off at better-than-usual odds today.

Comment: The good prices obtainable with some of the choices of this system would not be sacrificed by addition of a distance rule. Moreover, a player familiar with the fluctuations of Thoroughbred form could safely relax the ten-day rule.

Suggestions: Break ties by going to the higher-class animal.

SYSTEM 55

Principle: Play a horse that lost its last race provided that (1) the jockey has won with it at today's exact distance but in better company than today's and (2) the jockey is either a national leader or ranks among the top riders at the current meeting.

Reasoning: This is another fairly reasonable effort to get occasionally higher mutuels than one might expect when a leading jockey is aboard a class horse.

Comment: Recent races and workouts would make this more reassuring and, in fact, would permit elimination of the rule requiring a leading rider.

Suggestions: Note how often horses of this type come to life when switched from an apprentice or a rank-and-file journeyman to a leading reinsman or one who has won with the animal in the past.

SYSTEM 56

Principle: Play the horse listed at lowest odds in the track program's morning line, provided that it is ridden by one of the two leading jockeys of the meeting.

Reasoning: Hot jockey, hot horse.

Comment: The morning-line favorite does not always turn out to be the public's choice, but seldom pays better than 5 to 2. The stinginess of the odds are compensated by a good winning percentage.

Suggestion: The player may not believe that the jockeys listed at the head of the official "leading riders" tabulation are the best on the grounds. And he is probably correct. If he prefers, he can use the two jocks with the highest winning averages, or the two whom he regards most highly. But, since trainers tend to assign their best horses to the riders with the best reputations, the player had better not depart too far from that group.

Tote-Board Systems

The handicapper usually gains confidence in his bet when he notices significant tote-board activity on the horse. Certain system players omit the handicapping and look for omens on the tote board. Here are some of the more sensible systems that depend on betting trends.

SYSTEM 57

Principle: Using any reliable selection method, favor one of the top five horses in the race when the tote board shows that disproportionately high sums are being bet on it to win, by comparison with what is being bet on it to place or show.

Reasoning: Horsemen do not fool around with place and show betting. When they bet, they bet to win.

Comment: If the bets on a horse account for 20 percent of the win pool and only 15 percent of the place pool, it is obvious that someone is loading up on the front end. Indeed, if the place bets account for 17 percent of that pool a similar supposition is warranted. The only time place or show bets should be high in proportion to win bets is when the horse is odds-on. In such circumstances, lots of money, smart and otherwise, goes on place and show tickets.

Suggestions: If you like the horse and notice even slight overactivity in the win pool, it is safe to assume that some big bettors also like the horse. It is more than merely conceivable that these bettors include the owner and trainer and those who follow their tips.

SYSTEM 58

Principle: Bet on a horse whose tote-board odds a minute before post-time are less than 50 percent of the odds given in the track's morning line.

Reasoning: If the track handicapper thought the horse would go off at 8 to 1 and the crowd makes it 4 to 1, some smart money is on the animal.

Comment: The morning line is an effort by the track to forecast the final odds. At many tracks, the job is done by clerks with no particular qualifications. Moreover, late scratches can undermine even the canniest morning line. And so can the predictions of newspaper handicappers and tip sheets and the effects of wild rumor.

Suggestions: If none of the four top morning-line contenders is scratched, and if the track morning line is relatively competent, you can assume that a horse bet down to half of the morning odds is thought to be alive and well. If you plan to risk money on these suppositions, the best chances of profit lie in confining play to animals listed at 8 to 1 or less in the morning line.

SYSTEM 59

Principle: Bet on a horse that lost its last race and steps up in class today but goes to the post at lower odds than in the cheaper, losing race.

Reasoning: The insiders must have a coup cooking.

Comment: Ordinarily such a horse should be running at higher odds today. If the player's handicapping suggests that the animal is in shape, the lower odds may indeed be a sign of inside action.

Suggestions: Don't bother with this unless you have confidence in your handicapping.

SYSTEM 60

Principle: If one horse is heavily bet and its odds fall below 8 to 5, any horse whose odds do not rise is worth backing.

Reasoning: When the odds on the favorite drop, the odds on the other horses should rise. If the 4 to 1 or 5 to 1 shot holds steady when the favorite drops from 5 to 2 to 7 to 5, you know that many people have been buying tickets on the longer-priced animal.

Comment: Again, good handicapping is the key. If the favorite looks to you like a sucker horse, and you like the other, the steadiness of its odds are an indication that other smart players feel the same way.

Suggestions: Nothing but grief awaits the person who plays this system without bothering to examine the records of the horses.

SYSTEM 61

Principle: In the second race of the day, play a horse on which proportionately

more money was bet in the daily double than is being bet in the win pool of the race.

Reasoning: Rather than drive down the odds on his entrant in the second race, many a trainer or owner buys daily-double tickets on it. After the first race, the track posts the mutuel price that the double will pay on each horse in the second race. If the daily-double price on a horse is lower than it should be, considering the odds at which the horse is held in the win pool of the race itself, somebody must have plunged on the double.

Comment: Such things happen. If the stable holds a sufficient number of daily-double tickets which couple its horse with the winner of the first race, and if the daily-double price is right, the boys can sweeten the profit with only modest bets on the win end. Modest bets at high odds. This is preferable to betting a wad on the horse, driving the odds down, and collecting peanuts later.

Suggestions: Two minutes before post-time for the second race, divide the posted daily-double price on each horse by the latest tote-board quotation. Thus, if the daily-double price is $200 and the present odds against the horse are 20 to 1, the answer would be 10. If the daily-double price on another entrant is $24 and the odds against it to win the second race are 2 to 1, the answer in its case is 12. Clearly, the longshot was heavily backed in the daily double. Horses of this kind win once in a while. Not often enough to show a profit, however. The time to bet one is when its record offers some explanation for the vigor with which people bet on it in the double.

Public Selectors

Thousands of systems handicap the newspaper handicappers. Starting with the assumption that a good public selector, or a consensus of several, names horses with legitimate chances to win, the systems deploy simple handicapping procedures in an attempt to avoid the losers. Some of these systems produce lengthy strings of winners at low prices. Like other systems, they perform best when the track is fast.

SYSTEM 62

Principle: Play the "Form" or "Telegraph" consensus choice in an allowance, handicap or stakes races, provided that the horse (1) has won a third of its races since the beginning of last year and (2) either was in the money in its last race or lost by not more than two lengths and (3) has been in the money in at least

Veterinarian takes saliva sample for chemical testing.

The new Belmont Park clubhouse, where system players will do their arithmetic and squander their money in unprecedented comfort.

NEW YORK RACING ASSN.

five of its last seven races and (4) carries not more than 124 pounds, unless the race is a weight-for-age stakes.

Reasoning: Not only do the experts like it, but it clearly is an outstanding Thoroughbred.

Comment: A system like this hits few losers, and few payoffs above $4. Profits are possible.

Suggestions: Beware of cheaper allowance races at secondary tracks.

SYSTEM 63

Principle: Play the consensus ("Form" or "Telegraph") choice, provided that it has had a race and one workout within seven days.

Reasoning: A high proportion of winners have had a race and a workout in seven days. When the racing paper's consensus favors a horse with those qualifications, it ought to have a splendid chance.

Comment: This system has been around for years. It finds about one play a day at a typical major track, and is quite reliable.

Suggestions: Test it at your own track.

SYSTEM 64

Principle: Play "Trackman's" best bet of the day whenever the "Form" or "Telegraph" consensus selection (1) is another horse and (2) is picked by another selector as his best bet.

Reasoning: The racing paper representative known as Trackman is on the scene, where the racing is. Also, he often is a topnotch handicapper. If the consensus picks another horse and, moreover, that horse is highly enough regarded to be the best bet of some selector other than Trackman, better-than-usual payoffs reward Trackman's winning choice.

Comment: The logic is flawless. The system produces profits if the player does a little handicapping of his own.

Suggestions: At the very least, apply some consistency rules. Also, it helps to insist on a winning rider.

SYSTEM 65

Principle: Bet the consensus choice when no other horse in the field has raced more recently or is more consistent or has earned a higher speed rating in its last three races.

Reasoning: Consistency, fitness, overall speed and the high regard of experts should produce winners.

Comment: Do not be surprised if this one produces seven or eight short-priced winners in succession—at the rate of one play every ten days or so.

Suggestions: Try a prolonged dry run at your own track.

SYSTEM 66

Principle: Play any horse named by Trackman, provided that no other "Form" or "Telegraph" selector picks it to finish in the money.

Reasoning: Trackman has the advantage of being there every day to see the animals with his own eyes. If he thinks that a horse has improved enough to get part of a purse, and if no other selector thinks so, the odds may be magnificent.

Comment: The same idea can be applied to the choices of any other competent public selector. Prices are excellent, profits nil—unless the player does some handicapping.

Suggestions: On a casual outing to the track, this kind of play is easy fun.

SYSTEM 67

Principle: Play any horse picked to win by all selectors listed in the "Telegraph" consensus, provided that the "Form" consensus awards it at least 25 points. Or play any horse picked to win by all selectors in the "Form" consensus, provided that the "Telegraph" consensus awards it at least 30 points.

Reasoning: Such unanimity must be deserved.

Comment: One play every two weeks is a lot for this system, but it usually is profitable in the long haul. The reason for demanding 30 points of the *Telegraph* consensus is that it involves six selectors, as against the *Form's* five. Five points are awarded to each first choice, 2 points for second and 1 for third. The horse named as a selector's best bet of the day gets 7 points.

Suggestions: A good way to sharpen your skills is to study the past-performance records of horses that lose after being chosen by this system. Also note the kind of animals that beat them. Do not expect a pattern to emerge quickly, but pay special attention to the effects of high weight in distance races and long layoffs in allowance races.

SYSTEM 68

Principle: Using a graded handicap such as that of "Hermis" or "Sweep," determine whether it predicts odds of 3 to 1 or higher on its first choice in the first

and/or second race of the day. If so, cross out such a horse or horses. Now buy nine daily-double tickets which pair the top three remaining choices in the first race with the remaining top three in the second.

Reasoning: A horse held so lightly that the handicapper thinks it may go off at 3 to 1 is a good candidate for defeat. Pairing the other top animals in the double is an excellent way to hit a stout mutuel in circumstances of this kind.

Comment: If you insist on playing the double, this is as good a way as any.

Suggestions: Another comparatively plausible approach is to use any of the other systems in this chapter and, after three horses are found in each race, pair them in every possible combination—an $18 investment.

SYSTEM 69

Principle: Clip the "Horses to Watch" column which appears in the "Telegraph" and "Form" on Mondays. Play each horse three times or until it wins—whichever occurs sooner.

Reasoning: These are tips from clockers and other experts.

Comment: Profits are conceivable for a player who makes sure the animals are properly placed.

Suggestions: Do a dry run in which no paper bet is made unless the horse has had a race or a workout within a week, is entered at a suitable distance, and is assigned a leading jockey.

SYSTEM 70

Principle: Play any consensus choice that rates at least 25 points above the consensus second choice in the race, provided that the top choice (1) was favorite in its last race but lost, or (2) won its last race.

Reasoning: Only formidable animals achieve large margins in the consensus. A beaten favorite must be especially well placed to merit such esteem. The same is true of a horse that won its last race.

Comment: Lots of long winning streaks, the profits from which are annulled by only a few losers.

Suggestions: The remarks made in connection with System 67 apply here as well.

Arithmetical Systems

I now offer some methods that require paper work. The more elaborate are comprehensive enough to qualify as legitimate handicapping procedures. The reader may find one a pleasant way station between straight system play and independent handicapping.

SYSTEM 71

In 1964, Robert Rowe offered *American Turf Monthly* followers a selection method in which weighted percentages reflected the relative importance of each handicapping factor. It was not the first system of its kind (I have seen a few that employed algebraic equations), but it is by far the simplest and most sensible. It takes time but is logical and orderly enough to fall well within the grasp of any player.

Rowe recommended that the system be used only on fields of seven or fewer horses, where the purse was at least $5,000. The limitation on the size of the field saves work, and the minimum purse size strengthens the possibility that the system's choice will be a good, reliable animal.

The procedure applies the following table of values:

Current Condition	25%
Class	20
Consistency	15
Sex	10
Weights	6
Jockey	6
Distance	6
Liking for Track Condition	6
Age	6

The player deals with the race as if he were an old-time bookmaker. He works up booking percentages proportionate to the winning chances of each horse. He begins with the statistically valid assumption that, until further information arises, each horse must be granted an equal chance to win. In a five-horse field, therefore, each horse would have one chance in five. The natural odds against it would be 4 to 1, expressed in a percentage figure of 20. In a six-horse field, the percentage would be 17 per horse (obtained by dividing the number of horses into 100). The player's worksheet for a five-horse field would now look like this:

A	20%
B	20
C	20
D	20
E	20

From here on, the player decides which horses qualify as contenders in terms of each handicapping factor. If, for example, he feels that three of the five have shown positive signs of winning condition, he credits each of the three and penalizes the other two. Condition, as shown above, is worth 25 percent in this method. If three horses are in condition, each is awarded 8 percentage points—its share of the 25. The two animals that seem to be out of condition are each penalized by 12 points—25 divided by 2.

The list now has changed:

A	28%
B	28
C	28
D	8
E	8

Note that the sum of the percentages remains 100, or close to it. Therefore, the percentage finally earned by each horse is an approximation of its actual chance in the race. Whether it is a good approximation or not depends entirely on how carefully and knowingly the player appraises the animals in terms of each handicapping factor.

Rowe suggested that the class, consistency and weight factors should be handled as follows:

Class: Add the total earnings of the field, using this year's and last year's records. Divide the sum by the number of horses in the field, producing an average. Horses with earnings above the average are the class of the field. Divide the 20 points among them. Each horse below the average is penalized by whatever number of points represents its share of the 20. Thus, if Horses "A" and "C" were regarded as the class of the race, each would get 10 points, whereas 7 each would be taken from "B," "D," and "E." The list would now look like this:

A	38%
B	21
C	38
D	1
E	1

Consistency: Add all starts made by the entrants this year. Divide by the total number of times they have run in the money. Use the resultant average as in handling the class factor.

Weight: Add the weights assigned to the horses, and determine the average weight by dividing the number of entrants into the total. Horses carrying less than the average get credit. Those above the average are penalized.

If all entrants are male or female, no adjustment is made on grounds of sex. But if there were a female in a five-horse field, she would be penalized 10 points, and each of the others would get 2. Similar procedures would subtract 6 points from the only three-year-old running against older horses, or 3 points from each of two three-year-olds in such a fix. Another 6 points might be redistributed if one or more of the entrants were ridden by other than leading jockeys, or if one or more were a sprinter entered in a route race or a router in a sprint, or if the track were muddy and some of the horses were uncomfortable on such footing.

Rowe postulates a situation in which the final figures make "A" best with 41 percent, followed by "B" with 22. He suggests that the player calculate each horse's proper odds on the basis of these percentages, but allowing a fat 20 percent for take and breakage. Thus, assuming that the betting pool has been reduced to 80 percent, of which 41 represents "A's" chances, the proper odds against the animal's victory become 39 to 41—or almost exactly even money. The odds against "B" are 58 to 22, or 3 to 1.

The player should not, says Rowe, regard "A" as a good bet if the crowd sends it to the post at less than 3 to 1! Indeed, if "A" goes off at 5 to 2, and "B" at 10 to 1, the horse to bet is "B." Only by waiting until the actual odds are at least 200 percent better than those calculated by the system can the player be sure of having the percentages on his side, argues Rowe.

It's all a matter of individual taste, really. A player is unlikely to worry too much about the odds on any single bet if his handicapping cranks out a satisfactory percentage of winners at prices large enough to produce a comfortable profit. For such a player, some horses are worth backing at 2 to 5, and others are a waste of money at 20 to 1. The real merit of the Rowe system and, in fact, of all the others in this chapter, is not in its rules but in the concepts from which the rules develop. I imagine that the only unchangeable part of this system is the business of assigning each horse an equal percentage chance of winning, and then increasing or diminishing that chance according to values found in the horse's record.

Surely, many readers will prefer to modify every other rule of the system, especially the handicapping procedures used on each factor. In doing so, and testing the results, the experimenter will not only refine his handicapping skills but take a huge step toward developing a winning method that bears his own imprint.

SYSTEM 72

In 1958, Robert Saunders Dowst, the daddy of class-consistency handicapping and the first purveyor of betting advice to reach the general public with books and articles, published an extremely simple rating system in *American Turf Monthly*. It went like this.

Class: If the horse has never raced in a claimer, give it a 1. If it has raced in a mixture of claimers and non-claimers, give it a 2. If it has raced only in claimers, it gets 3.

Consistency: Winning average is calculated on the basis of ten or more races run this year. If the horse has been in fewer than ten this year, use this year's and last year's totals together. An animal that has won 70 percent of its races gets 1. For 40 to 70 percent, 2. For 20 to 40 percent, 3. For less than 20 percent, 4.

Using the same minimum number of starts, the player then computes the percentage of races in which the horse has finished in the money. The same percentages and point awards are used.

Weights: Using the Jockey Club Scale of Weights, add to each horse's assigned weight whatever sex and age allowances it should be getting on the scale. Horses whose adjusted weights fall into the middle range of the field get 2 points. Horses carrying a good deal less get 1. Horses carrying much more—giving as much as eight pounds to members of the middle group—get 3.

Form: Obvious non-contenders that have not been in contention for months get 3. Horses that have run poorly in their recent starts, but have done better in the past get 2. Everything else gets 1. Dowst was never much of a believer in form. He thought that class and consistency told the real story.

Picking the Winner: Add the five figures. Play the horse with the lowest total, provided it is not a female running against males.

The best bets are horses that earn ratings of 9 or less. A player who cares to jigger around with this system—especially in an effort to make it more realistic about the importance of current condition—should be able to hit a satisfactory percentage of winners with it.

SYSTEM 73

A fascinating, highly workable basis for almost any selection system starts with the assumption that a second-place finisher in a twelve-horse field has accomplished more than a second-place finisher in a smaller field. When the class of the race is incorporated into this idea, ratings can be assigned.

The system assumes that a winner deserves a rating of 100, regardless of the size of the field it may have beaten. The following ratings are used for other horses:

Horses in Race	Finish Position												
	2	3	4	5	6	7	8	9	10	11	12	13	14
5	67	43	25	0									
6	71	50	33	20	0								
7	75	56	40	27	17	0							
8	78	60	45	33	23	14	0						
9	80	64	50	38	29	20	13	0					
10	82	67	54	43	33	25	18	11	0				
11	83	70	57	47	38	29	22	16	10	0			
12	85	72	60	50	41	33	26	20	14	9	0		
13	87	74	63	53	44	37	29	24	17	12	8	0	
14	89	76	65	55	46	40	31	27	19	14	11	7	0

After eliminating any horse entered at an unsuitable distance or clearly unready to win, the player assigns each a class rating based on the price at which it was entered when it ran its best race at today's distance during the past month or two. If it was entered at $4,000, the class rating would be 400. If another was entered at $3,750, its class rating would be 375.

The second step is to use the chart of finishing positions and field sizes to modify the class rating. For example, if the animal entered at $4,000 in its good race ran third in a nine-horse field on that day, its rating would be 400 + 64 = 464. If the $3,750 horse ran second in a field of ten, its rating would be 375 + 82 = 457.

A logical sequence of additional steps might be:

1. Calculate winning percentage this year, or this year plus last, and add it to the rating.
2. Calculate percentage of starts in the money and add it to the rating.
3. Calculate average earnings per start and add it.
4. Add the speed rating earned in the good race.
5. Add 5 points for each plus factor (See Chapter 16).
6. Add or subtract the difference between today's weight and the poundage that the horse carried in its good race.
7. Add 2 points for each workout and 4 points for each race in the past two weeks.

Players unwilling to rely on their own evaluations of the distance factor could remain in the ball game by rating only those animals that have run in the money at today's distance, or at a distance within half a furlong of today's. Those who prefer mechanical rules to personal analysis of the form factor could survive by rating the horse's three most recent races, and adding the total, provided that the latest race had taken place not more than two weeks ago and all three had occurred in the past month.

SYSTEM 74

Here is a simple, arithmetical method which catches a fair percentage of winners in wide-open races among animals of indifferent consistency and obscure current form. It is especially useful during the first weeks of the Florida and New York seasons, when each field includes horses that have not raced recently at the local track:

1. Eliminate all entrants except those whose last races took place at today's track within the past nine days, at today's distance or shorter.

2. Now eliminate all those that did not finish within five lengths of the winner of that recent, local race.

3. Assign each remaining contender a class rating equal to $\frac{1}{100}$ of the price at which it was entered in that latest race. A horse entered at $7,500 would get a rating of 75. A horse entered at $4,250 would get a rating of 43. A horse entered at $10,500 rates 105.

4. To the class rating add ten times the number of lengths each horse gained in the stretch of its race. If a horse gained 3½ lengths, add 35. If it gained 2¼ lengths, add 23. If it gained 1¾ lengths, add 18.

5. If a horse led at the stretch call and won its race while increasing its lead, multiply its winning margin by ten and add that to the class rating. Do not use the stretch-gain figure for a horse of that kind.

6. If a horse led at the stretch call and *lost* ground in the stretch, multiply its margin at the stretch call by ten and add that to the class rating.

7. If the horse carries more weight today than in its last race, deduct the number of extra pounds from the rating. If the horse carries less weight, add the number of pounds.

8. Play the horse with the highest rating.

Players who wish to take on animals whose last races were at longer distances than today's can do so by using Item 6 above, especially if the horse ran at seven furlongs last time and today's race is at six, or if the horse ran at a mile and an eighth last time and goes at a mile today. If today's distance is more than a furlong shorter than the distance of the last race, the player should make sure that the horse is properly placed. If it has never run a good race at today's distance, it should be eliminated.

In claiming races which produce no play for this system, System 6 works especially well. Look it up.

SYSTEM 75

Here is one for players who have copies of "The American Racing Manual." Without requiring the player to do any handicapping of his own, it puts him on the consistent horse, trainer and jockey.

Obtain the following figures:

1. The horse's percentage of victories in all its starts this year and last.

2. The horse's in-the-money percentage this year and last (combined).

3. The jockey's current winning average, as shown in the official track tabulation of leading riders at the meeting. If the jockey is not listed, eliminate the horse.

4. The jockey's winning average last year, as shown in *The American Racing Manual*.

5. The trainer's current winning average, as shown in the official track tabulation of leading trainers at the meeting. Eliminate any horse whose trainer is not listed.

6. The trainer's winning average last year, as shown in *The American Racing Manual*.

7. Add all the percentages. Play the animal with the largest total.

The player who confines play to animals with a recent race and with proved ability at today's distance will be rewarded with a high percentage of winners. If he adds 5 points for each plus factor shown in the horse's record (see Chapter 16), results will improve even more.

SYSTEM 76

Now comes one of the oldest of all systems. It commands undying loyalty among thousands of players throughout the country.

1. Look at the horse's finishing position in each of its last three races. Give it 30 points for each victory, 20 points for a second, and 10 for a third. Anything worse than third gets no credit.

2. Add the points.

3. Subtract the total from today's assigned weight.

4. Play the horse with the lowest net figure.

This system improves when the player eliminates horses that have not raced within three weeks (a month for stakes and handicap animals), and is careful to demand a recent workout of any horse that has not raced in twelve days or more. Another great help is a rule confining play to animals that have proved their ability at today's distance. A search for plus factors also boosts profits.

SYSTEM 77

This, the last but not the least useful of our systems, gets upward of 40 percent winners for anyone patient enough to use it. Not more than two plays a week will be found. Most of the choices are favorites, although a surprisingly high mutuel occurs every now and again.

Play is confined to high-class races with purses in excess of $8,000. Races for two-year-olds are not suitable.

Contenders are picked on the following bases:

1. Qualify the three entrants that earned the highest speed ratings in their last outings. If two or more tie and you find yourself with more than three horses, no harm is done.

2. Qualify any other horse if it has won a third of all its races this year and last.

To separate the contenders, award points as follows:

1. Two points for a winning average of 20 percent in all races this year and last.

2. Two points for finishing in the money in half of all races this year and last.

3. Two points to each contender whose average earnings per start are among the top three averages in the field. Compute average earnings on the basis of total races this year and last.

4. Two points to any contender that has finished in the money in each race for which a running line is shown in the past-performance record. Do not count races run over off-tracks.

5. One point to any contender that has been out of the money not more than twice in the races listed in the record.

6. One point to the contender that has run in the most stakes races at major tracks. If a tie, award a point to each horse involved in the tie.

7. One point to any contender that has finished in the money in two of its last three races.

8. One point to the contender or contenders that ran on the most recent date.

9. One point to any contender that worked out yesterday.

10. One point to the contender or contenders that have gone to the post as favorites most often in the past four months.

11. One point to each contender for every race it has won when ridden by today's jockey. Three points to the contender ridden by the leading jockey at the current meeting, or by a recognized national leader.

12. One point to the contender chosen as winner by the "Telegraph" or "Form" consensus. Two points if named as Consensus Best Bet.

13. One point to each contender for each plus factor, as explained in Chapter 16.

14. Play the horse with the highest total. In case of tie, pass the race, or play the tied horse that goes postward at 5 to 2 or better.

The seventy-seven systems described in this chapter are food for years of recreational thought. Some will win money as is. Others need tinkering to bring them into phase with the individual track and the individual temperament. Thousands of variations are possible. Have fun.

19 The Rules of Racing

The rules of the sport vary slightly, but insignificantly, from state to state. Here are the rules of the Jockey Club of New York.

PART I.
Definitions and Interpretations

1. A recognized meeting is:

(a) A meeting held with the sanction of the Commission upon a race course operated by a duly licensed Association, for the time and at the place where such meeting is licensed to be held.

(b) A meeting held in other portions of the United States, or in any foreign country, with the sanction of any turf authority whose jurisdiction over racing of any nature is recognized by The Jockey Club and which gives effect to sentences imposed by The Jockey Club upon those guilty of improper turf practices.

2. An "Association" is a person, or persons, or a corporate body, conducting a recognized meeting.

3. A "Horse" includes mare, gelding, colt and filly.

4. A horse is "bred" at the place of his birth.

5. The age of a horse is reckoned as beginning on the first of January in the year in which he is foaled.

6. A "Maiden" is a horse which, at the time of starting, has never won a race on the flat in any country.

7. A "Race" includes a stake, a purse, a sweepstakes, a private sweepstakes, a match or an overnight event, but does not include a steeplechase or hurdle race.

8. A "Purse" is a race for money or other prize to which the owners of the horses engaged do not contribute.

9. A "Sweepstakes" is a race in which stakes are to be made by the owners of the horses engaged, and it is still a sweepstakes when money or other prize is added, but, within the meaning of this rule, no overnight race, whatever its conditions, shall be considered to be a sweepstakes.

10. A "Private Sweepstakes" is one to which no money or other prize is added and which, previous to closing, has not been advertised, either by publication, or by circular, or entry blank, or in any other way.

11. A "Match" is a race between two horses the property of two different owners on terms agreed upon by them and to which no money, or other prize, is added; it is void if either party die.

12. An "Overnight Race" is one for which the entries close seventy-two hours (exclusive of Sundays), or less, before the time set for the first race of the day on which such race is to be run.

13. A "Handicap" is a race in which the weights to be carried by the horses

are adjusted by the handicapper for the purpose of equalizing their chances of winning.

14. A "Free Handicap" is one in which no liability is incurred for entrance money, stake or forfeit, until acceptance of the weight, either directly or through omission to declare out.

15. A "Highweight Handicap" is one in which the top weight shall not be less than 140 pounds.

16. A "Post Race" is one in which the subscribers declare, at the usual time before a race for declaring to start, the horse or horses they are to run, without limitations of choice other than that prescribed by the rules of racing or the conditions of the race.

17. A "Produce" Race is one to be run for by the produce of horses named or described at the time of entry.

18. An untried horse is one whose produce are maidens.

19. (a) A "Claiming Race" is one in which every horse running therein may be claimed in conformity to the rules.

(b) An "Optional Claiming Race" is a race restricted to horses entered to be claimed for a stated claiming price and to those which have started previously for that claiming price or less. In the case of horses entered to be claimed in such a race, the race will be considered, for the purposes of these rules, a claiming race.

20. The "Nominator" is the person in whose name a horse is entered for a race.

21. "Owner" includes part owner or lessee, and singular words include the plural, except where the context otherwise requires.

22. The "Breeder" of a horse is the owner of his dam at the time of foaling.

23. (a) An "Authorized Agent" is a person appointed by a document, accompanied by a fee of $1, signed by the owner and lodged annually at the office of The Jockey Club and approved by it, or if for a single meeting only, with the Clerk of the Course for transmission to The Jockey Club.

(b) An authorized agent may appoint a Sub-Agent only when authorized so to do by the document lodged as above and when the appointment, approved by The Jockey Club, of the Sub-Agent is lodged as above, accompanied by a fee of $1.

Rule 24 (a) and (b). (Stricken out.)

25. "Weight for Age" means standard weight according to these Rules. A "weight for age" race is one in which all horses carry weight according to the scale without penalties or allowances.

26. A "Walkover" is when two horses in entirely different interests do not run for a race.

27. The publications of The Jockey Club are the Racing Calendar and the Stud Book, and such other publications as hereafter may be designated by The Jockey Club.

PART II.
Calculation of Time

28. (a) When the last day for doing anything under these Rules falls on a Sunday, it may be done on the following Monday, unless a race to which such act relates is appointed for that day, in which case it must be done on the previous Saturday.

(b) "A month" means a calendar month; "a day" means twenty-four hours.

PART III.
Regulations for Race Meetings

29. After May 31st in each year, only four overnight events for a distance less than a mile for horses three years old and upwards shall be given on any race day, except upon approval by the Stewards.

30. After June 30th in each year, there shall be no race less than five furlongs.

31. The number of starters in overnight races shall be limited by the width of the track at the starting post, the

maximum number to be determined by the Stewards. The number of starters in such overnight races, except handicaps, shall be reduced to the proper number by lot, or by division, also by lot, of the race, at the option of the Association. The division of overnight handicaps shall be made by the Racing Secretary in his entire discretion.

32. By permission of the Stewards of The Jockey Club, races may be run over a race course other than the one over which they have been announced to be run.

33. (a) If a horse runs at any unrecognized meeting, he is disqualified for all races to which these rules apply.

(b) Any person owning, training or riding horses which run at any unrecognized meeting is disqualified, as are also all horses owned by or in charge of any such person.

(c) Any person acting in any official capacity at any unrecognized meeting may be disqualified.

PART IV.
Powers of the Stewards of The Jockey Club

34. (a) The Stewards of The Jockey Club have power, at their discretion, to grant and to withdraw the approval of The Jockey Club to Associations in the conduct of meetings.

(b) The appointment of a general Racing Secretary, the handicapper, clerk of the scales, starter and judge or judges and all minor racing officials shall be made by the Stewards of The Jockey Club subject, when required by the rules of the Racing Commission, or by the laws, of any State, to the approval of said Racing Commission.

35. The Stewards of The Jockey Club have charge of the forfeit list, the registry office, and the registration of partnerships and other documents required by Rule 86 or other Rules to be registered or filed with The Jockey Club.

36. The Stewards of The Jockey Club have power to make inquiry into and to deal with any matter relating to racing, and to rule off, or otherwise less severely punish, any person concerned in any improper turf practice.

37. The Stewards of The Jockey Club shall hear cases on appeal as provided for in these Rules.

PART V.
Stewards

38. Whenever the word "Steward" or "Stewards" is used, it means Steward or Stewards of the Meeting, or their duly appointed deputy or deputies.

39. (a) There shall be three Stewards to supervise each race meeting. One of such Stewards shall be appointed by the State Racing Commission, one shall be appointed by The Jockey Club, and one shall be appointed by the Association conducting such race meeting.

(b) The Jockey Club may designate one of its members to visit each race meeting in an honorary capacity in association with the Stewards.

40. Each Steward may appoint a deputy to act for him at any time. If there be but one Steward present, he shall, in case of necessity, appoint one or more persons to act with him. If none of the Stewards are present, the officers of the Association shall request two or more persons to act during the absence of such Stewards.

41. In case of emergency, the Stewards may, during a meeting, appoint a substitute to fill any of the offices for that meeting only.

42. Every complaint against an official shall be made to the Stewards in writing signed by the complainant.

43. The Stewards have power, as they think proper, to make and, if necessary, to vary all arrangements for the conduct of the meeting, as well as power to put off any race from day to day until a Sunday intervenes.

44. The Stewards have control over, and they and the Stewards of The Jockey Club and members of the State Racing Commission of the State wherein the racing is being conducted, or their

duly appointed representatives, have free access to all stands, weighing rooms, enclosures and all other places within the grounds of the Associations.

45. (a) The Stewards shall exclude from all places under their control every person who is warned or ruled off.

(b) They may so exclude any person who, by the turf authorities of any country, or by the Stewards of any recognized meeting, has been declared guilty of any improper turf practice.

46. The Stewards have supervision over all entries and declarations.

47. The Stewards have power to regulate and control the conduct of all officials, and of all owners, trainers, jockeys, grooms and other persons attendant on horses.

48. If the Stewards shall find any person has violated these Rules of Racing or has been involved in any improper turf practice, they may impose a punishment no greater than the exclusion of such person from the grounds, or any portion of such grounds, of the association conducting the meeting, for a period not exceeding the remainder of the meeting, or the suspension of such person from acting or riding for a period not exceeding twenty racing days after the meeting, or by fine not exceeding two hundred dollars, or by more than one of such punishments; and if they consider necessary any further pun-ishment, they shall immediately refer the matter to the Stewards of The Jockey Club. Whenever under these Rules of Racing a matter has been referred to the Stewards of The Jockey Club, they shall take such action as they shall deem proper and appropriate.

49. The Stewards have power to determine all questions arising in reference to racing at the meeting, subject to appeal under Part XIX. Should no decision have been arrived at by the Stewards within seven days of an objection being lodged, the Clerk of the Course shall then report the case to the Stewards of The Jockey Club, who may at their discretion decide the matter, and who, if they consider there has been negligence, may order any additional expense arising therefrom, to be defrayed out of the funds of the meeting at which the case occurred.

50. The Stewards have power to call for proof that a horse is neither itself disqualified in any respect, nor nominated by, nor the property, wholly or in part, of a disqualified person, and in default of such proof being given to their satisfaction, they may declare the horse disqualified.

51. The Stewards have power at any time to order an examination, by such person or persons as they think fit, of any horse entered for a race, or which has run in a race.

PART VI.
Officials of Meetings

52. (a) The Secretary of the Association, or his deputy, shall be Clerk of the Course. He shall discharge all duties, expressed or implied, required by the Rules of Racing, and he shall report to the Stewards all violations of the Rules of Racing or of the regulations of the meeting.

(b) He shall keep a complete record of all races.

(c) He shall receive all stakes, forfeits, entrance moneys, fines, fees, including jockeys' fees.

(d) Within fourteen days, exclusive of Sundays, from the close of the meeting, he shall pay, to the persons en-titled to it, all the money collected by him; and at the expiration of the same period he shall notify The Jockey Club of all arrears then remaining unpaid, and all arrears not then reported shall be regarded as having been assumed by the Association.

(e) Before acceptance, he shall submit to The Jockey Club, all entries and transfers of engagements for all races except those opened and decided during the meeting.

53. The handicapper shall append to the weights for every handicap the day and hour from which winners will be liable to a penalty and no alteration

shall be made after publication except in case of omission, through error, of the name or weight of a horse duly entered, in which cases by permission of the Stewards the omission may be rectified by the handicapper.

54. (a) The Clerk of the Scales shall exhibit the number (as allotted on the official card) of each horse for which a jockey has been weighed out, and shall forthwith furnish the starter with a list of such numbers.

(b) Any extra or special weight declared for any horse, or any declaration to win, or any alteration of colors shall be exhibited by the Clerk of the Scales upon the Notice Board.

(c) He shall in all cases weigh in the riders of the horses, and report to the Stewards any jockey not presenting himself to be weighed in.

(d) He shall, at the close of each day's racing, send a return to the office of the Secretary of The Jockey Club, of the weights carried in every race, and the names of the jockeys, specifying overweight, if any.

55. (a) The Judge or Judges must occupy the Judge's box at the time the horses pass the winning post, and their sole duty shall be to place the horses. They must announce their decisions promptly, and such decisions shall be final, unless objection to the winner or any placed horse is made and sustained. Provided, that this rule shall not prevent the Judges from correcting any mistake, such correction being subject to confirmation by the Stewards.

(b) A camera approved by the Stewards of The Jockey Club may be used to make a photograph or photographs of the horses at the finish to assist in determining their positions as exclusively indicated by their noses.

56. The official time of each race shall be determined by the official timer. The time recorded when the first horse crosses the finish line shall be the official time of the race.

57. The Judge or Judges shall, at the close of each day's racing, sign and send a report of the result of each race to the office of The Jockey Club.

58. The Judge or Judges shall determine the order of finishing of as many horses as they may think proper.

PART VII.
Registry Office and Registration of Horses

59. Except as provided in section (b) of this Rule, no horse may start in any race unless duly registered in the Registry Office and duly named.

(b) If for any reason ineligible for registration, or pending inquiry as to eligibility, a horse foaled outside of the United States or its possessions, Canada, Cuba or Mexico, and imported into the United States, may be submitted by the owner for approval solely for racing purposes if the application is accompanied by such information as the Stewards of The Jockey Club shall require; whereupon if said Stewards shall consider that the horse has an outstanding racing record and that the application and accompanying information meet the requirements prescribed by said Stewards, they may direct the Executive Secretary or other person authorized by them to issue a permit granting racing privileges only for such horse. Application for such a permit for such a horse must be made to The Jockey Club within thirty days of the original arrival of the horse in the United States—the application to be accompanied by a fee of $50, which will include the permit if granted. In case of failure to apply for a permit within the thirty-day period, and upon proof that failure to do so was unintentional or accidental, application for such a permit may be made within three months after original arrival. Such application shall be accompanied by a fee of $200, which will include the permit if granted.

60. The Registry Office, which is the office of The Jockey Club, is established for the identification of all race horses, whether foaled in the United States or its possessions or in other countries, and for the certification of their pedigrees.

61. Except as provided in Rule 65, horses foaled in the United States or its possessions, Canada, Cuba or Mexico must be registered with the Registry Office before October 1st of the year in which they are foaled.

62. (a) The registration shall comprise the name, if any; the color and marks, if any; whether a horse, mare or gelding; and the names of its sire and dam. If the mare was covered by more than one stallion, the names or descriptions in full must be stated.

(b) In any case of doubt regarding the true parentage or identification of an animal, blood tests may be required, and, taking into consideration the results of such tests and/or such other information as may be available, the Stewards may authorize such corrections in the records as may be determined to be necessary or appropriate.

63. The registration fee shall be $30 for each animal, which will include certificate.

64. Only those horses are eligible for registry which authentically trace, in all of their lines, to animals recorded in the American Stud Book or in a Stud Book of another country recognized by The Jockey Club, and which are eligible under the rules and regulations from time to time adopted by the Stewards of The Jockey Club. A horse born in the United States or its possessions, Canada, Cuba or Mexico may not be registered unless both its sire and dam have been previously registered in The American Stud Book. The only exception to this rule is a foal imported in utero whose dam is properly registered in The American Stud Book after importation, and whose sire was not imported but is properly recorded in the Stud Book of a country recognized by The Jockey Club.

65. Upon failure to register a horse before October 1st of the year of his birth, he may be registered prior to January 1st of his three-year-old year by special permission of the Stewards of The Jockey Club, but not thereafter. If the application to register be made prior to the January 1st next following his birth, the payment of a fee of $60 will be required; if made after that date and prior to January 1st of his two-year-old year the required fee will be $150; and if made after that date and prior to January 1st of his three-year-old year, $300.

66. A name for each horse may be claimed gratis through the Registry Office before January 1st of his two-year-old year. On or after that date, a horse may be named upon payment of a fee of $50 and then only if the name is claimed and allowed at least two days before the date of his first start.

67. (a) All names are subject to approval or disapproval by the Stewards of The Jockey Club.

(b) No name that has been used during the previous fifteen years, either in the stud or on the turf, shall be duplicated, and no name may be claimed for any unregistered horse.

68. By special permission of the Stewards of The Jockey Club a name may be changed but only upon the payment of a fee of $100, except that when a horse's name is changed before January 1st of his two-year-old year, permission is not necessary and the fee is only $10. However, no change of name will be permitted after a horse has started.

69. (a) No horse foaled out of the United States or its possessions, Canada, Cuba or Mexico, shall be registered until the owner has filed in the Registry Office a certificate stating age, color, sex, distinguishing marks, if any, and pedigree as recorded in the recognized Stud Book of its native country or of that country from which it is exported; or unless, in respect of the age and identity of the horse, the owner has otherwise satisfied the Stewards of The Jockey Club. In both cases there must be filed after importation a veterinarian's certificate of identification.

(b) All such applications must be accompanied by a certified copy of the horse's complete racing record in all countries; such record to state date, the type race, distance and the amount of money won in each race.

(c) This registration must be made at the Registry Office within sixty days after the horse's original landing in the United States or its possessions, Canada, Cuba or Mexico and the registration fee shall be $30 for each horse, which will include certificate of registration.

(d) If it be proved to the satisfaction of the Stewards of The Jockey Club that the failure to apply for the registration of a horse within the 60-day period provided in paragraph (c) of this rule was the result of an excusable inadvertence, such registration may be permitted thereafter, provided, however, that such application to register is made within two years after original arrival in the United States or its possessions, Canada, Cuba or Mexico and provided further that the Stewards are furnished with such authenticated information, in respect of the age and identity of the horse and other relevant matters, as they may require.

If the application to register be made within six months after the original arrival, the fee will be $100 for each horse; if made within one year after original arrival, the fee will be $400.

PART VIII.
Entries, Subscriptions, Declarations and Acceptances for Races

70. Every person subscribing to a sweepstake or entering a horse in a race to be run under these Rules accepts the decision of the Stewards or the decision of the Stewards of The Jockey Club or the decision of the State Racing Commission, as the case may be, on any question relating to a race or to racing.

71. At the discretion of the Stewards of The Jockey Club or of the Stewards or of the Association, and without notice, the nominations or entries of any person or the transfer of any nomination or entry may be cancelled or refused.

72. A horse is not qualified to run in any race unless he is duly entered for that race.

73. No horse shall be permitted to start unless his certificate of registration or his racing permit is on file at the Identification Office of The Jockey Club, except that the Stewards, in their discretion, for good cause, waive this requirement if the horse is otherwise properly identified.

74. No horse is qualified to be entered or run which is wholly or partly the property of or leased to or from, or in any way under the care or superintendence of, a disqualified person. Disqualification of a husband or wife from racing horses applies equally to both.

75. Any horse which has been the subject of improper practice may be disqualified for such time and for such races as the Stewards shall determine.

76. (a) Entries and declarations shall be made in writing signed by the owner of the horse or of the engagement or by his authorized agent or some person deputed by him; and in order to secure privacy all entries to overnight races must be made at a specially designated booth.

(b) Entries and declarations by telegraph are binding if promptly confirmed in writing.

(c) Entrance money is not returned on the death of a horse nor on his failure to start, whatever be the cause of the failure.

(d) Entries to all races, excepting those which are opened and decided during the meeting, must be posted on the bulletin boards at the track where the meeting is being held.

77. (a) A horse of a partnership cannot be entered or run in the name, whether real or stable name, of an individual partner in accordance with Rule 87, unless that individual's interest or property in the racing qualities of that horse is equal to at least 25 per cent.

(b) All horses owned wholly or in part by the same person or the spouse of any such person or trained by the same trainer, must be coupled and run as an entry.

(c) Not more than one horse owned by the same person or two horses trained by the same person shall be drawn into any overnight race, or on the also eligible list, to the exclusion of another horse.

(d) For purposes of paragraphs (b) and (c) of this Rule 77, a horse shall be deemed "owned wholly or in part" by a particular person or "owned" by a particular person if that person holds the entire property interest in the horse or if, by lease or ownership, he controls the racing qualities of the horse or if he holds a proportionate interest of 25 per cent or more in a partnership which either holds the property interest in the horse or, by lease or ownership, controls the racing qualities of the horse.

(e) No licensed or authorized trainer shall have any interest, either by ownership of the horse or by lease of its racing qualities in a horse of which he is not the trainer and which may be racing at the same track where the trainer is licensed or authorized and currently racing.

78. (a) The list of entries for overnight races shall be closed at the advertised time and no entry shall be admitted after that time, except that, in case of an emergency, the Racing Secretary may, with the consent of a Steward, grant an extension of time.

(b) The list of entries for all other races shall be closed at the advertised time and no entry shall be admitted after that time unless the nominator can prove to the Stewards that the entry was mailed before the advertised time of closing; and starters must be named through the entry box by the usual time of closing on the day preceding the race.

79. (a) Except as provided in paragraph (b) of this Rule, entries shall be in the name of one person or a stable name, and shall state the name, or the stable name, of the owner, the name or description of the horse, if unnamed, and if the race be for horses of different ages, the age of the horse entered.

(b) Entries may be made in the name of a corporation or a partnership, but, in order to remain eligible, such entries must be transferred to one name on or before January 1st of the two-year-old year of the horse or horses entered.

80. (a) In entering a horse for the first time, it shall be identified by stating its name (if it has any), its color and sex and the name or description of its sire and dam as recorded in the Stud Book. If the dam was covered by more than one stallion, the names or description of all must be stated.

(b) Except as provided in Rule 81, this description must be repeated in every entry until a description of the horse with his name has been published in the Racing Calendar or in the program or the list of entries of an Association.

(c) In every entry after such publication, his name and age will be sufficient.

81. If a horse be entered with a name for the first time, in several races for the same meeting, closing at the same place on the same day, the description need not be added in more than one of the entries.

82. Upon any change of name of a horse which has run in any country, his old name as well as his new name must be given in every entry until he has run three times under his new name over the course of an Association.

Produce Races

83. In making an entry for a produce race, the produce is entered by specifying the dam and the sire or sires.

84. If the produce of a mare is dropped before the 1st of January, or if there is no produce, or if the produce is dead when dropped, or if twins are dropped, the entry of such mare is void.

85. In produce races, allowance for the produce of untried horses must be claimed before the time of closing, and are not lost by subsequent winnings.

Partnerships and Stable Names

86. (a) A horse may be owned by an individual or by a partnership of any number of persons, but no horse shall be entered and run by an owning partnership if it contains more than four members or if the proportionate interest of any member is less than 25 per cent.

(b) A horse owned by a partnership in which the number of members or proportionate interest of any member does not meet the requirements of paragraph (a) of this Rule 86 may be entered and run only by a lessee of its racing qualities, which lessee shall be an individual or a partnership in which the number of members and the proportionate interest of every member meets the requirements of paragraph (a) of this Rule 86. In such a case, the lessee may be a member of or may include one or more members of the owning partnership.

(c) All partnerships having any property, ownership or racing interest in a horse, and the name and address of every individual having any such interest in a horse, the relative proportions of such interest, and the terms of any sale with contingencies, of any lease or of any arrangement, must be signed by all the parties or by their authorized agents and be lodged annually at the office of The Jockey Club or with the Clerk of the Course for transmission to that office, and must be approved by The Jockey Club and a fee of $1.00 per horse be paid, before any horse which is a joint property or which is sold with contingencies or is leased can start in any race.

(d) In the case of a partnership which, by ownership or lease, controls the racing qualities of a horse, all of the partners and each of them shall be jointly and severally liable for all stakes and obligations.

(e) No statement of partnership of a partnership which proposes, by ownership or lease, to control the racing qualities of any horse will be accepted unless proportionate interest of each such partner is at least 25 per cent.

(f) The Jockey Club shall not be required to lodge under paragraph (c) of this Rule 86 any lease of the racing qualities of a horse or horses which is contrary to the law or officially declared public policy of any State in which racing is authorized to be conducted. As a condition of the acceptance of a lease, The Jockey Club may require lessors and lessees to supply such information concerning the identity of their members or participants as is reasonably necessary to insure compliance with this paragraph.

(g) The Jockey Club reserves the right to disapprove any partnership, sale with contingencies, lease, or other arrangements required to be lodged with and approved by The Jockey Club pursuant to paragraph (c) of this Rule 86 when, in the opinion of The Jockey Club, the effect of the partnership, sale, lease, or other arrangement would be to deceive or improperly mislead the public as to the identity of the persons holding an interest in a horse.

87. All statements of partnerships, of sales with contingencies, of leases, or of arrangements, shall declare in whose name the horse will run, to whom winnings are payable (which must be the name of the nominator), and with whom rests the power of entry.

88. In cases of emergency, authority to sign declarations of partnership may be given to The Jockey Club by a telegram promptly confirmed in writing.

89. No member of a partnership which owns a horse or leases the racing qualities of a horse shall assign his share or any part of it without the written consent of the other partners lodged and approved by paragraph (c) of Rule 86. No assignment of an interest in a partnership, which, by ownership or lease, control the racing qualities of a horse will be accepted, if the effect of the assignment would be to create a partnership, which would not be accepted under the terms of paragraph (c) of Rule 86.

90. (a) An individual may adopt a stable name under which to race horses by registering it annually with The Jockey Club and by paying annually a fee of $100. Such a registration shall be

effective only during the calendar year for which it is made, and all such names shall be subject to the approval or disapproval of The Jockey Club.

(b) An individual cannot have registered more than one stable name at the same time, and, so long as an individual has a stable name registered, he shall not use or permit the use of his real name to identify the ownership interest in the racing qualities of any horse.

(c) A partnership which, by ownership or lease, controls the racing qualities of a horse or horses shall race such horses under the name, either real or stable name, of a member of the partnership whose proportionate interest in the horse meets the requirements of paragraph (a) of Rule 77. All horses the racing qualities of which are controlled by a given partnership shall be raced under the same name.

(d) A stable name may be changed at any time by registering a new stable name and by paying the fee of $100.

(e) An individual cannot register as a stable name one which has been already registered, or one which is the name of a race horse, or one which is the real name of an owner.

91. Any individual who has registered a stable name may at any time abandon it by giving written notice at the office of The Jockey Club; notice of such abandonment shall be published in the next Racing Calendar, after which all entries which have been made in the stable name shall be altered as may be approved by The Jockey Club.

92. No trainer of race horses shall register a stable name, but the partnership of which a trainer is a member may use the stable name of another member, provided the use of such other member's stable name is otherwise authorized by these Rules.

93. (Stricken out.)

94. Provided the identity of the horse is satisfactorily established, incorrect or imperfect description in the entry of a horse or failure to register a partnership, may be corrected at any time before the horse is announced as a starter and his number exhibited for the race concerned; or in a handicap before

the weights are announced; but this rule shall not be construed so as to allow any horse to start in any race for which he is not otherwise completely qualified under these Rules of Racing.

95. Except in overnight races, if the hour for closing of entries or for declarations be not stated, it is understood to be midnight of the day specified.

96. In the absence of notice to the contrary, entries and declarations of forfeit, due on the eve of and during a meeting, are due at the office of the Clerk of the Course where the race is to be run.

97. A person who subscribes to a sweepstakes may, after approval by the Stewards, transfer his subscription.

98. An entry of a horse in a sweepstakes is a subscription to the sweepstakes. Such an entry or subscription may, before the time of closing, be altered or withdrawn.

99. Subscriptions and all entries or rights of entry under them shall not become void on the death of the person in whose name they were made or taken. All rights, privileges and obligations shall attach to the continuing owners including the legal representatives of the decedent.

100. No horse shall be considered as struck out of any of his engagements until the owner or his authorized agent shall have given notice, in writing or by telegram, promptly confirmed in writing, to the Clerk of the Course where the horse is engaged.

101. (a) The striking of a horse out of an engagement is irrevocable.

(b) Omission by the vendor to strike a horse out of an engagement, not sold or transferred with him, does not entitle his owner to start him, or to the stakes if he wins.

102. (Stricken out.)

103. (a) If a horse is sold by private treaty, or at public auction, or claimed out of a claiming race (unless the conditions of the claiming race stated otherwise) the written acknowledgment of both parties is necessary to prove the fact that it was transferred with its engagements.

(b) When a horse is sold with his

engagements, or any part of them, the seller cannot strike the horse out of any such engagements.

(c) If only certain engagements be specified, those only are transferred with the horse.

104. A sale to a person ruled off, or to an unqualified or disqualified person, will not entitle such person to be recognized as an owner under these Rules of Racing.

PART IX.
Stakes, Subscriptions, Etc.

105. In the absence of conditions or notice to the contrary, entries for overnight races are to be made at the office of the Clerk of the Course by 2 P.M. on the day before the race.

106. Every horse shall be considered as having started and be liable for whatever is due for so doing, when its jockey has been weighed and its number displayed, unless the Stewards shall otherwise determine.

107. (Stricken out.)

108. No horse shall be allowed to start for any race and no jockey shall be weighed out for any horse until there have been paid or guaranteed to the Clerk of the Course

(a) Any stake or entrance money due by the owner in respect to that race.

(b) The jockey's fee.

PART X.

Rules 109 through 116 were repealed by The Jockey Club years ago.

PART XI.
Qualifications of Starters

117. (a) A horse shall not be qualified to start in any race unless, not less than 30 minutes before the time set for the race, his presence on the grounds of the Association be reported to the paddock judge, he be announced to the Clerk of the Scales as a starter, and the name of his jockey given to the latter official.

(b) Any subsequent change of jockeys must be sanctioned by the Stewards, who, if no satisfactory reason is given for the change, may fine or suspend any person they may think culpable in the matter.

(c) All horses must be saddled in the paddock.

(d) The paddock judge shall be in charge of the paddock and inspect all race horses and their equipment prior to each race, and shall report forthwith

to a Steward any violation observed by him.

(e) No one not actually connected with its stable shall touch a horse while in the paddock preparatory to starting a race, except as provided in Rule 117(f).

(f) A representative of the Association conducting a meeting shall inspect the plating and bandaging of each horse as it enters the paddock before the race, and record the plating on a board provided for the purpose in the paddock.

118. The Stewards may permit or direct the withdrawing of a horse after weighing out.

119. The time fixed for the first race shall be printed on the program.

Post time is the time designated by the Stewards at which horses are to arrive at the post for each race, and such time shall be shown on the dial provided for that purpose.

PART XII.
Weights, Penalties and Allowances

120. (a) The following weights are carried when the weights are not stated in the conditions of the race:

Scale of Weights for Age

Distance	Age	Jan.	Feb.	Mar.	April	May	June	July	Aug.	Sept.	Oct.	Nov.	Dec.
Half Mile	Two years	x	x	x	x	x	x	x	105	108	111	114	114
	Three years	117	117	119	119	121	123	125	126	127	128	129	129
	Four years	130	130	130	130	130	130	130	130	130	130	130	130
	Five years & up	130	130	130	130	130	130	130	130	130	130	130	130
Six Furlongs	Two years	x	x	x	x	x	x	x	102	105	108	111	111
	Three years	114	114	117	117	119	121	123	125	126	127	128	128
	Four years	129	129	130	130	130	130	130	130	130	130	130	130
	Five years & up	130	130	130	130	130	130	130	130	130	130	130	130
One Mile	Two years	x	x	x	x	x	x	x	x	96	99	102	102
	Three years	107	107	111	111	113	115	117	119	121	122	123	123
	Four years	127	127	128	128	127	126	126	126	126	126	126	126
	Five years & up	128	128	128	128	127	126	126	126	126	126	126	126
One and a Quarter Miles	Two years	x	x	x	x	x	x	x	x	x	x	x	x
	Three years	101	101	107	107	111	113	116	118	120	121	122	122
	Four years	125	125	127	127	127	126	126	126	126	126	126	126
	Five years & up	127	127	127	127	127	126	126	126	126	126	126	126
One and a Half Miles	Two years	x	x	x	x	x	x	x	x	x	x	x	x
	Three years	98	98	104	104	108	111	114	117	119	121	122	122
	Four years	124	124	126	126	126	126	126	126	126	126	126	126
	Five years & up	126	126	126	126	126	126	126	126	126	126	126	126
Two Miles	Three years	96	96	102	102	106	109	112	114	117	119	120	120
	Four years	124	124	126	126	126	126	126	125	125	124	124	124
	Five years & up	126	126	126	126	126	126	126	125	125	124	124	124

(b) In races of intermediate lengths, the weights for the shorter distance are carried.

(c) In races exclusively for three-year-olds or four-year-olds, the weight is 126 lbs., and in races exclusively for two-year-olds, it is 122 lbs.

(d) In all races except handicaps and races where the conditions expressly state to the contrary, the scale of weights is less, by the following: for fillies two years old, 3 lbs.; for mares three years old and upward, 5 lbs. before September 1, and 3 lbs. thereafter.

(e) Welter weights are 28 lbs added to the weight for age.

(f) In all overnight races except handicaps, not more than six pounds may be deducted from the scale of weights for age, except for allowances, but in no case shall the total allowances of any type reduce the lowest weight below 101 lbs., except that this minimum weight need not apply to two-year-olds or three-year-olds when racing with older horses.

(g) In all handicaps which close more than 72 hours prior to the race the top weight shall not be less than 126 lbs., except that in handicaps for fillies and mares, the top weight shall not be less than 126 lbs. less the sex allowance at the time the race is run; and scale weight for fillies and mares or three-year-olds may be used for open handicaps as minimum top weight in place of 126 lbs.

(h) In all overnight handicaps and in all claiming handicaps, the top weight shall not be less than 122 lbs.

(i) In all overnight races for two-year-olds, for three-year-olds, or for four-year-olds and upward the minimum weight shall be 112 pounds, subject to sex and apprentice allowances. This rule shall not apply to handicaps, nor to races for three-year-olds and upward.

Estimated Winnings

121. (a) In estimating the value of a race to the winner, there shall be deducted only the amount of money payable to the owners of the other horses and to other persons out of the stakes and out of the added money.

(b) In estimating foreign winnings, the current rate of exchange at the time of such winnings shall be adopted.

(c) The value of prizes not in money will not be estimated in the value of the race to the winner.

(d) In estimating the value of a series of races in which an extra sum of money is won by winning two or more races, the extra sum shall be estimated in the last race by which it was finally won.

122. In all races, should there be any surplus from entries, or subscriptions over the advertised value, it shall be paid the winner, unless stated by the conditions to go to other horses in the race.

123. (a) Winnings during the year shall include all prizes from the 1st of January preceding to the time appointed for the start, and shall apply to all races in any country; and winning shall include dividing or walking over.

(b) Winning of a fixed sum is understood to be winning it in one race, unless specified to the contrary.

124. (a) In a case of a walkover, one-half of the money offered to the winner is given.

(b) When a walkover is the result of arrangement by owners of horses engaged, no portion of the added money nor any other prize need be given.

125. Any money or prize which by the conditions is to go to the horse placed second, or in any lower place in the race, shall, if the winner has walked over or no horse has been so placed, be dealt with as follows:

(a) If part of the stake, it shall go to the winner; or

(b) If a separate donation from the Association or any other source, it shall not be given at all; or

(c) If entrance money for the race, it shall go to the Association.

126. If a race never be run or be void, all moneys paid by an owner in respect to that race shall be returned.

127. A race may be declared void if no qualified horse covers the course according to rule.

Penalties

128. No horse shall carry extra weight, nor be barred from any race for having run second or in any lower place in a race.

129. When the winners of claiming races are exempted from penalties, the exemption does not apply to races in which any of the horses running are not subject to being claimed.

130. Penalties and allowances are not cumulative, unless so declared by the conditions of the race.

Allowances

131. (a) Any male between the ages of sixteen and twenty-five years who has never previously been licensed as a jockey in any country, and has of his own free will and, if under age, with the written consent of his parents or guardian, bound himself to an owner or trainer for a term of not less than three nor more than five years (subject to written extension if made for less than five years) by written contract approved by and filed with The Jockey Club, and after at least one year service with a racing stable, may claim in all overnight races, except handicaps, the following allowances:

(1) Ten pounds until he has ridden five winners and seven pounds until he has ridden an additional 30 winners; if he has ridden 35 winners prior to the end of one year from the date of riding his fifth winner, he shall have an allowance of five pounds until the end of that year.

(2) After the completion of conditions above, for one year he may claim three pounds when riding horses owned or trained by his original contract employer provided his contract has not been permanently transferred or sold since he rode his first winner.

(3) The holder of the contract at the time the boy rides his first winner shall be considered the original contract employer.

(b) All holders of apprentice contracts shall be subject to investigation as to character, ability, facilities and financial responsibility; and shall, at the time of making the contract, own in good faith a minimum of three horses in training, or, if a trainer, shall operate in good faith a stable of at least three horses.

(c) Contracts for apprentice jockeys shall provide for fair remuneration, adequate medical attention and suitable board and lodging for the apprentice; and approved provision shall be made for savings out of his earnings.

(d) Under exceptional circumstances which would prevent an apprentice jockey from riding during the full periods specified above, such as (a) service in the armed forces of the United States; (b) personal injuries suffered in the course of his occupation or otherwise; (c) a disabling illness; (d) restrictions on racing; (e) or other valid reason, the Stewards may extend said period and the term of his contract to compensate therefor.

(e) No apprentice shall be permitted to acquire his own contract.

(f) All apprentice contracts described in this rule shall be filed with The Jockey Club within thirty days after execution thereof or upon filing application for license with the New York State Racing Commission.

(g) The failure of an owner or trainer to file such contract or to obtain the approval of The Jockey Club thereto, may subject such owner or trainer to the revocation or suspension of his license or to such other disciplinary action by the Commission as in its judgment may seem proper.

132. No horse shall receive allowance of weight, or be relieved from extra weight, for having been beaten in one or more races; provided that this rule shall not prohibit maiden allowances, or allowances to horses that have not won within a specified time, or that have not won races of a specified value.

PART XIII.
Weighing Out

133. (a) Every jockey must be weighed for a specified horse not less than 30 minutes before the time fixed for the race, and the number of the horse shall be exhibited officially as soon as possible.

(b) Only equipment specifically approved by the Stewards shall be worn or carried by a jockey or a horse in a race.

(c) Every jockey, apprentice jockey and other rider, whether in a race or when exercising or ponying a Thoroughbred horse, shall wear a safety helmet of a type approved in writing by the Stewards; and no change shall be made in any such helmet without the approval of the Stewards.

134. If a horse run in muzzle, martingale, breastplate or clothing, it must be put on the scale and included in the jockey's weight.

135. No whip, or substitute for a whip, blinkers or number cloth shall be allowed on the scales, nor shall any bridle or safety helmet approved by the Stewards be weighed.

136. If a jockey intends to carry overweight, he must declare the amount thereof at the time of weighing out, or if in doubt as to his proper weight, he may declare the weight he intends to carry.

137. If a jockey intends to carry overweight exceeding by more than two pounds the weight which his horse is to carry, the owner or trainer consenting, he must declare the amount of overweight to the Clerk of the Scales at least 45 minutes before the time appointed for the race, and the Clerk shall cause the overweight to be stated on the Notice Board immediately. For failure on the part of a jockey to comply with this Rule he may be punished as provided by Rule 48.

138. No horse shall carry more than five pounds overweight except in races confined exclusively to amateurs or to riders who are Officers of the United States Army or Navy or of the National Guard.

139. The owner is responsible for the weight carried by his horse.

PART XIV.
Starting

140. (a) The Starter shall give all orders necessary for securing a fair start.

(b) He shall report to the Stewards by whom or by what cause any delay was occasioned, and any cases of misconduct by jockeys when under his orders.

141. If a horse whose number has been exhibited or whose starting is obligatory does not start and run in the race, the Stewards may fine or suspend any person or persons responsible therefor.

142. After the horses are ordered to the starting post, and until the Stewards direct the gates to be reopened, all persons except the racing officials shall be excluded from the course to be run over.

143. A bell shall be rung to indicate the time to saddle and a bugle sounded to indicate the time to go to the post.

144. (a) All horses shall parade and, under penalty of disqualification, shall carry their weight from the paddock to the starting post, such parade to pass the finish line.

(b) When by permission of the paddock judge and upon payment of $10 a horse is led to the post, he is excused from parading with the other horses, but nevertheless he must, on his way to the post, pass the Steward's stand.

145. (a) The position of horses when starting shall be determined by a lot, i.e., a numbered ball shall be drawn from a bottle by the Clerk of the Scales.

(b) The Starter may place vicious and unruly horses on the outside and behind the line.

(c) A horse in the hands of the Starter shall receive no further care from anyone at the starting post except the assistant starters, provided that if any accident happen to a jockey, his horse or his equipment, the Starter may permit any jockey or jockeys to dismount and the horses to be cared for during the delay; otherwise no jockey shall dismount.

146. (a) Except in cases provided for in paragraph (b) of this Rule, all races shall be started by a starting gate selected by the Association conducting the meeting if approved by the Stewards of The Jockey Club.

(b) By permission of the Stewards, a race may be started without a gate.

(c) When a race is started without a starting gate, the start shall not be official until, and there shall be no recall after, the recall flag has been dropped in answer to that of the starter.

147. A start in front of the post is void, and the horses must be started again.

148. All horses shall be schooled properly before starting and, upon the report of the Starter, the Stewards may fine or suspend any trainer who, after being notified, shall start any unruly horse.

149. The horses shall be started as far as possible in a line, but may be started at such reasonable distance behind the starting post as the Starter thinks necessary.

150. (a) The Starter may fine or suspend a jockey for disobedience of his orders at the starting gate or for attempting any unfair advantage; and the Starter may impose upon an offender a fine not exceeding $200 and suspension not exceeding ten days, with or without reference to the Stewards for further action, but such suspension shall not take effect until after the last race of the day of his suspension.

(b) All fines and suspensions by the Starter must be reported in writing by him to the Clerk of the Course, and they may be modified or remitted by the Stewards only.

151. The concurrent statements of the Starter and his assistant as to incidents of the start are conclusive.

PART XV.
Rules of the Race

152. An owner running two or more horses in a race may declare to win with one of them, and such declaration must be made at the time of weighing out, and it is to be immediately posted on the Notice Board. A jockey riding a horse with which his owner has not declared to win must on no account stop such horse except in favor of the stable companion on whose behalf declaration to win has been made.

153. (a) When clear, a horse may be taken to any part of the course provided that crossing or weaving in front of contenders may constitute interference or intimidation for which the offender may be disciplined.

(b) A horse crossing another so as actually to impede him is disqualified, unless the impeded horse was partly in fault or the crossing was wholly caused by the fault of some other horse or jockey.

(c) If a horse or jockey jostle another horse, the aggressor may be disqualified, unless the impeded horse or his jockey was partly in fault or the jostle was wholly caused by the fault of some other horse or jockey.

(d) If a jockey wilfully strike another horse or jockey, or ride wilfully or carelessly so as to injure another horse which is in no way in fault or so as to cause other horses to do so, his horse is disqualified.

(e) When a horse is disqualified under this rule, every horse in the same race belonging wholly or partly to the same owner, in the discretion of the Stewards, may be disqualified.

(f) Complaints under this rule can only be received from the owner, trainer or jockey of the horse alleged to be aggrieved, and must be made to the Clerk of the Scales or to the Stewards before or immediately after his jockey has passed the scales. But nothing in this rule shall prevent the Stewards taking cognizance of foul riding.

(g) Any jockey against whom a foul is claimed shall be given the opportunity to appear before the Stewards before any decision is made by them.

(h) A jockey whose horse has been disqualified or who unnecessarily causes his horse to shorten his stride with a view to complaint, or an owner, trainer or jockey who complains frivolously that his horse was crossed or jostled, may be fined or suspended.

(i) The extent of disqualification shall be determined by the Stewards as in these rules provided.

154. If the Stewards at any time are satisfied that the riding of any race was intentionally foul or that any jockey was instructed or induced so to ride, all persons guilty of complicity shall be suspended and the case shall be reported to the Stewards of The Jockey Club for such additional action as they may consider necessary.

155. If a horse leaves the course, he must turn back and run the course from the point at which he left it.

156. If a race has been run by all the horses at wrong weights or over a wrong course or distance, and an objection be made before official confirmation of the number of the horses placed in the race, or if a Judge is not in the stand when the horses pass the winning post, the race shall be run again after the last race of the day, but in no case less than 30 minutes after the finish of the wrongly run race.

Walking Over

157. In a sweepstake, if only one horse remains to start, the Stewards may dispense with a walkover.

PART XVI.
Weighing In

158. Every jockey must, immediately after pulling up, ride his horse to the place of weighing, dismount only after obtaining permission from the official in charge, and present himself to be weighed by the Clerk of the Scales; provided that if a jockey be prevented from riding to the place of weighing by reason of accident or illness by which he or his horse is disabled, he may walk or be carried to the scales.

159. Except by special permission of the official in charge, every jockey must, upon pulling up, unsaddle his own horse, and no attendant shall touch the horse, except by his bridle. Upon the returning of a jockey to the winner's circle to dismount after a race has been run, no one may touch the equipment of the jockey until he has been weighed in, except upon the approval of the official in charge.

160. If a jockey does not present himself to weigh in, or if he be more than one pound short of his weight, or if he be guilty of any fraudulent practice with respect to weight or weighing, or, except as provided in Rule 158, if he dismount before reaching the scales, or dismount without permission, or if he touch (except accidentally) before weighing in any person or thing other than his own equipment, his horse may be disqualified and he himself may be fined or suspended, as provided by Rule 48.

161. If a horse carry more than two pounds over his proper or declared weight, his jockey shall be fined, suspended or ruled off, unless the Stewards are satisfied that such excess weight has been caused by rain or mud.

PART XVII.
Dead Heats

162. When a race results in a dead heat, the dead heat shall not be run off, owners shall divide, except where division would conflict with the conditions of the race.

When two horses run a dead heat for first place, all prizes to which first and second horses would have been entitled shall be divided equally between them; and this applies in dividing prizes, whatever the number of horses running a dead heat and whatever places for which the dead heat is run. Each horse shall be deemed a winner and liable to

penalty for the amount he shall receive.

When a dead heat is run for second place and an objection is made to the winner of the race, and sustained, the horses which ran the dead heat shall be deemed to have run a dead heat for first place.

163. If the dividing owners cannot agree as to which of them is to have a Cup or other prize which cannot be divided, the question shall be determined by lot by the Stewards.

164. On a dead heat for a match, the match is off.

PART XVIII.
Claiming Races

165. (a) In claiming races any horse may be claimed for its entered price by any owner presently registered in good faith for racing at that meeting who has nominated a starter up to or including the race in which the claim is made, or by his authorized agent, but for the account only of the owner making the claim, or for whom the claim was made by the agent; provided, however, that no person shall claim his own horse or

cause his horse to be claimed directly or indirectly for his own account.

(b) The minimum price for which a horse may be entered in a claiming race shall be twelve hundred dollars, but in no case shall it be entered for less than the value of the purse to the winner.

(c) If a horse is claimed, it shall not start in a claiming race for a period of 30 days from date of claim for less than

25% more than the amount for which it was claimed.

(d) If a horse is claimed, it shall not be sold or transferred to anyone wholly or in part, except in a claiming race, for a period of 30 days from date of claim, nor shall it, unless reclaimed, remain in the same stable or under control or management of its former owner or trainer for a like period, nor shall it race elsewhere until after the close of the meeting at which it was claimed.

166. All claims shall be in writing, sealed and deposited in a locked box provided for this purpose by the Clerk of the Course, at least fifteen minutes before post time. No money shall accompany the claim. Each person desiring to make a claim, unless he shall have such amount to his credit with the Association, must first deposit with the Association the whole amount of the claim in cash, for which a receipt will be given. All claims shall be passed upon by the Stewards, and the person determined at the closing time for claiming to have the right of claim shall become the owner of the horse when the start is effected whether it be alive or dead, sound or unsound, or injured before or during the race, or after it. If more than one person should enter a claim for the same horse, the disposition of the horse shall be decided by lot by the Stewards. An owner shall not be informed that a claim has been made until after the race has been run, and any horse so claimed shall then be taken to the paddock for delivery to the claimant.

167. No person shall claim more than one horse in a race.

168. Each horse shall run for the account of the person in whose name it starts.

169. When a claim has been lodged with the Secretary or Clerk of the Course, it is irrevocable, and is at the risk of the claimant.

170. In case of a dead heat, each of the dividing horses is the winner for the purpose of these rules.

171. (a) Should the Stewards be of the opinion that any person is claiming a horse collusively for the benefit of another interest or in order to evade the provisions of Rule 165, they may require him to make an affidavit that he is not so doing, and if upon proof it is ascertained that he made a false affidavit he shall be referred to the Stewards of The Jockey Club for further action.

(b) Should the Stewards within twenty-four hours after the running of a race be of the opinion that the lease or the entry of a horse was not made in good faith but was made for the purpose of obtaining the privilege of entering a claim, then in each case they may disallow or cancel any such claim and order the return of a horse that may have been delivered and refer the case to the Stewards of The Jockey Club for further action.

172. A horse's liability to be claimed is not affected by his walking over, but he shall receive all the money offered by the conditions of the race to the winner.

173. No horse shall be delivered except on a written order from the Secretary or Clerk of the Course.

174. Any person refusing to deliver a claimed horse shall be suspended and his case may be referred to the Stewards of The Jockey Club. The horse is disqualified until he is delivered to the purchaser.

175. (a) When a stable has been eliminated by claiming, the owner so affected, if he has not replenished his stable before the close of the meeting, may obtain a certificate from the Stewards of the meeting, and on presentation thereof the owner shall be entitled to claim during the next thirty racing days at any recognized meeting operating under the jurisdiction of The Jockey Club, until he has claimed a horse. Stables eliminated by fire or other hazards may also be permitted to claim under this Rule by the discretion of the Stewards.

(b) Any person who shall attempt to prevent another person from claiming any horse in a claiming race, or any owners running in claiming races who may make any agreement for the claiming of each other's horses, may be fined or suspended by the Stewards and referred to the Stewards of The Jockey Club for further action.

PART XIX.
Disputes, Objections, Appeals, Etc.

176. When a race is in dispute, both the horse that finished first and any horse claiming the race shall be liable to all the penalties attaching to the winner of that race until the matter is decided.

177. Every objection shall be decided by the Stewards, but the decisions shall be subject to appeal to the Stewards of The Jockey Club so far as relates to points involving the interpretation of these rules, or to any question other than a question of fact, on which there shall be no appeal unless by leave of the Stewards and with the consent of the Stewards of The Jockey Club. Notice of appeal must be given in writing to the Clerk of the Course within forty-eight hours of the decision being known.

Objections, When and Where Made

178. Every objection must be made by the owner, trainer or jockey of some horse engaged in the race, or by the officials of the course, to the Clerk of the Scales or to one of the Stewards, or an objection may be made by any one of the Stewards.

179. All objections except claims of interference during a race must be in writing signed by the objector.

180. An objection cannot be withdrawn without leave of the Stewards.

181. All costs and expenses in relation to determining an objection or conducting an inquiry shall be paid by such person or persons, and in such proportions as the Stewards shall direct.

182. Before considering an objection, the Stewards may require a deposit of $25, which shall be forfeited if the objection is decided to be frivolous or vexatious.

183. If an objection to a horse engaged in a race be made not less than 15 minutes before the time set for the race, the Stewards may require the qualification to be proved before the race, and in default of such proof being given to their satisfaction, they must declare the horse disqualified.

184. An objection to any decision of the Clerk of the Scales must be made at once.

185. An objection to the distance of a course officially designated must be made not less than 15 minutes before the race.

186. An objection to a horse on the ground of his not having run the proper course, or of the race having been run on a wrong course, or of any other matter occurring in the race, must be made before the numbers of the horses placed in the race are confirmed officially.

187. (a) An objection on the ground

(1) Of misstatement, omission or error in the entry under which a horse has run; or

(2) That the horse which ran was not the horse nor of the age which he was represented to be at the time of entry; or

(3) That he was not qualified under the conditions of the race or by reason of default; or

(4) That he has run in contravention of the rules of partnership or registration, may be received up to 48 hours exclusive of Sunday after the last race of the last day of the meeting.

(b) In any other case an objection must be within 48 hours of the race being run, exclusive of Sunday, save in the case of any fraud or willful misstatement, when there shall be no limit to the time of objecting provided the Stewards are satisfied that there has been no unnecessary delay on the part of the objector.

188. The Stewards are vested with the power to determine the extent of disqualification in case of fouls. They may place the offending horse behind such horses as in their judgment it interfered with, or they may place it last, and they may disqualify it from participation in any part of the purse.

189. If by reason of an objection to

a horse a race or place is awarded to another horse, the money for such race shall be distributed in accordance with the final placing, and the owner of a horse to which the race or place is finally awarded can recover the money from those who wrongfully received it.

190. Pending the determination of an objection any prize which the horse objected to may have won or may win in the race, or any money held by the association holding the meeting, as the price of a horse claimed (if affected by the determination of the objection) shall be withheld until the objection is determined.

PART XX.

Licenses or Authorizations for Participants in Racing

191. Except as provided in Rule 192, no person shall be allowed to start, ride or train horses, and no person may pursue any other occupation or be employed at race meetings, in any State where it is or shall be required that such person be licensed, or obtain an authorization, in order to pursue his occupation or employment upon the grounds of an Association, unless such person shall have been licensed or shall have obtained such authorization.

192. Unless otherwise provided by the rules of the Racing Commission, or by the laws, of the State concerned:

(a) No jockey license or authorization shall be granted to anyone less than sixteen years of age;

(b) Each owner, to be eligible for a license or authorization, shall be required to submit an affidavit, as to his ownership or lease of all horses in his possession;

(c) Boys never having ridden in a race may be allowed to ride twice, if approved by the Stewards, before applying for a license or authorization; but a license or authorization shall not be granted to boys who have never ridden in a race;

(d) In an emergency, the Stewards may permit owners, trainers, assistant trainers and jockeys and others to start, train or ride or pursue their other occupations or employments pending action on their applications; and

(e) Any amateur wishing to ride in races on even terms with jockeys shall obtain leave, good until revoked, from the Stewards of The Jockey Club;

(f) No person shall be eligible for an owner's or trainer's license or authorization, if, during the term of such license or authorization, he would practice as farrier or veterinarian with horses racing under the jurisdiction of The Jockey Club; provided, however, that a duly licensed or authorized owner may personally shoe a horse owned by him upon applying for and receiving a certificate of fitness therefor from the Stewards;

193. Trainer and assistant trainers are responsible for the condition of horses in their care and are presumed to know these Rules.

Jockeys' Betting, Etc.

194. (a) No jockey shall bet on any race except through the owner of and on the horses which he rides, and any jockey who shall be proved to the satisfaction of the Stewards to have any interest in any race horse, or to have been engaged in any betting transaction except as permitted by this Rule, or to have received presents from persons other than the owner, may be punished as provided by Rule 48.

(b) Any person knowingly acting in the capacity of part owner or trainer of any horse in which a jockey possesses any interest, or making any bet with or in behalf of any jockey except as provided in Rule 194(a), or otherwise aiding or abetting in any breach of these Rules of Racing, may be punished as provided by Rule 48.

195. (a) No jockey shall be the owner of any race horse.

(b) A jockey may not ride in any race against a starter of his contract employer unless his mount and his contract employer's starter are both in the hands of the same trainer.

196. (a) A jockey or trainer under

suspension in any state or foreign country, shall not be permitted to train or ride in a race for anyone during the period of his suspension. Any person who shall employ a jockey or trainer in contravention of this Rule may be punished as provided by Rule 48.

ished as provided by Rule 48.

(b) All fines imposed upon jockeys must be paid by the jockeys themselves. Any other person found paying the same shall be punished as well as the jockey.

197. In the absence of a specific contract, jockey's fees shall be as follows:

Purse	Winner	Second	Third	Loser	Purse	Winner	Second	Third	Loser
$ 400	$25.00	$15.00	$12.00	$10.00	1,200-1,300	42.00	27.00	23.00	18.00
500	26.00	16.00	13.00	11.00	1,400-1,500	44.00	29.00	24.00	19.00
600	27.00	17.00	14.00	12.00	1,600-1,700	47.00	32.00	25.00	20.00
700	34.00	21.00	19.00	15.00	1,800-1,900	50.00	35.00	27.00	22.00
800- 900	37.00	22.00	21.00	17.00	2,000 & up	50.00	40.00	30.00	25.00
1,000-1,100	39.00	24.00	22.00	17.00					

198. (a) The terms of all contracts between jockeys and their employers shall be filed with The Jockey Club, accompanied by a fee of $1, and must be approved by it (in the cases of apprentices, before a license or authorization be granted), and such contracts shall contain a provision that in case a jockey's license or authorization be revoked or suspended, the salary of the jockey shall in the former case cease, and in the latter case cease during the time of his suspension. The terms of all contracts between jockeys and jockey agents shall be filed with The Jockey Club accompanied by a fee of $1 and must be approved by it before being effective.

(b) A jockey shall be compensated and insured by either the owner or trainer of the horse according to which one is the employer as defined by the applicable Workmen's Compensation Law.

199. If a jockey engaged for a race, or for a specified time, refuses to fulfill his engagement, he may be punished as provided by Rule 48.

200. Employers retaining the same jockey have precedence according to the priority of the retainers as specified in the contracts.

201. Conflicting claims for the services of a jockey shall be decided by the Stewards.

Stable Employees

202. No owner or trainer shall engage any person who has not a written discharge from his last employer, but any person prevented by this rule from obtaining or retaining employment shall have the right of appeal to the Stewards

against the person withholding his written discharge.

203. Any owner or trainer employing a person in violation of any of Rules 191 to 202, inclusive, may be punished as provided by Rule 48.

PART XXI.
Racing Colors and Numbers

204. (a) Racing colors shall be registered annually on payment of $5, or for five years on payment of $15. Colors so registered shall not be taken by any other person. All disputes as to the right to particular colors shall be settled by the Stewards of The Jockey Club.

(b) No person shall run a horse in

colors other than those registered in his own or a stable name without special permission of the Stewards.

205. Jockeys must wear a number on the saddle cloths corresponding to the numbers of the horses as exhibited after weighing out.

206. Any deviation from the recorded

colors of the owner that may be granted by the Stewards is to be immediately posted on the Notice Board.

207. Under special circumstances, a horse may be permitted by the Stewards to run in colors not those of the owner.

PART XXII.
Corrupt Practices and Disqualifications of Persons

208. (a) If any person give, offer or promise, directly or indirectly, any bribe in any form to any person having official duties in relation to any race or race horse, or to any trainer, jockey or agent, or to any other person having charge of, or access to, any race horse; or

(b) If any person having official duties in relation to any race track, race or race horse, or if any trainer, jockey, agent or other person having charge of, or access to, any race horse, solicit, accept, or offer to accept any bribe in any form; or

(c) If any licensed person, or person permitted within the grounds of any Association, shall be approached with an offer or promise of a bribe or with a request or a suggestion for a bribe or for any improper, corrupt or fraudulent act or practice in relation to a race or racing, or that any race shall be conducted otherwise than fairly and in accordance with these Rules of Racing, and if such licensed or other person shall not immediately report the matter to the Stewards; or

(d) If any person wilfully enter, or cause or permit to be entered, or to start, in any race a horse which he knows or has reason to believe to be disqualified; or

(e) If any person shall have in his possession in or about any race track, or shall use, appliances—electrical, mechanical, or otherwise—other than the ordinary equipment, of such nature as could affect the speed or racing condition of a horse; or

(f) If any person be guilty of any improper, corrupt or fraudulent act or practice in relation to racing in this or in any other country, or shall conspire with any other person to commit, or shall assist in the commission of, any such act or practice;

Any person found by the Stewards to have violated Rule 208.(a), (b), (c),

(d), (e) or (f) shall have such penalty imposed upon him and the Stewards shall take such other action in the matter as they may deem proper under any Rules of Racing, including reference to the Stewards of The Jockey Club.

(g) If the Stewards shall find that any drug has been administered or attempted to be administered, internally or externally, to a horse before a race, which is of such a character as could affect the racing condition of the horse in such a race, such Stewards shall impose such penalty and take such other action as they may deem proper under any of these Rules of Racing (including reference to the Stewards of The Jockey Club) against every person found by them to have administered, or to have attempted to administer or to have caused to be administered or to have caused an attempt to administer, or to have conspired with another person to administer such drug.

The trainer, groom, and any other person, having charge, custody or care of the horse, are obligated properly to protect the horse and guard it against such administration or attempted administration and, if the Stewards shall find that any such person has failed to show proper protection and guarding of the horse, they shall impose such penalty and take such other action as they may deem proper under any of the Rules of Racing, including reference to the Stewards of The Jockey Club.

The owner or owners of a horse so found to have received such administration shall be denied, or shall promptly return, any portion of the purse or sweepstakes, and any trophy in such race, and the same shall be distributed as in the case of a disqualification. If a horse shall be disqualified in a race because of the infraction of this Rule 208(g), the eligibility of other horses which ran in such race and which have started in a subsequent race before announcement of such disqualification, shall not be in any way affected.

(h) No person within the grounds of a racing Association where race horses are lodged or kept, shall have in or upon the premises which he occupies or has the right to occupy, or in his personal property or effects, any hypodermic syringe, hypodermic needle, or other device which could be used for the injection or other infusion into a horse of a drug without first securing written permission from the Stewards. Every racing Association, upon the grounds of which race horses are lodged or kept, is required to use all reasonable efforts to prevent the violation of this Rule. Every such racing Association, the Commission, and the Stewards, or any of them, shall have the right to permit a person or persons authorized by any of them to enter into or upon the buildings, stables, rooms or other places within the grounds of such an Association and to examine the same and to inspect and examine the personal property and effects of any person, within such places; and every licensed person and person authorized to pursue his occupation or employment within the grounds of any Association, by accepting his license or accepting such authorization, does consent to such search and to the seizure of any such hypodermic syringes, hypodermic needles or other devices, and any drugs apparently intended to be used in connection therewith, so found. If the Stewards shall find that any persons have violated this Rule 208(h), they shall impose such penalty and take such other action as they may deem proper under any of the Rules of Racing, including reference to the Stewards of The Jockey Club.

(i) Every person ruled off the course of a recognized Association is ruled off wherever these rules have force.

(j) Anyone who has been ruled off or who has been suspended, whether temporarily for investigation or otherwise, and anyone penalized as above by the highest official regulatory racing body having jurisdiction where the offense occurred, shall be denied admission to all race tracks until duly reinstated.

(k) A person whose license or authorization has been revoked or has been suspended, whether temporarily for investigation or otherwise, and so long as his exclusion or suspension continues shall not be qualified, whether acting as agent or otherwise, to subscribe for or to run any horse for any race, either in his own name or in that of any other person.

(l) All horses in the charge of a trainer who has been ruled off or has been suspended, whether temporarily for investigation or otherwise shall be automatically suspended from racing during the period of the trainer's exclusion or suspension. Permission may be given by the Stewards for the transfer of such horses to another trainer during such period, and upon such approval such horses shall again be eligible to race.

(m) In the event that a horse establishes a track or other record in a race and it should be determined by competent authority that the chemical analysis of any sample taken from such horse shows the presence of a drug which is of such character as could affect the racing condition of the horse in such race, then such record shall be null and void.

PART XXIII.
Discretionary Powers

209. If any case occurs which is not or which is alleged not to be provided for by these Rules, it shall be determined by the Stewards or by the Stewards of The Jockey Club, as the case may be, in such manner as they think just and conformable to the usages of the turf.

210. These Rules of Racing or any rules, not consistent therewith, made by the State Racing Commission of the State concerned, supersede the conditions of a race or regulations of a meeting when they conflict.

211. The Stewards shall not entertain any disputes relating to bets.

212. The Jockey Club may contract with racing authorities, racing Associations and other bodies for the rendition of such advisory or other services as may be desired.

PART XXIV.
New Rules

213. No new Rules of Racing can be adopted by The Jockey Club nor can any of its Rules be rescinded or altered unless the proposed new rule, rescission or alteration shall have been previously advertised twice in the Racing Calendar nor unless notice shall have been given in such advertisement of the meeting of The Jockey Club at which it is to be acted upon, except that:

(a) In the event of an "Emergency," so declared by the Stewards of The Jockey Club, new rules may be passed and any existing rule rescinded or altered at a meeting of The Jockey Club called upon twenty-four hours' notice, which notice shall contain the reason for the meeting.

(b) The Stewards of The Jockey Club may sanction variations in these Rules to conform with local conditions.

20 How to Read Charts and Past Performances

Not one racegoer in a thousand is fully conversant with the symbols and abbreviations that *The Morning Telegraph* and *Racing Form* use in their result charts and past-performance records. Spending a few minutes with the *Form* or *Telegraph* sections of this chapter is highly recommended.

Sample Result Chart

This sample Official Result Chart illustrates how completely every factor pertaining to a race is covered by the expert trackmen and statistical staffs of **The Morning Telegraph**.

FIRST RACE
GS - 22601
January 1, 1965

6 FURLONGS (Chute). (I Appeal, May 21, 1955, 1.08$\frac{4}{5}$, 4, 112.)
Purse $4,000. 4-year-olds and upward. Claiming. Weights, 4-year-olds, 120 lbs., older 122 lbs. Non-winners of two races since Nov. 30 allowed 3 lbs., Sept. 16, 5 lbs., a race since Aug. 27, 7 lbs. Claiming price, $10,000. If entered for less, 2 lbs. allowed for each $500 down to $8,000.
Value to winner $2,400, second $850, third $475, fourth $275. Mutuel pool $231,802.

Index	Horse	Eqt A Wt PP St	1/4	1/2	Str	Fin	Jockey	Cl'g Pr	Owner	Odds $1
22301GS[1]	—Autumn Gold	b 4 120 5 1	3[1]	3[3]	1[1]	1[1]	G L Smith†	10000	Autumn Farm	2.20
21101Aqu[3]	—Crown Seal	b 5 114 2 7	4[1]	4[1]	4½	2½	S Boulmetis	8000	Sunset Stable	3.30
22002Lrl[2]	—[D]Indulger	6 113 3 3	2h	2h	2h	3h	W Hartack	9000	R J Hinds	[D]-3.50
21406CD[4]	—Prelude	b 4 111 7 9	8½	7½	5[1]	41¼	J Ruane[5]	9000	F–M Stable	15.40
22309SP[6]	—Mercurius	b 7 112 1 2	1[1]	1[1]	31½	5[1]	R Sterling[3]	9500	M O'Connor	a–6.80
20811Suf[6]	—[DH]PrairieMoon	9 117 1C 10	10[2]	8[2]	71½	6	W Blum	10000	H Brown	[DH]–f–20.10
22340Bow[5]	—[DH]Foxland	b 6 122 6 8	7[2]	6[1]	6[2]	62½	H B Wilson	10000	C Jones	[DH]–90.20
20812Del[10]	—Promptitude	7 111 9 5	5½	5½	8[5]	8[3]	T Atkinson	8500	Lewis Bros	14.00
21704Pim[3]	—Western Glow	b 5 108 8 6	9[3]	9[1]	9[1]	9[1]	J McNeil[10]	9000	E Franks	f–20.10
22407SA[9]	—Rowladdie	6 102 4 4	6h	10[1]	10[1]	10[no]	C Bradford[7]	8000	J Gardner	a–6.80
22312TrP[12]	—Go It Alone	b 5 113 14 12	11[1]	11½	11½	11[nk]	J Culmone	8500	Rivers Farm	b–63.60
22411FG[2]	—Ripple Fox	b 4 114 12 14	14[2]	13[1]	12½	12[1]	W M Cook	8500	F Linderman	47.20
23110P[2]	—Fantail	b 6 109 11 13	13[1]	14[1]	14[1]	13[2]	J Polion[5]	8000	B Smith	f–20.10
22418GP[8]	—Why Talk	8 108 13 11	12[1]	12[3]	13[1]	14½	O Scurlock	8000	Rivers Farm	b–63.60
22316Hia[7]	—Missy Lou	b 6 106 15 15	15	15	15	15	S Cole	8000	H Allen	31.80

† Five pounds apprentice allowance waived.
[D]–Disqualified and placed fourth. [DH]–Dead-heat. f–Mutuel field.
a–Coupled—Mercurius and Rowladdie, b–Go It Alone and Why Talk.
Time .22$\frac{4}{5}$, .45$\frac{1}{5}$, 1.10$\frac{4}{5}$. Track fast.

Official Program Numbers↘

$2 Mutuel Prices:
4–AUTUMN GOLD	6.40	4.60	3.20
3–CROWN SEAL		4.80	3.60
6–PRELUDE			6.80

Ch. c, by Autumn—Falling Leaves, by Gold Sun. Trainer F. J. Peters. Bred by Autumn Farm.
IN GATE AT 1.31. OFF AT 1.31½ EASTERN STANDARD TIME. Start good. Won driving.

AUTUMN GOLD, away fast, raced forwardly placed to the stretch, assumed command when settled for the drive, and, continuing gamely under strong urging, held CROWN SEAL safe. The latter, in hand early, drifted to the middle of the track at the stretch turn, closed strongly when straightened but could not reach the winner. INDULGER, a strong factor from the start, swerved suddenly in midstretch, then, when straightened, went well to the finish. INDULGER was disqualified for interfering with PRELUDE and was placed fourth. PRELUDE, sluggish early, was making a strong run at the leaders when INDULGER swerved in front of him, forcing his rider to take up. MERCURIUS took an early lead, set the pace to the stretch under urging, then faltered in the drive. PRAIRIE MOON lacked early foot and could not threaten the leaders when set down for the drive. FOXLAND had no mishap. PROMPTITUDE was caught in close quarters entering the stretch. ROWLADDIE, fractious in the post parade, flashed brief speed and tired. The others were outrun from the start and were never in contention.

No whip—Fantail
Scratched—Demolition, Engineer.
Overweights—Why Talk 1 pound, Rowladdie 2. Corrected weight— Promptitude 111 pounds.
Crown Seal was claimed by Mrs. F. J. Smith, trainer R. P. Scott.

How to Read Charts

This complete Official Result Chart, as it would appear in **The Morning Telegraph,** contains a wealth of information. The value of this data can best be illustrated by breaking the chart down into its component parts and explaining each figure, abbreviation and symbol.

Race, Track Index Number, Date

FIRST RACE
GS - 22601
January 1, 1965

FIRST RACE means just that—this event was first on the day's program at (GS) Garden State Park. (Note: A complete list of North American track abbreviations appear on page 461.) 22601 is the index number assigned this particular race by The Morning Telegraph. The next time each starter runs, his name in the chart will be preceded by index number and track abbreviation, **22601GS,** making possible easy reference to this race in either back copies of The Morning Telegraph or in Daily Racing Form Monthly Chart Books. **January 1, 1965,** indicates the date the race was run.

Distance, Track Record

6 FURLONGS (Chute). (I Appeal, May 21, 1955, 1.08⅘, 4, 112.)

6 FURLONGS is the distance at which the race was run. A furlong is one-eighth of a mile or 220 yards. **(Chute)** indicates that the race was started and raced in its earliest stages on a straightaway extension of the main track. **(I Appeal, May 21, 1955, 1.08⅘, 4, 112)** shows that the track record at Garden State for six furlongs was established by I Appeal on May 21, 1955, that he ran the distance in 1.08⅘ (one minute, eight and four-fifths seconds), when he was four years old (4) and that he carried 112 pounds (112).

Conditions of Race

Purse $4,000. 4–year–olds and upward. Claiming. Weights, 4–year–olds, 120 lbs., older 122 lbs. Non–winners of two races since Nov. 30 allowed 3 lbs., Sept. 16, 5 lbs., a race since Aug. 27, 7 lbs. Claiming price, $10,000. If entered for less, 2 lbs. allowed for each $500 down to $8,000.

These are the "conditions" of the race, written in advance by the track's racing secretary and published in a "condition book." They set down the specific conditions for this race, fixing the requirements a horse must meet to be eligible to compete and the weight each starter shall carry. In this instance the weights are based on the claiming prices and certain allowances.

A breakdown of the conditions reveals that the track offered a purse of $4,000 (**Purse $4,000**); only horses who are four years old and older (**4-year-olds and upward**) were eligible to compete; it was a claiming race (**Claiming**); the weight each starter carried had been decreed by the racing secretary (under the heading **Weights**), with provisions made for less weight to be carried if a horse met certain requirements.

(NOTE: See "Explanation of Various Races" beginning on page 443 for definitions of claiming races and all other types of contests run at recognized tracks.)

Purse Split, Mutuel Pool

Value to winner $2,400, second $850, third $475, fourth $275. Mutuel pool $231,802.

This line shows that the owner of the winner received **$2,400** as his share of the $4,000 purse; that **$850** was paid to the owner of the second horse, **$475** to the owner of the horse officially placed third and **$275** to the owner of the horse officially placed fourth. **Mutuel pool $231,802** gives the total amount of money wagered in the totalisator on all starters in this race (win, place and show).

Index Number

Index Number of Last Previous Race Superior figure 1 shows finish position	Name of Horse	Equipment Carried Age of Horse Weight Carried Post Position	at Start	Positions in Race and Lengths Ahead of Next Following Horse			Jockey	Claiming Price	Owner	Equivalent Odds to $1
				at ¼	at ½	at Stretch	at Finish				
22301GS¹	—Autumn Gold	b 4 120 5	1	3¹	3³	1¹	1¹	G L Smith	10000	Autumn Farm	2.20

22301GS¹ is the index number of the chart of Autumn Gold's last previous race and the track at which the race was run. The Morning Telegraph assigns an index number to the chart of each race run at a recognized North American track. Thus it is simple to check a horse's record in either back copies of The Morning Telegraph or in Daily Racing Form Monthly Chart Books. The superior figure ¹ indicates that Autumn Gold finished first in race number **22301** at Garden State Park. If he had finished second, the superior figure would have been 2; if third, 3; fourth, 4, etc. If the track abbreviation is not followed by a superior figure, the horse did not finish the race, or was disqualified and unplaced from actual finish position.

Equipment

22301GS¹ —Autumn Gold b 4 120 5 1   3¹ 3³ 1¹ 1¹ G L Smith   10000 Autumn Farm   2.20

b indicates that Autumn Gold was wearing blinkers (**b**). If his rider had also been equipped with spurs, the letter (**s**) would have been added. NOTE: All riders are equipped with whips unless the chart footnotes indicate otherwise.

Age

22301GS¹ —Autumn Gold b 4 120 5 1   3¹ 3³ 1¹ 1¹ G L Smith   10000 Autumn Farm   2.20

   4 is Autumn Gold's age. He is four years old. A horse's age is reckoned at beginning on January 1 of the year in which he was foaled. In other words, a horse foaled (born) in March, 1957, becomes one year old on January 1, 1958.

Weight

22301GS¹ —Autumn Gold. b 4 120 5 1   3¹ 3³ 1¹ 1¹ G L Smith   10000 Autumn Farm   2.20

   120 is the weight Autumn Gold carried. This includes the weight of his rider, the jockey's equipment and whatever lead slabs were necessary to bring the total weight up to the assigned impost.

Post Position

22301GS¹ —Autumn Gold · b 4 120 5 1   3¹ 3³ 1¹ 1¹ G L Smith   10000 Autumn Farm   2.20

   5 is Autumn Gold's post position. Post positions are drawn by lot and numbered from the inside rail outward.

Running Positions

22301GS¹ —Autumn Gold b 4 120 5 1   3¹ 3³ 1¹ 1¹ G L Smith   10000 Autumn Farm   2.20

   1 is Autumn Gold's position at the start of the race, immediately after the field had left the start gate.

   (NOTE: In races at one mile and one-quarter or longer each horse's position after the field has run a quarter of a mile is substituted for his position at the start.)

22301GS¹ —Autumn Gold b 4 120 5 1   3¹ 3³ 1¹ 1¹ G L Smith   10000 Autumn Farm   2.20

   3¹ shows that Autumn Gold was third, one length in front of the fourth horse, after running a quarter-mile.

22301GS¹ —Autumn Gold b 4 120 5 1   3¹ 3³ 1¹ 1¹ G L Smith   10000 Autumn Farm   2.20

   3³ reveals that Autumn Gold was third, three lengths in front of the fourth horse, after running a half-mile.

22301GS¹ —Autumn Gold b 4 120 5 1   3¹ 3³ 1¹ 1¹ G L Smith   10000 Autumn Farm   2.20

   1¹ indicates that Autumn Gold was in front by one length in the stretch. The stretch call is usually made one-eighth of a mile from the finish line.

22301GS[1] —Autumn Gold b 4 120 5 1   3[1] 3[3] 1[1] 1[1] G L Smith   10000 Autumn Farm   2.20

▲

1[1] shows that Autumn Gold won the race by one length.

The number of running positions given in a chart and the point in the race at which these "calls" were made will vary according to the distance of the race. However, these points of call always appear directly above the running positions of the winning horse.

(NOTE: The complete finish of each race at every major track is confirmed by a photo finish camera.)

Jockey

22301GS[1] —Autumn Gold b 4 120 5 1   3[1] 3[3] 1[1] 1[1] G L Smith   10000 Autumn Farm   2.20

▲

G L Smith is the name of the jockey who rode Autumn Gold. Weight allowances claimed for apprentice riders are indicated by superior figures following the jockey's name, as illustrated below:

R. Sterling[3]   **J Ruane[5]**
3-pound apprentice allowance   5-pound apprentice allowance

C Bradford[7]   **J McNeil[10]**
7-pound apprentice allowance   10-pound apprentice allowance

(NOTE: Apprentice allowances vary in different states. The apprentice allowance is actually a reduction in the weight the horse would have had to carry if ridden by a full-fledged jockey not entitled to a concession. For example, Autumn Gold, in sample chart 15401, carried 120 pounds. If a three-pound apprentice allowance had been claimed for his rider, he would have carried only 117 pounds; if a five-pound allowance had been claimed, he would have carried 115 pounds, etc.)

Claiming Price

22301GS[1] —Autumn Gold b 4 120 5 1   3[1] 3[3] 1[1] 1[1] G L Smith   10000 Autumn Farm   2.20

▲

10000 is the amount for which Autumn Gold was entered to be claimed. In races other than claiming this space is blank.

(NOTE: Claiming rules vary from state to state. However, the general claiming procedure in most states follows the pattern outlined in the Rules of Racing adopted by The Jockey Club:

("In claiming races any horse may be claimed for its entered price by any owner presently registered in good faith for racing at that meeting who has nominated a starter up to or including the race in which the claim is made, or by his authorized agent, but for the account only of the owner making the claim, or for whom the claim was made by the agent; provided, however, that no person shall claim his own horse or cause his horse to be claimed directly or indirectly for his own account.")

"Claiming" a horse actually is buying him. When an owner starts a horse in a claiming event, he does so with the express understanding that any owner eligible to make a claim at that meeting may acquire him for his entered price. All claims must be in writing, sealed and deposited in a locked box provided for that purpose by the Clerk of the Course at a stipulated time before the race is run. When there is more than one claim for the same horse, the new owner is decided by lot. All claims are passed upon by the stewards, and the new owner takes possession of the horse after the race no matter if he is dead or alive, sound or unsound, or injured during or after the race.

Owner

22301GS[1] —Autumn Gold b 4 120 5 1   3[1] 3[3] 1[1] 1[1] G L Smith   10000 Autumn Farm   2.20
                                                                                  ▲

Autumn Farm is the owner of Autumn Gold.

Equivalent Odds

22301GS[1] —Autumn Gold b 4 120 5 1   3[1] 3[3] 1[1] 1[1] G L Smith   10000 Autumn Farm   2.20
                                                                                  ▲

2.20 is Autumn Gold's odds to $1 in the pari-mutuel win pool.

Entries

When two or more horses starting in the same race are trained by the same person, regardless of their ownership, or are owned by one interest, even though conditioned by different trainers, they constitute an entry at most tracks. The horses comprising the entry are "coupled" in the wagering and run as one betting interest. Holders of winning pari-mutuel tickets on the entry collect regardless of which member of the coupling finishes in the money, because entries are treated as one horse in the betting. The following lines from Sample Chart 22601 show how entries are designated by the letters a, b, etc., preceding each horse's equivalent odds to $1:

22309SP[6] —Mercurius   b 7 112 1 2   1[1] 1[1] 31½ 5[1] R Sterling[3]   9500 M O'Connor   a–6.80
22407SA[9] —Rowladdie   6 102 4 4   6[h] 10[1] 10[1] 10[no] C Bradford[7] 8000 J Gardner   a–6.80
22312TrP[12]—Go It Alone b 5 113 14 12   11[1] 11½ 11½ 11[nk] J Culmone   8500 Rivers Farm   b–63.60
22418GP[8] —Why Talk   8 108 13 11   12[1] 12[3] 13[1] 14½ O Scurlock   8000 Rivers Farm   b–63.60

Each member of an entry receives the same identifying letter. For further clarity, the letter designating each entry and the names of the horses coupled in each entry are repeated at the bottom of the chart, directly under the line giving the running positions of the last horse in the race.

(NOTE: There is an exception to the general entry rule in some States where the rules provide that in **stake races only** the coupling or uncoupling of separately owned or trained horses for purposes of pari-mutuel wagering shall be at the discretion of the stewards.)

Field Horses

At most tracks, when more than 12 horses owned by 12 different interests start in a race, all horses in excess of 11 are coupled in the betting as the "mutuel field." As in the case of entries, a wager on one horse in the field is a wager on all. The mutuel field has been instituted because the pari-mutuel equipment at most tracks is geared to handle wagers on no more than 12 interests, although this number may vary at different tracks. At some tracks, the field horses are designated by the track handicapper, while at others all horses having the outside post positions may be grouped in the field. The following lines from Sample Chart 22601 show how the field horses are designated in the chart by the letter **f** preceding each horse's equivalent odds to $1.00.

The following horses are members of the mutuel field in Sample Chart 22601 which appears on page 6.

20811Suf^{6}	—[DH]PrairieMoon		9	117	10	10	10^{2}	8^{2}	7$^{1\frac{1}{2}}$	6	W Blum	10000	H Brown	[DH]f–20.10
21704Pim^{3}	—Western Glow	b	5	108	8	6	9^{3}	9^{1}	9^{1}	9^{1}	J McNeil^{10}	9000	E Franks	f–20.10
22311OP^{2}	—Fantail	b	6	109	11	13	13^{1}	14^{1}	14^{1}	13^{2}	J Polion^{5}	8000	B Smith	f–20.10

Fractional Times, Track Conditions

Time .22⅘, .45⅕, 1.10⅘. Track fast.

This line in the chart gives the running time of the leading horse at each point in the race clocked. In this six-furlong race, the positions at which clockings were taken are quarter-mile (.22⅘), half-mile (.45⅕) and the finish of the six furlongs (1.10⅘). The number of fractional times given in the chart and the point at which they were taken will vary, depending upon the distance of the race.

Track fast indicates that the racing surface of the track for this race was classified as fast. Other classifications for conditions of dirt tracks, as opposed to turf, or grass courses, are **frozen, good, slow, sloppy, muddy** and **heavy**. For races run on turf courses, the track condition classifications are **hard firm, good** and **soft.**

Program Numbers, Mutuel Prices

Official Program Numbers↘

$2 Mutuel Prices:				
	4–AUTUMN GOLD	6.40	4.60	3.20
	3–CROWN SEAL		4.80	3.60
	6–PRELUDE			6.80

Official Program Numbers are just that: the number assigned each horse in the official track program to facilitate pari-mutuel wagering and to prevent errors due to the mispronunciation of horses' names, etc. (Obviously it is easier to say "Number Two" than "Fauchelevant.") The official program numbers frequently correspond with the post position numbers but late scratches, entries or a mutuel field may take them differ completely.

Mutuel Prices are the across-the-board pay-offs to holders of win, place or show mutuel tickets on the horses officially placed first, second and third. (NOTE: Odds to $1.00 are determined by deducting the $2.00 paid for the ticket from the official mutuel price and dividing the remainder in half. For example, winning $2.00 tickets on Autumn Gold paid $6.40. Deduct $2.00 for the cost of the ticket and you have winnings of $4.40. This is the net profit for a $2.00 wager. Divide $4.40 in half and you get $2.20, Autumn Gold's "equivalent odds to $1.00.")

Pedigree of Winner

Ch. c, by Autumn—Falling Leaves, by Gold Sun. Trainer F. J. Peters. Bred by Autumn Farm.

This is the pedigree, or breeding, of the winning horse, revealing that Autumn Gold is a chestnut (**ch**) colt (**c**) sired by **Autumn**, that his dam was **Falling Leaves**,

and that the sire of his dam was **Gold Sun**. This line also gives the name of the winner's present trainer, **F. J. Peters**, and the name of his breeder, **Autumn Farm**. In this case, Autumn Gold's breeder is also his present owner, but this is not always so. The breeder of a horse, as defined in The Jockey Club's Rules of Racing, "is the owner of his dam at the time of foaling."

In the charts of all 2-year-old races of 1965 the name of the state (abbreviated) in which the thoroughbred was foaled is shown directly after the name of the breeder in the pedigree line of the winner. The place of origin for 2-year-old winners foaled in Canada, Mexico or Puerto Rico is also indicated.

(NOTE: A complete list of color and sex abbreviations used in The Morning Telegraph's Official Result Charts and Past Performances appears on page 440.)

Post and Off Time

IN GATE AT 1.31. OFF AT 1.31¼ EASTERN STANDARD TIME. Start good. Won driving.

Virtually self-explanatory, this line shows that the entire field of 15 horses was locked in the starting gate at 31 minutes after 1 o'clock, Eastern Standard Time, and that the race was officially begun precisely 30 seconds later, that the field got away to a good start and the winner was "driving."

Footnotes

AUTUMN GOLD, away fast, raced forwardly placed to the stretch, assumed command when settled for the drive, and, continuing gamely under strong urging, held CROWN SEAL safe. The latter, in hand early, drifted to the middle of the track at the stretch turn, closed strongly when straightened but could not reach the winner. INDULGER, a strong factor from the start, swerved suddenly in midstretch, then, when straightened, went well to the finish. INDULGER was disqualified for interfering with PRELUDE and was placed fourth. PRELUDE, sluggish early, was making a strong run at the leaders when INDULGER swerved in front of him, forcing his rider to take up. MERCURIUS took an early lead, set the pace to the stretch under urging, then faltered in the drive. PRAIRIE MOON lacked early foot and could not threaten the leaders when set down for the drive. FOXLAND had no mishap. PROMPTITUDE was caught in close quarters entering the stretch. ROWLADDIE, fractious in the post parade, flashed brief speed and tired. The others were outrun from the start and were never in contention.

This is the chart-caller's expert description of the running which supplements the chart itself by relating in minute detail how most of the starters ran at various stages of the contest and calling attention to interference and other factors which have a bearing on performance. Among other important details, the footnotes point out that Indulger swerved in the stretch, blocking Prelude, for which he was disqualified.

Scratches

Scratched—Demolition, Engineer.

Listed here are the names of the horses who were originally entered in the race but did not start.

Waived Apprentice Allowance

†Five pounds apprentice allowance waived.

This notation indicates that Autumn Gold's trainer waived—or voluntarily relinquished—his privilege of a five-pound weight allowance had the horse been ridden by an apprentice jockey. In the entries filed the day before the race, an apprentice allowance was claimed for Autumn Gold, with the horse scheduled to carry 115 pounds, five pounds less than the 120 he would have had to carry with a full-fledged jockey up. By substituting G. L. Smith, a rider not entitled to the apprentice allowance, Autumn Gold's trainer gave up his claim to the five-pound concession and the horse carried his original assignment of 120 pounds.

Overweights

Overweights—Why Talk 1 pound, Rowladdie 2.

This line reveals that Why Talk carried one pound more and Rowladdie two pounds more than the conditions of the race, including apprentice allowances, required of them. In almost all cases, overweight is carried by a horse because the jockey is unable to "make" the stipulated weight. For example, Why Talk had one pound overweight because, although he was required to carry only 107 pounds, jockey O. Scurlock weighed 108 pounds. This, of course, included his saddle, etc.

Corrected Weight

Corrected weight—Promptitude 111 pounds.

Promptitude actually carried 111 pounds in the race, but this line shows that this weight has been corrected from the assignment originally announced for the horse. This situation arises when a weight allowance is either overlooked or mistakenly claimed by a trainer when the horse is entered. The corrected weight line is printed to indicate that this error was discovered before the race and the horse carried his required weight. The actual weight carried in the race by each horse appears in the chart and takes into account all allowances, overweight and corrections.

Claims

Crown Seal was claimed by Mrs. F. J. Smith, trainer R. P. Scott.

Self-explanatory, this reveals that Crown Seal was claimed by Mrs. F. J. Smith and that the horse's new trainer is R. P. Scott. Crown Seal's claiming price—the amount paid for him by his new owner—follows the jockey's name in the chart.

Symbols Infrequently Used in Charts

Disqualifications and dead-heats are not rare, but they are infrequent. However, The Morning Telegraph's Official Result Charts clearly indicate them when they do occur, as shown in the following lines from Sample Chart GS 22601.

Disqualifications:

22002Lrl² —ⒹIndulger   6 113 3 3   2ʰ 2ʰ 2ʰ 3ʰ W Hartack   9000 R J Hinds   Ⓓ3.50

Ⓓ before a horse's name and equivalent odds shows that he was disqualified. The symbol is repeated farther down in the chart under the running positions of the last horse, followed by an explanation of where the horse was placed, as follows:

ⒹDisqualified and placed fourth.

Dead-heats:

20811Suf⁶ —ⒹⴴPrairieMoon 9 117 10 10   10² 8² 7¹¹₂ 6   W Blum   10000 H Brown   ⴴf–20.10
22340Bow⁵ —ⴴFoxland b 6 122 6 8   7² 6¹ 6² 6²₂ H B Wilson 10000 C Jones   ⴴ90.20

The ⴴ symbol shows that Prairie Moon and Foxland finished in a dead-heat (tie). The ⴴ symbol appears before the name of each horse involved in the dead-heat and again before his equivalent odds. For further clarity, it is repeated directly above the fractional times in the chart, as follows:

ⴴDead–heat.

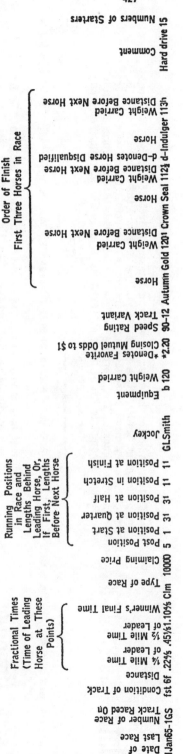

How to Read Past Performances

Past Performances are a statistical record of a horse's race, giving his position at the various calls in addition to considerable other data. A series of past performance lines is in effect a graph of all his most recent races, revealing his traits and his capabilities. The past performance line stems from the official result chart, containing the same important details in a slightly altered style. The sample past performance line below covers the race run by Autumn Gold in Sample Chart GS 22601. It is the story of a race in a line of type—and if you can read one line you can read them all. This illustrates how very simple it is to read that one line:

The sample past performance line, with labels:

Date of Last Race	1Jan65-1GS
Number of Race	
Track Raced On	
Condition of Track	fst
Distance	6f
Fractional Times (Time of Leading Horse at These Points)	.22⅖ .45½ 1.10⅘
¼ Mile Time of Leader	
½ Mile Time of Leader	
Winner's Final Time	
Type of Race	Clm
Claiming Price	10000
Post Position	5
Running Positions in Race and Lengths Behind Leading Horse, Or, If First, Lengths Before Next Horse — Position at Start	1
Position at Quarter	3¹
Position at Half	3¹
Position in Stretch	1¹
Position at Finish	1¹
Jockey	GLSmith
Equipment	b
Weight Carried	120
*Denotes Favorite / Closing Mutuel Odds to $1	*2.20
Speed Rating	90
Track Variant	-12
Order of Finish — First Three Horses in Race:	
Horse	Autumn Gold
Weight Carried	120
Distance Before Next Horse	1
Horse	Crown Seal
Weight Carried	112½
Distance Before Next Horse	¾
d–Denotes Horse Disqualified / Horse	d–Indulger
Weight Carried	113
Distance Before Next Horse	h
Comment	Hard drive
Numbers of Starters	15

1Jan65-1GS fst 6f .22⅘ .45⅕1.10⅘ Clm 10000 5 1 3^{1} 3^{1} 1^{1} 1^{1} GLSmith b 120 *2.20 90-12 Autumn Gold 120^{1} Crown Seal 112½ d-Indulger 113^{h} Hard drive 15

Date, Race, Track

1Jan65-1GS indicates that the race was run January 1, 1965. It was the first event on the program at Garden State Park (1GS). The date and the track given in the past performances make possible easy reference to the actual charts of the races either in back copies of The Morning Telegraph or in Daily Racing Form Monthly Chart Books. A complete list of track abbreviations used in The Morning Telegraph past performances appears on page 461.

1Jan65-1GS fst 6f .22⅘ .45⅕1.10⅘ Clm 10000 5 1 3^{1} 3^{1} 1^{1} 1^{1} GLSmith b 120 *2.20 90-12 Autumn Gold 120^{1} Crown Seal 112½ d-Indulger 113^{h} Hard drive 15

Track Condition

Track conditions may change during the course of one racing program. The fst notation in the past performance line indicates that the track was fast for this particular race.

Other track conditions are indicated in the past performances as follows:

14Mar64-1LD fr 7f .24⅘ .49⅗1.29 Clm 2000 1 4 $1^{1\frac{1}{2}}$ $1^{2\frac{1}{2}}$ 1^{1} 1no OHeadley 114 *1.90 82-15 Cellero 114no Scarlet Ibis 114^{8} Danny O. $112^{2\frac{3}{4}}$ Held on stubbornly 8

fr—Track frozen.

11May64-3Pim gd 6f .24⅕ .48⅗1.12 Allowance 5 4 3^{1} 2^{2} 1^{1} 1^{4} SPalumbo b 114 3.60 90-14 Will'gHands 114^{4} RedBarn 115^{nk} LineScore 113no Drew out handily 8

gd—Track good.

15Apr64-1Bow sl 6f .24 .49⅕1.15⅕ Clm 5000 3 8 5^{7} 8^{8} 9^{9} 9^{12} HGrant b 115 55.50 63-24 Best Dress 110^{3} Old Union $113^{2\frac{1}{2}}$ Green Hat 114^{nk} Fell back early 10

sl—Track slow.

1Jun62-3Bel sly 7f .22⅘ .46⅗1.24 Allowance 5 1 3^{1} 3^{4} 5^{7} 8^{10} WBoland b 115 16.60 80-15 Prof. Higgins 115^{3} Pickering 114^{1} Foolish Fancy 112^{h} Tired 10

sly—Track sloppy.

22May64-3Del my 1¼.50⅗1.16⅗2.12⅗ Clm 4000 6 2 1^{1} 1^{2} 1^{4} 1^{6} SArmstrong b 113 *0.80 55-33 By the Book 113^{6} Rigid 115^{4} Righteous 110^{1} Drew out easily 9

my—Track muddy.

14Apr64-2Atl hy 1⅛.51 1.14⅗1.53⅕ Handicap 3 1 1^{3} 1^{3} 1^{3} 1^{4} WLester b 117 3.25 80-21 Valdina Maiden 114^{4} Going Great $114^{2\frac{1}{2}}$ Show Award 119^{1} Driving 8

hy—Track heavy.

Track conditions for races contested over the turf, hurdle and steeplechase courses are indicated as follows:

11Sep62-3Bel fm*2 S'chase 3.42⅕ Allowance 5 4 4^{10} 5^{8} 3^{6} 2^{5} FDAdams sb 154 4.50 —— Over Hill 157^{5} Wishing Well 154^{2} Coming In 135^{5} Finished well 8

fm—Course firm.

11Jly 63-3Aqu gd $1\frac{1}{8}$ TC 1.13⅘ 1.49 Handicap 1 4 2^{3} $2^{1\frac{1}{2}}$ $2^{2\frac{1}{2}}$ 1^{nk} JDJohn b 114 *1.70 90– 8 Johnnie J. 114^{nk} Sol R. 118^{2} Fred G. 113^{2} Up in last strides 10

Gd—Course good.

3Jun63-5Del sf $1\frac{1}{2}$ Hurdles 2.50 Clm 4000 4 7 2^{1} 3^{5} 4^{8} 8^{10} CPeoples b 135 45.50 —— June J. 131no Willybill 143^{nk} Prim Glow 133^{3} Early speed, tired 10

sf—Course soft.

8Jan63-4SA hd $1\frac{1}{4}$ TC 1.59 Allowance 1 5 5^{5} $6^{6\frac{1}{2}}$ 6^{13} 6^{19} GTaniguchi 114 7.00 80–10 Louisa Kid 114^{3} Sand Dunes 114^{6} Johnny Macan 111^{2} Fell far back 12

hd—Course hard.

1Jan65-1GS fst 6f .22⅘ .45⅕ 1.10⅘ Clm 10000 5 1 3^{1} 3^{1} 1^{1} 1^{1} GLSmith b 120 *2.20 90–12 Autumn Gold 120^{1} Crown Seal $112^{\frac{1}{2}}$ d–Indulger 113^{h} Hard drive 15

Distance of Race

6f shows that the distance of the race was six furlongs (three-quarters of a mile). At some tracks, races are run over certain courses which may be several feet longer or shorter than the accepted standard distance. Races at these "about" distances are indicated by an asterisk, as indicated below. In this instance, the race was at "about six furlongs."

1Jan65-1GS fst*6f .22⅘ .45⅕ 1.10⅘ Clm 10000 5 1 3^{1} 3^{1} 1^{1} 1^{1} GLSmith b 120 *2.20 90–12 Autumn Gold 120^{1} Crown Seal $112^{\frac{1}{2}}$ d–Indulger 113^{h} Hard drive 15

Special Courses

At many tracks, races are run over courses other than the main dirt racing strip. Special identification of these courses is made in the past performance lines following the distance of the race, as follows:

6Jun63–8Was fm$1\frac{1}{16}$TC 1.12 1.43 Handicap 1 5 2^{3} 3^{4} $7^{8\frac{1}{4}}$ $7^{7\frac{1}{2}}$ JAdams 120 2.50 92– 2 Sir Tribal $119^{2\frac{1}{4}}$ Bozi $110^{\frac{1}{2}}$ Hasseyampa $120^{1\frac{1}{2}}$ Lacked racing room 9

tc indicates that the race was contested over the track's turf (grass) course.

30Aug64-5Sar sf*2½ S'chase 5.16⅗ SarStplH 2 6 $6^{7\frac{1}{2}}$ $6^{6\frac{1}{2}}$ $4^{5\frac{1}{2}}$ $2^{2\frac{3}{4}}$ JMurphy 143 3.00 —— Mighty Mo $138^{2\frac{3}{4}}$ Carthage 143^{2} Basilia 130^{h} Strong stretch bid 6

S'chase indicates that the race was contested over the steeplechase course. A steeplechase is a race on grass in which the horses must jump over a certain number of obstacles placed at specified intervals.

2Aug64-3Mth fm*1¾ Hurdles 3.20⅕ Clm 4000 7 2 $2^{\frac{1}{2}}$ $1^{\frac{1}{2}}$ 1^{h} 1^{h} MHoey 146 *1.90 —— Hurst Park 146^{h} Get Lost 136^{4} Marcheast 145^{4} Fully extended 7

Hurdles indicates the race was run over the hurdle course. A hurdle race is similar to a steeplechase in that they are both raced over the grass and over obstacles. However, the required height of the obstacles in a hurdle race is less than that for a steeplechase event.

Fractional Times

The fractional times in past performances vary, hinging on the distance of the race. In events under one mile, fractional times are given for the quarter-mile, half-mile and finish. In races at one mile or more, the fractional times are for the half-mile, three-quarters and finish. The sample past performance line printed below pertains to a race at six furlongs (three-quarters of a mile), thus the fractional times are for the quarter, half and finish, as illustrated:

1Jan65-1GS fst 6f .22⅘ .45⅕ 1.10⅘ Clm 10000 5 1 3[1] 3[1] 1[1] 1[1] GLSmith b 120 *2.20 90-12 Autumn Gold 120[1] Crown Seal 112½ d-Indulger 113[h] Hard drive 15

.22⅘ is the running time of the horse in front at the quarter.

.45⅕ is the running time of the horse in front at the half.

1.10⅘ is the running time of the horse in front at the finish of the six-furlong race. (Note: In the event of a disqualification, this is the running time of the horse in front at the finish, even though he is not the official winner.)

To determine the approximate running time of a horse who finished other than first, add one-fifth of a second for each length he was beaten to the wire. For example, if a horse finished nine lengths behind Autumn Gold, who completed the six furlongs in 1.10⅘, his approximate time would be 1.12⅗ (nine lengths equals one and four-fifths seconds). NOTE: In computing the approximate running time of beaten horses, fractions of one-half length or more are considered as one full length or one-fifth second in time.

1Jan65-1GS fst 6f .22⅘ .45⅕ 1.10⅘ Clm 10000 5 1 3[1] 3[1] 1[1] 1[1] GLSmith b 120 *2.20 90-12 Autumn Gold 120[1] Crown Seal 112½ d-Indulger 113[h] Hard drive 15

Class of Race

Clm 10000 indicates that the race was a claiming race and the price for which Autumn Gold was entered to be claimed was $10,000. If Autumn Gold had been claimed out of this race, the letter (c) would precede his claiming price in the past performance line as follows:

1Jan65-1GS fst 6f .22⅘ .45⅕ 1.10⅘ Cl c-10000 5 1 3[1] 3[1] 1[1] 1[1] GLSmith b 120 *2.20 90-12 Autumn Gold 120[1] Crown Seal 112½ d-Indulger 113[h] Hard drive 15

1Jan65-1GS fst 6f .22$\frac{4}{5}$ .45$\frac{1}{5}$1.10$\frac{4}{5}$ Clm 10000 5 1 3^1 3^1 1^1 1^1 GLSmith b 120 *2.20 90-12 Autumn Gold 120^1 Crown Seal $112\frac{1}{2}$ d-Indulger 113^h Hard drive 15

Post Position

5 was Autumn Gold's post position, meaning that he occupied the fifth stall from the rail in the starting gate.

1Jan65-1GS fst 6f .22$\frac{4}{5}$ .45$\frac{1}{5}$1.10$\frac{4}{5}$ Clm 10000 5 1 3^1 3^1 1^1 1^1 GLSmith b 120 *2.20 90-12 Autumn Gold 120^1 Crown Seal $112\frac{1}{2}$ d-Indulger 113^h Hard drive 15

Position at Start

1 indicates that Autumn Gold was in first place shortly after the field left the starting gate. (NOTE: In races of one mile or more, the position at the start is eliminated and the horse's position at the next point of call — quarter-mile — is substituted for the start call.)

1Jan65-1GS fst 6f .22$\frac{4}{5}$ .45$\frac{1}{5}$1.10$\frac{4}{5}$ Clm 10000 5 1 3^1 3^1 1^1 1^1 GLSmith b 120 *2.20 90-12 Autumn Gold 120^1 Crown Seal $112\frac{1}{2}$ d-Indulger 113^h Hard drive 15

At the Quarter

3^1 indicates that Autumn Gold was running third at the completion of a quarter-mile, one length behind the leading horses at that point.

1Jan65-1GS fst 6f .22$\frac{4}{5}$ .45$\frac{1}{5}$1.10$\frac{4}{5}$ Clm 10000 5 1 3^1 3^1 1^1 1^1 GLSmith b 120 *2.20 90-12 Autumn Gold 120^1 Crown Seal $112\frac{1}{2}$ d-Indulger 113^h Hard drive 15

At the Half

3^1 shows that Autumn Gold was still running third after the completion of one-half mile of the race, one length behind the leading horses at that point. This position is also known as the "pre-stretch call."

1Jan65-1GS fst 6f .22$\frac{4}{5}$ .45$\frac{1}{5}$1.10$\frac{4}{5}$ Clm 10000 5 1 3^1 3^1 1^1 1^1 GLSmith b 120 *2.20 90-12 Autumn Gold 120^1 Crown Seal $112\frac{1}{2}$ d-Indulger 113^h Hard drive 15

In the Stretch

1^1 reveals that Autumn Gold moved up to take the lead in the stretch, usually one-eighth of a mile from the finish line, and was one length in front of the second horse.

1Jan65-1GS fst 6f .22⅘ .45⅕1.10⅘ Clm 10000 5 1 3¹ 3¹ 1¹ 1¹ GLSmith b 120 *2.20 90-12 Autumn Gold 120¹ Crown Seal 112½ d-Indulger 113h Hard drive 15

At the Finish

1¹ indicates that Autumn Gold maintained his lead and reached the finish line one length in front of the second horse.

Various Points Of Call

The points of call of the five running positions (excluding the post position but including the start) given in the past performances vary according to the distance of the race. The following table lists the points of call of the running positions for the most frequently raced distances:

Distance of Race	1st Position at	2nd Position at	3rd Position at	4th Position at	5th Position at
2 Furlongs	Start	—	—	Stretch	Finish
5/16 Mile	Start	—	—	Stretch	Finish
3 Furlongs	Start	—	—	Stretch	Finish
4 Furlongs	Start	—	¼ mile	Stretch	Finish
4½ Furlongs	Start	—	¼ mile	Stretch	Finish
5 Furlongs	Start	3/16 mile	⅜ mile	Stretch	Finish
5½ Furlongs	Start	¼ mile	½ mile	Stretch	Finish
6 Furlongs	Start	¼ mile	½ mile	Stretch	Finish
6½ Furlongs	Start	¼ mile	½ mile	Stretch	Finish
7 Furlongs	Start	¼ mile	½ mile	Stretch	Finish
1 Mile	¼ mile	½ mile	¾ mile	Stretch	Finish
1 Mile, 70 Yds	¼ mile	½ mile	¾ mile	Stretch	Finish
1 1/16 Miles	¼ mile	½ mile	¾ mile	Stretch	Finish
1⅛ Miles	¼ mile	½ mile	¾ mile	Stretch	Finish
1 3/16 Miles	¼ mile	½ mile	¾ mile	Stretch	Finish
1¼ Miles	¼ mile	½ mile	1 mile	Stretch	Finish
1 5/16 Miles	¼ mile	½ mile	1 mile	Stretch	Finish
1⅜ Miles	¼ mile	½ mile	1⅛ miles	Stretch	Finish
1½ Miles	¼ mile	½ mile	1¼ miles	Stretch	Finish
1⅝ Miles	¼ mile	½ mile	1⅜ miles	Stretch	Finish
1¾ Miles	¼ mile	½ mile	1½ miles	Stretch	Finish

1Jan65-1GS fst 6f .22⅘ .45⅕1.10⅘ Clm 10000 5 1 3¹ 3¹ 1¹ 1¹ GLSmith b 120 *2.20 90-12 Autumn Gold 120¹ Crown Seal 112½ d-Indulger 113h Hard drive 15

Jockey

GLSmith reveals that Autumn Gold was ridden by jockey G. L. Smith. Apprentice weight allowances are indicated by a superior figure, denoting the amount of the allowance, following the jockey's name ($^{3\ 5\ 7\ 10}$). Thus, if Autumn Gold had been ridden by an apprentice for whom a weight allowance of three pounds had been claimed, his past performance line would appear as follows:

1Jan65-1GS fst 6f .22⅘ .45⅕1.10⅘ Clm 10000 5 1 3¹ 3¹ 1¹ 1¹ GLSmith³ b 120 *2.20 90-12 Autumn Gold 120¹ Crown Seal 112½ d-Indulger 113h Hard drive 15

1Jan65-1GS fst 6f .22⅘ .45⅕1.10⅘ Clm 10000 5 1 3¹ 3¹ 1¹ 1¹ GLSmith b 120 *2.20 90-12 Autumn Gold 120¹ Crown Seal 112½ d-Indulger 113h Hard drive 15

Equipment

b reveals that Autumn Gold was equipped with blinkers (b). If the rider wore spurs, this would be indicated by the letter s. NOTE: All riders are equipped with whips unless the chart footnotes indicate otherwise.

1Jan65-1GS fst 6f .22⅘ .45⅕1.10⅘ Clm 10000 5 1 3¹ 3¹ 1¹ 1¹ GLSmith b 120 *2.20 90-12 Autumn Gold 120¹ Crown Seal 112½ d-Indulger 113h Hard drive 15

Weight

120 reveals that Autumn Gold carried 120 pounds.

1Jan65-1GS fst 6f .22⅘ .45⅕1.10⅘ Clm 10000 5 1 3^1 3^1 1^1 1^1 GLSmith b 120 *2.20 90–12 Autumn Gold 120^1 Crown Seal 112½ d–Indulger 113^h Hard drive 15

Equivalent Odds

***2.20** was Autumn Gold's equivalent odds—his closing odds to $1.00—in the win pool of the pari-mutuel betting. The star (*) preceding the equivalent odds indicates that he was the favorite in the wagering.

SYMBOLS DENOTING ENTRIES, FIELD HORSES, ETC.

Entries, field horses, dead-heats and disqualifications are indicated by various symbols before the equivalent odds. They are shown in the past performances as follows:

1Jan65-1GS fst 6f .22⅘ .45⅕1.10⅘ Clm 10000 5 1 3^1 3^1 1^1 1^1 GLSmith b 120 *2.20e 90–12 Autumn Gold 120^1 Crown Seal 112½ d–Indulger 113^h Hard drive 15

e is the symbol used to indicate horse was a member of a stable entry.

1Jan65-1GS fst 6f .22⅘ .45⅕1.10⅘ Clm 10000 5 1 3^1 3^1 1^1 1^1 GLSmith b 120 *2.20f 90–12 Autumn Gold 120^1 Crown Seal 112½ d–Indulger 113^h Hard drive 15

f is the symbol used to indicate horse was a member of the mutuel field.

1Jan65-1GS fst 6f .22⅘ .45⅕1.10⅘ Clm 10000 5 1 3^1 3^1 1^1 1^1 GLSmith b 120 •*2.20 90–12 •Autumn Gold 120^1 Crown Seal 112½ d–Indulger 113^h Hard drive 15
1Jan65 –•–Dead heat.

• is the symbol used to indicate horse finished in a dead-heat. For further emphasis, the date of the race, symbol and words "Dead-heat," are repeated directly below the past performance line.

1Jan65-1GS fst 6f .22⅘ .45⅕1.10⅘ Clm 10000 3 3 2^1 2^1 2^1 3^{1½} WHartack w 113 d–3.50 88–12 Autumn Gold 120^1 Crown Seal 112½ d–Indulger 113^h Swerved out 15
1Jan65 –d–Disqualified and placed fourth.

d preceding the equivalent odds indicates that the horse was disqualified from the position in which he actually finished. The disqualification symbol (d) is repeated beneath the past performance line for that date followed by an explanation of where the horse was placed.

When a horse is moved up too a higher finishing position because of the disqualification of another horse, this is indicated by a footnote under the past performance line for that race, as follows:

1Jan65-1GS fst 6f .22⅘ .45⅕1.10⅘ Clm 10000 7 9 8^{5¾} 7^{6½} 5^3 4^{1½} JRuane b 111 15.40 88–12 Autumn Gold 120^1 Crown Seal 112½ d–Indulger 113^h Blocked 15
1Jan65–Placed third through disqualification.

1Jan65-1GS fst 6f .22⅘ .45⅕1.10⅘ Clm 10000 5 1 3¹ 3¹ 1¹ 1¹ GLSmith b 120 *2.20 90–12 Autumn Gold 120¹ Crown Seal 112½ d–Indulger 113h Hard drive 15

Speed Rating

90 is Autumn Gold's speed rating. The speed rating is a comparison of the horse's running time with the track record for the distance which was in effect at the opening of the meeting. The track record time receives the standard rating of 100. For each one-fifth of a second a horse betters or runs slower than the track record, one point is added to or subtracted from 100 to determine his speed rating for that particular race. Thus, if a horse equals the track record his speed rating for that race would be 100. If he breaks the track record by two-fifths of a second, his speed rating would be 102. In Autumn Gold's instance, his time of 1.10⅘ was two full seconds (10 fifths) slower than the track record of 1.08⅘, necessitating a deduction of 10 points from the standard of 100 to give him a speed rating of 90. No speed ratings are given for steeplechase or hurdle events, or for races of less than three furlongs.

(NOTE: In races for which The Morning Telegraph prints its own time—in addition to the official track time—the speed rating is computed on the basis of the official track time.)

1Jan65-1GS fst 6f .22⅘ .45⅕1.10⅘ Clm 10000 5 1 3¹ 3¹ 1¹ 1¹ GLSmith b 120 *2.20 90–12 Autumn Gold 120¹ Crown Seal 112½ d–Indulger 113h Hard drive 15

Track Variant

12 is the track variant for the day. The track variant shows how many points below par the track was that day on the basis of the times for all of the races run. The track record is par (100) and each race is scored according to the number of points (one point is equivalent to one-fifth of a second) it is off the record. In other words, the score for each race is the speed rating of the winner. Thus, a race run two seconds slower than the track record is a "90" race. The average for all the races of the day is taken and the difference between this average and 100 is the track variant. If the track condition changes during the course of the program, races run over fast, frozen and good strips are used in striking one average, while races run on slow, sloppy, muddy and heavy strips are brought together in another average. If all the races are run in either one or the other of these two general classifications, then only one average is computed. For instance, if the average of eight races all run on fast, frozen or good strips is 88, then the track variant for the day is 12. This figure could reflect the condition of the track and the grade of horses who ran in all races that day. No track variant is given for steeplechase or hurdle events.

NOTE: A separate track variant is computed for races run on the turf (grass) course, and for races of less than five furlongs.

1Jan65-1GS fst 6f .22⅘ .45⅕1.10⅘ Clm 10000 5 1 3[1] 3[1] 1[1] 1[1] GLSmith b 120 *2.20 90-12 Autumn Gold 120[1] Crown Seal 112½ d-Indulger 113[h] Hard drive 15

First Three Finishers

Autumn Gold 120[1] Crown Seal 112½ d-Indulger 113[h] are the first three horses in the order of finish. Following each horse's name is the weight carried. The superior figure after the weight is the horse's margin in front of the next horse following. Thus Autumn Gold finished first, carried 120 pounds, and was one length before Crown Seal. Crown Seal ran second, carried 112 pounds, and was one-half length before Indulger. Indulger carried 113 pounds and was a head in front of the fourth horse. The letter d before Indulger's name indicates that he was disqualified from this position. If one or more of the first three finishers was in a dead-heat, the dead-heat symbol (•) will precede the name of the horses involved.

1Jan65-1GS fst 6f .22⅘ .45⅕1.10⅘ Clm 10000 5 1 3[1] 3[1] 1[1] 1[1] GLSmith b 120 *2.20 90-12 Autumn Gold 120[1] Crown Seal 112½ d-Indulger 113[h] Hard drive 15

Comment

Hard drive is a condensation of the chart maker's comment on Autumn Gold's performance as it originally appeared in the chart footnotes. The comment will also note if the horse was involved in any untoward incidents or if he broke down, bled, appeared sore, etc.

1Jan65-1GS fst 6f .22⅘ .45⅕1.10⅘ Clm 10000 5 1 3[1] 3[1] 1[1] 1[1] GLSmith b 120 *2.20 90-12 Autumn Gold 120[1] Crown Seal 112½ d-Indulger 113[h] Hard drive 15

Size of Field

15 reveals that 15 horses started in the race.

Special Footnotes

All races run at recognized North American tracks are timed separately by a member of The Morning Telegraph's staff of clockers. When the time recorded for the race by The Morning Telegraph clocker differs from the track's official time, special note of this is made in the chart and it appears in the past performance line as follows:

```
1Jan65-1GS  fst 6f .22⅘ .45⅕1.10⅘ Clm 10000 5 1 3^1 3^1 1^1 1^1 GLSmith  b 120 *2.20 90-12 Autumn Gold 120^1 Crown Seal 112^1/2 d-Indulger 113^h   Hard drive 15
   1Jan65--The Morning Telegraph time, 1.11⅕.
```

In cases where a horse is disqualified and only the distribution of the purse is affected—rulings which usually are made several days after the running of the race—this is indicated by a special footnote under the past performance line as follows:

```
1Jan65-1GS  fst 6f .22⅘ .45⅕1.10⅘ Clm 10000 3 3 2^1 2^1 2^1 3^1 1/2 WHartack  113 3.50 88-12 Autumn Gold 120^1 Crown Seal 112^1/2 d-Indulger 113^h   Swerved out 15
   1Jan65--Disqualified from purse money.
1Jan65-1GS  fst 6f .22⅘ .45⅕1.10⅘ Clm 10000 7 9 8^5 3/4 7^6 1/2 5^3 4^1 1/2 JRuane  b 111 15.40 88-12 Autumn Gold 120^1 Crown Seal 112^1/2 d-Indulger 113^h   Blocked 15
   1Jan65--Awarded third purse money.
```

Occasionally, special races are held on which there is no betting, but which are included in a horse's past performances. When no wagering is held on a race, a dash appears in place of the closing mutuel odds, with an explanatory footnote under the past performance line, as follows:

```
1Jan65-1GS  fst 6f .22⅘ .45⅕1.10⅘ Clm 10000 5 1 3^1 3^1 1^1 1^1 GLSmith  b 120 —— 90-12 Autumn Gold 120^1 Crown Seal 112^1/2 d-Indulger 113^h   Hard drive 6
   1Jan65-Special Race—Run between fourth and fifth races. No wagering.
```

Autumn Gold's Past Performances

While the condensations of the charts of several of Autumn Gold's races are the most important part of his past performances, much other vital data is included when these past performances are printed in The Morning Telegraph on the day the horse is entered in a race. Following is how Autumn Gold's past performances, with seven hypothetical races, would appear in The Morning Telegraph:

```
Autumn Gold *   $12,500   Ch. c (1961), by Autumn—Falling Leaves, by Gold Sun          115   1965  1  1  0  0   $2,400
                          Autumn Farm     F. J. Peters            (Autumn Farm)             1964  6  3  0  2  $16,980
1Jan65-1GS   fst 6f .22⅘ .45⅕1.10⅘ Clm 10000 5 1 3^1 3^1 1^1 1^1 GLSmith  b 120 *2.20 90-12 Autumn Gold 120^1 Crown Seal 112^1/2 d-Indulger 113^h   Hard drive 15
22May64-4GS  sly 6f .23⅕ .46⅖1.11⅗ Clm  9000 6 3 3^3 1^no 1^nk 1^3 GLSmith  b 117 3.40 86-16 AutumnGold117^3 Wavering115^nk CrownSeal 115^2 Driving, drew clear 9
13May64-6GS  fst 6f .22⅖ .45  1.10⅖ Allowance 9 4 2^2 4^5 4^7 5^8 HGrant  b 114 5.70 84-11 Honshu 114^3 Hornbrook 117^2 Laurens 115^nk   Early speed, tired 10
   13May64- The Morning Telegraph time, 1.10⅘.
20Mar64-6GP  fst 6f .22⅕ .44⅗1.10⅖ Handicap 3 2 2^2 2^1 2^nk 3^1 GLSmith  b 118 4.40 92-15 Madrigal 111^no Pentathlon 119^1 Autumn Gold 118^3   Faltered 9
29Jan64-4Hia fst 6f .22⅕ .45⅗1.11⅗ Clm 10000 6 1 1^1 1^3 1^5 1^8 GLSmith  b 116 *0.90 82-16 Autumn Gold 116^8 Reparations 113^2 1/2 Rushville 113^nk   Easily 10
9Jan64-6TrP  fst 6f .21⅘ .45  1.10⅕ Allowance 1 1 1^1 1^1 1^1 1/4 1^1 3/4 GLSmith  b 113 2.50 89-14 Autumn Gold 113^1 3/4 Breakwater 115^1/2 Mangrove 115^3   Hard drive 8
1Jan64-5TrP  fst 6f .21⅗ .44⅘1.10  Allowance 5 5 1^1 1^2 2^nk 3^3 GLSmith  b 115 6.30 87-11 Breakwater 114^no Lankester 118^3 Autumn Gold 115^2 1/4   Weakened 9
LATEST WORKOUTS   Dec 30 GS 3f fst .37 h   Dec 26 GS 4f fst .51 b   Dec 20 GS 3f fst .36⅗ h   Dec 17 GS 5f fst 1.01⅕ h
```

Pedigree, Owner, Trainer, Weight, Record

NOTE: (*) preceding a horse's name indicates that he was bred in a foreign country. (with the exception that no notation is made for horses bred in Canada or Mexico.)

The figure to the right of the horse's name ($12,500) is the claiming price for which he is entered. If the race is not a claiming event, this space is left blank.

The asterisk(✳) following Autumn Gold's name denotes that on the basis of his past performances he has been classified as a fair mud runner. The symbol ✕ denotes a good mud runner; ⊗ a superior mud runner. The absence of a symbol suggests that the horse has shown no particular preference for an "off" track.

Ch. c (1961), by Autumn—Falling Leaves, by Gold Sun		115	1965	1 1 0 0	$2,400
Autumn Farm F. J. Peters	(Autumn Farm)		1964	6 3 0 2	$16,980

This is Autumn Gold's color, sex, year foaled and pedigree, showing that he is a chestnut (**ch.**) colt (**c**),foaled in 1961, by **Autumn** from the mare **Falling Leaves**, who in turn, was sired by **Gold Sun**. This portion of his past performances also lists the present owner of Autumn Gold (**Autumn Farm**), his trainer (**F. J. Peters**) and, in parentheses, his breeder (**Autumn Farm**.)

Effective with the racing of 1965, the pedigree line of all 2-year-olds (foals of 1963) includes the name of the state (abbreviated) in which the thoroughbred was foaled. The place of origin of 2-year-olds foaled in Canada, Mexico and Puerto Rico is also indicated.

The large figure to the right (**115**) is the weight, with all allowances taken into consideration, Autumn Gold is scheduled to carry in this particular race. The superior figure (3), (5), (7) or (10) after the weight would indicate the number of pounds claimed for apprentice rider.

At the extreme right is Autumn Gold's race and earnings record for the past two years. This reveals that in 1964 he started 6 times; winning **three** races and finishing third **twice**, and that he earned **$16,980**. In 1965, up to the date of this race, he started **once** and won that race, earning **$2,400**. If a horse is a maiden, the letter **M** will appear in his record line. If **M** appears only in the previous year's record column it indicates that the horse was still a maiden at the end of that year.

LATEST WORKOUTS Dec 30 GS 3f fst .37 h Dec 26 GS 4f fst .51 b Dec 20 GS 3f fst .36⅗ h Dec 17 GS 5f fst 1.01⅕ h

Latest Workouts

Directly under Autumn Gold's past past performances are his **latest workouts.** Using his most recent workout as an example, it is noted that this trial took place on December 30 at Garden State Park **(GS)**, that the distance of the workout was three furlongs **(3f)**, the track was fast **(fst)**, the time of the workout was 37 seconds **(.37)** and that he accomplished his trial handily **(h)**. Abbreviations for the track and track conditions, for workouts, are the same as those used in the past performances. When a track has more than one course, the abbreviation **tr.t.** after the name of the track indicates the workout was over the training track; **m.t.** indicates the workout was over the main track and **t.c.** indicates the workout was over the turf course. All workouts are on the main track unless otherwise indicated. The following abbreviations are used after the time of the workout to indicate the manner in which the horse accomplished his move: **h**-handily, **b**-breezing, **e**-easily, **d**-driving, **u**-eased up, **o**-all out, **ro**-ran out. If any of these symbols is followed by the letter g, it indicates the horse began his workout by breaking from the starting gate.

Past Performances Of Foreign Races

In recent years, many horses who were bred and raced in foreign countries have come to the United States to compete. When such a horse is entered in a race here, The Morning Telegraph publishes past performance lines for those events in which he raced abroad. Although charts of European races are incomplete by American standards, The Morning Telegraph has made arrangements with foreign jockey clubs and racing organizations to obtain whatever such information is available. These limited past performances appear in The Morning Telegraph as follows:

9Nov56-Curragh (Ire.)	sf 1	1.46⅘TC	Beresford Stakes (Flat)	4$1\frac{1}{4}$	ABrabazon	131	8.00	——	Viviptic 116no Star Prince 125$1\frac{1}{4}$ Sail Aniar 126^{h}	Went well 11
6Oct56-Curragh (Ire.)	sf*6½f	1.23⅖TC	Nat'l Produce Stks (Flat)	1^{2}	TPBurns	118	6.00	——	El Minzah 118^{2} Spelling Bee 121^{1} No.Complaint 136^{nk}	Going away 14
29Sep56-Leopardstown(Ire.)	sf*7f	1.36⅖TC	Laragh Plate (Flat)	2^{2}	MKennedy	125	6.00	——	Ballymoss 126^{2} El Minzah 125^{4} Sun Invasion 126^{1}	Closed fast 16

These past performances follow the same general style as those used for races run in America, but fractional times, running positions, speed rating and track variant are omitted. From left to right, the past performance lines for races run at foreign tracks show the date of the race, track raced on, country, condition of track, distance, time of winner, name of race, whether race was on the flat or over jumps, position at finish with winning or beaten margin, jockey, weight carried, closing odds, first three finishers, comment and number of starters.

Color Abbreviations

The following abbreviations are used in The Morning Telegraph Official Result Charts and Past Performances to indicate the colors of thoroughbreds. The descriptions of the colors which follow have been provided by The Jockey Club:

B.—Bay. Bay varies from a light yellowish tan (light bay) to a dark rich shade, almost brown, and between these, a bright mahogany (blood bay). Bays always have black mane and tail, black points.

Br.—Brown. Brown is sometimes difficult to tell from black to dark bay, but can be distinguished by noting the fine tan or brown hairs on the muzzle or flanks.

Blk.—Black. If any doubt arises in distinguishing between dark brown and black, the black can be determined by noting the fine black hair on the muzzle.

Ch.—Chestnut. Chestnut varies from a dark liver color to a light washy yellow, between which comes the brilliant red gold and copper shades. A chestnut never has a black mane, tail or points.

Gr.—Gray. Gray is a mixture of white hairs and black, sometimes scarcely distinguishable from black at birth, getting lighter with age.

Ro.—Roan. There are two classes of roan—red, or strawberry, produced by intermingling of red, white and yellow hairs, and the blue, produced by intermingling of black, white and yellow hairs.

(NOTE: The predominant color among thoroughbreds is bay, about 46 per cent being of that coat. About 30 per cent are chestnuts, 18 per cent browns, 3 per cent blacks, 2 per cent grays and 1 per cent roans.)

Sex Abbreviations

Sex abbreviations used in The Morning Telegraph Official Result Charts and Past Performances are as follows:

c—colt. An entire male through four years of age.

h—horse. An entire male five years old or older.

g—gelding. A male of any age who has been unsexed.

f—filly. A female through four years of age.

m—mare. A female five years old or older.

rig—ridgling. A male of any age with one or both organs of reproduction absent from the sac.

Explanation Of Different Races

Claiming races predominate at most tracks but racing secretaries have a variety of other events in their condition books. The abbreviation for each of these races is printed where the claiming price normally appears in the past performances. The following examples show the abbreviations used for these other races, with a brief outline of what they are:

Note: Races exclusively for fillies or fillies and mares are indicated by the letter "f" before race classification. Example, f-15000—filly or filly and mare race—entered for $15,000. Other examples shown in parenthesis in explanation below.

1Jan63-1GS fst 6f .22⅘ .45⅕1.10⅘ Md Sp Wt 5 1 3^1 3^1 1^1 1^1 GLSmith b 120 *2.20 90-12 Autumn Gold 120^1 Crown Seal 112½ d-Indulger 113^h Hard drive 15

▲ **Md Sp Wt**—Maiden Special Weight race. A race exclusively for maidens who are to carry the special weight listed in the conditions. (A maiden is a horse of either sex who, at time of starting, has never won a race on the flat in any country other than a match or private sweepstakes. A maiden who has been disqualified after having finished first is still a maiden.) (f-MdSpWt).

1Jan63-1GS fst 6f .22⅘ .45⅕1.10⅘ Md Allow 5 1 3^1 3^1 1^1 1^1 GLSmith b 120 *2.20 90-12 Autumn Gold 120^1 Crown Seal 112½ d-Indulger 113^h Hard drive 15

▲ **Md Allow**—Maiden Allowance race. A race restricted to maidens who have previously started in a claiming race. (f-MdAlw).

1Jan63-1GS fst 6f .22⅘ .45⅕1.10⅘ Spec'l Wt 5 1 3^1 3^1 1^1 1^1 GLSmith b 120 *2.20 90-12 Autumn Gold 120^1 Crown Seal 112½ d-Indulger 113^h Hard drive 15

▲ **Spec'l Wt**—Special Weight race. A race in which the weights are fixed by the racing secretary in the conditions of the race. (f-Specl Wt).

1Jan63-1GS fst 6f .22⅘ .45⅕1.10⅘ Allowance 5 1 3^1 3^1 1^1 1^1 GLSmith b 120 *2.20 90-12 Autumn Gold 120^1 Crown Seal 112½ d-Indulger 113^h Hard drive 15

▲ **Allowance**—Allowance race. An event in which the entrants receive weight allowances for not having won a designated amount of money or number of races over a stated period of time. (f-Allow) For example, here are the actual conditions written by Racing Secretary F. E. Kilroe for an allowance race at Belmont Park:

> "4-year-olds and upward. For non-winners of two races of $4,125 each since March 31, 1956. Weight, 122 lbs. Non-winners of two races of any kind since March 30 or a race of $7,000 in 1956-57 allowed 3 lbs., a race of $3,900 since March 30 or two such races since July 7, 6 lbs., a race of $3,500 at one mile or over since July 7, 9 lbs."

1Jan63-1GS fst 6f .22⅘ .45⅕1.10⅘ Handicap 5 1 3^1 3^1 1^1 1^1 GLSmith b 120 *2.20 90-12 Autumn Gold 120^1 Crown Seal 112½ d-Indulger 113^h Hard drive 15

▲ **Handicap**—Overnight Handicap. A race in which the weights to be carried by the horses are assigned by the track handicapper to equalize their chances of winning. Entries for "overnight" events close 72 hours or less—exclusive of Sundays—before the day of the race. (f-H'dicap).

1Jan63-1GS fst 6f .22⅘ .45⅕1.10⅘ Md 10000 5 1 3^1 3^1 1^1 1^1 GLSmith b 120 *2.20 90-12 Autumn Gold 120^1 Crown Seal 112½ d-Indulger 113^h Hard drive 15

▲ **Md 10000**—Maiden Claiming race. A race for maidens who are entered to be claimed for a stipulated sum (in this case $10,000). (f-M 10000).

1Jan63-1GS fst 6f .22⅘ .45⅕1.10⅘ Hcp 8000 5 1 3^1 3^1 1^1 1^1 GLSmith b 120 *2.20 90-12 Autumn Gold 120^1 Crown Seal 112½ d-Indulger 113^h Hard drive 15

▲ **Hcp 8000**—Handicap Claiming race. A race run under handicap conditions but with a claiming clause. Entrants subject to be claimed for amount stipulated (in this case $8,000). (f-H 8000).

1Jan63-1GS fst 6f .22⅘ .45⅕1.10⅘ Clm 8000^0 5 1 3^1 3^1 1^1 1^1 GLSmith b 120 *2.20 90-12 Autumn Gold 120^1 Crown Seal 112½ d-Indulger 113^h Hard drive 15

▲ **Clm 8000^0**—Optional Claiming race with horse entered TO BE claimed for amount shown. (Superior letter ^{0} folows the claiming price.) (f-8000^0).

1Jan63-1GS fst 6f .22⅘ .45⅕1.10⅘ Clm ^{08000} 5 1 3^1 3^1 1^1 1^1 GLSmith b 120 *2.20 90-12 Autumn Gold 120^1 Crown Seal 112½ d-Indulger 113^h Hard drive 15

▲ **Clm ^{08000}**—Optional Claiming race with horse entered NOT to be claimed. (Superior letter ^{0} precedes the claiming price.) (f-^{08000}).

NOTE: An **Optional Claiming** race is restricted to horses entered or having previously run for a stated claiming price. However, the owner has the option of entering his horse in either category—eligible to be claimed or not to be claimed. If an owner does not want to enter his horse to be claimed, the horse must meet the "optional" conditions for the race. A horse who races in an optional claiming event but is not entered to be claimed must have raced at some time for a specified claiming price to obtain a classification. He must again race for a claiming price if the owner wishes to reclassify him in a lower category. A winner of an optional claiming race, if he was entered NOT to be claimed, cannot be eligible for the same class of race in his next start unless entered as eligible to be claimed. If a horse is entered NOT to be claimed, the claiming price given represents the highest amount stipulated in the conditions of the race for those entered to be claimed.

1Jan63-1GS fst 6f .22⅘ .45⅕1.10⅘ Hcp 8000^0 5 1 3^1 3^1 1^1 1^1 GLSmith b 120 *2.20 90-12 Autumn Gold 120^1 Crown Seal 112½ d-Indulger 113^h Hard drive 15

▲ **Hcp 8000^0**—Optional Claiming Handicap with horse entered TO BE claimed for amount shown. (Superior letter ^{0} follows the claiming price.) This is an optional claiming race as explained above but run under handicap conditions, with the weights assigned by the track handicapper. (f-H 8000^0).

1Jan63-1GS fst 6f .22⅘ .45⅕1.10⅘ Hcp ^{08000} 5 1 3^1 3^1 1^1 1^1 GLSmith b 120 *2.20 90-12 Autumn Gold 120^1 Crown Seal 112½ d-Indulger 113^h Hard drive 15

▲ **Hcp ^{08000}—Optional Claiming Handicap with horse entered NOT to be claimed. (Superior letter ^{0} precedes the claiming price.) (f-H ^{08000}).**

1Jan63-1GS fst 6f .22⅘ .45⅕1.10⅘ Alw 9000s 5 1 3^1 3^1 1^1 1^1 GLSmith b 120 *2.20 90-12 Autumn Gold 120^1 Crown Seal 112½ d-Indulger 113^h Hard drive 15

▲ **Alw 9000s**—Starter Allowance race. An event run under allowance conditions restricted to horses who have previously started for the designated claiming price, or less, stated in the conditions of the race. (In this case, the horse must previously have run for a claiming price of $9,000 or less.) Horses entered in "starter" races are not subject to claim. (f-Alw 9000s).

1Jan63-1GS fst 6f .22⅘ .45⅕1.10⅘ Hcp 9000s 5 1 3^1 3^1 1^1 1^1 GLSmith b 120 *2.20 90-12 Autumn Gold 120^1 Crown Seal 112½ d-Indulger 113^h Hard drive 15

▲ **Hcp 9000s**—Starter Handicap race. Same as above, but race is contested under "handicap" instead of "allowance" conditions. (f-Hp9000s).

1Jan63-1GS fst 6f .22⅘ .45⅕1.10⅘ Spw 9000s 5 1 3^1 3^1 1^1 1^1 GLSmith b 120 *2.20 90-12 Autumn Gold 120^1 Crown Seal 112½ d-Indulger 113^h Hard drive 15

▲ **Spw 9000s**—Starter Special Weight race. A starter race as explained above, only run under "special weight" conditions. (f-Spw 9000s).

1Jan63-1GS fst 6f .22⅘ .45⅕1.10⅘ Alw——s 5 1 3^1 3^1 1^1 1^1 GLSmith b 120 *2.20 90-12 Autumn Gold 120^1 Crown Seal 112½ d-Indulger 113^h Hard drive 15

▲ **Alw———s**—Starter Allowance race. (f-Alw—s). A race as previously explained, but open to horses who have started for a claiming price of any amount since no stipulated figure is given in the conditions. For these races, dashes are substituted where the claiming price usually appears. Starter Handicap and Starter Special Weight races of this type are indicated in the past performances as follows:

▼

1Jan63-1GS fst 6f .22⅘ .45⅕1.10⅘ Hcp——s 5 1 3^1 3^1 1^1 1^1 GLSmith b 120 *2.20 90-12 Autumn Gold 120^1 Crown Seal 112½ d-Indulger 113^h Hard drive 15
1Jan63-1GS fst 6f .22⅘ .45⅕1.10⅘ Spw——s 5 1 3^1 3^1 1^1 1^1 GLSmith b 120 *2.20 90-12 Autumn Gold 120^1 Crown Seal 112½ d-Indulger 113^h Hard drive 15

Stakes Races

For stakes races, the name of the race, or an abbreviation of the name, is given in the Class of Race column, as follows:

18May57-7Pim fst 1$\frac{3}{16}$ .46⅖1.10⅗1.56⅕ Preakness 1 5 4^5 4$^{5\frac{1}{2}}$ 6^{11} 6^{15} JCulmone b 126 20.60 77-13 Bold Ruler 126^2 Iron Liege 126^{nk} Inside Tract 126$^{2\frac{1}{4}}$ No mishap 7

▲ **Preakness** identifies the race as the famed Preakness Stakes.

30May57-7Bel fst 7f .22⅕ .45⅖1.23 Carter H 2 11 11^{19}11^{13} 7^8 4$^{3\frac{3}{4}}$ CMcCreary 116 9.10 92-13 Portersville 111^h Dedicate 126^{nk} Jutland 112^3 Was away sluggishly 11

▲ **Carter H**—Carter Handicap. When the capital letter **H** follows the name of the race it indicates the event was a handicap, with the track handicapper assigning the weight for each horse. **f-KyOaks**—A stakes for fillies or fillies and mares.

NOTE: There are several types of "stakes races." A stake—which is the popular contraction for the term "sweepstakes"—may be run under handicap, allowance, special weight, scale weight or weight-for-age, conditions. However, a race may be classified as a stake only if it meets the following standard adopted by The Jockey Club in its Rules of Racing:

"A sweepstakes is a race in which stakes are to be made by the owners of the horses engaged, and it is still a sweepstakes when money or other prize is added, but, within the meaning of this rule, no overnight race, whatever its conditions, shall be considered to be a sweepstakes."

The Jockey Club's interpretation of an "overnight race" follows:

"An 'overnight race' is one for which the entries close 72 hours (exclusive of Sundays), or less, before the time set for the first race of the day on which such race is to be run."

A "handicap stake" is a stake run under handicap conditions, in which the weights to be carried by the horses are assigned by the track handicapper in an effort to equalize their chances.

An "allowance stake" is a stake in which the weights to be carried by the horses are determined by the conditions set forth by the racing secretary, which may call for less weight (allowances) for certain horses if they have not won a prescribed amount of money or races.

A "special weight stake" is a stake in which the weights are fixed by the racing secretary.

A "scale weight stake" is a stake in which horses carry fixed weights as determined in most states, by The Jockey Club's Scale of Weights—in races exclusively for 2-year-olds, 122 pounds; for 3-year-olds and 4-year-olds, 126 pounds, less sex allowances. The Kentucky Derby, Preakness and Belmont, for example, are scale weight stakes.

A "weight-for-age stake" is a stake in which the weights to be carried by the horses vary with their ages, distance and the time of year, less sex allowances.

Sample Result Chart

This sample DAILY RACING FORM Official Result Chart reveals how exhaustively every factor pertaining to any race is covered.

FIRST RACE
BM - 16301
April 1, 1963

6 FURLONGS (chute). (Ole Fols, Jan. 9, 1959. 1:08⅘, 3, 120). Purse $4,500. 4-year-olds and upward. Claiming. Weights, 4-year-olds, 121 lbs.; older, 122 lbs. Non-winners of one race since Dec. 25 or two races since Oct. 25 allowed 3 lbs.; one race since Oct. 25, 6 lbs. Claiming price, $8,000; if for less, 2 lbs. allowed for each $500 to $7,000.

Value to winner $2,475; second, $900; third, $675; fourth, $450. Mutuel Pool, $414,850.

Index	Horses	Eq't A Wt PP St	¼	½	Str	Fin	Jockeys	Cl'gPr	Owners	Odds to $1
16001SA⁵	—Sea Falcon	sb 4 112 4 4	5h	4h	3¹½	1½	H Morenot†	7000	Franchuk Stable	28.00
1016SA¹	ⒹWallchain	5 111 5 3	2h	1h	1¹	2¹	M Green⁵	8000	Mrs F W Brester	Ⓓ-14.35
16223SA⁴	—Bill Nixon	5 116 6 6	1h	2h	2¹½	3ⁿᵏ	R York	8000	R W Nixon	2.40
16299BM²	—Count Indigo	b 4 108 10 9	7¹	6h	4h	4³½	R Yaka⁵	7500	R'ddr Br's-R McD'n'l Co	21.50
1936SA³	—Regally Yours	4 113 2 5	4h	7³	55	5½	J Longden	7000	Mrs C J Dorfman	7.10
10225SA⁶	—Khalex	4 113 3 7	10²	10³	7h	6¾	R Griffiths	7500	J N Crofton	a-62.95
14260P²	ⒹⒽWise Jax	6 116 9 1	6²	5³	6½	7	G Glisson	8000	M D Allen	ⒹⒽ-4.20
4722SP⁴	ⒹⒽShape Burner	b 4 115 8 8	9¹½	8½	9½	7¹½	D Pierce	8000	Reliable Stable	ⒹⒽ-35.95
5207BM³	—Regradi	b 4 110 7 2	3¹½	3¹	8h	9⁵	W Sh'mak'r	8000	Thiessen Stable	3.05
5201BM¹	—Dusky Spark	4 111 11 11	11	11	11	10¹½	W Harmatz	7000	C J Sebastian	a-62.95
10320SA⁹	—Traveling Man	b 5 114 1 10	8¹½	9h	10½	11	E Arcaro	7500	Triple K Stable	f-10.30

Ⓓ Disqualified and placed third.   a-Coupled, Khalex and Dusky Spark.   ⒹⒽ Dead-heat.   f-Mutuel field
†Five pounds apprentice allowance waived.

Time, :22⅖, :45⅖, 1:11⅖, Track fast.

Official Program Numbers ↘

$2 Mutuel Prices :

4-SEA FALCON	58.00	19.30	11.30
6-BILL NIXON		4.50	3.20
5-WALLCHAIN			6.70

B. g. by Noor—Sea Gold, by Seabiscuit. Trainer, C. A. Comiskey. Bred by Ridgewood Company (Calif.)

IN GATE—2:16. OFF AT 2:16½ PACIFIC STANDARD TIME. Start good. Won driving.

SEA FALCON moved to strong contention nearing the stretch turn and, continuing strongly on the outside through the stretch, was up to win in the last thirty yards. WALLCHAIN had speed while racing on the inside of BILL NIXON and bore out in front of the latter in the stretch run for which he was disqualified from second position and placed third following a stewards' inquiry. BILL NIXON displayed good early speed, was bothered by WALLCHAIN in the stretch and was awarded second place when the latter was disqualified. COUNT INDIGO made up some ground in the stretch. WISE JAX was unable to keep up. REGRADI had speed to the stretch and then tired.

Scratched—Infinity Sheik, June J.

Overweights—Regally Yours, 2 pounds; Sea Falcon, 1. No whip—Sea Falcon.

Sea Falcon claimed by J. N. Croft, trainer W. Jones.

How to Read Charts

To illustrate the wealth of information contained in DAILY RACING FORM Official Result Charts we explain the meaning of each figure, abbreviation and symbol, beginning with the material contained in the "chart head."

Race, Track, Index Number, Date

FIRST   RACE

BM - 16301

April 1, 1963

"FIRST RACE" shows that this event was first on the program. "BM - 16301" is the track abbreviation and index number of this particular race. The next time each starter runs, his name in the chart will be preceded by index number 16301BM, making possible easy reference to the race in either back copies of DAILY RACING FORM or in DAILY RACING FORM Monthly Chart Books. "April 1, 1963" reveals that the race was run on April 1, 1963.

NOTE: A complete list of track abbreviations appears on page 461.

Track Record, Conditions of Race

6 FURLONGS (chute). (Ole Fols, Jan. 9, 1959, 1:08⅘, 3, 120).
Purse $4,500. 4-year-olds and upward. Claiming. Weights, 4-year-olds, 121 lbs.; older, 122 lbs. Non-winners of one race since Dec. 25, or two races since Oct. 25 allowed 3 lbs.; one race since Oct. 25, 6 lbs. Claiming price, $8,000; if for less, 2 lbs. allowed for each $500 to $7,000.

This part of the "chart head" tells a complete story in itself. "6 FURLONGS" is the distance of the race. "Chute" indicates that the race was started and raced in its earliest stages on a straightaway extension of the main track. "Ole Fols, Jan. 9, 1959, 1:08⅘, 3, 120" shows that the track record for six furlongs was established by Ole Fols on January 9, 1959, that he ran the distance in 1:08⅘, when he was three years old (3) and that he carried 120 pounds (120).

"Purse $4,500. 4-year-olds and upward. Claiming. Weights, 4-year-olds, 121 lbs.; older, 122 lbs. Non-winners of one race since Dec. 25 or two races since Oct. 25 allowed 3 lbs.; one race since Oct. 25, 6 lbs. Claiming price, $8,000; if for less, 2 lbs. allowed for each $500 to $7,000."

These are the "conditions" of the race which determine how much weight each starter shall carry. See "Abbreviations for Various Races" on page 455 for explanations of claiming events and all other classes of races carded at recognized tracks.

Purse Division, Mutuel Pool

"Value to winner $2,475; second, $900; third, $675; fourth, $450. Mutuel Pool, $414,850." shows that the owner of the winner received $2,475 from the track management as his share of the $4,500 purse; that $900 went to the owner of the second horse, $675 to the owner of the third horse and $450 to the owner of the fourth horse. The money wagered in the totalisator ("Mutuel Pool, $414,850") on all the starters in this race (straight, place and show) totaled $414,850.

Index Number

Index number for reference to chart of Sea Falcon's prior start. Superior figure 5 following index number and track abbreviation denotes position of finish in prior start.	Name of horse.	Equipment (Jockey wore spurs. Sea Falcon was equipped with blinkers).	Sea Falcon's age.	Weight carried by Sea Falcon.	Post position.	Position at start.	Position at quarter mile. (Indicates Sea Falcon was fifth, a head before the sixth horse.)	Position at half mile. (Sea Falcon was running fourth, a head before the fifth horse.)	Position in stretch. (Indicates Sea Falcon was third, one and one-half lengths in front of the fourth horse.)	Position at finish. (Indicates Sea Falcon won by a half-length.)	Jockey who rode Sea Falcon.	Claiming price for which Sea Falcon was entered.	Owner of Sea Falcon.	Sea Falcon's equivalent odds to $1.00.
16001SA[5] —Sea Falcon		sb	4	112	4	4	5h	4h	31½	1½	H Moreno	7000	Franchuk Stable	28.00

"16001SA[5] is the "index number" of the chart of Sea Falcon's last previous race. Each chart is numbered, making it comparatively easy to check back on a horse's record in either DAILY RACING FORM charts or in DAILY RACING FORM Monthly Chart Books. If he had finished first the track abbreviation shown after his index number would have been followed by the superior figure[1]. If he had finished second, the superior figure would have been[2]. If he had finished third, the superior figure would have been[3]. If he had finished fourth, the superior figure would have been[4], etc. If no superior figure appears after track abbreviation, horse was disqualified and unplaced from actual finish position or did not finish the race.

Equipment

16001SA[5] —Sea Falcon sb 4 112 4 4 5h 4h 31½ 1½ H Moreno 7000 Franchuk Stable 28.00

"sb" indicates that Sea Falcon's rider wore spurs (s) and the horse was equipped with blinkers (b). Note: All riders carry whips (w) unless indicated in footnote to chart—"No whip-Sea Falcon."

Age

16001SA[5] —Sea Falcon sb 4 112 4 4 5h 4h 31½ 1½ H Moreno 7000 Franchuk Stable 28.00

"4" is Sea Falcon's age. He is four years old. The age of a horse is reckoned as beginning on the first of January in the year in which he is foaled. In other words, a horse foaled (born) in April, 1958, becomes one year old on January 1, 1959.

Weight

16001SA[5] —Sea Falcon sb 4 112 4 4 5h 4h 31½ 1½ H Moreno 7000 Franchuk Stable 28.00

"112" is the weight Sea Falcon carried. This includes the weight of his rider, the latter's equipment and whatever lead was necessary to bring the impost up to the required poundage.

Post Position

16001SA[5] —Sea Falcon sb 4 112 4 4 5h 4h 31½ 1½ H Moreno 7000 Franchuk Stable 28.00

"4" is Sea Falcon's post position. NOTE: Post positions are drawn by lot.

Running Positions

16001SA⁵ —Sea Falcon sb 4 112 4 <u>4</u>   5ʰ   4ʰ   31½   1½ H Moreno 7000 Franchuk Stable   28.00

"4" shows that Sea Falcon was fourth at the start.

NOTE: In races at one mile and one quarter or more each horse's position at the quarter-mile is substituted for the start call.

16001SA⁵ —Sea Falcon sb 4 112 4 4   <u>5ʰ</u>   4ʰ   31½   1½ H Moreno 7000 Franchuk Stable   28.00

"5ʰ" shows that Sea Falcon was fifth, a head before the sixth horse after running a quarter-mile.

16001SA⁵ —Sea Falcon sb 4 112 4 4   5ʰ   <u>4ʰ</u>   31½   1½ H Moreno 7000 Franchuk Stable   28.00

"4ʰ" shows that Sea Falcon was fourth, a head before the fifth horse after he had run a half-mile.

16001SA⁵ —Sea Falcon sb 4 112 4 4   5ʰ   4ʰ   <u>31½</u>   1½ H Moreno 7000 Franchuk Stable   28.00

"31½" shows that Sea Falcon was third, a length and one-half before the fourth horse in the stretch (at the furlong pole—one furlong from the finish). The length of the stretch varies at different tracks and is shown in the chart head and over each set of past performances.

16001SA⁵ —Sea Falcon sb 4 112 4 4   5ʰ   4ʰ   31½   <u>1½</u> H Moreno 7000 Franchuk Stable   28.00

"1½" shows that Sea Falcon won the race by one-half length.

Jockey

16001SA⁵ —Sea Falcon sb 4 112 4 4   5ʰ   4ʰ   31½   1½ <u>H Moreno</u> 7000 Franchuk Stable   28.00

"H Moreno" is the name of the jockey who rode Sea Falcon. Apprentice allowances claimed for riders are indicated by superior figures which appear after jockeys' names. For illustrative purposes, we list the names of two riders in Sample Chart BM - 16301.

5-pound apprentice allowance   M Green⁵   R Yaka⁵

NOTE: Apprentice allowances vary in different states. The "apprentice" allowance is actually a reduction in the weight the horse would have to carry if ridden by a jockey not entitled to a weight concession.

Claiming Price

16001SA⁵ —Sea Falcon sb 4 112 4 4   5ʰ   4ʰ   31½   1½ H Moreno <u>7000</u> Franchuk Stable   28.00

"7000" is the sum for which Sea Falcon was entered to be claimed. In races which do not carry the claiming clause this space is blank.

NOTE: Claiming rules vary in different states. However, the general claiming procedure in most states follows the pattern outlined in the Rules of Racing adopted by The Jockey Club.

"In claiming races any horse may be claimed for its entered price by any owner presently registered in good faith for racing at that meeting who has nominated a starter up to or including the race in which the claim is made, or by his authorized agent, but for the account only of the owner making the claim, or for whom the claim was made by the agent; provided, however, that no person shall claim his own horse or cause his horse to be claimed directly or indirectly for his own account."

"Claiming" a horse is actually buying him. When an owner starts a horse in a claiming event, he does so with the express understanding that any owner eligible to make a claim under the rules of the association staging the meeting may "buy" him for his entered price. All claims must be in writing, sealed and deposited in a locked box provided for that purpose by the Clerk of Course at a stipulated time BEFORE the race is run. When there is more than one claim for a horse the owner who "wins" him is determined by lot. The money the horse earns in the race from which he is claimed belongs to his original owner. All claims are passed upon by the stewards and the person determined at the closing time for claiming to have the right of claim becomes the owner of the horse, be it alive or dead, sound or unsound, or injured during of after the race. Owners are not informed that a claim has been made until after the race is run, when the claimed horse is taken to the paddock for delivery to the claimant.

Owner

16001SA⁵ —Sea Falcon   sb   4 112   4 4   5ʰ   4ʰ   31¼   1½ H Moreno   7000   <u>Franchuk Stable</u>   28.00

"Franchuk Stable" is Sea Falcon's owner.

Equivalent Odds

16001SA⁵ —Sea Falcon   sb   4 112   4 4   5ʰ   4ʰ   31¼   1½ H Moreno   7000   Franchuk Stable   <u>28.00</u>

"$28.00"—Sea Falcon's equivalent odds—his closing price to $1.00 in the mutuel pool.

(NOTE: Odds to $1.00 are determined by deducting the $2.00 paid for mutuel ticket and dividing remainder in half. For example, winning $2.00 mutuel tickets on Sea Falcon paid $58.00. Deduct $2.00 for cost of ticket and you have a net gain of $56.00. Divide this in half and you get $28.00, his "equivalent odds to $1.00.")

Waived Apprentice Allowances

Waived apprentice allowances are pointed out by symbols which immediately follow jockeys' names. These symbols are repeated, and then explained, directly under the line giving the running positions of the last horse in the chart, as follows:

16001SA⁵ —Sea Falcon   sb   4 112   4 4   5ʰ   4ʰ   31¼   1½ H Moreno†   7000   Franchuk Stable   28.00

†Five pounds apprentice allowance waived.

NOTE: Apprentice allowances may be waived—passed up—at the discretion of each horse's trainer. For example, after claiming a five-pound apprentice allowance, he may decide to use a full-fledged jockey, for whom no concessions can be claimed. He first must receive the permission of the stewards. The final weight carried by each horse is shown in the chart and takes into consideration deductions (apprentice allowances), additions (apprentice allowances waived), and overweights.

Entries

When two or more horses start in the same race and are conditioned by the same trainer, regardless of their ownership, or are owned by one party, even though conditioned by different trainers, they constitute an entry at most tracks. (Holders of mutuel tickets on horses in an entry collect regardless of which member of the combination wins because entries are treated as one horse in the machines—"coupled in the wagering.") The following lines from Sample Chart BM 5601 show how entries are designated by initials preceding each horse's equivalent odds to $1.00:

10225SA⁶ —Khalex   4 113   3 7   10² 10³ 7ʰ 6¾ R Griffiths   7500   J N Crofton   <u>a-62.95</u>
5201BM¹—Dusky Spark   4 111 11 11   11 11 11 10½¼ W Harmatz   7000   C J Sebastian   <u>a-62.95</u>

"Field" Horses

Because pari-mutuel machines are equipped to handle wagers on no more than twelve horses in most instances (the number varies), some horses are coupled (combined as in an entry) in the wagering as a "mutuel field." At some tracks the "field" horses are designated by the track handicapper, at others they may be all horses having the outside post positions (like post positions ten, eleven and twelve, etc.). The following lines from Sample Chart BM 16301 show how "field" horses are designated by the letter "f" preceding each horse's equivalent odds to $1.00:

10320SA⁹ —Traveling Man   b 5 114 1 10   8½ 9ʰ 10¼ 11   E Arcaro   7500 Triple K Stable   f-10.30

Fractional Times

"Time, :22⅖, :45⅘, 1:11⅖. Track fast." This gives the running time of the first horse at each position clocked (quarter-mile, half-mile and three-quarter mile) and shows that the track was fast.

(NOTE: Fractional times vary, depending upon the distance of the race.)

Official Program Numbers and Mutuel Prices

Official Program Numbers ↘

$2 Mutuel Prices :

4-SEA FALCON	58.00	19.30	11.30
6-BILL NIXON		4.50	3.20
5-WALLCHAIN			6.70

"Official Program Numbers" are just that—the numbers printed in the track program to assure the rapid, errorless sale of pari-mutuel tickets.

NOTE: Official program numbers do not necessarily correspond with post position numbers, being affected by stable couplings and mutuel fields.

Mutuel Prices are the official tote returns across the board (first, second and third, or straight, place and show).

Pedigree of Winner

"B. g, by Noor—Sea Gold, by Seabiscuit" reveals that Sea Falcon, winner of the race, is a bay (b) gelding (g) sired by Noor, that his dam was Sea Gold, and that the sire of his dam was Seabiscuit. This line also gives the name of the winner's present trainer, C. A. Comiskey, and the name of his breeder, Ridgewood Company. The breeder of a horse is the owner of his dam at the time of foaling.

NOTE: Effective with the racing of 1965, the pedigree of each two-year-old of 1965 includes the state in which the thoroughbred was foaled, the state (abbreviated and parenthesized) appearing directly after the breeder's name.

For complete list of color and sex abbreviations see page 458.

In Gate and Off Time

"IN GATE—2:16. OFF AT 2:16½" shows that the field was locked in the starting gate at sixteen minutes after two o'clock and that the official start was effected at sixteen and one-half minutes after two o'clock. "Start good. Won driving" indicates the field was off to a good start and that the winner was under a drive at the finish.

Footnotes

SEA FALCON moved to strong contention nearing the stretch turn and, continuing strongly on the outside through the stretch, was up to win in the last thirty yards. WALLCHAIN had speed while racing on the inside of BILL NIXON and bore out in front of the latter in the stretch run for which he was disqualified from second position and placed third following a stewards' inquiry. BILL NIXON displayed good early speed, was bothered by WALLCHAIN in the stretch and was awarded second place when the latter was disqualified. COUNT INDIGO made up some ground in the stretch. WISE JAX was unable to keep up. REGRADI had speed to the stretch and then tired.

This is a description of the running, giving in minute detail pertinent facts about how most of the starters ran at various stages of the race—revealing, among other important things, that Wallchain bothered Bill Nixon and was disqualified from second position by the stewards.

Scratches

Scratched—Infinity Sheik, June J.

This names the horses who were originally entered in the race but did not start.

Overweights

Overweights —Regally Yours, 2 pounds; Sea Falcon, 1.

"Overweights—Regally Yours, 2 pounds; Sea Falcon, 1" shows that Regally Yours carried two pounds more than the conditions of the race called for and that Sea Falcon carried one pound more.

NOTE: In most cases these "overweights" are carried because the jockey in each instance could not "make" the stipulated weight.

Claims

Sea Falcon claimed by J. N. Croft, trainer W. Jones.

"Sea Falcon claimed by J. N. Croft" means just what it says: that he was claimed by J. N. Croft, whose horses are trained by W. Jones. The price for which he was claimed follows the jockey's name in the chart.

How to Read Past Performances

The information contained on Sea Falcon in the sample DAILY RACING FORM Result Chart is condensed to occupy a single line, two columns wide, in DAILY RACING FORM'S Past Performances.

Here is Sea Falcon's Past Performance line:

Date of Last Race	Number of Race and Track Raced on	Distance	Time of Winner	Condition of Track	Closing Odds *Denotes Favorite	Weight Carried	First Call After Start	Pre-Stretch	In Stretch	At Finish	Jockey and	Post Position	Denotes Claim Type of Race or Claiming Price Speed Rating	FIRST THREE HORSES IN ORDER OF FINISH WITH WEIGHT CARRIED BY FIRST TWO FINISHERS.	Starters in Race

Position in Race and Lengths Behind Leading Horse.

Apr 1-63¹B.M   6 f 1:11⅖ft 28   112   5¹¾ 4¹¼ 3²½ 1½   M'renoH⁴ c7000 87 SeaFalcon 112 Wallchain 111 BillNixon 11

Date, Race, Track

Apr 1-63¹B.M   6 f 1:11⅖ft 28   112   5¹¾ 4¹¼ 3²½ 1½   M'renoH⁴ c7000 87 SeaFalcon 112 Wallchain 111 BillNixon 11

"Apr. 1-63¹BM" indicates the race was run on April 1, 1963, and that it was the first event at Bay Meadows. The date and track in the past performances make possible easy reference to the actual charts, either in back copies of DAILY RACING FORM or DAILY RACING FORM Monthly Chart Books. A complete list of track abbreviations is printed on page 461. These abbreviations are used in DAILY RACING FORM entries and past performances.

Distance, Time, Track Condition

Apr 1-63¹B.M   6 f 1:11⅖ft 28   112   5¹¾ 4¹¼ 3²½ 1½   M'renoH⁴ c7000 87 SeaFalcon 112 Wallchain 111 BillNixon 11

"6 f 1:11⅖ft" indicates the distance of the race was six furlongs, that the winner (Sea Falcon in this instance) was timed in 1:11⅖ over a fast (ft) track. The running time of the winner of each race is always given in DAILY RACING FORM past performances. To determine the approximate running time of the horses who have been defeated, simply compute the number of lengths they were beaten by the winner and add one-fifth of a second to the winner's time for each length.

In other words, Wallchain, beaten one-half length by Sea Falcon, who ran the six furlongs in 1:11⅖, covered the distance in 1:11⅗ (one-half length or one-fifth of a second behind him). Note: In computing the approximate running time of beaten horses, fractions of one-half length or more are considered as one full length or one fifth second in time.

When the distance of the race is approximate, not exact, the past performance line reveals that fact as follows:

Apr 1-63^{1}B.M a 6 f 1:11⅖ft 28 112 5^{1¾} 4^{1¼} 3^{2½} 1½ M'renoH^{4} c7000 87 SeaFalcon 112 Wallchain 111 BillNixon 11

"a" is the abbreviation for "about." The distance is "about 6 furlongs." When the letter "f" follows the distance, as per the example below, it means furlongs. This is used for races at two, three, four, five, five and a half furlongs, etc., as follows:

May 4-63^{7}C.D 5½ f 1:07⅖ft 3 ▲126 8^{16} 4^{2} 1^{3} 1^{8} ArcaroE^{4} 3500 90 Klondike123 Curator122 Starling 11

Special Courses

Races on turf courses are designated as follows, with the letters "tc" immediately preceding the distance in the past performance line:

Aug22-63^{6}Atl tc 1 1:37⅕hd 27 108 9^{12} 8^{5¾} 2^{h} 1^{3½} BurrC^{3} HcpS 95 Armag'd'n121 Potpourri 114 Rol'lGov'r 10

Track Condition Abbreviations

We reproduce below several past performance lines illustrating the abbreviations used for all track conditions:

Aug 4-63^{4}Suf 6 f 1:12⅗ft 15 116 7^{10} 6^{8} 3^{1½} 4^{5¼} WilsonJ^{6} Alw 79 BestDress110 BonnieBeryl 116 Axiom 7

"ft"—track fast.

Aug16-63^{7}Was 1 1-8-1:53⅗gd 9 120 6^{3} 3^{1½} 3½ 4^{3} GrohsO^{11} Alw 73 Galap'x120 K.DoeDoe109 Sig'lsBloke 11

"gd"—track good.

Aug17-63^{7}Was 1 1:41 sl 14 111 1^{2} 1^{2} 1^{1½} 3^{2½} Thom'nB^{7} Alw 70 Val'aMaiden111 Bl'kPep'r113 Damos 8

"sl"—track slow.

Jly 26-63^{6}G.S 1$\frac{1}{16}$ 1:46 sy 2½ ▲116 6^{10} 6^{10} 6^{10} 6^{12} Long'nJ^{3} c7000 74 OldUnion113 R'hRonan113 Gr'nApples 6

"sy"—track sloppy.

Jly 7-63^{5}Suf 6 f 1:14⅘m 4 111 3^{3} 3^{1½} 3^{1½} 1^{2} TrentT^{1} 4500 71 TopTransit112 Vim116 MaybeMiss 5

"m"—track muddy.

Aug 6-63^{3}Was 7 f 1:29⅗hy 6½ 116 6^{5} 3^{4½} 5^{5} 6^{8} BaileyW^{3} Alw 55 Anoth'rNight112 C'yTrifle118 ShutEye 7

"hy"—track heavy.

Mar18-63^{1}Bow 6 f 1:13⅗fr 30 116 2^{1} 3^{2} 2½ 1^{2½} ServoS^{2} 2500 83 Frosty 116 Mr. Man 112 Jab Me 12

"fr"—track frozen.

Jan21-63^{7}Lrl tc 1 7:39⅘hd 3 114 3^{1} 3^{1½} 2^{1} 1^{3} GobbV^{3} Alw 92 Trask114 Cyson110 Grubrow 12

"hd"—track hard (used only for races run on grass).

Jan21-63^{8}Hia tc 1⅛ 1:52⅖fm 8 118 5^{3½} 5^{1¾} 4^{5} 3^{5} ErbD^{5} 5500 84 Fugitive107 Sw'pSon112 Q'ter-M'ster 12

"fm"—track firm (used only for races run on grass).

Oct 9-63^{5}Bel a 3 3:45⅕sf 2¼ 160 4^{5½} 2^{4½} 2^{3} 2^{4½} McD'dR^{3} HcpS [S HisBoots141 MightyMo132 SunSh'w'r 11

"sf"—track soft (used only for races run on grass).

Approximate Odds

Apr 1-63^{1}B.M 6 f 1:11⅖ft 28 112 5^{1¾} 4^{1¼} 3^{2½} 1½ M'renoH^{4} c7000 87 SeaFalcon 112 Wallchain 111 BillNixon 11

"28" indicates that Sea Falcon paid approximately 28-1. A triangle (▲) would reveal that he was favorite.

If Sea Falcon had been coupled in the betting (part of an entry) with another horse, his past performance line would have appeared as follows:

Apr 1-63^{1}B.M 6 f 1:11⅖ft 28e 112 5^{1¾} 4^{1¼} 3^{2½} 1½ M'reno^{4} c7000 87 SeaFalcon 112 Wallchain 111 BillNixon 11

"28e" would indicate Sea Falcon was approximately 28-1 and was part of an entry (e).

If Sea Falcon had been a member of the mutuel field, this would have been indicated as follows in his past performances:

Apr 1-63^{1}B.M 6 f 1:11⅖ft 28f 112 5^{1¾} 4^{1¼} 3^{2½} 1½ Mor'noH^{4} c7000 87 SeaFalcon 112 Wallchain 111 BillNixon 11

"28f" would indicate Sea Falcon was approximately 28-1 and was a member of the mutuel field (f).

Weight Carried

Apr 1-63¹B.M   6 f 1:11⅖ft 28 112 51¾ 41¼ 32½ 1½ M'renoH4 c7000 87 SeaFalcon 112 Wallchain 111 BillNixon 11

"112" shows that Sea Falcon carried 112 pounds.

Apprentice Allowances

If Sea Falcon had been ridden by an apprentice for whom a three-pound allowance had been claimed, his past performance line would have appeared as follows:
Apr 1-63¹B.M   6 f 1:11⅖ft 28 112§ 51¾ 41¼ 32½ 1½ Mor'noH4 c7000 87 SeaFalcon 112 Wallchain 111 BillNixon 11

If Sea Falcon had been ridden by an apprentice for whom a five-pound allowance had been claimed, his past performance line would have appeared as follows:
Apr 1-63¹B.M   6 f 1:11⅖ft 28 112* 51¾ 41¼ 32½ 1½ Mor'noH4 c7000 87 SeaFalcon 112 Wallchain 111 BillNixon 11

If Sea Falcon had been ridden by an apprentice for whom a seven-pound allowance had been claimed, his past performance line would have appeared as follows:
Apr 1-63¹B.M   6 f 1:11⅖ft 28 112‡ 51¾ 41¼ 32½ 1½ Mor'noH4 c7000 87 SeaFalcon 112 Wallchain 111 BillNixon 11

If Sea Falcon had been ridden by an apprentice for whom a ten-pound allowance had been claimed, his past performance line would have appeared as follows:
Apr 1-63¹B.M   6 f 1:11⅖ft 28 112⁂51¾ 41¼ 32½ 1½ Mor'noH4 c7000 87 SeaFalcon 112 Wallchain 111 BillNixon 11

NOTE: Apprentice allowances vary in different states.

Position at First Call

Apr 1-63¹B.M   6 f 1:11⅖ft 28 112 51¾ 41¼ 32½ 1½ M'renoH4 c7000 87 SeaFalcon 112 Wallchain 111 BillNixon 11

"51¾"—Sea Falcon's position at the first call after the start (at the quarter-mile in this instance). "51¾" reveals that Sea Falcon was fifth at the quarter, 1¾ lengths behind the first horse.

NOTE: The first call after the start varies, depending upon the distance of the race. To determine the exact position of the first call check the actual chart of the race.

Pre-Stretch

Apr 1-63¹B.M   6 f 1:11⅖ft 28 112 51¾ 41¼ 32½ 1½ M'renoH4 c7000 87 SeaFalcon 112 Wallchain 111 BillNixon 11

"41¼" indicates Sea Falcon was fourth when one-half mile of the race had been run, and that he was 1¼ lengths behind the leader.

NOTE: Pre-stretch indicates call before stretch. Position of this call varies with distance of race. In virtually every race the pre-stretch call is made one-quarter mile from the finish.

Stretch

Apr 1-63¹B.M   6 f 1:11⅖ft 28 112 51¾ 41¼ 32½ 1½ M'renoH4 c7000 87 SeaFalcon 112 Wallchain 111 BillNixon 11

"32½" reveals that Sea Falcon was third 2½ lengths behind leader in the stretch.
NOTE: In most races the stretch call is made one furlong from the finish.

Finish

Apr 1-63¹B.M   6 f 1:11⅖ft 28 112 51¾ 41¼ 32½ 1½ M'renoH4 c7000 87 SeaFalcon 112 Wallchain 111 BillNixon 11

"1½" reveals that Sea Falcon won by one-half length.

Jockey and Post Position

Apr 1-63¹B.M   6 f 1:11⅖ft 28   112   5¹¾ 4¹¼ 3²½ 1½   M'renoH⁴ c7000 87 SeaFalcon 112 Wallchain 111 BillNixon 11

"MorenoH⁴" reveals that Sea Falcon was ridden by H. Moreno and that he broke from post position number 4. When a horse breaks from outside the gate his original post position is shown in a circle ④.

Type of Race

Apr 1-63¹B.M   6 f 1:11⅖ft 28   112   5¹¾ 4¹¼ 3²½ 1½   M'renoH⁴ c7000 87 SeaFalcon 112 Wallchain 111 BillNixon 11

"c7000" is the price for which Sea Falcon was entered to be claimed. Knowing the type of race in which the horse ran is highly important to all handicappers. This item in the past performance line covers every conceivable type of contest.

As Sea Falcon was claimed, a lower case (small) "c" preceded his claiming price in the past performance line.

Every type of race in which horses compete is clearly indicated in DAILY RACING FORM'S past performances, eliminating all possibility of confusion in determining the quality of the starters. The various classes of races are denoted by the following simple abbreviations:

Mdn—Maidens.
AlwM—Maiden allowance.
M5000—Maiden claiming race.
Alw—Allowance.
A5000—Starter allowance.
S5000—Starter special weight.
AlwS—Allowance stake.
HcpO—Overnight handicap.

H5000—Starter handicap.
SpwS—Special weight stake.
HcpS—Handicap stake.
Wfa—Weight-for-age.
WfaS—Weight-for-age stake.
ScwS—Scale weight stake.
SplW—Special weight.
Mtch—Match race.

The amount for which each horse is entered to be claimed, regardless of whether it is an overnight purse, stake, handicap, etc., is printed following the jockey's name and post position (H5000). Optional claiming races are indicated by a superior "0" immediately preceding or following the claiming price. The "0" before the claiming price denotes the horse WAS NOT entered to be claimed; "0" after claiming price indicates horse WAS entered to be claimed. Where the capital letter "A," "H" or "S" precedes a claiming price, a "Starter Race" is indicated. A detailed explanation of the various type races follows:

Abbreviations for Various Races

May 4-63⁷C.D   1 1-4 2:03⅖ft   3 ▲126   8¹⁶ 4² 1³ 1⁸   ArcaroE⁴ Mdn 90 Klondike123   Curator122   Starling 11

"Mdn" race exclusively for maidens. (A "maiden" is a horse who, at time of starting, has never won a race on the flat in any country.)

May 4-63⁷C.D   1 1-4 2:03⅖ft   3 ▲126   8¹⁶ 4² 1³ 1⁸   ArcaroE⁴ AlwM 90 Klondike123   Curator122   Starling 11

"AlwM" race exclusively for maidens, but with certain allowances.

May 4-63⁷C.D   1 1-4 2:03⅖ft   3 ▲126   8¹⁶ 4² 1³ 1⁸   ArcaroE⁴ M5000 90 Klondike123   Curator122   Starling 11

"M5000" Maiden claiming race. A race exclusively for maidens entered to be claimed for the amount shown.

May 4-63⁷C.D   1 1-4 2:03⅖ft   3 ▲126   8¹⁶ 4² 1³ 1⁸   ArcaroE⁴ Alw 90 Klondike123   Curator122   Starling 11

"Alw" an allowance race (events in which the weights carried by the contestants are determined by the conditions as set forth by the racing secretary). Here are the conditions for one of Racing Secretary Frank E. Kilroe's allowance events at Jamaica: "For non-winners of two races. Weights: 3-year-olds, 113 pounds; older, 120 pounds. Non-winners at one mile and a quarter or over allowed two pounds; maidens, seven pounds."

May 4-637C.D   1 1-4 2:03⅗ft   3 ▲126   8¹⁶ 4²   1³   1⁸   ArcaroE4   <u>A5000</u> 90 Klondike123   Curator122   Starling 11

"A5000" starter allowance. An event run under allowance conditions restricted to horses who have previously started for the designated claiming price or less stated in the conditions of the race. (In this case the horse must have previously run for a claiming price of $5,000 or less). Horses in "Starter Races" are not subject to be claimed.

May 4-637C.D   1 1-4 2:03⅗ft   3 ▲126   8¹⁶ 4²   1³   1⁸   ArcaroE4   <u>S5000</u> 90 Klondike123   Curator122   Starling 11

"S5000" Starter special weight. A starter race as defined above, only run under "Special Weights" conditions. Where no claiming price is specified in the "Starter" conditions—the race being open to horses who have previously started for a claiming price of any amount—dashes will be substituted for the claiming price: "A—"; "H—"; or "S—."

May 4-637C.D   1 1-4 2:03⅗ft   3 ▲126   8¹⁶ 4²   1³   1⁸   ArcaroE4   <u>AlwS</u> 90 Klondike123   Curator122   Starling 11

"AlwS" allowance stake. (The Jockey Club's "Rules of Racing" defines a stake as follows: "A 'Sweepstakes' is a race in which stakes are to be made by the owners of the horses engaged, and it is still a sweepstakes when money or any other prize is added, but within the meaning of this rule, no overnight race whatever its conditions shall be considered to be a sweepstakes.")

May 4-637C.D   1 1-4 2:03⅗ft   3 ▲126   8¹⁶ 4²   1³   1⁸   ArcaroE4   <u>HcpO</u> 90 Klondike123   Curator122   Starling 11

"HcpO" overnight handicap. (A "Handicap" is a race in which the weights to be carried by the horses are assigned by the handicapper for the purpose of equalizing their chances of winning. An "Overnight Handicap" is one for which the entries close seventy-two hours—exclusive of Sundays—or less before the time set for the first race of the day on which such race is to be run.)

May 4-637C.D   1 1-4 2:03⅗ft   3 ▲126   8¹⁶ 4²   1³   1⁸   ArcaroE4   <u>H5000</u> 90 Klondike123   Curator122   Starling 11

"H5000" Starter Handicap. Similar to starter allowance race only race was run under "handicap" conditions.

May 4-637C.D   1 1-4 2:03⅗ft   3 ▲126   8¹⁶ 4²   1³   1⁸   ArcaroE4   <u>SpwS</u> 90 Klondike123   Curator122   Starling 11

"SpwS" special weight stake. Stake race with weights fixed by the racing secretary.

May 4-637C.D   1 1-4 2:03⅗ft   3 ▲126   8¹⁶ 4²   1³   1⁸   ArcaroE4   <u>HcpS</u> 90 Klondike123   Curator122   Starling 11

"HcpS" handicap stake.

May 4-637C.D   1 1-4 2:03⅗ft   3 ▲126   8¹⁶ *2   1³   1⁸   ArcaroE4   <u>Wfa</u> 90 Klondike123   Curator122   Starling 11

"Wfa" weight-for-age. The imposts the horses carry vary with their ages, distance, and the seasons, less sex allowances.

May 4-637C.D   1 1-4 2:03⅗ft   3 ▲126   8¹⁶ 4²   1³   1⁸   ArcaroE4   <u>WfaS</u> 90 Klondike123   Curator122   Starling 11

"WfaS" weight-for-age stake.

May 4-637C.D   1 1-4 2:03⅗ft   3 ▲126   8¹⁶ 4²   1³   1⁸   ArcaroE4   <u>ScwS</u> 90 Klondike123   Curator122   Starling 11

"ScwS" scale weight stake. (Contestants carry a fixed scale weight. In races exclusively for three-year-olds or four-year-olds, 126 pounds; exclusively for two-year-olds, 122 pounds, less sex allowances. The Kentucky Derby, for example, is a scale weight stake.)

May 4-637C.D   1 1-4 2:03⅗ft   3 ▲126   8¹⁶ 4²   1³   1⁸   ArcaroE4   <u>SplW</u> 90 Klondike123   Curator122   Starling 11

"SplW" special weights. (The weights fixed by the racing secretary, not necessarily scale weights.)

May 4-637C.D   1 1-4 2:03⅗ft   3 ▲126   8¹⁶ 4²   1³   1⁸   ArcaroE4   <u>⁰5000</u> 90 Klondike123   Curator122   Starling 11

"⁰5000" optional claiming race. (Entered NOT to be claimed.)

May 4-637C.D   1 1-4 2:03⅗ft   3 ▲126   8¹⁶ 4²   1³   1⁸   ArcaroE4   <u>5000⁰</u> 90 Klondike123   Curator122   Starling 11

"5000⁰" optional claiming race. (Entered TO BE claimed.) An optional claiming race is a race restricted to horses running for a claiming price, or who have previously run for a claiming price. The term OPTIONAL CLAIMING means just what the name implies, the owner having the option of entering his horse for a price (eligible to be claimed) or not entering his horse for a price (not eligible to be claimed). If an owner does not want to enter his horse to be claimed, his horse must meet the "optional" conditions set down by the racing secretary in order to be eligible to compete. These conditions appear in the past performances preceding each race. All horses who race in optional claimers, but are not entered to be claimed, must have raced at some time for a specified claiming price to obtain a classification, and they must again race for a claiming price if the owner wishes to reclassify his horse in a lower category. Also, winners of optional claiming races when entered NOT to be claimed, can not be eligible for the same class of race next time out unless entered eligible to be claimed.

May 4-63⁷C.D 1 1-4 2:03⅖ft 3 ▲126 8¹⁶ 4² 1³ 1⁸ ArcaroE⁴ <u>Mtch</u> 90 Klondike123   Curator122   Starling 11

"Mtch" match race, usually between two horses.

May 4-63⁷C.D 1 1-4 2:03⅖ft 3 ▲126 8¹⁶ 4² 1³ 1⁸ ArcaroE⁴ <u>3500</u> 90 Klondike123   Curator122   Starling 11

"3500" the price for which the horse was entered to be claimed. (See "Claiming Prices" in chart explanation for a more detailed account of races of this type.)

May 4-63⁷C.D 1 1-4 2:03⅖ft 3 ▲126 8¹⁶ 4² 1³ 1⁸ ArcaroE⁴ <u>c3500</u> 90 Klondike123   Curator122   Starling 11

"c3500" shows the horse was claimed for $3,500.

May 4-63⁷C.D 1 1-4 2:03⅖ft 3 ▲126 8¹⁶ 4² 1³ 1⁸ ArcaroE⁴ <u>Alw ⦋S</u> Klondike123   Curator122   Starling 11

"Alw⦋S" allowance steeplechase.

May 4-63⁷C.D 1 1-4 2:03⅖ft 3 ▲126 8¹⁶ 4² 1³ 1⁸ ArcaroE⁴ <u>Alw ⦋H</u> Klondike123   Curator122   Starling 11

"Alw⦋H" allowance hurdle.

Speed Rating

Apr 1-63¹B.M   6 f 1:11⅖ft 28 112 5¹³ 41¼ 32½ 1½ M'renoH⁴ c7000 <u>87</u> SeaFalcon 112 Wallchain 111 BillNixon 11

"87" is Sea Falcon's speed rating. DAILY RACING FORM'S speed ratings are based on a comparison of each horse's running time with the track record established prior to the opening of the current meeting (with the exception of inaugural meetings, or when a new distance is being run, for which speed ratings will be computed and assigned during the course of the meeting as adequate time standards are established). The track record receives a standard rating of 100. Thus a horse equalling the record receives a rating of 100. One point is deducted for each one-fifth second slower than the track record. For example, Sea Falcon ran his six furlongs in 1:11⅖. The track record was 1:08⅘. Therefore, Sea Falcon was timed two and three-fifths seconds (or 13 fifths) slower than the record, necessitating a deduction of 13 points and giving him a speed rating of 87 (100 minus 13). Speed ratings, in races where DAILY RACING FORM adds a footnote listing a running time that varies with the official track time, will be computed on the official track time and not the time taken by the DAILY RAC-ING FORM. No speed ratings are computed for races of less than three furlongs.

(NOTE: When a horse breaks the track record, his speed rating exceeds the standard rating of 100 by one point for each one-fifth second he is timed faster than the track record. Thus, if the record is 2:01⅖ and a horse is timed in 2:01 his speed rating is 102.)

First Three Finishers

Apr 1-63¹B.M   6 f 1:11⅖ft 28 112 5¹³ 41¼ 32½ 1½ M'renoH⁴ c7000 87 <u>SeaFalcon 112 Wallchain 111 BillNixon 11</u>

"Sea Falcon 112 Wallchain 111 Bill Nixon 11" are the first three horses in the order of finish. Following the first and second horse's name is the weight carried. The figure following the third horse's name (11) reveals that 11 horses started in the race.

Sea Falcon's Past Performances

The actual races themselves are only a part of each horse's past performances. We are reproducing on the following page six theoretical races by Sea Falcon to illustrate other important details.

Sea Falcon ⁎ **118** B. g, (1959), by Noor—Sea Gold, by Seabiscuit.
Breeder, Ridgewood Company (Calif.) 1963.. 1 1 0 0 $2,475
Owner, J. N. Croft. Trainer, W. Jones. $7,000 1959.. 2 0 0 0 $500

Apr 1-63[1]B.M	6 f	1:11$\frac{2}{5}$	ft	28	112	$5^{1\frac{3}{4}}$	$4^{1\frac{1}{4}}$	$3^{2\frac{1}{2}}$	$1^{\frac{1}{2}}$	M'renoH[4]	c7000	87	SeaFalcon112	Wallchain111	BillNixon	11
Jan24-59[3]S.A	6$\frac{1}{2}$ f	1:17	ft	9$\frac{1}{4}$	111	$7^{2\frac{1}{2}}$	$4^{2\frac{1}{2}}$	$6^{2\frac{3}{4}}$	$4^{1\frac{1}{2}}$	MorenoH[9]	7000	91	Flav'sBoy 113	Rhin 110	PrizeQuestion	12
Jan 9-59[8]S.A	1$\frac{1}{16}$	1:43	ft	43	112	$2^{1\frac{1}{2}}$	3^{2}	$6^{4\frac{3}{4}}$	8^{11}	M'renoH[6]	7000[0]	78	Tippecanoe108	HomeFl'tll.116	Honest	11
Jan21-58[7]Lrl	tc 1	1:39$\frac{4}{5}$	shd	3	114	3^{1}	$3^{1\frac{1}{2}}$	2^{1}	1^{3}	GobbV[3]	Alw	92	SeaFalcon 114	Cyson 110	Grubrow	12
Apr11-58[6]G.G	6 f	1:10$\frac{1}{5}$	ft	4-5	▲120	4^{nk}	$5^{3\frac{1}{2}}$	8^{12}	8^{12}	NevesR[3]	Alw	77	HighP'f'ce120	L'dF'tl'ry120	T'one G'ns	8
Mar21-58[7]G.G	6 f	1:12	m	3$\frac{3}{4}$	122	3^{1}	$4^{4\frac{1}{2}}$	3^{8}	3^{5}	Val'nz'la[2]	Alw	75	Bl'ckSign'l 119	Tabm'c 119	Sea Falcon	7
Mar12-58[7]G.G	6 f	1:09	ft	4e	110	$5^{4\frac{1}{2}}$	$6^{8\frac{1}{2}}$	$5^{9\frac{1}{2}}$	$4^{7\frac{3}{4}}$	TrejosR[4]	Hcp0	87	PrizeHost 122	Crasher 114	CircleLea	6

Mar 29 BM 3-8 ft :35$\frac{3}{5}$h Mar 22 BM 3-8 ft :36h Mar 20 BM 1-2 ft :51b

You will note that, in addition to Sea Falcon's past performances, the weight he is to carry (118) on the day he is entered is given, plus his pedigree, owner, trainer, breeder, the price for which he is entered is $7,000, and his record of starts and money earned for the last two years in competition. The symbol ⁎ next to his name indicates that he is a fair mud runner. If an × follows a horse's name, it denotes that he is a good mud runner. ⊗ denotes that he is a superior mud runner. An asterisk before a horse's name indicates he or she was bred in a foreign country. The country of origin is listed immediately after the breeder's name.

NOTE: Effective with the racing of 1965, the pedigree of each two-year-old of 1965 includes the state in which the thoroughbred was foaled, the state (abbreviated and parenthesized) appearing directly after the breeder's name.

His starts and earnings record reveal that he started once in 1963, winning that race and earning $2,475. In 1959 he started twice and failed to place first, second or third, earning $500 for finishing fourth.

Sex Abbreviations

The following abbreviations are used in DAILY RACING FORM Past Performances to specify the sex of the various contestants:

"c" colt (an entire male through four years of age).

"h" horse (an entire male five years old or older).

"g" gelding (a male horse who has been unsexed).

"f" filly (a female through four years of age).

"m" mare (a female five years old or older).

"rig" ridgling (a half-castrated male horse or a horse with one or both organs of reproduction absent from the sac).

Color Abbreviations

"b" bay (varies from a light yellowish tan [light bay] to a dark rich shade, almost brown, and, between these, a bright mahogany [blood bay]. A bay always has a black mane and tail).

"br" brown (sometimes difficult to tell from black or dark bay, but can be distinguished by noting the fine tan or brown hairs on the muzzle or flanks).

"blk" black (if any doubt arises in distinguishing between dark brown and black, the black can be determined by noting the fine black hairs on the muzzle).

"ch" chestnut (varies from a dark liver color to a light washy yellow, between which comes the brilliant red gold and copper shades. A chestnut never has black mane, tail or points).

"dk b or br" describes horses whose color is marginal, as well as those which are brown.

"gr" gray (mixture of white hairs and black, sometimes scarcely distinguishable from black at birth, getting lighter with age).

"ro" roan (there are two classes—red or strawberry, produced by intermingling of red, white and yellow hairs, and the blue, produced by intermingling of black, white and yellow hairs).

NOTE: Effective with the registration of foals of 1963, individual designations as "dark bay" and "brown" have been dropped, and the term "dark bay or brown" has been adopted.

Workouts

Mar 29 BM 3-8 ft :35⅗h **Mar 22 BM 3-8 ft :36h** **Mar 20 BM 1-2 ft :51b**

The last line of Sea Falcon's past performances gives his workouts, including the track over which he was trained, the condition of the strip, the date of the trial, the time, and the manner in which the trial was accomplished.

The track abbreviatons used in workouts are the same as those used in the Past Performances. When the letters "trt" follow the track abbreviation they indicate that the workout took place over the training track. All workouts are on the main tracks unless otherwise designated.

The following letter symbols are used to describe how each horse worked:

"h"—handily "b"—breezing "d"—driving "e"—easily
"o"—all out "u"—eased up "g"—worked from gate
"bo"—bore out "ro"—ran out

NOTE: In addition to the workouts carried in Past Performances, DAILY RACING FORM offers complete lists of workouts at all major tracks, graded alphabetically.

Symbols Infrequently Used in Charts

Disqualifications and dead-heats are not rare, but they are comparatively infrequent. However, DAILY RACING FORM Result Charts point out every unusual happening. We reproduce below a portion of a Sample Chart showing how disqualifications and dead-heats are indicated. The DH which precedes the names of the first two horses and is repeated before the odds to $1 means dead-heat, and is virtually self-explanatory, while the D before Zacawon and repeated before the odds to $1 means that he was disqualified.

FIRST RACE
Bel - 7001
Sept'ber 1, 1960

1 MILE. (Count Fleet, Oct. 10, 1952, 1:34⅘, 2, 116.)
Purse, $4,000. 3-year-olds and upward. Maidens. Claiming. Weights, 3-year-olds, 122 lbs.; older, 126 lbs. Claiming price $5,000; if for less, 3 lbs. allowed for each $500 to $3,000.
Value to winners, $1,700 each; third, $400; fourth, $200. Mutuel Pool, $370,950,

Index	Horse	Eq't	A	Wt	PP	St	¼	½	¾	Str	Fin	Jockeys	Cl'gPr	Owners	Odds to $1
6895Bel^2	DH Fall Flight		3	119	12	4	3^1	4^3	$2^{1\frac{1}{2}}$	1^5	1	D Gorman	5000	V Sheskier	DH-a-2.85
6659Atl^4	DH Wise Sun	b	3	112	3	6	8^h	5^h	5^3	3^1	1^3	T Atkinson	3500	B F Spach	DH-1.70
6292GS^3	D Zacawon		3	112	8	10	12^4	9^{nk}	8^4	$4^{\frac{1}{2}}$	3^5	E Arcaro	4000	M MacSchwebel	D-3.25
6094Aqu	—Wherrie	b	3	106	5	8	11^1	12^4	7^1	7^4	4^1	R Permane	3000	B Tetterberg	3.45
4653Del	—Big Sun	b	4	126	4	5	4^h	3^1	3^h	5^h	5^h	J Zubrinic†	5000	Mrs E Mulrenan	a-2.85

DH Dead-heat. D Disqualified and placed last.

a-Coupled, Fall Flight and Big Sun. †Three pounds apprentice allowance waived.

Time, :23⅕, :47⅖, 1:13⅕, 1:39⅗. Track fast.

Official Program Numbers↘

$2 Mutuel Prices:

1-FALL FLIGHT (Dead-heat)(a-Entry)	4.20	3.70	3.40
4-WISE SUN (Dead-heat)	3.40	3.20	2.70
6-WHERRIE			5.90

Fall Flight, ch. f, by Sickle—So Rare, by Stimulus. Trainer, H. Shillick. Bred by A. B. Hancock. Wise Sun, ch. g, by Wise Counsellor—Sun Maiden, by Sunridge. Trainer, W. A. Crawford. Bred by J. R. Neville Co.

IN GATE—1:48. OFF AT 1:48½ EASTERN STANDARD TIME. Start good. Won driving.

FALL FLIGHT raced in nearest pursuit of the early pace, assumed command rounding the stretch turn, but tired suddenly and just lasted to dead-heat with WISE SUN. The latter improved his position steadily and, under a vigorous drive in the stretch run, was up to finish on even terms with FALL FLIGHT. ZACAWON was slow to settle in stride, closed fast under a hard drive after rounding the final bend, but swerved into BIG SUN, forcing the latter to take up sharply, and was disqualified for foul. WHERRIE showed a good effort throughout. BIG SUN was unable to regain his stride after interference.

Dead-Heats, Disqualifications in Past Performances

Nothing is left to the imagination in DAILY RACING FORM Past Performances. When a horse finishes in a dead-heat, or is disqualified, a dagger (†) precedes his jockey's name in the Past Performances followed by an explanatory line which tells what happened to him. Officials have discretionary power to position the disqualified horse. Thus, in both Charts and Past Performances the word "disqualified" is used with reference to placing.

The five Past Performance lines below are taken from the Sample Chart Bel-7001. They show exactly how dead-heats and disqualifications are treated.

FALL FLIGHT

Sep 1-60^{1}Bel	1	1:39$\frac{3}{5}$ft	2$\frac{3}{4}$e	119	3^{2}	$2^{\frac{1}{2}}$	1^{5}	1^{3}	†G'rm'nD^{12}	5000	76	FallFlight 119	WiseSun 112	Zacawon 14

†Dead-heat.

WISE SUN

Sep 1-60^{1}Bel	1	1:39$\frac{3}{5}$ft	9-5	▲112	8^{6}	5^{4}	3^{5}	1^{3}	†Atk'onT^{3}	c3500	76	FallFlight 119	WiseSun 112	Zacawon 14

†Dead-heat.

ZACAWON

Sep 1-60^{1}Bel	1	1:39$\frac{3}{5}$ft	3$\frac{1}{4}$	112	12^{12}	$8^{8\frac{1}{4}}$	4^{6}	3^{3}	†ArcaroE^{8}	4000	73	FallFlight 119	WiseSun 112	Zacawon 14

†Disqualified and placed last.

WHERRIE

Sep 1-60^{1}Bel	1	1:39$\frac{3}{5}$ft	3$\frac{1}{2}$	106	11^{10}	$7^{7\frac{1}{4}}$	7^{7}	4^{8}	†Perma'eR^{5}	3000	68	FallFlight 119	WiseSun 112	Zacawon 14

†Placed third through disqualification.

BIG SUN

Sep 1-60^{1}Bel	1	1:39$\frac{3}{5}$ft	2$\frac{3}{4}$e	126	4^{3}	3^{2}	$5^{6\frac{1}{2}}$	5^{9}	†ZubrinicJ^{4}	5000	67	FallFlight 119	WiseSun 112	Zacawon 14

†Placed fourth through disqualification.

The style used in Past Performances for disqualifications which affect only the purse distribution—usually made several days after the running—is herewith illustrated:

†Disqualified from purse money.
†Awarded first purse money.
†Awarded second purse money.
†Awarded third purse money.
†Awarded fourth purse money.

Foreign Past Performances

The number of imported horses is increasing each year. To provide readers with up-to-date records of the performances of these thoroughbreds in their native lands, the publishers of DAILY RACING FORM have made arrangements with turf authorities and publications of recognized standing in several foreign countries for an exchange of racing information and statistics. This official information is transposed into DAILY RACING FORM past performances to best reveal the quality of the importees. As an example, we reproduce below the complete past performances of the Irish-bred *Stephanotis:

***Stephanotis** **126** B. h (1959), by Stardust—Shello, by Donatello II.
Breeder, The Limestone Stud (Ireland). 1957 . . 6 2 0 1 $10,180
Owner, Mrs. A. Plesch. Trainer, J. M. Rogers. 1956 . . 6 3 0 1 $7,258

Oct30-57 New	1 1-8	1:54$\frac{2}{5}$gd	17	117	Cambridgeshire	1$\frac{3}{4}$	CarrH	Stk	Stephanotis117	Heritiere112	F'ryStone 38
Oct19-57 Cur	1 1-48	hy	9-5	▲147	Irish	5	BurnsTP	Stk	BushW'k 106	Taip'c 116	M'd ofGal'way 12
Aug20-57 Yor	1	1:42$\frac{3}{5}$hy	7	115	Rose of York	4^{3}	CarrW	Hcp	Counsel 114	RiverLine 86	FairyStone 19
Aug10-57 PhP	1	1:47$\frac{1}{5}$sgd	6-5	▲125	North Wall	1^{3}	BurnsTP	Hcp	Stephanotis125	Ant'h'rS'ly101	Calv'ro 6
May 4-57 PhP	1	1:41$\frac{4}{5}$fm	6$\frac{1}{2}$	133	Enniskerry	$3^{4\frac{1}{2}}$	BurkeW	Hcp	Lon'nSc'tish117	D'coVol'te110	Step'tis 12
Apr 6-57 Cur	1	1:53 hy	25	133	Irish Lincolnsh'e	$5^{4\frac{1}{2}}$	BurkeW	Hcp	EndMoney 116	Gladness 140	ButWhy 20
Jun21-56 Ast	1$\frac{1}{2}$	2:35$\frac{2}{5}$sgd	25	129	King George V.	Unp.	Get'nK	HcpS	Donald114	Affiliat'nOrd'r124	GayBal'd 20
Jun 6-56 Epm	1$\frac{1}{2}$	2:36$\frac{2}{5}$fm	33	126	Derby	Unp.	GethinK	Stk	Lavandin 126	Montaval 126	Roistar 27
May25-56 Lfd	1$\frac{1}{4}$	2:11$\frac{1}{5}$sgd	1-6	▲133	Godstone Plate	1^{2}	GethinK		Stephanotis133	Notus 123	Ky.Belle 4
May10-56 Chs	a 1$\frac{1}{4}$	2:10$\frac{2}{5}$	2$\frac{1}{4}$	▲124	Ormonde	1^{nk}	GethinK	Stk	Stephanotis124	Dionisio124	Montauk 8
Apr28-56 San	1	1:47$\frac{2}{5}$gd	3	126	Marcus Beresf'd	1^{2}	GethinK	Stk	Stephanotis126	Articul'te126	F'stLi'ht 24
Apr18-56 New	1	1:43$\frac{3}{5}$gd	9-5	▲126	Wood Ditton	3^{4}	GethinK	Stk	FullM'sure126	FairyCr've123	Steph'otis 11

You will note that only the horse's finishing position is given, since in most foreign countries the positions of the horses are recorded only as they cross the finish line. In place of the missing calls the name of the race is substituted. The letters "Unp" indicate that the horse was unplaced.

NOTE: All foreign-bred horses are identified by an asterisk (*) placed before the horse's name atop the past performance chart. The country of origin is shown after breeder's name.

Track Abbreviations FOR NORTH AMERICAN TRACKS

Abbreviations below designate tracks in DAILY RACING FORM entries and past performances.

AC	— (Agua) Caliente, Mex.	GG	— Golden Gate Fields, Calif.	Pln	— Pleasanton, Calif.
Aks	— Ak-Sar-Ben, Nebr.	Gln	— Glyndon Hunt, Md.	PM	— Portland Meadows, Ore.
Alb	— Albuquerque, N. Mex.	GM	—*Green Mountain Park, Vt.	Pom	—*Pomona, Calif.
Ali	—*Alliance, Neb. (Sandhillo)	GmP	—*Gresham Park, Ore.	PP	— Pikes Peak Meadows, Colo.
AP	— Arlington Park, Ill.	GN	— Grand National Hunt, Md.	PR	— Puerto Rico
Aqu	— Aqueduct, N. Y.	GP	— Gulfstream Park, Fla.	Pre	—*Prescott, Ariz.
Asc	—*Ascot Park,Ohio	Grd	—†*Greenwood, Can.	Pur	— Purchase, N. Y.
AsD	— Assiniboia Downs, Can.	GS	— Garden State Park, N. J.	PW	— Percy Warner Hunt, Tenn.
Atl	— Atlantic City, N. J.	Hag	—*Hagerstown, Md.	Ran	— Randall Park, Ohio
Ato	—*Atokad, Neb.	Haw	— Hawthorne, Ill.	RaP	—*‡Raceway Park, Ohio
BB	—*Blue Bonnets, Can.	Hia	— Hialeah Park, Fla.	RB	— Red Bank Hunts, N. J.
BD	—*Berkshire Downs, Mass.	Hol	— Hollywood Park, Calif.	RD	— River Downs, Ohio
Bel	— Belmont Park, N. Y.	HP	—*Hazel Park, Mich.	Reg	—*Regina, Can.
Beu	— Beulah Park, Ohio	JnD	— Jefferson Downs, La.	Ril	—*Rillito, Ariz.
BF	—*Brockton Fair, Mass.	Jua	— Juarez, Mex.	Rkm	— Rockingham, N. H.
Bil	—*Billings, Mont.	Kee	— Keeneland, Ky.	Roy	— Royalton Hunt, Ind.
Blr	—*Bel Air, Md.	LaM	—*La Mesa Park, N. Mex.	Rui	—*Ruidoso, N. Mex.
BM	— Bay Meadows, Calif.	Lat	—*Latonia, Ky.	SA	— Santa Anita Park, Calif.
Bmf	— Bay Meadows Fair, Calif.	LaV	— Las Vegas, Nev.	Sac	— Sacramento, Calif.
Bml	— Balmoral, Ill.	Lbg	—*Lethbridge, Can.	Sal	—*Salem, Ore.
Bow	— Bowie, Md.	LD	—*Lincoln Downs, R. I.	San	— Sandown Park, B. C., Can.
Cam	— Camden Hunt,,S. C.	Lga	— Longacres, Wash.	Sar	— Saratoga, N. Y.
CD	— Churchill Downs, Ky.	Lig	—*Ligonier Hunt, Pa.	Sas	—*Saskatoon, Can.
Ceg	— Calgary, Can. (Victoria Pk.)	LnN	—*Lincoln State Fair, Neb.	ScD	—*Scarborough Downs, Me.
Cen	— Centennial Race Track, Colo.	LP	— Lansdowne Park, Can.	ShD	—*Shenandoah Downs, W. Va.
CF	—*Cumberland Fair, Md.	Lrl	— Laurel Park, Md.	Sol	— Solano, Calif.
Cka	—*Cahokia Downs, Ill.	Mad	—*Madison, Neb.	SoP	— Southern Pines Hunt, N. C.
Clm	— Clemmons, N. C.	Mal	—*Malvern Hunt, Pa.	Spt	—*Sportsman's Park, Ill.
Cls	—*Columbus, Neb.	Mar	—*Marlboro, Md.	SP	— Sunshine Park, Fla.
Col	— Columbia, S. C.	Mch	—*Mitchell, Neb.	SR	—*Santa Rosa, Calif.
Crn	—*Cranwood Park, Ohio	Med	—*Media, Pa.	Stk	—*Stockton, Calif.
CT	—*Charles Town, W. Va.	Mem	—*Memorial Park, Colo.	Suf	— Suffolk Downs, Mass.
Del	— Delaware Park, Del.	Mex	—*Mexico City, Mex.	Sun	— Sunland Park, N. Mex.
Det	— Detroit, Mich.	MF	—*Marshfield Fair, Mass.	Tan	— Tanforan, Calif.
Dmr	— Del Mar, Calif.	Mid	— Middleburg Hunt, Va.	Tdn	— ThistleDown Park, Ohio
DR	—*Deep Run Hunt, Va.	Mon	— Monkton Hunt, Md.	ThD	— Thunderbird Downs, Nev.
EIP	— Ellis Park, Ky.	MP	—*Miles Park, Ky.	Tim	—*Timonium, Md.
EP	—*Exhibition Park, Can.	Mth	— Monmouth Park, N. J.	TrP	— Tropical Park Fla.
Fai	— Fair Hill Hunt, Md.	Mtp	—*Montpelier Hunt, W. Va.	Try	—*Tryon Hunt,N. C.
Fax	— Fairfax Hunt, Va.	Nar	—*Narragansett Park, R. I.	TuP	— Turf Paradise, Ariz.
FE	— Fort Erie, Can.	Nmp	—*Northampton, Mass.	Uni	— Unionville Hunt, Pa.
Fer	— Ferndale, Calif.	NP	—*Northlands Park, Can.	War	— Warrenton Hunt, Va.
FG	— Fair Grounds, La.	Oak	— Oak Brook Hunt, Ill.	Was	— Washington Park, Ill.
FH	— Far Hills, N. J.	OG	— Oak Grove, Tenn.	Wat	— Waterford Park, W. Va.
FL	— Finger Lakes, N. Y.	OP	— Oaklawn Park, Ark.	Wey	—*Weymouth Fair, Mass.
Fno	— Fresno, Calif.	Oxm	— Oxmoor Hunt, Ky.	Whe	—*Wheeling Downs, W. Va.
Fon	— Fonner Park, Neb.	Pim	— Pimlico, Md.	WmV	—*Whitemarsh Val. Hunt, Pa.
FP	— Fairmount Park, Ill.	Pin	— Pinehurst Hunt, N. Car.	WO	— Woodbine, Can.
GBF	—*Great Barrington, Mass.	PJ	—*Park Jefferson, S. D.	YM	— Yakima Meadows, Wash.
GF	—*Great Falls, Mont.	Pla	— Playfair, Wash.		

Tracks marked with an asterisk (*) are less than one mile in circumference. The new abbreviations contained in the table above are shown here in bold face, with those formerly used shown in parenthesis **RaP** (RaT)— *Raceway Park, Toledo, Ohio; **Grd** (OW)—*†Formerly Old Woodbine, changed to Greenwood. Toronto, Can. **NP** (Edm)—*‡Formerly named Edmonton, Can.

Markings

STAR—Small patch of white hair on the forehead. It is never called a "white" star, the adjective being assumed.

BLAZE—A larger white patch. If spread over the entire face the horse could be described as having a "white face."

STRIP—White running part-way down the face.

STRIPE—Thin narrow mark running down the face to bridge of nose or below.

SNIP—Small patch on the lip or nose. This may be either white or flesh-colored.

One also omits the term "white" in describing the markings of a coronet or fetlock unless one speaks of white socks or stockings, the meaning of which is obvious.

There are other white body markings. Some of these are congenital, others the result of an injury over which the hair has grown white.

ABBREVIATIONS FOR FOREIGN TRACKS

Track	Abbr.	Track	Abbr.	Track	Abbr.
Aberdeen, Aus.	AbA	Galway, Ire.	Gal	Ostend, Belgium	Ost
Africa	Af	Goodwood, Eng.	Gwd	Otaki Maori, N. Z.	OtM
Aintree, Eng.	Ain	Gosford, Aus.	GoA	Palermo, Arg.	Pal
Aix-En-Provence, Fr.	AEP	Gowran Park, Ire.	GoP	Panama	Pan
Alexandra Park, Eng.	Alx	Hamburg, Ger.	Ham	Perth, Scot.	Per
Amiens, Fra.	Amie	Hamilton, Scot.	Hml	Phoenix Park, Ire.	PhP
Andelys, Fra.	And	Hanshin, Japan	Han	Plumpton, Eng.	Plu
Angers, Fra.	Ang	Hawkes Bay, N. Z.	H.B	Pompadour, Fra.	Pomp
Ascot, Eng.	Ast	Haydock Park, Eng.	Hay	Pontefract, Eng.	Pon
Auckland, N. Z.	Auc	Hazeldean, Aus.	HnA	Powerstown Park, Ire.	Pow
Australia	Aus	Hereford, Eng.	Hfd	Punchestown, Ire.	Pun
Auteuil, Fra.	Aut	Hipodromo Argentino, S. A.	HAr	Queensland, Aus.	QdA
Ayr, Scot.	Ayr	Hipodromo Chile, Chile	HCh	Rafaela, Arg.	Raf
Baden Baden, Ger.	BaB	Horst-Emscher, Ger.	Hor	Randwick, Aus.	Rand
Baldoyle, Ire.	Bal	Hurst Park, Eng.	HuP	Redcar, Eng.	Red
Bangor-on-Dee, Eng.	Bo-D	Iffezheim-Baden, Ger.	If-Ba	Reims, Fra.	Rei
Bath, Eng.	Bat	Isle Sorgue, Fra.	I.S	Rennes, Fra.	Rei
Beaudesert, Aus.	BtA	Jamaica, B. W. I.	BWI	Rinconada, Vza.	Rin
Belgium	Belg	Kelso, Scot.	Kel	Rio de Janiero, Brazil	R.J
Bellestown, Ire.	Bell	Kembia Grange, Aus.	K.G.	Ripon, Eng.	Rip
Berlin, East Germany	BlnE	Kempton Park, Eng.	Kem	Rome, Italy	Rom
Bernay, Fra.	Bern	Kilbeggan, Ire.	Kilb	Rosario, Arg.	Rio
Beverley, Eng.	Bev	Killarney, Ire.	Kill	Roscommon, Ire.	Rmn
Biarritz-Bayonne, Fra.	Brtz	Knutsford Park, B. W. I.	Kfd	Rosehill, Aus.	Ros
Birmingham, Eng.	Bir	Koin, Ger.	Koi	Rouen, Fra.	Rou
Bogota, Col.	Bgta	Krefeld, Ger.	Kre	Saint-Cloud, Fra.	StC
Bogside, Scot.	Bog	Kretein, Ger.	Kret	Salisbury, Eng.	Sby
Boiktort, Belgium	Boik	Kyoto, Japan	Kyo	Sandown, Eng.	Sdn
Bordeaux, Fra.	Bor	La Capelle, Fra.	LaC	San Felipe, Peru	SF:
Brazil	Braz	Lanark, Scot.	Lan	San Isidro, Arg.	S.I.
Brighton, Eng.	Bri	La Plata, S. A.	LaP	Santiago, Chile	Sant
Brisbane, Aus.	Bris.	Layton, Ire.	Layt	Sedgefield, Eng.	Sed
Brussels, Belgium	Bru	Leghorn, Italy	Lgn	Sligo, Ire.	Sli
Buckfastleigh, Eng.	Bgh	Leicester, Eng.	Lei	South Africa	SthA
Budapest, Hungary	Bda	Leopardstown, Ire.	Leo	Southwell, Eng.	Sll
Cagnes, Fra.	Cgs	Le Tremblay, Fra.	Tre	St. Malo, Fra.	StM
Canterbury, Aus.	Can	Lewes, Eng.	Lew	Stockel, Belgium	Stkl
Caracas, Venez.	Cara	Lima, Peru	Peru	Stockholm, Sweden	Stock
Carlisle, Eng.	Car	Limerick Junction, Ire.	LimJ	Stockton, Eng.	Stn
Catterick, Eng.	Ctk	Lincoln, Eng.	Lin	Stratford-on-Avon, Eng.	SoA
Caulfield, Aus.	Cau	Lingfield, Eng.	Lfd	Sydney, Aus.	Syd
Cavaillon, Fra.	Cav	Listowell, Ire.	List	Taunton, Eng.	Tau
Cessnock, Aus.	CeA	Liverpool, Eng	Liv	Thirsk, Eng.	Tsk
Chantilly, Fra.	Cha	Longchamp, Fra.	Lon	Thurles, Ire.	Thur
Cheltenham, Eng.	Che	Loudeac, Fra.	Lou	Tokyo, Japan	Tok
Cheltenham, Aus.	ChA	Ludlow, Eng.	Lud	Toowoomba, Aus.	ToA
Chepstow, Eng.	Chep	Lvov, Ukrania	Lvov	Toulouse, Fra.	Toul
Chester, Eng.	Chs	Lyons, Fra.	Lyon	Touquest, Fra.	Tou
Cidare Jardim, Brazil	CiJ	Maissons-Laffitte, Fra.	Mai	Towcester, Eng.	Tow
Clairfontaine, Fra.	Cla	Mallow, Fra.	Mall	Tralee, Ire.	Tra
Clarendon, Aus.	Cln	Manchester, Eng.	Man	Tramore, Ire.	Trm
Club Hipico de Santiago, Chile	HdS	Marseille, Fra.	Msl	Turin, Italy	Tur
Cologne, Ger.	Clqe	Masterton, N. Z.	Mas	Uruguay	Uru
Columbia, S. A.	CSA	Manawatu, N. Z.	Mtu	Uttoxetter, Eng.	Utx
Compiegne, Fra.	Com	Mendoza, Arg.	Mda	Valparaiso, Chile	Val
Cordoba, Arg.	Cor	Merano, Italy	Mer	Vannes, Fra.	Van
Cote d'Azur, Fra.	Cd'A	Milan, Italy	Mil	Varese, Italy	Var
Craon, Fra.	Cra	Monterrico, Peru	Mto	Vernon, Fra.	Ver
Croise-Laroche, Fra.	C-L	Moonee Vly, Aus.	MVA	Vichy, Fra.	Vich
Curragh, Ire.	Cur	Mornington, Aus.	Mor	Victoria, Aus.	Vic
Deauville, Fra.	Dea	Morphetville, Aus.	Mrpt	Vienna, Austria	Vna
Devon-Exeter, Eng.	Dev	Moscow, Russia	Mos.	Waikato, N. Z.	Wto
Dieppe, Fra.	Diep	Mulheim, Ger.	Muh	Wanganui, N. Z.	Wan
Doncaster, Eng.	Don	Mullinger, Ire.	Mul	Warsaw, Poland	Wsw
Dortmund, Ger.	Dor	Naas, Ire.	Naas	Warwick, Eng.	Wak
Down Royal, Ire.	DRoy	Nakayama, Japan	Nak	Warwick Farm, Aus.	WarF
Duindigt, Holland	Ddt	Nantes, Fra.	Nan	Waterford-Tramore, Ire.	Wa-T
Dundalk, Ire.	Dun	Naples, Italy	Nap	Wellington, N. Z.	Wel
Dusseldorf, Ger.	Dus	Navan, Ire.	Nav	Werribee, Aus.	Wer
Edinburgh, Scot.	Edn	Neuss, Ger.	Nus	Wetherby, Eng.	Wet
Elbeut, Fra.	Elb	Newbury, Eng.	Nby	Windsor, Eng.	Win
Enghien, Fra.	Eng	Newcastle, Aus.	NeA	Wolverhampton, Eng.	Wolv
Epsom, Eng.	Epm	Newcastle, Eng.	Nec	Woodend, Aus.	Wdn
Esk, Australia	Esk	Newmarket, Eng.	New	Worcester, Eng.	Wor
Fairyhouse, Ire.	Fy	Newton Abbott, Eng.	Ntn	Wye, Eng.	Wye
Flemington, Aus.	FlA	New Zealand	N.Z	Wyong, Aus.	Wvo
Folkestone, Eng.	Fol	Nort Erdre, Fra.	NoE	Yarmouth, Eng.	Yar
Fontainebleau, Fra.	Font	Nottingham, Eng.	Not	York, Eng.	Yor
Fontwell, Eng.	Fwl	Orleans, Fra.	Orl	Yugoslavia	Yugo
Frankfort, Ger.	Fra	Oslo, Norway	Oslo		

21 The Racegoer's Dictionary

Acey deucy—Riding style in which right stirrup is shorter than left, enabling jockey to balance more easily on turns.

Across the board—Three bets—win, place and show—on one horse.

Added money—Purse money with which track management supplements stakes posted by owners and breeders.

Aged—Of a horse, aged seven or older.

Airing—A workout; a racing performance in which horse runs as if it were only out for exercise.

All-out—Maximum exertion.

Allowance race—A non-claiming affair in which published conditions stipulate weight allowances according to previous purse earnings and/or number or type of victories.

Also eligible—Official entrants that will not run unless other horses are scratched and vacancies occur in field.

Also-ran—Horse that finished out of the money.

Alter—To castrate, geld.

Ankle boot—Protective covering for fetlock, usually leather or rubber.

Ankle cutter—Horse that cuts a fetlock with opposite foot while running.

Apprentice—Student jockey.

Apprentice allowance—Weight concession granted animal ridden by apprentice.

Arm—Foreleg, between elbow and knee; forearm.

Armchair ride—Easy victory without urging by rider.

Baby—Two-year-olds, especially during first months of year.

Baby race—Two-, three- or four-furlong race for two-year-olds, early in year.

Back at the knee—Defective conformation in which foreleg bends slightly backward at knee.

Backstretch—Straight part of track on far side; stable area.

Back up—Slow down noticeably.

Bad actor—Fractious horse.

Bad doer—Horse that lacks appetite, usually because of illness, pain, fatigue, nervousness or loneliness.

Badger—Cheap horse that qualifies owner for track privileges; "badge horse."

Bald—Of a horse, with a white face.

Ball—Pill; physic.

Bandage—Leg wrapping.

Bangtail—Tail bobbed or tied short; journalese for horse.

Bar plates—Horseshoes with bars across rear.

Barrel—Horse's torso.

Barrier—Starting gate.

Baseball—Daily-double play in which bettor couples a horse in one race with all horses in the other; "wheeling."

Bat—Whip (a term used by writers, not jockeys).

Bay—Brown or tan horse with black mane and tail.

Bear in—Running toward inside rail instead of straight.

Bear out—Running toward outside, especially on turns.

Beef—Protest, usually by jockey about another's riding tactics.

Bell—Signals start of race and termination of betting.

Bend—A turn of the track.

Big Apple—A major racing circuit.

Bill Daly—Rider who takes lead as soon as possible is "on the Bill Daly." Famous trainer, "Father Bill" Daly, used to tell jockeys, "Get on top right away and improve your position."

Bit—Metal mouth bar to which reins are attached.

Blanket finish—Extremely close finish.

Blaze—Large white marking on horse's face.

Bleeder—Horse that bleeds during heavy exertion, usually from ruptured blood vessels of nose.

Blind switch—In which rider finds his mount pocketed behind horses and must decide whether to hope for an opening or take back and go around.

Blinkers—Eye pieces that limit a horse's vision and sometimes help him to concentrate on running.

Blister—Treatment of damaged tissue with chemical irritant or heat, causes blistering and encourages development of scar tissue.

Block heel—Horseshoe with raised heel, to prevent running down.

Bloodline—Pedigree.

Blow out—Short exercise to limber a horse before its race.

Blue roan—Horse with coat of black, white and yellow hairs, producing blue-gray effect.

Boat race—A fixed race.

Bobble—Stumble; break stride clumsily.

Bog Spavin—Puffy swelling on inside of hock. Caused by strain.

Bold eye—Prominent eye, supposedly sign of courage.

Bold front—Long, well-muscled neck, another sign of courage.

Bolt—To run off in wrong direction, as when horse tries to return to barn instead of going to starting gate.

Bone spavin—Bony swelling, usually below the hock joint.

Book—Jockey's schedule of riding assignments; bookmaker; bookmaker's tally of amounts bet on each horse and odds necessary to assure him of profit.

Boot—To kick horse, as when booting it home in race; rubber or leather anklet.

Boots and Saddles—Bugle call sounded when riders mount and when horses enter track for post parade.

Bottom—Equine stamina; horse assigned outside post position and listed last in program of race; sub-surface of racing strip.

Bottom line—Bottom, or female side of pedigree.

Bow—When strained sheath of flexor tendon ruptures, allowing tendon to stand out behind cannon bone like string of a bow.

Boy—Jockey.

Brace—Horse liniment.

Brackets—Victory, because index numbers with which official result charts identify previous race of each horse are enclosed in brackets if horse won that race.

Break—Start of race; accustoming young horse to saddle, bridle and rider.

Breakage—Difference between true mutuel odds and lesser, rounded amounts given to winning players. The resultant millions usually are divided between track and state.

Break down—Become unable to race because of lameness or injury.

Break in the air—Leap upward at the start, instead of hustling forward.

Break maiden—When horse or rider wins first race of career.

Breastplate—Leather passed across chest of horse and fastened to each side of saddle, keeping it in place. Used on thin horses.

Breather—Restraining horse to rest and relax it before stretch drive.

Breed—To mate horses.

Breeder—Owner of mare at time she drops foal.

Breeze—Running under a stout hold, easily, without encouragement.

Bridge-jumper—Bettor who specializes in large show bets on odds-on favorites.

Brisket—Area of horse's body between forelegs.

Brittle feet—Hooves that chip easily and are difficult to shoe.

Broken knees—Skin lesions at knee.

Broken wind—When overstrained lung tissue breaks down, causing breathing problems; "heaves."

Broodmare—Female Thoroughbred used for breeding.

Broodmare dam—Mare whose female offspring become good broodmares.

Broodmare sire—Male horse whose female offspring become good broodmares.

Bruce Lowe system—A method of identifying Thoroughbred families by number, according to the female ancestor from which each family descends.

Brushing—Horse scrapes fetlock with opposite shoe. Caused by improper balance, poor shoes or fatigue.

Bucked shins—Shins painfully inflamed by overstrain.

Bug boy—Apprentice jockey, because of asterisk with which newspapers identify apprentice in entry lists.

Bull ring—Small track, because of sharp turns.

Bushes—Small-time, bush-league racing.

Buy the rack—Purchase every possible daily-double ticket.

Buzzer—Battery-powered oscillator or vibrator used illegally to frighten horse into running.

Calculator—Clerk who computes parimutuel odds.

Calk—Horseshoe cleat for greater purchase in mud or on grass.

Call—To announce progress of race for purposes of official result charts (chart-caller); to describe race to audience; stage of race at which running positions are recorded, like "half-mile call."

Canker—Foot infection that softens the hoof.

Cannon—Foreleg between knee and ankle. Rear leg between hock and ankle.

Canter—Slow gallop; lope.

Capped—Swollen, as of elbow or hock rubbed or bumped in stall.

Card—Program of racing.

Car fit—Severe fright while being shipped in van, train or plane.

Carry the target—Run last all the way.

Cast—Fallen and unable to rise, as of a horse; lost or "thrown," as of a horseshoe.

Chalk horse—Betting favorite.

Chalk player—Bettor on favorites.

Challenge—To vie for lead.

Chart—Result chart.

Chase—Steeplechase.

Chestnut—Brown or tan horse with brown tail and mane; horny growth ("night eyes") on inside of horse's legs.

Choppy—Of stride, shortness, often reveals soreness.

Chute—Extension of stretch to permit long, straight run from starting gate to first turn.

Circuit—Geographical grouping of tracks whose meetings are coordinated to run in sequence.

Claim—To buy horse in claiming race.

Claimer—Claiming race; horse that runs in such races.

Claiming box—Where claims are deposited before race.

Clerk of the scales—Weighs riders and tack before and after race.

Clever—Of a horse, kindly, easily managed, able.

Client—Purchaser of betting information from horseman or other tipster.

Climb—To run with unusually high motion of forelegs, usually when flustered or tired.

Clocker—Person who times workouts, usually for betting information.

Close—Of final odds on horse ("closed at 2 to 1"); to gain ground on leader.

Close-coupled—Of a horse, short-backed.

Close fast—Finish fast, gaining on leader.

Clothes—Horse blanket.

Clubhouse turn—Turn of track nearest clubhouse; first turn of races that begin on homestretch.

Coffin bone—Main bone in equine foot.

Cold—Of a horse, unreadiness to win because of physical condition or stable's intentions.

Cold-blooded—Of a non-Thoroughbred horse.

Colors—Distinctively patterned rider's costumes identifying owner.

Colt—Unaltered male horse aged four or less.

Combination—Across-the-board bet for which a single mutuel ticket is issued.

Come back to—Of a horse, to tire and slow down, allowing other horse to close gap.

Condition—Equine form or fitness; to train a horse.

Condition book—Publication in which track announces purses, terms of eligibility and weight formulas of races.

Conditions—Terms of race, including

purse size, eligibility for entry, and weight concessions.

Connections—Owner, trainer and other custodians of horse.

Consolation double—When horse is scratched from second race after daily-double betting begins, money is set aside to pay those who have bought tickets pairing horse with winner of first race.

Contract rider—Jockey on whose services an owner, by contract, has first call.

Cooler—Covering draped on horse while it cools out after race or workout; horse that is restrained to prevent it from running well.

Corn—Horny callus caused by irritation from horseshoes.

Coronet—Area just above hoof; "crown of hoof."

Cover—Of a stallion, act of coupling with a mare.

Cow hocks—Hocks that turn toward each other, like cow's.

Cresty—Of horse, thick-necked and probably not nimble.

Cribber—Horse that bites parts of its stall, sucking air into lungs; "windsucker"; "crib-biter."

Cropper—Spill, usually in jump race.

Croup—Top hindquarters of horse.

Crowd—To race too close to another horse, forcing its rider to take up or change course.

Cryptorchid—Male horse with undescended testicle.

Cuff—Horse anklet; credit ("on the cuff").

Cull—Unwanted horse disposed of by owner.

Cup—Type of blinker.

Cup horse—Good router.

Cuppy—Of a track, when surface breaks into clods and shows hoofprints.

Curb—Sprain at back of hock; a powerful bit equipped with extra strap or chain beneath horse's chin.

Cushion—Subsurface of track.

Cut down—Of a horse, injured during race by shoe of another horse or by striking itself with own shoe.

Daily double—Form of mutuel betting in which player attempts to pick winners of two races, buying a single ticket on the double choice.

Dam—Horse's mother.

Dark—Of a track at which or a day on which there is no racing.

Dark horse—Underrated animal that wins or has good prospects of winning.

Dash—Sprint race.

Dead heat—When two or more horses reach finish wire simultaneously.

Dead weight—Lead slabs carried in saddle to increase weight of jockey and tack.

Declaration to win—Public announcement by owner of more than one entrant in a race that he will try to win with one but not with the others.

Declare—To withdraw horse from race.

Deep—Of racing surface recently harrowed or to which extra top soil has been added, increasing holding qualities.

Derby—Stakes race for three-year-olds.

Destroy—To kill a horse.

Disqualify—To lower horse's actual finishing position by official act after deciding it interfered with others during race, or carried improper weight or was drugged.

Distaff side—Female ancestry, shown in lower half of pedigree.

Distance of ground—A route race.

Division—When too many entries are made in an important race, track may divide it into two races.

Doer—Of a horse, eater.

Dog—Obstructions placed near rail when track is muddy, to prevent horses from running there and kicking up the surface during workouts; cheap horse; quitter.

Dope—Information about races or horses; drugs.

Draw Away—To win going away; "draw clear"; "draw out."

Drench—To give horse liquid medicine.

Drive—All-out exertion, under heavy punishment, especially in homestretch.

Drop—Give birth to foal.

Dun—Mousy, grayish color in brown to gold range, usually with black mane and tail.

Dutch—To take advantage of booking percentages by eliminating heavily bet non-contenders, betting on others in exact proportions necessary to yield profit no matter which wins.

Dwell—Of a horse that breaks slowly from the gate.

Early foot—Good speed at beginning of race.

Ease up—To slow horse's stride, sparing it exertion.

Easy ride—Performance in which jockey fails to try.

Eggs (walking on)—Of a sore horse.

Eighth—Furlong; 220 yards; 660 feet.

Eighth pole—Colored post at the inside rail exactly one furlong from finish wire.

Empty—Of a horse that lacks energy for finishing drive.

English Stud Book—Official repository of English Thoroughbred records.

Entire—Of an unaltered male horse.

Entry—Two or more horses owned by same interests, or trained by same person, entered in same race and coupled in the betting.

Ewe-necked—Of a horse with concave neck, a sign of clumsiness.

Exacta—Form of betting in which player attempts to pick winner and second horse, buying one mutuel ticket on the double choice.

Excused—Permitted to withdraw horse after official scratch time.

Exercise boy—Rider in training workouts.

Extend—To force horse to go all out.

Fade—To tire and drop out of contention.

False quarter—Horizontal crack in hoof, caused by coronet injury.

Falter—To tire badly.

Farrier—Horseshoer.

Fast track—Dry, hard strip on which horses run fastest; a track at which typical running times are relatively fast by comparison with most other tracks.

Feather—Extremely light weight.

Fetlock—Horse's ankle.

Field—All entrants in race; in parimutuel betting, two or more lightly regarded horses grouped as a single betting entry.

Filly—Female horse, aged four or less.

Film patrol—Crew that records running of each race on movie film or television tape, for possible review by stewards when questions arise about behavior of horse or rider.

Fire—Cauterization of ailing tissue with red-hot needle or firing iron.

Fit—Of a horse, physical readiness.

Five-eighths pole—Post at inside rail, exactly five furlongs from finish wire.

Flag—Signal held by official flag man a few yards in front of the gate, where race actually starts. Timing begins when horses reach that point and he drops flag.

Flag down—To wave at an exercise rider to indicate horse is working too hard.

Flash—Change of odds information on tote board.

Flat—Conventional racing surface, contrasted with grass or jump course.

Flatten out—Of an exhausted horse that stops, often dropping its head flat-level with body.

Foal—Newborn horse; of a mare, to give birth.

Foot—Speed; soft tissue beneath hoof.

Footing—Condition of track surface.

Forearm—Horse's foreleg between elbow and knee.

Forked—Of horse's conformation where forelegs join body.

Form—Of a horse, current condition; *Daily Racing Form.*

Form player—Bettor who makes selections from past-performance records.

Fractions—Clockings at quarter-mile intervals in races and workouts.

Free lance—Jockey not under contract to one stable.

Freemartin—Filly twin of a colt.

Freshener—Layoff designed to restore energies of overworked horse.

Frog—Triangular fleshy cushion on sole of horse's foot.

Front runner—Horse that prefers to run in front.

Furlong—One eighth of a mile.

Futurity—Race in which horses are entered before birth.

Gad—Jockey's whip.

Gait—Equine walk, trot or gallop; horse's action or "way of going."

Gallop—Fastest gait; workout; an easy race or workout, compared with one in which horse is urged.

Garrison finish—Victory by a come-from-behind horse, such as those ridden by the famous Snapper Garrison.

Gaskin—Hind leg between thigh and hock.

Gate—Starting gate; entrance to track.

Gelding—Castrated male horse.

Gentleman jockey—Amateur rider.

Get—Offspring of stallion.

Getaway day—Last day of race meeting.

Get into—Of a rider, to whip horse.

Gimpy—Of a lame, sore, "ouchy" horse.

Girth—Saddle band.

Go—Of a stable or horse, to start in a race; an effort to win.

Going—Condition of racing surface; of a horse, its stride ("way of going").

Going away—Winning while increasing the lead.

Good bone—Impressive bone structure indicative of weight-bearing ability and ruggedness.

Good doer—Of a horse, a hearty eater.

Go on—Of a horse, to win at a new, longer distance. "I think he'll go on."

Goose-rumped—Of a horse, high hindquarters with a sharp slope at base of tail.

Grab—To catch foreleg with a hind foot, because of faulty conformation. Causes stumbling, loss of stride.

Graded race—One in which eligibility is limited to horses in one or another classification, as determined by racing secretary. Graded allowances and grade handicaps are common.

Graduate—To break maiden.

Grandam—Equine grandma.

Grandsire—Equine grandpa.

Gray—Equine color composed of black and white hairs.

Groom—Stable employee who tends horse, brings it to paddock for race.

Grounded—Of a jockey, suspended from competition for infractions of rules.

Grunter—Horse whose noisy breathing indicates unreadiness for hard exertion.

Guinea—Stablehand, because winning British owners used to tip the groom a guinea.

Gumbo—Heavy mud.

Gun—All-out effort by jockey.

Gypsy—Itinerant owner-trainer; "gyp."

Half—Half-mile; time "to the half" is fractional time after half a mile of running.

Half brother—Male horse out of same dam as, but by different sire than another horse.

Half-mile pole—Vertical pole at infield rail exactly four furlongs from finish line.

Half-miler—A track of that distance; horse that prefers such a track.

Half sister—Female horse out of same dam as, but by different sire than another horse.

Halter—Hand-held rope or strap by which horses are led; to claim a horse.

Halter man—Owner or trainer who specializes in buying horses from claiming races.

Hand—Four inches of equine height.

Handicap—Race in which racing secretary or track handicapper assigns weights designed to equalize winning chances of entrants; to study horses' records in effort to determine winner of race.

Handicap Triple Crown—Mythical award to horse that wins the three classic handicaps—the Brooklyn, Suburban and Metropolitan—in one season.

Handily—Of a comparatively easy victory achieved without hard urging; of a fairly strenuous workout under a hand ride without whipping.

Handle—Total sum bet on a race or in a day or some other period.

Hand ride—Urging horse toward longer, faster, more rhythmic stride by rolling hands on its neck, lifting its head at beginning of stride.

Handy—Of a nimble, trappy, light-footed, easily guided horse.

Hang—Of a horse unable to produce the expected finishing kick and therefore unable to improve its position in the stretch.

Hardboot—A Kentucky horseman of the old school, because of the legendary mud caked on his boots.

Hat trick—The winning, usually by a jockey, of three races on a single program.

Have one in the boot—To ride a horse whose owner or trainer has made bets, including one for the rider.

Hayburner—Horse that fails to pay its own feed bill; "oatburner."

Headed—Beaten by a head to the wire.

Head of the stretch—End of the final turn; top of the stretch.

Heat—A race.

Heavy-fronted—Of a horse with extremely wide, muscular chest. Supposedly a sign of poor quality.

Heavy-headed—Of a horse that fights the reins, responds slowly to guidance, or prefers to run with its head low.

Heavy-topped—Of a horse with an unusually large, muscular body by comparison with its legs. A sign of susceptibility to soreness and lameness.

Heavy track—A running surface drier than muddy, and often slower.

Height—Of a horse, distance from ground to withers.

Herd—To alter horse's course so as to prevent another from improving its position.

Herring-gutted—A poor doer with practically no depth of abdomen.

Hind sticker—Horseshoe similar to mud calk, except that cleat is on outside edge.

Hip number—Identification number attached to horse's hip at Thoroughbred sales.

Hock—Hind elbow joint between gaskin and cannon.

Homebred—Horse foaled in state where it races.

Homestretch—Straight part of track from final turn to finish wire.

Honest—Of a kind, reliable horse.

Hood—Head covering containing blinkers.

Hop—To drug a horse illegally.

Horse—Technically, any entire male aged five or more.

Horseman—An owner or trainer.

Horseman's Benevolent and Protective Association—Trade association of owners and trainers.

Horsing—Of a mare in heat.

Hot—Of a horse expected to win; of a jockey or stable on a winning streak; of a horse overheated from exertion.

Hot-walker—Stablehand who walks horse while it cools out after a race or workout.

Hunt—Amateur racing, mainly on grass and over jumps.

Hurdle race—A race over low obstacles.

Ice—To anesthetize a horse's painful feet or legs by standing it in ice.

Impost—Weight carried by horse.

In-and-outer—Inconsistent horse that "runs hot and cold."

Index—Number that identifies a specific result chart. When printed in racing papers, directs player to chart of horse's most recent race.

Infield—The area on the inner circumference of the track, where grass and jump races are run and the tote board is found.

In hand—Of a horse running under restraint.

In light—Carrying relatively little weight.

Inquiry—Official investigation of the running of a race to see whether it was fairly won.

In shape—Of a horse ready to win.

Inside—Anything to the left of a horse during the race; position closest to the rail.

Inside rail—Fence separating racing strip from infield.

Interfere—Of a horse, to strike a leg with opposite hoof; to impede another horse in the race.

In the can—An out-of-the-money finish; "in the crapper," etc.

In the money—Technically, a finish in the first four, entitling the owner to a share of the purse; among bettors, a finish in the first three, resulting in a mutuel payoff.

In tough—Of a horse entered with animals it is unlikely to beat.

Irons—Stirrups.

Jail—Of the first month that a claimed horse is in the new barn, when racing law requires it to run at a 25 percent higher claiming price or remain idle.

Jam—Traffic jam during a race.

Jockey—Race rider; to maneuver for position during a race.

Jockey agent—Person who helps rider obtain mounts in return for 20 percent or more of the rider's earnings.

Jockey Club—Name taken by organizations that operate tracks; New York organization that maintains the American Stud Book and approves Thoroughbred names and registry; the governing body of British racing.

Jockeys' Guild—National association of race riders.

Jog—Slow, easy gait, similar to a trot.

Jostle—To bump another horse during a race.

Journeyman—A full-fledged professional jockey.

Jumper—Horse that runs in steeplechase or hurdle races.

Jump up—Of a horse that wins in a surprising reversal of form.

Juvenile—Two-year-old.

Kiss the eighth pole—Of a horse, to finish far behind.

Kitchen—Horsemen's restaurant in backstretch area.

Knee spavin—Bony growth behind knee, caused by blow or overstrain. More serious than hock spavin.

Laminitis—Serious inflammation of equine foot.

Lay—To occupy a certain running position deliberately, while waiting to make strategic move. "Lay fourth, off the pace."

Lead pad—Saddle pocket in which lead weights can be placed.

Lead pony—Horse on which outrider escorts Thoroughbreds to the post.

Leaky roof circuit—Minor tracks.

Leather—A whip.

Leathers—Stirrup straps.

Leg lock—When jockey illegally hooks legs with another rider, impeding the other horse.

Leg up—To build horse's speed and stamina with work; a jockey's riding assignment.

Length—Eight or nine feet.

Light over the kidney—Of a horse, slender-loined; wasp-waisted.

Line—Pedigree; male side of the pedigree as contrasted with family, or female side.

Live weight—The weight of the jockey, as contrasted with dead weight.

Loaded shoulder—Unusually thick shoulder and unimpressive withers, making for an awkward gait.

Loafer—Horse unwilling to run well without hard urging.

Lob—A cooler or stiff.

Lock—A sure thing.

Look for hole in fence—Of a quitter that acts as if it would rather run back to the barn than continue in the race.

Look of eagles—The proud look in the eyes of many good horses, as if they knew they were good.

Loose-coupled—Opposite of close-coupled; slack-coupled.

Loose mount—Horse that continues running after losing rider.

Lug in—Bear in.

Machine—Battery.

Machines—The mutuels.

Maiden—Of a horse or jockey, a non-winner; of a race, one for non-winners.

Make a run—Of a horse that turns on the speed, makes a move, makes a bid.

Marathon—A race longer than 1¼ miles.

Mare—A female horse of five or older.

Martingale—Straps attached to bit or noseband and girth, preventing horse from rearing.

Match race—A race between two horses, winner-take-all.

Maturity—A race for four-year-olds in which entries are made before their birth.

Meant—Of a horse whose stable intends to win; "well-meant."

Meat ball—Cathartic pill.

Meet—Race meeting.

Middle distance—Of a race longer than seven furlongs but less than 1⅛ miles.

Mile pole—Colored post at infield rail exactly a mile from finish wire.

Minus pool—In pari-mutuel betting, a situation in which so much money is bet on a horse (usually to show) that the pool is insufficient, after take and breakage, to pay holders of winning tickets the legal minimum odds of 1 to 10 or 20. The track is required to make up the difference from its own funds.

Monkey crouch—Riding style popularized by Tod Sloan in which jockey bends forward over horse's withers; "monkey-on-a-stick."

Morning glory—Horse that runs well in workouts but not in races.

Morning line—Forecast of probable odds.

Move up—Gain ground; run in a higher-class race.

Muck out—Clean a horse's stall.

Mudder—Horse that prefers muddy going; "mudlark."

Muddy track—Soft, wet and holding.

Mutuel pool—Total amount bet to win, place or show in a race; total amount bet on daily double, exacta, quinella, etc.

Muzzle—Straps that keep horse's mouth closed, prevent it from biting.

Name—To enter a horse in a race.

Nape—Top of horse's neck; poll.

Navicular disease—A crippling, sometimes fatal ulcer which corrodes the navicular bone of the foot. Usually found in forefoot.

Near side—Horse's left side.

Neck—About ¼ length.

Nerve—To remove a nerve, eliminating pain but not the infirmity that causes it. Illegal in major racing.

Nick—To nerve a horse; a supposedly strategic feature of a pedigree, representing a particular mating or cross-breeding worthy of repetition.

Nightcap—Last race on the program.

Nod—Lowering of head; permission to a jockey to dismount after race.

Nom de course—Stable name.

Nose—The narrowest possible winning margin.

Number ball—Numbered ball drawn from number box to assign post positions.

Nursery race—Baby race.

Oaks—Stakes race for three-year-old fillies.

Oatburner—Hayburner.

Objection—Complaint by jockey that a foul has been committed.

Odds board—Tote board.

Odds man—At tracks where electronic computers are not in use, an employee who calculates changing odds as betting progresses.

Odds on—Odds of less than even money.

Off—The start, or the time of the start; difference between track record and final clocking of a race; slowness of a horse, expressed in a time comparison or a lengths comparison between its current performance and what it should do, or what other horses have done or are likely to do. "He's off at least three lengths."

Off side—Right side of a horse.

Off the board—Of a horse so lightly bet that its odds exceed 99 to 1; failure to finish in the money.

Off the pace—To run behind the early leaders.

Off the top—Of the practice of deducting a fixed "take" percentage from the mutuel pool before paying holders of winning tickets.

Off track—A racing surface other than fast; of betting conducted away from the track.

On edge—Nervous; sharply conditioned.

On the bit—Of a horse eagerly straining against the bit.

On the chin strap—Winning by·a wide margin.

On the ground—Of a suspended jockey.

On the nose—A bet that horse will win.

On the rail—Running close to the infield rail.

On top—In the lead.

One-run—Of a horse that expends all its energy in a single burst of speed, usually in stretch.

Open race—A race with lenient eligibility conditions, permitting entry of a wide variety of horses.

Optional claimer—A race for horses entered to be claimed at a fixed price or a price within a limited range, and open also to horses that have run at such a price in the past but are not entered to be claimed today.

Osselets—Bony growths on injured membrane of ankle joint.

Ouchy—Sore.

Out of—In discussing a horse's parentage,

one says that it is "by" a sire "out of" a dam.

Outrider—Mounted employee who escorts horses to post.

Over at the knee—The foreleg curves forward at the knee.

Overland—Of the course followed by a horse that runs wide on the turns, losing ground.

Overlay—Horse whose odds are high by comparison with its good winning chances.

Overnight race—One for which entries close less than three days before the start of the program.

Overnights—Tomorrow's entries, as released by the racing secretary's office.

Overreach—To strike a forefoot with a hind shoe while running.

Overweight—Pounds that a horse carries in excess of officially assigned weight, because jockey is too heavy.

Pace—The speed of the leaders at each stage of the race.

Paddock—Saddling enclosure.

Pari-mutuels—From Paris ("Paree") Mutuels, system invented by Frenchman, whereby winning bettors get all money wagered by losers, after deduction of house percentage.

Pasteboard track—Fast racing strip, so-called because thin and hard.

Pastern—Area between fetlock and coronet.

Peacocky—High-headed, flighty horse.

Periodic ophthalmia—Periodic loss of vision by horse; "moonblindness."

Pigeye—Small equine eye, supposed sign of meanness.

Pinched back—Caught in a jam and forced back during race.

Pink—Uniformed Pinkerton guard at track.

Pipe opener—Short workout; blow out.

Plater—Horseshoer, farrier; claiming horse, because of silver plates formerly awarded to winners of such races.

Pocket—Racing predicament in which horse is surrounded by others and unable to increase speed until opening occurs.

Points—In Thoroughbred conformation, a physical feature; the lower legs

of a horse, especially in describing color ("Dark brown or bay horses always have black points").

Poll—Top of horse's head.

Pony—Any workhorse at a track, such as lead pony.

Pool—Total amount bet for win, place or show, or in daily double, etc.

Post—Starting gate.

Powder—Minor physical contact between horses during race.

Preferred—Of horses given preference in entry for particular race, usually previous winners or horses bred or foaled in the local jurisdiction.

Prepotent—Of horse whose offspring breed comparatively true to type, inheriting the desired characteristics.

Prod—Illegal battery, as in cattleprod.

Produce—Offspring of mare.

Prop—Refusing to break at start; standing flat-footed.

Public stable—Enterprise of "public trainer" who handles horses on free-lance basis, as contrasted with one who trains stock of only one owner.

Puett gate—Widely used brand of starting gate.

Pull—To restrain horse deliberately, preventing it from winning; to "stiff."

Pull in the weights—A weight advantage.

Pull up—To stop or slow a horse during or after race or workout.

Punter—Horseplayer.

Quarter—Quarter-mile; two furlongs; side of hoof.

Quarter crack—Separation of inner and outer walls of hoof in quarter area.

Quarter horse—Extremely speedy breed used for ranch work and racing up to a quarter-mile.

Quarter pole—Colored post at infield rail exactly two furlongs from finish wire.

Quinella (quiniela; quinela)—Form of mutuel betting in which player tries to pick first two finishers, regardless of order.

Racing plate—Shoe worn for racing purposes.

Racing secretary—Official who prescribes conditions of races at his track and usually serves as track handicapper, assigning weights to entrants in handicap races.

Racing sound—Of a horse able to race, although not necessarily in prime health.

Rack up—To interfere with several other horses so severely that they all slow down.

Rail runner—Horse that prefers to run along inside rail.

Raised bar—Bar plate which helps prevent running down.

Rank—Of a fractious horse, especially when, "running rank," it refuses to be rated early in race.

Rate—To restrain a horse early in race, conserving its energies for later challenges.

Receiving barn—Where horses stabled at other tracks are kept before they go to the paddock for their races.

Red roan—Of a horse whose coat consists of red, yellow and white hairs.

Refuse—Of a horse that fails to break at the start or, in jump races, fails to attempt one of the fences.

Ridden out—Of a horse that wins under an active but not a driving ride, and probably has racing energy left; sometimes, contradictorily, a winner whose jockey parcels out its energy so that none is left after it passes finish line.

Ride short—To ride with short stirrup leathers.

Ridgling—Partly castrated horse; "rigling."

Right price—Among players, mutuel odds high enough to warrant risking a bet on a particular animal; among horsemen, odds high enough to warrant an all-out try with horse.

Rim—Horseshoe with long cleat or grab on outer rim, sometimes helps horses with bad tendons.

Ringbone—Bony overgrowth at top of hoof or near pastern bones, found often in horses with straight pasterns. Formerly treated by nerving.

Ringer—Of a horse entered under another's name.

Roan—Striking reddish or grayish color.

Roar—Of a horse, noisy breathing like coughing.

Rogue—Chronically fractious horse.

Rogue's badge—Blinkers.

Romp—An easy race.

Roping—Training or exercising a horse by having it move in circles at end of a tether.

Route—A relatively long race.

Router—Horse that does its best in races of 1⅛ miles or longer.

Rug—Heavy horse blanket.

Rule off—To bar from racing.

Run down—Of a horse, to scrape the flesh of the heels on the track surface while racing. Associated with weak pasterns; "run down behind."

Run in—To win unexpectedly.

Runner—Messenger to and from mutuel windows for occupants of clubhouse boxes.

Run out—To finish out of the money; to run toward outside rail.

Run-out bit—Bit that gives rider extra leverage on one side, helping prevent animal from lugging in or bearing out.

Run wide—To race far from inside rail, covering extra ground.

Saddlecloth—Piece of fabric between saddle and horse.

Saliva test—Chemical analysis of horse's saliva, routinely performed on in-money finishers, in attempt to see whether animal was dosed with illegal drugs.

Salute—Of jockey who raises whip in greeting to stewards after race, in customary request to dismount.

Sand crack—Vertical crack on hoof from coronet downward.

Sanitary ride—Of a horse that did not try its best in a race, or of a jockey that took the animal wide to avoid tight spots or flying mud, harming its chances.

Savage—Of a horse, to bite.

Save ground—To cover the shortest possible distance in a race, hugging the rail on turns, running in direct, straight line on stretches.

Scale of weights—Official tabulation of correct weights for various age groups at all distances and all times of year; "the scale."

Scale weights—Weights carried in an official weight-for-age race.

Scenic route—When a horse loses ground by running far from rail; overland.

School—To train a horse, especially at the gate, in the paddock or over jumps.

Score—To win a race or a bet; a victory.

Scratch—To withdraw an entrant from its race.

Scratch sheet—Daily publication that includes graded handicaps, tips, scratches.

Season—The period in which racing is conducted on a particular circuit or at a particular track; of a filly or mare, the period of estrus or "heat."

Seat—The posture of a rider on a horse.

Second dam—Horse's maternal grandmother.

Second sire—Horse's paternal grandfather.

Selling plater—Claiming horse; plater.

Selling race—Claiming race; type of race that antedated claimers and no longer is run, in which rules required that winner be auctioned off afterward.

Send—To enter a horse in a race; of a horseman, to try to win with the horse.

Send away—Of an official starter, opening the gate and beginning the race.

Sesamoiditis—Bone inflammation above and behind fetlock.

Set down—To suspend horseman, rider, stablehand from racing for a period; to shake up a horse and ask it for speed in a race or workout.

Sex allowance—Weight concession given female horses in races against males.

Shadow roll—Sheepskin or cloth cylinder strapped across horse's nose to bar its vision of ground, prevent it from shying at shadows.

Shake up—To hit a horse in effort to make it run.

Shank—Rope or strap attached to halter or bridle, for leading a horse by hand.

Sheath—Fleshy pocket containing genital organs of male horse.

Shed row—Racetrack barns; the backstretch community.

Ship—To transport a horse.

Shipping fever—Respiratory ailment of horses, associated with move from one climate to another.

Shoe board—Sign that tells what kind of shoes each entrant wears.

Shoo in—A supposed cinch bet or guaranteed victor; a fixed race.

Short—Of a horse that tires in stretch after long layoff, demonstrating need for more work.

Short price—Small mutuel payoff.

Show wear—Fetlocks swollen by overwork.

Shuffle—Of jockey who hand rides, pumping his hands and moving his feet.

Shuffled back—Of a horse that loses ground or racing position because of jams.

Shut off—To cross in front of another horse during race, forcing it to take up or go around.

Shut out—What happens to the player who gets on the betting line too late and is still waiting when the window closes.

Silks—Nylon or other costume worn by rider in race.

Sire—Horse's father.

Sit-still—A type of riding dependent more on patience, knowledge of pace than active, "whoop-de-doo" whipping; of a jockey who loses the race through inactivity with the whip.

Sixteenth pole—Vertical post on infield rail exactly half a furlong from finish wire.

Skin—To make a track faster by rolling and hardening the surface.

Skittish—Of a nervous horse.

Slab-sided—Of a horse with flat, narrow rib cage, indicative of poor lung capacity.

Slack of rib—Of a horse whose last rib is not close to its hip, indicating a long, weak back.

Sleeper—An underrated horse that could, or does, surprise.

Sloppy track—When racing strip is covered with puddles, but is not yet muddy, the surface remaining hard.

Slot—Post position.

Slow pill—Drug that dulls horse's nervous system, preventing it from performing alertly.

Slow track—A track wetter than good, not as thick as muddy.

Smart money—Insiders' bets, insiders themselves.

Snatch—Any violent, sudden action with reins or halter; "snatch up," "snatch around."

Snip—White or flesh-colored marking on horse's nose.

Snug—To keep a tight hold on horse while rating it during race; "snug back," "snug hold."

Socks—White ankles, allegedly a sign of weakness.

Solid—Of a ready horse, suitably placed.

Sophomore—Three-year-old.

Spanish bit—Type of bit that causes pain under pressure of reins. Used as last resort in schooling rebellious horses.

Spark—To use a battery in a race.

Spavin—Bony outcropping caused by inflammation of equine joints.

Special weights—Even weights, except for sex and apprentice allowances, assigned by racing secretary without recourse to official weight scale. Used mainly in races for better maidens.

Speedy cut—Leg injury caused by blow from opposite foot while running.

Spit out the bit—When an exhausted horse "backs up" and stops pressing against the bit.

Splint—Bony growth on horse's shin.

Split race—When an oversubscribed race is divided into two.

Sponge—To insert a piece of sponge or other foreign substance in a horse's nostrils, impeding its breathing and preventing it from performing well.

Spot—To concede weight to another horse.

Spot play—Type of play in which bettor risks money only on types of races and horses which seem relatively worthwhile risks.

Spring halt—Nerve-muscle ailment causing spasmodic elevation of rear legs.

Sprint—Short race, seven furlongs or less.

Stake—Commission paid winning jockey, trainer or groom.

Stakes—A race in which purse consists of nomination, entrance and starting fees plus money added by track itself. Improperly called "stake" race.

Stale—Of a jaded, overworked horse; of a horse, to urinate.

Stall gate—Starting gate in which each horse has its own compartment.

Stallion—Entire male horse.

Stall walker—Horse that paces its stall, consuming energy.

Stand—Of a stallion, to be at stud.

Star—White marking on horse's forehead.

Starter's list—List of horses ruled out of action by official starter because of chronic misbehavior at gate and, therefore, ineligible for racing until bad habits are corrected.

Stayer—A reliable, determined router.

Steeplechase—A race over jumps higher and broader than hurdles.

Stewards—The three duly-appointed arbiters of racing law who judge human and equine conduct at a race meeting.

Stick—Whip; to whip.

Sticker—Cleat on a horseshoe.

Stick horse—Horse that runs better when whipped.

Stiff—To prevent a horse from winning by deliberately riding poorly or by drugging it or training it inappropriately; an unfit or outclassed horse; a horse that has been stiffed.

Stifle—Foreward area of horse's thigh.

Sting—To use a battery in a race.

Stirrup—Where jockey's feet go when he is mounted; irons.

Stockings—White leg markings, longer than socks.

Stooper—One of several dozen Americans who make a precarious living picking up discarded mutuel tickets at tracks and cashing those that have been thrown away by mistake.

Straight—Another term for a bet to win; "straight, place and show."

Straight as a string—Of a horse going all-out; "strung out."

Straightaway—Straight part of a race course; stretch.

Stretch call—Position in stretch where call is made for charting purposes. Usually a furlong from the wire.

Stretch turn—The turn into the homestretch.

Stride—Of a horse, its way of running or the ground it covers after each foot has been in contact with the track once.

String—The horses owned by one stable or handled by one trainer.

Strip—Racing strip; narrow white marking on horse's face.

Stripe—Marking similar to strip, but longer.

Stud—Stallion; breeding farm; horses at a breeding farm.

Studbook—Official registry of Thoroughbreds; a stallion's date book.

Stud fee—What the stallion's owner gets for its breeding services.

Subscription—Fees required of owner who enters horse in stakes race.

Sulk—Of a horse that refuses to run or respond to jockey's guidance.

Surcingle—Buckled strap that holds blanket on horse.

Suspension—Punishment, usually temporary, that declares jockey, horseman or stablehand ineligible for participation in sport.

Swamp fever—Infectious equine anemia.

Sweat the brass—To overwork a horse.

Sweepstakes—Stakes race.

Tack—What goes on the horse in addition to the rider.

Tag—Claiming price.

Tail female—Horse's female ancestry on dam's side.

Tail male—Horse's male ancestry on sire's side.

Take—Money deducted from each mutuel pool for track revenue and taxes.

Take back—To restrain a horse, either to rate it or prevent running into trouble.

Take care of—Of a jockey, to give the works to another in a race.

Take down—To disqualify a horse after it has finished in the money. Its number literally is removed from the list of early finishers.

Take out—Track take.

Take up—To slow sharply in effort to avoid collision or other racing trouble.

Tea—Any illegal chemical used to drug a horse and worsen or improve its performance.

Teaser—Stallion that tests mare's readiness for mating.

Teletimer—Electronic timer that flashes the fractional and final times of races on the tote board.

Tenderfoot—Sore-footed horse.

Thief—Unreliable horse that runs worst when its chances seem best.

Third sire—Horse's paternal great-grandfather.

Thoroughbred Racing Association—Trade association of track owners and managers.

Thoroughbred Racing Protective Bureau—The TRA's FBI, an intelligence network which combats corruption by investigating suspected evildoers and exposing those it catches.

Thoroughpins—A larger version of bog spavin that often goes right through the upper hock.

Three-eighths pole—Colored pole at inside rail, exactly three furlongs from finish wire.

Three-quarters pole—Colored pole at inside rail, exactly six furlongs from finish wire.

Throat latch—Upper part of horse's throat.

Thrush—Inflammation of the frog.

Tied on—Reins knotted and crossed, for stouter hold.

Tight—Fit and ready.

Tightener—A race intended to bring a horse to its peak.

Timber—Hurdle or other obstacle in jump race.

Timber rider—Steeplechase jockey.

Timber topper—A horse that runs in jump races.

Toe plate—Horseshoe with cleat in front, prevents sliding.

Tongue strap—Leather or cloth band that holds horse's tongue down to prevent horse from swallowing it during race or workout.

Top horse—Horse listed first in program of the race.

Top line—Male side of Thoroughbred pedigree.

Top weight—Heaviest impost in race.

Totalisator—Automated pari-mutuel machine which records bets as soon as tickets are dispensed at betting windows.

Tout—To give or sell betting advice; one who does so.

Trackmaster—Employee in charge of maintaining racing strip.

Training track—Separate track where workouts are held.

Trappy—Of a nimble, kind Thoroughbred.

Travel in straw—To travel with the horses in shipping vans, as stablehands do.

Trial—A preparatory race; a workout in which horse is asked for speed.

Triple Crown—Mythical award to any three-year-old that wins Kentucky Derby, Preakness Stakes and Belmont Stakes.

Trouble line—Words at end of each past-performance line in *The Morning Telegraph,* appraising horse's effort or stating any legitimate excuse it might have had for losing.

Turf course—A grass-covered track.

Turn out—To send a horse to the farm for pasturage and rest.

Twitch—Noose that can be tightened painfully around horse's nose and upper lip, keeping it quiet in starting gate, elsewhere "tongs."

Under wraps—Of a horse showing less than its best, probably because trainer does not want to extend it.

Untrack—What a horse is said to do to itself when it finally generates momentum and shows its talent.

Unwind—To taper off a horse's training preparatory to resting it.

Up—Of a jockey's assignment ("Buckpasser, Baeza up"), or an order to jockeys ("Riders, up!").

Urine test—Chemical analysis of horse's urine in effort to tell whether animal was drugged.

Used up—Of an exhausted horse.

Valet—Employee who takes care of jockey's clothing, carries his tack.

Van—A motor truck in which horses are shipped.

Veer—Of a horse, to swerve.

Vet's list—List of ill or injured horses declared ineligible for racing by the track veterinarian.

Vice—Any undesirable habit of a horse.

Walking ring—Oval near paddock enclosure, where horses walk and riders mount before start of post parade.

Walkover—A race from which all but one horse are scratched, permitting the horse to win by walking the distance.

Walk-up start—In contrast with the standing start at the stall gate, a start in which riders walk horses toward the starting point, and begin to run at the starter's command.

Warm up—Pre-race gallop.

Washy—Of a nervously sweating horse.

Water out—To water horse while it cools out after exertion.

Weanling—A newly weaned horse.

Weave—Of a horse, to move with a swaying, rocking motion in stall, or to pursue erratic course during a race.

Webfoot—A mudder.

Weigh in—Of jockeys, to be weighed with tack after race.

Weigh out—Of jockeys, to be weighed with tack before race.

Weight-for-age race—In which horses carry weights as prescribed by the official scale of weights.

Well let down—Of a horse with long, arched ribs, long forearms and short cannon bones, signifying good lung capacity and an easy, long stride.

Well ribbed up—Of a horse whose last rib is close to its hip, signifying a short, strong back.

Well-sprung ribs—Full, arched ribs for maximum lung capacity.

Welterweights—Weights 28 pounds over the official scale of weights, to test weight-bearing ability of entrants.

Wheel—Of a horse, to turn sharply, almost pinwheeling; a form of betting in which daily-double, perfecta or quinella player makes every possible combination bet on his favored horse or horses.

Whistle—Noisy equine breathing, like a whistle, caused by overstrained respiratory system.

Whoop-de-doo—A riding style that stresses an effort to get the lead immediately and run as fast as possible, with much whip action and little effort at rating; "whoop-de-hoo."

Wind sucker—Of a horse that swallows air, often with spasmodic motions of chin.

Winter—To spend the winter away from competition.

Wound up—Of a fit, ready horse.

Index

798.4   35705
AIN

Ainslee
Ainslee's complete guide to
thoroughbred racing.

DATE DUE
